FORMAL MODELS, LANGUAGES AND APPLICATIONS

SERIES IN MACHINE PERCEPTION AND ARTIFICIAL INTELLIGENCE*

Editors: **H. Bunke** (Univ. Bern, Switzerland)
P. S. P. Wang (Northeastern Univ., USA)

Vol. 51: Automatic Diatom Identification
(Eds. *H. du Buf and M. M. Bayer*)

Vol. 52: Advances in Image Processing and Understanding
A Festschrift for Thomas S. Huwang
(Eds. *A. C. Bovik, C. W. Chen and D. Goldgof*)

Vol. 53: Soft Computing Approach to Pattern Recognition and Image Processing
(Eds. *A. Ghosh and S. K. Pal*)

Vol. 54: Fundamentals of Robotics — Linking Perception to Action
(*M. Xie*)

Vol. 55: Web Document Analysis: Challenges and Opportunities
(Eds. *A. Antonacopoulos and J. Hu*)

Vol. 56: Artificial Intelligence Methods in Software Testing
(Eds. *M. Last, A. Kandel and H. Bunke*)

Vol. 57: Data Mining in Time Series Databases y
(Eds. *M. Last, A. Kandel and H. Bunke*)

Vol. 58: Computational Web Intelligence: Intelligent Technology for Web Applications
(Eds. *Y. Zhang, A. Kandel, T. Y. Lin and Y. Yao*)

Vol. 59: Fuzzy Neural Network Theory and Application
(*P. Liu and H. Li*)

Vol. 60: Robust Range Image Registration Using Genetic Algorithms and the Surface Interpenetration Measure
(*L. Silva, O. R. P. Bellon and K. L. Boyer*)

Vol. 61: Decomposition Methodology for Knowledge Discovery and Data Mining: Theory and Applications
(*O. Maimon and L. Rokach*)

Vol. 62: Graph-Theoretic Techniques for Web Content Mining
(*A. Schenker, H. Bunke, M. Last and A. Kandel*)

Vol. 63: Computational Intelligence in Software Quality Assurance
(*S. Dick and A. Kandel*)

Vol. 64: The Dissimilarity Representation for Pattern Recognition: Foundations and Applications
(*Elżbieta Pękalska and Robert P. W. Duin*)

Vol. 65: Fighting Terror in Cyberspace
(*Eds. M. Last and A. Kandel*)

Vol. 66: Formal Models, Languages and Applications
(Eds. *K. G. Subramanian, K. Rangarajan and M. Mukund*)

*For the complete list of titles in this series, please write to the Publisher.

Series in Machine Perception and Artificial Intelligence – Vol. 66

FORMAL MODELS, LANGUAGES AND APPLICATIONS

Editors

K. G. Subramanian
Madras Christian College, India

K. Rangarajan
Madras Christian College, India

M. Mukund
Chennai Mathematical Institute, India

World Scientific

NEW JERSEY • LONDON • SINGAPORE • BEIJING • SHANGHAI • HONG KONG • TAIPEI • CHENNAI

Published by

World Scientific Publishing Co. Pte. Ltd.

5 Toh Tuck Link, Singapore 596224

USA office: 27 Warren Street, Suite 401-402, Hackensack, NJ 07601

UK office: 57 Shelton Street, Covent Garden, London WC2H 9HE

British Library Cataloguing-in-Publication Data
A catalogue record for this book is available from the British Library.

FORMAL MODELS, LANGUAGES AND APPLICATIONS
Series in Machine Perception and Artificial Intelligence — Vol. 66

ISBN 981-256-889-1

Printed in Singapore by B & JO Enterprise

PREFACE

This volume of contributed papers commemorates the 75th birthday of Prof. Rani Siromoney, one of the foremost theoretical computer scientists in India and a leading authority on Formal Languages and Automata Theory. Over a period spanning four decades, she has made tremendous technical contributions to the field through her research. She has also inspired generations of students in Chennai with her teaching and has been responsible for building up a community of dedicated teachers and researchers in this part of India to carry forward her vision.

Prof. Siromoney has served on the Editorial Board of the journals *Theoretical Computer Science* and *International Journal of Foundations of Computer Science* and has headed several international collaborative research projects. She also served on the Programme Committee for the first ten editions of the international conference *Foundations of Software Technology and Theoretical Computer Science*, one of the leading theoretical computer science conferences in the world. She is currently Professor Emeritus at Madras Christian College, the illustrious institution where she has spent most of her professional life. She continues to play an active role in research and teaching as Adjunct Professor at Chennai Mathematical Institute.

The contributions in this volume span a wide range of subjects, thematically connected by the use of concepts from formal languages and automata theory. The areas explored in this volume include compiler construction, computational complexity theory, formal modelling of concurrent systems, codes and image analysis. The contributors are leading researchers in computer science from all parts of the world, all of whom have been associated with Rani Siromoney during the course of her long and productive career.

We thank all the authors for readily accepting to contribute to this volume. We also thank the staff of World Scientific for their assistance and cooperation that have been crucial for the successful completion of this project.

K.G. Subramanian
K. Rangarajan
Madhavan Mukund

CONTENTS

CHAPTER 1

FINITE ARRAY AUTOMATA AND REGULAR ARRAY GRAMMARS

Adrian Atanasiu

Faculty of Mathematics, Bucharest University,
Str. Academiei 14, sector 1, 70109 Bucharest, Romania
E-mail: aadrian@pcnet.ro

K. G. Subramanian

Department of Mathematics, Madras Christian College,
Tambaram, Chennai 600 059, India
E-mail: kgsmani1948@yahoo.com

K. Rangarajan

Department of Mathematics, Bharath Institute of Higher Education,
Selaiyur, Chennai 600 059, India

P. S. P. Wang

College of Computer Science, Northeastern University,
Boston, MA 02115, USA
E-mail: pwang@ccs.neu.edu

A recognition device, called Finite Array Automaton, accepting a class of picture arrays, is introduced and it is shown that this device is equivalent to the $n-$dimensional regular array grammar. Regular (string) languages, called spreading languages, are associated to the corresponding $n-$dimensional array regular languages in order to deal with certain decision problems. Also the effect of controlling the application of rules of regular array grammars is brought out.

1. Introduction

Picture languages generated by array grammars or accepted by array automata have been studied by researchers and various models have been proposed in the literature, motivated by problems arising in the framework of syntactic methods of pattern recognition and image processing.[6,8,9] Freund[4] has made an extensive and deep study of array grammars in a general setting of $n-$dimensions. Many different aspects of these grammars such as regulated rewriting,[2,3] cooperating systems,[5] contextual features[4] and so on have been investigated. $k-$head finite array automata,[1] have also been considered to characterize certain families of array languages.

In this paper, an explicit construction of a recognition device, called a Finite Array Automaton equivalent to an $n-$dimensional Regular Array Grammar is made. A class of regular string languages, called Spreading languages is associated to the finite array automaton which is useful in certain decision problems. In the case of two dimensions ($n = 2$), the effect of controlling the application of rules of a Regular array grammar is brought out.

2. Preliminaries

For notions of formal languages we refer to Refs. 7 and 10; for basic notions, notations and results about array grammars to Ref. 4.

Let V be a finite and nonempty alphabet. Let Z denote the set of integers and N denote the set of positive integers and let $n \in N$. For $x = (x_1, x_2, \dots, x_n) \in Z^n$, we shall define

$$\|x\| = \sum_{i=1}^{n} x_i^2 .$$

A $n-$dimensional array A over an alphabet V is a function $A : Z^n \longrightarrow V \cup \{\#\}$ with finite support, supp(A), defined by

$$\text{supp}(A) = \{u \in Z^n \mid A(u) \neq \#\} ;$$

is called the blank symbol, which is not in V. Usually we write

$$A = \{(u, A(u)) \mid u \in \text{supp}(A)\} .$$

In each location $u \in Z^n$ of the grid an element from $V \cup \{\#\}$ is placed by the function $A : Z^n \to V \cup \{\#\}$. Moreover, the set

$$\text{supp}(A) = \{u \in Z^n / A(u) \neq \#\}$$

is finite and nonempty. We require that for any $u \in \text{supp}(A)$, $A(v) \neq \#$ for at least one v with $\|u - v\| = 1$.

The set of all $n-$dimensional arrays over V is denoted by V^{*n}. Any subset of V^{*n} is called a $n-$dimensional array language.

Let $u \in Z^n$. Then the translation $\tau_u : Z^n \longrightarrow Z^n$ is defined by $\tau_u(v) = v + u$ for all $v \in Z^n$; for any array $A \in V^{*n}$ we define $\tau_u(A)$, the corresponding n–dimensional array translated by u, by

$$\tau_u(A(v)) = A(v + u), \quad \forall\, v \in Z^n .$$

The vector $(0, 0, \ldots, 0) \in Z^n$ shall be often denoted by Ω_n.

Usually, arrays are regarded as equivalence classes with respect to linear translations, i.e. only the relative positions of the symbols from supp(A) are taken into account.

The equivalence class $[A]$ of an array $A \in V^{*n}$ is defined by

$$[A] = \{B \in V^{*n} \mid \exists\, u \in Z^n, B = \tau_u(A)\} .$$

For any element $u \in \text{supp}(A)$, we define the frame

$$W_u = \{(u, v)/v \in Z^n, \|u - v\| = 1\} .$$

If $u = \Omega_n$, then the frame $W_0 = \{(\Omega_n, v)/\|v\| = 1\}$ is called the initial frame. Obviously, W_0 has $2n$ elements.

Let us consider the operation of translation $\tau_x(W_u) = \{(u+x, v+x) \mid v \in Z^n\} = W_{u+x}$. Then, any frame can be obtained by the translation of the initial frame: $W_u = \tau_u(W_0)$ (or $W_0 = \tau_{-u}(W_u)$).

A n–dimensional array production over V is a triple $P = (W, A_1, A_2)$ where $W \subset Z^n$ is a finite set and A_1, A_2 are mappings from W to $V \cup \{\#\}$.

In such a writing, all positions in W together with their associated symbols must be listed for representing A_1 and A_2, by

$$A_i = \{(u, A_i(u)) \mid u \in W\}, \quad 1 \le i \le 2 .$$

This representation is general, for the infinite set of equivalent n–dimensional array productions of the form $(\tau_u(W), \tau_u(A_1), \tau_u(A_2))$ with $u \in Z^n$. Hence without loss of generality, it can be assumed that $\Omega_n \in W$. Moreover, the set W can be omitted because it can be uniquely reconstructed from the description of the mappings A_1, A_2. A n–dimensional array production $p = (W, A_1, A_2)$ is regular if:

(1) $W = \{\Omega_n, u\} \subset Z^n, \|u\| = 1$ and $A_1 = \{(\Omega_n, B), (u, \#)\}$,
$A_2 = \{(\Omega_n, a), (u, C)\}, B, C \in V_N, a \in V_T$, or
(2) $W = \{\Omega_n\}, A_1 = \{(\Omega_n, B)\}, A_2 = \{(\Omega_n, b)\}$, where $B \in V_N, b \in V_T$.

If B_1, B_2 are two n–dimensional arrays, we shall write $B_1 \Rightarrow B_2$ if and only if there exist $u \in Z^n$ and a production $p = (W, A_1, A_2)$ such that the restrictions of B_i to $\tau_u(W)$ are $A_i (i = 1, 2)$.

In other words, the array $B_2 \in V^{*^n}$ is directly derivable from the array $B_1 \in V^{*^n}$ by the $n-$dimensional production (W, A_1, A_2) if and only if the subarray of B_1 corresponding to A_1 is replaced by A_2, yielding B_2.

A $n-$dimensional array grammar is a quintuple $G = (n, V_N, V_T, P, \{v_s, S)\}, \#)$, where

- V_N is the alphabet of nonterminal symbols, V_T is the alphabet of terminal symbols, $V_N \cap V_T = \phi$;
- P is a finite non-empty set of $n-$dimensional array productions over $V_N \cup V_T$;
- $\{(v_s, S)\}$ is the start array ($S \in V_N$ is the start symbol, $v_s \in Z^n$ is the start location).

The array $B_2 \in V^{*n}$ is directly derivable from the array $B_1 \in V^{*n}$ in G, denoted $B_1 \Rightarrow_G B_2$ if and only if there exists a $n-$dimensional array production $p = (W, A_1, A_2)$ in P such that $B_1 \Rightarrow B_2$. If $\Rightarrow^*$ is the reflexive and transitive closure of $\Rightarrow_G$, then the array language generated by G is defined by

$$L(G) = \{A \in V_T^{*n} / (v_s, S) \Rightarrow^* A\} .$$

The corresponding $n-$dimensional array language of equivalence classes with respect to linear translation is $[L(G)] = \{[A]/A \in L(G)\}$.

The $n-$dimensional array grammar G is called regular if every production in P is regular; in this case $L(G)$ is called a $n-$dimensional regular array language. The family of $n-$dimensional regular array languages will be denoted by $L(n, \text{reg})$ and the family of regular array languages of equivalence of classes of arrays will be denoted by $[L(n, \text{reg})]$.

3. Finite Array Automata

Let V be a finite and non-empty alphabet. Let $V^1 = \{a_1/a \in V\}$ be another alphabet, distinct from V. The set of strings over $V(V^1)$ is denoted as usual by $V^*(V^{1*}$ respectively) with the difference that the identity will be considered # (blank symbol).

Definition 1: Let A be a $n-$dimensional array over the alphabet V. A n-Finite Array Automaton (n-FAA in short) is a 7-tuple, $M = (n, Q, V, \delta, q_o, v_0, F)$,

- $n \geq 1$.
- Q and V are finite and nonempty sets of "states" and "input characters" respectively.
- $\delta : (Q \times Z^n) \times V \to 2^{Q \times z^n}$ is the transition map, satisfying the invariance property $(p, v) \in \delta((q, u), a) \Leftrightarrow (p, \tau_x(v)) \in \delta(q, \tau_x(u), a), \forall\ x \in Z^n$.
- $q_0 \in Q$ is the "initial state".
- $v_0 \in Z^n$ is the start location; if $v_0 = \Omega_n$ this element can be ignored.
- $F \subseteq Q, (F \neq \phi)$ is the set of "final states".

$(p, v) \in \delta((q, u), a)$ is defined only if the following constraint is fulfilled:

$$p, q \in Q, u, v \in Z^n, \|u - v\| = 1, a \in V\,.$$

We interpret these restrictions in the following way: if the automaton M is in the state q and finds a symbol $a \in V$ in the location u, then it will pass on to a state p and in another location v in its neighborhood.

Otherwise $\delta((q, u), a) = \phi$.

After such a rule is applied relating to a location u, the element $a \in V$ from this location is replaced by $a^1 \in V^1$ (in order to avoid the possibility of the automaton passing a second time through the location u).

The content of the location v is not important at this moment, but we remark that δ cannot be applied if in the current location u there is # or an element from V^1.

Remark 1: $(p, -u) \notin \delta((q, u), a)$ unless $u = \Omega_n$ or $p \in F$ (otherwise this rule cannot be applied).

The property of invariance assures a homogenous behaviour of the transition map δ on the grid Z^n. Therefore it is enough to define the transition map of a $n-$dimensional finite array automaton only for the initial frame:

$$(p, v) \in \delta((q, u), a) \Leftrightarrow (p, v - u) \in \delta((q, \Omega_n), a)\,.$$

In the following we shall consider, without loss of generality, only the case $v_0 = \Omega_n$.

The transition map δ can be extended recursively to $\delta^\wedge : (Q \times Z^n) \times V^* \to 2^{Q \times Z^n}$ as follows:

$$\delta^\wedge((q, u), \#) = \{(q, u)\}, \forall\ q \in Q, u \in Z^n\,,$$
$$\delta^\wedge((q, u), \alpha a) = \cup_{(p,v) \in \delta^\wedge((q,u),\alpha)} \delta((p, v), a), \forall\ p, q \in Q, a \in V, \alpha \in V^*\,.$$

For $\alpha = \#$ we obtain $\delta^\wedge((q, u), \#a) = \delta((q, u), a)$; so, $\delta^\wedge$ is a natural extension of δ because the invariance assures that $\#a = a$. In the following we shall denote $\delta^\wedge$ also by δ.

Proposition 1: $\delta((q,u),\alpha\beta) = \delta(\delta((q,u),\alpha),\beta)$.

Proof: Straightforward to prove, by induction on the length of β. Now, we give the definition of the array language accepted by a $n - FAAM = (Q, V, \delta, q_0, V_0, F)$: $L(M)$ contains all the sequences $(v_0, a_0), (v_1, a_1), \ldots, (v_n, a_n)$ which satisfy the constraints:

(1) $\exists q_1, \ldots, q_{n+1} \in Q$ with $(q_{i+1}, v_{i+1}) \in \delta((q_i, v_i)a_i), 0 \le i \le n$;
(2) $(v_i, v_{i+1}) \in W_{v_i}, 0 \le i \le n$;
(3) $q_{n+1} \in F$.

Let us denote by $\tau_x(L(M))$ the language accepted by the same automaton but with the start location $v_0 + x$ and let $L_0(M) = \tau_{-v_0}(L(M))$ Then the general language accepted by the automaton $M = (Q, V, \delta, q_0, v_0, F)$ is

$$[L(M)] = \bigcup_{u \in Z^n} \tau_u(L_0(M))\,.$$

Let $pro : Z^n \times V \to V$ be the function projection, defined by $pro((u,a)) = a, \forall\ a \in V, u \in Z^n$. This function can be extended to a morphism; now, another language, which is a projection in a 1-dimensional array of the language $L_0(M)$, can be defined:

$$pro(L(M)) = \{\alpha \in V^* | \exists\ q \in F, \exists\ v \in Z^n, (q,v) \in \delta((q_0, v_0), \alpha)\}\,.$$

It is clear that $pro(L(M))$ is a regular string language (in terms of formal languages).
□

Example 1: Let $n = 2$, $Q = \{q_0, q_1, q_2\}$, $V = \{a, b, c\}$, $v_0 = \Omega_n$, $F = \{q_0\}$ and $\delta((q_0, \Omega_n), a) = \{(q_1, (1,0))\}$, $\delta((q_1, \Omega_n), b) = \{(q_2, (0,1))\}$, $\delta((q_2, \Omega_n), c) = \{(q_0, (0,1))\}$. The language accepted by this 2-FAA contains all the arrays having the structure shown below:

$$\begin{array}{llllll} & & & & & c \\ & & & & a & b \\ & & & \cdots & & \\ & & & c & & \\ & & a & b & & \\ & c & & & & \\ a & b & & & & \end{array}$$

Thus $[L(M)] = \{((i,2i),a)((i+1,2i),b)((i+1,2i+1),c)\cdots((j,2j),a),((j+1,2j),b),((j+1,2j+1),c)|i,j \in Z, i \le j\}$ and $pro(L(M)) = (abc)^+$.

Example 2: If we take $n = 1$, $Q = \{q_0, q_1\}$, $V = \{x\}$, $v_0 = (0) = \Omega_1$, $F = \{q_0\}$ and $\delta((q_0, \Omega_1), x) = (q_1(1))$, $\delta((q_1, \Omega_1), x) = (q_0, (-1))$, the language accepted by this 1-FAA has only one sequence: $L_0(M) - \{((0), x)((1), x)\}$.

Indeed for the string xx, after the second x is accepted the sequence will have the form x^1x^1 and the current location becomes again Ω_1 where the symbol is now x^1. Because the current state is the final state q_0, this string is accepted and the automaton stops.

If $F = \{q_1\}$, then $L_0(M) = \{((0), x)\}$.

Remark 2: The usual Finite Automata accepting strings can be considered as a special case 1-FAA, where the frames used by the transition map are only $(i, i+1) \in W_i$, $i = 0, 1, 2, \ldots$.

Theorem 1: The class of languages accepted by n-FAA is $[L(n, \text{reg})]$.

Proof: Let L be a $n-$dimensional regular array language. Thus, there is a $n-$dimensional regular array grammar $G = (n, V_N, V_T, P, \{(v_s, S)\}, \#\}$ with $[L(G)] = L$. We shall construct the n-$FAAM = (n, Q, V, \delta, q_0, v_0, F)$ as follows:

- $Q = V_N \cup \{X\}$, $q_0 = S$, $F = \{X\}$ where $X \notin V_N \cup V_T$;
- $V = V_T$;
- $v_0 = v_o$;
- The transition map δ is defined as follows:

For a production $\{A_1 = \{(\Omega_n, B), (v, \#)\}, A_2 = \{(\Omega_n, a), (v, C)\}\}$, the rule $(C, v) \in \delta((B, \Omega_n,), a)$ is generated by keeping the same initial frame.

For a production $\{A_1 = \{(\Omega_n, B), A_2 = \{(\Omega_n, b)\}\}$, we consider an arbitrary initial frame $(\Omega_n, b) \in W_0$ we generate the rule $(X, v) \in \delta((B, \Omega_n), b)$.

The equality $[L(M)] = L$ can be proved, by the induction on the number of production rules used in a derivation.

Let M be a n-FAA and $L = [L(M)]$ be the array language accepted. We define a $n-$dimensional regular array grammar $G = (n, V_N, V_T, P, \{(v_s, S)\}, \#\}$ as follows:

- $V_N = Q$, $V_T = V$;
- $S = q_0$; $v_s = v_0$;
- The set P of productions will contain:

$\{A_1 = \{(\Omega_n, q), (v, \#)\}$, $A_2 = \{(\Omega_n, a), (v, p)\}\}$, for any rule $(p, v) \in \delta((q, \Omega_n), a)$; the frame W is the same for the automaton rule and for the grammar production.

For any $q_f \in F$ we look for the rules $(q_f, v) \in \delta((q, \Omega_n), a)$; each such rule will generate a production $\{A_1 = \{(\Omega_n, q), \} A_2 = \{\Omega_n, a)\}\}$ where its associated frame is restricted to $W = \{\Omega_n\}$.

The proof of the equality $L = [L(G)]$ is now straightforward. □

Example 3: For the 2-dimensional finite array automaton defined in Example 1, the regular array grammar which will generate the same language has the rules

$$\{\{((0,0), q_0), ((1,0), \#)\}, \{((0,0), a), ((1,0), q_1)\}\},$$
$$\{((0,0), q_1), ((0,1), \#)\}, \{((0,0), b), ((0,1), q_2)\}\},$$
$$\{((0,0), q_2), ((0,1), \#)\}, \{((0,0), c), ((0,1), q_0)\}\},$$
$$\{((0,0), q_2), ((0,0), c)\}\}.$$

3.1. *The spreading languages*

As in the case of regular languages, it is possible to associate an oriented graph Γ to a n-FAA. The construction of Γ is the following:

Let $M = (n, Q, V, \delta, q_0, v_0, F)$ be a $n-$dimensional finite array automaton.

- The nodes of the graph Γ will be labelled by states; q_0 will be the initial node and the nodes labelled by F are final nodes.
- The labels of the edges are the elements of the set $E = \{a_u | a \in V, u \in W_0\}$.

For any rule $(p, u) \in \delta((q, \Omega_n), a)$, an edge from q to p, labelled by a_u is drawn. So, at most $2n$ edges can leave every node of this graph.

Example 4: For the 2-FAA of Example 1, the graph associated is.

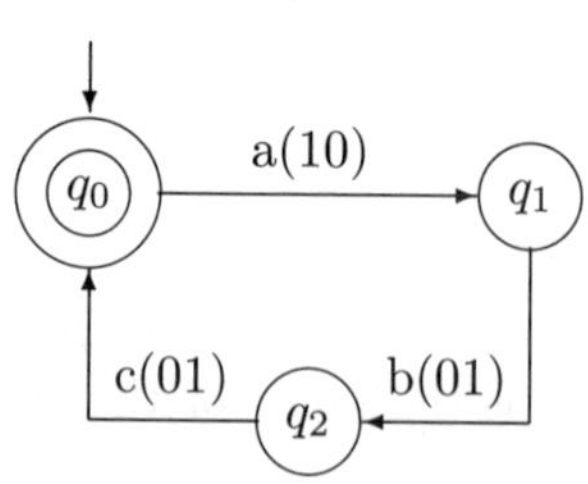

Example 5: For the Example 2, the graph associated is

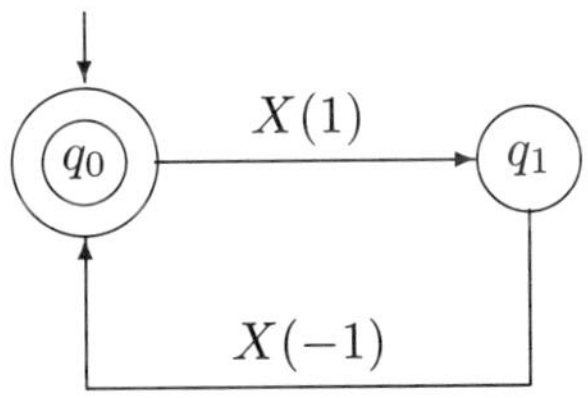

This graph Γ designs a finite automaton and thus a regular language.

Let $\overline{M} = (Q, \overline{V}, \overline{\delta}, q_0, F)$ be the finite automaton defined by the graph Γ, where

- $\overline{V} = \{a_u | a \in V, u \in W_0\}$;
- $p \in \overline{\delta}(q, a_u) \Leftrightarrow (p, u) \in \delta((q, \Omega_n), a)$.

Let $\overline{L} = \overline{L}(M)$be the regular language accepted by the regular automaton M. This language will be called the spreading language of L.

For every word $w = (\Omega_n, a_0)(v_1, a_1) \cdots (v_k, a_k) \in L(M)$ there is a path in Γ designed by the sequence $\overline{w} = (a_0)_{v'_1}, (a_1)_{v'_2} \cdots (a_{k-1})_{v'_k}, (a_k)_{v'_{k+1}} \in \overline{V}^*$ from the initial state q_0 to a final state q with $(q, v_{k+1}) \in \delta((p, v_k), a_k)$; we have denoted by $v'_i = \tau_{-v_i - 1}(v_i)(2 \leq i \leq k+1), v_{1'} = v_1$.

Let $\phi : L \to \overline{L}$ be the mapping defined by $\phi(w) = \overline{w}$. In this way, for every word in a $n-$dimensional array regular language corresponds a word in a regular language. The language $\phi(L)$ is regular sublanguage of $\overline{L}$. Sometimes the mapping ϕ is surjective (like for the 2-dimensional array language defined in Example 1), but this property does not hold always; the 1-dimensional regular language defined in Example 2 is finite, but the graph Γ constructed in Example 5 accepts the infinite language $\overline{L} = (xx)^*$. So, in this case $\phi(L) \subset \overline{L}$; But it is possible to find if a given sentence $\overline{w} \in L$ is in $\phi(L)$ or not.

Theorem 2: Let L be a $n-$dimensional regular array language and $\overline{L}$ its spreading language, with $\phi(L) \subset \overline{L}$ Let $w \in \overline{L}$. We can decide recursively whether $w \in \phi(L)$ or not.

Proof: Let $M = (n, Q, V, \delta, q_0, v_0, F)$ be a n-FAA with $L = L(M)$ and $\overline{L}$ its spreading language. The algorithm will have as input a sentence $w = a_{u_0} a_{u_1} \cdots a_{u_{k-1}} \in \overline{L}$, $(a_u \in \overline{V}, u \in W_0, 0 \leq i \leq k-1)$. The steps are:

(1) $m_0 := \{v_0\}$, $i = 1$;
(2) $v_i : -v_{i-1} + u_{i-1}$; $M_i := M_{i-1} \cup \{v_{i-1}\}$;

(3) If $(M \neq M_{i-1})$ and $(i < k)$ then $i := i + 1$, go to 2;
(4) If $i = k$ then $w \in \phi(L)$, otherwise $w \in \overline{L} \setminus \phi(L)$.

The algorithm tries to find a word $z \in L$ so that $\phi(z) = w$. So it iteratively builds the locations where the symbols of z can be placed. If these locations do not overlap, such a construction is possible from the point of view of finite array automaton M. The formal details are easy to be supplied. □

Example 6: Let us consider the 2-dimensional finite array automaton $M = (2, Q, V, \delta, q_0, F)$ with $Q = \{q_0, q_1, q_2, q_3\}$, $F = \{q_3\}$, $V = \{a\}$ and the transition map:

$$\delta((q_0, \Omega_2), a) = \{(q_0, (1,0)), (q_1, (1,0))\},$$
$$\delta((q_1, \Omega_2), a) = \{(q_1, (0,1)), (q_2, (-1,0))\},$$
$$\delta((q_2, \Omega_2), a) = \{(q_2, (-1,0)), (q_3, (0,-1))\},$$
$$\delta((q_3, \Omega_2), a) = \{(q_3, (0,-1)), (q_0, (1,0))\},$$

We shall construct the graph Γ designed by this automaton:

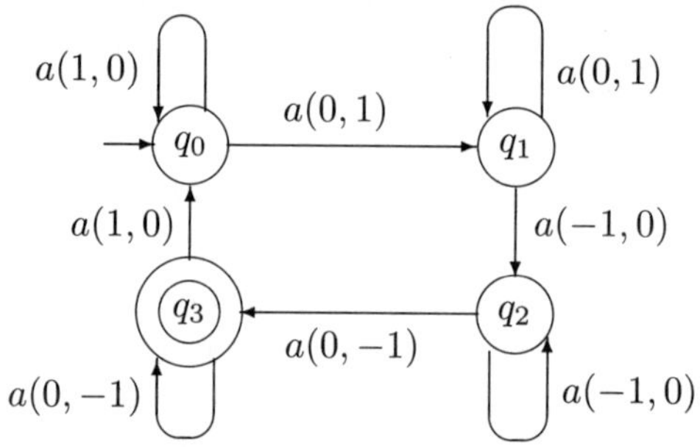

The spreading language is $L = (a^+_{(1,0)} a^+_{(0,1)} a^+_{(-1,0)} a^+_{(0,-1)})^+ \in L$.

Let us select for instance the sentence $w = a_{(1,0)}\ a_{(1,0)}\ a_{(0,1)}\ a_{(-1,0)}\ a_{(0,-1)}\ a_{(0,-1)} \in \overline{L}$.

Thus $k = 6$ and the algorithm will generate:

(1) $v_0 = (0,0)$, $M_0 = \{(0,0)\}$;
(2) $v_1 = (0,0) + (1,0) = (1,0)$, $M_1 = \{(0,0), (1,0)\}$;
(3) $v_2 = (1,0) + (1,0) = (2,0)$, $M_2 = \{(0,0), (1,0), (2,0)\}$;
(4) $v_3 = (2,0) + (0,1) = (2,1)$, $M_3 = \{(0,0), (1,0), (2,0), (2,1)\}$;
(5) $v_4 = (2,1) + (-1,0) = (1,1)$, $M_4 = \{(0,0), (1,0), (2,0), (2,1), (1,1)\}$;
(6) $v_5 = (1,1) + (0,-1) = (1,0)$, $M_5 = \{(0,0), (1,0), (2,0), (2,1), (1,1)\} = M_4$;

Since $i = 5$ and $5 \neq k$, the answer is $w \notin \phi(L)$: if we wish to draw the array of this word in a 2-dimensional grid, the location (1, 0) will appear twice.

But, if we consider the word $w = a_{(1,0)}\ a_{(1,0)}\ a_{(0,1)}\ a_{(-1,0)}\ a_{(0,-1)} \in L$, it will be accepted, because although $M_5 = M_4$, we have $i = k = 5$. The sentence $z \in L$ with $\phi(z) = w$ is $z = (\Omega_2, a)\ ((1,0), a)\ ((2,0), a)\ ((2,1), a)\ ((1,1), a)$ with the array representation shown below:

$$\begin{array}{ccc} \# & a & a \\ a & a & a \end{array}$$

4. Regular Array Languages and Pumping Lemma

Let M be a $n-$dimensional finite array automaton, $L = L(M)$ be the regular array language accepted by M and $\overline{L}$ its spreading language. Since $\overline{L}$ is a regular language and $\phi(L) \subseteq \overline{L}$, we can use the pumping lemma in order to decide whether or not some n-array languages are regular.

Proposition 2:

(1) *The 2-dimensional array language of all hollow rectangles is not regular.*
(2) *The 2-dimensional array language of all hollow squares is not regular.*

Proof: (1) Let L be the 2-dimensional array language of all rectangles. Let us suppose that this is a regular array language and let $\overline{L}$ be its spreading language. Since any rectangle has four sides with opposite sides equal, we have

$$\overline{L} = \{w/w = a^n_{(1,0)} a^m_{(0,1)} a^n_{(-1,0)} a^m_{(0,-1)}, m, n \geq 1\}$$

where $a \in V$ is the symbol used by drawing the rectangles.

But the pumping lemma for regular languages shows that a language of type $\{a^n b^m c^n d^m | m, n \geq 1\}$ is not a regular language[4]; thus $\overline{L}$ is not regular, a contradiction.

(2) If the 2-dimensional language of all squares would be a regular language, the spreading language associated will be

$$\overline{L} = \{w/w = a^n_{(1,0)} a^n_{(0,1)} a^n_{(-1,0)} a^n_{(0,-1)}, n \geq 1\};$$

but a language of type $\{a^n b^n c^n d^n | n \geq 1\}$ is not regular, so $\overline{L}$ cannot be a spreading language, contradiction. □

Remark: It is known[11] that hollow rectangles and hollow squares cannot be generated by regular array grammars although solid rectangles and solid squares can be generated. The Proposition 2 gives a different approach to this question. We have chosen to reduce the decision of finding if a language is not regular, from the $n-$dimensional array languages area to formal regular languages area. This problem arises because the pumping lemma is not easy to be established in array languages.

Let us recall the following lemma (Lemma 4.1[10]):

Lemma 1: *Let R be a regular language over V. Then there is a constant k, depending on R, such that for each $w \in R$ with $|w| \geq k$ there exist x, y, $z \in V^*$ such that $w = xyz$ and:*

(1) $|xy| \leq k$;
(2) $|y| \geq 1$;
(3) $xy^iz \in R$ for all $i \geq 0$.

We suppose that this pumping lemma is true also for $n-$dimensional regular array languages; we try to apply it to the language L generated by the 2-FAA built in Example 6. Let us consider the word w designed by

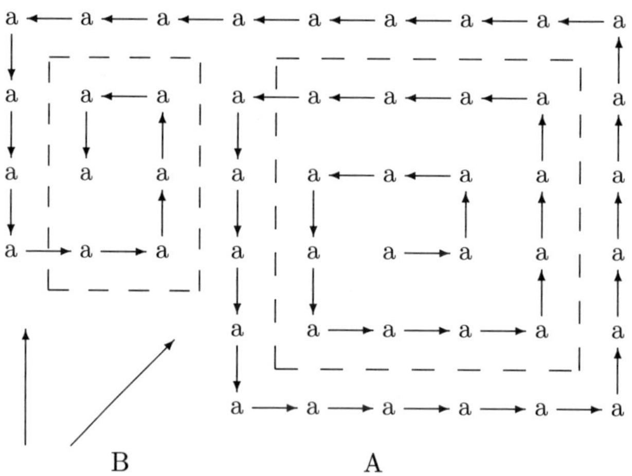

(blank symbols were ignored) where in the zone A there are more than k "a"-s. In the decomposition $w = xyz$, the subword y has to be in the zone A; but here there is no possibility of erasing or of pumping another subwords of $y - s$. If we relax the condition (1) by replacing it by (1) $|y| \leq k$, then we can find the sequence y somewhere outside the zones A and B. In this case the pumping lemma will be true for all assertions, except the case $i = 0$ in

(3): there is no word in L of the form xz, because overlaps will arise in all variants.

5. Control on Regular Array grammars

We examine now the effect of controlling the application of rules of a regular array grammar by prescribed sequences of their applications, constituting a control language. We consider the case $n = 2$ here.

In the two dimensional case the array productions can be depicted in a more simple way as given below:

$$A\# \to aB, \#A \to Ba, \begin{array}{c}\#\\A\end{array} \to \begin{array}{c}B\\a\end{array}, \begin{array}{c}A\\\#\end{array} \to \begin{array}{c}a\\B\end{array}, A \to a\,.$$

The concept of control on the application of the rules in a grammar is standard in the string language theory. The rules of a grammar are given labels and the control word is a sequence of such labels. A derivation in the grammar is obtained from the start symbol by applying the productions corresponding to the labels that occur in order from left to right in a given control word. The terminal words obtained in this way constitute the language generated. The control words themselves constitute a language, called the control language. Here we consider regular, context-free or context-sensitive control languages. We denote a 2-dimensional regular array grammar with control by $G = (2, V_N, V_T, P, \{(v_s, S), \#\}, Lab(P), C)$ where $Lab(P)$ is the set of labels of productions in P and $C \subseteq (Lab(P))^*$ is the control language.

As in string language theory regular control does not increase the generative power of regular array grammars but CF and CS controls do increase.

Proposition 3: *Given a 2-dimensional regular array grammar*

$$G = (2, V_N, V_T, P, \{(v_s, S), \#\}, Lab(P), C) \text{ with control } C\,,$$

the array language generated by G is regular if $C \subseteq (Lab(P))^*$ is a regular string language. But if C is context-free or context-sensitive then the array langauge generated need not be regular.

Proof: When C is regular generated by rules of the forms $X \to fY$, $Z \to g$ where f, g belong to $Lab(P)$ and X, Y, Z are nonterminals in the regular grammar generating C and if f is the label of a rule in G of the form, say, $A\# \to aB$, then we form a regular array rule of the form $(A, X)\# \to$

$a(B, Y)$ (likewise for other types of regular array rules). If g is the label of a rule in G (which will be a terminal rule) of the form $A \to a$, then we form a regular array rule of the form $(A, Z) \to a$. It can be easily seen that the 2-dimensional array language generated by the new regular array productions is the same as the 2-dimensional array language of G. In fact the effect of the control word is taken care of by the second component of the new nonterminals formed.

When C is context-free or context-sensitive, that the generative capacity of G is increased can be seen from the following examples.

We give only the rules of the regular array grammar G_1 and the context-free control language C_1. The rules are

$$f_1 : \#S \to Sa\,, \quad f_2 : \begin{matrix} \# \\ S \end{matrix} \to \begin{matrix} S \\ a \end{matrix}\,, f_3 : S \to a$$

and context-free control language

$$C = \{f_1^{n-1} f_2^{n-1} f_3 / n \geq 1\}\,.$$

G_1 generates arrays over $\{a\}$ which describe "token L" with equal arms of all sizes. For instance, for $n = 5$, the control word is $f_1^4 f_2^4 f_3$. Applying rules with label f_1 four times followed by f_2 four times and finally f_3, we obtain the array as

$$\begin{matrix} a & & & & \\ a & & & & \\ a & & & & \\ a & & & & \\ a & a & a & a & a \end{matrix}$$

It can be seen that these arrays describing token L cannot be generated by a regular array grammar as the "arms" of equal sizes cannot be maintained by regular array grammar rules.

When the rules are the following

$$f_1 : S\# \to aS\,, \quad f_2 : \begin{matrix} \# \\ S \end{matrix} \to \begin{matrix} S \\ a \end{matrix}\,, \qquad f_3 : \#S \to Sa\,,$$

$$f_4 : \begin{matrix} S \\ \# \end{matrix} \to \begin{matrix} a \\ S \end{matrix}\,, \quad f_5 : S \to a$$

and the context-sensitive control language $C = \{f_1^{m-1} f_2^{n-1} f_3^{m-1} f_4^{n-2}$ $f_5 / m, n \geq 1\}$ then the grammar generates arrays over $\{a\}$ which describe hollow rectangles. □

6. Final Remarks

The recognition device proposed here, namely, the $n-$dimensional finite array automaton equivalent to the $n-$dimensional regular array grammar, represents a natural extension of the usual finite automaton and recognizes $[L(n, \text{reg})]$. There are some problems that remain to be solved. For example, each regular language R is spreading a family of $n-$dimensional finite array languages. What are the properties of thus family? It not empty because R is spreading by itself. Is it possible to establish a pumping lemma regarding n-FAA? This will help us to solve some decidability problems (i.e. emptiness, finiteness). It would also be interesting to study the deterministic behavior of n-FAA. For example, we can consider that a n-FAA is non-deterministic if and only if there are p, q, $r \in Q$, $y \in W_0$, $a \in V$ with (p, y), $(r, y) \in \delta((q, \Omega_n), a)$ but $p \neq r$. This type of definition for non-deterministic n-FAA can be eliminated in the same way as we do for usual NFA(see[4]). But, What happens if (p, y), $(r, z) \in \delta((q, \Omega_n), a)$ but $y \neq z$? These questions and other problems regarding $n-$dimensional finite array automata remain to be solved in forthcoming papers.

References

1. H. Fernau, R. Freund and M. Holzer, Character recognition with K-head finite array automata, *SSPR'98, Sydney, Australia*, 1998.
2. H. Fernau, R. Freund and M. Holzer, Regulated array grammars of finite index, Parts I and II: Theoretical investigations in I and Syntactic pattern recognition in II, *In "Grammatical models of multi-agent systems", Gh. Paun, A. Salomaa (Eds.) Gordon and Breach, Reading, UK*, 1998.
3. R. Freund, Control mechanism on # context-free array grammars, *In Gh. Paun (Ed.), Mathematical aspects of Natural and Formal Languages, World Scientific, Singapore*, 97–137, 1994.
4. R. Freund, Array grammars, *XI Tarragona Seminar on Formal Syntax and Semantics, FS and S, Tech. Report 15/00*, 2000.
5. R. Freund, Array Grammar Systems, *Journal of Automata, Languages and Combinatorics 5*, 13–20, 2000.
6. K. S. Fu, Syntactic Methods in Pattern Recognition, *Academic Press, New York*, 1974.
7. M. A. Harrison, Introduction to Formal Language Theory, *Addison Wesley, Reading Cliffs, MA*, 1978.
8. A. Rosenfeld, Picture Languages, *Academic Press, New York*, 1979.
9. A. Rosenfeld and R. Siromoney, Picture Languages — A Survey, *Languages of design 1*, 229–245, 1999.
10. G. Rozenberg and A. Salomaa (Eds.), Handbook of Formal Languages, *Springer-Verlag*, 1997.

11. Y. Yamamoto, K. Morita and K. Sugata, Context-sensitivity of two-dimensional regular array grammars, *In P. S. P. Wang (Ed.) Array Grammars, Patterns and Recognizers, WSP Series in Computer Science, Vol. 18*, 1989.

CHAPTER 2

L-CONVEX POLYOMINOES: A SURVEY

Giusi Castiglione and Antonio Restivo
University of Palermo, Dipartimento di Matematica e Applicazioni,
Via Archirafi 34, 90123 Palermo, Italy
E-mail: {giusi, restivo}@math.unipa.it

In the present paper we give a survey about the family of L-convex polyominoes, recently introduced as the first level in a classification of convex polyominoes. We show their relevance in the fields of study of polyominoes such as, for example, enumeration and discrete tomography.

1. Introduction

A *polyomino*[16] is a finite union of elementary cells (unitary square) of the lattice $\mathbb{Z}^2$. Polyominoes are well-known objects related to a series of problems such as tiling[14,15] and enumeration.[2] Equivalent objects called animals[11,19] are studied in physics, they are obtained by taking the center of the cells of a polyomino. Polyominoes have been investigated also in discrete tomography as particular discrete sets in which each discrete point is represented as a cell (unitary square). Many of the general problems are very difficult to solve and are still open. In order to obtain a simplification several subclasses were defined by combining the geometrical notion of convexity and the more recent notion of directed growth.

In the present paper we will be concerned with polyominoes that satisfy a particular convexity property called L-convexity, recently introduced by the authors.[3] The so called L-convex polyominoes are at the first level of a classification of convex polyominoes presented in the same paper. Successively they have been considered by several points of view with nice results. Here we want to give a survey about L-convex polyominoes showing as they reveals to be relevant in the classical fields of investigation about polyominoes, in particular enumeration and discrete tomography. Furthermore we study the subpicture order defined on the space of matrices over a finite alphabet and its behavior on the subclass of L-convex polyominoes.

2. Definitions and Preliminaries on L-convex Polyominoes

A *discrete set* P is a finite subset of the lattice $\mathbb{Z}^2$ defined up to translation. We denote by $\mathcal{D}$ the class of discrete sets. Let $P \in \mathcal{D}$, and $m \times n$ be the size of the minimal bounding rectangle, so P can be represented as a binary matrix $(P_{ij})_{m \times n}$ such that

$$P_{ij} = \begin{cases} 1 & \text{if } (i,j) \in P \\ 0 & \text{otherwise} \end{cases} .$$

In what follows we denote by (i, j) a generic element of the lattice and by $P(i, j)$ a generic element of P (i.e. such that $P_{ij} = 1$) that we call *cell* of P and we represent by a unitary square. Two cell $P(i, j)$ and $P(i', j')$ are *adjacent* if ($i' = i \pm 1$ and $j' = j$) or ($i' = i$ and $j' = j \pm 1$).

A particular class of discrete sets is the class of *polyominoes*. A *polyomino* is a finite union of elementary cells of the lattice $\mathbb{Z}^2$, whose interior is connected (see Fig. 1(a)). The class of polyominoes is here denoted by $\mathcal{P}$. The most studied parameter about polyominoes are the perimeter (i.e. the length of the border) and the area (i.e. the number of cells).

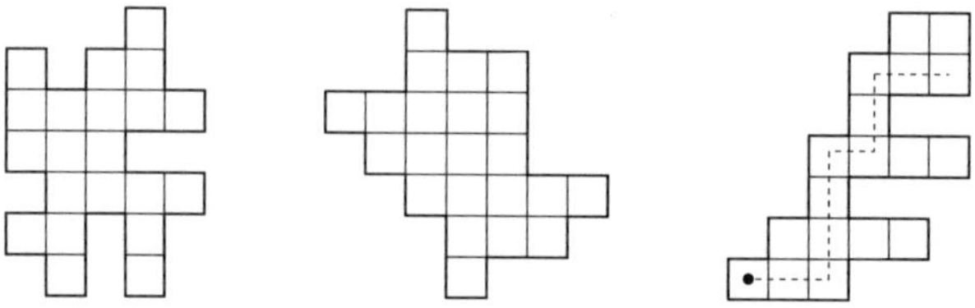

(a) (b) (c)

Fig. 1. (a) a polyomino; (b) a convex polyomino and (c) a directed (not convex) polyomino.

In a polyomino we will define a *path* as a self-avoiding sequence of unitary steps of four types: *north* (0, 1), *south* (0, −1), *east* (1, 0), and *west* (−1, 0). A path connecting two distinct cells A and B, starts from the center of A, and ends in the center of B (see Fig. 2(a)). We say that a path is *monotone* if it is constituted of at most two type of steps (see Fig. 2(b)).

Given a path $w = u_1 \cdots u_k$, each pair of steps $u_i u_{i+1}$ such that $u_i \neq u_{i+1}$, $0 < i < k$, is called a *change of direction.*

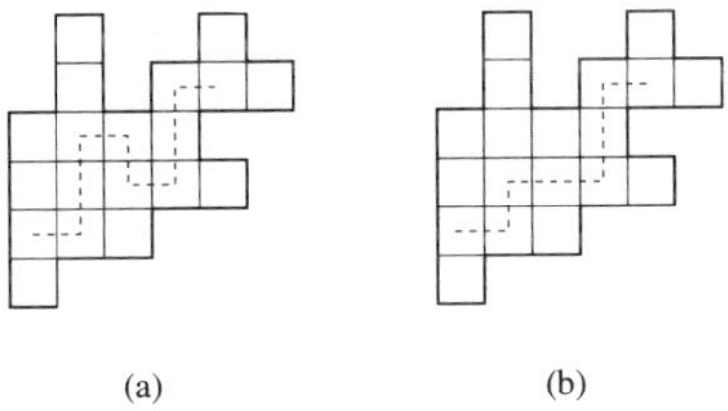

Fig. 2. (a) a path between two cells in polyomino; (b) a monotone path made only of north and east steps.

The most frequently investigated poyominoes are *convex* polyominoes and *directed* polyominoes. A polyomino is said to be *h-convex* (resp. *v-convex*) if every its row (resp. column) is connected. A polyomino is said to be *hv-convex*, or simply *convex*, if it is both h-convex and v-convex (see Fig. 1(b)). We will denote by $\mathcal{C}$ the class of convex polyominoes. A polyomino P is said to be *directed* if there exist a cell called *root* that can be connected to each other cell of P by a path using only north and east steps (see Fig. 1(c)). In Fig. 3(d) a directed and convex polyomino is depicted. Three classical families of directed and convex polyominoes are Ferrer diagrams (see Fig. 3(a)), stack polyominoes (see Fig. 3(b))and parallelogram polyominoes (see Fig. 3(c)). In the class of convex polyominoes they are characterized by the fact that two or three vertices of the minimal bounding rectangle of the polyomino must also belong to the polyomino itself.

The following Proposition 1,[3] states a particular property of convex polyominoes that give rise, in natural manner, to a classification of the elements of $\mathcal{C}$.

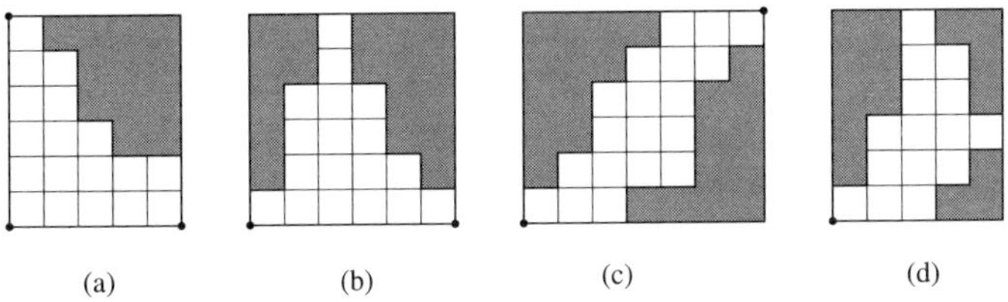

Fig. 3. (a) A Ferrer diagram; (b) a stack polyomino; (c) a parallelogram polyomino and (d) a directed-convex polyomino.

Proposition 1: *A polyomino P is convex iff every pair of cells is connected by a monotone path of cells of P.*

We call *k-convex* a convex polyomino such that every pair of cells can be connected by a monotone path with at most k changes of direction. Figure 4 shows an example of polyomino which is 3-convex, but not 2-convex, since there exist two cells that can be connected only by some paths with at least three changes of direction.

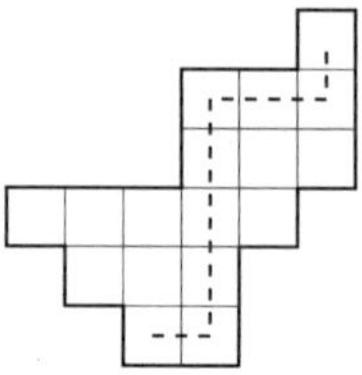

Fig. 4. A 3-convex polyomino.

As a consequence, in the same paper it is proposed a classification of convex polyominoes with respect to maximal number of changes of direction that monotone paths, connecting two cells, must have. At first level of this classification we have *1-convex* polyominoes called *L-convex* polyominoes introduced and studied[3] and that are object of our investigation in this paper.

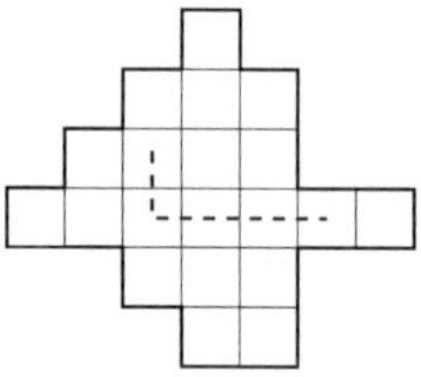

Fig. 5. L-convex Polyomino.

Definition 1: An L-convex polyomino P is a convex polyomino in which every pair of cells is connected by a path, of cells of P, with at most one change of direction, for its shape called *L-path* (see Fig. 5).

We denote by $\mathcal{L}$ the class of L-convex polyominoes. Now, we present the first characterization of L-convex polyominoes that gives an idea of the

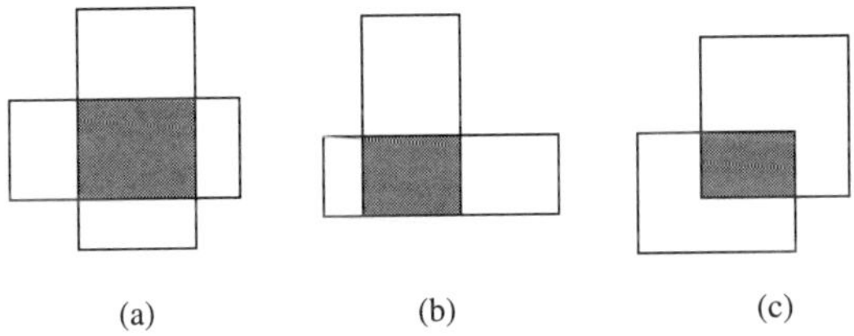

Fig. 6. (a) and (b) are examples of crossing intersection, (c) is not.

structure of these objects. This involves the position of rectangles that we can inscribe in a polyomino.

A *rectangle*, that we denote by $[x, y]$, with $x, y \in \mathbb{N} \setminus \{0\}$, is a rectangular polyomino whose dimensions are x and y (x rows and y columns).

Definition 2: We say $[x, y]$ to be *maximal* in P if

$$\forall [x', y'], \quad [x, y] \subseteq [x', y'] \subseteq P \Rightarrow [x, y] = [x', y'] .$$

Given two occurrences of the rectangles $[x, y]$ and $[x'y']$ in a polyomino P, respectively, we say that they have a *crossing intersection*, if their intersection is a rectangle with basis the smallest of two basis and height the smallest of two heights. See Fig. 6 for an example.

Theorem 1: A convex polyomino P is L-convex iff every pair of its maximal rectangles has a crossing intersection.

From Theorem 1, it immediately follows that each maximal rectangle of a L-convex polyomino P is contained in it only once. The same result allows to characterize a L-convex polyomino as one of the overlapping of its maximal rectangles.

Vice versa, each overlapping of rectangles $[x_1, y_1]$, $[x_2, y_2], \ldots, [x_n, y_n]$ such that

$$x_1 > x_2 > \cdots > x_n \quad \text{and} \quad y_1 < y_2 < \cdots < y_n .$$

with the property that any pair of them has a crossing intersection, determines a L-convex polyomino (see Fig. 7 for an example).

We call *horizontal basis* (resp. *vertical basis*) the maximal rectangle $[x, y]$ such that x (resp. y) is maximal.

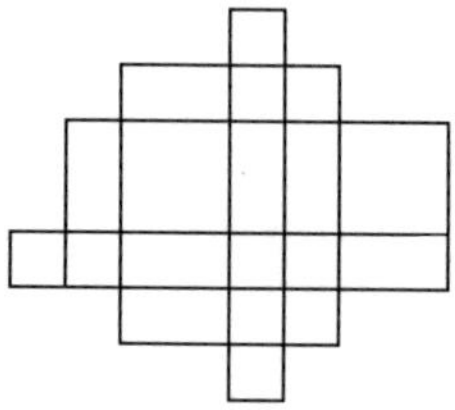

Fig. 7. L-convex polyomino overlapping of four rectangles.

3. Discrete Tomography

To each discrete set P, we can associate two integer vectors $H = (h_1, \ldots, h_m)$ and $V = (v_1, \ldots, v_n)$ such that

$$h_i = \sum_{j=1}^{n} P_{ij} \; \forall \, 1 \leq i \leq m \tag{1}$$

and

$$v_j = \sum_{i=1}^{m} P_{ij} \; \forall \, 1 \leq j \leq n \,. \tag{2}$$

The defined vectors H and V are called the *horizontal* and *vertical projections* of P. Given two vectors H and V, we will indicate with $\mathcal{U}(H, V)$ the class of discrete sets having H and V as projections.

A discrete set P is *unique* (with respect to H and V) if $\mathcal{U}(H, V) = \{P\}$. In that case H and V are said to be *unique* as well.

Let $\mathcal{G}$ be a class of discrete sets. We say that $Q \in \mathcal{G}$ is *determined* by projections (H, V) if $\mathcal{U}(H, V) \cap \mathcal{G} = \{Q\}$.

Fundamental problems of discrete tomography regards uniqueness and reconstruction of discrete sets from their projections. Many authors studied reconstruction problem in the various classes of discrete sets. Ryser[28] proved that in $\mathcal{D}$ the reconstruction problem can be solved in $O(mn)$ time and gave an algorithm of reconstruction. Woeginger[30] posed his attention to the class $\mathcal{P}$ proving that in this class the problem is NP-complete. With regards to class $\mathcal{C}$, the authors[1] gave an algorithm that reconstructs convex polyominoes from (H, V) in polynomial time.

As regards uniqueness, we know that in the general case the knowledge of the horizontal and vertical projections of a discrete set are not sufficient to univocally determine it (see Fig. 8), so a problem of ambiguity is posed.

An operator whose successive application allows to transform an element of $\mathcal{U}(H, V)$ into each other in the same class exists. This operator is based on the concept of *switching component*.[27] A switching component of a discrete set P is a set of four cells (i_1, j_1), (i_1, j_2), (i_2, j_1) and (i_2, j_2) such that:

$$P_{i_1 j_1} = P_{i_2 j_2} = 1 - P_{i_1 j_2} = 1 - P_{i_2 j_1} .$$

Elementary switching operator, or simply *switching*, transforms all the 0's of the switching component in 1's and viceversa.

The following basic result holds:

Theorem 2: (Ryser's Theorem) A discrete set is nonunique (with respect to its horizontal and vertical projections) if and only if it has a switching component.

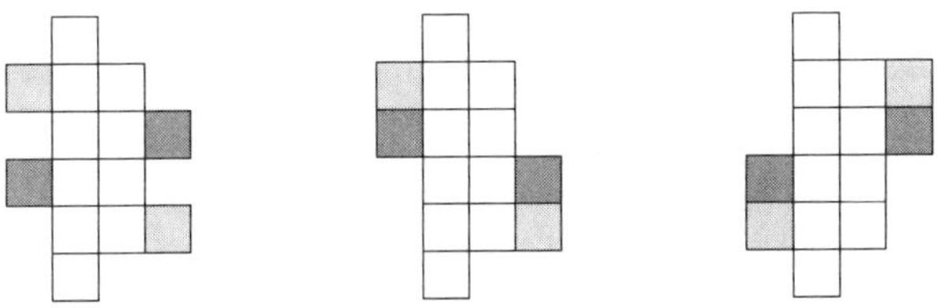

a) *b)* *c)*

Fig. 8. Three polyominoes belonging to the class $\mathcal{U}(H, V)$, with $H = (1, 3, 3, 3, 3, 1)$ and $V = (2, 6, 4, 2)$.

The discrete sets in Fig. 8 have the same projections, furthermore *b*) and *c*) are obtained from *a*) by performing the highlighted switchings.

The problem of reducing ambiguity has been also studied by considering some restriction suh as convexity and directed growth. But, with regards to convex polyominoes the ambiguity can be exponential.[9] However, it is proved[23] that directed h-convex (or v-convex) sets are determined by their orthogonal projections.

3.1. *A characterization theorem for L-convex polyominoes*

We see now what is the role of L-convex polyominoes in this field by reporting some results obtained.[6] There we give a theorem that is both a result of uniqueness in $\mathcal{D}$ and a characterization of L-convex polyominoes.

We can easily convince ourselves that L-convex polyominoes have not any switching components, thus we have the following lemma.

Lemma 1: *A L-convex polyomino P is unique with respect to its horizontal and vertical projections.*

We define an integer vector $X = (x_1, \ldots, x_k)$ to be *unimodal*, if there exists $0 \leq i \leq k$, such that $x_1 \leq x_2 \leq \ldots, \leq x_i$ and $x_i \geq x_{i+1} \geq \cdots \geq x_k$. Hence, we have the principal theorem.

Theorem 3: Let $H \in \mathbb{N}^m$, $V \in \mathbb{N}^n$ be two unimodal vectors.

$$\mathcal{U}(H, V) = \{P\} \Leftrightarrow P \text{ is L-convex polyomino}.$$

As a simple consequence we have:

Remark 1: Let P be a discrete set.

$$P \text{ is convex and unique } \Leftrightarrow P \text{ is a L-convex polyomino}.$$

In this way, we have again a polynomial solution for the reconstruction problem.

3.2. *Extension to measurable plane sets*

All these result can be extended to the continuum by introducing the L-convex plane sets and refering to switching theory in the continuum.[22]

A set P of $\mathbb{R}^2$ is called *h-convex* (resp. *v-convex*) if, for each pair of points (x, y), $(u, v) \in P$, with $y = v$ (resp. $x = u$), the horizontal (resp. vertical) line segment which join them is entirely contained in P. We call *hv-convex* the plane sets that are both h-convex and v-convex.

Furthermore, a *step polygon* is a polygonal curve consisting of horizontal and vertical line segments and having no self-intersections. A step polygon joining two distinct points (x, y), $(u, v) \in \mathbb{R}^2$ can be expressed as a finite sequence of vertices

$$((x, y) = (x_0, y_0), (x_1, y_1), \ldots, (x_k, y_k) = (u, v))$$

such that each vertex is connected by a line segment to the next one. These line segments are the continuum counterpart of the four kinds of steps defined in Section 2 for the discrete lattice, and so they can be classified as north, south, east and west segments as well. A step polygon is called *monotone* if it is composed of at most two different kinds of these segments.

Hence, we have the following natural generalization of Proposition 1 to convex plane sets:

Proposition 2: *A plane set P is convex iff every pair of points in P can be joined by a monotone step polygon lying in P.*

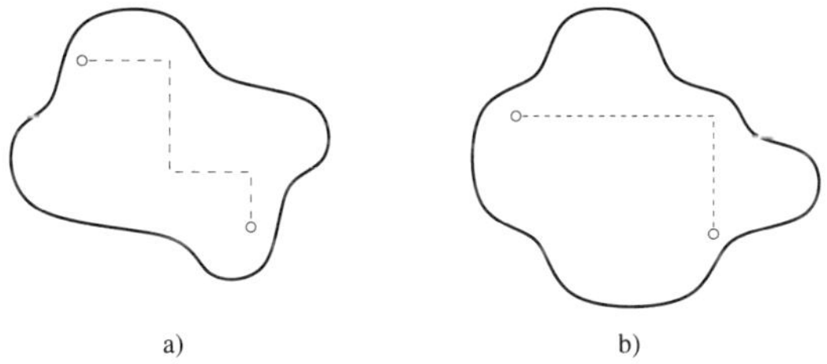

Fig. 9. a) A hv-convex plane set; b) A L-convex plane set.

Now we can finally define a plane set P to be *L-convex* if each pair of its points can be joined by a monotone step polygon with at most three vertices, and entirely contained in P. Figure 9(a) shows a hv-convex plane set and a monotone step polygon lying in it. In Fig. 9(b) a L-convex plane set is depicted with an example of step polygon with three vertices.

It is well known that a function f, defined in the interval $[a, b] \subset \mathbb{R}$, is *unimodal* if there exists $\overline{x} \in [a, b]$ (called *mode*) such that f increases from a to $\overline{x}$ and decreases from $\overline{x}$ to b.

Let $P \subseteq \mathbb{R}^2$ be a measurable set such that $\lambda_2(S) < \infty$ (λ_2 being the two dimensional Lebesgue measure), and let $f(x, y)$ be its characteristic function. Using well known notations and definitions,[22] we call *horizontal projection* of P the function

$$f_x(y) = \int_{-\infty}^{\infty} f(x, y)dx \tag{3}$$

and *vertical projection* of P the function

$$f_y(x) = \int_{-\infty}^{\infty} f(x, y)dy\,. \tag{4}$$

These functions exist almost everywhere on $\mathbb{R}$ and they are integrable (Fubini's theorem).

A notion of switching components in the continuum which is very similar to the one defined for discrete sets, is given.[22] Also in this case the existence of some switching components characterizes non-unique measurable plane sets with finite measure.

Finally, L-convexity of a plane set causes the existence of a mode both in its horizontal and in its vertical projections:

Lemma 2: *If a plane set is L-convex, then both its horizontal and its vertical projections are unimodal.*

As a consequence we can obtain, for the continuous case, the same characterization result as for discrete sets:

Theorem 4: Let f_x and f_y be projection functions defined in $\mathbb{R}^2$ of a plane set S. It holds that

$$\left.\begin{array}{l} f_x \text{ and } f_y \text{ are unimodal} \\ f_x \text{ and } f_y \text{ are unique} \end{array}\right\} \Leftrightarrow S \text{ is L-convex}.$$

We conclude,[22] a different and interesting characterization of unique plane sets is provided. Let S be a measurable plane set of finite measure. The rectangle $X \times Y$ is *measurably inscribed* (briefly m-inscribed) in S if

$$X \times Y \subseteq S \quad \text{and} \quad \overline{X} \times \overline{Y} \subseteq \overline{S}.$$

The set S is *m-inscribable* if it is the union of m-inscribed rectangles. We can immediately argue that the presence of m-inscribed rectangles inside the set S is similar to the presence of maximal rectangles inside an L-convex polyomino.

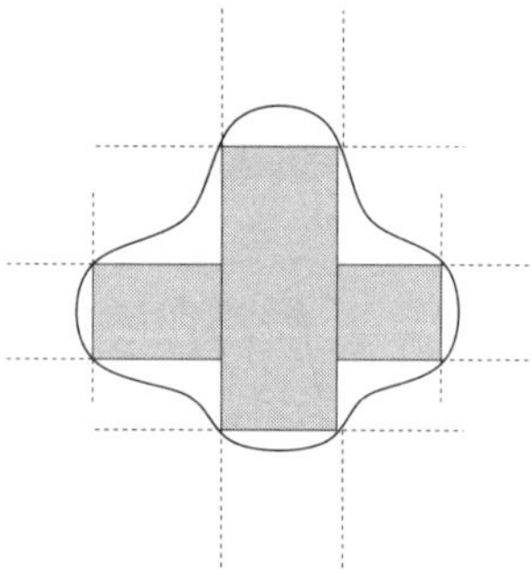

Fig. 10. Two m-inscribed rectangles inside a L-convex plane set.

This idea is strengthened by the fact that in the same paper the following theorem is proved.

Theorem 5: A measurable plane set having finite measure is uniquely determined by its projection functions iff it is m-inscribable.

We want to observe that the notion of crossing intersection in the continuum environment, leads to the equivalence between L-convex plane sets and m-inscribable plane sets. In fact, at the same time, we obtain a nice generalization of theorem Theorem 1 and an uniqueness result.

Theorem 6: Let S a measurable plane set. It holds that S is L-convex iff S is m-inscribable by rectangles with crossing intersection.

4. L-convex Polyominoes with Respect to Subpicture Order

Let $\mathcal{M}$ be the set of matrices (or picture) over a finite alphabet. In Matz[25]) a binary relation on $\mathcal{M}$ is given as follows and is called *subpicture* order.

Definition 3: Let P, $Q \in \mathcal{M}$ such that P has dimension $m \times n$. $P \preceq Q$ (or P is *subpicture* of Q) if there are strictly monotone functions $r : \{1, \ldots, n\} \to \mathbb{N}_{\geq 1}$ and $c : \{1, \ldots, m\} \to \mathbb{N}_{\geq 1}$ such that $P_{ij} = Q_{r(i)c(j)}$ for all $(i, j) \in \{1, \ldots, n\} \times \{1, \ldots, m\}$.

Example 1: P and Q are two matrices over the finite alphabet $\Sigma = \{a, b, c\}$.

$$P = \begin{pmatrix} a & b & c \\ a & b & b \\ c & b & b \end{pmatrix} \quad Q = \begin{pmatrix} a & b & b & c \\ b & b & a & b \\ a & a & b & b \\ c & a & b & b \end{pmatrix}$$

If we consider the strictly monotone functions r, $c : \{1, 2, 3\} \to \{1, 2, 3, 4\}$ such that $r(1) = c(1) = 1$, $r(2) = c(2) = 3$, $r(3) = c(3) = 4$, we have that $P_{ij} = Q_{r(i)c(j)}$, $\forall\ (i, j) \in \{1, 2, 3\} \times \{1, 2, 3, 4\}$, then $P \preceq Q$.

In simple way, we can say that $P \preceq Q$ if P can be obtained from Q by deleting some rows and/or columns. In the previous example P is obtained from Q by deleting the second row and the second column.

In case of binary alphabet we have an order relation between discrete sets and, in particular, polyominoes. With our notation we can, easily, say that if P and Q are two discrete sets such that P has dimension $m \times n$, then $P \leq Q$ if there are strictly monotone functions $r : \{1, \ldots, n\} \to \mathbb{N}_{\geq 1}$ and $c : \{1, \ldots, m\} \to \mathbb{N}_{\geq 1}$ such that $(i, j) \in P \Leftrightarrow (r(i), c(j)) \in Q$, for all $(i, j) \in \{1, \ldots, n\} \times \{1, \ldots, m\}$.

In a previous work[4] we studied the closure properties, with respect to $\preceq$, of the various families of polyominoes here considered. The main theorem (Theorem 7) gives a characterization of L-convex polyominoes in terms of the order $\preceq$: we prove that a polyomino is L-convex iff its down-set is contained in $\mathcal{P}$.

Definition 4: Let us consider the ordering $(\mathcal{D}, \preceq)$ and $\mathcal{S}$ a generic subset of $\mathcal{D}$. $\mathcal{S}$ is a down-set, with respect to $\preceq$, if it satisfies the following condition:

$$if\ S \in \mathcal{S} \quad \text{and} \quad T \preceq S\,, \quad \text{then}\ T \in \mathcal{S}\,.$$

We denote by $Down(\mathcal{S})$ the *down-set* of $\mathcal{S}$ in $(\mathcal{D}, \preceq)$:

$$Down(\mathcal{S}) = \{T \in \mathcal{D} | \ \exists \ S \in \mathcal{S} \text{ such that } T \preceq S\}.$$

If $S = \{P\}$ we denote by $Down(P)$ the down-set of S.

For any $\mathcal{S} \subseteq \mathcal{D}$ we have, in general, that $\mathcal{S} \subseteq Down(\mathcal{S})$ and we have that $\mathcal{S}$ is a down-set if $Down(\mathcal{S}) = \mathcal{S}$.

Our question is whether the families of polyominoes introduced in Section 2 are down-sets of $(\mathcal{D}, \preceq)$.

Figure 11 shows that $\mathcal{C}$ and $\mathcal{P}$ are not down sets of $(\mathcal{D}, \preceq)$. Actually, one can proves that $Down(\mathcal{C}) \cap \mathcal{P} = \mathcal{C}$ that is all the polyominoes that are subpictures of a convex polyomino are convex too.

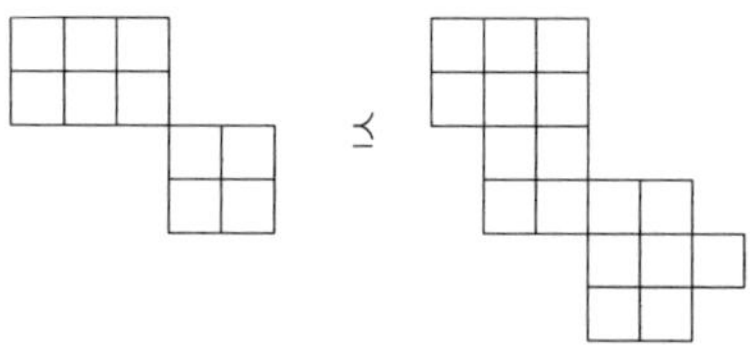

Fig. 11. A discrete set comparable with a convex polyomino.

As regards to L-convex polyominoes we have the following proposition.

Proposition 3: *$\mathcal{L}$ is a down-set of $(\mathcal{D}, \preceq)$, i.e. $Down(\mathcal{L}) = \mathcal{L}$.*

Thus we have another characterization of L-convex polyominoes.

Theorem 7: Let $P \in \mathcal{D}$. P is L-convex if and only if $Down(P) \subseteq \mathcal{P}$.

In the same paper we investigated whether Higman's theorem can be extended to two-dimensional words (matrices). In particular, a negative answer is given for the class of convex polyominoes, with the partial-order here considered. Indeed, we can find out an infinite antichain. However, we proved that the class of L-convex polyominoes is well-ordered. Such a theorem provides a non trivial generalization of Higman's theorem to an important class of bidimensional objectsand shows more and on the interest of the notion of L-convex polyomino.

4.1. *Well-ordering*

We call *antichain* a set of pairwise incomparable elements. A partial-ordering $(\mathcal{A}, \leq)$ is *well partial-ordering* if for every infinite sequence A_1,

A_2, $A_3, \ldots$ of elements of $\mathcal{A}$ there exist integers i, j such that $1 \leq i < j$ such that $A_i \leq A_j$.

There exist many equivalent conditions of well partial-ordering, in particular we have the following theorem.[20]

Theorem 8: Let $(\mathcal{A}, \leq)$ be a quasi-ordering. $(\mathcal{A}, \leq)$ is a well partial-ordering iff every infinite sequence of elements of $\mathcal{A}$ has an infinite ascending subsequence.

A basic theorem in the theory of well partial-ordering is Higman's theorem,[20] which states, in particular, that subword order is a well partial-order in the set of words over a finite alphabet.

Definition 5:[24] Let Σ be a finite alphabet and $u = a_1 \cdots a_n$, $v = b_1 \cdots b_m$ with a_i, $b_j \in \Sigma$ for all i, j. We say that $u \preceq v$ (u is a *subword* of v) iff $\exists\, 1 < k_1 < \cdots < k_n \leq m$ such that $a_i = b_{k_i} \forall\, i$.

Example 2: Let $\Sigma = \{a, b, c\}$. We have that $abcc \preceq abbcaccb$ with $k_1 = 1$, $k_2 = 2$, $k_3 = 4$ and $k_4 = 6$.

Theorem 9: $(\Sigma^*, \preceq)$ is a well partial-ordering.

Higman's theorem has been extended to structures more general than the words as, for instance, labelled trees[21] and infinite words.[13] It is worth noting that there exist many papers devoted to applications of well ordering to formal language theory.[12,8]

Let us note that subpicture order restricted to matrix of size $m \times 1$ is the subword order above defined, for this reason we use the same notation. Furthermore, this observation leads to investigate whether there exists some extension of Higman's theorem to the set of picture. We consider the following hierarchy of partially ordered sets:

$$(\mathcal{L}, \preceq) \subseteq (\mathcal{C}, \preceq) \subseteq (\mathcal{P}, \preceq) \subseteq (\mathcal{D}, \preceq) \subseteq (\mathcal{M}, \preceq)\,.$$

Remark 2: Recall that, if $(X, \leq)$ is a well-ordering and $Y \subseteq X$, then $(Y, \leq)$ is a well-ordering too.

Proposition 4: $(\mathcal{C}, \preceq)$, $(\mathcal{P}, \preceq)$, $(\mathcal{D}, \preceq)$ *and* $(\mathcal{M}, \preceq)$ *are not well-ordering.*

By previous remark, it suffices to prove that $(\mathcal{C}, \leq)$ is not a well-ordering. Let us consider $\{A_n\}_{n \geq 6}$ the infinite family of symmetric square matrices

A_n, of size $n \times n$, with entries $a_n(i,j)$, i, $j \leq n$ defined as follows

$$a_n(i,j) = \begin{cases} 1 & i-1 \leq j \leq i+1 \\ 1 & (i,j) \in \{(1,3),(3,1),(n-2,n),(n,n-2)\} \\ 0 & \text{otherwise} \end{cases} .$$

One can easily proves that this family is an infinite antichain.

The main theorem of the cited work[4] states that:

Theorem 10: $(\mathcal{L}, \preceq)$ is a well-ordering.

5. Enumerating L-Convex Polyominoes

The enumeration of self-avoiding walks on a regular lattice is one of the most famous problems in combinatorics. A closely related problem is the open problem of the enumeration of polyominoes. For some particular types of polyominoes is known the exact formulas with respect to on parameter. Also in this case, polyominoes satisfying convexity properties are largely investigated. It is well known that Delest and Viennot[10] enumerated convex polyominoes with respect to the perimeter by constructing a bijection with words of an algebraic language. This means that generating function for the number of convex polyominoes with fixed perimeter is algebraic.

Theorem 11: The generating function for the numbers p_{2n} of convex polyominoes with perimeter $2n$ is

$$\sum_{n \geq 2} p_{2n} t^{2n} = \frac{t^4(1-6t^2+11t^4-4t^6)}{(1-4t^2)^2} - 4t^8(1-4t^2)^{-3/2} . \quad (5)$$

Enting and Guttmann[17] found the same result. As regards to the enumeration according to the area the problem is more difficult and there exist any asymptotic results[18]. An interesting approach in this sense can be to consider enumeration of k-convex polyominoes. Solution to the problem[5,7] is given for L-convex polyominoes (i.e. k=1) with the nice result of a rational generating function with respect to the semiperimeter. In particular we have the following.

Theorem 12: The generating function for the numbers l_n of L-convex polyominoes with semiperimeter $n+2$ is

$$\sum_{n \geq 2} l_n t^n = \frac{(1-t)^2}{1-4t+2t^2} . \quad (6)$$

Let us denote by L_n the set of L-convex polyominoes having semi-perimeter $n+2$. In a previous paper,[5] using the ECO method, it was proved that the numbers $l_n = |L_n|$ satisfy the recurrence relation:

$$l_{n+2} = 4l_{n+1} - 2l_n \quad (n \geq 1) \tag{7}$$

with $l_0 = 1$, $l_1 = 2$, $l_2 = 7$.

5.1. *L-convex polyominoes, integer partitions and stack polyominoes*

We want to conclude this section by showing some connection between L-convex polyominoes, integer partitions and stack polyominoes. Furthermore, we remark a characteristic of recurrence relations of these combinatorial objects whose combinatorial explanation we are investigating.

As already observed,[26] stack polyominoes, defined in Section 2, can be seen as particular L-convex polyominoes in which any two cells can be connected by an L-path that is chosen from only two orientation of the elle (for example, down and across, or up and across). Furthermore, a representation of L-convex polyominoes as stacks[7] whose rows have two colors is given as follows.

We start from an L-convex polyomino that we consider to be white colored. We give black color to the rows placed below the horizontal basis. Then we vertically translate them above the basis respecting condition that for any fixed length, the black rows precede the white ones having the same length.[7]

Furthermore, every integer partition $\lambda = (p_1, \ldots, p_l)$, with $p_1 \geq p_2 \geq \cdots \geq p_l$, can be represented as a *Ferrer diagram* made of l rows such that the i-th row has p_i cells. In Fig. 3(a) a Ferrer diagram representing the partition (5, 5, 3, 2, 2, 1) is depicted.

The number p_n of Ferrer diagrams having semi-perimeter equal to $n+2$ is easily proved to satisfy the recurrence relation:

$$p_n = 2p_{n-1}\,, \quad n \geq 1\,. \tag{8}$$

The number s_n of stack polyominoes having semi-perimeter equal to $n+2$ satisfies the recurrence relation:

$$s_n = 3s_{n-1} - s_{n-2}\,, \quad n \geq 2\,. \tag{9}$$

The sequence s_n is well known as the *bisection of Fibonacci sequence.*[29]

We have that the number f_n of L-convex polyominoes having semiperimeter $n+2$ satisfies recurrence (7). We can easy observe that recurrence relations (8), (9) and (7) have the form:

$$x_n = (u+2)x_{n-1} - ux_{n-2}\,, \quad n \geq u+1\,, \tag{10}$$

with $u = 0$, 1, 2 respectively. Thus, the question of determining some class of polyominoes for which the recurrence (10) holds with $u = 3$ is natural.

References

1. E. Barcucci, A. Del Lungo, M. Nivat, R. Pinzani: Reconstructing convex polyominoes from horizontal and vertical projections. *Theoret. Comput. Sci.* **155** (1996) 321–347.
2. M. Bousquet-Mèlou: A method for the enumeration of various classes of column-convex polygons. *Dis. Math.* **154** (1996) 1–25.
3. G. Castiglione, A. Restivo: Reconstruction of L-convex Polyominoes. *Electronic Notes in Discrete Mathematics* **12**, Elsevier Science (2003).
4. G. Castiglione, A. Restivo, Ordering and Convex Polyominoes, in M. Margenstern (ed.): Machines, Computations and Universality (MCU 2004), *Lecture Notes in Comp. Sci.* **3354** 128–139.
5. G. Castiglione, A. Frosini, A. Restivo, S. Rinaldi: Enumeration of L-convex Polyominoes, *Theor. Comput. Sci.* **347**(1–2) (2005) 336–352.
6. G. Castiglione, A. Frosini, A. Restivo, S. Rinaldi, A Tomographical Characterization of L-convex Polyominoes, (DGCI 2005), *Lecture Notes in Comp. Sci.* **3429** (2005) 115–125.
7. G. Castiglione, A. Frosini, E. Munarini A. Restivo, S. Rinaldi: Enumeration of L-convex Polyominoes, II. Bijection and area, FPSAC 2005, Taormina, June 20–25, 2005.
8. D'Alessandro, F., Varricchio, S.: Well quasi-orders on languages. *Lecture Notes in Comp. Sci.* **2710** (2003) 230–241.
9. A. Del Lungo, M. Nivat, R. Pinzani: The number of convex polyominoes reconstructible from their orthogonal projections. *Discrete Math.* **157** (1996) 65–78.
10. M. P. Delest, G. Viennot: Algebraic languages and polyominoes enumeration. *Theoret. Comput. Sci.* **34** (1984) 169–206 North-Holland.
11. D. Dhar: Equivalence of two-dimensional directed animal problem to a one-dimensional path problem. *Adv. in Appl. Math.* **9** (1988) 959–962.
12. A. Ehrenfencht, D. Haussler, G. Rozenberg: On regularity of context-free languages. *Theoret. Comput. Sci.* **27** (1983) 311–332.
13. A. Finkel: Une Généralisation des théorèmes de Higman et de Simon aux Mots Infinis. *Theoret. Comput. Sci.* **38** (1985) 137–142.
14. D. Girault-Beauquier, M. Nivat: Tiling the plane with one tile, Proceedings of the sixth annual symposium on Computational geometry, Berkley, California, United States june 07-09, 1990.

15. S. W. Golomb: Polyominoes: Puzzles, Patterns, Problems and Packing, Princeton Academic Press, 1996.
16. S. W. Golomb: Polyominoes. Scribner, New York (1965).
17. A. J. Guttmann, I. G. Enting: The number of convex polygons on the square and honeycomb lattices. *J. Phys. A: Math. Gen.* **21** (1988) 464–474.
18. A. J. Guttmann: On the number of lattice animals embedable in the square lattice. *J. Phys. A: Math. Gen.* **15** (1982) 1987–1990.
19. V. Hakim, J. P. Nadal: Exact result for 2D directed lattice animals on a strip of finite width, *J. Phys. A: Math. Gen.* **16** (1983) L213–L218.
20. G. H. Higman: Ordering by divisibility in abstract algebra. Proc. London Math. Soc. **2** (1952) 326–336.
21. J. B. Kruskal: Well-quasi-ordering, the Tree Theorem, and Vazsonyi's conjecture. *Trans. Amer. Math. Soc.* **95** (1960) 210–225.
22. A. Kuba, A. Volčič: Characterization of measurable plane sets which are reconstructable from their two projections, *Inverse Problems*, **4**, (1988) 513–527.
23. A. Kuba, E. Balogh: Reconstruction of convex 2D discrete sets in polynomial time, *Theoret. Comput. Sci.* **283** (2002) 223–242.
24. M. Lothaire: Combinatorics on Words. Encyclopedia of Mathematics and its Applications, **17**, Addison-Wesley, Reading, MA, (1983)
25. O. Matz: On piecewise testable, starfree, and recognizable picture languages.Foundations of Software Science and Computation Structures **1378**(1998).
26. S. Rinaldi, D. G. Rogers: How the odd terms in the Fibonacci sequence stack up, *Math. Gaz.*, to appear.
27. H. J. Ryser: Combinatorial properties of matrices of zeros and ones, *Canad. J. Math.*, **9** (1957) 371-377.
28. H. J. Ryser: Combinatorial Mathematics. The Carus Mathematical Monographs Vol.14 (The Mathematical Association of America, Rahway, 1963).
29. N. J. A. Sloane: The On-Line Encyclopedia of Integer Sequences, published electronically at *http://uuu.research.att.com/~ njas/sequences/*.
30. G. J., Woeginger: The Reconstruction of Polyominoes from their Orthogonal Projections (1996) Preprint.

CHAPTER 3

ON ORIENTED LABELLING PARAMETERS

Daniel Gonçalves, André Raspaud and M. A. Shalu*

LaBRI UMR CNRS 5800, Université Bordeaux I,
33405 Talence Cedex, France
E-mail: raspaud@labri.fr

We introduce two notions, (i) $L(p,q)$ labelling for oriented graphs and (ii) oriented $L(p,q)$ labelling, to explore frequency assignment problem under half-duplex setting and compute bounds of oriented labelling of special classes of graphs: trees, bipartite graphs and planar graphs. Moreover we prove that the span of the $L(p,1)$ labelling for oriented graphs is bounded by $\left\lfloor \frac{\Delta^2}{2} \right\rfloor + p\Delta$.

1. Introduction

The frequency assignment problem (FAP) arises in wireless communication systems. There are several models based on genetic algorithms, neural networks, constrained programming and combinatorial enumeration to explore and optimize different features of FAP such as available frequencies and limiting interference among radio signals. In 1970, Metzger[15] introduced graph coloring techniques as a tool to optimize the frequency spectrum used in FAP. Motivated by FAP, Hale[11] developed the concept of T-coloring and it lead to many indepth graph theoretical results. A common feature of all these graph theoretical models of FAP is that they assume communication is viable in both direction (duplex) between two radio trasmitters and hence model FAP as a non-oriented graph. This is far away from reality. In fact, Aardal et al emphasised the importance of "direction/orientation" of transmission in their recent survey (for details see Ref. 1 page 4) on FAP.

*This work has been done during a visit of the third author at LaBRI. This visit was sponsored by the french ministry of education and research.

In this paper, we explore FAP under half-duplex setting (i.e., there are radio transimitters in a network in which at most one way transimission is effective between any two of them). Hence FAP can be modeled as an oriented multi graph. As a preliminary step, we focus on oriented simple graphs.

2. Oriented Vertex Partitioning Problems

The partitioning of the vertex set of a non-oriented graph into minimum number of subsets in which each subset possesses a special property is a fundamental graph theory problem with many applications. For example: vertex coloring, star (vertex) coloring and clique cover problem. We suggest a general frame work to incorporate "orientation" into various vertex partitioning problems. Two subsets A, B of the vertex set of an oriented graph is called *one way oriented* if all edges with one end vertex in A and other in B are oriented from A (respectively B) to B (respectively A).

Oriented vertex partitioning problem: Partition the vertex set of an oriented graph into minimum number of pairwise one way oriented subsets in which each set possesses a special property.

Oriented coloring is a well known oriented vertex partitioning problem.[17,18]

3. Notation and Terminology

In this paper, we consider only finite (oriented and non-oriented) simple graphs. As usual, $N^+(v) = \{u : \overrightarrow{vu} \in E(\vec{G})\}$ and $N^-(v) = \{u : \overrightarrow{uv} \in E(\vec{G})\}$. A proper k-coloring of the vertices of a non-oriented graph G is an assignement f of integers (or labels), using at most k colors (or labels), to the vertices of G such that $f(u) \neq f(v)$ if the vertices u en v are adjacent in G. The chromatic number of a graph G is the smallest integer k such that G has a proper k-coloring. A proper k-coloring of the vertices of a non-oriented graph is called *acyclic* if the subgraph induced by the vertices of any two color classes has no cycle. The acyclic chromatic number of a graph G is the smallest integer k such that G has an acyclic k-coloring. We will say that a graph G is k-acyclic if its acyclic chromatic number is at most k. The length of the shortest path joining two vertices x, y in a non-oriented graph is called distance between x and y. A path with an orientation such that all internal vertices have both in-degree and out-degree one is called an *oriented path*. The length of a shortest oriented path joining two vertices x, y in an oriented graph is called *oriented distance* between x and y. The *girth* of a non-oriented graph G is the length of its smallest cycle. Let $\vec{G} = (V, A)$ and $\vec{H} = (U, B)$ be two oriented graphs. A homomorphism from $\vec{G}$ to $\vec{H}$ is a map $f : V \longrightarrow U$ which preserves adjacency, that is for any arc $\overrightarrow{xy} \in A$, the corresponding arc $\overrightarrow{f(x)f(y)} \in B$.

Oriented coloring[17,18]: Let $\vec{G} = (V, A)$ be an oriented graph. A map $c : V \longrightarrow \{1, 2, \ldots, k\}$ is called a k-oriented coloring of $\vec{G}$ if it satisfies the following conditions:

(i) For any edge of $\vec{G}$, $\overrightarrow{xy}$, $c(x) \neq c(y)$.
(ii) There are no two edges of $\vec{G}$, $\overrightarrow{xy}$, $\overrightarrow{uv}$ such that $c(x) = c(v)$ and $c(y) = c(u)$.

The least integer k in which $\vec{G}$ has k-oriented coloring is called the oriented chromatic number $\vec{\chi}(\vec{G})$ of $\vec{G}$. The *oriented chromatic number* $\vec{\chi}(G)$ of a non-oriented graph G is defined as max $\{\vec{\chi}(\vec{G}) : \vec{G}$ is an orientation of $G\}$.

Note that the condition (i) of oriented coloring ensures that adjacent vertices do not belong to same color class. The condition (ii) guarantees that any two color classes preserve one way oriented property in an oriented graph. Moreover, $\chi(G) \leq \vec{\chi}(G)$ where $\chi(G)$ denotes the chromatic number of G. Since $\vec{\chi}(K_{n,n}) = 2n$, $\vec{\chi}(G)$ has no upper bound as a function of $\chi(G)$. Raspaud and Sopena[18] proved that the oriented chromatic number of a planar graph is at most 80.

A suggestion of Roberts to distinguish close and very close transmitters in a wireless communication system led Griggs and Yeh[10] to propose a variation of FAP as labelling the vertices of a non-oriented graph with a condition at a distance two (known as $L(2, 1)$-labelling). Georges and Mauro[8] generalized this as follows:

$L(p, q)$-Labelling: Let $G = (V, E)$ be a non-oriented graph and p, q be two positive integers. A map $L : V \longrightarrow \{0, 1, \ldots, k\}$ is called a k-$L(p, q)$-labelling if it satisfies the following.

(i) For any edge $xy \in E$, $|L(x) - L(y)| \geq p$.
(ii) For any pair of vertices x, y at a distance 2, $|L(x) - L(y)| \geq q$.

The *span*, $\lambda_{p,q}(G)$, of G is defined as min $\{k : G$ has a k-$L(p, q)$-labelling$\}$. For convenience, we prefer $\lambda_p(G)$ to $\lambda_{p,1}(G)$.

We cite a few known results in $L(p, q)$-labelling problems.

(1) $L(2, 1)$-labelling problem is NP-complete.[10]
(2) For a tree T with maximum degree Δ, $\Delta + 1 \leq \lambda_2(T) \leq \Delta + 2$.[10]

(3) For a graph G with maximum degree Δ, $\lambda_p(G) \leq \Delta^2 + (p-1)\Delta - 2$.[9]

4. Two Oriented Variations of $L(p,q)$-Labelling

In this section, we extend $L(p,q)$-labelling to oriented graphs and propose a new oriented vertex partitioning problem.

$L(p,q)$-Labelling for oriented graphs: Let $\vec{G} = (V, A)$ be an oriented graph and p, q be two positive integers. A map $L : V \longrightarrow \{0, 1, \ldots, k\}$ is called a k-$L(p,q)$-labelling of $\vec{G}$ if it satisfies the following.

(i) For any edge $\vec{xy} \in A$, $|L(x) - L(y)| \geq p$.
(ii) For any pair of vertices x, y at an oriented distance 2, $|L(x) - L(y)| \geq q$.

The *span*, $\lambda^o_{p,q}(\vec{G})$, of $\vec{G}$ is defined as min $\{k : \vec{G}$ has a k-$L(p,q)$-labelling$\}$. The *span* of a non-oriented graph G, $\lambda^o_{p,q}(G)$, is defined as max $\{\lambda^o_{p,q}(\vec{G}) : \vec{G}$ is an orientation of $G\}$. For convenience (when $q = 1$), we denote $\lambda^o_{p,1}(G) = \lambda^o_p(G)$.

This notion is already studied by Chang *et al.*[6] They give interesting bounds for the span of oriented graphs with a specified longest dipath length.

Oriented $L(p,q)$-Labelling: Let $\vec{G} = (V, A)$ be an oriented graph and p be a positive integer. A map $l : V \longrightarrow \{0, 1, \ldots, k\}$ is called a k-oriented $L(p,q)$-labelling if it satisfies the following.

(i) For any edge $\vec{xy} \in A$, $|l(x) - l(y)| \geq p$.
(ii) For any pair of vertices x, y at an oriented distance 2, $|l(x) - l(y)| \geq q$.
(iii) There are no two edges $\vec{xy}$, $\vec{uv}$ such that $l(x) = l(v)$ and $l(y) = l(u)$.

The *span*, $\vec{\lambda}_{p,q}(\vec{G})$, of $\vec{G}$ is defined as min $\{k : \vec{G}$ has a k-oriented $L(p,q)$-labelling$\}$. The *span* of a non-oriented graph G, $\vec{\lambda}_{p,q}(G)$, is defined as max $\{\vec{\lambda}_{p,q}(\vec{G}) : \vec{G}$ is an orientation of $G\}$. For convenience (when $q = 1$), we denote $\vec{\lambda}_{p,1}(G) = \vec{\lambda}_p(G)$.

Remarks: There is a distinction between the $L(p,q)$-labelling of oriented graphs and the oriented $L(p,q)$-labelling. Note that any two oriented $L(p,q)$-labelling color classes (i.e. set of vertices with same label) are one way oriented. But $L(p,q)$-labelling doesn't guarantee one way orientedness of its color classes. A pair of color classes in a $L(p,q)$-labelling can be viewed as a union of two (disconnected) pairs of one way oriented sets (see Fig. 1). Hence, an oriented $L(p,q)$-labelling of an oriented graph $\vec{G}$ is also a $L(p,q)$-labelling of $\vec{G}$. The graph $\vec{H}$ in Fig. 1, with $\lambda^o_1(\vec{H}) = 3$ and $\vec{\lambda}_1(\vec{H}) = 4$, shows that the converse is not true.

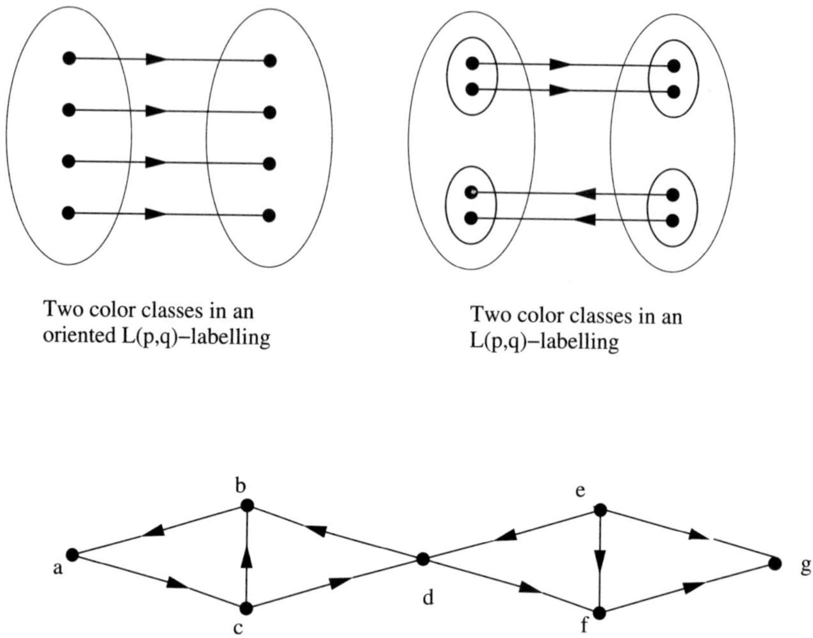

Fig. 1. Oriented color classes and the graph $\vec{H}$.

Let H be a subgraph of G. Then $\vec{\lambda}_p(H) \leq \vec{\lambda}_p(G)$. Oriented $L(p,q)$-labelling is a generalization of oriented coloring. In particular, $\vec{\lambda}_1(\vec{G}) = \vec{\chi}(\vec{G}) - 1$ (we do allow '0' as a label). Let $I_0, I_1, \ldots, I_{\vec{\chi}-1}$ be a set of oriented color classes of $\vec{G}$. We produce a $(\vec{\chi}(\vec{G})-1)p$-oriented $L(p,p)$-labelling of $\vec{G}$ by assigning the label jp to each vertex in the set I_j for $0 \leq j \leq \vec{\chi}(\vec{G}) - 1$. It is easy to see that if there is a homomophism $h : \vec{G} \rightarrow \vec{H}$, then $\vec{\lambda}_{p,q}(\vec{G}) \leq \vec{\lambda}_{p,q}(\vec{H})$. Indeed, given a k-oriented $L(p,q)$-labelling l_H of $\vec{H}$, we define a k-oriented $L(p,q)$-labelling l_G of $\vec{G}$, by $l_G(v) = l_H(h(v))$, for all $v \in V_G$. We also note that a $L(p,q)$-labelling of a non-oriented graph G is a $L(p,q)$-labelling of any orientation of G. By definition, an oriented $L(p,q)$-labelling of an oriented graph is also its $L(p,1)$-labelling. These remarks prove the following lemma.

Lemma 1: *Let G be a non-oriented graph. Then*

(i) *For $p \geq q > 0$, $\vec{\chi}(G) - 1 \leq \vec{\lambda}_{p,q}(G) \leq (\vec{\chi}(G) - 1)p$.*
(ii) $\lambda^o_{p,q}(G) \leq \lambda_{p,q}(G)$.
(iii) $\lambda^o_{p,q}(G) \leq \vec{\lambda}_{p,q}(G)$.

There is no trivial relation between $\lambda_{p,q}$ and $\vec{\lambda}_{p,q}$. Indeed, the graphs H_1 and H_2 depicted in Fig. 2 are such that $\lambda_{p,q}(H_1) < \vec{\lambda}_{p,q}(H_1)$ and $\lambda_{p,q}(H_2) > \vec{\lambda}_{p,q}(H_2)$.

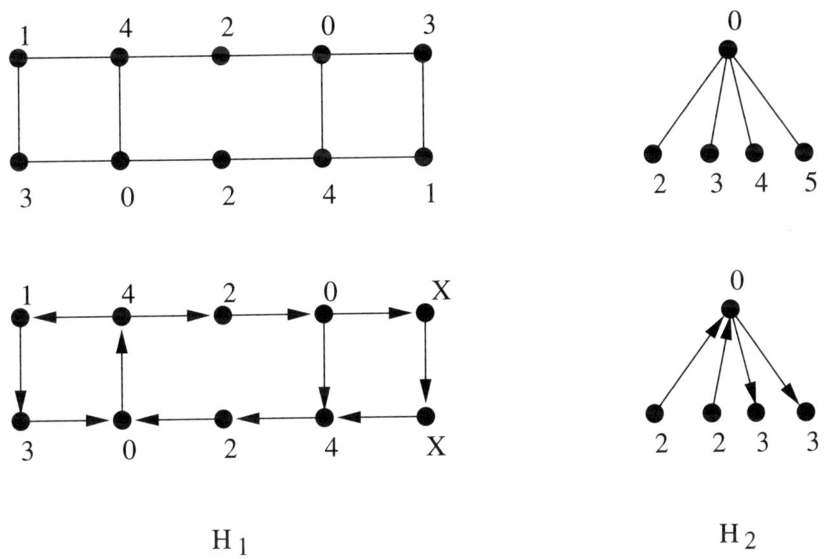

Fig. 2. The graphs H_1 and H_2.

For a compelete graph K_n, $\vec{\lambda}_p(K_n) = (\vec{\chi}(K_n) - 1)p$. Moreover, $\vec{\lambda}_2(C_5) = 4 = \vec{\chi}(C_5) - 1$. Though the bounds in the Lemma 1 (i) is tight for certain graphs, we could significantly improve this result for the class of trees.

5. Oriented $L(p,q)$-Labelling for Trees

A *star*, S, is a tree with a special vertex x and all other vertices of S are adjacent to x. A *double star*, D, is a tree with a special pair of adjacent vertices x, y and all other vertices of D are adjacent to either x or y (see Fig. 3).

We denote P_k the paths with k vertices. Any tree $T \neq K_1$, K_2 has a P_3 as a subgraph. A tree T ($\neq K_1, K_2$) with no P_5 as a subgraph is either a star or a double star. The minimal span for the oriented $L(p,q)$-labelling of an unoriented tree T is easily computable with the following theorem.

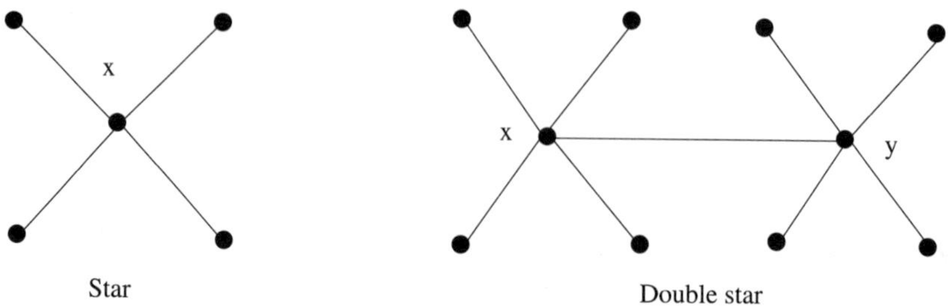

Fig. 3. Star and Double Star.

Theorem 1: Let T be an unoriented tree. Then

$$\vec{\lambda}_{p,q}(T) = \begin{cases} 0 & \text{if } T = K_1\,, \\ p & \text{if } T = K_2\,, \\ p+q & \text{if } T \text{ is a star or a double star}\,, \\ p+2q & \text{else (i.e. } P_5 \text{ is a subgraph of } T)\,. \end{cases}$$

The two first cases are trivial. We begin by proving that in the two last cases the span cannot be decreased. Since $\vec{\lambda}_{p,q}(H) \leq \vec{\lambda}_{p,q}(G)$ if H is a subgraph of G, we just have to note that $\vec{\lambda}_{p,q}(P_3) = p+q$ and $\vec{\lambda}_{p,q}(P_5) = p+2q$. Now we show how to label the trees.

Case 1: Let T be a star with a special vertex x. We construct an oriented $L(p,q)$-labelling of $\vec{T}$ by assigning 0 to the special vertex x, p to all vertices of $N^+_{\vec{H}}(x)$, and $p+q$ to all vertices of $N^-_{\vec{H}}(x)$.

Case 2: Let T be a double star with special vertices x, y. Without loss of generality, assume that $\vec{xy} \in E(\vec{H})$. We construct an oriented $L(p,q)$-labelling of $\vec{H}$ by assigning 0 to all vertices of $N^-_{\vec{H}}(y)$, q to all vertices of $N^+_{\vec{H}}(y)$, p to all vertices of $N^-_{\vec{H}}(x)$, and $p+q$ to all vertices of $N^+_{\vec{H}}(x)$.

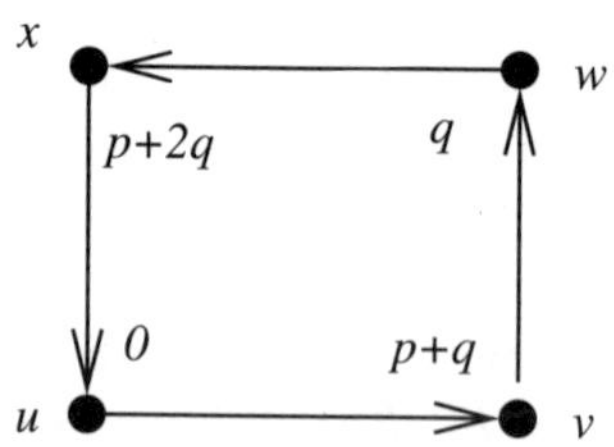

Fig. 4. The graph $\vec{C_4}$.

Case 3: Let $\vec{T}$ be an orientation of T. To prove the upperbound, we construct a homomorphism $f : \vec{T} \longrightarrow \vec{C_4}$. In Fig. 4, u, v, w, and w are vertices of $\vec{C_4}$ and 0, $p+q$, q, $p+2q$ are their respective labels in a $p+2q$-oriented $L(p,q)$-labelling of $\vec{C_4}$. First, we pick an arbitaray vertex a of $\vec{T}$ and map a to u (i.e., $f(a) = u$). Then, we map the vertices of $N^+_{\vec{T}}(a)$ (respectively $N^-_{\vec{T}}(a)$) into $N^+_{\vec{C_4}}(u) = \{v\}$ (respectively $N^-_{\vec{C_4}}(u) = \{x\}$). We continue this process until all vertices of $\vec{T}$ are mapped into $V(\vec{C_4})$.

6. Oriented $L(p,1)$-Labelling of Bipartite Graphs

Lemma 2: *For a complete bipartite graph* $K_{m,n}$ $(m, n \geq 1)$, $\vec{\lambda_p}(K_{m,n}) \leq m+n+p-2$.

Proof: Let $V(K_{m,n}) = A \cup B$ where $A = \{u_1, u_2, \ldots, u_m\}$ and $B = \{v_1, v_2, \ldots, v_n\}$. We construct an oriented $(m+n+p-2)$-labelling of an arbitrary orientation of $K_{m,n}$ by a function $l : V(K_{m,n}) \longrightarrow \{0, 1, \ldots, m+n+p-2\}$ defined as $l(u_i) = i-1$ for $1 \leq i \leq m$ and $l(v_j) = m+j+p-2$ for $1 \leq j \leq n$. Hence $\vec{\lambda_p}(K_{m,n}) \leq m+n+p-2$. □

It is not hard to show that the upper bound in the Lemma is tight if $m = n$, i.e., $\vec{\lambda_p}(K_{n,n}) = 2n+p-2$. Note that every bipartite graph is a subgraph of a complete bipartite graph. Hence, for a bipartite graph G, $\vec{\lambda_p}(G) \leq |V(G)| + p - 2$.

7. Oriented $L(p,1)$-Labelling and the Acyclic Chromatic Number

In this section, we supply an upperbound of $\vec{\lambda_p}$ of planar graphs based on a method developed by Alon, Marshall, Nesetril, Raspaud and Sopena.[2,16,18] In fact, they found a homorphism from any oriented k-acyclic graph to a special graph, $\vec{M_k}$.

Special graph $\vec{M_k}$: Let $\vec{M_k}$ be an oriented graph with vertex set $V(M_k) = \{(i, a_1, a_2, \ldots, a_{i-1}, a_{i+1}, \ldots, a_k) : 1 \leq i \leq k \text{ and } a_j \in \{0,1\}\}$. The edge set of $\vec{M_k}$ is defined as follows. Let $x = (i, a_1, a_2, \ldots, a_{i-1}, a_{i+1}, \ldots, a_k)$ and $y = (l, b_1, b_2, \ldots, b_{l-1}, b_{l+1}, \ldots, b_k)$, $1 \leq i < l \leq k$, be two vertices. Then (i) $\vec{xy} \in E(\vec{M_k})$ if $\overrightarrow{a_l b_i} \in E(\vec{T})$ and (ii) $\vec{yx} \in E(\vec{M_k})$ if $\overrightarrow{b_i a_l} \in E(\vec{T})$ (see Fig. 5 for $\vec{T}$).

Theorem 2:[16] Let $\vec{G}$ be an orientation of a k-acyclic graph G. Then there exists a homomorphism from $\vec{G}$ to $\vec{M_k}$.

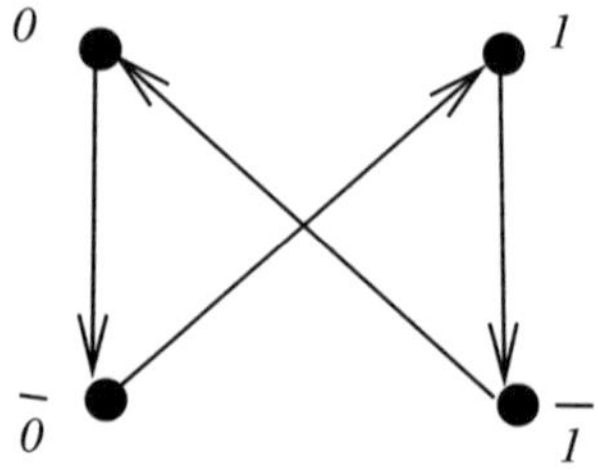

Fig. 5. The graph $\vec{T}$.

Lemma 3: $\vec{\lambda}_p(\vec{M}_k) \leq k(2^{k-1}-1)+p(k-1)$.

Proof: Let $V(\vec{M}_k) = \cup_{i=1}^{k} V_i$, where $V_i = \{(i, a_1, a_2, \ldots, a_{i-1}, a_{i+1}, \ldots, a_k) : a_j \in \{0,1\}\}$. Note that $|V_i| = 2^{k-1}$. Then we re-label the vertices of V_i as $\{v_{i,j} : 1 \leq j \leq 2^{k-1}\}$, $1 \leq i \leq k$. Now, it is easy to see that the map $f : V(\vec{M}_k) \longrightarrow \{0, 1, \ldots, k2^{k-1} + (k-1)(p-1) - 1\}$ such that $f(v_{i,j}) = (i-1)(2^{k-1}+p-1)+j-1, 1 \leq i \leq k$ and $1 \leq j \leq 2^{k-1}$, is an oriented $L(p,1)$-labelling of $\vec{M}_k$. Indeed, f is an oriented labelling (coloring), it follows that vertices at distance 2 have different colors, moreover if u and v are adjacent vertices we have $|f(u) - f(v)| \geq p$. Hence $\vec{\lambda}_p(\vec{M}_k) \leq k(2^{k-1}-1)+p(k-1)$ □

Theorem 3: Let G be a k-acyclic graph. Then $\vec{\lambda}_p(G) \leq k(2^{k-1}-1) + p(k-1)$.

Proof: Let $\vec{G}$ be an orientation of G. By Theorem 2, there exists a homomorphism from $\vec{G}$ to $\vec{M}_k$. Then $\vec{\lambda}_p(\vec{G}) \leq \vec{\lambda}_p(\vec{M}_k)$. Since $\vec{G}$ is an arbitrary orientation of G, $\vec{\lambda}_p(G) \leq \vec{\lambda}_p(\vec{M}_k)$. By Lemma 3, $\vec{\lambda}_p(G) \leq k(2^{k-1}-1)+p(k-1)$. □

A well-known result of Borodin[3] states that any planar graph is 5-acyclic colorable. In Ref. 5, the authors proved that planar graphs with girth at least 5 (resp. 7) are 4-acyclic colorable (resp. 3-acyclic colorable). Moreover it is well known that graphs with treewidth k are $(k+1)$-acyclic colorable. So we have the following corollary.

Corollary 1: *If G is a planar graph, then $\vec{\lambda}_p(G) \leq 75 + 4p$.*
If G is a planar graph with girth at least 5, then $\vec{\lambda}_p(G) \leq 28 + 3p$.
If G is a planar graph with girth at least 7, then $\vec{\lambda}_p(G) \leq 9 + 2p$.
If G is a graph with treewidth k, then $\vec{\lambda}_p(G) \leq (k+1)(2^k - 1) + pk$.

8. $L(p, q)$-Labelling of Oriented Graphs

In Ref. 10, the authors conjectured that for an unoriented graph G, $\lambda_{2,1}(G) \leq \Delta^2$, where Δ is the maximum degree of G. Much work[7,14,9] have been done on bounding $\lambda_{p,q}$ by a function of Δ. Here, we prove a similar result for oriented graphs.

Theorem 4: For every directed graph $G = (V, A)$ with maximal degree Δ, $\lambda^o_{p,1}(G) \leq \left\lfloor \frac{\Delta^2}{2} \right\rfloor + p\Delta$.

In a directed graph $G = (V, A)$, u is a 2-*neighbor* of v if there is a directed 2-path between u and v. Given a directed graph $G = (V, A)$, its 2-*paths graph* $G^2 = (V, E)$ is an unoritented graph with the same vertex set. There is an edge uv in this graph if and only if there is a directed 2-path in G linking u and v. The next lemma gives an interesting property of these graphs.

Lemma 4: *For every directed graph $G = (V, A)$ with maximal degree Δ, its 2-paths graph $G^2 = (V, E)$ is $\left\lfloor \frac{\Delta^2}{2} \right\rfloor$-degenerate.*

Proof: We prove that for any $S \subseteq V$, the induced graph $G^2[S]$ has minimal degree at most $\left\lfloor \frac{\Delta^2}{2} \right\rfloor$. We do so, using a discharging method.

Let the initial charge $\gamma(v)$ of the vertices be $\frac{\Delta^2}{2}$ if $v \in S$, or 0 if $v \notin S$. The total charge of the graph is $\frac{\Delta^2}{2}|S|$. Then we proceed to the following discharging step, every vertex of S gives the charge $\frac{\Delta}{2}$ to each of its neighbors. We denote γ^* the new charge of the vertices of G. Note that a vertex v with k neighbors in S has charge $\gamma^*(v)$ at least $\frac{k\Delta}{2}$.

Now consider the number of oriented 2-paths going through a vertex $v \in V(G)$ and linking two vertices in S. Let us denote this number $\pi_S(v)$. Note that for a vertex v with k neighbors in S, we have that $\pi_S(v) \leq \max\{i \times j, i + j = k\} = \left\lfloor \frac{k^2}{4} \right\rfloor$, where i and j are respectively the number of incoming and outgoing arcs.

Since $k \leq \Delta$ we have that $\pi_S(v) \leq \left\lfloor \frac{k^2}{4} \right\rfloor \leq \frac{k\Delta}{4} \leq \frac{\gamma^*(v)}{2}$. This implies that the number of edges in $G^2[S]$, $\sum_{v \in V(G)} \pi_S(v)$, is at most $\frac{1}{2} \sum_{v \in V(G)} \gamma^*(v)$. Since the discharging does not change the total charge of the graph, we have that $\sum_{v \in V(G)} \pi_S(v) \leq \frac{1}{2} \sum_{v \in V(G)} \gamma(v) = \frac{1}{2} \times \frac{\Delta^2}{2}|S|$. So we have that the sum of the degrees in $G^2[S]$ is at most $\frac{\Delta^2}{2}|S|$, which implies that there is a vertex with degree at most $\left\lfloor \frac{\Delta^2}{2} \right\rfloor$ in $G^2[S]$. □

Proof of Theorem 4. This lemma implies that there is an order v_1, $v_2, \ldots, v_n$ on the vertices of $G = (V, A)$, such that for every $i \leq n$, the vertex v_i has at most $\left\lfloor \frac{\Delta^2}{2} \right\rfloor$ 2-neighbors v_j, with $j < i$. Given this order on the vertices, we consider the following algorithm:

```
i = 0 ;
while there are unlabelled vertices do
    for v_j = v_1 to v_n do
        if v_j is unlabelled and v_j can be labelled i then
            let v_j be labelled i;
        end
    end
    i = i + 1;
end
```

Now consider the last vertex being labelled by this algorithm, say v with label k. What could prevent it to be labelled with the value $x < k$, when the algorithm considered the possibility (i.e. when $i = x$ and $v_j = v$)? It is either a neighbor of v that was already labelled with the label l, with $x - p < l \leq x$, or a 2-neighbor of v that was labelled x. Note that if a 2-neighbor of v is labelled x before the possibility was offered to v, it implies that this 2-neighbor appears before v in the order. So the 2-neighbors of v posterior to v in the order cannot prohibit a value to v. Since v has at most Δ neighbors and at most $\left\lfloor \frac{\Delta^2}{2} \right\rfloor$ 2-neighbors appearing before v in the order, at most $\left\lfloor \frac{\Delta^2}{2} \right\rfloor + p\Delta$ values were refused to v. This implies that $k \leq \left\lfloor \frac{\Delta^2}{2} \right\rfloor + p\Delta$. □

Note that this implies that the algorithm labels the graph in time $O(\Delta^2 n)$.

9. Conclusion

In this article, we have explored the role of "orientation" in FAP by extending $L(p, q)$-labelling to oriented graphs and introducing oriented $L(p, q)$-labelling. We have computed upper bounds of oriented $L(p, q)$-labelling of trees, bipartite graphs and planar graphs. Note that bounds of $L(p, q)$-labelling of a tree depends on its maximum degree but bounds of oriented

$L(p, q)$-labelling depends on its structure (see Theorem 1). It indicates that an oriented version of labelling may provide more structrual information of concerned network of FAP than its non-oriented version.

References

1. K. I. Aardal, S. P. M. V. Hossel, A. M. C. A. Koster, C. Mannino and A. Sassano, *Models and Solution Techniques for Frequency Assignment Problems*,(available at http://fap.zib.de/survey/)
2. N. Alon and T. H. Marshall, *Homomorphisms of edge-coloured graphs and Coxeter groups*, J. Algebraic Combin. **8** (1998) 5-13.
3. O. V. Borodin, *On acyclic colorings of planar graphs*, Discrete Math. **26** (1979), 211-236.
4. O. V. Borodin, A. V. Kostochka, J. Nešetřil, A. Raspaud and E. Sopena, *On the maximum average degree and the oriented chromatic number of a graph*, Discrete Math. **206** (1999) 77-89.
5. O. V. Borodin, A. V. Kostochka, and D. R. Woodall, *Acyclic colourings of planar graphs with large girth*, J. London Math. Soc. (2). **60** (1999) 344-352.
6. G. J. Chang, J. Cheng, D. Kuo, *Distance-two labelings of digraphs*, Tech. Report 2004-011, National Center for Theoritical Sciences at Taipei.
7. G. J. Chang, Wen-Tsai Ke, D. Kuo, D. D. F. Liu and R. K. Yeh, *On L(d,1)-labelling of graphs*, Discrete Math. **220** (2000) 57-66.
8. J. P. Georges and D. W. Mauro, *Generalized vertex labelings with a condition at a distance two*, Congr. Numer., **109** (1994), 141-159.
9. D. Gonçalves, *On the L(d,1)-labelling of graphs*, submitted.
10. J. R. Griggs and R. K. Yeh, *Labelling graphs with a condition at a distance two*, SIAM J. Discrete Math., **5** (1992), 586-595.
11. W. K. Hale, *Frequency assignment : Theory and application,* Proc. IEEE, **68** (1980), 1497-1514.
12. J. C. M. Janssen, *Channel assignment and graph labeling*, Handbook of Wireless Networks and Mobile Computing(Editor : Ivan Stojmenvoic), John Wiley and Sons,Inc., Chapter 5, (2002) 95-117.
13. A. V. Kostochka, E. Sopena and X. Zhu, *Acyclic and oriented chromatic numbers of graphs*, J. Graph Theory **14**, No.4 (1997) 331-340.
14. D. Král and R. Škrekovski, *A theorem about the channel assignement problem*, SIAM J.Discrete Math., 16 (2003), pp. 426-43.
15. B. H. Metzger, *Spectrum management technique*, Fall 1970, Presentation at 38th National ORSA meeting (Detroit, MI)
16. J. Nešetřil and A. Raspaud, *Colored homomorphisms of colored mixed graphs*, J. Combin. Theory Ser. B, *80* (2000) 147-155.
17. J. Nešetřil, A. Raspaud and E. Sopena, *Colorings and girth of oriented planar graphs*, Discrete Math.**165, 166**, Nos. 1-3 (1997), 519-530.
18. A. Raspaud and E. Sopena, *Good and semi-strong colorings of oriented planar graphs*, Inform. Process. Lett. **51** (1994) 171-174.
19. E. Sopena, *The chromatic number of oriented graphs*, J. Graph Theory **25** (1997) 191-205.

CHAPTER 4

ON A VARIANT OF PARALLEL COMMUNICATING GRAMMAR SYSTEMS WITH COMMUNICATION BY COMMAND

Erzsébet Csuhaj-Varjú and György Vaszil

Computer and Automation Research Institute,
Hungarian Academy of Sciences,
Kende u. 13-17, H-1111 Budapest, Hungary
E-mail: {csuhaj, vaszil}@sztaki.hu

We introduce the notion of a parallel communicating grammar system with communication by command and with finite sets of axioms (an FCCPC grammar system) which consists of a finite number of Chomsky grammars generating and communicating to each other finite sets of strings in a synchronized manner with the assistance of so-called filter languages. The notion is an extension of the concept of a CCPC grammar system, a parallel communicating grammar system with communication by command. We show that these constructs with two regular grammars are able to generate non-regular languages and prove that any recursively enumerable language can be obtained with an FCCPC grammar system with at most three regular component grammars. We also demonstrate how two well-known NP-complete problems, the satisfiability problem of propositional formulas (SAT) and the Hamiltonian Path Problem (HPP, can effectively be solved with these constructs, in a constant number of derivation steps.

1. Introduction

Parallel communicating grammar systems with communication by command (CCPC grammar systems, for short) represent the first models of networks of language processors where communication is performed through filters.[6] These architectures were motivated by known paradigms of distributed computation, as the WAVE paradigm,[11,17] the Boltzmann machine,[12] and the Connection Machine.[18]

A CCPC grammar system consists of a finite set of Chomsky grammars defined over a common nonterminal alphabet and a common terminal alphabet. Each component grammar is located at a node of a virtual complete graph together with a so-called filter or selector language which is a regular language. The system functions by alternating rewriting and communication steps. The grammars start working from their own start symbols. A rewriting step in these systems is defined as follows: each grammar generates its own string until it has no more applicable productions. Then the components communicate their strings to each other in the following manner: every grammar tries to send a copy of its own string to each of the other grammars, but only those strings are accepted at a component which pass the filter associated with it, that is, which are elements of the associated regular language. The strings arriving at the nodes as results of a successful communication are concatenated in the sequence ordered by the growing index of the sender nodes. If the component does not receive any string but it successfully communicates its own string to some other node, then the grammar returns to its start symbol. If the grammar neither receives any string, nor can successfully communicate its own string, then the string of the component remains unchanged. The language of the system is the set of terminal words that appear during a derivation at a distinguished component, the master, after a rewriting step. These constructs are powerful computational devices: CCPC grammar systems even with three regular grammars as components are as powerful as the Turing machines.[13]

Since CCPC grammar systems realize a rather simple and elegant way of information generation and transmission in networks, several variants of networks of language processors have been developed from the generic model, with different motivations or with different ways of rewriting or communication. For the concept of the general paradigm and summaries on some developments in the field, the reader is referred to Refs. 3 and 8. In the theory of networks of language processors, models inspired by biology, as test tube systems based on splicing, networks of Watson-Crick $D0L$ systems, networks of parallel language processors, and networks of evolutionary processors are of particular importance. Test tube systems based on splicing operate on sets of strings. Their basic operation, splicing, is motivated by the recombinant behaviour of DNA.[5] The grammars in networks of Watson-Crick $D0L$ systems are developmental systems over a special, so-called DNA-like alphabet (each symbol has a complementary symbol) operating on sets or multisets of strings. In these systems both rewriting and communication are controlled by a condition which mimics the well-known property of the DNA helix, the Watson-Crick complementarity.[9,10]

Networks of parallel language processors are developmental (Lindenmayer) systems which function over sets or multisets of strings in a synchronized manner and communicate strings to each other through filters given by different types of context-conditions.[7] As further developments of the idea, networks of evolutionary processors were introduced, which constructs are synchronously working and communicating generative devices where the basic operations are point mutations (an insertion, or a deletion, or a replacement of a symbol), the components operate on sets or multisets of strings, and the filters are given by random context conditions.[1,2] Although all these constructs are networks of language generating devices with communication by command through filters, they significantly differ from CCPC grammar systems in one feature of the communication. Namely, the successfully communicated strings are not concatenated but any string received by a component belongs to the new set of strings at the node.

These constructs are computationally complete devices, certain types of them even with a number of components bounded by a small constant are able to determine any recursively enumerable language. Moreover, these constructs can be used for deciding NP-complete problems in polynomial time.

In this paper, we adopt some ideas from the above constructs, by extending the notion of a CCPC grammar system as follows. Firstly, the grammars start their work from a non-empty finite set of axiom words (not necessarily from a single symbol). Secondly, the new set of strings at a component resulted in a successful communication to this node is the finite language that is obtained as a concatenation of the finite sets of strings successfully communicated by the other components to this node, in the previously mentioned, growing order of the index of the sender nodes. We call these systems FCCPC grammar systems.

We demonstrate that this way of functioning provides much power and efficiency: FCCPC grammar systems with three regular grammars are computationally complete (as it is expected) and they are able to determine non-context-free languages even with only two regular components. Moreover, FCCPC systems with context-free components can effectively be used for deciding NP-complete problems, for example, the satisfiability problem of propositional formulas (SAT) and the Hamiltonian Path Problem (HPP) can be solved by these constructs in a constant number of derivation steps. We close the paper by we stating some open problems and proposing some new topics for further research.

2. Basic Notions and Definitions

Throughout the paper we assume that the reader is familiar with the basic notions of formal language theory. For further details and unexplained notions consult.[14,15]

The set of non-empty strings over an alphabet Σ is denoted by Σ^+; if the empty string, λ, is included, then we use notation Σ^*. A set of strings $L \subseteq \Sigma^*$ is said to be a language over alphabet Σ. The number of elements of a finite set A is denoted by card(A). We denote a phrase-structure grammar by $G = (N, T, P, S)$, where N and T are the disjoint sets of nonterminals and terminals, P is the set of productions, and S is the start symbol. The direct derivation relation in G is denoted by $\Longrightarrow_P$, the transitive and reflexive closure of $\Longrightarrow_P$ is denoted by $\Longrightarrow_P^*$.

The class of regular, context-free, and recursively enumerable languages is denoted by REG, CF, and RE, respectively. If no confusion arises, we use the notations REG and CF for the class of regular grammars and the class of context-free grammars, respectively.

Definition 1: A parallel communicating grammar system with communication by command and with finite sets of axioms or an FCCPC grammar system (of degree n) is a construct

$$\Gamma = (N, T, (F_1, P_1, R_1), \dots, (F_n, P_n, R_n)), \quad n \geq 1,$$

where

- N and T are disjoint finite alphabets; N is called the nonterminal alphabet and T is called the terminal alphabet of the system,
- (F_i, P_i, R_i), $1 \leq i \leq n$, is a component of Γ, the ith component, where
  - — $F_i \subset (N \cup T)^*$ is a non-empty finite set, the set of the axioms of the component,
  - — P_i is a finite set of rewriting rules over $(N \cup T)$, and
  - — R_i is a regular language with $R_i \subseteq (N \cup T)^*$, called the selector language or the filter of the ith component.

The first component is designated as the master.

If no confusion arises, we may refer to P_i, above, as the ith component.

Throughout the paper, we consider FCCPC grammar systems with components of a certain type of grammars in the Chomsky hierarchy. We call an FCCPC grammar system $\Gamma = (N, T, (F_1, P_1, R_1), \dots, (F_n, P_n, R_n))$, $n \geq 1$, regular, context-free, or phrase-structure if the rules in P_i, $1 \leq i \leq n$, are rules of a regular, a context-free, or a phrase-structure grammar, respectively, with nonterminal alphabet N and terminal alphabet T.

Definition 2: By a configuration (a state) of an FCCPC grammar system $\Gamma = (N, T, (F_1, P_1, R_1), \ldots, (F_n, P_n, R_n))$, $n \geq 1$, we mean an n-tuple $(L_1, \ldots, L_n)$, where $L_i \subset (N \cup T)^*$, $1 \leq i \leq n$, are finite languages. $(F_1, \ldots, F_n)$ is called the initial configuration (the initial state) of Γ.

FCCPC grammar systems function by changing their configurations. This is realized by alternating rewriting and communication steps.

Definition 3: Let $\Gamma = (N, T, (F_1, P_1, R_1), \ldots, (F_n, P_n, R_n))$, $n \geq 1$, be an FCCPC grammar system and let $C_1 = (L_1, \ldots, L_n)$ and $C_2 = (L'_1, \ldots, L'_n)$ be two configurations of Γ. We say that C_2 is derived from C_1 by a rewriting step, denoted by

$$(L_1, \ldots, L_n) \Longrightarrow_\Gamma (L'_1, \ldots, L'_n),$$

if for all i, $1 \leq i \leq n$,

$$L'_i = \{y | x \Longrightarrow^*_{P_i} y, x \in L_i \text{ and there is no } z \in (N \cup T)^* \text{ such that } y \Longrightarrow_{P_i} z\}.$$

Notice that if $x \in L_i \cap T^*$, then $x \in L'_i$.

If no confusion arises, we may omit Γ from the notation $\Longrightarrow_\Gamma$.

Thus, after a rewriting step, the new set of strings consists of all words which can be generated with zero or more derivation steps in the grammar from the strings of the component and the grammar has no rule applicable to any of these strings. The reader can easily observe that the synchronization of the rewriting steps is done at the level of the FCCPC grammar system, the individual components may perform a different number of rewriting steps on the different strings.

Definition 4: Let $\Gamma = (N, T, (F_1, P_1, R_1), \ldots, (F_n, P_n, R_n))$, where $n \geq 1$, be an FCCPC grammar system and let $C_1 = (L_1, \ldots, L_n)$ and $C_2 = (L'_1, \ldots, L'_n)$ be two configurations of Γ. We say that C_2 is derived from C_1 by a communication step, denoted by

$$(L_1, \ldots, L_n) \vdash_\Gamma (L'_1, \ldots, L'_n),$$

if the following conditions hold.

Let the set of strings sent by the ith component to the jth one be defined as

$$\delta(L_i, j) = \begin{cases} \{\lambda\}, & \text{if } L_i \cap R_j = \emptyset \text{ or } i = j, \\ L_i \cap R_j, & \text{otherwise}, \end{cases}$$

for $1 \leq i, j \leq n$.

Let

$$\Delta(j) = \delta(L_1, j)\delta(L_2, j)\cdots\delta(L_n, j),$$

be the concatenation of the sets of strings sent to the jth component, for $1 \leq j \leq n$, i.e. the "total message" received by the jth component, and let

$$\delta(i) = \delta(L_i, 1)\delta(L_i, 2)\cdots\delta(L_i, n),$$

for $1 \leq i \leq n$, represent the "string transferring capacity" of the ith component. Then, for $1 \leq i \leq n$, we define

$$L'_i = \begin{cases} \Delta(i), & \text{if } \Delta(i) \neq \{\lambda\}, \\ L_i, & \text{if } \Delta(i) = \{\lambda\} \text{ and } \delta(i) = \{\lambda\}, \\ F_i, & \text{if } \Delta(i) = \{\lambda\} \text{ and } \delta(i) \neq \{\lambda\}. \end{cases}$$

If no confusion arises, we may omit Γ from the notation $\vdash_\Gamma$.

After a communication step, the obtained language, L'_i, is either the concatenation of the received sets of strings, or it is the previous language, when this component is not involved in communication, or it is equal to F_i, if this component successfully sends strings to the other components but it does not receive any string. Observe that a component is not allowed to send strings to itself.

A sequence of alternating rewriting steps and communication steps determines a computation (a derivation) in Γ; we may also refer a rewriting step and a communication step as a computation (a derivation) step.

The language of an FCCPC grammar system is the set of terminal words which appear at the master during a computation after performing a rewriting step.

Definition 5: The language $L(\Gamma)$ generated by an FCCPC grammar system $\Gamma = (N, T, (F_1, P_1, R_1), \ldots, (F_n, P_n, R_n))$, $n \geq 1$, is defined as follows:

$$L(\Gamma) = \{w \in T^* | (F_1, \ldots, F_n) \Longrightarrow_\Gamma (L_1^{(1)}, \ldots, L_n^{(1)}) \vdash_\Gamma (L_1^{(2)}, \ldots, L_n^{(2)}) \Longrightarrow_\Gamma$$
$$(L_1^{(3)}, \ldots, L_n^{(3)}) \vdash_\Gamma (L_1^{(4)}, \ldots, L_n^{(4)}) \Longrightarrow_\Gamma \cdots \Longrightarrow_\Gamma (L_1^{(s)}, \ldots, L_n^{(s)}),$$
$$\text{for some } s \geq 1 \text{ such that } w \in L_1^{(s)}\}.$$

Example 1: Consider the FCCPC grammar system with two regular components $\Gamma = (N, T, (F_1, P_1, R_1), (F_2, P_2, R_2))$, where

$$N = \{A, B, C, A', B', C', A'', B'', C'', S, S'\},$$

$T = \{a, b, c\}$ and

$$F_1 = \{ABC\},$$

$$P_1 = \{A \to aA', B \to bB', C \to cC', A'' \to \lambda, B'' \to \lambda, C'' \to \lambda\},$$

$$R_1 = a^+Ab^+Bc^+C \cup a^+A''b^+B''c^+C'',$$

$$F_2 = \{S\},$$

$$P_2 = \{S \to S', A' \to A, B' \to B, C' \to C, A' \to A'', B' \to B'', C' \to C''\},$$

$$R_2 = a^+A'b^+B'c^+C'.$$

The first few steps of the derivation are as follows.

$$(\{ABC\}, \{S\}) \Longrightarrow (\{aA'bB'cC'\}, \{S'\}) \vdash (\{ABC\}, \{aA'bB'cC'\}) \Longrightarrow (\{aA'bB'cC'\}, w),$$

where w is of the form $aXbYcZ$, with $X \in \{A, A''\}$, $Y \in \{B, B''\}$, $Z \in \{C, C''\}$. This word can only be successfully communicated to the first component if it is either of the form $w = aAbBcC$ or $w = aA''bB''cC''$. In the latter case the next rewriting steps results in terminal word abc at the master component, while in the first case the derivation can be continued with $a^2A'b^2B'c^2C'$ at the first component. Analyzing the possible further derivation steps, it is easy to see $L(\Gamma) = \{a^nb^nc^n | n \geq 1\}$ which is a non-context-free language.

Notation 1: We denote by $FCCPC_n(X)$ the family of languages generated by FCCPC grammar systems of type X with at most n components, where $n \geq 1$, and $X \in \{REG, CF\}$. When the number of the components is not specified, then we write $FCCPC_\infty(X)$.

3. On the Power of FCCPC Grammar Systems

In Ref. 6 it was shown that CCPC grammar systems with two regular components determine the class of regular languages, while these systems with two context-free grammars are as powerful as the phrase-structure grammars. In Ref. 13 the authors proved that CCPC grammar systems with three regular components are able to generate any recursively enumerable language. In the case of FCCPC grammar systems, systems with two regular components are sufficient to generate a non-context-free, thus non-regular language, and as it is expected, systems with three regular grammars are computationally complete. We present here a proof based on ideas different from that of the proof of the corresponding statement in Ref. 13. Note that by definition, $FCCPC_n(X) \subseteq FCCPC_{n+1}(X)$ for $X \in \{REG, CF\}$ and $n \geq 1$.

Theorem 1: $REG = FCCPC_1(REG) \subset FCCPC_2(REG)$.

Proof: FCCPC grammar systems with one regular component are as powerful as the regular grammars; the result is a consequence of the closure properties of regular languages. A non-regular language generated by an FCCPC grammar system with two regular components is presented the example in the previous section. □

Theorem 2:

$$FCCPC_3(REG) = FCCPC_n(REG) = FCCPC_\infty(REG) = RE\,, \quad n \geq 4\,.$$

Proof: Let L be a recursively enumerable language generated by a phrase-structure grammar $G = (N, T, P, S)$ in a Penttonen normal form, that is, with productions of the forms $AB \to AC$, $A \to BC$, $A \to a$, and $A \to \lambda$, where A, B, C are nonterminals and a is a terminal letter. We construct a regular FCCPC grammar system Γ with three components such that Γ generates L.

The derivations of Γ simulate the derivations of G by using the rotate-and-simulate method. In its original form, the rotate-and-simulate method means that the words found in the nodes of Γ are involved in either the rotation of the rightmost symbol of a sentential form in G (the rightmost symbol of the word is moved to the beginning of the word) or a simulation of the application of a rule of P. The context-free rules in P are applied to the rightmost symbol of the string, the context-sensitive rules are applied by replacing the leftmost symbol, supposing that the rightmost symbol is the one which appears at the first position of the left-hand side (and also at the right-hand side) of the given rule. To guarantee the correct simulation, a marker symbol, \$, is introduced for indicating the beginning of the rotated word, which is removed at the end of the computation provided that it is the leftmost symbol. This method is adapted to FCCPC grammars systems for our purposes: since the grammar system has only regular rules, the simulation of the context-free rules is done in different way from the above described one.

In more details, the proof idea is the following: the sentential forms at the second component represent sentential forms uv of G, where u, $v \in (N \cup T)^*$, in the form $v\$u$. The second component either prepares the string for further rewriting or it indicates that the string is guessed to be a terminal word. If the derivation of the string will be continued, then the second component indicates by marking the rightmost letter of the string whether the rotation of this symbol or the application of a production to this symbol is intended to be performed. (If the production is of the form $AB \to AC$, then the first letter of this string is marked, too.) The first component meantime generates symbols which are marked letters indicating the rotation of symbols in $(N \cup \{\$\} \cup T)^*$, and marked versions of letters C on the right-hand side of productions of the form $A \to BC$, and two auxiliary letters, E, K. Then, the strings at the first and the second component are sent to the third component and their copies are concatenated in such way that a copy of each string at the first component is concatenated with a copy of each string of the second component. The third component either generates a terminal string from the new string obtained by communication, or it prepares the string for further rewriting. In the latter case, the component "colours" the string, that is, it rewrites it to its double-primed version and then communicates the obtained word to the second component. The filter of the second component is defined in such way that only strings representing a correct simulation of the planned action (the rotation of a symbol or the application of a production) are accepted by the component. For example, if we would like to simulate the rotation of symbol A in the sentential form $z\$wA$, z, $w \in (N \cup T)^*$ at the second component, then the string arriving back must be of the form $A''^{(l-\mathrm{rot})}z''\$''w''A''^{(r-\mathrm{rot})}$, where letters $A''^{(l-\mathrm{rot})}$ and $A''^{(r-\mathrm{rot})}$ refer to the rotation, furthermore $A^{(l-\mathrm{rot})}$ was a symbol sent by the first component to the third one in the previous communication step. After the performed communication, the second component prepares the next action or makes preparations to select the terminal strings which are obtained at the third component.

Before defining the components of Γ, we introduce some notations. Let $V = N \cup \{[a] | a \in T\}$, and let $\$$, K, S_3, E, $[\lambda]$ be symbols not in $(N \cup T)$. ($[\lambda]$ is used for representing the empty word.) Let $\mathrm{card}(P) = h$, and let us order a unique label from the set $Lab(P) = \{1, \ldots, h\}$ to each production p in P. Let us define $V^{(l-\mathrm{rot})} = \{X^{(l-\mathrm{rot})} | X \in V \cup \{\$\}\}$ and $V^{(r-\mathrm{rot})} =$

$\{X^{(r-\mathrm{rot})}|X \in V \cup \{\$\}\}$. These symbols assist the rotation of symbols from $V \cup \{\$\}$, letter l refers to the first letter from the left-hand side and letter r refers to the first letter from the right-hand side of the word, that is, to the last letter. Let $V_P = \{X^{(r)}|X \in (V \cup [\lambda]), r \in Lab(P)\}$. These letters indicate which production is planned to be applied. Finally, let V', $V'^{(l-\mathrm{rot})}$, $V'^{(r-\mathrm{rot})}$, V'_P and V'', $V''^{(l-\mathrm{rot})}$, $V''^{(r-\mathrm{rot})}$, V''_P be the alphabets consisting of the primed and the double-primed versions of the elements of V, $V^{(l-\mathrm{rot})}$, $V^{(r-\mathrm{rot})}$, V_P, respectively.

Now we define Γ as follows: let

$$\Gamma = (N_\Gamma, T, (F_1, P_1, R_1), (F_2, P_2, R_2), (F_3, P_3, R_3)),$$

where $N_\Gamma = V \cup V' \cup V'' \cup V^{(l-\mathrm{rot})} \cup V^{(r-\mathrm{rot})} \cup V_P \cup V'^{(l-\mathrm{rot})} \cup V'^{(r-\mathrm{rot})} \cup V'_P \cup V''^{(l-\mathrm{rot})} \cup V''^{(r-\mathrm{rot})} \cup V''_P \cup \{\$, \$', \$'', \bar{\$}, K, K', K'', S_3, S'_3, E, E'\} \cup \{[\bar{a}]\}|a \in T\} \cup \{[\lambda], [\lambda]', [\lambda]'', [\bar{\lambda}]$ and let

$$F_1 = V'^{(l-\mathrm{rot})} \cup V'_P \cup \{K', E'\}, \quad P_1 = \{X' \to X | X \in F_1\}, \quad R_1 = \emptyset .$$

This component is used for appending a nonterminal indicating either the rotation of the rightmost symbol in the simulated sentential form or the application of a production to that word.

$$\begin{aligned}
F_2 &= \{\$''B''C''|S \to BC \in P\} \cup \{\$''[a]''|S \to a \in P\} \cup \\
&\quad \{\$''[\lambda]''|S \to \lambda \in P\}, \\
P_2 &= \{X \to X', X \to X^{(r-\mathrm{rot})}|X \in V \cup \{\$\}\} \cup \\
&\quad \{A \to B^{(r)}|r : A \to BC \in P\} \\
&\quad \{A \to A^{(s)}, B \to C^{(s)}|s : AB \to AC \in P\} \cup \\
&\quad \{A \to [a]^{(q)}|q : A \to a \in P\} \cup \{A \to [\lambda]^{(z)}|z : A \to \lambda \in P\} \cup \\
&\quad \{a'' \to [a]|a \in T\} \cup \{\$'' \to \bar{\$}, [\lambda]'' \to [\bar{\lambda}]\} \cup \\
&\quad \{X'' \to X, X''^{(l-\mathrm{rot})} \to X, X''^{(r-\mathrm{rot})} \to \lambda | X \in V \cup \{\$\}\} \cup \\
&\quad \{X''^{(s)} \to X | X^s \in (V_P \setminus \{[\lambda]\}, s \in Lab(P)\} \cup \\
&\quad \{[\lambda]''^{(z)} \to \lambda | z : A \to \lambda \in P\} \cup \{K'' \to \lambda\}, \\
R_2 &= \{X''^{(l-\mathrm{rot})}\alpha X''^{(r-\mathrm{rot})}|X \in V \cup \{\$\}, \alpha \in (V'' \cup \{\$''\})^*\} \cup \\
&\quad \{C''^{(r)}\alpha B''^{(r)}|r : A \to BC \in P, \alpha \in (V'' \cup \{\$''\})^*\} \cup \\
&\quad \{K''C''^{(s)}\alpha A''^{(s)}|s : AB \to AC \in P, \alpha \in (V'' \cup \{\$''\})^*\} \cup
\end{aligned}$$

$$\{K''\alpha[a]''^{(q)}|q : A \to a \in P, \alpha \in (V'' \cup \{\$''\})^*\} \cup$$
$$\{K''\alpha[\lambda]''^{(z)}|z : A \to \lambda \in P, \alpha \in (V'' \cup \{\$''\})^*\}.$$

This component is used for indicating the rotation of the rightmost symbol in the current sentential form or making preparations to the simulation of a production in P, by marking symbols with production labels. In addition, this component indicates that the string represents a terminal word.

Let

$$F_3 = \{S_3\}$$

$$P_3 = \{X' \to X''|X \in V \cup \{\$\}\} \cup \{K \to K''\} \cup \{S_3 \to S_3'\} \cup$$
$$\{X^{l-\text{rot}} \to X''^{(l-\text{rot})}, X^{(r-\text{rot})} \to X''^{(r-\text{rot})}| \in V \cup \{\$\}\} \cup$$
$$\{X^{(r)} \to X''^{(r)}|X^{(r)} \in V_P, r \in Lab(P)\} \cup$$
$$\{[\bar{a}] \to a|a \in T\} \cup \{X \to \lambda|X \in \{\bar{\$}, [\bar{\lambda}], E\}\},$$

$$R_3 = V^{(l-\text{rot})} \cup V_P \cup \{K\} \cup \{\alpha X^{(r-\text{rot})}|X \in V \cup \{\$\}, \alpha \in (V' \cup \{\$'\})^*\} \cup$$
$$\{\alpha X^{(r)}|X^r \in V_P, r \in Lab(P)\} \cup \{\bar{\$}\alpha|\alpha \in \{[\bar{a}]|a \in T\}^+\} \cup \{\bar{\$}, [\bar{\lambda}]\}.$$

This component is the master component. It receives strings from the first and the second component by communication. These words are guessed to correspond to the leftmost symbol and the remaining symbols in a string representing a sentential form of G together with the indication of an action to be performed on it. The action can be the rotation of a symbol or the application of a production. After being concatenated with some other string and rewritten to a double-primed version, the obtained new string is communicated to the second component. The filter of the second component is defined in such way that only strings corresponding to sentential forms of G are accepted, thus the correctness of the simulation is guaranteed.

This component also serves for selecting the terminal words which were prepared by the second component by removing the priming and introducing barred versions of symbols \$, $[\lambda]$ and $[a]$, for $a \in T$. If such a sentential form corresponding to a terminal word arrives from the second component and it is concatenated with the symbol E arriving from the first one, then a terminal word which can also be generated by the grammar G, is produced. If it is concatenated with other letters, then no terminal word is obtained from the string. We note that without the loss of the generality we might choose the third component to be the master.

We show that $L(\Gamma) = L(G)$ holds. The functioning of Γ starts with the initial state (F_1, F_2, F_3). After the first rewriting step in the system, the first component will contain a marked copy of each symbol in $V \cup \$$ indicating the rotation of this symbol (the marked symbol will be appended to the left-end of the string), or indicating the application of a production (with reference to the production to be applied), and two additional symbols, K and E. The second component will have all the strings which are obtained from the double-primed versions of the strings that can be derived in one step from the start symbol in G. First it rewrites the axioms to their unprimed version and then marks them at the right-hand end or changes the string for its corresponding barred version, supposing that a single terminal letter or the empty word can be derived from the start symbol of G. The third component rewrites S_3 to S_3'.

Then, by the next communication, the strings of the first and the second component are sent to the third component where they are concatenated with each other, that is, a copy of each string of the first component is concatenated with the copy of each string of the second component.

The first and the second components return to their axiom sets. Then, by the following rewriting steps, the first two components generate the same sets as before and the third component rewrites its strings either to a double-primed string or to a terminal word. After the following communication, the second component will have those strings from the third component which correspond to strings representing the application of a correct simulation of an action on a sentential form and only these strings. If no such word exists, then the component will have its axioms. The third component, as previously, will receive the strings of the first and the second component, and the first component will return to its axiom set. After any following communication step, the first component will return to its axiom, the second component will have all the strings which represent a correct simulation of the application of an action on a sentential form at the corresponding derivation step in G, and the third component will have strings with markers or auxiliary letters at the two ends indicating that the string is planned to be further rewritten or that the strings are guessed to represent terminal words G. Repeating the procedure, all strings of $L(G)$ can be obtained in this manner at the third component, and since the above steps are the only possible derivation steps in Γ, no more terminal strings can be obtained. □

There have been several questions left open. Although we know that the power of FCCPC grammar systems with two regular components exceeds the power of the regular grammars, the exact place of their language class in the Chomsky hierarchy is not known. Similarly, it would be interesting to know what about the power of the so-called free regular or context-free FCCPC grammar systems, that is, FCCPC grammar systems where the filter language is the set of all words over the total (nonterminal and terminal) alphabet of the system. The question, how much power can be obtained with FCCPC grammar systems with different restricted variants of regular filters, for example, those ones which correspond to random context conditions, is also of interest.

4. On the Efficiency of FCCPC Grammar Systems

In the following we demonstrate that FCCPC grammar systems can effectively be used for solving NP-complete problems. The reason of this fact is that these constructs are able to create an exponentially growing number of strings in linear time. By our method, starting from a given instance of a decision problem, we construct an FCCPC grammar system such that the result of the computation in this system in a known number of steps gives an answer to this problem. The result is obtained at the master component; for decision problems the answer is yes if and only if after this derivation step the master contains a specified string (a set of specified strings).

We first show that the satisfiability problem for propositional formulas can be solved by FCCPC grammar systems in a constant number of steps, independently of the number of clauses and variables in the formula.

It is well known that the satisfiability problem SAT of propositional formulas is NP-complete[14,16] We consider propositional formulas in conjunctive normal form, thus, a formula is a conjunction of disjunctions whose terms are literals, that is, variables or their negations. The disjunctions are referred to as clauses. We assume that the formula contains n variables and m clauses. A formula γ is satisfiable if there is a truth-value assignment for the variables (that is, an assignment of T or F) giving γ the value T.

Theorem 3: For any $m, n \geq 1$, the satisfiability of a propositional formula in conjunctive normal form consisting of m clauses and n variables can be decided in five derivation steps by a context-free FCCPC grammar system which can effectively be constructed.

Proof: Let us consider a propositional formula $\gamma = C_1 \wedge \cdots \wedge C_m$ in conjunctive normal form with m clauses C_i, $1 \leq i \leq m$, and n variables x_k, $1 \leq k \leq n$, where $C_j = y_{j,1} \vee \cdots \vee y_{j,k_j}$, $1 \leq j \leq m$, with $y_{j,i} \in \{x_l, \neg x_l | 1 \leq l \leq n\}$, $1 \leq i \leq k_j$. Let $N_C = \{C_1, \ldots, C_m\}$.

For each i, $1 \leq i \leq n$, let us denote by $\mathrm{true}(\gamma, T_i)$ the string $C_{i_1} C_{i_2} \cdots C_{i_s}$ indicating the clauses in γ which contain x_i and by $\mathrm{true}(\gamma, F_i)$ the string $C_{j_1} C_{j_2} \cdots C_{j_t}$ of clauses in γ which contain $\neg x_i$ (therefore, these strings are over the alphabet N_C). Notice that these strings can be empty strings.

We construct the FCCPC grammar system Γ deciding whether or not γ is satisfiable as follows: Let

$$\Gamma = (N, T, (F_1, P_1, R_1), \ldots, (F_{n+2}, P_{n+2}, R_{n+2})),$$

where $N = \bigcup_{i=1}^{n} \{S_{i_1}, S_{i_2}, T_i, F_i\} \cup N_C \cup \{S_{n+1}, S_{n+2}, S'_{n+1}, S'_{n+2}, S''_{n+2}\}$, $T = \{c\}$, and

$$F_i = \{S_{i_1}, S_{i_2}\}, \quad P_i = \{S_{i_1} \to T_i, S_{i_2} \to F_i\}, \quad R_i = \{S'_{n+1}\},$$

for $1 \leq i \leq n$,

$$F_{n+1} = \{S_{n+1}\},$$

$$P_{n+1} = \{S_{n+1} \to S'_{n+1}\} \cup \{T_i \to \mathrm{true}(\gamma, T_i), \ F_i \to \mathrm{true}(\gamma, F_i) | 1 \leq i \leq n\},$$

$$R_{n+1} = \bigcup_{i=1}^{n} \{T_i, F_i\} \cup \{S''_{n+2}\}, \text{ and finally},$$

$$F_{n+2} = \{S_{n+2}\},$$

$$P_{n+2} = \{S_{n+2} \to S'_{n+2}, S'_{n+2} \to S''_{n+2}\} \cup \{C_i \to c | 1 \leq i \leq n\},$$

$$R_{n+2} = \bigcap_{j=1}^{m} N_C^* C_j N_C^* .$$

Without the loss of the generality we may assume that the master component is the $(n+2)$th component.

We prove that γ is satisfiable if and only if the $(n+2)$th component contains a terminal word over c at the fifth step.

The system starts its work from the initial state

$$(\{S_{1_1}, S_{1_2}\}, \ldots, \{S_{n_1}, S_{n_2}\}, \{S_{n+1}\}, \{S_{n+2}\}).$$

After the first rewriting step, the obtained new configuration will be

$$(\{T_1, F_1\}, \ldots, \{T_n, F_n\}, \{S'_{n+1}\}, \{S'_{n+2}\}).$$

After performing the first communication step, the system enters the following state:

$$(\{S'_{n+1}\},\dots,\{S'_{n+1}\},\{T_1,F_1\}\{T_2,F_2\}\cdots\{T_n,F_n\},\{S'_{n+2}\})\,.$$

By this step, strings corresponding to all truth assignments are obtained at the $(n+1)$th component. The next rewriting step results in

$$(\{S'_{n+1}\},\dots,\{S'_{n+1}\},\\ \{\text{true}(\gamma,T_1),\text{true}(\gamma,F_1)\}\cdots\{\text{true}(\gamma,T_n),\text{true}(\gamma,F_n)\},\{S''_{n+2}\})\,.$$

After the following communication only those strings over N_C will arrive at the $(n+2)$th component that have at least one occurrence of C_i, for each i, $1 \le i \le n$, that is, which represent a truth assignment satisfying γ. If no such string exist, then the formula is not satisfiable. Supposing that γ is satisfiable, the next rewriting step leads to the configuration

$$(\{S'_{n+1}\},\dots,\{S'_{n+1}\},\{S''_{n+2}\},L_C)\,,$$

where $L_C \subset \{c\}^+$ is a nonempty finite set.

If γ is not satisfiable, instead of the configuration above, we obtain

$$(\{S'_{n+1}\},\dots,\{S'_{n+1}\},\{S''_{n+2}\},\{S_{n+2}\})\,,$$

and the system enters an infinite computation as

$$\begin{aligned}
&(\{S'_{n+1}\},\dots,\{S'_{n+1}\},\{S''_{n+2}\},\{S_{n+2}\})\\
&\quad\Rightarrow(\{S'_{n+1}\},\dots,\{S'_{n+1}\},\{S''_{n+2}\},\{S'_{n+2}\})\\
&\quad\vdash(\{S'_{n+1}\},\dots,\{S'_{n+1}\},\{S''_{n+2}\},\{S'_{n+2}\})\\
&\quad\Rightarrow(\{S'_{n+1}\},\dots,\{S'_{n+1}\},\{S''_{n+2}\},\{S''_{n+2}\})\\
&\quad\vdash(\{S'_{n+1}\},\dots,\{S'_{n+1}\},\{S''_{n+2}\},\{S_{n+2}\})\,.
\end{aligned}$$

Then, the procedure is repeated. If no string over N_C is communicated to the $(n+2)$th component at the 4th step, then no such string will ever be communicated to that, thus the formula is not satisfiable. Since the above procedure is the only way of functioning of Γ, the statement of the theorem holds.

The reader might notice that Γ is a context-free FCCPC grammar system. □

In the following we show how another well-known NP-complete problem, namely the Hamiltonian Path Problem (HPP) can be solved in constant time by FCCPC grammar systems. We present an FCCPC grammar system which decides whether a given directed graph $\gamma = (V, E)$, where V is the set of vertices or nodes of γ and E denotes the set of its edges, contains a path which starts from a given node v_{in} and ends at a given node v_{out} visiting each node of the graph exactly once.

Theorem 4: For any directed graph γ, a context-free FCCPC grammar system can effectively be constructed which decides in five derivation steps whether or not γ contains a Hamiltonian path. Moreover, if γ has a Hamiltonian path, then any word in the language generated by the system corresponds to a unique description of a Hamiltonian path, and all Hamiltonian paths are represented by a terminal word.

Proof: Let $\gamma = (V, E)$ be with vertices $V = \{V_1, \ldots, V_n\}$, $n \geq 1$, and with a set of edges E. The context-free FCCPC grammar system Γ, deciding whether γ contains a Hamiltonian path starting from V_1 and ending in V_n is constructed as follows. Let

$$\Gamma = (N, T, (F_1, P_1, R_1), \ldots, (F_{n+2}, P_{n+2}, R_{n+2}))\,,$$

where $N = \{V_i, V_i', V_i'' | 1 \leq i \leq n\} \cup \{S_{n+1}, S_{n+1}', S_{n+2}, S_{n+2}', S_{n+2}''\}$, $T = \{v_1, \ldots, v_n\}$, and let us denote by $V' = \{V_1', \ldots, V_n'\}$ and by $V'' = \{V_1'', \ldots, V_n''\}$.

Let

$$F_i = V\,, \quad P_i = \{V_i \to V_i' | 1 \leq i \leq n\}\,, \quad R_i = \{S_{n+1}'\}\,,$$

for $1 \leq i \leq n$,

$$\begin{aligned} F_{n+1} &= \{S_{n+1}\}\,, \\ P_{n+1} &= \{S_{n+1} \to S_{n+1}'\} \cup \{V_i' \to V_i'' | 1 \leq i \leq n\}\,, \\ R_{n+1} &= V' \cup \{S_{n+2}''\}\,, \end{aligned}$$

and

$$\begin{aligned} F_{n+2} &= \{S_{n+2}\}\,, \\ P_{n+2} &= \{S_{n+2} \to S_{n+2}', S_{n+2}' \to S_{n+2}''\} \cup \{V_i'' \to v_i | 1 \leq i \leq n\}\,, \\ R_{n+2} &= \left(\bigcap_{i=1}^{n} V''^* V_i'' V''^*\right) \bigcap \left(V''^* \Big\backslash \left(\bigcup_{(V_i, V_j) \notin E} V''^* V_i'' V_j'' V''^*\right)\right) \\ &\quad \cap (V_1'' V''^* V_n'')\,. \end{aligned}$$

The master component of Γ is the $(n+2)$th component.

We prove that if γ has a Hamiltonian path, then the language generated by Γ is not empty and any word over T that can be found at the master component is a unique description of a Hamiltonian path where letter v_i, $1 \le i \le n$, corresponds to vertex V_i in γ, and moreover, all Hamiltonian paths of γ are represented by a word over T at this component.

The computation in Γ starts with the initial state

$$(V, \dots, V, \{S_{n+1}\}, \{S_{n+2}\}) .$$

After performing a rewriting step, the new configuration will be

$$(V', \dots, V', \{S'_{n+1}\}, \{S'_{n+2}\}) ,$$

which after the following communication enters the state

$$(\{S'_{n+1}\}, \dots, \{S'_{n+1}\}, V'V' \cdots V', \{S'_{n+2}\}) .$$

After this step, the $(n+1)$th component will have the description of all possible paths of length n in a graph with the set of vertices V. Performing a rewriting step again, we obtain the configuration

$$(\{S'_{n+1}\}, \dots, \{S'_{n+1}\}, V''V'' \cdots V'', \{S''_{n+2}\}) .$$

The following communication step selects those strings which are paths in γ visiting each node only once starting from node V_1 and ending at node V_n. Namely, the new configuration will either be

$$(\{S'_{n+1}\}, \dots, \{S'_{n+1}\}, \{S''_{n+2}\}, L_{V''}) ,$$

where $L_{V''}$ is the nonempty set of strings corresponding to the Hamiltonian paths in γ, or

$$(\{S'_{n+1}\}, \dots, \{S'_{n+1}\}, \{S''_{n+2}\}, \{S_{n+2}\}) .$$

In the latter case γ does not have Hamiltonian path and Γ enters an infinite computation repeating the steps

$$\begin{aligned}
&(\{S'_{n+1}\}, \dots, \{S'_{n+1}\}, \{S''_{n+2}\}, \{S_{n+2}\}) \\
&\quad \Rightarrow (\{S'_{n+1}\}, \dots, \{S'_{n+1}\}, \{S''_{n+2}\}, \{S'_{n+2}\}) \\
&\quad \vdash (\{S'_{n+1}\}, \dots, \{S'_{n+1}\}, \{S''_{n+2}\}, \{S'_{n+2}\}) \\
&\quad \Rightarrow (\{S'_{n+1}\}, \dots, \{S'_{n+1}\}, \{S''_{n+2}\}, \{S''_{n+2}\}) \\
&\quad \vdash (\{S'_{n+1}\}, \dots, \{S'_{n+1}\}, \{S''_{n+2}\}, \{S_{n+2}\}) .
\end{aligned}$$

If $L_{V''}$ is not empty, then by the next rewriting step, all words of $L_{V''}$ are rewritten to words over T representing the Hamiltonian path in γ. It is also obvious, that $L_{V''}$ identifies all Hamiltonian paths and the following derivation steps do not result in further words over T. □

5. Final Remarks

Analyzing the above proofs, it can be seen that some of the results remain valid for networks of parallel language processor or networks of evolutionary processors if we modify the notion of their functioning in such way that the successfully communicated strings are concatenated in the same way as in the case of FCCPC grammar systems. Since these constructs can be considered as models of biological sequences, these new variants might be of interest, since they can be considered as models of sequence assembly in biologically inspired networks. We plan to return to these topics in the future.

References

1. J. Castellanos, C. Martín-Vide, V. Mitrana and J. Sempere, in *IWANN 2001*, Eds., J. Mira and A. Prieto (Lecture Notes in Computer Science, Vol. 2084, Springer-Verlag, Berlin, 2001), p. 621.
2. J. Castellanos, C. Martín-Vide, V. Mitrana and J. Sempere, *Acta Inform.*, **39(6-7)**, 517 (2003).
3. E. Csuhaj-Varjú, *EATCS Bull.*, **63**, 134 (1997).
4. E. Csuhaj-Varjú, in *Proc. Workshop Algebraic Systems, Languages and Computations, March 21-23, 2000, Kyoto,* Ed. M. Ito (RIMS Kokyuroku 1116, Kyoto, 2000), p. 43.
5. E. Csuhaj-Varjú, L. Kari, and Gh. Păun, Test tube distributed systems based on splicing. *Comput. and Artif. Intell.*, **15(2-3)**, 211 (1996).
6. E. Csuhaj-Varjú, J. Kelemen, and Gh. Păun, *Comput. and Artif. Intell.*, **15(5)**, 419 (1996).
7. E. Csuhaj-Varjú and A. Salomaa, in *New Trends in Formal Languages; Control, Cooperation, and Combinatorics*, Eds. Gh. Păun and A. Salomaa (Lecture Notes in Computer Science, Vol. 1218, Springer-Verlag, Berlin, 1997), p. 299.
8. E. Csuhaj-Varjú and A. Salomaa, *EATCS Bull.*, **66**, 122 (1998).
9. E. Csuhaj-Varjú and A. Salomaa, in *Words, Languages & Combinatorics III*, Ed. M. Ito and T. Imaoka (World Scientific, Singapore, 2003), p. 134.
10. E. Csuhaj-Varjú and A. Salomaa, in *Aspects of Molecular Computing. Essays Dedicated to Tom Head on the Occasion of His 70th Birthday.*, Eds. N. Jonoska, Gh. Păun, and G. Rozenberg (Lecture Notes in Computer Science, Vol. 2950, Springer, Berlin, 2004), p. 106.
11. L. Errico, C. Jesshope, in *Proc. Conf. Artificial Intelligence and Information-Control Systems of Robots '94*, Ed. I Plander (World Scientific, Singapore, 1994), p. 31.
12. S. E. Fahlman, G. E. Hinton, T. J. Seijnowski, in *Proc. AAAI National Conf. on AI*, (William Kaufman, Los Altos, 1983), p. 109.
13. L. Ilie and A. Salomaa, *Acta Cybern.*, **12(4)**, 411 (1996).

14. G. Rozenberg and A. Salomaa, Eds., *Handbook of Formal Languages*, (Springer, Berlin-Heidelberg, 1997)
15. A. Salomaa, *Formal Languages*, (Academic Press, New York, 1973).
16. A. Salomaa, *Computation and Automata*, (Cambridge University Press, Cambridge, London, New York, 1985.)
17. P. S. Sapaty, *The WAVE Paradigm, Internal Report 17/92*, (Dept. Informatics, University of Karlsruhe, 1992).
18. Thinking Machines Corporation, *Connection Machine Model CM-2 Technical Summary.* (Thinking Machines Corporation, Cambridge, Mass., 1987).

CHAPTER 5

SOME REMARKS ON HOMOGENEOUS GENERATING NETWORKS OF FREE EVOLUTIONARY PROCESSORS

Jürgen Dassow

Faculty of Computer Science, University of Magdeburg,
P.O.Box 4120, D-39016, Magdeburg, Germany
E-mail: dassow@iws.cs.uni-magdeburg.de

Carlos Martín-Vide

Research Group in Mathematical Linguistics, Rovira i Virgili University,
Pça. Imperial Tarraco 1, 43005, Tarragona, Spain
E-mail: carlos.martin@urv.net

Victor Mitrana

Faculty of Mathematics and Computer Science, University of Bucharest,
Str. Academiei 14, 010014, Bucharest, Romania
and
Research Group in Mathematical Linguistics, Rovira i Virgili University,
Pça. Imperial Tarraco 1, 43005, Tarragona, Spain
E-mail: mitrana@fmi.unibuc.ro

This work is a first step of an investigation regarding homogeneous generating networks of free evolutionary processors (HGNFEP for short). HGNFEP is an extremely simple variant of generating hybrid networks of evolutionary processors showed to be a computationally complete model in Ref. 9. Two simplifications are considered: all filters are completely removed such that words can freely navigate in the networks and all evolutionary operations are applied uniformly. In our view, this variant seems most suitable for a possible biological implementation. We prove that such networks with two nodes only are able to generate non-regular languages and give an upper limit for the computational power of these devices: each language generated by a HGNFEP can be accepted by a normalized generalized partially blind one-way multicounter machine. As a direct consequence, the membership problem for HGNFEPs is decidable.

1. Introduction

The line of research discussed in this paper lies among a wide range of language based approaches rooted in molecular biology. A very few of them are briefly discussed in what follows. Although biologists have long made use of linguistic metaphors in describing processes involving nucleic acids, protein sequences, cellular phenomena, since 1980's molecular sequences started to be investigated with the methods and tools derived from Chomsky's legacy.[24–26] Some surveys present various applications of Chomsky grammars or derivatives of them in biology.[27,28] Computational biology led on the other hand, in the context of formal languages based modelling, to the emergent area of natural computing, which investigates new computational paradigms rooted in biology.[20]

Treating chromosomes and genomes as words and languages raises the possibility to generalize and investigate the structural information contained in biological sequences by means of the formal language theory methods. It is suggested[26] that both syntactical and functional structure of formal grammars can be modelled by sets of nucleotides and hybridization experiments, respectively. Chromosomal rearrangements including pericentric and paracentric inversions, intrachromosomal as well as interchromosomal transpositions, translocations are modelled as operations on languages.[24,10,29] A language generating mechanism based on the operations suggested by all mutations mentioned above is introduced[10] and some properties studied.[1]

A few words about the history of introducing the model discussed here. A rather well-known architecture for parallel and distributed symbolic processing, related to the Connection Machine[15] as well as the Logic Flow paradigm[11] consists of several processors, each of them being placed in a node of a virtual complete graph, which are able to handle data associated with the respective node. Each node processor acts on the local data in accordance with some predefined rules, and then local data becomes a mobile agent which can navigate in the network following a given protocol. Only that data which can pass a filtering process can be communicated to the other processors. This filtering process may require to satisfy some conditions imposed by the sending processor, by the receiving processor or by both of them. All the nodes send simultaneously their data and the receiving nodes handle also simultaneously all the arriving messages, according to some strategies, see, e.g., Refs. 12 and 15.

Starting from the premise that data can be given in the form of words, Csuhaj-Varjú & Salomaa introduced in Ref. 6 a concept called network of parallel language processors with the aim of investigating this concept in terms of formal grammars and languages. Networks of parallel language processors are closely related to grammar systems,[5] more specifically to parallel communicating grammar systems.[19] The main idea is that one can place a language generating device (grammar, Lindenmayer system, etc.) in each node of an underlying graph. Each device rewrites the words existing in the corresponding node and then the words are communicated to the other nodes. Words can be successfully communicated if they pass some output and input filters. More recently,[8] introduced networks whose nodes are (standard) Watson-Crick D0L systems which communicate each other either the correct or the corrected words.

In Ref. 2, this concept was modified in a way inspired from cell biology. Each processor placed in the nodes of the network is a very simple processor, an evolutionary processor. This is not a real, existing object but a mathematical concept. By an evolutionary processor it is meant a processor which is able to perform very simple operations, namely formal language theoretic operations that mimic the point mutations in a DNA sequence (insertion, deletion or substitution of a pair of nucleotides). More generally, each node may be viewed as a cell having genetic information encoded in DNA sequences which may evolve by local evolutionary events, namely point mutations. Each node is specialized just for one of these evolutionary operations. Furthermore, the data in each node is organized in the form of multisets of words (each word appears in an arbitrarily large number of copies), and all copies are processed in parallel such that all the possible events that can take place do actually take place. From the biological point of view, it cannot be expected that the components of any biological organism evolve sequentially or the cell reproduction may be modelled within a sequential approach. Cell state changes are modelled by rewriting rules like in formal grammars. The parallel nature of the cell state changes is modelled by the parallel execution of the symbols rewriting according to the rules applied. Consequently, hybrid networks of evolutionary processors might be viewed as bio-inspired computing models. Obviously, the computational process described here is not exactly an evolutionary process in the Darwinian sense. But the rewriting operations we have considered might be interpreted as mutations and the filtering process might be viewed as a selection process. Recombination is missing but it was asserted that evolutionary and functional relationships between genes can be captured by taking only local mutations into consideration.[23] Furthermore, we are not concerned here with a possible biological implementation, though a matter of great importance.

Our mechanisms introduced in Ref. 2 are further considered in a series of subsequent works as language generating and their computational power in this respect is investigated. Furthermore, filters based on the random-context conditions used in Ref. 6 are generalized in some versions defined in Refs. 2 and 3. More precisely, the new filters are based on different types of random-context conditions which seem to be more appropriate for an automated or biological implementation. In the aforementioned papers, the filters of all nodes are defined by the same random-context condition type. Moreover, the rules are applied in the same manner in all the nodes. These restrictions are discarded in Refs. 18 and 17. By this reason, these networks are called hybrid. On the other hand, this model is considered as an accepting device in Ref. 17, where a new characterization of **NP** is obtained, as well as a problem solver in Refs. 18 and 16, where a few NP-complete problems are solved in linear time with polynomially bounded resources.

A similar concept is the one introduced in Ref. 7 inspired by the evolution of cell populations, which might model some properties of evolving cell communities at the syntactical level. Cells are represented by words which describe their DNA sequences. Informally, at any moment of time, the evolutionary system is described by a collection of words, where each word represents one cell. Cells belong to species and their community evolves according to mutations and division which are defined by operations on words. Only those cells are accepted as surviving (correct) ones which are represented by a word in a given set of words, called the genotype space of the species.

This feature parallels with the natural process of evolution. It is worth mentioning that any recursively enumerable language is a language of a species of an evolutionary system with point mutations of restricted forms. In the aforementioned paper, a connection between Lindenmayer systems (language theoretical models of developmental systems) and evolutionary systems is established, namely the growth function of any deterministic 0L system can be obtained from the population growth relation of some (deterministic) evolutionary system.

The aforementioned models, besides the mathematical motivation, may also have a biological one. Cells always form tissues and organs interacting with each other either directly or via the common environment. In this context, our approach is closely related to "tissue-like" or "neural-like" membrane systems, see, e.g., the Chapter 6 in Ref. 21.

In this paper we start an investigation on a variant of generating network of evolutionary processors twofold motivated:

(i) Firstly, the considered variant is an extreme simplification of the models studied in Refs. 4, 9 and 18, showed to be computationally complete in Ref. 9. Thus, all filters are completely removed such that words can freely navigate in the networks and all evolutionary operations are applied uniformly.

(ii) Secondly, this variant seems most suitable to be biologically implemented.

2. Basic Definitions

We first summarize the notions we shall use throughout the paper; for the notions undefined here the reader is referred to Ref. 22. An *alphabet* is a finite and nonempty set of symbols. The cardinality of a finite set A is written as card(A). A sequence of symbols from an alphabet V is called a *word* over V. The set of all words over V is denoted by V^* and the empty word is denoted by ε; we use $V^+ = V^* - \{\varepsilon\}$. The length of a word x is denoted by $|x|$, while we denote the number of occurrences of a letter a in a word x by $|x|_a$. For an alphabet $V = \{a_1, a_2, \ldots, a_k\}$, the Parikh mapping associated with V is a homomorphism ψ_V from V^* into the monoid of vector addition on $\mathbb{N}^k$, defined by $\Psi_V(s) = (|s|_{a_1}, |s|_{a_2}, \ldots, |s|_{a_k})$.

We say that a rule $a \to b$, with $a, b \in V \cup \{\varepsilon\}$ is a *substitution rule* if both a and b are different from ε; it is a *deletion rule* if $a \neq \varepsilon$ and $b = \varepsilon$; and, it is an *insertion rule* if $a = \varepsilon$ and $b \neq \varepsilon$. The set of all substitution, deletion, and insertion rules over an alphabet V are denoted by Sub_V, Del_V, and Ins_V, respectively. Given a rule σ, as above, and a word $w \in V^*$, we define the following *actions* of σ on w:

— If $\sigma \equiv a \to b \in Sub_V$, then

$$\sigma^*(w) = \begin{cases} \{ubv : \exists\, u, v \in V^*(w = uav)\}, \\ \{w\}, \quad \text{otherwise} \end{cases}$$

— If $\sigma \equiv a \to \varepsilon \in Del_V$, then

$$\sigma^*(w) = \begin{cases} \{uv : \exists\, u, v \in V^*(w = uav)\}, \\ \{w\}, \quad \text{otherwise} \end{cases}$$

$$\sigma^r(w) = \begin{cases} \{u : w = ua\}, \\ \{w\}, \quad \text{otherwise} \end{cases} \qquad \sigma^l(w) = \begin{cases} \{v : w = av\}, \\ \{w\}, \quad \text{otherwise} \end{cases}$$

— If $\sigma \equiv \varepsilon \to a \in Ins_V$, then

$$\sigma^*(w) = \{uav : \exists\, u, v \in V^*(w = uv)\}, \quad \sigma^r(w) = \{wa\}, \quad \sigma^l(w) = \{aw\}.$$

Symbol $\alpha \in \{*, l, r\}$ denotes the way of applying an insertion or deletion rule to a word, namely, at any position ($\alpha = *$), in the left-hand end ($\alpha = l$), or in the right-hand end ($\alpha = r$) of the word, respectively. Note that a substitution rule can be applied at any position only. For every rule σ, action $\alpha \in \{*, l, r\}$, and $L \subseteq V^*$, we define the *α-action of σ on L* by $\sigma^\alpha(L) = \bigcup_{w \in L} \sigma^\alpha(w)$. For a given finite set of rules M, we define the *α-action of M* on a word w and on a language L by:

$$M^\alpha(w) = \bigcup_{\sigma \in M} \sigma^\alpha(w) \quad \text{and} \quad M^\alpha(L) = \bigcup_{w \in L} M^\alpha(w),$$

respectively.

In the following we shall refer to the rewriting operations defined above as *evolutionary operations*, since they may be viewed as formulations of local gene mutations in terms of formal languages.

A *generating network of free evolutionary processors* (GNFEP) is a 6-tuple $\Gamma = (V, G, \mathcal{N}, C_0, \alpha, i_0)$, where the following conditions hold:

- V is an alphabet.
- $G = (X_G, E_G)$ is an undirected graph with the set of vertices X_G and the set of edges E_G, each edge is given in the form of a set of two nodes. Note that G has no loop. G is called the *underlying graph* of the network.
- $\mathcal{N} : X_G \longrightarrow 2^{Del_V \cup Ins_V \cup Sub_V}$ is a mapping which associates with each node $x \in X_G$ the set $\mathcal{N}(x)$ of evolutionary rules, such that either $\mathcal{N}(x) \subseteq Sub_V$ or $\mathcal{N}(x) \subseteq Del_V$ or $\mathcal{N}(x) \subseteq Ins_V$. Note that every processor is dedicated to one type of the above evolutionary operations only.
- $C_0 : X_G \longrightarrow V^*$ is a mapping which identifies the initial configuration of the network. It associates a finite set of words with each node of the graph G.
- $\alpha : X_G \longrightarrow \{*, l, r\}$; $\alpha(x)$ gives the action mode of the rules of node x on the words occurring in that node.
- $i_0 \in X_G$ is the *output node* of the GNFEP.

We say that card(X_G) is the *size* of Γ. If $\alpha(x) = \alpha(y)$ and $\beta(x) = \beta(y)$ for any pair of nodes x, $y \in X_G$, then the network is said to be *homogeneous*. Note that in a homogeneous GNFEP (HGNFEP for short), the way of applying the evolutionary rules is $*$ for all nodes. If the set of rules in every node consists of at most one rule, then the network is said to be *elementary*.

The central object of investigation of this work is the HGNFEP. In the theory of networks some types of underlying graphs are common, these are for example, rings, stars, grids, paths, etc. We shall investigate networks of evolutionary processors with these underlying graphs. Thus, a (H)GNFEP is said to be a *star, ring, path or complete* (H)GNFEP if its underlying graph is a star, ring, path or complete graph, respectively. The star, ring, path, and complete graph with n vertices is denoted by S_n, R_n, P_n, and K_n, respectively.

A *configuration* of an (H)GNFEP Γ as above is a mapping $C : X_G \longrightarrow V^*$ which associates a set of words with each node of the graph. A component $C(x)$ of a configuration C is the set of words that can be found in the node x in this configuration, hence a configuration can be considered as the sets of words which are present in the nodes of the network at a given moment. A configuration can change either by an *evolutionary step* or by a *communication step*. When changing by an evolutionary step, each component $C(x)$ of the configuration C is changed in accordance with the set of evolutionary rules $\mathcal{N}(x)$ associated with the node x and the way of applying these rules $\alpha(x)$. Formally, we say that the configuration C' is obtained in *one evolutionary step* from the configuration C, written as $C \Longrightarrow C'$, iff

$$C'(x) = \mathcal{N}(x)^{\alpha(x)}(C(x)) \quad \text{for all} \quad x \in X_G .$$

When changing by a communication step, each node processor $x \in X_G$ sends a copy of each of its words to every node processor which is connected with x and receives all the words which are sent by the node processors connected with x. Formally, we say that the configuration C' is obtained in *one communication step* from configuration C, written as $C \vdash C'$, iff

$$C'(x) = \bigcup_{\{x,y\} \in E_G} C(y) \text{ for all } x \in X_G .$$

Let Γ a (H)GNFEP, a *computation* in Γ is a sequence of configurations C_0, $C_1, C_2, \ldots$, where C_0 is the initial configuration of Γ, $C_{2i} \Longrightarrow C_{2i+1}$ and $C_{2i+1} \vdash C_{2i+2}$, for all $i \geq 0$. The generated language is the set of all words which appear in the output node in a configuration of a computation in the network. Formally, the *language* generated by Γ is

$$L(\Gamma) = \bigcup_{s \geq 0} C_s(i_0) .$$

Some remarks are worth mentioning here. In GHNEPs (generating hybrid networks of evolutionary processors), as they were considered in Refs. 2–4, 9 and 18, each processor is endowed with both an input and output filter which actually are predicates based on *random-context conditions* defined by two sets P (*permitting contexts/symbols*) and F (*forbidding contexts/symbols*). Informally, these conditions applied to a word w require that either

— all permitting symbols are and no forbidding symbol is present in w, or
— all symbols of w are permitting ones, or
— some forbidding symbols may appear in w but not all of them, or
— at least one permitting symbol appears in w.

In a communication step of a GHNEP each node processor $x \in X_G$ sends one copy of each word it has, which is able to pass the output filter of x, to all the node processors connected to x and receives all the words sent by any node processor connected with x providing that they can pass its input filter.

Therefore, HGNFEPs defined above are very particular variants of GHNEPs in which filters are ignored which means that at any moment each string can pass both input and output filter of any node. Furthermore, all rules of any processor are applied in the same manner. In our view an investigation of the computational power of HGNFEPs is naturally motivated by one of the main results from Ref. 9 which states that any recursively enumerable language can be generated by an elementary complete or star GHNEP.

3. Computational Power of HGNFEPs

We present a few remarks about the computational power of HGNFEPs regardless the underlying graph structure. Clearly, the language generated by any HGNFEP of size 1, which is actually a GHNEP, is regular. But not all regular languages can be generated by HGNFEPs of size 1, see, e.g., Ref. 4 where one further proves that one can algorithmically decide whether or not a given regular language can be generated by a HGNFEP. As we shall see below, there are HGNFEPs of size 2 generating non-regular languages. Since the underlying structure of any HGNFEP of size 2 is the same we have the following result:

Proposition 1: *There are elementary and complete/star/ring/path HGNFEPs generating non-regular languages.*

Proof: It is sufficient to take a homogeneous, elementary GNFEP Γ with two nodes x, y both being insertion nodes. Assume that in x the symbol a

is inserted while in y the symbol b is inserted. If one starts with the empty word in x and x is the output node, then

$$L(\Gamma) = \{w \in \{a,b\}^* || w|_a = |w|_b \text{ or } |w|_a = |w|_b + 1, |w|_b \geq 0\}$$

which is not a regular language. □

As we have seen HGNFEPs with two nodes are able to generate non-regular languages; on the other hand we have:

Proposition 2: *There are regular languages, even over the unary alphabet, which cannot be generated by any HGNFEP.*

Proof: The regular language $L = \{a^{2n} | n \geq 1\}$ is such a language. Assume that L can be generated by a HGNFEP $\Gamma = (V, G, \mathcal{N}, C_0, i_0)$ with the nodes labelled by $1, 2, \ldots, n$. Let $j_1, j_2, \ldots, j_k$ be the nodes of G such that $C_0(j_t) \neq \emptyset$ for all $1 \leq t \leq k$. Since the language generated by Γ is infinite, there exists a path $r_1, r_2, \ldots, r_m$ in G such that the following conditions are satisfied:

(i) $r_1 = j_t$ for some $1 \leq t \leq k$ and $r_m = i_0$.
(ii) there exists $1 \leq p \leq m-1$ such that if $\varepsilon \to b \in \mathcal{N}(j_p)$ for some $b \in V$, then either j_{p+1} is not a deletion node or $b \to \varepsilon$ is not the only rule of $\mathcal{N}(j_{p+1})$.

Clearly, if $p = m-1$, then we get a contradiction since as soon as a^{2s}, for some $s > 0$, is in i_0, $a^{2s}b$ will be in i_0 after three steps. Therefore, we can take $p < m-1$. We distinguish two cases:

Case 1. $\varepsilon \to b \in \mathcal{N}(j_p)$ and $b \neq a$.

The path

$$j_m, j_{m-1}, \ldots, \underbrace{\underbrace{j_{p+1}, j_p}, \underbrace{j_{p+1}, j_p}, \ldots, \underbrace{j_{p+1}, j_p}}_{m \text{ times}}\ j_{p+1}, j_{p+2}, \ldots, j_m$$

can transform a^{2s} into a word containing the symbol $b \neq a$, a contradiction.

Case 2. $\varepsilon \to a \in \mathcal{N}(j_p)$.

By our assumption, either j_{p+1} is not a deletion node or $a \to \varepsilon$ is not the only rule of $\mathcal{N}(j_{p+1})$. It follows that one of the paths

$$j_m, j_{m-1}, \ldots, \underbrace{\underbrace{j_{p+1}, j_p}, \underbrace{j_{p+1}, j_p}, \ldots, \underbrace{j_{p+1}, j_p}}_{s \text{ times}}\ j_{p+1}, j_{p+2}, \ldots, j_m$$

$$j_m, j_{m-1}, \ldots, \underbrace{\underbrace{j_{p+1}, j_p}, \underbrace{j_{p+1}, j_p}, \ldots, \underbrace{j_{p+1}, j_p}}_{s+1 \text{ times}}\ j_{p+1}, j_{p+2}, \ldots, j_m$$

can transform a^{2s} into a word of odd length, a contradiction. □

Now we recall the definition of an automaton introduced in Ref. 13, which is a generalization of the partially blind automaton introduced in Ref. 14, in order to give an upper bound for the computational power of HGNFEPs. First, some preliminaries are needed. For a vector σ of the monoid of vector addition $\mathbb{N}^k$ we denote by $\sigma(i)$ the ith component of σ, $1 \leq i \leq k$. For a given k we denote by $\pi_i^{(k)}$ and λ_k the vector of size k having 1 on the ith position and 0 in rest, for each $1 \leq i \leq k$, and the empty vector of size k, respectively. For two vectors σ, $\tau \in \mathbb{N}^k$ we define $\sigma \sqsubseteq \tau$ iff $\sigma(i) \leq \tau(i)$ for all $1 \leq i \leq k$.

A *generalized partially blind one-way k-counter machine* (kGPBCM for short) is a construct $\Theta = (k, Q, V, f, q_0, \sigma)$, where $k \geq 1$ is the number of counters, Q and V are finite non-empty sets (the set of states and the input alphabet, respectively), $q_0 \in Q$ is the initial state, $\sigma \in \mathbb{N}^k$ is the initial contents of the counters, and $f : Q \times (V \cup \varepsilon) \times \mathbb{N}^k \to \mathcal{P}_f(Q \times \mathbb{N}^k)$ is the transition function. Θ is called *normalized*, if

$$f : Q \times (V \cup \varepsilon) \times \{\lambda_k, \pi_1^{(k)}, \pi_2^{(k)}, \ldots, \pi_k^{(k)}\} \to \mathcal{P}_f(Q \times \{\lambda_k, \pi_1^{(k)}, \pi_2^{(k)}, \ldots, \pi_k^{(k)}\}).$$

The behavior of a kGPBCM as above is described by transitions between configurations (instantaneous descriptions). A *configuration* of Θ is a triple $[q, x, \alpha]$, where $q \in Q$ is the current state of Θ, $x \in V^*$ is the contents of the input tape which is to be read, and $\alpha \in \mathbb{N}^k$ is the contents of its counters. A transition between two configurations $[q_1, ax, \alpha]$ and $[q_2, x, \beta]$ of Θ, with q_1, $q_2 \in Q$, $a \in V \cup \{\varepsilon\}$, $x \in V^*$, α, $\beta \in \mathbb{N}^k$, is defined by

$$[q_1, ax, \alpha] \vdash_\Theta [q_2, x, \beta]$$

iff there exist two vectors δ, γ of size k such that $(q_2, \gamma) \in f(q_1, a, \delta)$ and either $\delta \sqsubseteq \alpha$ and $\beta = \alpha - \delta + \gamma$, or $\delta \not\sqsubseteq \alpha$, $a = \varepsilon$, and $\beta = \alpha$. We denote by $\overset{*}{\vdash}_\Theta$ the reflexive and transitive closure of $\vdash_\Theta$.

The language recognized by Θ (by empty counters) is:

$$L_\lambda(\Theta) = \{w \in V^* | [q_0, w, \sigma] \overset{*}{\vdash} [q, \varepsilon, \lambda_k]\} .$$

The next result provides an upper bound for the computational power of HGNFEPs.

Proposition 3: *The language generated by any HGNFEP can be recognized by a normalized generalized partially blind one-way multicounter machine.*

Proof: Let $\Gamma = (V, G, \mathcal{N}, C_0, i_0)$ be a HGNFEP with $1, 2, \dots, n$ the labels of the underlying graph nodes. We define the normalized $nGPBCM\Theta = (n, V, Q, f, q_0, \lambda_n)$, where

$$Q = \{q_0\} \cup \left\{ q_f^x | x \text{ is a scattered subword of } w \in \bigcup_{i=1}^{n} C_0(i) \right\} \cup$$

$$\left\{ q_i^x | x \text{ is a scattered subword of}, 1 \le i \le n, w \in \bigcup_{j=1}^{n} C_0(j) \right\} \cup$$

$$\{\langle\tau\rangle_w^i | \tau \sqsubseteq \Psi_V(w), w \in C_0(i), 1 \le i \le n\} .$$

We informally describe the computation of this automaton on an input word w.

(1) From the initial state q_0 the automaton chooses nondeterministically a state $\langle\Psi_V(w)\rangle_w^i$ for some $w \in C_0(i)$, $1 \le i \le n$.

(2) Using states from $\{\langle\tau\rangle_w^i | \tau \sqsubseteq \Psi_V(w), w \in C_0(i)\}$ the automaton makes the content of the counters to be $\Psi_V(w)$ and enters q_i^w.

(3) The automaton follows a copy of w through the underlying graph G of Γ as described below. Let us suppose that our current word is z which lies in the node j, the current state of the automaton is q_i^y, and the current content of the counters is α. The following conditions are fulfilled:

(i) $i = j$,
(ii) y is a scattered subword of z,
(iii) $\alpha = \Psi_V(z)$.

Any application of a rule from a node to the current word, provided that the word lies in that node, transforms the content of the counters accordingly and may or may not transform the word stored in the state. Thus, at any moment, the index of the current state identifies the node in which the current word lies, the counter contents is exactly the Parikh image of this word and the word stored in the current state is a scattered subword of the current word.

Nondeterministically, when the current state is $q^y_{i_0}$, the automaton enters the state q^y_f.

(4) The automaton remains in states from $\{q^x_f | x$ is a scattered subword of $w \in \bigcup_{i=1}^{n} C_0(i)\}$ for the rest of the computation. It checks, reading effectively the input word, whether the Parikh image of the input word is exactly the counter contents as well as whether the word y, stored in the initial state q^y_f of this final part of computation, is a scattered subword of the input word. The input word is accepted if and only if both conditions are satisfied.

By these explanations it easily follows that the language accepted by Θ by empty counters is exactly $L(\Gamma)$. The reader interested to write formally the automaton Θ can do this following the above explanations. □

Clearly, this upper bound is rather unsatisfactory, a sharper limit being desirable. However, by this results, one can infer that the membership problem for HGNFEPs is decidable since the membership problem is decidable for generalized partially blind one-way multicounter machines.

4. Conclusion

This work is just the first step of an investigation regarding HGNFEPs. HGNFEP is an extremely simple variant of GHNEP showed to be computationally complete in Ref. 9. Thus, filters are completely removed such that words can freely navigate in the networks and all evolutionary operations are applied uniformly. Furthermore, in our view, this variant seems to offer more chances for a possible biological implementation.

We showed that such networks with two nodes only were able to generate non-regular languages and gave an upper limit for the computational power of these devices. Each language generated by a HGNFEP can be accepted by a normalized generalized partially blind one-way multicounter machine. There are plenty of natural problems for which we do not have an answer yet. A subjective list of such problems includes:

(1) Are there non-context-free languages which can be generated by HGNFEPs? If the answer is affirmative, which is the minimal size of such a HGNFEP?

(2) Are all languages generated by HGNFEPs semilinear?

(3) The membership problem is decidable while the emptiness problem is rather trivial. What other decidable properties do HGNFEPs posses? What is the membership complexity?

Since we consider that these devices deserve further investigation, we intend to return to these topics in other works.

References

1. I. Ardelean, M. Gheorghe, C. Martín-Vide and V. Mitrana, *BioSystems*, **76**, 1-3 (2004).
2. J. Castellanos, C. Martín-Vide, V. Mitrana and J. Sempere, *International Workshop on Artificial and Neural Networks IWANN 2001*, Eds. J. Mira and A. Prieto, (LNCS 2084, Springer-Verlag, Berlin, 2001), p. 621.
3. J. Castellanos, C. Martí n-Vide, V. Mitrana and J. Sempere, *Acta Informatica*, **39** (2003).
4. J. Castellanos, P. Leupold and V. Mitrana, *Theoret. Comput. Sci.* **330**, 2 (2005).
5. E. Csuhaj-Varjú, J. Dassow, J. Kelemen and G. Păun, *Grammar Systems*, (Gordon and Breach, London, 1993).
6. E. Csuhaj-Varjú and A. Salomaa, in *New Trends in Formal Languages*, Eds. G. Păun and A. Salomaa, (LNCS 1218, Springer Verlag, Berlin, 1997), p. 299.
7. E. Csuhaj-Varjú and V. Mitrana, *Acta Informatica*, **36** (2000).
8. E. Csuhaj-Varjú and A. Salomaa, in *Proc. International Conference Words, Languages & Combinatorics III*, Eds. M. Ito and T. Imaoka, (World Scientific, Singapore, 2003), p. 134.
9. E. Csuhaj-Varjú, C. Martín-Vide and V. Mitrana, *Acta Informatica*, **41**, 4-5 (2005).
10. J. Dassow, V. Mitrana and A. Salomaa, *Theoret. Comput. Sci.* **270**, 1-2 (2001).
11. L. Errico and C. Jesshope, in *Artificial Intelligence and Information-Control Systems of Robots '94*, Ed. I. Plander, (World Scientific, Singapore, 1994), p. 31.
12. S. E. Fahlman, G. E. Hinton and T. J. Seijnowski, in *Proc. AAAI National Conf. on AI*, (William Kaufman, Los Altos, 1983), p. 109.
13. R. Gramatovici, C. Martín-Vide and Mitrana, manuscript, 2005.
14. S. A. Greibach, *Theoret. Comput. Sci.* **7** (1978).
15. W. D. Hillis, *The Connection Machine*, (MIT Press, Cambridge, 1985).
16. F. Manea, C. Martín-Vide and V. Mitrana, in *Proc. of MCU 2004*, (LNCS 3354, Springer Verlag, Berlin, 2005), p. 269.
17. M. Margenstern, V. Mitrana and M. Perez-Jimenez, in *Proc. of DNA 10*, (LNCS 3384, Springer Verlag, Berlin, 2005), p. 107.
18. C. Martín-Vide, V. Mitrana, M. Perez-Jimenez and F. Sancho-Caparrini, in *Proc. of GECCO 2003*, (LNCS 2723, Springer Verlag, Berlin, 2003), p. 401.

19. G. Păun and L. Sântean, *Ann. Univ. Bucharest, Ser. Matem.-Inform.* **38** (1989).
20. G. Păun, G. Rozenberg and A. Salomaa, *DNA Computing. New Computing Paradigms*, (Springer-Verlag, Berlin, 1998).
21. G. Păun, *Membrane Computing. An Introduction*, (Springer Verlag, Berlin, 2002).
22. G. Rozenberg and A. Salomaa, Eds. *Handbook of Formal Languages* (Springer Verlag, Berlin, 1997).
23. D. Sankoff, G. Leduc, N. Antoine, B. Paquin, B. F. Lang and R. Cedergren, *Proc. Natl. Acad. Sci. USA*, **89** (1992).
24. D. B. Searls, in *Proc. of the 7th National Conference on Artificial Intelligence*, (American Assoc. Artif. Intell. 1988), p. 386.
25. D. B. Searls, in *Artificial Intelligence and Molecular Biology*, Ed. L. Hunter (AAAI Press, The MIT Press, 1993), p. 47.
26. D. B. Searls, in *IEEE Symp on Intelligence in Neural and Biological Systems*, (IEEE Computer Society Press, 1995), p. 30.
27. D. B. Searls, *Bioinformatics* **13** (1997).
28. D. B. Searls, *Nature* **420** (2002).
29. T. Yokomori and S. Kobayashi,*IEEE Symp. on Intelligence in Neural and Biological Systems* (IEEE Computer Society Press, 1995), p. 38

CHAPTER 6

HEXAGONAL CONTEXTUAL ARRAY P SYSTEMS

K. S. Dersanambika*, K. Krithivasan*, H. K. Agarwal† and J. Gupta†

*Department of Computer Science and Engineering,
Indian Institute of Technology Madras,
Chennai 600 036, India
E-mail: kamala@iitm.ernet.in

†Department of Electrical Engineering,
Indian Institute of Technology Madras,
Chennai 600 036, India

In this paper external and internal hexagonal array grammars and external and internal hexagonal array contextual P systems, which generate hexagonal arrays are defined. Some properties of these systems are discussed.

1. Introduction

P systems are a class of distributed parallel computing devices of a biochemical type introduced in Ref. 10, which can be seen as a general computing architecture where various types of objects can be processed by various operations. In the basic model one considers a membrane structure consisting of several cell-like membranes placed inside a main membrane, called the skin membrane. If a membrane does not contain any other membrane it is called an elementary membrane. Graphically a membrane structure is represented by a Venn diagram without intersection and with a unique superset. The membranes delimit regions, where we place objects, elements of a finite set. In this paper, we use array objects.

Starting from an initial configuration and using the evolution rules, we get a computation. We consider a computation complete when it halts, i.e., no further rule can be applied. Two ways of assigning a result to a computation were considered, one by designating an internal membrane as the output membrane, and the other by reading the result outside the system. We deal here with the latter variant.

There have been many pioneering works, in suggesting and applying a linguistic model in picture processing.[3,13,14] Contextual grammars were introduced by S. Marcus[7] as an intrinsic generation mechanism, without using auxiliary symbols and based not on rewriting but on the fundamental linguistic operation of adjoining contexts according to a selection procedure.

In ordinary context-free grammars, from a string xAy, by applying a rule $A \to w$, a string xwy can be derived. In contextual grammars the string xwy is derived by attaching the contexts (x, y) to the string w. Thus in a contextual grammar, the derivation steps occur in a somewhat reverse order compared to the steps of the context-free grammar.

Contextual P systems were considered in Ref. 5 and array contextual grammars were considered in Ref. 4. In this paper, we define contextual hexagonal array P systems, in which the rules consist of attaching contexts to hexagonal arrays depending upon a choice mapping. We consider some variants of contextual grammars and prove that contextual hexagonal array P systems with rules of the types corresponding to these variants are more powerful than the usual hexagonal array contextual grammars and their variants.

In Section 2, we give some prerequisites and also define external and internal hexagonal array grammars. In Section 3, external and internal hexagonal array contextual P systems are defined and some examples are given. One-sided contextual hexagonal array P systems are also defined. Some properties of hexagonal array contextual P systems are discussed in Section 5. The paper ends with a brief concluding remark in Section 7.

2. Preliminaries

Let I be an alphabet, a finite nonempty set of symbols. The set of all hexagonal arrays over I (including the empty array Λ) is denoted by I^{**H} and $I^{++H} = I^{**H} - \{\Lambda\}$.

The size of the hexagonal array is defined by parameters LU (Left Upper), LL (Left Lower), RU (Right Upper), RL (Right Lower), U (Upper), L (Lower) as shown in the Fig. 1.

For $X \in V^{**H}$ the length of Left Upper side of X is denoted by $|X|_{LU}$; similarly we define $|X|_{LL}$, $|X|_{RU}$, $|X|_{RL}$, $|X|_U$ and $|X|_L$.

For hexagonal arrays, three types of concatenation, viz. $\nearrow$, $\nwarrow$ and $\to$ catenation are defined.

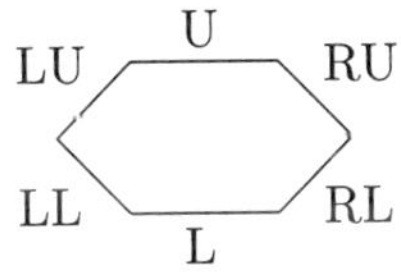

Fig. 1. Hexagonal array.

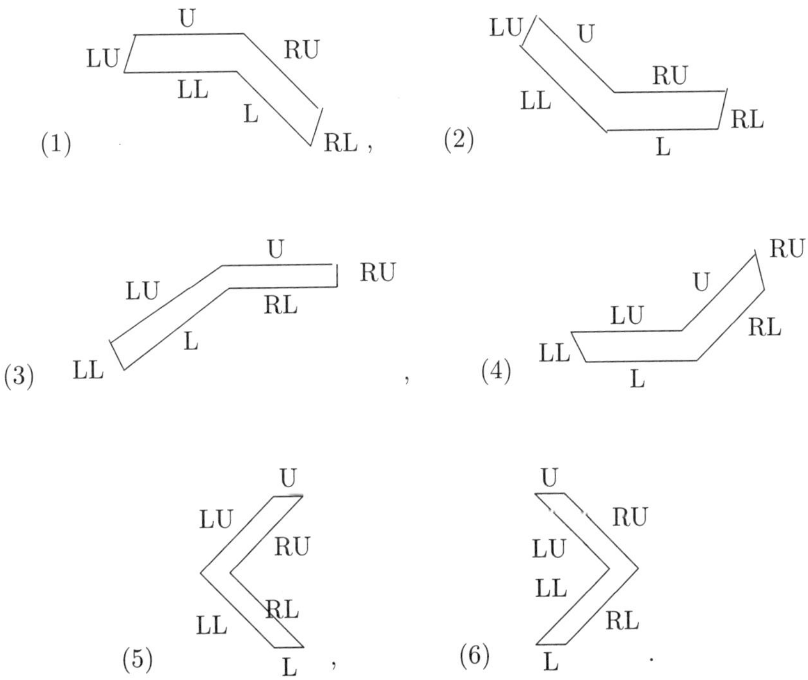

Fig. 2. Different arrowheads.

The hexagonal arrays in the form of arrowheads are given in Fig. 2. Six types of arrowheads are shown in the figure. It can be easily seen that, a hexagonal array of the form given in Fig. 1 can be concatenated with any one of the arrowheads to get a resultant hexagonal array.

Definition 1: For a hexagonal array X and an arrowhead Y of type 1, the $\nearrow$ catenation $X \oslash Y$ is defined if $|X|_U = |Y|_{LL}$, $|X|_{RU} = |Y|_L$ and the alignment of Upper and Right Upper side of X, and Left Lower and Lower side of Y should be such that the resultant is a hexagonal array.

For an arrowhead Y of type 2 and a hexagonal array X, the $\nearrow$ catenation $Y \oslash X$ is defined if $|X|_L = |Y|_{RU}$, $|X|_{LL} = |Y|_U$ and the alignment of Lower and Left Lower side of X, and Right Upper and Upper side of arrowhead Y should be such that the resultant is a hexagonal array.

Similarly, the $\nwarrow$ catenation and the $\rightarrow$ catenation can be defined.

For $x \in V^{**H}$, we denote the number of a's in the array x as $n_a(x)$. The set of arrays in the form of arrowheads 2 and 1 having thickness of 1 in $\nearrow$ direction are denoted by $(\backslash \underline{a})^n$ or $(\overline{a}\,\backslash)^n$ depending on the arrowhead. Similarly, we can proceed for other directions. We denote the set of all proper subarrays of x as $PSub(x)$.

For details regarding contextual grammar, the reader is referred to Refs. 9 and 12.

We now consider hexagonal arrays, and informally recall arrowhead catenation, since arrowhead catenation to a hexagon results in a hexagon. Adding a context in the $\nearrow$ direction would mean, informally speaking.

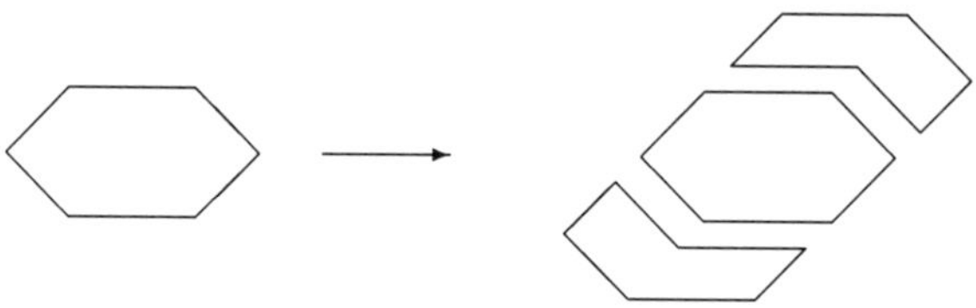

Similarly we can define adding context for the other two directions.
Some definitions for the case of hexagonal array contextual grammars are given below.

Definition 2: An external hexagonal array contextual grammar with choice ($EHACGC$) is a 6-tuple, $G = (V, B, L_{\oslash}, L_{\obslash}, L_{\ominus}, \varphi)$, where

(1) V is a finite nonempty set of symbols called the alphabet;
(2) B is a finite subset of V^{**H}, called the axioms;
(3) $L_{\oslash}$ — is a finite set of languages $\{\rho_1, \rho_2, \ldots, \rho_r\}$, each ρ_i consisting of arrowheads of type 1 or 2 of bounded thickness in the direction $\nearrow$;
(4) $L_{\obslash}$ — is a finite set of languages $\{\rho'_1, \rho'_2, \ldots, \rho'_s\}$, each ρ'_i consisting of arrowheads of type 3 or 4 of bounded thickness in the direction $\nwarrow$;
(5) $L_{\ominus}$, — is a finite set of languages $\{\rho''_1, \rho''_2, \ldots, \rho''_t\}$, each ρ''_i consisting of arrowheads of type 5 or 6 of bounded thickness in the direction $\rightarrow$;
(6) $\varphi_i : V^{**H} \rightarrow 2^{L_{\oslash} \cup L_{\obslash} \cup L_{\ominus}}$.

ρ_i's, ρ_i''s and ρ_i'''s are sets of arrays of the form of arrow heads. Derivation is defined as follows. For α, $\beta \in V^{**H}$, we say that α derives β, that is $\alpha \Rightarrow_{ex} \beta$, if:

Case I: $\beta = u\varnothing\ \alpha\varnothing\ v$ where u is an arrowhead of type 2 and v is an arrow head of type 1 and

$$|v|_{LL} = |\alpha|_U\,, \quad |v|_L = |\alpha|_{RU}\,, \quad |u|_U = |\alpha|_{LL}\,, \quad |u|_{RU} = |\alpha|_L$$

and $\varphi(\alpha)$ contain $\rho_i\$\rho_j$, $u \in \rho_i$, $v \in \rho_j$.

Case II: $\beta = u\Diamond\ \alpha\Diamond\ v$ where u, $v \in V^{**H}$, $\varphi(\alpha)$ contains ρ_i', $u\$v \in \rho_i'$, $\rho_i' \in L_{\Diamond}$ and

$$|v|_{RL} = |\alpha|_U\,, \quad |v|_L = |\alpha|_{LU}\,, \quad |u|_U = |\alpha|_{RL}\,, \quad |u|_{LU} = |\alpha|_L$$

Case III: $\beta = u\ominus\ \alpha\ominus\ v$ where u, $v \in V^{**H}$, $\varphi(\alpha)$ contains ρ_i'', $u\$v \in \rho_i''$, $\rho_i'' \in L_{\ominus}$ and

$$|v|_{RU} = |\alpha|_{LU}\,, \quad |u|_{RL} = |\alpha|_{LL}\,, \quad |v|_{LU} = |\alpha|_{RU}\,, \quad |v|_{LL} = |\alpha|_{RL}$$

Definition 3: The language generated by an $EHACGC$, G is defined as

$$L(G) = \{w \in V^{**H} | \alpha \Rightarrow_{ex}^{*} w, \alpha \in B\}\,.$$

By $EHACC$ we denote the family of languages generated by $EHACGC$.

Definition 4: An internal hexagonal array contextual grammar with choice ($IHACGC$) is a 6-tuple $G = (V, B, L_{\varnothing}, L_{\Diamond}, L_{\ominus}, \varphi)$, where V, B, $L_{\varnothing}$, $L_{\Diamond}$, $L_{\ominus}$, φ_i, are as in Definition 2.6.

For α, $\beta \in V^{**H}$, we say that α derives β, that is $\alpha \Rightarrow_{\text{in}} \beta$, if:

Case I: $\alpha = \alpha_1\varnothing\ \alpha_2\varnothing\ \alpha_3$, $\beta = \alpha_1\varnothing\ u\varnothing\ \alpha_2\varnothing\ v\varnothing\ \alpha_3$, where α_1, u are arrowheads of type 2, α_3, v are arrowheads of type 1, and $\alpha_2 \in V^{**H}$,

$$|\alpha_1|_U = |u|_{LL}\,, \quad |\alpha_1|_{RU} = |u|_L\,, \quad |u|_U = |\alpha_2|_{LL}\,, \quad |u|_{RU} = |\alpha_2|_L\,,$$

$$|\alpha_2|_U = |v|_{LL}\,, \quad |\alpha_2|_{RU} = |v|_L\,, \quad |v|_U = |\alpha_3|_{LL}\,, \quad |v|_{RU} = |\alpha_3|_L\,.$$

Similarly we define the other two cases.

Definition 5: The language generated by an $IHACGC$, G is defined as

$$L(G) = \{w \in V^{**H} | \alpha \Rightarrow_{\text{in}}^{*} w, \alpha \in B\}\,.$$

The family of languages generated by $IHACGC$ is denoted by $IHACC$.

In the previous definitions of $EHACGC$ and $IHACGC$, if the choice function is omitted, then the grammars are denoted by $EHACG$ and $IHACG$ respectively and the family of languages generated by them are denoted by $EHAC$ and $IHAC$ respectively.

Definition 6: A regulated external hexagonal array contextual grammar ($REHACG$) is a 6-tuple $G = (V, B, L_{\oslash}, L_{\obslash}, L_{\ominus}, R)$, where V, B, $L_{\oslash}, L_{\obslash}, L_{\ominus}$ are defined as in the definitions of $EHACGC$ and $IHACGC$, and R is a $PSL(REG, CFL, CSL)$ over set of rules R.

Here PSL, CSL, CFL and REG correspond to families of type 0, 1, 2 and 3 languages respectively.[12]

For α, $\beta \in V^{**H}$, we say that α derives β through the rule r, that is $\alpha \Rightarrow_{ex}^{r} \beta$, if

Case I: With the rules of the form $r : \rho_i \$ \rho_j$, ρ_i, $\rho_j \in L_{\oslash}$, $\beta = u \oslash \alpha \oslash v$, where $u \in \rho_i$, $v \in \rho_j$, $\alpha \in V^{**H}$ and $|v|_{LL} = |\alpha|_U$, $|v|_L = |\alpha|_{RU}$, $|u|_U = |\alpha|_{LL}$, $|u|_{RU} = |\alpha|_L$.

Similarly we define the other two cases.

The language generated by a $REHACG$ G is defined as $L(G) = \{x \in V^{**H} | \exists$ a sequence of steps $w \Rightarrow_{r_{i_1}} w_1 \Rightarrow_{r_{i_2}} \cdots \Rightarrow_{r_{i_n}} w_n = x$ and r_{i_1}, $r_{i_2}, \ldots, r_{i_n} \in R$, where $w \in B\}$.

The family of languages generated by $REHACG$ is denoted by $REHAC$. Similarly we define regulated internal hexagonal array contextual grammar which are denoted by $RIHACG$. The family of languages generated by $RIHACG$ is denoted by $RIHAC$.

3. External and Internal Hexagonal Array Contextual P Systems

In this section we define external and internal hexagonal array contextual P systems and give some examples.

Definition 7: An external contextual hexagonal array P system is a construct

$$\Pi = (V, T, \mu, M_1, M_2, \ldots, M_n, L_{\oslash}, L_{\obslash}, L_{\ominus}, R_1, R_2, \ldots, R_n, \varphi_1, \varphi_2, \ldots, \varphi_n),$$

where:

- V is the finite nonempty set of symbols called the total alphabet;
- $T \subseteq V$ is the set of terminal alphabet;
- μ is the membrane structure;

- M_i is a finite subset of V^{**H} whose elements are called axioms, representing the hexagonal arrays initially present in the region i, $1 \leq i \leq n$;
- $L_{\oslash}$ is a finite set of languages $\{\rho_1, \rho_2, \ldots, \rho_r\}$, each ρ_i containing arrowheads of bounded thickness in the direction $\nearrow$ (type 1 and 2);
- $L_{\otimes}$ is a finite set of languages $\{\rho'_1, \rho'_2, \ldots, \rho'_s\}$, each ρ'_i containing arrowheads of bounded thickness in the direction $\nwarrow$ (type 3 and 4);
- $L_{\ominus}$, is a finite set of languages $\{\rho''_1, \rho''_2, \ldots, \rho''_t\}$, each ρ''_i containing arrowheads of bounded thickness in the direction $\rightarrow$ (type 5 and 6);
- $\varphi_i : V^{**H} \rightarrow 2^{R_i}$.
- R_i are finite sets of rules of the form $(\rho_j \$ \rho_k, tar)$ or $(\rho_j \$ \rho_k, tar)\delta$ where $\rho_j, \rho_k \in L_{\oslash}$, or $\rho_j, \rho_k \in L_{\otimes}$, or $\rho_j, \rho_k \in L_{\ominus}$ and $tar \in \{\text{here}, \text{in}, \text{out}\}$ is a target indication, specifying the region where the result of the rewriting should be placed in the next step; "here" says that the result remains in the same membrane where the rule was applied, "out" says that the array has to be sent out of the region where it has been produced, and "in" says that the array should go to one of the directly inner membranes if any exists. Moreover, if the target is "in$_j$" then the array should go to the inner membrane j. ρ_i's , ρ'_i's and ρ''_i are sets of arrays over V^{**H}. If $(\rho_j \$ \rho_k, tar)$ is a rule where ρ_j, $\rho_k \in L_{\oslash}$ then ρ_j consist of arrowheads of type 2 and ρ_k consist of arrowheads of type 1. Similarly for the other two directions.

For α, $\beta \in V^{**H}$, we say that α derives β, i.e., $\alpha \Rightarrow_{ex} \beta$ if:

Case I: $\beta = u \oslash \alpha \oslash v$, where u, $v \in V^{**H}$, $\varphi_i(\alpha)$ contains $(\rho_j \$ \rho_k, tar)$ where ρ_j, $\rho_k \in L_{\oslash}$. The length of the sides of u, v, α should be such that it is possible to perform arrowhead catenation on α to get a proper hexagonal array β, i.e., $|v|_{LL} = |\alpha|_U$, $|v|_L = |\alpha|_{RU}$, $|u|_U = |\alpha|_{LL}$, $|u|_{RU} = |\alpha|_L u \in \rho_j$ and $v \in \rho_k$.

Similarly for the other two cases.

The membrane structure and the arrays in Π constitute the initial configuration of the system. We can pass from one configuration to another one by using the evolution rules. This is done in parallel: all arrays from all membranes, which can be the subject of local evolution rules should evolve simultaneously.

A sequence of transitions between configurations of a given P system Π is called a computation with respect to Π. A computation is successful if and only if it halts, that is there is no rule applicable to the terminal array present in the last configuration. The result of a successful computation is the set of hexagonal arrays which are sent out of the system during the computation (that is, only the arrays over T which are ejected out of the skin membrane are taken into account).

The family of languages generated by contextual P systems of degree at most n is denoted by $ECHAPC_n$ where the degree of the system is the total number of membranes in the system.

Example 1: Let us consider the system

$$\Pi = (V, T, \mu, M, L_{\oslash}, L_{\obslash}, L_{\ominus}, R, \varphi),$$

with: $V = T = \{X, a\}$, $\mu = [\ ]_1$,

$$M = \begin{array}{ccccc} & \mathrm{a} & & \mathrm{a} & \\ \mathrm{a} & & \mathrm{X} & & \mathrm{a} \\ & \mathrm{a} & & \mathrm{a} & \end{array},$$

$$L_{\oslash} = \{\rho_1, \rho_{11}\}, \quad \rho_1 = \{(\backslash\underline{a})^n | n \geq 1\}, \quad \rho_{11} = \{(\bar{a}\backslash)^n | n \geq 1\},$$

Here $(\backslash\underline{a})^n$ denotes an arrowhead of width one made up of n a's. Similarly for other arrowheads.

$$L_{\obslash} = \{\rho_2, \rho_{22},\}, \quad \rho_{22} = \{(/\bar{a})^n | n \geq 1\}, \quad \rho_2 = \{(\underline{a}/)^n | n \geq 1\},$$

$$L_{\ominus} = \{\rho_3, \rho_{33}\}, \quad \rho_3 = \{(< a)^n | n \geq 1\}, \quad \rho_{33} = \{(a >)^n | n \geq 1\},$$

$$R = \{(\rho_1 \$ \rho_{11}, \text{here}), (\rho_2 \$ \rho_{22}, \text{here}), (\rho_3 \$ \rho_{33}, \text{here}), (\rho_3 \$ \rho_{33}, \text{out})\},$$

$$\varphi(\alpha) = \{(\rho_1 \$ \rho_{11}, \text{here})\}, \varphi(\{(\backslash\underline{a})^n \oslash \alpha \oslash (\bar{a}\backslash)^n | n \geq 1\}) = \{(\rho_2 \$ \rho_{22}, \text{here})\},$$

$$\varphi((\underline{a}/)^n \obslash (\backslash\underline{a})^n \oslash \alpha \oslash (\bar{a}\backslash)^n \obslash (/\bar{a})^n | n \geq 1\})$$
$$= \{(\rho_3 \$ \rho_{33}, \text{here}), (\rho_3 \$ \rho_{33}, \text{out})\},$$

Here α is a hexagonal array of size $(2k, 2k, 2k)$, $k \geq 1$.

This hexagonal array P system generates arrays of size $(2n, 2n, 2n)$ with all "cells" marked with a, and with X in the center.

Definition 8: An internal hexagonal array contextual P system is a construct

$$\Pi = (V, T, \mu, M_1, M_2, \ldots, M_n, L_{\oslash}, L_{\obslash}, L_{\ominus}, R_1, R_2, \ldots, R_n, \varphi_1, \varphi_2, \ldots, \varphi_n),$$

where V, T, μ, M_i, $L_{\oslash}$, $L_{\obslash}$, $L_{\ominus}$, φ_i, R_i are as defined earlier, and with the derivation defined as follows. For α, $\beta \in V^{**H}$, we say that α derives

β, i.e., $\alpha \Rightarrow_{\text{in}} \beta$ if:

Case I: $\alpha = \alpha_1 \oslash \alpha_2 \oslash \alpha_3$, $\beta = \alpha_1 \oslash u \oslash \alpha_2 \oslash v \oslash \alpha_3$, where α_1, α_2, α_3, u, $v \in V^{**H}$, $\varphi_i(\alpha)$ contains $(\rho_j \$ \rho_k, tar)$ where ρ_j, $\rho_k \in L_{\oslash}$ and

$$|\alpha_{1_U} = |u|_{LL}\,, \quad |\alpha_1|_{RU} = |u|_L\,, \quad |u|_U = |\alpha_2|_{LL}\,, \quad |u|_{RU} = |\alpha_2|_L\,,$$

$$|\alpha_2|_U = |v|_{LL}\,, \quad |\alpha_2|_{RU} = |v|_L\,, \quad |v|_U = |\alpha_3|_{LL}\,,$$

$$|v|_{RU} = |\alpha_3|_L\,, \quad u \in \rho_j\,, \quad v \in |\rho_k\,.$$

The other two cases can be defined similarly.

Like external hexagonal array contextual P systems, the internal hexagonal array contextual P systems also work provided in evolution rules the contexts are internal.

The family of all languages generated by internal hexagonal array contextual P systems of degree at most n, $n \geq 1$ is denoted by $IHACPC_n$.

Example 2: Consider the system

$$\Pi = (\{X, a\}, \{X, a\}, [\,]_1, M, L_{\oslash}, L_{\obslash}, L_{\ominus}, R, \varphi)$$

$$M = \begin{array}{ccccc} & \text{x} & & \text{x} & \\ \text{x} & & \text{X} & & \text{x} \\ & \text{x} & & \text{x} & \end{array}$$

Consider the following arrowheads

$L_{\oslash} = \{\rho_1, \rho_{11}\}$, where $\rho_1 = \{$set of all arrowheads of types 2 in Fig. 3$\}$, $\rho_{11} = \{$set of all arrowheads of types 1 in Fig. 4$\}$, $L_{\obslash} = \{\rho_2, \rho_{22}\}$, where $\rho_2 = \{$set of all arrowheads of types 4 in Fig. 6$\}$, $\rho_{22} = \{$set of all arrowheads

$$\begin{array}{cccccc} \text{x} & & & & & \\ & \text{a} & & & & \\ & & \text{a} & \text{a} & \text{a} & \text{x} \end{array}$$

Fig. 3. sw-arrowhead.

$$\begin{array}{cccccc} \text{x} & \text{a} & \text{a} & \text{a} & & \\ & & & & \text{a} & \\ & & & & & \text{a} \\ & & & & & & \text{x} \end{array}$$

Fig. 4. ne-arrowhead.

		a	a	a	x
	a				
x					

Fig. 5. nw-arrowhead.

					x
				a	
x	a	a	a		

Fig. 6. se-arrowhead.

		x
	a	
a		
	a	
		x

Fig. 7. w-arrowhead.

x		
	a	
		a
	a	
x		

Fig. 8. e-arrowhead.

of types 3 in Fig. 5}, $L_{\ominus} = \{\rho_3, \rho_{33}\}$, where $\rho_3 = \{$set of all arrowheads of types 5 in Fig. 7$\}$, $\rho_{33} = \{$set of all arrowheads of types 6 in Fig. 8$\}$,

$$R = \{(\rho_1\$\rho_{11}, \text{here}), (\rho_2\$\rho_{22}, \text{here}), (\rho_3\$\rho_{33}, \text{here}), (\rho_3\$\rho_{33}, \text{out})\}\,.$$

α can be looked at as $\alpha_1 \oslash \alpha_2 \oslash \alpha_3$, in which case α_1 and α_3 are arrowheads of width 1 of type 2 and 1 respectively made up of x's and a's only.

Or $\alpha_1 \obslash \alpha_2 \obslash \alpha_3$, in which case α_1 and α_3 are arrowheads of width 1 of type 3 and 4 respectively made up of x's and a's only.

Or $\alpha_1 \ominus \alpha_2 \ominus \alpha_3$, in which case α_1 and α_3 are arrowheads of width 1 of type 5 and 6 respectively made up of x's and a's only.

The above P system generates hexagonal arrays of different proportions with X in the center surrounded by any number of a's, and bordered with one layer of x's.

4. Contextual Hexagonal Array P Systems with Erased Contexts

In a contextual P system we adjoin contexts; in a erased contextual P system we erase contexts. The two operations can be considered together in a P system which is able both to adjoin and to erase contexts. We give the definition of erased contextual P system as follows.

Definition 9: An external contextual hexagonal array P system of degree n with erased contexts is a construct

$$\Pi = (V, T, \mu, M_1, M_2, \ldots, M_n, L_{\varnothing}, L_{\otimes}, L_{\ominus}, R_1, R_2, \ldots, R_n, \varphi_1, \ldots, \varphi_n, \nu_1, \ldots, \nu_n)$$

where V, T, μ, M_i, $L_{\varnothing}$, $L_{\otimes}$, $L_{\ominus}$, R_i, and φ_i, $1 \leq i \leq n$ are as defined for contextual hexagonal array P system.

Here $\nu_i : V^{**H} \to 2^{R_i}$. This is written in the form $\nu_i(\alpha) = (\rho_j \$ \rho_k, tar)$ where $\rho_j, \rho_k \in L_{\varnothing}$ or ρ_j, $\rho_k \in L_{\otimes}$ or ρ_j, $\rho_k \in L_{\ominus}$ and $tar \in \{\text{here}, \text{in}_j, \text{out}\}$ where ρ_i's, are sets of arrays of the form of arrowheads.

Derivation for erased context is defined as follows. For α, $\beta \in V^{**H}$, we say α derives β, i.e.,

$$\alpha \Rightarrow_{ex} \beta \text{ if}$$

Case I: $\alpha = u\varnothing\ \beta\varnothing\ v$, where u, v are arrowheads $\nu_i(\alpha)$ contains $(\rho_j \$ \rho_k, tar)$ where ρ_j, $\rho_k \in L_{\varnothing}$ and $|v|_{LL} = |\beta|_U$, $|v|_L = |\beta|_{RU}$, $|u|_U = |\beta|_{LL}$, $|u|_{RU} = |\beta|_L$, $u \in \rho_j$, $v \in \rho_k$.

Similarly we define the other two cases.

Like external or internal hexagonal array contextual P systems, the external hexagonal array contextual P system with erased context also works provided in evolution rules, the contexts are either adjoined or erased. Here also the result of a successful computation is a set of arrays which are sent out of the system during the computation. The family of languages generated by external hexagonal array contextual P system with erased context of degree n is denoted by $EHACPEC_n$.

5. Some Properties of Hexagonal Array Contextual P Systems

Here we define some properties.

A language $L \subseteq V^{**H}$ has the external $\oslash$ bounded step ($E\oslash$ BS) property if there is a constant p such that for each $x \in L$ with $\max(|x|_{LU}, |x|_{RL}) > p$, there is y in L such that $x = u\oslash\, y\oslash\, v$ and $0 < \max(|u|_{LU} + |v|_{LU}, |u|_{RL} + |v|_{RL}) \leq p$.

Similarly, the $E\obslash$ BS property and the $E\ominus$ BS property are defined.

A language $L \subseteq V^{**H}$ has the internal $\oslash$ bounded step ($I\oslash$ BS) property if there is a constant p such that for each $x \in L$ with $\max(|x|_{LU}, |x|_{RL}) > p$, there is y in L such that $x = x_1\oslash\, u\oslash\, x_2\oslash\, v\oslash\, x_3$, $y = x_1\oslash\, x_2\oslash\, x_3$ and $0 < \max(|u|_{LU} + |v|_{LU}, |u|_{RL} + |v|_{RL}) \leq p$.

Similarly, the $I\obslash$ BS property and the $I\ominus$ BS property are defined.

A language $L \subseteq V^{**H}$ has the bounded $\oslash$ increase ($B\oslash$ I) property if there is a constant p such that for each $x \in L$ with $\max(|x|_{LU}, |x|_{RL}) > p$, there is $y \in L$ with $-p < \max(||x|_{LU} - |y|_{LU}|, ||x|_{RL} - |y|_{RL}|) \leq p$.

Similarly, the $B\obslash$ I property and the $B\ominus$ I property are defined.

Clearly, if a language has either the $E\oslash$ BS or the $I\oslash$ BS property, then it also has the $B\oslash$ I property. Also, if a language has either the $E\obslash$ BS or the $I\obslash$ BS property, then it also has the $B\obslash$ I property. Similarly, if a language has either the $E\ominus$ BS or the $I\ominus$ BS property, then it also has the $B\ominus$ I property.

The following statements are straightforward.

Theorem 1: The language generated by an external hexagonal array contextual P system satisfies the external $\oslash$ bounded step property ($E\oslash$ BS), external $\obslash$ bounded step property ($E\obslash$ BS) and external $\ominus$ bounded step property ($E\ominus$ BS) if the membrane structure consists of a single membrane and for every rule $(\rho_i\$\rho_j, \text{here})$ there should be a rule $(\rho_i\$\rho_j, \text{out})$.

Theorem 2: The language generated by an internal hexagonal array contextual P system satisfies the internal $\oslash$ bounded step property ($I\oslash$ BS), internal $\obslash$ bounded step property ($I\obslash$ BS) and internal $\ominus$ bounded step property ($I\ominus$ BS) if the membrane structure consists of a single membrane and for every rule $(\rho_i\$\rho_j, \text{here})$ there should be a rule $(\rho_i\$\rho_j, \text{out})$.

Theorem 3: If a language $L \subseteq V^{**H}$, satisfies the $E\oslash$ BS , $E\obslash$ BS and $E\ominus$ BS properties, then there is an external hexagonal array contextual P system which generates the language L.

Proof: Suppose $L \subseteq V^{**H}$ satisfies the $E\oslash$ BS property as well as $E\obslash$ BS and $E\ominus$ BS property. Now let us construct an external hexagonal array contextual P system which generates the language L.

Let the P system be

$$\Pi = (V, T, \mu, M, L_{\oslash}, L_{\obslash}, L_{\ominus}, R, \varphi)$$

where

$$T = V\,,$$

$$\mu = [\ ]_1\,,$$

$$M = \{x \in L \| x|_U, |x|_{RU}, |x|_{RL}, |x|_L, |x|_{LL}, |x|_{LU} \leq p\}\,,$$

$$L_{\oslash} = \{u \text{ is arrowhead of type 1 or 2} \mid \max(|u|_{LU}, |u|_{RL}) \leq p\}\,,$$

$$L_{\obslash} = \{u \text{ is arrowhead of type 3 or 4} \mid \max(|u|_{LL}, |u|_{RU}) \leq p\}\,,$$

$$L_{\ominus} = \{u \text{ is arrowhead of type 5 or 6} \mid \max(|u|_U, u_L) \leq p\}\,.$$

The choice function $\varphi : V^{**H} \to 2^R$ is

$$\begin{aligned} R = \{&(u\$v), \text{here})|0 < \max(|u|_{LU} + |v|_{LU}, |u|_{RL} + |v|_{RL}) \leq p\} \\ &\cup \{(u\$v), \text{out})|0 < \max(|u|_{LU} + |v|_{LU}, |u|_{RL} + |v|_{RL}) \leq p\} \\ &\cup \{(u\$v), \text{here})|0 < \max(|u|_{LL} + |v|_{LL}, |u|_{RU} + |v|_{RU}) \leq p\} \\ &\cup \{(u\$v), \text{out})|0 < \max(|u|_{LL} + |v|_{LL}, |u|_{RU} + |v|_{RU}) \leq p\} \\ &\cup \{(u\$v), \text{here})|0 < \max(|u|_U + |v|_U, |u|_L + |v|_L) \leq p\} \\ &\cup \{(u\$v), \text{out})|0 < \max(|u|_U + |v|_U, |u|_L + |v|_L) \leq p\}\,, \end{aligned}$$

$$\begin{aligned} \varphi(x) = &\{(u\$v, \text{here}), (u\$v, \text{out})|u, v \in L_{\oslash} \text{ and } u \oslash x \oslash v \in L\} \\ &\cup \{(u\$v, \text{here}), (u\$v, \text{out})|u, v \in L_{\obslash} \text{ and } u \obslash x \obslash v \in L\} \\ &\cup \{(u\$v, \text{here}), (u\$v, \text{out})|u, v \in L_{\ominus} \text{ and } u \ominus x \ominus v \in L\}\,. \end{aligned}$$

It is clear that the language constructed is an $EHACPC$. □

Theorem 4: If a language $L \subseteq V^{**H}$, satisfies $I\oslash\ BS$, $I\obslash\ BS$ and $I\ominus\ BS$ property, then there is an internal hexagonal array contextual P system which generates the language L.

The proof is similar.

During the computation in the contextual array P systems, we also get arrays which are not in the language generated, since the language generated by the contextual P systems consists of arrays which are coming out of the membrane structure. The arrays which are generated in intermediate steps in the process of generating an array belonging to the language generated are called array sentential forms.

Definition 10: A language $L \subseteq V^{**H}$ has the weak external $\oslash$ bounded step property ($WE\oslash\, BS$) if there is a constant p such that for each $x \in L$, $\max(|x|_{LU}, |x|_{RL}) > p$ there is an array sentential form y such that $x = u\oslash\, y\oslash\, v$ and $0 < \max(|u|_{LU} + |v|_{LU}, |u|_{RL} + |v|_{RL}) \leq p$.

Similarly we define ($WE\obslash\, BS$) and ($WE\ominus\, BS$) properties.

Definition 11: A language $L \subseteq V^{**H}$ is said to have weak internal $\oslash$ bounded step ($WI\oslash\, BS$) property if there is a constant p such that for each $x \in L$, $\max(|x|_{LU}, |x|_{RL}) > p$, there is an array sentential form y such that

$$x = x_1\oslash\, u\oslash\, x_2\oslash\, v\oslash\, x_3\,, \quad y = x_1\oslash\, x_2\oslash\, x_3$$

and

$$0 < \max(|u|_{LU} + |v|_{LU}, |u|_{RL} + |v|_{RL}) \leq p\,.$$

Similarly we define ($WI\obslash\, BS$) and ($WI\ominus\, BS$) properties.

In general external array contextual P systems need not satisfy the $E\oslash\, BS$, $E\obslash\, BS$ and $E\ominus\, BS$properties but it satisfies the following property.

Theorem 5: An external hexagonal array contextual P system satisfies the weak external $\oslash$ bounded step property ($WE\oslash\, BS$), weak external $\obslash$ bounded step ($WE\obslash\, BS$) and weak external $\ominus$ bounded step ($WE\ominus\, BS$) property.

Proof: Let

$$\Pi = (V, T, \mu, M_1, M_2, \ldots, M_n, L_{\oslash}, L_{\obslash}, L_{\ominus}, R_1, R_2, \ldots, R_n, \varphi_1, \varphi_2, \ldots, \varphi_n)$$

be an external hexagonal array contextual P system with $L_{\oslash} = \{\rho_1, \rho_2, \ldots, \rho_n\}$, $L_{\obslash} = \{\rho'_1, \rho'_2, \ldots, \rho'_n\}$ and $L_{\ominus} = \{\rho''_1, \rho''_2, \ldots, \rho''_n\}$. Let $p_1 = \max\{k_1 | \max(|x|_{LU}, |x|_{RL}) = k_1, (u\$v, tar) \in R_i, u, v \in L_{\oslash}\}$ and $p_2 = \max\{|\alpha|_{LU}, |\alpha|_{RL} | \alpha \in M_i\}$. Let $p = \max\{p_1, p_2\}$.

We have to prove that this external hexagonal array contextual P system satisfies the $WE\oslash\, BS$ property for p. If $z \in L_{ex}(G)$ with $\max(z_{LU}, z_{RL}) > p$ then $z \notin M_i$. Hence, $z = u\oslash\, z'\oslash\, v$ for some $u, v \in L_{\oslash}$ with $\max(|u|_{LU}+$

$|v|_{LU}, |u|_{RL}+|v|_{RL}) \leq p$ such that $(\varphi(z') = \{(u\$v, tar)\}$ and $(u\$v, tar) \in R_i$ and z' is an array sentential form.

Similarly, we can prove that this P system satisfies the $WE\obslash\, BS$ and $WE\ominus\, BS$ property. □

Theorem 6: An internal hexagonal array contextual P system satisfies the weak internal $\oslash$ bounded step property ($WI\oslash\, BS$), weak internal $\obslash$ bounded step ($WI\obslash\, BS$) and weak internal $\ominus$ bounded step ($WI\ominus\, BS$) property.

Since the proof is similar to that of the above theorem, it is omitted.

Theorem 7: If a language $L \subseteq V^{**H}$, satisfies $WE\oslash\, BS$, $WE\obslash\, BS$ and $WE\ominus\, BS$ property, then there is an external hexagonal array contextual P system which generates the language L.

Proof: Suppose $L \subseteq V^{**H}$ satisfies the $WE\oslash\, BS$, $WE\obslash\, BS$ and $WE\ominus\, BS$ property. Now let us construct an external hexagonal array contextual P system which generates the language L.

Let $x \in L$. Since L satisfies the $WE\oslash\, BS$, $WE\obslash\, BS$ and $WE\ominus\, BS$ property, there is a constant p such that for each $x \in L$,
(i) $\max(|x|_{LU}, |x|_{RL}) > p$ there is an array sentential form y such that $x = u\oslash\, y\oslash\, v$ and $0 < \max(|u|_{LU} + |v|_{LU}, |u|_{RL} + |v|_{RL}) \leq p$
(ii) $\max(|x|_{LL}, |x|_{RU}) > p$ there is an array sentential form y such that $x = u\obslash\, y\obslash\, v$ and $0 < \max(|u|_{LL} + |v|_{LL}, |u|_{RU} + |v|_{RU}) \leq p$
(iii) $\max(|x|_U, |x|_L) > p$ there is an array sentential form y such that $x = u\ominus\, y\ominus\, v$ and $0 < \max(|u|_U + |v|_U, |u|_L + |v|_L) \leq p$

Let the P system be

$$\Pi = (V, T, \mu, M, L_{\oslash}, L_{\obslash}, L_{\ominus}, R, \varphi)$$

where

$$T = V,$$

$$\mu = [\ ]_1,$$

$$M = \{x \in L \,||x|_U, |x|_{RU}, |x|_{RL}, |x|_L, |x|_{LL}, |x|_{LU} \leq p\},$$

$$L_{\oslash} = \{u \text{ is arrowhead of type 1 or 2} \mid \max(|u|_{LU}, |u|_{RL}) \leq p\},$$

$$L_{\obslash} = \{uu \text{ is arrowhead of type 3 or 4} \mid \max(|u|_{LL}, |u|_{RU}) \leq p\},$$

$$L_{\ominus} = \{uu \text{ is arrowhead of type 3 or 4} \mid \max(|u|_U, |u|_L) \leq p\}.$$

The choice function $\varphi : V^{**H} \to 2^R$ is

$$\begin{aligned} R = \{(u\$v), \text{here})|0 < \max(|u|_{LU} + |v|_{LU}, |u|_{RL} + |v|_{RL}) \leq p\} \\ \cup \{(u\$v), \text{out})|0 < \max(|u|_{LU} + |v|_{LU}, |u|_{RL} + |v|_{RL}) \leq p\} \\ \cup \{(u\$v), \text{here})|0 < \max(|u|_{LL} + |v|_{LL}, |u|_{RU} + |v|_{RU}) \leq p\} \\ \cup \{(u\$v), \text{out})|0 < \max(|u|_{LL} + |v|_{LL}, |u|_{RU} + |v|_{RU}) \leq p\} \\ \cup \{(u\$v), \text{here})|0 < \max(|u|_{U} + |v|_{U}, |u|_{L} + |v|_{L}) \leq p\} \\ \cup \{(u\$v), \text{out})|0 < \max(|u|_{U} + |v|_{U}, |u|_{L} + |v|_{L}) \leq p\} \,. \end{aligned}$$

$\varphi(y) = \{(u\$v, \text{out})\}$ if $y \in V^{**H}$, $u, v \in L_{\oslash}$ and $u \oslash y \oslash v \in L$ or $u, v \in L_{\obslash}$ and $u \obslash y \obslash v \in L$ or $u, v \in L_{\ominus}$ and $u \ominus y \ominus v \in L$, $\varphi(y) = \{(u\$v, \text{here})\}$ if $y \in V^{**H}$ and y and $u \oslash y \oslash v$ are array sentential forms or y and $u \obslash y \obslash v$ are array sentential forms or y and $u \ominus y \ominus v$ are array sentential forms.

Now we can say $x = u \oslash y \oslash v$ or $x = u \obslash y \obslash v$ or $x = u \ominus y \ominus v$ in L where $\varphi(y) = (u\$v, \text{out})$.

It is clear that the language generated by the above P system is nothing but the given language. □

6. Correspondence between External Array Contextual P Systems and External Hexagonal Array Contextual Grammars with Regular Control

In this section we consider both external hexagonal array contextual P systems with erased contexts and external hexagonal array contextual grammars with regular control and discuss the relation between them.

Generalized definition of normal forms for rewriting P systems were given in Ref. 6. We extend this definition in the case of hexagonal array P systems.

Definition 12: An array P system is in m-n-normal form if its depth is exactly m and in each membrane we have exactly n rules. If we put no restriction either on the depth or on the number of rules, then we replace the corresponding term with $\star$.

Theorem 8: For any external hexagonal array contextual P system of degree m, there exists an equivalent external hexagonal array contextual P system of degree $m + 1$ with erased context in 2-$\star$ — normal form.

Theorem 9: For any external hexagonal array contextual P system, there exists a regulated external hexagonal array contextual grammar

$$G = (V, B, L_{\nearrow\!\!\!\!\bigcirc}, L_{\nwarrow\!\!\!\!\bigcirc}, L_{\rightarrow\!\!\!\!\bigcirc}, R)\,,$$

where R is a regular set.

Theorem 10: For any regulated external hexagonal array contextual grammar G, with regular control, we can construct an external hexagonal array contextual P system with erased context which generates the same language

The proofs of Theorems 8, 9, 10 runs on the same lines as that in the case of rectangular arrays in Ref. 1. Hence it is omitted.

7. Concluding Remarks

In this paper we have considered hexagonal array contextual P systems which generate hexagonal arrays. We studied external and internal hexagonal array contextual P systems with choice functions. We studied some properties of these systems. As in the case of rectangular arrays we can define external hexagonal array contextual P systems with erased context and also noticed that similar results[1] are obtained in the case of the relation between external hexagonal array contextual P systems with erased context and external hexagonal array contextual grammars with regular control. The relation between other variants of P systems like internal hexagonal array contextual P systems and internal hexagonal array contextual grammars with various controls can be considered. Tissue P systems which generate hexagonal arrays using contextual rules can also be considered.

References

1. K. S. Dersanambika and K. Krithivasan, Contextual array P systems, *International Journal of Computer Mathematics*, 81, 2004, 955-969.
2. R. Freund, *Array Grammars, Technical Report No. 15/00*, Universitat Rovira i Virgili, september, 2000.
3. K. S. Fu, *Syntactic Pattern Recognition and Applications*, Prentice-Hall Inc., 1982.
4. K. Krithivasan, M. S. Balan and R. Rama, Array contextual grammars, In C. Martin-vide and Gh. Păun, editors, *Recent Topics in Mathematical and Computational Linguistics*, The Publishing house of the Romanian Academy, 2000, 154–168.
5. M. Madhu and K. Krithivasan, Contextual P systems, *Fundamenta Informaticae*, 49, 2002, 179–189.

6. M. Madhu and K. Krithivasan, Generalised normal forms for rewriting P systems, *Acta Informatica*, 38, 2002, 721–734.
7. S. Marcus, Contextual grammars, *Rev. Roum. Math. Pures Appl.*, 14, 1969, 1525–1534.
8. I. Petre, A normal form for P systems, *Bulletin of EATCS*, 67, 1999, 165–172.
9. Gh. Păun, *Marcus Contextual Grammar*, Kluwer Acad. Pub., 1997.
10. Gh. Păun, Computing with membranes, *Journal of Computer and System Sciences*, 61, 2000, 108–143.
11. Gh. Păun, *Membrane Computing An Introduction*, Springer Verlag, 2002.
12. G. Rozenberg and A. Salomaa, editors, *Hand book of Formal languages*, volume 1,2,3, Springer-Verlag, Berlin, 1997.
13. A. Rosenfeld, *Picture languages (formal models for picture recognition)*, Academic Press, New York, 1979.
14. A. Rosenfeld and R. Siromoney, Picture languages-a survey, *Languages of design*, 1, 1993, 229–244.
15. G. Siromoney and R. Siromoney, Hexagonal arrays and rectangular blocks, *Computer Graphics and Image Processing*, 5, 1976, 353–381.

CHAPTER 7

A q-ANALOGUE OF THE PARIKH MATRIX MAPPING

Ömer Eğecioğlu and Oscar H. Ibarra*

Department of Computer Science, University of California, Santa Barbara, CA 93106, USA

E-mail: {omer, ibarra}@cs.ucsb.edu

We consider an extension of the Parikh mapping called the *Parikh q-matrix mapping*, which takes its values in matrices with polynomial entries. The morphism constructed represents a word w over a k-letter alphabet as a k-dimensional upper-triangular matrix with entries that are nonnegative integral polynomials in variable q. We show that by appropriately embedding the k-letter alphabet into the $(k+1)$-letter alphabet and putting $q = 1$, we obtain the extension of the Parikh mapping to $(k+1)$-dimensional (numerical) matrices introduced by Mateescu, Salomaa, Salomaa, and Yu. The Parikh q-matrix mapping however, produces matrices that carry more information about w than the numerical Parikh matrix. The entries of the q-matrix image of w under this morphism is constructed by *q-counting* the number of occurrences of certain words as scattered subwords of w.

1. Introduction

Parikh's celebrated theorem says that every context-free language is "letter-equivalent" to a regular language.[8] More precisely, the commutative image of any context-free language is always a semilinear set, and is therefore also the commutative image of some regular set. Consider the alphabet $\Sigma_k = \{a_1 < a_2 < \cdots < a_k\}$ and for $w \in \Sigma^*$, define by $|w|_{a_i}$ the number of occurrences of a_i in w. The *Parikh mapping* is a morphism

$$\Psi : \Sigma^* \to \mathbb{N}^k$$

where $\mathbb{N}$ denotes nonnegative integers and $\Psi(w) = (|w|_{a_1}, |w|_{a_2}, \ldots, |w|_{a_k})$.

*Supported in part by NSF Grants CCR-0208595 and CCF-0430945.

The Parikh mapping is a very important concept in the theory of formal languages. Various languages accepted (generated) by automata (grammars) more powerful than pushdown automata (context-free grammars) have been shown to have effectively computable semilinear sets. For example, it is known that every language accepted by a pushdown automaton augmented with reversal-bounded counters (i.e., each counter can be incremented/decremented by one and tested for zero, but the number of alternations between nondecreasing and nonincreasing modes is bounded by a fixed constant) has a semilinear Parikh map.[5] The fact that the emptiness problem for semilinear sets is decidable implies that the emptiness problem for these automata (grammars) is decidable. This decidability of emptiness has been used to show the decidability of many decision questions in formal languages and formal verification.[4,6]

The *Parikh matrix mapping* introduced in Ref. 7 is a morphism

$$\Psi_{\mathcal{M}_k} : \Sigma^* \to \mathcal{M}_{k+1}$$

where $\mathcal{M}_{k+1}$ is a collection of $(k+1)$-dimensional upper-triangular matrices with nonnegative integral entries and unit diagonal. The classical Parikh vector $\Psi(w)$ appears in the image matrix as the second diagonal.

The *Parikh q-matrix mapping* introduced in this paper is a morphism

$$\Psi_q^k : \Sigma^* \to \mathcal{M}_k(q)$$

where $\mathcal{M}_k(q)$ is a collection of k-dimensional upper-triangular matrices with nonnegative integral polynomials in q as entries. The diagonal entries of $\Psi_q^k(w)$ are

$$(q^{|w|_{a_1}}, q^{|w|_{a_2}}, \ldots, q^{|w|_{a_k}})$$

which readily encodes the Parikh vector. Moreover if we embed Σ_k into Σ_{k+1} in the obvious way, and put $q = 1$, then we obtain the matrices of the Parikh matrix map of Ref. 7. Thus, viewing $w \in \Sigma_k$ as a word in Σ_{k+1} with $|w|_{a_{k+1}} = 0$, the Parikh q-matrix $\Psi_q^{k+1}(w)$ evaluated at $q = 1$ is precisely the $(k+1)$-dimensional numerical Parikh matrix $\Psi_{\mathcal{M}_k}(w)$.

It is a basic property of the Parikh matrix mapping that two words with the same Parikh matrix have the same Parikh vector, but two words with the same Parikh vector in many cases have different Parikh matrices.[1] Thus, the Parikh matrix gives more information about a word than the Parikh vector. The injectivity of the Parikh matrix mapping is investigated in Ref. 1. From our construction it is easy to see that two words with the same Parikh q-matrix have the same Parikh matrix (and therefore the same Parikh vector), but there are cases in which two words with the same Parikh matrix have different q-matrices. Thus the Parikh q-matrix gives more information about a word than the Parikh matrix.

The basic idea in the construction of the entries of the Parikh q-matrix image of w is *q-counting* the number of occurrences of certain words as scattered subwords of w.

This paper is an extension of the extended abstract in Ref. 3 and has five sections in addition to this section. Section 2 gives some basic notation and definitions. Section 3 recalls the notion of a Parikh matrix mapping introduced in Ref. 7 and the fundamental theorem concerning these mappings. Section 4 presents our new Parikh mapping, called q-matrix mapping, that generalizes the Parikh matrix mapping: whereas the latter produces matrices with nonnegative integer entries, the former produces matrices with nonnegative integral polynomials (in variable q) entries. This extended mapping produces matrices that carry more information about the mapped words than the numerical matrices produced by the Parikh matrix mapping. Section 5 presents the main results, including Theorem 2, which gives the main properties of a q-matrix mapping. Section 6 looks at some matrix operations such as injectivity and inverse concerning q-matrix mapping.

2. Definitions

We start with some basic notation and definitions. Most of these are as they appear in Refs. 7 and 1. The set of all nonnegative integers is denoted by $\mathbb{N}$. We denote by $\mathbb{N}[q]$ the collection of polynomials in the variable q with coefficients from $\mathbb{N}$. $\mathbb{Z}$ denotes integers, and $\mathbb{Z}[q]$ denotes the ring of polynomials in the variable q with integral coefficients. For an alphabet Σ, we denote the set of all words over Σ by Σ^* and the empty word by λ. We use "ordered" alphabets. An ordered alphabet is an alphabet $\Sigma = \{a_1, a_2, \ldots, a_k\}$ with a relation of order ("<") on it. If for instance $a_1 < a_2 < \cdots < a_k$, then we use the notation

$$\Sigma = \{a_1 < a_2 < \cdots < a_k\}.$$

If $w \in \Sigma^*$ then $|w|$ denotes the length of w. For $a_i \in \Sigma$ and $w \in \Sigma^*$ the number of occurrences of the letter a_i in w is denoted by $|w|_{a_i}$. Accordingly $|w| = |w|_{a_1} + |w|_{a_2} + \cdots + |w|_{a_k}$.

Let $\Sigma = \{a_1 < a_2 < \cdots < a_k\}$ be an ordered alphabet. The Parikh vector of $w \in \Sigma^*$ is the vector of occurrences $(|w|_{a_1}, |w|_{a_2}, \ldots, |w|_{a_k})$. The

Parikh mapping

$$\Psi : \Sigma^* \to \mathbb{N}^k$$

is defined by setting

$$\Psi(w) = (|w|_{a_1}, |w|_{a_2}, \ldots, |w|_{a_k}).$$

Let v, w be words over Σ. As defined in Ref. 7, the word v is called a *scattered subword* of w if there exists a word u such that $w \in u \sqcup\!\sqcup v$, where $\sqcup\!\sqcup$ denotes the shuffle operation. If $v, w \in \Sigma^*$, then the number of occurrences of v in w as a scattered subword is denoted by $|w|_{\text{scatt}-v}$. Partially overlapping occurrences of a word as a scattered subword of a word are counted as distinct occurrences. For example, $|acbb|_{\text{scatt}-ab} = 2$, $|acba|_{\text{scatt}-ab} = 1$.

Notation: We shall also find it useful to denote $|w|_{\text{scatt}-v}$ by $S_{w,v}$. Using this notation, we write $S_{acbb,ab} = 2$, $S_{acba,ab} = 1$, and $S_{w,a_i} = |w|_{a_i}$ for any letter $a_i \in \Sigma$.

Notation: Consider the ordered alphabet $\{a_1 < a_2 < \cdots < a_k\}$ where $k \geq 1$. As in Ref. 7, we denote by $a_{i,j}$ the word $a_i a_{i+1} \cdots a_j$ where $1 \leq i \leq j \leq k$.

For motivation and further issues about the Parikh mapping as well as language-theoretic notions not considered here, we refer the reader to Ref. 9.

3. Parikh Matrix Mapping

We first describe the extension of the Parikh mapping to matrices as originally defined in Ref. 7. The extension involves special types of triangular matrices. These are square matrices $m = (m_{i,j})_{1 \leq i,j \leq k}$ such that $m_{i,j} \in \mathbb{N}$, for all $1 \leq i, j \leq k$, $m_{i,j} = 0$, for all $1 \leq j < i \leq k$, and moreover, $m_{i,i} = 1$, for all $1 \leq i \leq k$. The set of all these matrices of dimension k is denoted by $\mathcal{M}_k$. Thus $\mathcal{M}_k$ is the collection $k \times k$ upper-triangular matrices with entries from $\mathbb{N}$ and unit diagonal. The set $\mathcal{M}_k$ is a monoid with respect to multiplication of matrices and has a unit which is the matrix I_k.

The main notion introduced in Ref. 7 is as follows:

Definition 1: Let $\Sigma = \{a_1 < a_2 < \cdots < a_k\}$ be an ordered alphabet, where $k \geq 1$. The Parikh matrix mapping, denoted by $\Psi_{\mathcal{M}_k}$, is the morphism:

$$\Psi_{\mathcal{M}_k} : \Sigma^* \to \mathcal{M}_{k+1}\,,$$

defined as follows:

If $\Psi_{M_k}(a_l) = (m_{i,j})_{1\le i,j\le(k+1)}$, then for each $1 \le i \le k+1$, $m_{i,i} = 1$, $m_{l,l+1} = 1$ and all other elements of the matrix $\Psi_{M_k}(a_l)$ are zero.

Example 1: Let Σ be the ordered alphabet $\{a < b < c\}$. Then the Parikh matrix mapping Ψ_{M_3} represents each word over Σ^* as a 4×4 upper triangular matrix with unit diagonal with nonnegative integral entries. We compute some special cases.

$$\Psi_{\mathcal{M}_3}(ab^2) = \Psi_{\mathcal{M}_3}(a)\Psi_{\mathcal{M}_3}(b)\Psi_{\mathcal{M}_3}(b)$$

and

$$\Psi_{\mathcal{M}_3}(abca) = \Psi_{\mathcal{M}_3}(a)\Psi_{\mathcal{M}_3}(b)\Psi_{\mathcal{M}_3}(c)\Psi_{\mathcal{M}_3}(a)\,.$$

Thus

$$\Psi_{\mathcal{M}_3}(ab^2) = \begin{bmatrix} 1&1&0&0\\ 0&1&0&0\\ 0&0&1&0\\ 0&0&0&1 \end{bmatrix} \begin{bmatrix} 1&0&0&0\\ 0&1&1&0\\ 0&0&1&0\\ 0&0&0&1 \end{bmatrix} \begin{bmatrix} 1&0&0&0\\ 0&1&1&0\\ 0&0&1&0\\ 0&0&0&1 \end{bmatrix}$$

$$= \begin{bmatrix} 1&1&2&0\\ 0&1&2&0\\ 0&0&1&0\\ 0&0&0&1 \end{bmatrix}$$

and

$$\Psi_{\mathcal{M}_3}(abca) = \begin{bmatrix} 1&1&0&0\\ 0&1&0&0\\ 0&0&1&0\\ 0&0&0&1 \end{bmatrix} \begin{bmatrix} 1&0&0&0\\ 0&1&1&0\\ 0&0&1&0\\ 0&0&0&1 \end{bmatrix} \begin{bmatrix} 1&0&0&0\\ 0&1&0&0\\ 0&0&1&1\\ 0&0&0&1 \end{bmatrix} \begin{bmatrix} 1&1&0&0\\ 0&1&0&0\\ 0&0&1&0\\ 0&0&0&1 \end{bmatrix}$$

$$= \begin{bmatrix} 1&2&1&1\\ 0&1&1&1\\ 0&0&1&1\\ 0&0&0&1 \end{bmatrix}$$

and consequently

$$\Psi_{\mathcal{M}_3}(ab^2abca) = \begin{bmatrix} 1&1&2&0 \\ 0&1&2&0 \\ 0&0&1&0 \\ 0&0&0&1 \end{bmatrix} \begin{bmatrix} 1&2&1&1 \\ 0&1&1&1 \\ 0&0&1&1 \\ 0&0&0&1 \end{bmatrix} = \begin{bmatrix} 1&3&4&4 \\ 0&1&3&3 \\ 0&0&1&1 \\ 0&0&0&1 \end{bmatrix}$$

Remark: The Parikh matrix mapping is not an injective mapping. For instance over the ordered alphabet $\{a < b < c\}$ one has

$$\Psi_{\mathcal{M}_3}(acb) = \Psi_{\mathcal{M}_3}(cab) = \begin{bmatrix} 1&1&1&0 \\ 0&1&1&0 \\ 0&0&1&1 \\ 0&0&0&1 \end{bmatrix}$$

Conditions for two words α and β to possess the same Parikh matrix was studied for the binary alphabet in Ref. 1. We will discuss some of these conditions later in the paper.

The main property of the Parikh matrix mapping proved in Ref. 7 is the following theorem:

Theorem 1: (Ref. 7, Theorem 3.1) Let $\Sigma = \{a_1 < a_2 < \cdots < a_k\}$ be an ordered alphabet, where $k \geq 1$ and assume that $w \in \Sigma^*$. The matrix $\Psi_{M_k}(w) = (m_{i,j})_{1 \leq i,j \leq (k+1)}$, has the following properties

(1) $m_{i,j} = 0$, for all $1 \leq j < i \leq (k+1)$,
(2) $m_{i,i} = 1$, for all $1 \leq i \leq (k+1)$,
(3) $m_{i,j+1} = S_{w,a_{i,j}}$ for all $1 \leq i \leq j \leq k$.

As a corollary

Corollary 1: (*Ref.* 7, *Corollary* 3.1) *Let* $\Sigma = \{a_1 < a_2 < \cdots < a_k\}$ *The matrix* $\Psi_{M_k}(w)$ *has the second diagonal (i.e., the vector* $(m_{1,2}, m_{2,3}, \ldots, m_{k,k+1})$*) the Parikh vector of* w*, i.e.,*

$$(m_{1,2}, m_{2,3}, \ldots, m_{k,k+1}) = \Psi(w) = (|w|_{a_1}, |w|_{a_2}, \ldots, |w|_{a_k}) .$$

4. q-Counting Scattered Subwords

Next we introduce a collection of polynomials $S_{w,a_{i,j}}(q)$ indexed by pairs of words $a_{i,j}$, $w \in \Sigma^*$, with $j \leq k-1$. These polynomials will "q-count" the quantities $S_{w,a_{i,j}}$ defined above for general v and w as will be explained shortly in the case $a_{i,j}$ is a scattered subword of w. To construct $S_{w,a_{i,j}}(q)$, we consider each factorization

$$w = u_i a_i u_{i+1} a_{i+1} \cdots u_j a_j u_{j+1} \tag{1}$$

with $u_s \in \Sigma^*$ for $i \leq s \leq j+1$, and construct the corresponding monomial

$$q^{|u_i|_{a_i} + |u_{i+1}|_{a_{i+1}} + \cdots + |u_j|_{a_j} + |u_{j+1}|_{a_{j+1}}} \tag{2}$$

in $\mathbb{N}[q]$, and add up these monomials. Note that $a_{j+1} \in \Sigma$ since $j < k$, so that the last term in the exponent in (2) is defined. Thus

$$S_{w,a_{i,j}}(q) = \sum_{w = u_i a_i \cdots u_j a_j u_{j+1}} q^{|u_i|_{a_i} + |u_{i+1}|_{a_{i+1}} + \cdots + |u_j|_{a_j} + |u_{j+1}|_{a_{j+1}}}. \tag{3}$$

Example 2: Suppose $\Sigma = \{a < b < c < d\}$ and $i = 2$, $j = 2$. Then $a_{i,j} = b$ and for $w \in \Sigma^*$,

$$S_{w,b}(q) = \sum_{w=xby} q^{|x|_b + |y|_c}.$$

For example for $w = baccbcdab$, the relevant factorizations of w are

$$(\lambda)b(accbcdab)\,, \quad (bacc)b(cdab)\,, \quad (baccbcda)b(\lambda)\,,$$

and therefore

$$S_{w,b}(q) = q^{0+3} + q^{1+1} + q^{2+0} = 2q^2 + q^3\,.$$

Example 3: Suppose $\Sigma = \{a < b < c < d\}$ and $i = 2$, $j = 3$. Then $a_{i,j} = bc$ and for $w \in \Sigma^*$,

$$S_{w,bc}(q) = \sum_{w=xbycz} q^{|x|_b + |y|_c + |z|_d}.$$

For example for $w = baccbcdab$, the relevant factorizations of w are

$$(\lambda)b(a)c(cbcdab)\,, \quad (\lambda)b(ac)c(bcdab)\,, \quad (\lambda)b(accb)c(dab)\,, \quad (bacc)b(\lambda)c(dab)\,,$$

and therefore

$$S_{w,bc}(q) = q^{0+0+1} + q^{0+1+1} + q^{0+2+1} + q^{1+0+1} = q + 2q^2 + q^3\,.$$

Example 4: Suppose $\Sigma = \{a < b < c < d\}$ and $i = 1$, $j = 3$. Then $a_{i,j} = abc$ and for $w \in \Sigma^*$,

$$S_{w,abc}(q) = \sum_{w=taxbycz} q^{|t|_a + |x|_b + |y|_c + |z|_d}.$$

For example for $w = baccbcdab$, the only relevant factorization of w is

$$(b)a(cc)b(\lambda)c(dab)\,,$$

and therefore

$$S_{w,abc}(q) = q^{0+0+1} = q\,.$$

Since the summation in the definition (3) is over all occurrences of $a_{i,j}$ in w as a scattered subword, the following proposition is immediate:

Proposition 1: *Let* $\Sigma = \{a_1 < a_2 < \cdots < a_k\}$ *and* $1 \le i \le j < k$. *Then*

$$S_{w,a_{i,j}}(1) = S_{w,a_{i,j}}(= |w|_{\mathrm{scatt}-a_{i,j}})\,.$$

This is the sense in which the polynomials $S_{w,a_{i,j}}(q)$ "q-count" the number of occurrences of $a_i a_{i+1} \cdots a_j$ as a scattered subword of w. These polynomials are the "q-analogues" of the numbers $S_{w,a_{i,j}}$.

We need the following properties of the polynomials $S_{w,a_{i,j}}(q)$:

Lemma 1: *Let* $\Sigma = \{a_1 < a_2 < \cdots < a_k\}$ *and suppose* $w = w'a_j$ *for some* $a_j \in \Sigma$, $j < k$. *Then*

(1) $S_{w,a_{i,j-1}}(q) = qS_{w',a_{i,j-1}}(q)$ *for* $1 \le i \le j$,
(2) $S_{w,a_{i,j}}(q) = S_{w',a_{i,j-1}}(q) + S_{w',a_{i,j}}(q)$ *for* $1 \le i < j$.

Proof: For the proof of (1), we note that there is a one-to-one correspondence between factorizations $w' = u'_i a_i u'_{i+1} a_{i+1} \cdots u'_{j-1} a_{j-1} u'_j$ of w' and factorizations $w = u_i a_i u_{i+1} a_{i+1} \cdots u_{j-1} a_{j-1} u_j$ of w in which $u'_k = u_k$ for $k = 1, 2, \ldots, j-1$, except $u_j = u'_j a_j$. Thus the exponents of the monomials in (2) that are summed up to construct $S_{w,a_{i,j-1}}(q)$ are one more than those of the monomials in the computation of $S_{w',a_{i,j-1}}(q)$. This means that $S_{w,a_{i,j-1}}(q) = qS_{w',a_{i,j-1}}(q)$.

For the proof of (2), we note that the factorizations of w of the form (1) with $u_{j+1} = \lambda$ contribute the monomials in $S_{w',a_{i,j-1}}(q)$ to the sum in (3), while the remaining factorizations of w contribute $S_{w',a_{i,j}}(q)$. □

5. Parikh q-Matrix Mapping

We denote by $\mathcal{M}_k(q)$ the collection of k-dimensional upper-triangular matrices with entries in $\mathbb{N}[q]$. Let I_k denote the identity matrix of dimension k. The matrix $\Psi_q(a_l)$ corresponding to a $a_l \in \Sigma$ is defined as the matrix obtained from I_k first by changing the lth diagonal element from 1 to q. Then if $l < k$, we also change the entry immediately to the right of the q from 0 to a (1). Thus if $\Psi_q(a_l) = (m_{i,j})_{1 \le i,j \le k}$, then

(1) $m_{l,l} = q$,
(2) $m_{i,i} = 1$ for $1 \leq i \leq k$, $i \neq l$,
(3) $m_{l,l+1} = 1$ if $l < k$,
(4) all other entries of the matrix $\Psi_q(a_l)$ are zero.

When the alphabet is $\Sigma = \{a < b < c\}$, then

$$\Psi_q(a) = \begin{bmatrix} q & 1 & 0 \\ 0 & 1 & 0 \\ 0 & 0 & 1 \end{bmatrix}, \quad \Psi_q(b) = \begin{bmatrix} 1 & 0 & 0 \\ 0 & q & 1 \\ 0 & 0 & 1 \end{bmatrix}, \quad \Psi_q(c) = \begin{bmatrix} 1 & 0 & 0 \\ 0 & 1 & 0 \\ 0 & 0 & q \end{bmatrix}$$

We extend the mapping from Σ to Σ^* by setting

(1) $\Psi_q(\lambda) = I_k$,
(2) $\Psi_q(w_1 w_2 \cdots w_n) = \Psi_q(w_1)\Psi_q(w_2) \cdots \Psi_q(w_n)$, $w_i \in \Sigma$, $1 \leq i \leq n$

We will refer to $\Psi_q = \Psi_q^k$ as the Parikh q-matrix mapping. Note that the parameter $k = |\Sigma|$ is implicit in our notation.

Remark: Just as the Parikh mapping is a morphism from the monoid $(\Sigma^*, \cdot, \lambda)$ to the monoid $(\mathbb{N}^k, +, (0, 0, \ldots, 0))$, the set of matrices $\mathcal{M}_k(q)$ is a monoid with respect to matrix multiplication and I_k as its unit.

Thus the Parikh q-matrix mapping is a morphism

$$\Psi_q : \Sigma^* \to \mathcal{M}_k(q).$$

As examples, we have

$$\Psi_q(ab^2) = \Psi_q(a)\Psi_q(b)\Psi_q(b) \quad \text{and} \quad \Psi_q(abca) = \Psi_q(a)\Psi_q(b)\Psi_q(c)\Psi_q(a).$$

Thus

$$\Psi_q(ab^2) = \begin{bmatrix} q & 1 & 0 \\ 0 & 1 & 0 \\ 0 & 0 & 1 \end{bmatrix} \begin{bmatrix} 1 & 0 & 0 \\ 0 & q & 1 \\ 0 & 0 & 1 \end{bmatrix} \begin{bmatrix} 1 & 0 & 0 \\ 0 & q & 1 \\ 0 & 0 & 1 \end{bmatrix} = \begin{bmatrix} q & q^2 & 1+q \\ 0 & q^2 & 1+q \\ 0 & 0 & 1 \end{bmatrix}$$

$$\Psi_q(abca) = \begin{bmatrix} q & 1 & 0 \\ 0 & 1 & 0 \\ 0 & 0 & 1 \end{bmatrix} \begin{bmatrix} 1 & 0 & 0 \\ 0 & q & 1 \\ 0 & 0 & 1 \end{bmatrix} \begin{bmatrix} 1 & 0 & 0 \\ 0 & 1 & 0 \\ 0 & 0 & q \end{bmatrix} \begin{bmatrix} q & 1 & 0 \\ 0 & 1 & 0 \\ 0 & 0 & 1 \end{bmatrix}$$

$$= \begin{bmatrix} q^2 & 2q & q \\ 0 & q & q \\ 0 & 0 & q \end{bmatrix}$$

Consequently, for $w = ab^2abca$, we compute that

$$\Psi_q(w) = \begin{bmatrix} q & q^2 & 1+q \\ 0 & q^2 & 1+q \\ 0 & 0 & 1 \end{bmatrix} \begin{bmatrix} q^2 & 2q & q \\ 0 & q & q \\ 0 & 0 & q \end{bmatrix}$$

$$= \begin{bmatrix} q^3 & 2q^2+q^3 & q+2q^2+q^3 \\ 0 & q^3 & q+q^2+q^3 \\ 0 & 0 & q \end{bmatrix}$$

Remark: For the Parikh q-matrix mapping it is not true that if $\mathcal{L}$ is a context-free language, then its image is some suitable extension of the notion of semilinearity to matrices over $\mathbb{N}[q]$. This is a direct consequence of Theorem 3 and the negative result concerning the Parikh matrix mapping (Ref. 7, Remark 3.2).

Proposition 2: *Let $\Sigma = \{a_1 < a_2 < \cdots < a_k\}$ and $w \in \Sigma^*$. Then the vector of diagonal entries of the matrix $\Psi_q(w)$ is*

$$(q^{|w|_{a_1}}, q^{|w|_{a_2}}, \ldots, q^{|w|_{a_k}}) \in \mathbb{N}[q]^k .$$

Proof: The matrices $\Psi_q(a_l)$ are all upper-triangular. It is easy to see that the diagonal entries of a product of two upper-triangular matrices depend only on the diagonal elements of each of the matrices. Since diagonal matrices commute, and each occurrence of the letter a_l in w has the effect of multiplying the lth diagonal entry of the k-dimensional identity matrix I_k by q, the result follows immediately. □

Remark: We note that the Parikh vector of w is given by the formal derivative of

$$(q^{|w|_{a_1}}, q^{|w|_{a_2}}, \ldots, q^{|w|_{a_k}}) \in \mathbb{N}[q]^k$$

with respect to q evaluated at $q = 1$.

Theorem 2: Let $\Sigma = \{a_1 < a_2 < \cdots < a_k\}$ be an ordered alphabet, where $k \geq 1$ and assume that $w \in \Sigma^*$. The matrix $\Psi_q(w) = (m_{i,j}(q))_{1 \leq i,j \leq k}$, has the following properties

(1) $m_{i,j} = 0$, for all $1 \leq j < i \leq k$,
(2) $m_{i,i} = q^{|w|_{a_i}}$, for all $1 \leq i \leq k$,
(3) $m_{i,j+1} = S_{w,a_{i,j}}(q)$ for all $1 \leq i \leq j < k$.

Proof: The proof of the parts (1) and (2) are immediate. We now prove property (3). Assume that $|w| = n$. The proof is by induction on n. If $n \leq 1$, the assertion holds. Assume now that part (3) holds for all words of length n and let w be of length $n+1$. Write $w = w'a_j$ where $|w'| = n$ and $a_j \in \Sigma$. Then

$$\Psi_q(w) = \Psi_q(w')\Psi_q(a_j)$$

Assume that

$$\Psi_q(w') = \begin{bmatrix} q^{|w'|_{a_1}} & m'_{1,2} & \cdots & \cdots & m'_{1,k} \\ 0 & q^{|w'|_{a_2}} & \cdots & \cdots & m'_{2,k} \\ \vdots & \vdots & \vdots & \vdots & \vdots \\ \vdots & \vdots & \vdots & \vdots & m'_{k-1,k} \\ 0 & 0 & \cdots & \cdots & q^{|w'|_{a_k}} \end{bmatrix} = M'$$

By the inductive hypothesis the matrix $\Psi_q(w')$ has property (3). The proof has two cases depending on whether $j = k$, or $j < k$. For $j < k$, we have

$$\Psi_q(a_j) = \begin{bmatrix} 1 & 0 & & \cdots & & 0 \\ \vdots & \vdots & \vdots & \vdots & \vdots & \vdots \\ 0 & \cdots & q & 1 & \cdots & 0 \\ \vdots & \vdots & \vdots & \vdots & \vdots & \vdots \\ 0 & 0 & & \cdots & & 1 \end{bmatrix}$$

where the matrix differs from I_k only in two entries: The entry in position (j, j) is q instead of 1, and the entry in position $(j, j+1)$ is 1 instead of 0. Let $M = \Psi_q(w)$. Then

$$M = \begin{bmatrix} q^{|w'|_{a_1}} & m'_{1,2} & \cdots & \cdots & m'_{1,k} \\ 0 & q^{|w'|_{a_2}} & \cdots & \cdots & m'_{2,k} \\ \vdots & \vdots & \vdots & \vdots & \vdots \\ \vdots & \vdots & \vdots & \vdots & m'_{k-1,k} \\ 0 & 0 & \cdots & \cdots & q^{|w'|_{a_k}} \end{bmatrix} \begin{bmatrix} 1 & 0 & & \cdots & & 0 \\ \vdots & \vdots & \vdots & \vdots & \vdots & \vdots \\ 0 & \cdots & q & 1 & \cdots & 0 \\ \vdots & \vdots & \vdots & \vdots & \vdots & \vdots \\ 0 & 0 & & \cdots & & 1 \end{bmatrix}$$

If $M = (m_{p,q})_{1 \leq p,q \leq k}$, then

$$m_{i,j} = qm'_{i,j} \text{ for } 1 \leq i \leq j\,,$$

$$m_{i,j+1} = m'_{i,j} + m'_{i,j+1} \text{ for } 1 \leq i \leq j$$

and for all other indices, $m_{p,q} = m'_{p,q}$. The two equalities for the altered entries of the matrix are equivalent to

$$S_{w'a_j,a_{i,j-1}}(q) = qS_{w',a_{i,j-1}}(q) \text{ for } 1 \leq i \leq j\,,$$

$$S_{w'a_j,a_{i,j}}(q) = S_{w',a_{i,j-1}}(q) + S_{w',a_{i,j}}(q) \text{ for } 1 \leq i < j\,,$$

which hold by Lemma 1. In the case $j = k$ the only change that appears in going from M' to M is that the last column M is obtained from M' by multiplying the elements of the last column of M' by q. This corresponds to the fact that the number of occurrences of a_k in u_{k+1} in any factorization of the form (1) is increased by 1: i.e.,

$$S_{w'a_k,a_{1,k-1}}(q) = qS_{w',a_{1,k-1}}(q)$$

and the proof follows by induction. □

Remark: The structure of how the polynomials in the matrix are indexed can be mnemonically recorded as shown below in the case of the four-letter alphabet $\Sigma = \{a_1 < a_1 < a_3 < a_4\}$:

$$\begin{array}{c} a_1 \\ a_2 \\ a_3 \\ a_4 \end{array} \begin{bmatrix} q^{|w|_{a_1}} & a_1 & a_1a_2 & a_1a_2a_3 \\ 0 & q^{|w|_{a_2}} & a_2 & a_2a_3 \\ 0 & 0 & q^{|w|_{a_3}} & a_3 \\ 0 & 0 & 0 & q^{|w|_{a_4}} \end{bmatrix}$$

As an example, the entry in second row and the fourth column is a shorthand for the polynomial $S_{w,a_2a_3}(q)$, the q-count of the number of occurrences of a_2a_3 as a scattered subword of w as developed in Sec. 4.

Proposition 3: *Let $\Sigma = \{a_1 < a_2 < \cdots < a_k\}$ and $w \in \Sigma^*$. Suppose the vector of super diagonal entries of the matrix $\Psi_q(w)$ is*

$$(m_{1,2}(q), m_{2,3}(q), \ldots, m_{k-1,k}(q)) \in \mathbb{N}[q]^{k-1}\,.$$

Then at $q = 1$, this vector evaluates to

$$(|w|_{a_1}, |w|_{a_2}, \ldots, |w|_{a_{k-1}})\,.$$

Proof: This proposition is a special case of a stronger result that characterizes the whole matrix $\Psi_q(w)$ at $q = 1$ that we give as Theorem 3. □

Theorem 3: Suppose $\Sigma = \{a_1 < a_2 < \cdots < a_k\}$ and $w \in \Sigma^*$. Consider w as a word over $\Gamma = \{a_1 < a_2 < \cdots < a_k < a_{k+1}\}$ and let $\Psi_q(w)$ be the resulting Parikh q-matrix in $\mathbb{N}[q]^{k+1}$. Then $\Psi_q(w)$ evaluated at $q = 1$ is the Parikh matrix $\Psi_{\mathcal{M}_k}(w)$.

Proof: Combine Theorem 2, Theorem 1, and Proposition 1. □

6. Injectivity, Inverse, and Further Remarks

Just as the Parikh matrix mapping, the Parikh q-matrix mapping is not an injective mapping either. For instance over the ordered alphabet $\{a < b < c\}$ one has

$$\Psi_q(acb) = \Psi_q(cab) = \begin{bmatrix} q & q & 1 \\ 0 & q & 1 \\ 0 & 0 & q \end{bmatrix}$$

However, there are instances in which two words can have the same Parikh matrix, but distinct Parikh q-matrices.

The injectivity of the Parikh matrix mapping was studied in Ref. 1. In particular it was proved that over a binary alphabet Σ, a pair of *palindromic amiable* words α, β have the same Parikh matrix image. The definition of palindromic amiable pair is as follows:

(1) Both α and β are palindromes,
(2) α and β have the same Parikh vector, i.e., $\Psi(\alpha) = \Psi(\beta)$.

For example the words $\alpha = aba^2ba$ and $\beta = ba^4b$ over $\Sigma = \{a < b\}$ are palindromic amiables. Therefore as proved in Ref. 1, they have the same 3×3 Parikh matrix image. We calculate directly that indeed

$$\Psi_{\mathcal{M}_2}(\alpha) = \begin{bmatrix} 1 & 4 & 4 \\ 0 & 1 & 2 \\ 0 & 0 & 1 \end{bmatrix} = \Psi_{\mathcal{M}_2}(\beta) \tag{4}$$

The corresponding matrices given by the Parikh q-matrix mapping Ψ_q are calculated over the alphabet $\{a < b < c\}$ in accordance with Theorem 3. These are also 3×3 upper-triangular matrices, but with entries from $\mathbb{N}[q]$. They are given by

$$\Psi_q(\alpha) = \begin{bmatrix} q^4 & 2q^2 + 2q^3 & 1 + 2q + q^2 \\ 0 & q^2 & 1 + q \\ 0 & 0 & 1 \end{bmatrix} \tag{5}$$

$$\Psi_q(\beta) = \begin{bmatrix} q^4 & q + q^2 + q^3 + q^4 & 1 + q + q^2 + q^3 \\ 0 & q^2 & 1 + q \\ 0 & 0 & 1 \end{bmatrix} \tag{6}$$

Clearly, these two distinct matrices reduce to $\Psi_{\mathcal{M}_2}(\alpha) = \Psi_{\mathcal{M}_2}(\beta)$ given in (4) as guaranteed by Theorem 3. Thus the matrices obtained by the Parikh q-matrix mapping contains finer information that is able to distinguish words that are equal under the ordinary Parikh matrix map. An alternate generalization of the Parikh matrix mapping with additional injectivity properties using a different q-analogue of scattered-subwords appears in Ref. 2.

The notion of the alternate (signed) Parikh matrix developed in Ref. 7 has the nice property that the inverse of the matrix $\Psi_{\mathcal{M}_k}(w)$ is the alternate Parikh matrix of the mirror image $mi(w)$ of w. This property also carries over to the case of the Parikh q-matrix mapping with some modifications. Let $\Sigma = \{a_1 < a_2 < \cdots < a_k\}$. We define a morphism (called the *alternate Parikh q-matrix mapping*) $\overline{\Psi}_q = \overline{\Psi}_q^k$ from Σ^* to a collection of k-dimensional upper-triangular matrices over $\mathbb{Z}[q]$. $\overline{\Psi}_q$ is defined on Σ as follows: If $\overline{\Psi}_q(a_l) = (m_{i,j})_{1 \le i,j \le k}$, then

(1) $m_{l,l} = 1$,
(2) $m_{i,i} = q$ for $1 \le i \le k$, $i \ne l$,
(3) $m_{l,l+1} = -1$ if $l < k$,
(4) all other entries of the matrix $\Psi_q(a_l)$ are zero.

Example 5: When the alphabet is $\Sigma = \{a < b < c\}$, then

$$\overline{\Psi}_q(a) = \begin{bmatrix} 1 & -1 & 0 \\ 0 & q & 0 \\ 0 & 0 & q \end{bmatrix}, \quad \overline{\Psi}_q(b) = \begin{bmatrix} q & 0 & 0 \\ 0 & 1 & -1 \\ 0 & 0 & q \end{bmatrix}, \quad \overline{\Psi}_q(c) = \begin{bmatrix} q & 0 & 0 \\ 0 & q & 0 \\ 0 & 0 & 1 \end{bmatrix}$$

Note that $\Psi_q(a)\overline{\Psi}_q(a) = \Psi_q(b)\overline{\Psi}_q(b) = \Psi_q(c)\overline{\Psi}_q(c) = qI_3$. As an example, for $w = ab^2abca$, we compute that

$$\overline{\Psi}_q(mi(w)) = \begin{bmatrix} q^4 & -2q^3 - q^4 & 2q^3 + 2q^4 + q^5 \\ 0 & q^4 & -q^4 - q^5 - q^6 \\ 0 & 0 & q^6 \end{bmatrix}$$

Then the following result holds.

Theorem 4: Suppose $\Sigma = \{a_1 < a_2 < \cdots < a_k\}$ and $w \in \Sigma^*$. If Ψ_q and $\overline{\Psi}_q$ are the Parikh q-matrix, and the alternate Parikh q-matrix mappings from Σ^* to upper-triangular integral matrices over $\mathbb{Z}[q]$, then the k-dimensional matrix identity

$$\Psi_q(w)\overline{\Psi}_q(mi(w)) = \begin{bmatrix} q^{|w|} & 0 & \cdots & & 0 \\ 0 & q^{|w|} & 0 & \cdots & 0 \\ \vdots & & \ddots & & \vdots \\ 0 & \cdots & & 0 & q^{|w|} \end{bmatrix} \tag{7}$$

holds.

Proof: From the definition of the matrices $\Psi_q(a_l)$ and $\overline{\Psi}_q(a_l)$, we have the the matrix product

$$\Psi_q(a_l)\overline{\Psi}_q(a_l) = qI_k$$

for any letter $a_l \in \Sigma$. If $|w| > 1$, write $w = w'a_j$ with $a_j \in \Sigma$. Then

$$\begin{aligned} \Psi_q(w)\overline{\Psi}_q(mi(w)) &= \Psi_q(w')\Psi_q(a_j)\overline{\Psi}_q(a_j)\overline{\Psi}_q(mi(w')) \\ &= \Psi_q(w')qI_k\overline{\Psi}_q(mi(w')) \\ &= qI_k\Psi_q(w')\overline{\Psi}_q(mi(w')) \end{aligned}$$

and the theorem follows by induction on $|w|$. □

It can also be shown that the identity (7) reduces to the matrix inverse identity of the Parikh matrix mapping of Ref. 7 when we extend the alphabet as in Theorem 3 and put $q = 1$.

References

1. A. Atanasiu, C. Martin-Vide and A. Mateescu, *Fundamenta Informaticae* **49**, 289 (2002).
2. Ö. Eğecioğlu, in *Proc. Int. Conf. on Computers and Communications (ICCC 2004)*, Oradea, Romania, 147 (2004).
3. Ö. Eğecioğlu and O. Ibarra, in *Proc. of IFIP World Computer Congress (WCC): 3rd IFIP International Conference on Theoretical Computer Science (TCS 2004)*, Toulouse, France, 133 (2004).
4. T. Harju, O. Ibarra, J. Karhumaki and A. Salomaa, *J. Computer and System Sciences* **65**, 278 (2002).
5. O. Ibarra, *J. Assoc. Comput. Mach.* **24**, 123 (1978).
6. O. Ibarra, J. Su, Z. Dang, T. Bultan and R. Kemmerer, *Theoretical Computer Science* **289**, 165 (2002).
7. A. Mateescu, A. Salomaa, K. Salomaa and S. Yu, *Theoretical Informatics and Applications* **35**, 551 (2001).
8. R. J. Parikh, *J. Assoc. Comput. Mach.* **13**, 570 (1966).
9. G. Rozenberg and A. Salomaa (eds), *Handbook of Formal Languages* (Springer, Berlin, 1997).

CHAPTER 8

CONTEXTUAL ARRAY GRAMMARS

Rudolf Freund*, Gheorghe Păun† and Grzegorz Rozenberg‡

** Vienna University of Technology, Institute of Computer Languages, Favoritenstr. 9–11, 1040 Wien, Austria*

† Institute of Mathematics of the Romanian Academy of Sciences, PO Box 1-764, 014700 Bucureşti, Romania
and
Research Group on Natural Computing, Department of Computer Science and Artificial Intelligence, University of Sevilla, Avda. Reina Mercedes s/n, 41012 Sevilla, Spain

‡ University of Leiden, Department of Computer Science, Niels Bohrweg 1, 2333 CA Leiden, The Netherlands

** E-mail: rudi@emcc.at*
† E-mail: gpaun@us.es
‡ E-mail: rozenber@liacs.nl

We consider the (d-dimensional) array counterpart of string contextual grammars in the sense of Marcus and investigate the power of such grammars, especially in comparison with context-free array grammars. The main result is that every array language generated by a context-free array grammar is the coding of an array language generated by a contextual array grammar. Moreover, we also show how an array language generated by a regular Siromoney matrix array grammar can be obtained as the coding of an array language generated by a two-dimensional contextual array grammar.

1. Introduction

Contextual grammars were introduced for the string case,[8] with motivations arising from descriptive linguistics. Basically, such a grammar consists of a finite set of strings (*axioms*) and a finite set of pairs (s, c), where s is a string and c is a *context*, i.e., a pair of strings, $c = (u, v)$, over the alphabet under consideration. Such a pair (s, c) is called *production*, and s is called its *selector*. Starting from an axiom, contexts iteratively are added as it is indicated by the productions, which yields new strings. There are two modes of adjoining contexts: at the ends of strings only (this case was named *external*;[8] infinitely many productions (s, c), with finitely many contexts, are usually used, otherwise the obtained language is finite), or in the interior of strings, bracketing one occurrence of a selector with the associated context (this case was named *interior*[9]). The generated language consists of all strings obtained in this way, by finitely but arbitrarily many context adjoinings.

Several variants of these grammars were considered;[3–5,10–12,19] one variant which we shall use also here concerns the way of defining the generated language: for a given grammar we can retain only the set of strings produced by blocked derivations, i.e., derivations which cannot be continued. This corresponds to the maximal mode of derivation (called t-mode) in cooperating grammar systems.[1]

The fundamental difference between contextual grammars and Chomsky grammars or Lindenmayer systems is that in contextual grammars we do not *rewrite* symbols, but we only *adjoin* symbols to the current string; once introduced, a symbol cannot be modified, it remains in the string to be finally generated.

The contextual style of generating strings can be extended to arrays in a natural way (see Section 3); in some sense, this case is even more natural than that of strings, because we no longer have to consider internal and external derivations, or pairs of adjoined strings, one to the left and one to the right of the selector: basically, we start from a given finite set of arrays (axioms) and apply to them productions (s, c) where both s and c are finite patterns; if in the current array we can identify a subarray identical with s in such a way that the places corresponding to c are empty, then c is adjoined, producing a new array. In the generated language we may retain either all the arrays produced in this way or only the arrays to which no production is applicable (maximal derivations).

The main results of the paper concern the relations between the families of array languages generated in this way (their generative power is investigated in Section 4) and array languages generated by context-free array grammars: in Section 5 we prove that every array language generated by a context-free array grammar is the coding of a language generated by a contextual array grammar in the maximal mode of derivation. Moreover, we show that another well-known generating mechanism for array languages can be simulated by contextual array grammars: Siromoney matrix array grammars were introduced as tools for describing two-dimensional picture languages of rectangular arrays ("matrices").[16–18] In Section 6 we show that an array language generated by a regular Siromoney matrix array grammar can be obtained as the coding of an array language generated by a two-dimensional contextual array grammar.

2. Array Grammars — Definitions and Examples

In the main part of this section we will introduce the definitions and notations for arrays and sequential array grammars[7,13,20] and give some explanatory examples. For the basic notions and results from the theory of formal languages the reader is referred to well-known tetxbooks.[14,15]

Let $\mathbb{Z}$ denote the set of integers, let $\mathbb{N}$ denote the set of positive integers, i.e., $\mathbb{N} = \{1, 2, \ldots\}$, and let $d \in \mathbb{N}$. Then a *d-dimensional array* $\mathcal{A}$ over an alphabet V is a function $\mathcal{A} : \mathbb{Z}^d \to V \cup \{\#\}$ where

$$\text{shape}(\mathcal{A}) = \{v \in \mathbb{Z}^d | \mathcal{A}(v) \neq \#\}$$

is finite and $\# \notin V$ is called the *background* or *blank symbol.* We usually write

$$\mathcal{A} = \{(v, \mathcal{A}(v)) | v \in \text{shape } (\mathcal{A})\} .$$

The set of all d-dimensional arrays over V is denoted by V^{*d}. The *empty array* in V^{*d} with empty shape is denoted by Λ_d. Moreover, we define $V^{+d} = V^{*d} - \{\Lambda_d\}$. Any subset of V^{+d} is called a Λ-free d-dimensional array language.

Let $v \in \mathbb{Z}^d$. Then the *translation* $\tau_v : \mathbb{Z}^d \to \mathbb{Z}^d$ is defined by $\tau_v(w) = w + v$ for all $w \in \mathbb{Z}^d$, and for any array $\mathcal{A} \in V^{*d}$ we define $\tau_v(\mathcal{A})$, the corresponding d-dimensional array translated by v, by $(\tau_v(\mathcal{A}))(w) = \mathcal{A}(w - v)$ for all $w \in \mathbb{Z}^d$. The vector $(0, \ldots, 0) \in \mathbb{Z}^d$ shall be denoted by Ω_d, the vector $(1, \ldots, 1)$ shall be denoted by E_d.

Usually[2,13,20,21] arrays are regarded as equivalence classes of arrays with respect to linear translations, i.e., only the relative positions of the symbols different from # in the plane are taken into account: the equivalence class $[\mathcal{A}]$ of an array $\mathcal{A} \in V^{*d}$ is defined by

$$[\mathcal{A}] = \{\mathcal{B} \in V^{*d} | \mathcal{B} = \tau_v(\mathcal{A}) \text{ for some } v \in \mathbb{Z}^d\} .$$

The set of all equivalence classes of d-dimensional arrays over V with respect to linear translations is denoted by $[V^{*d}]$ etc.

In order to be able to define the important notion of connectedness of d-dimensional arrays, we need the following definitions:

An (undirected) *graph* g is an ordered pair (K, E) where K is a finite set of nodes and E is a set of undirected edges $\{x, y\}$ with x, $y \in K$. A sequence of different nodes $x_0, x_1, \ldots, x_m$, $m \in \mathbb{N}$, is called a path of length m in g with the starting-point x_0 and the ending-point x_m if for all i with $1 \leq i \leq m$ an edge $\{x_{i-1}, x_i\}$ in E exists. A graph g is said to be *connected* if for any two nodes x, $y \in K$, $x \neq y$, a path in g with starting point x and ending point y exists. Observe that a graph $(\{x\}, \emptyset)$ with only one node and an empty set of edges is connected, too.

Let W be a non-empty finite subset of $\mathbb{Z}^d$. For any $k \in \mathbb{N} \cup \{0\}$, a graph $g_k(W) = (W, E_k)$ can be assigned to W such that E_k for $v, w \in W$ contains the edge $\{v, w\}$ if and only if $0 < \|v - w\| \leq k$, where the norm $\|u\|$ of a vector $u \in \mathbb{Z}^d$, $u = (u(1), \ldots, u(d))$, is defined by $\|u\| = \max\{\|u(i)\| | 1 \leq i \leq d\}$. Then W is said to be *k-connected* if $g_k(W)$ is a connected graph. Observe that W is 0-connected if and only if $\text{card}(W) = 1$, where $\text{card}(W)$ denotes the number of elements in the set W.

Now let V be a finite alphabet and $\mathcal{A}$ a d-dimensional array over V, $\mathcal{A} \neq \Lambda_d$. Then $\mathcal{A}$ (respectively $[\mathcal{A}]$) is said to be *k-connected* if $g_k(\text{shape}(\mathcal{A}))$ is a connected graph. Obviously, if $\mathcal{A}$ is k-connected then $\mathcal{A}$ is m-connected for all $m > k$, too. The *norm of* $\mathcal{A}$ is the smallest number $k \in \mathbb{N} \cup \{0\}$ such that $\mathcal{A}$ is k-connected, and is denoted by $\|\mathcal{A}\|$. Observe that $\|\mathcal{A}\| = 0$ if and only if $\text{card}(\text{shape}(\mathcal{A})) = 1$. For any $\mathcal{A} \in V^{+d}$ we define $\|[\mathcal{A}]\| = \|\mathcal{A}\|$.

Example 1: The d-dimensional array $\mathcal{E}(d, k) = \{(\Omega_d, a), (kE_d, a)\}$ in $\{a\}^{*d}$ is m-connected only for every $m \geq k$, and $\|\mathcal{E}(d, k)\| = \|[\mathcal{E}(d, k)]\| = k$.

A *d-dimensional array production* p over V is a triple $(W, \mathcal{A}_1, \mathcal{A}_2)$ where $W \subseteq \mathbb{Z}^d$ is a finite set and $\mathcal{A}_1$ and $\mathcal{A}_2$ are mappings from W to $V \cup \{\#\}$. We say that the array $\mathcal{C}_2 \in V^{*d}$ is *directly derivable* from the array $\mathcal{C}_1 \in V^{+d}$ by the d-dimensional array production $(W, \mathcal{A}_1, \mathcal{A}_2)$ if and only if there exists a vector $v \in \mathbb{Z}^d$ such that $\mathcal{C}_1(w) = \mathcal{C}_2(w)$ for all $w \in \mathbb{Z}^d - \tau_v(W)$ as well as $\mathcal{C}_1(w) = \mathcal{A}_1(\tau_{-v}(w))$ and $\mathcal{C}_2(w) = \mathcal{A}_2(\tau_{-v}(w))$ for all $w \in \tau_v(W)$, i.e., the subarray of $\mathcal{C}_1$ corresponding to $\mathcal{A}_1$ is replaced by $\mathcal{A}_2$, thus yielding $\mathcal{C}_2$; we also write $\mathcal{C}_1 \Longrightarrow_p \mathcal{C}_2$. Moreover we say that the array $\mathcal{B}_2 \in [V^{*d}]$ is *directly derivable* from the array $\mathcal{B}_1 \in [V^{+d}]$ by the d-dimensional array production $(W, \mathcal{A}_1, \mathcal{A}_2)$ if and only if there exist $\mathcal{C}_1 \in \mathcal{B}_1$ and $\mathcal{C}_2 \in \mathcal{B}_2$ such that $\mathcal{C}_1 \Longrightarrow_p \mathcal{C}_2$; we also write $\mathcal{B}_1 \Longrightarrow_p \mathcal{B}_2$.

In contrast to the representation of an array $\mathcal{A} \in V^{*d}$, which is uniquely described by $\{(v, \mathcal{A}(v)) | v \in \text{shape } (\mathcal{A})\}$, i.e., by listing every position v in $\mathbb{Z}^n$ occupied by a non-blank symbol $\mathcal{A}(v) \in V$ together with this symbol $\mathcal{A}(v)$, in a d-dimensional array production $(W, \mathcal{A}_1, \mathcal{A}_2)$ over V all positions in W together with their associated symbols must be listed for representing $\mathcal{A}_1$ and $\mathcal{A}_2$, respectively, by $\mathcal{A}_i = \{(v, \mathcal{A}_i(v)) | v \in W\}$, $1 \le i \le 2$. The norm of the d-dimensional array production $(W, \mathcal{A}_1, \mathcal{A}_2)$ is defined to be the norm of W, i.e., $\|(W, \mathcal{A}_1, \mathcal{A}_2)\| = \|W\|$. For the mappings $\mathcal{A}_1$ and $\mathcal{A}_2$ in the d-dimensional array production $(W, \mathcal{A}_1, \mathcal{A}_2)$ we define their shapes by shape $(\mathcal{A}_i) = \{v \in \mathbb{Z}^d | \mathcal{A}_i(v) \neq \#\}$, $1 \le i \le 2$. As can already be seen from the definitions of a d-dimensional array production, the conditions for an application to a d-dimensional array $\mathcal{B}$ and the result of an application to $\mathcal{B}$, a d-dimensional array production $(W, \mathcal{A}_1, \mathcal{A}_2)$ is a representative for the infinite set of equivalent d-dimensional array productions of the form $(\tau_v(W), \tau_v(\mathcal{A}_1), \tau_v(\mathcal{A}_2))$ with $v \in \mathbb{Z}^d$. Hence, without loss of generality, in the sequel we shall assume $\Omega_d \in W$. Moreover, we often will omit the set W, because it is uniquely reconstructible from the description of the two mappings $\mathcal{A}_1$ and $\mathcal{A}_2$ by $\mathcal{A}_i = \{(v, \mathcal{A}_i(v)) | v \in W\}$, $1 \le i \le 2$. Thus, in the sequel we will represent the d-dimensional array production $(W, \mathcal{A}_1, \mathcal{A}_2)$ also by writing $\mathcal{A}_1 \to \mathcal{A}_2$, i.e., $\{(v, \mathcal{A}_1(v)) | v \in W\} \to \{(v, \mathcal{A}_2(v)) | v \in W\}$.

A *d-dimensional array grammar* is a quintuple

$$G = (d, V_N, V_T, \#, P, S),$$

where V_N is the alphabet of *non-terminal symbols*, V_T is the alphabet of *terminal symbols*, $V_N \cap V_T = \emptyset$, $\# \notin V_N \cup V_T$; P is a finite non-empty set of d-dimensional array productions over $V_N \cup V_T$, and S is the *start symbol.*

We say that the array $\mathcal{B}_2 \in [V^{*d}]$ is *directly derivable* from the array $\mathcal{B}_1 \in [V^{+n}]$ in G, denoted $\mathcal{B}_1 \Longrightarrow_G \mathcal{B}_2$, if and only if there exists a d-dimensional array production $p = (W, \mathcal{A}_1, \mathcal{A}_2)$ in P such that $\mathcal{B}_1 \Longrightarrow_p \mathcal{B}_2$. Let $\Longrightarrow_G^*$ be the reflexive transitive closure of $\Longrightarrow_G$. Then the *(d-dimensional) array language generated by G*, $[L(G)]$, is defined by

$$[L(G)] = \{\mathcal{B} \in [V_T^{*d}] | [\{(\Omega_d, S)\}] \Longrightarrow_G^* \mathcal{B}\}.$$

The norm of the d-dimensional array grammar G is defined to be the maximum of the norms of the d-dimensional array productions in P, i.e.,

$$\|G\| = \max\{\|p\| | p \in P\}.$$

In this paper, we will call a d-dimensional array production $p = (W, \mathcal{A}_1, \mathcal{A}_2)$ in P

- *monotonic*, if shape $(\mathcal{A}_1) \subseteq$ shape $(\mathcal{A}_2)$;
- *context-free*, if p is monotonic and, moreover, card(shape $(\mathcal{A}_1)) = 1$ with $\mathcal{A}_1(\Omega_d) \in V_N$ as well as card(shape $(\mathcal{A}_2))$ = card (W); the condition

$\mathcal{A}_1(\Omega_n) \in V_N$ allows the representation of a context-free array production as

$$(A, \{(v, \mathcal{A}_2(v)) | v \in W\}) \text{ or } A \to \{(v, \mathcal{A}_2(v)) | v \in W\}$$

instead of

$$(W, \{(\Omega_d, A)\} \cup \{(v, \#) | v \in W - \{\Omega_d\}\}, \{(v, \mathcal{A}_2(v)) | v \in W\});$$

if card$(W) = 1$, we only write $A \to \mathcal{A}_2(\Omega_d)$; moreover, the condition card(shape $(\mathcal{A}_2)$) $=$ card(W) implies $\mathcal{A}_2(v) \in V_N \cup V_T$ for all $v \in W$.

G is called (recursively) enumerable, monotonic, and context-free, respectively, if every array production in P is an arbitrary, monotonic or context-free array production. The corresponding families of Λ-free d-dimensional array languages of equivalence classes of arrays are denoted by $[L(d, enum)]$, $[L(d, mon)]$, and $[L(d, cf)]$, respectively.

Like in the string case, the families of array languages defined above form a strict hierarchy.[7]

Proposition 1: *For all* $d \in \mathbb{N}$, $[L(d, cf)] \subsetneq [L(d, mon)] \subsetneq [L(d, enum)]$.

With respect to the norms of monotonic and context-free array grammars, respectively, for each $k \geq 1$ we can distinguish different families of array languages: for all d, $k \in \mathbb{N}$ the families of d-dimensional array languages (of equivalence classes of arrays) that can be generated by some monotonic or some context-free array grammar G with $\|G\| \leq k$ are denoted by $[L(d, mon, k)]$ and $[L(d, cf, k)]$, respectively; when no bound on the degree of connectedness is considered, we replace k by ∞. According to this definition, for $X \in \{mon, cf\}$, we have

$$\bigcup_{k \in \mathbb{N}} [L(d, X, k)] = [L(d, X, \infty)] = [L(d, X)].$$

Example 2: Consider the d-dimensional context-free array grammar

$$G(d, k) = (d, \{S\}, \{a\}, \#, \{S \to \mathcal{E}(d, k)\}, S)$$

where the $\mathcal{E}(d, k) = \{(\Omega_d, a), (kE_d, a)\}$ are the arrays already considered in Example 1 with $\|[\mathcal{E}(d, k)]\| = k$. For all $k \geq 2$, $[L(G(d, k))] = \{[\mathcal{E}(d, k)]\}$, hence, we have $[L(G(d, k))] \in ([L(d, cf, k)] - [L(d, mon, k - 1)])$.

As many results for d-dimensional arrays for a special d can be taken over immediately for higher dimensions, we introduce the following notion:

Let $n, m \in \mathbb{N}$ with $n \leq m$. For $n < m$, the natural embedding $i_{n,m} : \mathbb{Z}^n \to \mathbb{Z}^m$ is defined by $i_{n,m}(v) = (v, \Omega_{m-n})$ for all $v \in \mathbb{Z}^n$; for $n = m$ we define $i_{n,n} : \mathbb{Z}^n \to \mathbb{Z}^n$ by $i_{n,n}(v) = v$ for all $v \in \mathbb{Z}^n$. To an n-dimensional array $\mathcal{A} \in V^{+n}$ with $\mathcal{A} = \{(v, \mathcal{A}(v)) | v \in \text{shape } (\mathcal{A})\}$ we assign the m-dimensional array $i_{n,m}(\mathcal{A}) = \{(i_{n,m}(v), \mathcal{A}(v)) | v \in \text{shape } (\mathcal{A})\}$.

3. Contextual Array Grammars: Definitions and Examples

First we introduce the concept of contextual grammars for arrays:

A *d-dimensional contextual array grammar* ($d \in \mathbb{N}$) is a construct $G = (d, V, \#, P, A)$ where V is an alphabet not containing the blank symbol $\#$, A is a finite set of axioms, i.e., of d-dimensional arrays in $[V^{+d}]$, and P is a finite set of rules of the form $(U_\alpha, \alpha, U_\beta, \beta)$ where

(i) $U_\alpha, U_\beta \subseteq \mathbb{Z}^d$, $U_\alpha \cap U_\beta = \emptyset$, and U_α, U_β are finite and at least U_α is non-empty;

(ii) $\alpha : U_\alpha \to V \cup \{\#\}$, $\beta : U_\beta \to V$ such that card(shape $(\alpha)) \neq \emptyset$, where in the usual way we define shape $(\alpha) = \{w \in U_\alpha | \alpha(w) \in V\}$.

(U_α, α) corresponds with the *selector* and (U_β, β) with the *context* of the production $(U_\alpha, \alpha, U_\beta, \beta)$; U_α is called the *selector area*, and U_β is the *context area*. As the sets U_α and U_β are uniquely determined by α and β, we will also represent $(U_\alpha, \alpha, U_\beta, \beta)$ by (α, β) only.

For $\mathcal{C}_1, \mathcal{C}_2 \in V^{+d}$ we say that $\mathcal{C}_2$ is directly derivable from $\mathcal{C}_1$ by the contextual array production $p \in P$, $p = (U_\alpha, \alpha, U_\beta, \beta)$ (we write $\mathcal{C}_1 \Longrightarrow_p \mathcal{C}_2$), if there exists a vector $v \in \mathbb{Z}^d$ such that

- $\mathcal{C}_1(w) = \mathcal{C}_2(w) = \alpha(\tau_{-v}(w))$ for all $w \in \tau_v(U_\alpha)$,
- $\mathcal{C}_1(w) = \#$ for all $w \in \tau_v(U_\beta)$,
- $\mathcal{C}_2(w) = \beta(\tau_{-v}(w))$ for all $w \in \tau_v(U_\beta)$,
- $\mathcal{C}_1(w) = \mathcal{C}_2(w)$ for all $w \in \mathbb{Z}^d - \tau_v(U_\alpha \cup U_\beta)$.

Hence, if in $\mathcal{C}_1$ we find a subpattern that corresponds with the selector α and only blank symbols at the places corresponding with β, we can add the context β thus obtaining $\mathcal{C}_2$.

For every $\mathcal{B}_1$, $\mathcal{B}_2 \in [V^{+d}]$ we say that $\mathcal{B}_2$ is directly derivable from $\mathcal{B}_1$ by the contextual array production $p \in P$, $p = (U_\alpha, \alpha, U_\beta, \beta)$, denoted $\mathcal{B}_1 \Longrightarrow_p \mathcal{B}_2$, if and only if there exist $\mathcal{C}_1 \in \mathcal{B}_1$ and $\mathcal{C}_2 \in \mathcal{B}_2$ such that $\mathcal{C}_1 \Longrightarrow_p \mathcal{C}_2$. $\mathcal{B}_2$ is said to be directly derivable from $\mathcal{B}_1$ in G, denoted $\mathcal{B}_1 \Longrightarrow_G \mathcal{B}_2$, if and only if $\mathcal{B}_1 \Longrightarrow_p \mathcal{B}_2$ for some $p \in P$.

For every rule $(U_\alpha, \alpha, U_\beta, \beta)$ we define $\|(U_\alpha, \alpha, U_\beta, \beta)\| = \|U_\alpha \cup U_\beta\|$; the norm of the set of contextual array productions in G, $\|P\|$, is defined by

$$\|P\| = \max\{\|U_\alpha \cup U_\beta\| | (U_\alpha, \alpha, U_\beta, \beta) \in P\}.$$

Moreover, we define the norm of the set of axioms, $\|A\|$, by

$$\|A\| = \max\{\|\mathcal{A}\| | \mathcal{A} \in A\}$$

as well as the norm of the contextual array grammar G, $\|G\|$, by

$$\|G\| = \max\{\|P\|, \|A\|\}.$$

By $\Longrightarrow_G^*$ we denote the reflexive transitive closure of $\Longrightarrow_G$ and by $\Longrightarrow_G^t$ we denote the relation which, for arbitrary arrays $\mathcal{A}, \mathcal{B} \in [V^{+d}]$, is defined by $\mathcal{A} \Longrightarrow_G^t \mathcal{B}$ if and only if $\mathcal{A} \Longrightarrow_G^* \mathcal{B}$ and there is no $\mathcal{C} \in [V^{+d}]$ such that $\mathcal{B} \Longrightarrow_G \mathcal{C}$.

In that way, two array languages can be associated with G :

$$[L_*(G)] = \{\mathcal{B} \in [V^{+d}] | \mathcal{A} \Longrightarrow_G^* \mathcal{B} \text{ for some } \mathcal{A} \in A\},$$

$$[L_t(G)] = \{\mathcal{B} \in [V^{+d}] | \mathcal{A} \Longrightarrow_G^t \mathcal{B} \text{ for some } \mathcal{A} \in A\}.$$

The family of d-dimensional array languages generated by contextual array grammars of the form $G = (d, V, \#, P, A)$ with $\|G\| \leq k$ in the mode $f \in \{*, t\}$ is denoted by $[L(d, \text{cont}, k, f)]$; when no bound on the degree of connectedness is considered, we replace k by ∞, thus obtaining $[L(d, \text{cont}, \infty, f)]$.

In order to elucidate the definitions given above, let us consider some examples:

Example 3: Let L be a finite subset of $[V^{+d}]$. For the d-dimensional contextual array grammar $G_L = (d, V, \#, \emptyset, L)$ we obviously obtain

$$[L_*(G_L)] = [L_t(G_L)] = L \quad \text{and} \quad \|G_L\| = \|L\|.$$

As a special example, consider $L(d, k) = \{[\mathcal{E}(d, k)]\}$, where

$$\mathcal{E}(d, k) = \{(\Omega_d, a), (kE_d, a)\}$$

as in Example 2. Then

$$[L_*(G_{L(d,k)})] = [L_t(G_{L(d,k)})] = L(d, k)$$

and, as $\|G_{L(d,k)}\| = \|L(d, k)\| = k$, for all $k \geq 2$ we immediately obtain

$$L(d, k) \in (([L(d, \text{cont}, k, *)] \cap [L(d, \text{cont}, k, t)]) - ([L(d, \text{cont}, k-1, *)] \cup [L(d, \text{cont}, k-1, t])).$$

Example 4: Let $G = (2, \{a\}, \#, P, A)$ be a two-dimensional contextual array grammar with A containing the axiom

$$[\{((0,0),a),((0,1),a),((1,0),a)\}],$$

which in a more depictive way can be described by $\begin{array}{ll} a & \\ a & a \end{array}$, and P consisting of four productions p_1, p_2, p_3, p_4:

$$\begin{aligned} p_1 = (&\{(0,0),(0,1),(1,0)\},\{((0,0),a),((0,1),a),((1,0),a)\},\\ &\{(1,1),(1,2),(2,1)\},\{((1,1),a),((1,2),a),((2,1),a)\}),\\ p_2 = (&\{(0,0),(0,1),(1,0)\},\{((0,0),a),((0,1),a),((1,0),a)\},\\ &\{(1,1)\},\{((1,1),a)\}),\\ p_3 = (&\{(0,0),(1,0),(1,1)\},\{((0,0),a),((1,0),a),((1,1),a)\},\\ &\{(0,1)\},\{((0,1),a)\}),\\ p_4 = (&\{(0,0),(0,1),(1,1)\},\{((0,0),a),((0,1),a),((1,1),a)\},\\ &\{(1,0)\},\{((1,0),a)\}). \end{aligned}$$

As the selector area U_α and the context area U_β in a contextual array production of the form $(U_\alpha, \alpha, U_\beta, \beta)$ are disjoint, both α and β can be represented within only one pattern, i.e., p_1, p_2, p_3, p_4 in a more depictive way can be represented by the following patterns (the symbols of the selector are enclosed in boxes):

$$p_1 = \begin{array}{ccc} & a & \\ \boxed{a} & a & a \\ \boxed{a} & \boxed{a} & \end{array}, \quad p_2 = \begin{array}{cc} \boxed{a} & a \\ \boxed{a} & \boxed{a} \end{array}, \quad p_3 = \begin{array}{cc} a & \boxed{a} \\ \boxed{a} & \boxed{a} \end{array}, \quad p_4 = \begin{array}{cc} \boxed{a} & \boxed{a} \\ \boxed{a} & a \end{array}.$$

Let us examine the maximal derivations in G: The rule p_1 cannot be used after using p_2, the rules p_3, p_4 can be used as long as the array contains North-West or South-East "angles". We start from an array without angles in the South-West direction; the use of all rules preserves this property. After using p_2 no angle exists in the North-East direction. In sum, what we obtain by maximal derivations must be a rectangle. As when using p_1 and p_2 we go on a diagonal of such a rectangle, we obtain in fact a square. In conclusion, $L_t(G)$ is the language of all solid squares of side length at least 2; adding the square $\{((0,0),a)\}$ to $\mathcal{A}$ we can also get the 1×1 square, i.e. we obtain the set of all solid squares Sq (there even exists a regular array grammar generating Sq, which result[21] is based on the fact that even regular array productions make use of some #-sensing ability). Let us consider two maximal derivations in G:

$$(1)\quad \begin{array}{ll} a & \\ a & a \end{array} \Longrightarrow_G \begin{array}{ll} a & a \\ a & a \end{array};$$

$$(2)\quad \begin{array}{lll} & & \\ a & & \\ a & a & \end{array} \Longrightarrow_G \begin{array}{lll} & a & \\ a & a & a \\ a & a & \end{array} \Longrightarrow_G \begin{array}{lll} & a & a \\ a & a & a \\ a & a & \end{array} \Longrightarrow_G \begin{array}{lll} a & a & a \\ a & a & a \\ a & a & \end{array} \Longrightarrow_G \begin{array}{lll} a & a & a \\ a & a & a \\ a & a & a \end{array}; \text{ etc.}$$

The sequences of rules used in these maximal derivations in G are described by the strings p_2 and $p_1p_2p_3p_4$, respectively. In general, for $n \geq 0$, a derivation in G described by the sequence of rules $p_1^n p_2 p_3^{n(n+1)/2} p_4^{n(n+1)/2}$ generates a square of side length $n + 2$.

Two d-dimensional arrays $\mathcal{A}$ and $\mathcal{B}$ in $[V^{*d}]$ are called *shape-equivalent* if and only if shape $(\mathcal{A})$ = shape $(\mathcal{B})$. Two d-dimensional array languages L_1 and L_2 are called shape-equivalent if and only if

$$\{\text{shape } (\mathcal{A}) | \mathcal{A} \in L_1\} = \{\text{shape } (\mathcal{B}) | \mathcal{B} \in L_2\}.$$

4. The Power of Contextual Array Grammars

According to Example 3 we immediately obtain the following strict inclusions:

Lemma 1: *For any $f \in \{*, t\}$ as well as every $d \in \mathbb{N}$ and every $k \in \mathbb{N}$,*

$$[L(d, \text{cont}, k, f)] \subsetneq [L(d, \text{cont}, k+1, f)].$$

As d-dimensional contextual array productions never change a non-blank symbol, we obviously have the following results on the connectedness of arrays generated by contextual array grammars:

Lemma 2: *For any $f \in \{*, t\}$ as well as every $d \in \mathbb{N}$ and every $k \in \mathbb{N}$, every d-dimensional array in a d-dimensional array language from $[L(d, \text{cont}, k, f)]$ is k-connected.*

As contextual array grammars cannot rewrite symbols, especially they cannot rewrite a non-blank symbol to the blank symbol # again, the following two results are not surprising:

Theorem 1: For every $d \in \mathbb{N}$ and every $k \in \mathbb{N} \cup \{\infty\}$,

$$[L(d, \text{cont}, k, *)] \subseteq [L(d, mon, k)].$$

Proof: We start from a d-dimensional contextual array grammar

$$G = (d, V, \#, P, A)$$

and consider the d-dimensional monotonic array grammar

$$G' = (d, V_N, V_T, \#, P', S)$$

with $V_N = \{a' | a \in V\} \cup \{S\}$ and P' constructed as follows: take the coding φ defined by $\varphi(a) = a'$, $a \in V$, which can be extended in an obvious way to arrays; then P' contains the following array productions:

(1) $(S, \varphi(\alpha))$ for each $\alpha \in A$,
(2) $(U_\alpha \cup U_\beta, \varphi(\alpha) \cup \beta', \varphi(\alpha) \cup \varphi(\beta))$ for each $(U_\alpha, \alpha, U_\beta, \beta) \in P$, where $\beta' = \{(v, \#) | v \in U_\beta\}$ for $\beta = \{(v, \beta(v)) | v \in U_\beta\}$,
(3) $(a', \{(\Omega_d, a)\})$ for all $a \in V$.

The equality $[L_*(G)] = [L(G')]$ is obvious; moreover, by construction $\|G'\| = \|G\|$. □

Theorem 2: For every $d \in \mathbb{N}$ and every $k \in \mathbb{N} \cup \{\infty\}$,

$$[L(d, \text{cont}, k, t)] \subseteq [L(d, mon, k)] .$$

Proof: Take a d-dimensional contextual array grammar

$$G = (d, V, \#, P, A)$$

with $\|G\| = k$, and construct the d-dimensional monotonic array grammar

$$G' = (V_N, V, \#, P', S)$$

with P' containing the following (groups of) rules:

(1) $S \to \alpha'$ for each $\alpha \in A$, with α' obtained from α by replacing each $a \in V$ with a' except for replacing exactly one occurrence of some symbol $b \in V$ by $[b', X]$.
(2) $(\{\Omega_d, v\}, \{(\Omega_d, [a', X]), (v, b')\}, \{(\Omega_d, a'), (v, [b', X])\})$ for each $v \in \mathbb{Z}^d$ with $\|v\| \leq k$ and all a, $b \in V$. Using these rules, the symbol X freely circulates on the second component of markings of the current array. In every moment, exactly one occurrence of X is present and all symbols in V are primed (hence are non-terminal symbols from the point of view of G').

(3) $(U_\alpha \cup U_\beta, \alpha' \cup \beta'', \alpha' \cup \beta')$ for $(U_\alpha, \alpha, U_\beta, \beta) \in P$, where α', β' are obtained from α, β, respectively, by replacing each $a \in V$ with a' except for replacing one occurrence of some $b \in V$ in α with $[b, X]$ and one occurrence of $c \in V$ in β with $[c, X]$; moreover, β'' is equal to $\{(v, \#)|v \in U_\beta\}$ for $\beta = \{(v, \beta(v))|v \in U_\beta\}$.
In this way, the productions of G are simulated in the presence of X.

(4) $[a', X] \to [a', Y]$.
In some moment, X is replaced by Y; from now on, no rule of G can be simulated in G' any more.

(5) $(\{\Omega_d, v\}, \{(\Omega_d, [x, Y]), (v, y)\}, \{(\Omega_d, x), (v, [y, Y])\})$
for each $v \in \mathbb{Z}^d$ with $\|v\| \leq k$ and all x, $y \in V \cup \{a'|a \in V\}$.
The symbol Y freely circulates, paired both with symbols in V or with primed symbols.

(6) If the cell marked with $[a', Y]$, $a \in V$, cannot be part of an area where a rule from P could be applied, we want to replace a' by a. The symbol a can appear at different positions in the selector area of a contextual array production $(U_\alpha, \alpha, U_\beta, \beta)$ in P. Hence we consider a sequence $\mathcal{R}(a)$ of triples

$$\mathcal{R}(a, i) = (U_\alpha(a, i), \alpha(a, i), U_\beta(a, i)), 1 \leq i \leq m(a)$$

such that

- for each $(U_\alpha(a, i), \alpha(a, i), U_\beta(a, i))$ in the sequence $\mathcal{R}(a)$ there exists a contextual array production $(U_\alpha, \alpha, U_\beta, \beta)$ in P and some $u_0(a, i) \in U_\alpha$ such that $U_\alpha(a, i) = U_\alpha$, $\alpha(a, i)(u_0(a, i)) = [a', Y(i)]$, $\alpha(u_0(a, i)) = a$, $\alpha(a, i)(u) = \alpha(ud)$ for all $u \in U_\alpha - \{u_0(a, i)\}$, and $U_\beta(a, i) = U_\beta$;
- all possibilities of such triples corresponding to a contextual array production in P are covered by this sequence $\mathcal{R}(a)$ (observe that the sequence may also be empty).

Therefore, for each $a \in V$ we take the following array productions for P':

(a) $[a', Y] \to [a', Y(1)]$;

(b) for every i with $1 \leq i \leq m(a)$ we take
$(U_\alpha(a, i) \cup U_\beta(a, i),\ \alpha'(a, i) \cup \beta''(a, i),\ \alpha''(a, i) \cup \beta''(a, i))$ where $\beta''(a, i) = \{(v, \#)|v \in U_\beta(a, i)\}$, $\alpha'(a, i)(u_0(a, i)) = [a', Y(i)]$, $\alpha''(a, i)(u_0(a, i)) = [a', Y(i{+}1)]$, and $\alpha''(a, i)(u) = \alpha'(a, i)(u)$ for all $u \in U_\alpha(a, i) - \{u_0(a, i)\}$, but $\alpha'(a, i) \neq \alpha(a, i)$, for all such possible patterns $\alpha'(a, i)$.

Using these rules we can check whether some rule of P can be used "around" the cell marked with the symbol Y.

(c) $[a', Y(m+1)] \to [a, Y]$;
if no rule of P can be used, then a' from the cell marked with $[a', Y]$ can be replaced by the corresponding terminal symbol a.

The marker Y circulates across the current array and only when no rule of P can be used we obtain an array marked with terminals only except for one cell marked with $[a, Y]$.

(7) $[a, Y] \to a$ for all $a \in V$.

In conclusion, the derivation in G' yields a terminal array if and only if it corresponds to a maximal derivation in G, hence $[L_t(G)] = [L(G')]$.

From the array productions above we obtain the set of non-terminal symbols

$$V_N = \{S\} \cup \{a' | a \in V\} \\ \cup \bigcup_{a \in V} \{[a, Z], [a', Z] | Z \in \{X, Y\} \cup \{Y(i) | 1 \leq i \leq m(a) + 1\}\}.$$

By construction, $\|G'\| = \|G\|$. □

The following theorem establishes a connection between array languages generated by contextual array grammars working in the derivation mode $*$ and array languages generated by contextual array grammars working in the maximal derivation mode t:

Theorem 3: For every $d \in \mathbb{N}$ and every $k \in \mathbb{N} \cup \{\infty\}$, each language in $[L(d, \mathrm{cont}, k, *)]$ is the coding of a corresponding language in $[L(d, \mathrm{cont}, k, t)]$.

Proof: Let

$$G = (d, V, \#, P, A)$$

be a d-dimensional contextual array grammar, and let us assume the contextual array productions in P to be labelled by numbers $1, \dots, r$, where $r = \mathrm{card}\ (P)$, i.e., $P = \{i : (U_i, \alpha_i, W_i, \beta_i) | 1 \leq i \leq r\}$. Now consider the new alphabet

$$V' = V \times \{0, 1\}^F \text{ with} \\ F = \{(i, v) | 1 \leq i \leq r, v \in U_i\}.$$

The idea is to mark each non-blank cell of an array (generated in the $*$-mode by G) by a symbol (a, f), where a is the symbol from V marking the cell in the original array and f is a function assigning the values 0 or 1 to the pairs (i, v) : $f((i, v)) = 1$ indicates that the underlying cell may be used by a selector α_i at the position $v \in U_i$ of the contextual array production i, whereas $f((i, v)) = 0$ does not allow us to use the cell in this way. Thus, the function f associated with a cell controls the adjoining of contexts, selectively blocking the use of the contextual array production i, depending on the values of the $f(i, v)$, $v \in U_i$.

Take the finite substitution $\varphi : V^* \to 2^{V'^*}$ defined by

$$\varphi(a) = \{a\} \times \{0, 1\}^F , \quad a \in V ,$$

and consider the new contextual array grammar

$$G' = (d, V', \#, P', A')$$

with

$$A' = \bigcup_{\alpha \in A} \varphi(\alpha) ,$$

$$P' = \{(U_i, \alpha'_i, W_i, \beta'_i) | 1 \le i \le r, \alpha'_i \in \varphi(\alpha_i), \beta'_i \in \varphi(\beta_i) ,$$
$$\alpha'_i = \{(\alpha_i(v), f_v) | v \in U_i\}, f_v((i, v)) = 1 \text{ for all } v \subset U_i\} .$$

Defining the coding

$$h : V' \to V \text{ by } h((a, f)) = a, a \in V, f \in \{0, 1\}^F ,$$

we apparently obtain $[L_*(G)] = [h(L_t(G'))]$, i.e., $[L_*(G)]$ is a coding of $[L_t(G')]$.

The type of G, i.e., the degree of connectedness k, plays no rôle, because G' is of the same type, which observation completes the proof. □

Remark 1: For $d \ge 2$, the converse of Theorem 3 is not true, e.g., according to Example 4 the two-dimensional array language Sq of solid squares is in $[L(2, \text{cont}, 2, t)]$, but no language in $[L(2, \text{cont}, \infty, *)]$ is shape-equivalent with Sq: in any contextual grammar we start from a finite set of axioms, and in order to generate an arbitrarily large square we must pass through stages when the current array cannot be a square; yet such arrays would belong to $[L_*(G)]$ for any contextual array grammar G. Moreover, for $d \ge 2$, no array language in $[L(d, \text{cont}, \infty, *)]$ is shape-equivalent with $i_{2,d}(Sq)$.

5. Contextual Array Grammars and Context-free Array Grammars

We first show that the generative power of contextual array grammars can exceed that of context-free array grammars:

Example 5: There is a language L in

$$[L(2, \text{cont}, 2, t)]$$

such that there is no context-free array grammar generating an array language L' which is shape-equivalent with L:

Consider the set R_H of hollow rectangles with arbitrary side lengths p, $q \geq 3$. R_H can be generated by the contextual array grammar

$$G = \left(2, \{a, b\}, \#, P, \left\{\begin{array}{cc} a & \\ a & a \end{array}\right\}\right)$$

with P containing the contextual array productions

$$p_1 = \begin{array}{c} a \\ \boxed{a} \\ \boxed{a} \end{array}, \quad p_2 = \begin{array}{cc} b & b \\ \boxed{a} & \\ \boxed{a} & \end{array}, \quad p_3 = \begin{array}{ccc} \boxed{b} & \boxed{b} & b \\ & \boxed{\#} & \end{array},$$

$$p_4 = \begin{array}{ccc} \boxed{a} & \boxed{a} & a \end{array}, \quad p_5 = \begin{array}{ccc} & & b \\ \boxed{a} & \boxed{a} & b \end{array}, \quad p_6 = \begin{array}{cc} & b \\ \boxed{\#} & \boxed{b} \\ & \boxed{b} \end{array}.$$

Starting form the axiom $\mathcal{A}$, we can go up using the rule p_1 $p-3$ times and go to the right using the rule p_4 $q-3$ times, where p, $q \geq 3$ can be chosen arbtirarily. Then we turn to the right from the vertical line by once using the rule p_2 and turn up from the horizontal line by once using the rule p_5, respectively; in both cases symbols b are introduced at the ends of the growing lines, whereafter the rules p_1, p_2, p_3, and p_4 cannot be applied anymore.

As long as we can find two neighbouring cells occupied by symbols b in a horizontal line, where the right one of the two cells has an empty cell below it, we can use the rule p_3. As long as we can find two neighbouring cells occupied by symbols b in a vertical line, where the upper one has an empty cell on its left side, we can use the rule p_6.

These rules cannot be used any more whenever the rectangle has been completed, and this is the only case where the derivation is blocked. As each rectangle of side lengths p and q with $p,\, q \geq 3$ can be generated in that way, we conclude

$$R_H \in [L(2, \text{cont}, 2, *, 2)]\,.$$

In the following we give a typical example of a derivation yielding the rectangle with side lengths 5 and 4:

```
          a        a           a
a   ⟹G   a   ⟹G  a     ⟹G   a      ⟹G
a a       a a      a a a      a a a a
b b          b b             b b b
a            a              a
       ⟹G               ⟹G            ⟹G
a            a      b       a      b
a a a a      a a a a b      a a a a b
b b b b        b b b b        b b b b b
a              a      b       a      b
         ⟹G              ⟹G
a      b       a      b       a      b
a a a a b      a a a a b      a a a a b
```

Conversely, R_H cannot be generated by a context-free array grammar, which can easily be shown by extending arguments used for similar problems;[6] a detailed elaboration of the proof is left to the reader.

Before proving the main result of our paper, i.e., that every context-free array language in $[L(d, cf, k)]$ is the coding of a contextual array language in $[L(n, \text{cont}, k, t)]$, we establish a special normal form for context-free array grammars, which is also interesting for its own (in some sense it corresponds to the Greibach normal form for context-free string grammars).

Theorem 4: For every context-free array grammar

$$G = (d, V_N, V_T, \#, P, S)$$

there exists an equivalent context-free array grammar

$$G' = (d, V_N', V_T, \#, P', S')$$

with $[L(G')] = [L(G)]$ and $\|G'\| = \|G\|$ such that each of the context-free array productions in P' is of one of the following forms:

- $S' \to a,\ a \in V_T$;
- $S' \to \alpha$, $\text{card}(\text{shape}\ (\alpha)) \geq 2$,
  $\alpha = \{(u, \alpha(u)) | u \in U\}$, $\alpha(u) \in V_N \cup V_T - \{S'\}$ for all $u \in U$, $\alpha(\Omega_d) \in V_T$;

- $A \to \alpha$, $A \in V_N - \{S'\}$; card(shape $(\alpha)) \geq 2$,
  $\alpha = \{(u, \alpha(u)) | u \in U\}$, $\alpha(u) \in V_N \cup V_T - \{S'\}$ for all $u \in U$, $\alpha(\Omega_d) \in V_T$.

Proof: We will elaborate the desired normal form in 3 steps:

Step 1: We first eliminate all chain rules of the form $A \to B$, A, $B \in V_N$, from P, in order to obtain a context-free array grammar $G_1' = (d, V_N, V_T, \#, P_1', S)$ with $[L(G_1')] = [L(G)]$, where we define

$$P_1' = P - \{A \to B | A, B \in V_N\}$$

$\cup \{A \to a | A \in V_N, a \in V_T$,

and there is a non-recurrent derivation of the form

$$\{(\Omega_d, A)\} = \{(\Omega_d, B_1)\} \Longrightarrow_{p_1} \cdots \{(\Omega_d, B_k)\} \Longrightarrow_{p_k} \{(\Omega_d, a)\}$$

with $p_i \in P, B_i \in V_N, 1 \leq i \leq k, k \geq 1\}$

$\cup \{A \to \alpha | A \in V_N, \text{card (shape } (\alpha)) \geq 2$

and there is a non-recurrent derivation of the form

$$\{(\Omega_d, A)\} = \{(\Omega_d, B_1)\} \Longrightarrow_{p_1} \cdots \{(\Omega_d, B_k)\} \Longrightarrow_{p_k} \alpha$$

with $p_i \in P, B_i \in V_N,\ 1 \leq i \leq k, k \geq 1\}$.

As a consequence of this modification we find that no rule $A \to \alpha$ from P_1' can be used twice at the same cell of an array. It is obvious from this construction that $[L(G_1')] = [L(G)]$.

Step 2: Now a context-free array grammar $G_2' = (d, V_N, V_T, \#, P_2', S)$ can be constructed from G_1' such that $[L(G_2')] = [L(G_1')]$ and for each rule $A \to \alpha$ in P_2' we have $\alpha(\Omega_d) \in V_T$.

Indeed, if P_1' contains a rule $A \to \alpha$ with $\alpha(\Omega_d) \in V_N$, then the cell marked with A where we have applied $A \to \alpha$ now is marked with the non-terminal symbol $\alpha(\Omega_d)$; to this cell again a rule $\alpha(\Omega_d) \to \beta$ has to be applied etc. until finally a terminal symbol is assigned to the cell under consideration. However, at each step, where we use a rule of the form $B \to \gamma$ with $\gamma(\Omega_d) \in V_N$, in the neighbourhood of this cell at least one new non-blank symbol is generated, because P_1' contains no chain rules any more. As the number of cells in the $\|G\|$-neighbourhood of a cell is bounded by $(2\|G\| + 1)^d - 1$, after at most $(2\|G\| + 1)^d$ derivation steps affecting the chosen cell a terminal symbol must be assigned to this cell (or otherwise, the considered sequence of rules makes no sense as a part of a derivation in G' leading to a terminal array).

Hence, P_2' is obtained from P_1' by removing all rules of the form $A \to \alpha$ with $\alpha(\Omega_d) \in V_N$ from P_1', but adding all rules $A \to \beta$ with $\beta(\Omega_d) \in V_T$, where β is the result of a derivation as described above, i.e., of the form $\alpha_1 \Longrightarrow_{p_1} \cdots \alpha_k \Longrightarrow_{p_k} \beta$ where $\alpha_1 = \{(\Omega_d, A)\}$ and for $1 \leq i \leq k$, p_i is applied to the cell at the origin Ω_d, $\alpha_i(\Omega_d) \in V_N$, and $\beta(\Omega_d) \in V_T$.

The grammar G_2' obtained in this way is equivalent with G_1': Each new rule in P_2' corresponds to a sequence of rules from P_1'; the application of a rule from P_2' and the application of the corresponding sequence of rules from P_1' to an arbitrary array over $V_N \cup V_T$ yields the same result, hence $[L(G_2')] \subseteq [L(G_1')]$.

On the other hand, any derivation in G_1' not directly corresponding to a derivation in G_2' can be represented by a sequence of rules from P_1' in such a way that the rules rewriting the same cell can be put together in groups, yet each such block then must correspond to a rule in P_2', i.e., we obtain $[L(G_1')] \subseteq [L(G_2')]$, too. In conclusion, $[L(G_1')] = [L(G_2')]$.

The context-free array grammar G_2' has the useful property that in every derivation in G_2' each cell once marked with a non-terminal symbol in an intermediate array is used exactly once as the left-hand member of an array production during the whole derivation.

Step 3: In order to obtain the desired normal form for G', from P_2' all rules of the form $A \to b$, $A \in V_N$, $b \in V_T$, have to be eliminated. In order to be able to include terminal arrays of the form $[\{(\Omega_d, a)\}]$ with $a \in V_T$, we introduce a new start symbol S', i.e., we define $G' = (d, V_N \cup \{S'\}, V_T, \#, P', S')$ with

$$
\begin{aligned}
P' = {} & P_2' - \{A \to b | A \in V_N, b \in V_T\} \\
& \cup \{S' \to b | b \in V_T, S \to b \in P_2'\} \\
& \cup \{S' \to \alpha^* | S \to \alpha \in P_2', \text{card (shape } (\alpha)) \geq 2\,, \\
& \quad \alpha = \{(v, \alpha(v)) | v \in U\}, \alpha^* = \{(v, \alpha^*(v)) | v \in U\} \\
& \quad \text{where for all } v \in U \\
& \quad \alpha^*(v) = \alpha(v) \text{ or } \alpha^*(v) = c \text{ for some } c \in V_T \text{ with } \alpha(v) \to c \in P_2'\} \\
& \cup \{A \to \alpha^* | A \to \alpha \in P_2', A \in V_N, \text{card (shape } (\alpha)) \geq 2\,, \\
& \quad \alpha = \{(v, \alpha(v)) | v \in U\}, \alpha^* = \{(v, \alpha^*(v)) | v \in U\} \\
& \quad \text{where for all } v \in U \\
& \quad \alpha^*(v) = \alpha(v) \text{ or } \alpha^*(v) = c \text{ for some } c \in V_T \text{ with } \alpha(v) \to c \in P_2'\}\,.
\end{aligned}
$$

The equality $[L(G')] = [L(G_2')]$ is obvious.

In conclusion, we have constructed a context-free array grammar G' with $[L(G')] = [L(G)]$ and $\|G'\| = \|G\|$ where G' has the desired properties. □

Theorem 5: For every $d \in \mathbb{N}$ and every $k \in \mathbb{N} \cup \{\infty\}$, each context-free array language in $[L(d, cf, k)]$ is the coding of a contextual array language in $[L(d, \text{cont}, k, t)]$.

Proof: Let $L \in [L(d, cf, k)]$ be given by a context-free array grammar $G' = (d, V_N', V_T, \#, P', S')$, which, without loss of generality, we can assume to be in the normal form established in Theorem 4 and to have norm k. We now construct a contextual array grammar $G = (d, V, \#, P, A)$ and a coding $\varphi : V \to V_T$ such that $\varphi([L_t(G)]) = [L(G')]$.

The variables in V are triples (a, v, q) where $a \in V_T$, $v \in \mathbb{Z}^d$ with $\|v\| \leq k$, and $q \in \{\emptyset\} \cup \{\{p\} | p \in P'\}$; φ then projects each variable (a, v, q) on its first component a, i.e., we define $\varphi((a, v, q)) = a$. For the simulation of G' we now define the components of G as follows:

$$
\begin{aligned}
V = {} & \{(a, v, \emptyset) | a \in V_T, v \in \mathbb{Z}^d, \|v\| \leq k\} \\
& \cup \{(a, v, \{p\}) | a \in V_T, v \in \mathbb{Z}^d, \|v\| \leq k, \\
& \quad p \in P', p = X \to \alpha, \alpha(\Omega_d) = a\},
\end{aligned}
$$

$$
\begin{aligned}
A = {} & \{(a, \{\Omega_d\}, \emptyset) | S' \to a \in P', a \in V_T\} \\
& \cup \{\alpha' | S' \to \alpha \in P', \alpha = \{\alpha(v) | v \in U\}, \alpha' = \{\alpha'(v) | v \in U\} \text{ where}
\end{aligned}
$$

$$\alpha'(v) = (\alpha(v), v, \emptyset) \text{ for } v \in U \text{ and } \alpha(v) \in V_T \text{ as well as}$$

$$
\begin{aligned}
& \alpha'(v) = (a, v, \{p\}) \text{ for } v \in U \text{ and } \alpha(v) \in V_N', a \in V_T, \\
& \quad p \in P', p = \alpha(v) \to \beta \text{ with } \beta(\Omega_d) = a\},
\end{aligned}
$$

and P contains the following contextual array productions:

(1) $(\{\Omega_d\}, \{(\Omega_d, (a_0, v_0, \{p_0\}))\}, U - \{\Omega_d\}, \alpha')$ for every $v_0 \in \mathbb{Z}^d$ with $\|v_0\| \leq k$ and every context-free array production $p_0 \in P'$ where $p_0 = X \to \alpha$ such that $\alpha = \{\alpha(v) | v \in U\}$ for some U with $\{\Omega_d\} \neq\subset U \subseteq \mathbb{Z}^d$ and $\|U\| \leq k$, with $\alpha(\Omega_d) = a_0$, $a_0 \in V_T$, as well as for all $u \in U - \{\Omega_d\}$,
   - (a) $\alpha'(u) = (\alpha(u), u, \emptyset)$ for $\alpha(u) \in V_T$ and
   - (b) $\alpha'(u) = (b, u, \{q\})$ for any $q \in P'$ with $q = \alpha(u) \to \beta$ such that $\beta(\Omega_d) = b$ with $b \in V_T$.

(2) $(U, \alpha'', \emptyset, \emptyset)$ for every context-free array production $p \in P'$ with $p = X \to \alpha$, $\alpha = \{\alpha(v) | v \in U\}$, $\alpha'' = \{\alpha''(v) | v \in U\}$, $\alpha(\Omega_d) = a$, $\alpha''(\Omega_d) =$

$(a, v, \{p\})$, $a \in V_T$, $v \in \mathbb{Z}^d$, $\|v\| \leq k$, and for all $u \in U - \{\Omega_d\}$, $\alpha''(u) = (b(u), w(u), q(u))$ for some $b(u) \in V_T$, $w(u) \in \mathbb{Z}^d$, $\|w(u)\| \leq k$, and $q(u) \in \{\emptyset\} \cup \{\{p'\} | p' \in P'\}$, as well as for some $u_0 \in U - \{\Omega_d\}$,

(a) $\alpha(u_0) \in V_T$, but $\alpha''(u_0) \neq (\alpha(u_0), u_0, \emptyset)$, or
(b) $\alpha(u_0) \in V'_N$, but $\alpha''(u_0) \neq (b, u_0, \{q\})$ for some $q \in P'$ with $q = \alpha(u_0) \to \beta$ such that $\beta(\Omega_d) = b$ with $b \in V_T$.

The contextual array productions in the first group of rules allow for the simulation of the context-free array productions from P'. The non-blank cells in the arrays obtained in a derivation in G are marked by triples (a, v, q) where $a \in V_T$, $v \in \mathbb{Z}^d$ with $\|v\| \leq k$, and $q \in \{\emptyset\} \cup \{\{p\} | p \in P'\}$; in the triples $(a, v, \{p\})$ we remember the array production p which we have guessed to be used for deriving the terminal symbol a at this position as well as the position v from which this cell has been marked. The contextual array productions from the second group of rules then check the correct application of these array productions p; as they do not change the underlying array, we can never obtain a maximal derivation in G as long as such a rule can be applied. On the other hand, any maximal derivation in G ending up with an array $\mathcal{A}$ where each non-blank cell is marked with some triple (a, v, q) corresponds with a derivation in G' yielding a terminal array $\mathcal{A}'$, where $\mathcal{A}'$ is the coding of $\mathcal{A}$ with respect to $\varphi : V \to V_T$ defined by $\varphi((a, v, q)) = a$ for all $a \in V_T$, $v \in \mathbb{Z}^d$ with $0 \leq \|v\| \leq k$, and $q \in \{\emptyset\} \cup \{\{p\} | p \in P'\}$. Hence, we obtain the desired result $\varphi([L_t(G)]) = [L(G')]$. □

Corollary 1: *For every $d \in \mathbb{N}$ and every $k \in \mathbb{N} \cup \{\infty\}$, each context-free array language in $[L(d, cf, k)]$ is shape-equivalent with a contextual array language in $[L(d, \text{cont}, k, t)]$.*

Proof: The contextual array grammar G constructed in the proof of Theorem 5 in the maximal derivation mode yields an array language which is shape-equivalent with the array language generated by the given context-free array grammar. □

6. Contextual Array Grammars and Siromoney Matrix Array Grammars

In this section we show that an array language generated by a regular Siromoney matrix array grammar can be represented as the coding of an array language generated by a two-dimensional contextual array grammar.

A *regular Siromoney matrix array grammar* G is an $n+1$-tuple

$$(G_0, G_1, \ldots, G_n)$$

where all components G_i, $0 \leq i \leq n$, are regular string grammars with $G_i = (N_i, T_i, P_i, S_i)$, $0 \leq i \leq n$, such that, for some alphabet T, $T_i = T$ for all i with $1 \leq i \leq n$, and $T_0 = \{S_i | 1 \leq i \leq n\}$; moreover, we assume all alphabets of non-terminal symbols N_i, $0 \leq i \leq n$, to be mutually disjoint. The first grammar G_0 generates a horizontal line with the terminal objects being the start symbols S_i, $1 \leq i \leq n$, of the n regular grammars G_i, $1 \leq i \leq n$, which then in parallel generate the vertical lines (we can also assume that the productions of the G_i are applied sequentially, but then we only use those results that are rectangular arrays). In that way, G generates a set of two-dimensional rectangular arrays ("matrices").

Before proving the main result of this section, we elucidate the preceding definition by an example:

Example 6: Let $G = (G_0, G_1, G_2)$ be a regular Siromoney matrix array grammar with

$$G_0 = (\{S, S_1', S_2'\}, \{S_1, S_2\}, P_0, S),$$

$$P_0 = \{S \to S_1 S_1', S_1' \to S_2 S_2', S_2' \to S_1 S_1', S_2' \to S_1\};$$

$$G_1 = (\{S_1\}, \{a\}, P_2, S_1),$$

$$P_1 = \{S_1 \to a S_1, S_1 \to a\};$$

$$G_2 = (\{S_2, A, B\}, \{a, b\}, P_2, S_2),$$

$$P_2 = \{S_2 \to aB, B \to bA, A \to aB, A \to a\}.$$

Obviously, the first regular grammar G_0 generates a horizontal line that can be represented by strings from $\{S_1 S_2\}^+ \{S_1\}$, whereas the two regular grammars G_1 and G_2 generate strings from $\{a\}^+$ and $\{ab\}^+\{a\}$, respectively, which alternate in forming the vertical lines of lengths $2m+1$ for $m \geq 1$. In sum, we obtain rectangular pictures of the form:

$$\begin{array}{ccc} a\,a & & a \\ \vdots\,\vdots & & \vdots \\ a\,b & & a \\ a\,a & \cdots & a \end{array}, \text{ e.g., } \begin{array}{ccccccccc} a & a & a & a & a & a & a & a & a \\ a & b & a & b & a & b & a & b & a \\ a & a & a & a & a & a & a & a & a \\ a & b & a & b & a & b & a & b & a \\ a & a & a & a & a & a & a & a & a \\ a & b & a & b & a & b & a & b & a \\ a & a & a & a & a & a & a & a & a \end{array}$$

Theorem 6: Every array language generated by a regular Siromoney matrix array grammar is the coding of a contextual array language in $[L(2, \text{cont}, 1, t)]$.

Proof: Let $G = (G_0, G_1, \ldots, G_n)$ be a regular Siromoney matrix array grammar with regular grammars $G_i = (N_i, T_i, P_i, S_i)$, $0 \leq i \leq n$, such that, for some alphabet T, $T_i = T$ for all i with $1 \leq i \leq n$, and $T_0 = \{S_i | 1 \leq i \leq n\}$; moreover, without loss of generality, we assume all alphabets of non-terminal symbols N_i, $0 \leq i \leq n$, to be mutually disjoint and the G_i to be reduced, i.e., every non-terminal symbol from N_i takes part in a terminal derivation in G_i; finally, without loss of generality, we also assume that for each S_i, $1 \leq i \leq n$, there exists a terminal string generated by G_0 containing S_i. We now construct a two-dimensional contextual array grammar $G' = (2, V, \#, P, A)$ and a coding $\varphi : V \to T$ such that $\varphi([L_t(G')]) = [L(G)]$:

The variables in V are pairs of the form $(a, (\alpha))$ with $a \in T$; φ then projects each variable $(a, (\alpha))$ on its first component a, i.e., we define $\varphi((a, (\alpha))) = a$. For the simulation of G we distinguish between the following cases:

(1) The singleton arrays consisting of one non-blank cell only are encoded directly as axiom, i.e., for $S \to S_i \in P_0$ and $S_i \to a \in P_i$, $a \in T$, we take the axiom $(a, (S_i))$ into A.

(2) Single vertical lines start with the axioms $(a, (S_i, Y))$ in A for $S \to S_i \in P_0$ and $S_i \to aY \in P_i$, $a \in T$, $Y \in N_i$. The lines are continued in the vertical direction with the contextual array productions

$$\begin{array}{c} (b, (Y, Z)) \\ \boxed{(a, (X, Y))} \end{array}$$

with $X \to aY \in P_i$, $a \in T$, $Y \in N_i$, and $Y \to bZ \in P_i$, $b \in T$, $Z \in N_i \cup \{\lambda\}$. The derivation in G' ends with a symbol $(b, (Y, \lambda))$.

(3) Single horizontal lines start with the axioms $(a, (S, S_i, Y))$ in A for $S \to S_i Y \in P_0$ and $S_i \to a \in P_i$, $a \in T$, $Y \in N_0$. The lines are continued in the horizontal direction with the contextual array productions

$$\boxed{(a, (X, S_i, Y))}\ (b, (Y, S_j, Z))$$

with $X \to S_i Y \in P_0$, $S_i \to a \in P_i$, $a \in T$, X, $Y \in N_0$, and $Y \to S_j Z \in P_0$, $S_j \to b \in P_j$, $b \in T$, $Z \in N_0 \cup \{\lambda\}$. The derivation in G' ends with a symbol $(b, (Y, S_j, \lambda))$.

(4) The remaining pictures generated by G contain at least two horizontal and two vertical lines. The simulation of their generation starts with

the axioms $(a,(S,S_i,Y,U))$ in A for $S \to S_iY \in P_0$ and $S_i \to aU \in P_i$, $a \in T$, $Y \in N_0$, and $U \in N_i$. The first horizontal line is continued with the contextual array productions

$$\boxed{(a,(X,S_i,Y,U))}\ (b,(Y,S_j,Z,W))$$

with $X \to S_iY \in P_0$, $Y \to S_jZ \in P_0$, $S_i \to aU \in P_i$, $S_j \to bW \in P_j$, $a, b \in T$, $X, Y \in N_0$, $Z \in N_0 \cup \{\lambda\}$, $U \in N_i$, $W \in N_j$. The derivation of the first horizontal line ends with a symbol $(b,(Y,S_j,\lambda,W))$. Then the last vertical line can be generated by using the contextual array productions

$$\begin{array}{c} (b,(X,S_i,\lambda,W)) \\ \boxed{(a,(X,S_i,\lambda,U))} \end{array}$$

with $X \to S_i \in P_0$, $U'' \to aU \in P_i$, $U \to bW \in P_i$, $a, b \in T$, $X \in N_0$, $U, U'' \in N_i$, $W \in N_i \cup \{\lambda\}$. The derivation of the last vertical line ends with a symbol $(b,(Y,S_i,\lambda,\lambda))$.
The remaining parts of the rectangle ("matrix") now are filled up from right to left and from the bottom to the top, respectively, by using the contextual array productions

$$\begin{array}{ll} (b,(X,S_i,Y,W)) & \boxed{(c,(Y,S_j,Z,W'))} \\ \boxed{(a,(X,S_i,Y,U))} & \end{array}$$

with $X \to S_iY \in P_0$, $Y \to S_jZ \in P_0$, $U'' \to aU \in P_i$, $U \to bW \in P_i$, $U' \to cW' \in P_j$, $a, b, c \in T$, $X, Y \in N_0$, $Z \in N_0 \cup \{\lambda\}$, $U, U'' \in N_i$, $W \in N_i \cup \{\lambda\}$, $U' \in N_j$, $W' \in N_j \cup \{\lambda\}$, as well as with the additional condition for the uppermost horizontal line that $W = \lambda$ if and only if $W' = \lambda$. For the cases that this last condition $W = \lambda$ if and only if $W' = \lambda$ cannot be fulfilled (because there is no suitable production in P_i) we guarantee a non-terminating computation by the additional contextual array productions

$$\begin{array}{ll} (a,(\lambda,\lambda,\lambda,\lambda)) & \boxed{(c,(Y,S_j,Z,W'))} \\ \boxed{(a,(X,S_i,Y,U))} & \end{array} \quad \text{and} \quad \begin{array}{c} (a,(\lambda,\lambda,\lambda,\lambda)) \\ \boxed{(a,(\lambda,\lambda,\lambda,\lambda))} \end{array}.$$

The cases described above cover all derivations possible in G. By the given construction, the first symbol of the variables stores the value of the terminal symbol in each cell; finally, as the regular grammars G_i, $0 \le i \le n$, were assumed to be reduced, a derivation in G' terminates if and only if the corresponding derivation in G yields the same picture. Hence, we conclude $\varphi([L_t(G')]) = [L(G)]$. □

References

1. E. Csuhaj-Varjù, J. Dassow, J. Kelemen and Gh. Păun, *Grammar Systems. A Grammatical Approach to Distribution and Cooperation* (Gordon and Breach, London, 1994).
2. C. R. Cook and P. S.-P. Wang, A Chomsky hierarchy of isotonic array grammars and languages, *Computer Graphics and Image Processing* **8** (1978), pp. 144–152.
3. A. Ehrenfeucht, Gh. Păun and G. Rozenberg, On representing recursively enumerable languages by internal contextual languages, *Theoretical Computer Science* **205**, 1–2 (1998), pp. 61–83.
4. A. Ehrenfeucht, A. Mateescu, Gh. Păun, G. Rozenberg and A. Salomaa, On representing RE languages by one-sided internal contextual languages, *Acta Cybernetica* **12**, 3 (1996), pp. 217–233.
5. A. Ehrenfeucht, Gh. Păun and G. Rozenberg, The linear landscape of external contextual languages, *Acta Informatica* **35**, 6 (1996), pp. 571–593.
6. J. Dassow, R. Freund and Gh. Păun, Cooperating array grammar systems, *International Journal of Pattern Recognition and Artificial Intelligence* **9**, 6 (1995), pp. 1029–1053.
7. R. Freund, Control mechanisms on #-context-free array grammars, in Gh. Păun, Ed., *Mathematical Aspects of Natural and Formal Languages* (World Scientific, Singapore, 1994), pp. 97–137.
8. S. Marcus, Contextual grammars, *Rev. Roum. Math. Pures Appl.* **14** (1969), pp. 1525–1534.
9. Gh. Păun and X. M. Nguyen, On the inner contextual grammars, *Rev. Roum. Math. Pures Appl.* **25** (1980), pp. 641–651.
10. Gh. Păun, G. Rozenberg and A. Salomaa, Contextual grammars: erasing, determinism, one-sided contexts, in G. Rozenberg and A. Salomaa, Eds., *Developments in Language Theory* (World Scientific Publ., Singapore, 1994), pp. 370–388.
11. Gh. Păun, G. Rozenberg and A. Salomaa, Contextual grammars: parallelism and blocking of derivation, *Fundamenta Informaticae* **25** (1996), pp. 381–397.
12. Gh. Păun, *Marcus Contextual Grammars* (Kluver, Dordrecht, 1997).
13. A. Rosenfeld, *Picture Languages* (Academic Press, Reading, MA, 1979).
14. G. Rozenberg and A. Salomaa, Eds., *Handbook of Formal Languages* (3 volumes) (Springer-Verlag, Berlin, 1997).
15. A. Salomaa, *Formal Languages* (Academic Press, Reading, MA, 1973).
16. G. Siromoney, R. Siromoney and K. Krithivasan, Abstract families of matrices and picture languages, *Computer Graphics and Image Processing* **1** (1972), pp. 234–307.
17. G. Siromoney, R. Siromoney and K. Krithivasan, n-Dimensional array languages and description of crystal symmetry — I and II, *Proc. Indian Acad. Soc.* **78** (1973), pp. 72–88 and pp. 130–139.
18. R. Siromoney, K. G. Subramanian and K. Rangarajan, Parallel/sequential arrays with tables, *Int. J. Comput. Math.* **6A** (1977), pp. 143–158.

19. S. Vicolov-Dumitrescu, On parallel contextual grammars, in Gh. Păun, Ed., *Mathematical Linguistics and Related Topics*, The Publ. House of the Romanian Academy of Science (Bucharest, 1982), pp. 350–360.
20. P. S.-P. Wang, Some new results on isotonic array grammars, *Information Processing Letters* **10** (1980), pp. 129–131.
21. Y. Yamamoto, K. Morita and K. Sugata, Context-sensitivity of two-dimensional regular array grammars, in P. S.-P. Wang, Ed., *Array Grammars, Patterns and Recognizers*, WSP Series in Computer Science, Vol. **18** (World Scientific Publ., Singapore, 1989), pp. 17–41.

CHAPTER 9

CHARACTERIZING TRACTABILITY BY CELL-LIKE MEMBRANE SYSTEMS

Miguel A. Gutiérrez–Naranjo, Mario J. Pérez–Jiménez, Agustín Riscos-Núñez
Francisco J. Romero–Campero and Álvaro Romero–Jiménez

Research Group on Natural Computing,
Department of Computer Science and Artificial Intelligence,
Seville University, Avda. Reina Mercedes s/n, 41012 Seville, Spain
E-mail: {magutier, marper, ariscosn, fran, alvaro}@us.es

In this paper we present a polynomial complexity class in the framework of membrane computing. In this context, and using accepting transition P systems, we provide a characterization of the standard computational class **P** of problems solvable in polynomial time by deterministic Turing machines.

1. Introduction

The *Theory of Computation* deals with the *mechanical solvability* of problems, distinguishing clearly between problems for which there are algorithmic procedures solving them, and those for which there are none. But it is very important to clarify the difference between *solvability in theory* and *solvability in practice*; that is, studying procedures which can run using an amount of resources likely to be available. Roughly speaking, a problem is called *tractable* if it is mechanically solvable in practice.

Computational Complexity Theory tries to classify decision problems according to the amount of resources required for solving them in a *mechanical* way. A *complexity class* for a model of computation is a collection of problems that can be solved by some devices of this model with *similar* computational resources.

At the end of 1998, the area of *Membrane Computing* was initiated by Gh. Păun[7] coming from the observation that the processes which take place in the complex structure of a living cell can be considered as computations, and providing basic computing models consisting of distributed parallel devices processing multisets in the compartments defined by a cell-like hierarchy of membranes.

In this paper we present a *polynomial complexity class* in that framework, which allows us to detect some intrinsic difficulties of the resolution of a problem. In that context, a characterization of the standard computational class **P** of tractable problems (that is, problems solvable in polynomial time by deterministic Turing machines) is obtained.

The paper is organized as follows. In the next section some preliminary notions are given. In Section 3 we define the cellular framework (accepting cell-like membrane systems) in which a computational complexity theory will be developed. Section 4 introduces a polynomial complexity class associated with **P** systems. Sections 5 and 6 are devoted to characterize the standard class **P** through cellular computing models.

We work in this paper with cell-like membrane systems using symbol–objects.

2. Preliminaries

Roughly speaking, when we deal with *optimization problems* our goal is to find the *best* solution (according to a given criterion) among a class of possible (candidate or feasible) solutions.

Definition 1: An *optimization problem*, X, is a tuple (I_X, s_X, f_X) where: (a) I_X is a language over a finite alphabet; (b) s_X is a function whose domain is I_X and, for each $a \in I_X$, the set $s_X(a)$ is finite; and (c) f_X is a function (the objective function) that assigns to each instance $a \in I_X$ and each $c_a \in s_X(a)$ a positive rational number $f_X(a, c_a)$.

The elements of I_X are called *instances* of the problem X. For each instance $a \in I_X$, the elements of the finite set $s_X(a)$ are called *candidate* (or *feasible*) *solutions* associated with the instance a of the problem. The function f_X provides the criterion to determine the *best* solution.

Definition 2: Let $X = (I_X, s_X, f_X)$ be an optimization problem. An *optimal solution* for an instance $a \in I_X$ is a candidate solution $c \in s_X(a)$ associated with this instance such that either for all $c' \in s_X(a)$ we have $f_X(a, c) \leq f_X(a, c')$, or for all $c' \in s_X(a)$ we have $f_X(a, c) \geq f_X(a, c')$.

That is, an optimization problem seeks the best of all possible candidate solutions, according to a simple cost criterion given by the objective function.

An important class of combinatorial optimization problems is the class of decision problems, that is, problems that require a *yes* or *no* answer.

Definition 3: A decision problem, X, is a pair (I_X, θ_X) such that I_X is a language over a finite alphabet (whose elements are called *instances*) and θ_X is a total boolean function (that is, a predicate) over I_X.

There exists a natural correspondence between languages and decision problems in the following way. Each language L, over an alphabet Σ, has a decision problem, X_L, associated with it as follows: $I_{X_L} = \Sigma^*$, and $\theta_{X_L} = \{(u,1)|u \in L\} \cup \{(u,0)|u \in \Sigma^* - L\}$; reciprocally, given a decision problem $X = (I_X, \theta_X)$, the language L_X over the alphabet of I_X corresponding to it is defined as: $L_X = \{u \in I_X|\theta_X(u) = 1\}$.

Even though **NP**-completeness has been usually studied in the framework of decision problems, there are many abstract problems which are not of decision nature, for instance optimization problems, where some value has to be optimized (minimized or maximized). However, one can easily transform any optimization problem into a roughly equivalent decision problem by supplying a target/threshold value for the quantity to be optimized, and asking the question whether this value can be attained.

In order to specify the concept of solvability we work with an universal computing model: Turing machines.

Let M be a Turing machine such that the result of any halting computation is *yes* or *no*. If M is a *deterministic* device (with Σ as working alphabet), then we say that M *recognizes* a language L over Σ whenever, for any string a over Σ, if $a \in L$, then the answer of M on input a is *yes* (that is, M accepts a), and the answer is *no* otherwise (that is, M rejects a).

If M is a *non-deterministic* Turing machine, then we say that M *recognizes* L whenever, for any string a over Σ, $a \in L$ if and only if there exists a computation of M with input a such that the answer is *yes*. That is, an input string a is accepted by M if there is *an* accepting computation of M on input a. But now we do not have a mechanical criterion to reject an input string.

We say that a Turing machine M solves a decision problem X if M *recognizes* the language associated with X; that is, for any instance a of the problem: (1) in the deterministic case, the machine (with input a) outputs *yes* if the answer of the problem is *yes*, and the output is *no* otherwise; (2) in the non-deterministic case, there exists a computation of the machine (with input a) that outputs *yes* if and only if the answer of the problem is *yes*.

Due to the fact that we represent the instances of abstract problems as strings, we can consider their size in a natural manner: the size of an instance is the length of the string.

P is the class of all decision problems solvable by some deterministic Turing machine in a time bounded by a polynomial on the size of the input. Informally speaking, **P** corresponds to the class of problems having a *feasible* algorithm that gives an answer in a *reasonable* time; that is, problems that are realistically solvable on a machine (even for large instances of the problem).

NP is the class of all decision problems solvable in a polynomial time by non-deterministic Turing machines; that is, for every accepted instance there exists at least one accepting computation taking an amount of steps bounded by a polynomial on the length of the input.

These classes are *mathematically robust* in the following sense: they are invariant for all *reasonable* computational models because all of them are polynomially equivalent.

Every deterministic Turing machine can be considered as a non-deterministic one, so we have $\mathbf{P} \subseteq \mathbf{NP}$. The **P** versus **NP** problem is the problem of determining whether every problem solvable by some non-deterministic Turing machine in polynomial time can also be solved by some deterministic Turing machine in polynomial time.

The $\mathbf{P} \stackrel{?}{=} \mathbf{NP}$ question is one of the outstanding open problems in theoretical computer science. A negative answer to this question would confirm that the majority of current cryptographic systems are secure from a practical point of view. A positive answer would not only show the uncertainty about the secureness of these systems, but also this kind of answer is expected to come together with a general procedure that provides a deterministic algorithm solving most of **NP**–complete problems in polynomial time.

In the last years several computing models using powerful tools from nature have been developed (because of this, they are known as *bio-inspired* models) and several solutions in polynomial time to problems from the class **NP** have been presented, making use of non-determinism, massive parallelism and/or of an exponential amount of space. This is the reason why a practical implementation of such models (in biological, electronic, or other media) could provide a significant advance in the resolution of computationally hard problems.

3. Accepting Cell-like Membrane Systems

Membrane computing is a young branch of natural computing initiated by Gh. Păun in Ref. 7. It has been developed basically from a theoretical point of view.

Membrane systems are distributed parallel computing models inspired by the structure and functioning of living cells, as well as from the cooperation of cells in tissues, organs, and organisms.

Cell-like membrane systems (usually called **P** systems) have several *syntactic* ingredients: a *membrane structure* consisting of a hierarchical arrangement (a rooted tree) of membranes embedded in a *skin* membrane (the root of the tree), and delimiting *regions* or compartments (the nodes of the tree) where multisets of *objects* and sets (eventually empty) of (evolution) *rules* are placed.

Also, **P** systems have two main *semantic* ingredients: their inherent *parallelism* and *non-determinism.* The objects inside the membranes can evolve according to given rules in a synchronous (in the sense that a global clock is assumed), parallel, and non-deterministic manner.

In this paper we use membrane computing as a framework to attack the resolution of computationally hard problems. In order to solve this kind of problems and having in mind the relationship between the solvability of a problem and the acceptation of the language associated with it, we consider **P** systems as *language accepting* devices.

In the definitions of basic **P** systems initially considered, there is no membrane in which we can "introduce" objects before allowing the system to begin to work. So, the first results about *solvability* of **NP**–complete problems in polynomial time (even linear) by membrane systems were given by Gh. Păun,[5] C. Zandron *et al.*,[15] S. N. Krishna *et al.*,[3] and A. Obtulowicz[4] in the framework of **P** systems that lack an input membrane. Thus, the constructive proofs of such results design *one* system for *each* instance of the problem. We say that these are *semi-uniform* solutions.

However, it is easy to consider input membranes in this kind of computational devices.

Definition 4: A cell-like membrane system with input is a tuple (Π, Σ, i_Π), where: (a) Π is a **P** system, with working alphabet Γ and initial multisets $\mathcal{M}_1, \ldots, \mathcal{M}_p$ (associated with membranes labeled by $1, \ldots, p$, respectively); (b) Σ is an (input) alphabet strictly contained in Γ; (c) $\mathcal{M}_1, \ldots, \mathcal{M}_p$ are multisets over $\Gamma - \Sigma$; and (d) i_Π is the label of a distinguished membrane (input membrane).

Concerning the definition of the *result* (or *output*) of a cell-like membrane system, we can imagine that the internal processes are unknown, and that the information is obtained only via a multiset of objects that the system sends to the environment (in this case we say that the system has *external output*).

Definition 5: Let (Π, Σ, i_Π) be a cell-like membrane system with input and with external output. Let Γ be the working alphabet of Π, μ the membrane structure and $\mathcal{M}_1, \ldots, \mathcal{M}_p$ the initial multisets (over $\Gamma - \Sigma$) of Π. Let $m \in M(\Sigma)$ be a multiset over Σ. The initial configuration of (Π, Σ, i_Π) with input m is $(\mu, \mathcal{M}_0, \mathcal{M}_1, \ldots, \mathcal{M}_{i_\Pi} \cup m, \ldots, \mathcal{M}_p)$.

In the case of **P** systems with input and with external output, the concept of computation is introduced in a similar way as in the original model, but with a slight variant. The initial configuration must be the initial configuration of the system associated with an input multiset $m \in M(\Sigma)$, and in the configurations we do not work only with the membrane structure μ, but we incorporate information about the environment using an additional multiset (namely, $\mathcal{M}_0$ in Definition 5, initially empty).

Definition 6: An *accepting cell-like membrane system* is a P system with input and with external output such that: (a) the working alphabet contains two distinguished elements *yes* and *no*; and (b) if $\mathcal{C}$ is a halting computation of the system, then either the object *yes* or the object *no* (but not both) must have been released to the environment, and only in the last step of the computation.

We denote by $\mathcal{A}$ the class of accepting cell-like membrane systems.

The design of systems satisfying the above definition is usually a hard task, because the conditions are quite restrictive. We can make some technical changes to get a less restrictive variant, for example without loss of generality we will assume that an *accepting cell-like membrane system* is a P system with input and with external output such that: (a) the working alphabet contains three distinguished elements *yes*, *no* and #; and (b) if $\mathcal{C}$ is a halting computation of the system, then it sends out the symbol # only in the last step, and either some objects *yes* or objects *no* (but not both) must have been released to the environment along the execution.

In accepting P systems, we say that a halting computation $\mathcal{C}$ is an *accepting computation* (respectively, *rejecting computation*) if the object *yes* (respectively, *no*) appears in the environment associated with the corresponding halting configuration of $\mathcal{C}$.

If we want these kind of systems to solve decision problems capturing the classical algorithmic concept, it is necessary to require a condition of *confluence*; that is, the system (individualized by an appropriate input multiset) must always give the same answer.

In this context, a family of accepting **P** systems will solve a decision problem if for each instance of the problem,

(a) if *there exists an* accepting computation of the membrane system processing it, then the problem also answers *yes* for that instance (*soundness*);
(b) if the problem answers *yes*, then *there exists an* accepting computation of the membrane system processing that instance and, furthermore, *any* halting computation of such a system is an accepting one (*completeness*).

Next, we formalize these ideas in the following definition.

Definition 7: Let $X = (I_X, \theta_X)$ be a decision problem. Let $\mathbf{\Pi} = (\Pi(n))_{n\in\mathbb{N}}$ be a family of accepting P systems. A *polynomial encoding* of X in $\mathbf{\Pi}$ is a pair (cod, s) of polynomial time computable functions over I_X such that for each instance $w \in I_X$, $s(w)$ is a natural number and $cod(w)$ is an input multiset of the system $\Pi(s(w))$.

Definition 8: Let $X = (I_X, \theta_X)$ be a decision problem. Let $\mathbf{\Pi} = (\Pi(n))_{n\in\mathbb{N}}$ be a family of accepting **P** systems, and (cod, s) a polynomial encoding of X in $\mathbf{\Pi}$.

- We say that the family $\mathbf{\Pi}$ is *sound* with regard to (X, cod, s) whenever, for each instance of the problem $w \in I_X$, if there exists an accepting computation of $\Pi(s(w))$ with input $cod(w)$, then $\theta_X(w) = 1$.
- We say that the family $\mathbf{\Pi}$ is *complete* with regard to (X, cod, s) whenever, for each instance of the problem $w \in I_X$, if $\theta_X(w) = 1$ then there exists an accepting computation of $\Pi(s(w))$ with input $cod(w)$, and every halting computation of $\Pi(s(w))$ with input $cod(w)$ is an accepting one.

The soundness property means that if given an instance we obtain an *acceptance output* of the system associated with it through some computation, then the answer of the problem (for that instance) is *yes*. The completeness property means that if the instance of the problem has an *affirmative* response, then any halting computation of the system associated with it must be an accepting one.

4. Complexity Classes in Cell-like Membrane Systems

In this section we deal with accepting cell-like membrane systems and we propose to solve hard problems in an *uniform* way in the following sense: all instances of a decision problem that have the same *size* (according to a prefixed polynomial time computable criterion) are processed by the same system, to which an appropriate input, that depends on the specific instance, is supplied.

Now, we formalize these ideas in the following definition.

Definition 9: Let $X = (I_X, \theta_X)$ be a decision problem. We say that X is solvable in polynomial time by a family of accepting P systems $\mathbf{\Pi} = (\Pi(n))_{n\in\mathbb{N}}$, and we denote it by $X \in \mathbf{PMC}_{\mathcal{A}}$, if the following holds:

- The family $\mathbf{\Pi}$ is polynomially uniform by Turing machines; that is, there exists a deterministic Turing machine that constructs in polynomial time the system $\Pi(n)$ from $n \in \mathbb{N}$.
- There exists a polynomial encoding (cod, s) of X in $\mathbf{\Pi}$ such that:
  - — The family $\mathbf{\Pi}$ is polynomially bounded with regard to (X, cod, s); that is, there exists a polynomial function $p(n)$ such that for each $w \in I_X$ every halting computation of the system $\Pi(s(w))$ with input $cod(w)$ performs at most $p(|w|)$ steps.
  - — The family $\mathbf{\Pi}$ is sound and complete with regard to (X, cod, s).

Note that (according to the above definition) in order to decide about an instance, w, of a decision problem, first of all we need to compute the natural number $s(w)$, obtain the input multiset $cod(w)$, and construct the system $\Pi(s(w))$. This is properly a *pre-computation stage*, running in polynomial time expressed by a number of *sequential steps* in the framework of the Turing machines. After that, we execute the system $\Pi(s(w))$ with input $cod(w)$. This is properly the *computation stage*, also running in polynomial time, but now it is described by a number of *parallel steps* in the framework of membrane computing.

Polynomial time uniform solutions to some **NP**–complete problems can be found in the literature: e.g., *Satisfiability,*[12] *Knapsack,*[8] *Subset Sum,*[9] *Partition,*[2] *Clique,*[1] *Bin Packing,*[10] *Common Algorithmic Problem.*[11]

5. Simulating Turing Machines by P Systems

In this section we show how it is possible to attack the **P** versus **NP** problem within the framework of membrane computing.

First of all, in order to formally define what means that a family of P systems simulates a Turing machine, we shall introduce for each Turing machine a decision problem associated with it.

Definition 10: Let M be a Turing machine with input alphabet Σ_M. The *decision problem associated with* M is the problem $X_M = (I_M, \theta_M)$, where $I_M = \Sigma_M^*$, and for every $w \in \Sigma_M^*$, $\theta_M(w) = 1$ if and only if M accepts w.

Obviously, the decision problem X_M is solvable by the Turing machine M.

Definition 11: We say that a Turing machine M is simulated in polynomial time by a family of accepting P systems if $X_M \in \mathbf{PMC}_{\mathcal{A}}$.

In **P** systems, evolution rules, communication rules and rules involving dissolution are called *basic rules*. By applying this kind of rules the size of the membrane structures does not increase. Hence, it is not possible to construct an exponential working space (expressed by the number of membranes) in polynomial time using only basic rules in a P system.

Definition 12: An accepting **P** system that uses only basic rules, possibly using cooperative rules and priorities, is called accepting transition P system.

We denote by $\mathcal{T}$ the class of accepting transition P systems.

Next, we state that every deterministic Turing machine working in polynomial time can be simulated in polynomial time by a family of systems of the class $\mathcal{T}$.

Proposition 1: *Let M be a deterministic Turing machine working in polynomial time.. Then the decision problem associated with M belongs to* $\mathbf{PMC}_{\mathcal{T}}$.

Proof: Let M be a deterministic Turing machine working in polynomial time. Let $Q_M = \{q_N, q_Y, q_0, \ldots, q_n\}$ the set of states, $\Gamma_M = \{B, \triangleright, a_1, \ldots, a_m\}$ the working alphabet, $\Sigma_M = \{a_1, \ldots, a_p\}$, with $p \leq m$ the input alphabet, and $\delta_M(q_i, a_j) = (q_{Q(i,j)}, a_{A(i,j)}, D(i,j))$ the transition function. We denote $a_B = B$ (the blank symbol) and $a_0 = \triangleright$ (the first symbol).

Next, we describe a family of accepting transition P systems $\mathbf{\Pi}_M = (\Pi_M(k))_{k \in \mathbb{N}}$ that simulates the Turing machine M. For each $k \in \mathbb{N}$,

$$\Pi_M(k) = (\Sigma(k), \Gamma(k), \mu(k), \mathcal{M}_1(k), (R_1(k), \rho_1(k)), i(k))$$

where

$$\begin{aligned}
\Sigma(k) &= \{\langle a_i, j\rangle : 1 \le i \le p, 1 \le j \le k\} \\
\Gamma(k) &= \{\langle a_i, j\rangle : 1 \le i \le p, 0 \le j \le k\} \cup \{q_N, q_Y, h, h', s_E\} \\
&\cup \{q_i : 0 \le i \le n\} \cup \{a_i, a_i', a_i'', b_i : 0 \le i \le m\} \\
&\cup \{s_l, s_l^-, s_l^+ : l \in \{0, I_1, \dots, I_5, 1, \dots, 9\}\} \cup \{\#, Yes, No\} \\
\mu(k) &= [_1\,]_1 \\
\mathcal{M}_1(k) &= q_0 a_0 s_0 s_0^- s_{I_1}^- \cdots s_{I_5}^- s_1^- \cdots s_9^- \\
i(k) &= 1 \\
(R_1(k), \rho_1(k)) &= (R^0(k), \rho^0(k)) \cup (R^I, \rho^I) \cup (R^1, \rho^1) \cup (R^2, \rho^2) \\
&\cup (R^3, \rho^3) \cup (R^4, \rho^4)
\end{aligned}$$

The set of rules with their corresponding priorities is the following one:

- $(R^0(k), \rho^0(k)) = (R^{0_1}(k), \rho^{0_1}(k))$, with

$$(R^{0_1}(k), \rho^{0_1}(k)) \equiv \begin{cases} s_E s_0^- \to (\#, out) > s_0 s_0^- \to s_0^+ > s_0^- \to s_0^- > \\ \left\{ \begin{array}{ll} \langle a_i, j\rangle \to \langle a_i, j-1\rangle^2 & (1 \le i \le p, 1 \le j \le k) \\ \langle a_i, 0\rangle \to a_i & (1 \le i \le p) \end{array} \right\} > \\ s_0^+ \to s_0^- s_{I_1} \end{cases}$$

- $(R^I, \rho^I) = (R^{I_1}, \rho^{I_1}) \cup (R^{I_2}, \rho^{I_2}) \cup (R^{I_3}, \rho^{I_3}) \cup (R^{I_4}, \rho^{I_4}) \cup (R^{I_5}, \rho^{I_5})$, with

$$(R^{I_1}, \rho^{I_1}) \equiv \begin{cases} s_E s_{I_1}^- \to (\#, out) > s_{I_1} s_{I_1}^- \to s_{I_1}^+ > s_{I_1}^- \to s_{I_1}^- > \\ a_i s_{I_1}^+ \to a_i s_{I_1}^- s_{I_2} (1 \le i \le p) > s_{I_1}^+ \to s_{I_1}^- s_1 \end{cases}$$

$$(R^{I_2}, \rho^{I_2}) \equiv \begin{cases} s_E s_{I_2}^- \to (\#, out) > s_{I_2} s_{I_2}^- \to s_{I_2}^+ > s_{I_2}^- \to s_{I_2}^- > \\ \begin{cases} a_i \to a_i a_i' (1 \le i \le p) \\ s_{I_2}^+ \to s_{I_2}^- s_{I_3} \end{cases} \end{cases}$$

$$(R^{I_3}, \rho^{I_3}) \equiv \begin{cases} s_E s_{I_3}^- \to (\#, out) > s_{I_3} s_{I_3}^- \to s_{I_3}^+ > s_{I_3}^- \to s_{I_3}^- > \\ a_i'^2 \to a_i'' (1 \le i \le p) > a_i' s_{I_3}^+ \to a_i' s_{I_3}^- (1 \le i \le p) > \\ \begin{cases} a_i'' \to a_i' (1 \le i \le p) \\ s_{I_3}^+ \to s_{I_3}^- s_{I_4} \end{cases} \end{cases}$$

$$(R^{I_4},\rho^{I_4}) \equiv \begin{cases} s_E s_{I_4}^- \to (\#, out) > s_{I_4} s_{I_4}^- \to s_{I_4}^+ > s_{I_4}^- \to s_{I_4}^- > \\ a_i'^2 \to a_i''(1 \le i \le p) > a_i' a_j' s_{I_4}^+ \to a_i' a_j' s_{I_4}^- (1 \le i, j \le p, i \ne j) > \\ a_i' s_{I_4}^+ \to s_{I_4}^- s_{I_5} (1 \le i \le p) > s_{I_4}^+ \to s_{I_4}^- \end{cases}$$

$$(R^{I_5},\rho^{I_5}) \equiv \begin{cases} s_E s_{I_5}^- \to (\#, out) > s_{I_5} s_{I_5}^- \to s_{I_5}^+ > s_{I_5}^- \to s_{I_5}^- > \\ a_i'' \to a_i'(1 \le i \le p) > a_i' s_{I_5}^+ \to a_i' s_{I_5}^- s_{I_4} (1 \le i \le p) > \\ s_{I_5}^+ \to s_{I_5}^- s_1 \end{cases}$$

- $(R^1,\rho^1) = (R^{1_1},\rho^{1_1}) \cup (R^{1_2},\rho^{1_2}) \cup (R^{1_3},\rho^{1_3})$, with

$$(R^{1_1},\rho^{1_1}) \equiv \begin{cases} s_E s_1^- \to (\#, out) > s_1 s_1^- \to s_1^+ > s_1^- \to s_1^- > \\ \begin{cases} h \to hh' \\ a_i \to a_i a_i' (0 \le i \le m) \\ s_1^+ \to s_1^- s_2 \end{cases} \end{cases}$$

$$(R^{1_2},\rho^{1_2}) \equiv \begin{cases} s_E s_2^- \to (\#, out) > h' s_2 s_2^- \to s_2^+ > s_2 \to s_3 > \\ s_2^- \to s_2^- > a_i'^2 \to a_i'' (0 \le i \le m) > \begin{cases} a_i' \to \lambda (0 \le i \le m) \\ a_i'' \to a_i' (0 \le i \le m) \\ s_2^+ \to s_2^- s_2 \end{cases} \end{cases}$$

$$(R^{1_3},\rho^{1_3}) \equiv \begin{cases} s_E s_3^- \to (\#, out) > s_3 s_3^- \to s_3^+ > s_3^- \to s_3^- > \\ \begin{cases} a_i'^2 \to \lambda (0 \le i \le m) \\ s_3^+ \to s_3^- s_4 \end{cases} \end{cases}$$

- $(R^2,\rho^2) = (R^{2_1},\rho^{2_1}) \cup (R^{2_2},\rho^{2_2})$, with

$$(R^{2_1},\rho^{2_1}) \equiv \begin{cases} s_E s_4^- \to (\#, out) > s_4 s_4^- \to s_4^+ > s_4^- \to s_4^- > \\ \begin{cases} h \to hh' \\ s_4^+ \to s_4^- s_5 \end{cases} \end{cases}$$

$$(R^{2_2},\rho^{2_2}) \equiv \begin{cases} s_E s_5^- \to (\#, out) > s_5 s_5^- \to s_5^+ > s_5^- \to s_5^- > \\ \begin{cases} \text{Rules associated with the transition function} \\ s_5^+ \to s_5^- s_6 \end{cases} \end{cases}$$

The rules associated with the transition function, δ_M, are the following:

Case 1: State q_r, symbol $a_s \neq B$

Movement	Rules
left	$q_r a'_s h \rightarrow q_{Q(r,s)} a'_s b_{A(r,s)}$, if $A(r,s) \neq B$ $q_r a'_s h \rightarrow q_{Q(r,s)} a'_s$, if $A(r,s) = B$
equal	$q_r a'_s \rightarrow q_{Q(r,s)} a'_s b_{A(r,s)}$, if $A(r,s) \neq B$ $q_r a'_s \rightarrow q_{Q(r,s)} a'_s$, if $A(r,s) = B$
right	$q_r a'_s \rightarrow q_{Q(r,s)} a'_s b_{A(r,s)} h$, if $A(r,s) \neq B$ $q_r a'_s \rightarrow q_{Q(r,s)} a'_s h$, if $A(r,s) = B$

Case 2: State q_r, symbol $a_s = B$

Movement	Rules
left	$q_r h \rightarrow q_{Q(r,B)} b_{A(r,B)}$, if $A(r,B) \neq B$ $q_r h \rightarrow q_{Q(r,B)}$, if $A(r,B) = B$
equal	$q_r \rightarrow q_{Q(r,B)} b_{A(r,B)}$, if $A(r,B) \neq B$ $q_r \rightarrow q_{Q(r,B)}$, if $A(r,B) = B$
right	$q_r \rightarrow q_{Q(r,B)} b_{A(r,B)} h$, if $A(r,B) \neq B$ $q_r \rightarrow q_{Q(r,B)} h$, if $A(r,B) = B$

in order to avoid conflicts, each rule in case 1 has a greater priority than every rule in case 2.

- $(R^3, \rho^3) = (R^{3_1}, \rho^{3_1}) \cup (R^{3_2}, \rho^{3_2})$, with

$$(R^{3_1}, \rho^{3_1}) \equiv \begin{cases} s_E s_6^- \rightarrow (\#, out) > h' s_6 s_6^- \rightarrow s_6^+ > s_6 \rightarrow s_7 > \\ s_6^- \rightarrow s_6^- > \begin{cases} a'_i \rightarrow a'^2_i (0 \leq i \leq m) \\ b_i \rightarrow b_i^2 (0 \leq i \leq m) \\ s_6^+ \rightarrow s_6^- s_6 \end{cases} \end{cases}$$

$$(R^{3_2}, \rho^{3_2}) \equiv \begin{cases} s_E s_7^- \rightarrow (\#, out) > s_7 s_7^- \rightarrow s_7^+ > s_7^- \rightarrow s_7^- > \\ \begin{cases} a_i a'_i \rightarrow \lambda (0 \leq i \leq m) \\ b_i \rightarrow a_i (0 \leq i \leq m) \\ s_7^+ \rightarrow s_7^- s_8 \end{cases} \end{cases}$$

• $(R^4, \rho^4) = (R^{4_1}, \rho^{4_1}) \cup (R^{4_2}, \rho^{4_2})$, with

$$(R^{4_1}, \rho^{4_1}) \equiv \begin{cases} s_E s_8^- \to (\#, out) > s_8 s_8^- \to s_8^+ > s_8^- \to s_8^- > \\ \begin{cases} q_Y \to q_Y s_9 \\ q_N \to q_N s_9 \\ q_i \to q_i s_1 (0 \leq i \leq n) \\ s_8^+ \to s_8^- \end{cases} \end{cases}$$

$$(R^{4_2}, \rho^{4_2}) \equiv \begin{cases} s_E s_9^- \to (\#, out) > s_9 s_9^- \to s_9^+ > s_9^- \to s_9^- > \\ \begin{cases} q_Y \to (Yes, out) \\ q_N \to (No, out) \\ h \to \lambda \\ a_i \to \lambda (0 \leq i \leq m) \\ s_9^+ \to s_9^- s_E^{15} \end{cases} \end{cases}$$

Then we have the following:

(1) The family $\mathbf{\Pi}_M$ is polynomially uniform by Turing machines, because for $\Pi(k)$:
- The size of the input alphabet is $p \cdot k$.
- The size of the working alphabet is $p \cdot k + p + n + 4 \cdot m + 58$.
- The number of membranes of the system, the maximum length of the rules, and the size of the initial multisets, are constants.
- The total number of rules is linear in k.

where p, n, m are parameters only depending of M.

(2) We consider the functions *cod* and s over I_M given by $cod(a_{i_1} \cdots a_{i_t}) = \langle a_{i_1}, 1 \rangle \cdots \langle a_{i_t}, t \rangle$, and $s(w) = |w|$. Then, for each instance $w \in I_M$, $cod(w)$ is an input multiset of $\Pi_M(s(w))$. Moreover, the family $\mathbf{\Pi}_M$ is polynomially bounded, sound and complete with regard to (X_M, cod, s).

See Chapter 9 from Ref. 13 for more details. □

Theorem 1: $\mathbf{P} \subseteq \mathbf{PMC}_{\mathcal{T}}$.

Proof: Let X be a decision problem belonging to $\mathbf{P}$. Let M be a deterministic Turing machine working in polynomial time and solving X.

By Proposition 1, the problem X_M is in $\mathbf{PMC}_{\mathcal{T}}$. Then there exists a family $\mathbf{\Pi}_M = (\Pi_M(k))_{k \in \mathbb{N}}$ of accepting transition $\mathbf{P}$ systems simulating M

in polynomial time (with associated polynomial encoding (*cod*, s), being $s(w) = |w|$).

We consider the functions *cod'* and s' that are given by the restriction of cod and s to the set of instances of X. Then, the family $\mathbf{\Pi}_M$ is polynomially uniform by Turing machines, and polynomially bounded, sound and complete with regard to (X, cod', s'). Consequently, $X \in \mathbf{PMC}_{\mathcal{T}}$. □

Next, we are going to prove that if a decision problem can be solved in polynomial time by a family of accepting transition P systems, then it can also be solved in polynomial time by a deterministic Turing machine.

Theorem 2: $\mathbf{PMC}_{\mathcal{T}} \subseteq \mathbf{P}$.

Proof: Let X be a decision problem such that $X \in \mathbf{PMC}_{\mathcal{T}}$. Then, there exists a family of accepting transition **P** systems $\mathbf{\Pi} = (\Pi(n))_{n \in \mathbb{N}}$ such that:

(1) The family $\mathbf{\Pi}$ is polynomially uniform by Turing machines.
(2) There exist two polynomial time computable functions *cod* and s whose domain is I_X, such that for every $w \in I_X$, $s(w) \in \mathbb{N}$ and *cod*(w) is an input multiset of the system $\Pi(s(w))$. Moreover, the family $\mathbf{\Pi}$ is polynomially bounded, sound and complete with regard to (X, cod, s).

Next, let us associate with the system $\Pi(n)$ a deterministic Turing machine, $M(n)$, *with multiple tapes*, such that, given an input multiset m of $\Pi(n)$, the machine reproduces (only) *one* specific computation of $\Pi(n)$ with input m.

The input alphabet of the machine $M(n)$ coincides with that of the system $\Pi(n)$. On the other hand, the working alphabet contains, besides the symbols of the input alphabet of $\Pi(n)$ the following symbols: a symbol for each label assigned to the membranes of $\Pi(n)$; the symbols 0 and 1, that will allow to operate with numbers represented in base 2; three symbols indicating whether a membrane has not yet been dissolved, or has to be dissolved, or was already dissolved; and three symbols that will indicate whether a rule is awaiting, is applicable or is not applicable.

Subsequently, we specify the tapes of this machine.

- We have one *input tape*, that keeps a string representing the input multiset received.
- For each membrane of the system we have:
  - One *structure tape*, that keeps in the second cell the label of the parent membrane, and in the third cell one of the three symbols that indicate

if the membrane has not yet been dissolved, if the membrane must be dissolved, or if the membrane has been dissolved.

- For each object of the working alphabet of the system: (a) one *main tape*, that keeps the multiplicity of the object, in base 2, in the multiset contained in the membrane; and (b) one *auxiliary tape*, that keeps temporary results, also in base 2, of applying the rules associated with the membrane.
- One *rules tape*, in which each cell starting from the second one corresponds to a rule associated with the membrane (we suppose that the set of those rules is ordered), and keeps one of the three symbols that indicate whether the rule is awaiting, it is applicable, or it is not applicable.

• For each object of the output alphabet we have one *environment tape*, that keeps the multiplicity of the object, in base 2, in the multiset associated with the environment.

Next we describe the steps performed by the Turing machine in order to simulate the **P** system. Let us take into account that, making a breadth first search traversal (with the skin as source) on the *initial* membrane structure of the system $\Pi(n)$, we obtain a natural order between the membranes of $\Pi(n)$.

I. Initialization of the system. In the first phase of the simulation process followed by the Turing machine, the symbols needed to express the initial configuration of the computation with input m that is going to be simulated are included in the corresponding tapes.

II. Determine the applicable rules. To simulate a step of the **P** system, what the machine has to do first is to determine the set of rules that are applicable (each of them independently) to the configuration considered in the membranes they are associated with.

III. Apply the rules. Once the applicable rules are determined, they are applied in a maximal manner to the membranes they are associated with. The fact that the rules are considered in a certain order (using local maximality for each rule, according to that order) determines (only) *one specific* applicable multiset of rules, thus fixing the computation of the system that the Turing machine simulates. However, from our definition of complexity class it follows that the chosen computation is not relevant for the proof, due to the *confluence* of the system.

IV. Update the multisets. After applying the rules, the auxiliary tapes keep the results obtained, and then these results have to be moved to the corresponding main tapes.

V. Dissolve the membranes. To finish the simulation of one step of the computation of the P system it is necessary to dissolve the membranes according to the rules that have been applied in the previous phase and to rearrange accordingly the membrane structure.

VI. Check if the simulation has ended. Finally, after finishing the simulation of one transition step of the computation of $\Pi(n)$, the Turing machine has to check whether a halting configuration has been reached and, in that case, if the computation is an accepting or a rejecting one.

It is easy to check that the family $(M(n))_{n\in\mathbb{N}}$ can be constructed in an uniform way and in polynomial time from $n \in \mathbb{N}$.

Next, we consider the deterministic Turing machine $M_{\mathbf{\Pi}}$ working as follows:

Input: $w \in I_X$

— Compute $s(w)$
— Construct $M(s(w))$
— Compute $cod(w)$
— Simulate the functioning of $M(s(w))$ with input $cod(w)$

Then, we have the following:

(1) The machine $M_{\mathbf{\Pi}}$ works in polynomial time over $|w|$.
(2) Let us suppose that $M_{\mathbf{\Pi}}$ accepts the string w. Then *the* concrete computation of $\Pi(s(w))$ with input $cod(w)$ simulated by $M(s(w))$ is an accepting computation. Therefore $\theta_X(w) = 1$.
(3) Let us suppose that the problem X answers *yes* for the instance $w \in I_X$. Then every computation of $\Pi(s(w))$ with input $cod(w)$ is an accepting computation, in particular, also *the* computation simulated by $M(s(w))$. Hence $M_{\mathbf{\Pi}}$ accepts the string w.

Consequently, we have proved that the deterministic Turing machine $M_{\mathbf{\Pi}}$ solves X in polynomial time. That is, $X \in \mathbf{P}$. □

Corollary 1: $\mathbf{P} = \mathbf{PMC}_{\mathcal{T}}$.

Corollary 2: *The following statements are equivalent:*

(1) **P** = **NP**.
(2) *Any* ***NP****–complete problem is solvable in polynomial time by a family of accepting transition* **P** *systems.*
(3) *There exists an* ***NP****–complete problem that is solvable in polynomial time by a family of accepting transition* **P** *systems.*

Proof: (1) ⇒ (2) Let us suppose that **P** = **NP**. Let X be any **NP**–complete problem. Then $X \in$ **P**. From Theorem 1 we deduce that $X \in$ $\mathbf{PMC}_{\mathcal{T}}$.

(2) ⇒ (3) Obvious.

(3) ⇒ (1) Let X be an **NP**–complete problem solvable in polynomial time by a family of accepting transition P systems. From Theorem 2 we have $X \in$ **P**. Hence, **P** = **NP**. □

6. Conclusions

In this paper we have used membrane computing as a framework to address the solvability of computationally hard problems. For that, we deal with accepting cell–like membrane systems and we propose to solve **NP**–complete problems in an uniform way; that is, permitting that a P system processes a set of instances with the same *size*, and where each halting computation answers *yes* or *no*. In this context, polynomial complexity classes associated with these **P** systems has been defined.

The main result of the paper is a characterization of the standard computational class **P** of tractable problems (that is, problems solvable in polynomial time by deterministic Turing machines), through the solvability by accepting transition P systems in an uniform way.

This result provides a new tool to attack the conjecture **P** = **NP** in the framework of membrane computing.

Acknowledgments

The authors wish to acknowledge the support of the project TIC2002-04220-C03-01 of the Ministerio de Ciencia y Tecnología of Spain, cofinanced by FEDER funds.

References

1. A. Alhazov, C. Martín–Vide and L. Pan, Solving graph problems by P systems with restricted elementary active membranes, in *Aspects of Molecular*

Computing (N. Jonoska, Gh. Păun and G. Rozenberg, eds.), Lecture Notes in Computer Science **2950** (2004), 1–22.

2. M. A. Gutiérrez–Naranjo, M. J. Pérez–Jiménez and A. Riscos–Núñez, A fast P system for finding a balanced 2-partition, *Soft Computing* **9**, 9 (2005), 673–678.
3. S. N. Krishna and R. Rama, A variant of P systems with active membranes: Solving NP–complete problems, *Romanian Journal of Information Science and Technology* **2**, 4 (1999), 357–367.
4. A. Obtulowicz, Deterministic P systems for solving SAT problem, *Romanian Journal of Information Science and Technology* **4**, 1–2 (2001), 551–558.
5. Gh. Păun, P systems with active membranes: Attacking **NP**–complete problems, *Journal of Automata, Languages and Combinatorics* **6**, 1 (2001), 75–90.
6. Gh. Păun, *Membrane Computing. An Introduction*, Springer-Verlag, Berlin, 2002.
7. Gh. Păun Computing with membranes, *Journal of Computer and System Sciences* **61**, 1 (2000), 108–143, and *Turku Center for Computer Science-TUCS Report* Nr. 208, 1998.
8. M. J. Pérez–Jiménez and A. Riscos–Núñez, A linear time solution to the Knapsack problem using active membranes, in *Membrane Computing* (C. Martín-Vide, Gh. Păun, G. Rozenberg and A. Salomaa, eds.), Lecture Notes in Computer Science **2933** (2004), 250–268.
9. M. J. Pérez–Jiménez and A. Riscos–Núñez, Solving the Subset-Sum problem by P systems with active membranes, *New Generation Computing* **23**, 4 (2005), 367–384.
10. M. J. Pérez–Jiménez and F. J. Romero-Campero, An efficient family of P systems for packing items into bins, *Journal of Universal Computer Science* **10**, 5 (2004), 650–670.
11. M. J. Pérez–Jiménez and F. J. Romero-Campero, Attacking the Common Algorithmic problem by recognizer P systems, in *Machines, Computations and Universality, MCU'2004, Revised Papers* (M. Margenstern, ed.), Lecture Notes in Computer Science **3354** (2005), 304-315.
12. M. J. Pérez–Jiménez, A. Romero–Jiménez and F. Sancho–Caparrini, Complexity classes in models of cellular computing with membranes, *Natural Computing* **2**, 3 (2003), 265–285.
13. A. Romero-Jiménez, *Complexity and Universality in Cellular Computing Models*, PhD. Thesis, University of Seville, Spain, 2003.
14. A. Romero-Jiménez and M. J. Pérez Jiménez, Simulating Turing machines by P systems with external output, *Fundamenta Informaticae* **49**, 1–3 (2002), 273–287.
15. C. Zandron, C. Ferreti and G. Mauri, Solving NP-complete problems using P systems with active membranes, in *Unconventional Models of Computation, UMC'2K* (I. Antoniou, C. Calude, M.J. Dinneen, eds.), Springer-Verlag (2000), 289–301.

CHAPTER 10

A COSMIC MUSE

Tom Head
Department of Mathematical Sciences, Binghamton University,
Binghamton, New York 13902–6000, USA
tom@math.binghamton.edu

Does our cosmos provide more ladders for ascending to the discovery of its structure and dynamics than could have been anticipated? May we find a foundation of meaning in that classical mythology in which our cosmos is seen as the divine play of transcendental self–revelation?

"The eternal mystery of the world is its comprehensibility."
Albert Einstein.[4]

1. Introduction

Surely each of us occasionally hears from our depths the compound instruction: "Clothe the naked; feed the hungry; heal the sick." Perhaps we feel at times that we should eliminate, or minimize, the suffering of *all* life forms. Such feelings may arise from the recognition that each of us is an organ of our integrated planet-wide living system. Surely such feelings of union are a form of love. Knowledge may also be viewed as a form of love; as a union of the knower with the known. Indeed, in several traditions divine knowledge has been viewed through the imagery of the union of male and female.

Some of us hear a call to experience our cosmos as one grand unfurling blossom and to recognize ourselves as *channels* through which our cosmos is being known. The newly achieved awareness of the vast space and deep time of our cosmos has been the gift of our species. Migrating avian species have previously provided the awareness of the scale of our planet and have used the pattern of the stars as a tool of navigation. But surely our species is the first on our planet to extend awareness beyond even this pattern of stars, to pursue knowledge of the vast dynamic realm of the galaxies. This is a huge extension from Earth toward cosmic unification through knowledge and love.

2. Should the Scale of Our Cosmos Intimidate Us?

Earth is a small planet circling an undistinguished star in the outer provinces of one of the many spiral galaxies. The biospheric 'skin' of our planet may be only a few tens of kilometers thick. Should we conclude that life on our planet is an insignificant detail of our cosmos? *No.* Through expanding awareness, knowledge, and love, life progressively binds our cosmos in deeper and richer union. Thanks to (1) the wide separation between the stars and between the galaxies, (2) our location outside the center of our galaxy where the grand view is not obscured, and (3) our ability to design and construct tools, the vast volume of our cosmos is accessible to us. Moreover, thanks to the finiteness of the velocity of light, the deep recess of cosmic time can also be explored. The wonderful accessibility of our cosmos from our planet has been pointed out in Refs. 1, 2 and 12, but also in Ref. 6 which constitutes a prelude to and an evolutionary backbone for the present article. Earth life is well positioned for receiving the information from our space-time world that will allow unification through the construction of cosmic knowledge. No assumption is made that our species has arrived at a pinnacle of evolution for our planet, nor that it excels in comparison to life forms that may occur elsewhere.

3. The Dimension of the Eternal

In addition to the dimensions of space and time, our thought here is organized using a model in which we assume an extra dimension, *the dimension of the eternal.* In this imagery our cosmos is represented as a *several-dimensional surface* in a space with one additional dimension. Each point in our cosmos is then a point of incidence of a line in the dimension of the eternal with our space-time world. In this way the eternal is *transcendent* of the space-time world but also *imminent* at every point of that world. Since the dimension of the eternal is orthogonal to time as well as space, the mistake of confusing the eternal with an endless continuation of time is prevented. The apprehension of the "point of intersection of the timeless with time"[5] is possible at all points and times, although not routinely experienced. Perhaps our most fundamental prayer should be: "... please allow us the awareness of Your presence"?

4. Cosmoscopes

Each of us has an extensive internal life. Perhaps each internal life has a depth as great in extent as the depth of the external world in which we participate. We leave open the ancient, yet always current, question of whether the internal and the external constitute a duality or whether the apparent duality is an illusion masking an ultimate unity. We adopt a provisional duality and regard each organismic being as a *channel* between the internal and the external — a passageway through which information flows, allowing new constructions both inside and outside. All of this can be found consistent with the experience of silent concept-free meditation. Moreover, it seems that the interior may allow an opening facing into the dimension of the eternal. Each of us may then be an orifice through which our experience of, and knowledge of, our cosmos flows into the dimension of the eternal. We may be *cosmoscopes: tubes through which experience of our beautiful space-time world flow through to eternity.* Perhaps we life forms here on Earth are only beginning to shed complete opacity to this flow. Occasionally transmission through us may be only "as through a glass darkly". Can we make ourselves totally transparent, at least for short intervals? Can we become wide-open windows that allow the view from eternity to be crystal clear? Can such clarity be obtained by relaxing our servicing of the needs of the self which arise from its rootedness in the space-time world? It may be possible to clear our channel and experience the rush through us, toward eternity, of the beauty and magnificence of our cosmos. Perhaps the mysterious comprehensibility of our world is its essence.

5. Are all Eyes the Eyes of G-d?

Using "G-d" in preference to "God" recognizes that unfathomable mystery remains in all such references. "Eye" is used as the paradigm organ of information reception; "seeing" is used here in a sense intended to be inclusive of all modes of reception. Perhaps each of our companion life forms shares with us the role of being a passageway from our shared world into the dimension of the eternal. In this way G-d may participate from eternity in all aspects of our world; experiencing flying as a bat through a dark cave, wriggling as an earthworm through soft earth, singing as a whale in an ocean, and *deciphering as a human the light-encoded information that has traveled from the vast space and deep time of our cosmos.*[6] Perhaps the grand living system rises to the unification of our cosmos in a swelling of knowledge and love.

Is a billion years a long time? To life forms on our planet it seems long; perhaps even incomprehensible. As in time-lapse photography, we humans can see, in our minds, arbitrarily long scenarios in as little time as we wish. Ernst Mayr explains that a fundamental research procedure in the science of biological evolution consists of conjecturing scenarios and then testing them against all available evidence.[7] Likewise, cosmologists can mentally replay their various conjectured scenarios from the supposed Big Bang to the present. Conjectured scenarios are even underway that begin before the Big Bang, or that have no beginning at all. Since we have externalized our conjectures in formal models, our computers can rapidly display our billion year scenarios. Is a billion years a long time? Perhaps, from a cosmic perspective, the question is meaningless. Through mind, our species has loosened the grip of time and space. At least three billion years of evolution of life on our planet preceded the appearance our species. Does this deny our significance? *No.* Three billion years ago was yesterday. We are the first eyes on our planet through which awareness of the depths of space and time are being drawn into eternity.

6. Are all I's the I of G-d?

In both the Vedic/Upanishadic[3,8,9] and the Abrahamic traditions, mystical experience has continually suggested that each mind or spirit is finally identical with that of G-d. Mystics often find that fulfillment is achieved with a realization equivalent to: "G-d and I are One". Moreover, Erwin Schrödinger, a physicist who steeped himself in the Upanishads,[3] expressed in several major lectures[10,11] that mind must inevitably be understood in the singular and that each (apparent) mind should realize its identity with the one (universal) mind. The mystic's statement "I am G-d" has often lead to severe objections in Abrahamic communities. What is offered here is the much softer view that each of us (in fact, each life form) is a passageway between G-d and the space-time world. We clear our passageway by allowing our small self to temporarily dissolve. So again: Are all I's the I of G-d? Perhaps. But one may be more at ease regarding oneself as one of G-d's many cosmoscopes one of the orifices of flow linking eternity and the space-time world in which we participate.

References

1. S. Conway Morris, *Life's Solution — Inevitable Humans in a Lonely Universe*, Cambridge U. Press, Cambridge, UK (2003).

2. D. Darling, *Life Everywhere — the Maverick Science of Astrobiology*, Basic Books, NY (2001).
3. E. Easwaran, [Translator] *The Upanishads*, Nilgiri Press, Tomales, CA (1987).
4. A. Einstein, *Out of My Later Years*, Philosophical Library, NY (1950).
5. T. S. Eliot, *Four Quartets*, Harcourt B.J., Orlando, FL (1943/1971).
6. T. Head, Does light direct life toward cosmic awareness?, *Fundamenta Informaticae*, 64 (2005) 1–5. (Available from the author, if not otherwise.)
7. E. Mayr, *What Makes Biology Unique? — Considerations on the Autonomy of a Scientific Discipline*, Cambridge U. Press, NY (2004).
8. R. Panikkar, *The Vedic Experience*, Motilal Barnarsidass Pubs., Dehli (1977).
9. Patanjali (attribution), [Translation and commentary by B.S. Miller], *Yoga Discipline of Freedom*, U. Cal. Press, Berkeley (1995).
10. E. Schrödinger, *Mind and Matter*, Cambridge U. Press, NY (1958/1992).
11. E. Schrödinger, *My View of the World*, [Reprinted by] Ox Bow Press, Woodbridge, CN (1961/1983).
12. P. D. Ward and D. Brownlee, *Rare Earth — Why Complex Life Is Uncommon in the Universe*, Copernicus Springer–Verlag, NY (2000).

CHAPTER 11

SUBLOGARITHMICALLY SPACE-BOUNDED ALTERNATING ONE-PEBBLE TURING MACHINES WITH ONLY UNIVERSAL STATES

Katsushi Inoue, Akira Ito and Atsuyuki Inoue

Department of Computer Science and Systems Engineering, Faculty of Engineering, Yamaguchi University, Ube, 755-8611, Japan

E-mail: {inoue, ito, ainoue}@csse.yamaguchi-u.ac.jp

For any space function $L(n)$, let $USPACE^{peb}(L(n))$ denote the class of languages accepted by $L(n)$ space-bounded alternating one-pebble Turing machines with only universal states. This paper investigates some aspects of $USPACE^{peb}(L(n))$ with $\log\log n \leq L(n) \leq \log n$.

We first investigate a relationship between $USPACE^{peb}(L(n))$ and the class of languages accepted by two-way deterministic one-counter automata, and show that they are incomparable. Then we investigate a relationship between $USPACE^{peb}(L(n))$ and $ASPACE^{peb}(L(n))$, where $ASPACE^{peb}(L(n))$ denotes the class of languages accepted by $L(n)$ space-bounded alternating one-pebble Turing machines, and show that there exists a language in $ASPACE^{peb}(\log\log n)$, but not in $USPACE^{peb}(o(\log n))$. Furthermore, we investigate a space hierarchy, and show that for any one-pebble (fully) space constructible function $L(n) \leq \log n$, and any function $L'(n) = o(L(n))$, there exists a language in $USPACE^{peb}(L(n))$, but not in $USPACE^{peb}(L'(n))$. Finally, we investigate closure property of $USPACE^{peb}(L(n))$, and show that for any $\log\log n \leq L(n) = o(\log n)$, $USPACE^{peb}(L(n))$ is not closed under concatenation, Kleene closure, and length-preserving homomorphism.

1. Introduction

A Turing machine (Tm) considered here has a two-way read-only input tape and a semi-infinite (infinite to the right) storage tape.[5,8] A one-pebble Tm[8] is a Tm with the capability of using one-pebble which the finite control can use as a marker on the input tape. During the computation, the device can deposit (retrieve) a pebble on (from) any cell of the tape. The next move depends on the current state, the contents of the cells scanned by the input and storage tape heads, and on the presence of the pebble on the current input tape cell. See, e.g., Refs. 1, 3 and 8 for details of pebble automata. Blum and Hewitt[1] showed that one-pebble finite automata accept only regular sets. Chang *et al.*[3] strengthened this result, and showed that $o(\log\log n)$ space-bounded one-pebble Tm's accept only regular sets. Further, they showed in Ref. 3 that one pebble adds power, even when the input is restricted to a language over a unary alphabet, to Tm's whose space complexity lies between $\log\log n$ and $\log n$. Compared with many investigations of Tm's, there are not so many investigations of one-pebble Tm's. Recently, Inoue *et al.*[6] showed that (i) the class of languages accepted by deterministic two-way one-counter automata is incomparable with the class of languages accepted by $L(n)$ space-bounded nondeterministic one-pebble Tm's with $\log\log n \leq L(n) = o(\log n)$, (ii) nondeterminism is less powerful than alternation for $L(n)$ space-bounded one-pebble Tm's with $\log\log n \leq L(n) = o(\log n)$, and (iii) there is an infinite space hierarchy for the accepting powers of deterministic and nondeterministic one-pebble Tm's with spaces between $\log\log n$ and $\log n$.

This paper investigates some aspects of the accepting powers of alternating one-pebble Tm's with only universal states and with spaces between $\log\log n$ and $\log n$. Through the proofs of our results, we give a new technique for proving that some languages cannot be accepted by space-bounded alternating one-pebble Tm's with only universal states. Section 2 gives definitions and notations necessary for the subsequent sections. For any space function $L(n)$, let *strong(weak)-USPACE*$^{peb}(L(n))$ denote the class of languages accepted by strongly (weakly) $L(n)$ space-bounded alternating one-pebble Tm's with only universal states. Section 3 investigates a relationship between *strong(weak)-USPACE*$^{peb}(L(n))$ and the class of languages accepted by two-way deterministic one-counter automata, and shows that they are incomparable. Section 4 investigates a relationship between *strong(weak)-USPACE*$^{peb}(L(n))$ and *strong(weak)-ASPACE*$^{peb}(L(n))$, where *strong(weak)-ASPACE*$^{peb}(L(n))$ denotes the class of languages accepted by strongly (weakly) $L(n)$ space-bounded alternating one-pebble Tm's, and shows that there exists a language in *strong-ASPACE*$^{peb}(\log\log n)$, but not in *weak-USPACE*$^{peb}(o(\log n))$. Section 5 investigates a space hierarchy, and shows that for any one-pebble (fully) space constructible function $L(n) \leq \log n$, and any function $L'(n) = o(L(n))$, there exists a language in *strong-USPACE*$^{peb}(L(n))$, but not in *weak-USPACE*$^{peb}(L'(n))$. Section 6 investigates closure propertie of *strong(weak)-USPACE*$^{peb}(L(n))$, and show that for any $\log\log n \leq$

$L(n) = o(\log n)$, *strong(weak)*-$USPACE^{peb}(L(n))$ is not closed under concatenation, Kleene closure, and length-preserving homomorphism. Section 7 concludes this paper by giving open problems.

2. Definitions and Notations

Below, we denote a Turing machine by Tm. An *alternating* Tm M is a generalization of the nondeterministic Tm. M has a read-only input tape $\cent w\$$ (where $\cent$ is the left endmarker, \$ is the right endarker, and w is an input word) on which the input head can move right or left, and has one semi-infinite (infinite to the right) storage tape equiped with a storage head which can move right or left, and can read or write. All states of M are partitioned into *universal* and *existential* states. At each moment, M is in one of the states. Then it can read the contents of the scanned cells of both the input and storage tapes, change the contents of the scanned cell of the storage tape by writing a new symbol on it, move the input and storage tape heads in specified directions, and change its state. All these operations form a *step*, and are chosen from the possibilities defined by the transition function, as a function of the current state and symbols read from the tapes. M cannot write the blank symbols. A *storage state* of M is a combination of the (1) contents of the storage tape, (2) position of the storage head within the nonblank portion of the storage tape, and (3) state of the finite control. A *configuration* of M on an input w is a combination of the (1) storage state, and (2) position of the input head on $\cent w\$$. If q is the state associated with configuration c, then c is said to be a *universal (existential, accepting)* configuration if q is a universal (existential, accepting) state. The *initial* configuration of M is the configuration such that (i) the input head is on the left endmarker $\cent$, (ii) the finite control is in the initial state, (iii) each cell of the storage tape contains the blank symbol, and (iv) the storage tape head is on the leftmost cell of the storage tape. For each input word x, we write $c \vdash_{M,x} c'$, and say that c' is an *immediate successor* of c (of M on x), if configuration c' is derived from configuration c in one step of M on the input tape $\cent x\$$ according to the transition function. A configuration with no immediate successor is called a *halting* configuration. Below, we assume that every accepting configuration is a halting configuration.

We can view the computation of M as a tree whose nodes are labeled by configurations. A *computation tree* of M on an input w is a tree such that the root is labelled by the initial configuration and the children of any nonleaf node labelled by a universal (existential) configuration include all (one) of the immediate successors of that configuration. A computation tree is *accepting* if it is finite and all the leaves are labelled by accepting configurations. M accepts an inpu word w if there is an accepting computation tree of M on w. See Refs. 2 and 8 for the more detailed definitions of alternating Tm's.

A *one-pebble alternating* Tm is an alternating Tm with the capability of using one-pebble which the finite control can use as a marker on the input tape. During the computation, the device can deposit (retrieve) a pebble on (from) any cell of the tape. The next move depends on the current state, the contents of the cells scanned by the input and storage tape heads, and on the presence of the pebble on the current input tape cell. The concept of "storage state" for one-pebble alternating Tm's is defined as for alternating Tm's. A *configuration* of a one-pebble alternating Tm M on an input x is a combination of the storage state, the position of the input head, and the position of the pebble on $\cent x\$$. The *initial* configuration of M is the same as that of an alternating Tm, except that M starts with the pebble in the finite control. The concepts of "computation tree", "accepting computation tree", and "acceptance of an input word" for one-pebble Tm's are defined as for alternating Tm's.

A computation tree of a one-pebble alternating Tm M (on some input) is *lspace-bounded* if all nodes of the tree are labeled with configurations using at most l cells of the storage tape. Let $L(n) : N \to N$ be a function of the input length n, where N denotes the set of all the positive integers. M is *weakly*$L(n)$*space-bounded* if for every input w of length n, $n \geq 1$, that is accepted by M, there exists an $L(n)$ space-bounded accepting computation tree of M on w. M is *strongly*$L(n)$*space-bounded* if for every input w of length n (accepted by M or not), $n \geq 1$, any computation tree of M on w is $L(n)$ space-bounded. *One-pebble nondeterministic and one-pebble deterministic* Tm's are defined as usual. Let *weak-*$ASPACE^{peb}(L(n))$ (*weak-*$NSPACE^{peb}(L(n))$, *weak-*$DSPACE^{peb}(L(n))$) denote the class of languages accepted by weakly $L(n)$ space-bounded one-pebble alternating (nondeterministic, deterministic) Tm's, and let *strong-*$ASPACE^{peb}(L(n))$ (*strong-*$NSPACE^{peb}(L(n))$, *strong-*$DSPACE^{peb}(L(n))$) denote the class of languages accepted by strongly $L(n)$ space-bounded one-pebble alternating (nondeterministic, deterministic) Tm's. Further, let *weak*(*strong*)-$USPACE^{peb}(L(n))$ denote the class of languages accepted by weakly (strongly) $L(n)$ space-bounded alternating one-pebble Tm's with only universal states.

Let M be a one-pebble alternating Tm, and x be an input word. A sequence of configurations $c_1c_2\cdots c_m (m \geq 1)$ is called a *computation path of M on x* if $c_1 \vdash_{M,x} c_2 \vdash_{M,x} \cdots \vdash_{M,x} c_m$. For simplicity, we below call a computation path a *computation*. Let $c_1c_2\cdots c_m$ $(m \geq 1)$ be a computation of M on an input word x, and let l be a positive integer. Then, this computation is called:

- an l *space-bounded halting computation of M on x* if each c_i $(1 \leq i \leq m)$ is l space-bounded, $c_i \neq c_j$ for any $1 \leq i < j \leq m$, and c_m is a halting configuration other than any accepting confuguration,
- an l *space-bounded overflow computation of M on x* if each c_i $(1 \leq i \leq m-1)$ is l space-bounded, $c_i \neq c_j$ for any $1 \leq i < j \leq m-1$, and c_m uses $l+1$ cells of the storage tape,
- an l *space-bounded double-looping computation of M on x* if there exist some i $(1 \leq i \leq m-2)$ and some (possibly empty) sequence of confugurations s such that (i) $c_j \neq c_k$ for each $1 \leq j < k \leq i$, (ii) $c_1c_2\cdots c_m = c_1c_2\cdots c_{i-1}c_isc_isc_i$, and (iii) each configuration in c_is is different from each other, and different from each c_r $(1 \leq r < i)$, and
- an l *space-bounded rejecting computation of M on x* if the sequence $c_1c_2\cdots c_m$ is an l space-bounded halting, overflow, or double-looping computation.

A function $L : N \rightarrow N$ is *one-pebble space constructible (one-pebble fully space constructible)* if there exists a strongly $L(n)$ space-bounded deterministic one-pebble Tm M such that, for all $n \geq 1$ and for some (any) input word of length n, M will eventually halt having marked exactly $L(n)$ cells of the storage tape. We say that M *constructs (fully constructs)* $L(n)$.

In Section 5, we will use the following fact which was proved in Ref. 3.

Fact 1 $\lceil \log \log n \rceil$ is one-pebble fully space constructible.

A *two-way deterministic one-counter automaton* (2-dc) is a two-way deterministic pushdown automaton[4] which can use only one kind of symbol on the pushdown tape. Let 2-DC denote the class of languages accepted by 2-dc's.

Throughout this paper, we assume that the base of logarithm is 2. For any machine M, let $T(M)$ denote the set of words accepted by M. For any word w, $|w|$ denotes the length of w, and for any set S, $|S|$ denotes the cardinality of S. For any alphabet Σ and any integer $n \geq 1$, Σ^n denotes the set of all the words of length n over Σ. See Ref. 5 for undefined terms.

3. Incomparability with 2-*DC*

This section investigates a relationship between the accepting powers of 2-dc's and sublogarithmically space-bounded one-pebble alternating Tm's with only universal states.

Theorem 1: *strong*-$USPACE^{peb}(\log\log n) - 2\text{-}DC \neq \emptyset$.

Proof: It is shown in Ref. 7 that there is a language in *strong*-$DSPACE^{peb}(\log\log n)$, but not in 2-DC. This implies that the theorem holds. □

Theorem 2: $2\text{-}DC\text{-}weak\text{-}USPACE^{peb}(o(\log n)) \neq \emptyset$.

Proof: Let $T_1 = \{ww' | \exists\ n \geq 1[w, w' \in \{0,1\}^n w \neq w']\}$. It is an easy exercise to show that $T_1 \in 2\text{-}DC$. We below show that $T_1 \notin$ *weak*-$USPACE^{peb}(o(\log n))$. We suppose to the contrary that there is a weakly $L(n)$ space-bounded alternating one-pebble Tm with only universal states M which accepts T_1, where $L(n) = o(\log n)$. Let Q be the set of states of the finite control of M. We divide Q into two disjoint subsets Q^+ and Q^- which corresponds to the sets of states when M holds and does not hold the pebble in the finite control, respectively. M starts from the initial state in Q^+ with the input head on the left endmarker ¢. Below we shall consider the computations of M on words of length $2n$ for large n. Thus M uses at most $L(2n)$ cells of the storage tape. For each $n \geq 1$, let an *n-word* be a word over $\{0,1\}$ of length n, and $S(n)$ be the set of possible storage states of M using at most $L(2n)$ cells of the storage tape. Let $S^+(n) = \{s \in S(n)|$ the state component of s is in $Q^+\}$, $S^-(n) = \{s \in S(n)|$ the state component of s is in $Q^-\}$, and thus $S(n) = S^+(n) \cup S^-(n)$. Clearly $s^+(n) \triangleq |S^+(n)| = O(t^{L(2n)})$, $s^-(n) \triangleq |S^-(n)| = O(t^{L(2n)})$, and $s(n) \triangleq |S(n)| = O(t^{L(2n)})$ for some constant t depending only on M. Let x be any n-word that is supposed to be a subword of an input to M. Suppose that the pebble of M is not placed on the string ¢x (resp., $x\$$). Then, we define a mapping M_x^l (resp., M_x^r), which depends on M and x, from $S(n)$ to the power set of $S(n) \cup Q_{stop} \cup \{loop, overflow\}$ as follows (where Q_{stop} is the set of halting states other than accepting states, and *loop* and *overflow* are new symbols):

- for any s, $s' \in S^-(n)$, $s' \in M_x^l(s)$ (resp., $M_x^r(s)$) $\Leftrightarrow$ when M enters ¢x (resp., x§) in storage state s from the right (resp., left) edge of ¢x (resp., $x\$$), there exists a computation of M in which M eventually exits

$\not{c}x$ (resp., $x\$$) in storage state s' from the right (resp., left) edge of $\not{c}x$ (resp., $x\$$),

- for any $s \in S(n)$ and for any $q \in Q_{stop}$, $q \in M_x^l(s)$ (resp., $M_x^r(s)$) $\Leftrightarrow$ when M enters $\not{c}x$ (resp., $x\$$) in storage state s from the right (resp., left) edge of $\not{c}x$ (resp., $x\$$), there exists a computation of M in which M eventually enters state q in $\not{c}x$ (resp., $x\$$), and halts,
- for any $s \in S(n)$, $loop \in M_x^l(s)$ (resp., $M_x^r(s)$) $\Leftrightarrow$ when M enters $\not{c}x$ (resp., $x\$$) in storage state s from the right (resp., left) edge of $\not{c}x$ (resp., $x\$$), there exists a computation in which M enters a loop in $\not{c}x$ (resp., $x\$$), and
- for any $s \in S(n)$, $overflow \in M_x^l(s)$ (resp., $M_x^r(s)$) $\Leftrightarrow$ when M enters $\not{c}x$ (resp., $x\$$) in storage state s from the right (resp., left) edge of $\not{c}x$ (resp., $x\$$), there exists a computation of M in which M uses $L(2n) + 1$ cells of the storage tape for the first time in $\not{c}x$ (resp., $x\$$).

We say that two n-words x_1, x_2 are

- *M-equivalent* if two mappings $M_{x_1}^l$ and $M_{x_2}^l$ are equivalent, and two mappings $M_{x_1}^r$ and $M_{x_2}^r$ are equivalent, and
- *M^--equivalent* if for any s, $s' \in S^-(n)$ and for any $a \in \{l, r\}$, $s' \in M_{x_1}^a(s)$ if and only if $s' \in M_{x_2}^a(s)$.

(Note that if x_1 and x_2 are M-equivalent, then x_1 and x_2 are M^--equivalent.) Clearly, M-equivalence is an equivalence relation on n-words. There are 2^n n-words. Clearly, there are at most $e(n) = (2^{s(n)+d+2})^{s(n)}$, where $d = |Q_{stop}|$, M-equivalence classes of n-words. Let $P(n)$ be a largest M-equivalence class of n-words. Then we have $|P(n)| \geq \frac{2^n}{e(n)}$. Note that by a simple calculation, we can easily see that $|P(n)| \gg 1$ for large n, because $L(n) = o(\log n)$. Let w_1 and w_2 be in $P(n)$. For any computation $comp(w_1w_2)$ of M on w_1w_2, let

- $cross(comp(w_1w_2)) \stackrel{\triangle}{=}$ the sequence of storage states when M crosses the boundary between w_1 and w_2 from left to right or from righ t to left in $comp(w_1w_2)$, and
- $pebble\text{-}cross(comp(w_1w_2)) \stackrel{\triangle}{=}$ the sequence of storage states (in $S^+(n)$) when M crosses the boundary between w_1 and w_2 with the pebble in the finite control from left to right or from right to left in $comp(w_1w_2)$.

Of course, $pebble\text{-}cross(comp(w_1w_2))$ is a subsequence of $cross(comp(w_1w_2))$.

For each storage state s_i in $cross(comp(w_1w_2)) = s_1s_2\cdots s_i\cdots$, let

- $comp(w_1w_2)[-, s_i] \triangleq$ the sub-computation of $comp(w_1w_2)$ from the beginning of $comp(w_1w_2)$ to the moment of M crossing the boundary between w_1 and w_2 in storage state s_i, and
- $comp(w_1w_2)[s_i, -] \triangleq$ the sub-computation of $comp(w_1w_2)$ after the moment of M crossing the boundary between w_1 and w_2 in storage state s_i.

For any storage states s_i and $s_j (i < j)$ in $cross(comp(w_1w_2)) = s_1s_2\cdots s_i\cdots$, let

- $comp(w_1w_2)[s_i, s_j] \triangleq$ the sub-computation of $comp(w_1w_2)$ from the moment of M crossing the boundary between w_1 and w_2 in storage state s_i to the moment of M crossing again the boundary in storage state s_j.

For each $x \in P(n)$, xx is not in T_1, and so it must be rejected by M, and its length is $2n$. Therefore, it is easily seen that there exists an $L(2n)$ space-bounded rejecting computation of M on xx. Let "*recomp*(xx)" be such a fixed $L(2n)$ space-bounded rejecting computation of M on xx. It follows that the same storage state (in $S^+(n)$) appears at most five times in *pebble-cross*(*recomp*(xx)), because an $L(2n)$ space-bounded rejecting computation contains at most three same configurations. Therefore, the length of *pebble-cross*(*recomp*(xx)) is bounded by $5s^+(n)$. For each $n \gg 1$, let $PEBBLE\text{-}CROSS(n) = \{pebble\text{-}cross(recomp(xx)) | x \in P(n)\}$. From the observation above, it follows that $|PEBBLE\text{-}CROSS(n)| \leq (s^+(n))^{5s^+(n)}$. Since $L(n) = o(\log n)$, by a simple calculation, it follows that for large n, we have $|P(n)| \gg |PEBBLE\text{-}CROSS(n)|$. Thus, there must be two different words x and y in $P(n)$ such that *pebble-cross*(*recomp*(xx)) = *pebble-cross*(*recomp*(yy)). We below derive a contradiction by showing that a computation of M on xy which forces the word xy to be rejected can be constructed by combining *recomp*(xx) and *recomp*(yy), and thus xy would be rejected by M. We only consider the case where for some *odd* number $k \geq 1$,

(i) *pebble-cross*(*recomp*(xx)) = *pebble-cross*(*recomp*(yy)) = $s_1s_2\cdots s_k$ (each $s_i \in S^+(n)$),
(ii) $cross(recomp(xx)) = s^x_{01}s^x_{02}\cdots s^x_{0i_0}s_1s^x_{11}s^x_{12}\cdots s^x_{1i_1}s_2s^x_{21}s^x_{22}\cdots s^x_{2i_2}s_3 \cdots s_ks^x_{k1}s^x_{k2}\cdots s^x_{ki_k}$ ($i_0, i_1, \ldots, i_k \geq 0$, and each $s^x_{ij} \in S^-(n)$), and
(iii) $cross(recomp(yy)) = s^y_{01}s^y_{02}\cdots s^y_{0j_0}s_1s^y_{11}s^y_{12}\cdots s^y_{1j_1}s_2s^y_{21}s^y_{22}\cdots s^y_{2j_2}s_3 \cdots s_ks^y_{k1}s^y_{k2}\cdots s^y_{kj_k}$ ($j_0, j_1, \ldots, j_k \geq 0$, and each $s^y_{ij} \in S^-(n)$).

For other cases, a similar idea is used to derive a contradiction. Note that for each $w \in \{x, y\}$,

(i) in $recomp(ww)[-, s_1]$ and in $recomp(ww)[s_i, s_{i+1}]$ for each even number i, $2 \leq i \leq k-1$, the pebble is on the left segment $\cent w$ of the input $\cent ww\$$, and

(ii) in $recomp(ww)[s_i, s_{i+1}]$ for each odd number i, $1 \leq i \leq k-2$, and in $recomp(ww)[s_k, -]$, the pebble is on the right segment $w\$$ of the input $\cent ww\$$.

Since x and y are M-equivalent, it follows that we can construct a computation $comp(xy)$, which never enters any accepting state, of M on xy such that:

(i) $cross(comp(xy)) = s^x_{01}s^x_{02}\cdots s^x_{0i_0}s_1s^y_{11}s^y_{12}\cdots s^y_{1j_1}s_2s^x_{21}s^x_{22}\cdots s^x_{2i_2}s_3s^y_{31}$ $s^y_{32}\cdots s^y_{3j_3}s_4\cdots s_ks^y_{k1}s^y_{k2}\cdots s^y_{kj_k}$,

(ii) $pebble\text{-}cross(comp(xy)) = s_1s_2\cdots s_k$,

(iii) $comp(xy)[-, s^x_{01}] = recomp(xx)[-, s^x_{01}]$ ($comp(xy)[-, s_1] = recomp(xx)[-, s_1]$ if $i_0 = 0$), and

(iv) for each even number $l(0 \leq l \leq k-1)$,

 (a) $comp(xy)[s_l, s^x_{l1}] = recomp(xx)[s_l, s^x_{l1}]$ (where $l \neq 0$),

 (b) for each even number $r(2 \leq r \leq i_l - 1)$, $comp(xy)[s^x_{lr}, s^x_{l,r+1}] = recomp(xx)[s^x_{lr}, s^x_{l,r+1}]$,

 (c) $comp(xy)[s^x_{li_l}, s_{l+1}] = recomp(xx)[s^x_{li_l}, s_{l+1}]$, and

(v) for each odd number $l(1 \leq l \leq k)$,

 (a) $comp(xy)[s_l, s^y_{l1}] = recomp(yy)[s_l, s^y_{l1}]$,

 (b) for each even number $r(2 \leq r \leq j_l - 1)$, $comp(xy)[s^y_{lr}, s^y_{l,r+1}] = recomp(yy)[s^y_{lr}, s^y_{l,r+1}]$,

 (c) $comp(xy)[s^y_{lj_l}, s_{l+1}] = recomp(yy)[s^y_{lj_l}, s_{l+1}]$ (where $l \neq k$).

Note that since x and y are M-equivalent, it follows that

- for each even number $l(0 \leq l \leq k-1)$ and each odd number $r(1 \leq r \leq i_l - 1)$, $comp(xy)[s^x_{lr}, s^x_{l,r+1}]$ can be constructed owing to the fact that x and y are M^--equivalent, and for each odd number $l(1 \leq l \leq k)$ and each odd number $r(1 \leq r \leq j_l - 1)$, $comp(xy)[s^y_{lr}, s^y_{l,r+1}]$ can also be constructed owing to the fact that x and y are M^--equivalent,
- if $recomp(yy)$ is an $L(2n)$ space-bounded halting (resp., overflow) computation, then we can construct $comp(xy)[s^y_{kj_k}, -]$ ($comp(xy)[s_k, -]$ if $j_k = 0$) from $recomp(yy)[s^y_{kj_k}, -]$ ($recomp(yy)[s_k, -]$ if $j_k = 0$) so as for

comp(xy) to be an $L(2n)$ space-bounded halting (resp., overflow) computation, and

- if *recomp*(yy) is an $L(2n)$ space-bounded double-looping computation, then (i) we can construct *comp*(xy) so as for *comp*$(xy)[-, s^y_{kj_k}]$ (*comp*$(xy)[-, s_k]$ if $j_k = 0$) to have a loop, or (ii) we can construct *comp*$(xy)[s^y_{kj_k}, -]$ (*comp*$(xy)[s_k, -]$ if $j_k = 0$) from *recomp*$(yy)[s^y_{kj_k}, -]$ (*recomp*$(yy)[s_k, -]$ if $j_k = 0$) so as for *comp*(xy) to have a loop.

Clearly, this *comp*(xy) forces the input xy to be rejected by M, which contradicts the fact that xy is in T_1. This completes the proof of "$T_1 \notin$ *weak-USPACE*$^{peb}(o(\log n))$". □

From Theorems 1 and 2, we get the following theorem:

Theorem 3: For any $m \in \{strong, weak\}$ and any function $L(n)$ such that $\log\log n \leq L(n) = o(\log n)$, m-*USPACE*$^{peb}(L(n))$ is incomparable with 2-*DC*.

4. USPACE Versus ASPACE

This section investigates a relationship between the accepting powers of sublogarithmically space-bounded alternating one-pebble Tm's with only universal states and alternating one-pebble Tm's.

Lemma 1: *Let*

$$T_2 = \{B(1)\#B(2)\#\cdots\#B(n)cw_1cw_2c\cdots cw_kccu_1cu_2c\cdots cu_r \in \{0,1,c,\#\}^+ \\ |n \geq 2 \wedge k \geq 1 \wedge r \geq 1 \wedge \forall\, i(1 \leq i \leq k)[w_i \in \{0,1\}^{\lceil \log n \rceil}] \wedge \forall\, j(1 \leq \\ j \leq r)[u_j \in \{0,1\}^+] \wedge \exists\, l(1 \leq l \leq r)[\forall\, m(1 \leq m \leq k)[u_l \neq w_m]]\},$$

where for each positive integer i, $B(i)$ denotes the word over $\{0,1\}$ that represents the integer i in binary notation (with no leading zeros). Then,

(1) $T_2 \in$ *strong-ASPACE*$^{peb}(\log\log n)$, *and*
(2) $T_2 \notin$ *weak-USPACE*$^{peb}(L(n))$ *for any function* $\log\log n \leq L(n) = o(\log n)$

Proof: We first prove (1). T_2 is accepted by a strongly $\log\log n$ space-bounded alternating one-pebble Tm M which acts as follows. Suppose that an input string

$$\cent y_1\#y_2\#\cdots y_ncw_1cw_2c\cdots cw_kccu_1cu_2c\cdots cu_rc\$$$

(where $n \geq 2$, k, $r \geq 1$, and $y'_m s$, $w'_i s$, $u'_j s$ are all in $\{0,1\}^+$) is presented to M.(Input strings in the form different from the above can easily be rejected by M.) By using the well-known technique (see [5, Problem 10.2]), M first marks off $\log\log n$ cells of the storage tape when $y_m = B(m)$ for each $1 \leq m \leq n$. (Of course, M enters a rejecting state if $y_m \neq B(m)$ for some $1 \leq m \leq n$.)M then checks, by using $\log\log n$ cells of the storage tape,that $|w_1| = |w_2| = \cdots = |w_k| = \lceil \log n \rceil$. After that, M existentially chooses some l $(1 \leq l \leq r)$, puts the pebble on the symbol $'c'$ just before u_l, and universally checks that $u_l \neq w_m$ for each m $(1 \leq m \leq k)$. That is, for each $m(1 \leq l \leq r)$, in the mth universal branch, in order to check that $u_l \neq w_m$, M existentially stores some i_m $(1 \leq i_m \leq |w_m| = \lceil \log n \rceil)$ in binary notation on the storage tape, stores the i_mth symbol (from the left) of w_m in the finite control, and moves to the right until it meets the pebble (which is placed on the symbol $'c'$ just before u_l). Then, M picks up the i_mth symbol of u_l by using the integer i_m stored on the storage tape, and enters an accepting state only if the i_mth symbols of w_m and u_l are different. For these actions, $\log\log n$ cells of the storage tape are sufficient,and it is obvious that M accepts T_2.

We next prove (2). The proof is similar to that of "$T_1 \notin$ *weak-USPACE*$^{peb}(o(\log n))$" in the proof of Theorem 2. Suppose to the contrary that there is a weakly $L(n)$ space-bounded alternating one-pebble Turing machine with only universal states M which accepts T_2, where $L(n) = o(\log n)$. Let Q be the set of states of the finite control of M, and Q^+ and Q^- be defined as in the proof of Theorem 2. M starts from the initial state in Q^+ with the input head on the left endmarker ¢.

For each $n \geq 2$, let $V(n) = \{cw_1cw_2c\cdots cw_{p(n)}c | \forall\, i(1 \leq i \leq p(n))[w_i \in \{0,1\}^{\lceil \log n \rceil}]\}$, where $p(n) = 2^{\lceil \log n \rceil}$. For each $x = cw_1cw_2c\cdots cw_{p(n)}c \in V(n)$, let $contents(x) = \{u \in \{0,1\}^{\lceil \log n \rceil} | u = w_i \text{ for some } 1 \leq i \leq p(n)\}$. For any two words $x, y \in V(n)$, we say that x and y are *contents-equivalent* if $contents(x) = contents(y)$. Contents-equivalence is an equivalence relation on $V(n)$. There are $contents(n) = \binom{p(n)}{1} + \binom{p(n)}{2} + \cdots + \binom{p(n)}{p(n)} = 2^{p(n)} - 1$ contents-equivalence classes of $V(n)$. (Note that $contents(n)$ corresponds to the number of all the nonempty subsets of $\{0,1\}^{\lceil \log n \rceil}$.) We denote by $CONTENTS(n)$ the set of all the representatives, one for each contents-equivalence class, chosen arbitrarily. Of course, $|CONTENTS(n)| = contents(n)$. For each $n \geq 2$, let $W(n) = \{B(1)\#B(2)\#\cdots\#B(n)xy | x, y \in CONTENTS(n)\}$. Let $r(n)$ be the length of each word in $W(n)$. Note that $r(n) = O(n \log n)$. Below we consider the computations of M on words in

$W(n)$ for large n. Thus M uses at most $L(r(n))$ cells of the storage tape. For each $n \geq 2$, let $S(n)$ be the set of possible storage states of M using at most $L(r(n))$ cells of the storage tape, and let $S^+(n)$ and $S^-(n)$ be defined as in the proof of Theorem 2. Clearly $s^+(n) \triangleq |S^+(n)| = O(t^{L(r(n))})$, and $s(n) \triangleq |S(n)| = O(t^{L(r(n))})$ for some constant t depending only on M. Let x be a word in $CONTENTS(n)$ that is supposed to be a subword of an input word (in $W(n)$) to M. Suppose that the pebble of M is not placed on the string $\cent B(1)\#B(2)\#\cdots\#B(n)x$ (resp., $x\$$). Then, we define a mapping M_x^l (resp., M_x^r), which depends on M and x, from $S(n)$ to the power set of $S(n) \cup Q_{stop} \cup \{loop, overflow\}$ as in the proof of Theorem 2, except that "$\cent x$" is replaced by "$\cent B(1)\#B(2)\#\cdots\#B(n)x$". We say that two words x_1, $x_2 \in CONTENTS(n)$ are *M-equivalent* if two mappings $M_{x_1}^l$ and $M_{x_2}^l$ are equivalent, and two mappings $M_{x_1}^r$ and $M_{x_2}^r$ are equivalent. Clearly, M-equivalence is an equivalence relation on $CONTENTS(n)$, and there are at most $e(n) = (2^{s(n)+d+2})^{s(n)}$, where $d = |Q_{stop}|$, M-equivalence classes of $CONTENTS(n)$. Let $P(n)$ be a largest M-equivalence class of $CONTENTS(n)$. Then we have $|P(n)| \geq \frac{|CONTENTS(n)|}{e(n)} = \frac{contents(n)}{e(n)} \simeq \frac{2^{p(n)}}{e(n)}$. Note that by a simple calculation, we can easily see that $|P(n)| \gg 1$ for large n, because $L(n) = o(\log n)$. For each $x \in P(n)$, $B(1)\#B(2)\#\cdots\#B(n)xx$ is not in T_2, and in $W(n)$, and so it must be rejected by M, and its length is $r(n)$. Therefore, it is easily seen that there exists an $L(r(n))$ space-bounded rejecting computation of M on $B(1)\#B(2)\#\cdots\#B(n)xx$. Let "$recomp(xx)$" be such a fixed $L(r(n))$ space-bounded rejecting computation of M on $B(1)\#B(2)\#\cdots\#B(n)xx$, and let $pebble\text{-}cross(recomp(xx))$ be the sequence of storage states (in $S^+(n)$) when M crosses the boundary between the left x and the right x with the pebble in the finite control from left to right or from right to left in $recomp(xx)$. Furthermore, for each $n \gg 1$, let $PEBBLE\text{-}CROSS(n) = \{pebble\text{-}cross(recomp(xx)) | x \in P(n)\}$. "$L(n) = o(\log n)$" and an observation similar to that in the proof of "$T_1 \notin weak\text{-}USPACE^{peb}(o(\log n))$" (in the proof of Theorem 2) imply that for large n, $|P(n)| \gg |PEBBLE\text{-}CROSS(n)|$, and thus there must be two different words x and y in $P(n)$ such that $pebble\text{-}cross(recomp(xx)) = pebble\text{-}cross(recomp(yy))$. We assume without loss of generality that $contents(y) - contents(x) \neq \phi$. By using the same idea as in the proof of "$T_1 \notin weak\text{-}USPACE^{peb}(o(\log n))$", it follows that we can construct a computation which forces the word $B(1)\#B(2)\#\cdots\#B(n)xy$ to be rejected by M, which contradicts the fact that $B(1)\#B(2)\#\cdots\#B(n)xy$ is in T_2, because $contents(y) - contents(x) \neq \phi$. This completes the proof of "$T_2 \notin weak\text{-}USPACE^{peb}(o(\log n))$". □

From Lemma 1, we have the following theorem:

Theorem 4: For any function $\log\log n \leq L(n) = o(\log n)$ and for any $m \in \{strong, weak\}$, $m\text{-}USPACE^{peb}(L(n)) \subset m\text{-}ASPACE^{peb}(L(n))$.

5. Space Hierarchy

This section investigates a space hierarchy of the accepting powers of sublogarithmically space-bounded alternating one-pebble Tm's with only universal states.

Our main result of this section is:

Theorem 5: Let $L(n) : N \rightarrow N$ be a one-pebble fully space constructible function such that $L(n) \leq \log n (n \geq 1)$ and let $L'(n) : N \rightarrow N$ be any function such that $L'(n) = o(L(n))$. Then $strong\text{-}USPACE^{peb}(L(n))\text{-}weak\text{-}USPACE^{peb}(L'(n)) \neq \emptyset$.

Proof: Let $T(L) = \{wc^i w' | \ \exists\ n \geq 1[w, w' \in \{0,1\}^{2^{L(n)}} \wedge w \neq w' \wedge i = n - 2 \times 2^{L(n)}]\}$ be the language depending on the function $L(n)$ in the theorem. It is easy to show that $T(L)$ is in $strong\text{-}DSPACE^{peb}(L(n))$, and thus in $strong\text{-}USPACE^{peb}(L(n))$. On the other hand, by using an idea similar to that of the proof of "$T_1 \notin weak\text{-}USPACE^{peb}(o(\log n))$", we can show that "$T(L) \notin weak\text{-}USPACE^{peb}(L'(n))$" for $L'(n) = o(L(n))$. The proof is omitted here. □

From the fact (Fact 1) that $\lceil \log\log n \rceil$ is one-pebble fully space constractible, we can easily see that for any integer $k \geq 1$, $\lceil \log\log n \rceil^k$ is one-pebble fully space constractible. From this and from Theorem 5, we get the following corollary:

Corollary 1: *For any* $m \in \{strong, weak\}$ *and for any integer* $k \geq 1$, $m\text{-}USPACE^{peb}(\lceil \log\log n \rceil^k) \subset m\text{-}USPACE^{peb}(\lceil \log\log n \rceil^{k+1})$.

We can easily strengthen Theorem 5 as follows (the proof is omitted here):

Corollary 2: *Let* $L(n)$ *be a one-pebble space constractible function such that* $L(n) \leq \log n (n \geq 1)$, *and* $L'(n)$ *be any function such that* $L'(n) = o(L(n))$. *Then,* $strong\text{-}USPACE^{peb}(L(n))\text{-}weak\text{-}USPACE^{peb}(L'(n)) \neq \phi$.

6. Closure Property

This section investigates closure property of sublogarithmically space-bounded alternating one-pebble Tm's with only universal states.

It is easy to see that the following lemma holds, and so the proof is omitted here.

Lemma 2: *Let*

$$T_3 = \{B(1)\#B(2)\#\cdots\#B(n)cw_1cw_2c\cdots cw_kccu_1cu_2c\cdots cu_rc \in \{0,1,c,\#\}^+ \\ |n \geq 2 \wedge k \geq 1 \wedge r \geq 1 \wedge \forall\, i(1 \leq i \leq k)[w_i \in \{0,1\}^{\lceil \log n \rceil}] \wedge \\ \forall\, j(1 \leq j \leq r)[u_j \in \{0,1\}^+] \wedge \forall\, l(1 \leq l \leq k)[u_r \neq w_l]\},$$

$$T_4 = \{B(1)\#B(2)\#\cdots\#B(n)cw_1cw_2c\cdots cw_kcc_1u_1c_2u_2\cdots c_ru_rc \in \{0,1,c,d,\#\}^+ \\ |n \geq 2 \wedge k \geq 1 \wedge r \geq 1 \wedge \forall\, i(1 \leq i \leq k)[w_i \in \{0,1\}^{\lceil \log n \rceil}] \wedge \\ \forall\, j(1 \leq j \leq r)[u_r \in \{0,1\}^+] \wedge \exists\, l(1 \leq l \leq r)[c_l = d \wedge \forall\, m(1 \leq m \leq k) \\ [u_l \neq w_m] \wedge \forall\, p(1 \leq p \leq r, p \neq l)[c_p = c]]\},$$

$$T_5 = \{wc \in \{0,1,c\}^+ | w \in \{0,1\}^+\}^*,$$

and

$$T_6 = \{y_1\#y_2\#\cdots\#y_ncw_1cw_2c\cdots cw_kccu_1cu_2c\cdots cu_rc \in \{0,1,c,\#\}^+ |n \geq 2 \wedge \\ k, r \geq 1 \wedge \forall\, s(1 \leq s \leq n)\forall\, i(1 \leq i \leq k)\forall\, j(1 \leq j \leq r)[y_s, w_i, u_j \in \{0,1\}^+]\}.$$

Then, T_3, T_4, T_5, $T_3 \cup T_5$, and T_6 are all in strong-$DSPACE^{peb}(\log\log n)$ and thus in weak-$DSPACE^{peb}(\log\log n)$, strong-$USPACE^{peb}(L(n))$, and weak-$USPACE^{peb}(L(n))$.

From Lemmas 1(2) and 2, we can get the following theorem:

Theorem 6: For any function $\log\log n \leq L(n) = o(\log n)$, any $X \in \{D, U\}$, and any $m \in \{strong, weak\}$, m-$XSPACE^{peb}(L(n))$ is not closed under concatenation, Kleene closure, and length-preserving homomorphism.

Proof: Let T_2 be the language described in Lemma 1, and T_i, $i \in \{3,4,5,6\}$, be the languages described in Lemma 2.

Concatenation: Nonclosure under concatenation follows from the fact that $T_3T_5 = T_2$, and from Lemmas 1(2) and 2.

Kleene closure: It follows that $(T_3 \cup T_5)^* \cap T_6 = T_3T_5 = T_2$. From this, from Lemmas 1(2) and 2, and from the obvious fact that m-$XSPACE^{peb}(L(n))$ is closed under intersection for any $m \in$

$\{strong, weak\}$, any $X \in \{D, U\}$, and any function $L(n)$, nonclosure under Kleene closure follows.

Length-preserving homomorphism: Nonclosure under length-preserving homomorphism follows from Lemmas 1(2) and 2, and from the fact that $h(T_4) = T_2$, where $h : \{0, 1, c, d, \#\} \to \{0, 1, c, \#\}$ is a length-preserving homomorphism such that $h(0) = 0$, $h(1) = 1$, $h(\#) = \#$, $h(c) = h(d) = c$□

7. Conclusion

We conclude this paper by posing several open problems. Below, let $L(n)$ be any function such that $\log\log n \le L(n) = o(\log n)$.

(1) 2-*DC*-*weak* (or *strong*)-$ASPACE^{peb}(o(\log n)) = \emptyset$?

(2) For any $m \in \{strong, weak\}$:

- m-$DSPACE^{peb}(L(n)) \subset m$-$NSPACE^{peb}(L(n))$?
- m-$DSPACE^{peb}(L(n)) \subset m$-$USPACE^{peb}(L(n))$?
- What is a relationship between m-$NSPACE^{peb}(L(n))$ and m-$USPACE^{peb}(L(n))$?

(3) Let $L(n)$ be a one-pebble (fully) space constructible function and let $L'(n) = o(L(n))$. Then *strong*-$DSPACE^{peb}(L(n))$-*weak*-$ASPACE^{peb}(L'(n)) \neq \emptyset$?

(4) For any $m \in \{strong, weak\}$ and for any $X \in \{N, A\}$, is m-$XSPACE^{peb}(L(n))$ closed under concatenation, Kleene closure, and length-preserving homomorphism?

References

1. M. Blum and C. Hewitt, "Automata on a 2-dimensional tape", IEEE Symp. on Switching and Automata Theory, pp. 155–160, 1967.
2. A. K. Chandra, D. C. Kozen and L. J. Stockmeyer, "Alternation", J. Assoc. Comput. Mach., Vol. 28, No. 1, pp. 114–133, 1981.
3. J. H. Chang, O. H. Ibarra, M. A. Palis and B. Ravikumar, "On pebble automata", *Theoret. Comput. Sci. 44*, pp. 111–121, 1986.
4. Z. Galil, "Some open problems in the theory of computation as questions about two-way deterministic pushdown automata languages", Math. Systems Theory 10, pp. 211–228, 1977.
5. J. E. Hopcroft and J. D. Ullman, Introduction to Automata Theory, Languages and Computation, Addison-Wesley, Reading, MA, 1979.
6. A. Inoue, A. Ito, K. Inoue and T. Okazaki, "Some properties of one-pebble Turing machines with sublogarithmic space", ISAAC 2003, LNCS 2906, pp. 635–644, 2003.

7. T. Okazaki, L. Zhang, K. Inoue, A. Ito and Y. Wang, "A relationship between two-way deterministic one counter automata and one-pebble deterministic Turing machings with sublogarithmic space", IEICE Trans.INF. & SYST., Vol. E82-D, No. 5, pp. 999–1004, 1999.
8. A. Szepietowski, "Turing machines with sublogarithmic space", Lecture Notes in Computer Science 843, 1994.

CHAPTER 12

VERIFICATION OF CLOCK SYNCHRONIZATION IN TTP

K. Kalyanasundaram and R. K. Shyamasundar
School of Technology and Computer Science,
Tata Institute of Fundamental Research,
Mumbai 400 005, India
E-mail: {kalyan, shyam}@tcs.tifr.res.in

Time-triggered architectures are being widely deployed in safety-critical systems such as automotive systems. TTP and FlexRay are two widely used protocols for these applications. These protocols have much in common and are based on *a priori* fixed schedule of interaction of processes at known intervals of time and thus depend heavily on the correctness and tightness of clock synchronizations of the underlying processes. In this paper, we shall model TTP in LUSTRE — a widely used synchronous programming language and establish the correctness of the protocol. We have focussed our attention on establishing the correctness of clock synchronization properties such as bounded drift, precision and accuracy. Further, we show that the model enables us to establish bounds on clock drifts in processes other than that identified for clock synchronization in the TTP.

1. Introduction

Real-time computer control systems must process information reliably and in a timely manner. Most of these systems are distributed for reasons of performance and reliability. "Distributed real-time system"[6] as they are called, consist of a cluster of autonomous subsystems (also called "nodes") which collect critical information, and share it with other nodes in the cluster. There are fundamentally two paradigms for the design of such distributed systems — *Event-Triggered* architectures and *Time-Triggered* architectures. In event-triggered architectures, all system activities are initiated as a consequence of events that happen in the system. In time-triggered architectures, all activities are initiated by the progress of global time. The subsystems are triggered by individual clocks. The autonomous subsystems sample the events at *a priori* determined points in time, defined by their local clocks that must be synchronized in order to have a global time base for reliable communication. The reliability of these systems depends on fault-tolerant clock synchronization, which is provided by the underlying communication protocol. The Time-Triggered Protocol (TTP)[7] is an integrated communication protocol for time-triggered architectures, providing many tightly integrated services, including fault-tolerant clock synchronization. TTP differs from other communication protocols in the sense that there are no special acknowledgment and synchronization messages.

There has been an immense interest in time-triggered architectures, as a methodology for the design of safety-critical systems, due to its applications in the automotive industry. FlexRay[19] and TTP/C[1] are two prominent protocols in this context. As mentioned already, clock synchronization plays a crucial role in both these protocols to achieve fault-tolerance. Clock synchronization and issues of fault-tolerance have been widely studied in literature.[8,13–18] Clock synchronization as relevant to TTP has been studied in Refs. 2, 3, 4 and 7. In Ref. 2, the authors have established correctness of clock synchronization as used in TTP using the theorem prover PVS. In Ref. 12, the authors provide a methodology of using the industrial programming environment SCADE of LUSTRE along with SIMULINK for generating code for distributed embedded applications. In this paper, we use the synchronous approach for the modelling and verification of TTP.

The contributions of the paper are summarized below:

(1) Modelling and verification of TTP
   - Specifically, clock synchronization properties like bounded drift, precision and accuracy have been established through the verification environment.
   - Function of *Bus Guardian* is also established.

(2) Arriving at a bound on the clock drift of non-accurate clocks through the simulation environment SIM2CHRO of LUSTRE.

Establishing (2) through the integrated environment is advantageous as that enables one to arrive at a true bound on the drift of a non-accurate clock in a cluster. Note that as the bound on the drifts has a bearing on the cost of the system, it is one of the strong points for modelling and analyzing using LUSTRE. It may further be noted that the model is parameterized

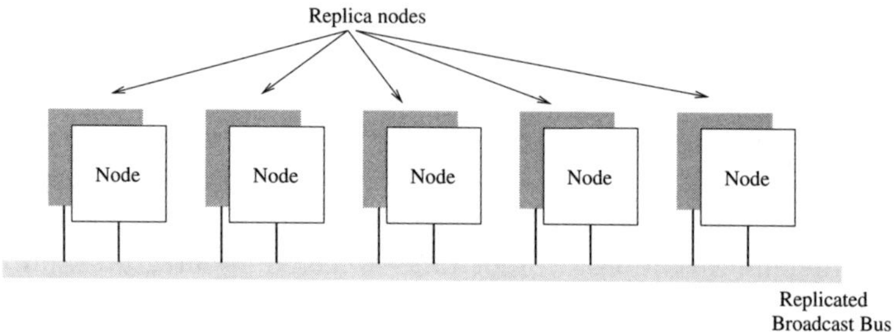

Fig. 1. TTA — Nodes and the broadcast bus.

in such a manner that it can be easily adapted for different number of processes, clock drifts as well as TDMA cycles.

Rest of the paper is organized as follows: Section 2 gives an introduction to TTP. Modelling of TTP in LUSTRE is given in Section 3. The properties of clock synchronization and verification of the same forms the subject of Section 4. The paper ends with a discussion in Section 5.

2. Time-Triggered Protocol

Time-triggered systems consist of a number of autonomous subsystems ("processes" or "nodes"), communicating with each other through a broadcast bus, as shown in Fig. 1. As the name suggests, the system activities are triggered by the progress of time as measured by a local clock in each node. Each node in the system is alloted time-slots to send messages over the bus. These time-slots are determined by a Time Division Multiple Access (TDMA) scheme, which is pre-compiled into each node in the cluster. In each node, the TDMA schedule is embedded in a structure called *MEssage Descriptor List (MEDL)*, which has global information pertaining to all the nodes in the cluster. Thus, the system behaviour is known to all the nodes in the cluster.

Each time-slot determined by TDMA can be visualized to consist of two phases — the *communication phase* during which a node sends message over the bus, and the *computation phase* during which each node changes its internal state (i.e., updates the values of the state variables); the duration of these phases are denoted by *comm_phase* and *comp_phase* respectively, as shown in Fig. 2. These phases roughly correspond to the "receive window", during which a node awaits a message, and the "inter-frame gap" during which there is silence on the bus, respectively.

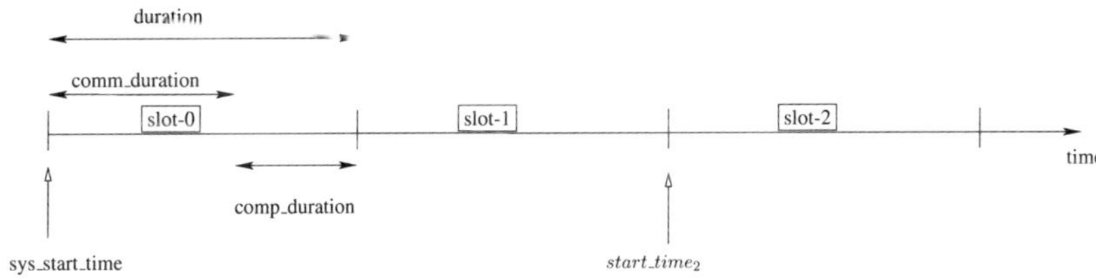

Fig. 2. Communication slots in a TTA.

The Time-Triggered Protocol (TTP) is the heart of the communication mechanism in time-triggered systems. Each node sends a message over the bus during its alloted time-slot, while the remaining nodes listen to the bus waiting for the message, for a specified period of time, the *receive window*. Since the system behaviour is known to all the nodes (through MEDL), there are no special acknowledgment messages sent on successful receipt of a message, and the arrival of the message during the corresponding "receive window" of a node itself suffices to consider the sending node as active. A complete round during which every node has had access to the bus once is called a *TDMA round*. After a TDMA round is completed, the same communication pattern is repeated over and over again. TTP uses clock synchronization, and *Bus Guardian* to achieve a robust fault-tolerant system. We shall delve into these aspects below.

2.1. *Clock synchronization*

Each node in TTP initiates activities according to its own physical clock, implemented by a crystal oscillator and a discrete counter. As no two crystal oscillators resonate with exactly the same frequency, the clocks of the nodes drift apart. Since the system activities crucially depend on time, it is important that the clocks of the nodes are synchronized enough so that the nodes agree on the given time-slot and access the bus at appropriate times to send messages. TTP uses an averaging algorithm for clock correction and it is different from other synchronization algorithms in the sense that there are no special synchronization messages involved. The drift of a particular node's clock is measured by the delay in the arrival of the message from the expected arrival time. Further, such time deviations for computing the average are collected from only four *a priori* determined nodes in the cluster, (in a sense, these four are the most accurate clocks) even if the cluster consists of more than four nodes.

Clock synchronization is the key issue of reliability in any time-triggered architecture. It is the task of the clock synchronization algorithms to compute the adjustments for the clocks and keep them in agreement with other nodes' clocks, in order to guarantee reliable communication, even in the presence of faulty nodes in the cluster. Since there are no explicit acknowledgment messages sent on receipt of a message by a node, it is very likely that the fault propagates in the cluster during message transfer.

TTP uses Fault-Tolerant Average (FTA) algorithm, an *averaging algorithm*,[a] for clock correction. Averaging algorithms typically operate by collecting clock deviations from the nodes and computing their average to be the correction for the individual clocks. In TTP the clock deviations are collected only from an ensemble of four *a priori* known clocks of high quality resonators. So, in the minimal configuration, it requires at least four nodes in order to tolerate a single Byzantine fault $((3m+1); m=1)$. The timing deviations of the messages from the expected arrival time are stored only if the *SYF* Flag (for *SYnchronization Frame*) is set in the MEDL for the particular slot. These flags are set when the sending node is one among the four nodes whose clock readings are used for correction. If the *CS* Flag (for *Clock Synchronization*) is set for a particular slot, then the clock correction is computed by applying FTA on the time deviations collected. In short, the clock synchronization operates as follows:

(1) If *SYF* flag is set for the current slot, the time difference value is stored in the node.
(2) If *CS* flag is set for the current slot, the FTA is applied, correction factor computed and the clock is corrected.

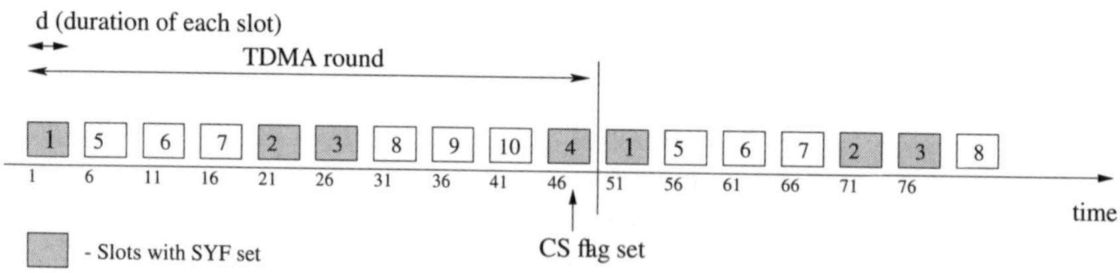

Fig. 3. TDMA round.

[a] *Non-averaging* algorithms operate by applying a fixed adjustment to clock values and *averaging algorithms* apply varying adjustments at fixed intervals. TTP uses FTA and FlexRay uses FTM (Fault-Tolerant Midpoint) algorithm which are averaging algorithms.

Consider a TTP cluster with ten nodes and communication pattern shown in Fig. 3. Here, there are four slots per TDMA round with *SYF* flag set. In TTP, the clocks are corrected only when four time difference values are obtained, i.e., when there are at least four slots with the *SYF* flag set. In this case, the clock will be corrected during the tenth slot, when the *CS* flag is set.

2.2. *Bus guardian*

Due to cost considerations, clocks with low quality resonators are also used in time-triggered systems. Due to the presence of such non-accurate clocks, the clock readings of the nodes in the system are not uniform. Since the nodes access the bus at particular time as read by their individual clocks, the varying clock drifts may lead to a disturbance in the schedule. To prevent a node from sending messages out of its turn, the bus interface is guarded by a *Bus Guardian*, that has independent information about the system and gives access to the nodes only at appropriate times. It plays an important role in maintaining the correct schedule for communication in the system. The TTP, besides fault-tolerant clock synchronization, also offers other tightly integrated services like group membership, redundancy management, etc.

The main characteristics of TTP are summarized below:

(1) The communication is through TDMA scheme which is pre-compiled into every node in the cluster.
(2) The system behaviour is known to all the nodes in the cluster and hence there are no special acknowledgment messages.
(3) The clock synchronization provided by TTP (using Fault-Tolerant Average or FTA algorithm) differs from other synchronization algorithms, as there are no separate synchronization messages involved.
(4) The time deviations from only four clocks in the cluster is considered for computing clock correction. These deviations are collected during slots where the *SYF* flag is set.
(5) The FTA algorithm is used to compute the correction factor for the clocks during slots where the *CS* flag is set.
(6) TTP guarantees reliable operation in the presence of at most one faulty node in the cluster.

3. Modelling TTP in lustre

We consider a TTP cluster with a fixed set of nodes, say ten[b] for the sake of simplicity. Let the communication pattern in the TDMA cycle be as shown in Fig. 3. The shaded slots indicate the slots where the *SYF* flag is set and the numbers inside the boxes indicate the node that is participating in the particular slot. In this model, during each slot, a node k sends a message, while the remaining $(10 - k)$ nodes (all assumed to be active), listen to the bus waiting for the message. The slots are equally divided, and when every node has had access to the bus once, the communication pattern is repeated again, as shown in Fig. 3. As highlighted already, clock synchronization is the crux of TTP; our modelling of TTP in LUSTRE will also confine to this aspect.

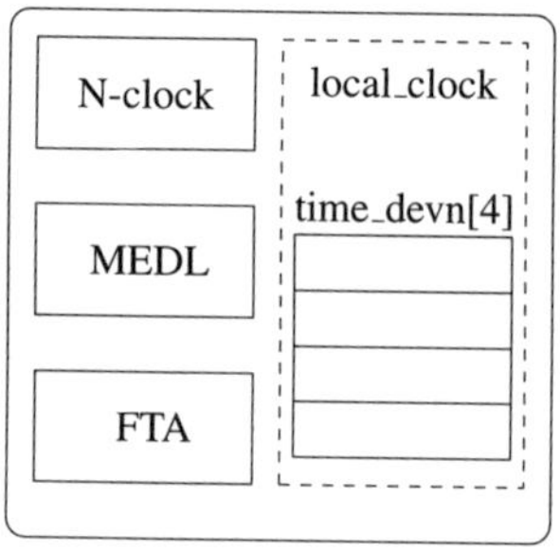

Fig. 4. Structure of a TTP node.

Each TTP node will have a structure shown in Fig. 4. The items inside the dotted box in Fig. 4 are derived during the communication process. We shall use the following data structure for a TTP Node:

- Two counters $(node\_clock)_k$ and $(local\_clock)_k$, which denote the physical clock, and the corresponding adjusted physical clock of node k.
- A counter $(slot\_count)_k$ that maintains the number of the current slot.
- An array $(timedevn)_k$ of size four for storing the time difference values.
- A variable $(clock\_correction)_k$ for storing the correction value of the current slot or the most recent slot.

and the following functions:

[b]We have experimented using a cluster of 25 nodes. In automotive applications, which this is intended for, the number of ECUs is roughly around this value.

(1) N-clock — It is a simple counter that takes the increment rate for the clock as input and generates clock with the increment rate as drift rate. By using different increment values, clocks of varying drift rates can be generated.
(2) FTA — this implements the Fault-Tolerant Average algorithm, which is used for clock correction. It takes four time deviation values, and computes their average, after ignoring the maximum and minimum deviations.
(3) MEDL — this maintains the TDMA schedule for each node. By fixing the duration of each slot, duration of a TDMA round, and the number of nodes, it simulates the repeating behaviour of the TDMA. It takes the drift rate of the corresponding node as input and generates the schedule for the node.

Each of the above functions is described in detail below.

3.0.1. *N-clock*

In order to simulate TTP nodes, we need to generate clocks with different drift rates. The module `N-clock` is an initialized counter with an increment value and a "reset" parameter, which is set to "false". The increment value can be changed to obtain clocks with different rates. The corresponding LUSTRE code is given in Table 1.

Table 1. N-clock module.

```
const init=1.0; -- initial value of the clock
const incr= x;  -- increment rate for the counter
node N-clock(in: real) returns (lc: real);
let
        lc = COUNTER(init,incr,false);
tel
```

3.0.2. *Fault-Tolerant Average (FTA) algorithm*

TTP uses FTA, an averaging algorithm for computing clock correction. It operates by computing the average of four time deviation values collected during a TDMA round. The algorithm makes periodic adjustments to the physical clocks of the nodes to keep them sufficiently close to each other. Let $(local\_clock)_k$ denote the adjusted physical clock of node k, $LC_k(t)$, its reading at time t and adj_i, the clock correction made during slot i of

TDMA round, we have

$$LC_k(t) = PC_k(t) + adj_i \tag{1}$$

In a TDMA round of n slots, for each node k with a local clock reading LC_k, and for slots i $(1 \leq i \leq n)$:

$$(timedevn)_k[1..4] = \begin{cases} [(LC_k - LC_p^i) & \text{if } SYF_i = \text{true} \\ [pre((LC_k - LC_p^i)) & \text{if } SYF_i = \text{false} \end{cases}$$

where LC_p^i is the clock reading of sending node p that is active during slot i when SYF flag is set, and $pre(x)$ denotes the previous value of x. Now, if the CS flag is set for a particular slot i, for a node k, the clock correction in the current TDMA round denoted $clock\_correction_k$ is given by:

$$\begin{aligned} clock\_correction_k = &\left(\left(\sum_{i=1}^{4} timedevn\right)_k [i]\right) \\ &- \max(timedevn)_k - \min(timedevn)_k/2) \\ &\text{if } CS_i = \text{true} \end{aligned} \tag{2}$$

where $\max(timedevn)_k$ and $\min(timedevn)_k$ denote the maximum and minimum values of the array $(timedevn)_k$ of time deviation values. These new values of the local clocks will be used by the nodes for further communication. The corresponding LUSTRE code given in Table 2 shows the averaging algorithm for tolerating "`f`" faults. TTP can be considered as a special case where `f` equals "1", since it can tolerate at most one Byzantine fault.

Table 2. The FTA module.

```
const k=4;   -- Number of time difference values
const f=1;  -- Number of faults to be tolerated

node FTA (time_diff: real^k) returns (avg_devn: real);
var NF,NFMIN: real^f;

let
   NF[0..(f-1)]=MAXFINDER(time_diff);
   NFMIN[0..(f-1)]=MINFINDER(time_diff);
   avg_devn = (TOTAL(k,time_diff)
- (with f>1 then TOTALNEW(fi,NF[0..(f-1)])
-             else NF[0])
- (with f>1 then TOTALNEW(fi,NFMIN[0..(f-1)])
-             else NFMIN[0]))/(k-2*f);
tel
```

where TOTAL returns the sum of k time deviation values, and MINFINDER and MAXFINDER are functions that return the minimum and maximum values of the arguments.

3.0.3. *MEssage Descriptor List (MEDL)*

MEDL contains the TDMA schedule information of all the nodes in the cluster, like sending times of the node, the identity of the sending node and the slots where *SYF* flags are set. The corresponding LUSTRE module is given in Table 3. S (a, b) is true when a and b do not differ by more than a particular value, that characterizes the drift. R_STABLE (n, x) is a function that sustains the true value of n for x time units. This x may be considered as the "receive window" of the node.

Table 3. MEDL module.

```
--      sc       - counter maintaining slot number
--      tx_time  - sending time of the nodes in the cluster
--      dc       - counter maintaining the duration of each TDMA slot
--  i1,i2,i3,i4 - slots where SYF flag is set
const init=1.0; - initial value of the counters used
const no=4;     - number of nodes with good clocks
const tn=10.0;  - total number of nodes
const t=5.0;    - duration of each slot
const mx=tn*t;  - duration of TDMA round
const i1=1.0; const i2=5.0; const i3=6.0; const i4=10.0;

node MEDL(incr: real) returns (syf_: bool;count: int);
var     bs, sc, dc, j, tx_time, ock, nc: real;
        reset, reset_1, reset_2: bool;

let
    nc = 0.0 -> COUNTER(init,incr,pre nc >= mx);
    j = 1.0 -> if pre ock >= mx then pre j + 1.0
                else pre j;
    tx_time = mx*(j-1.0) + [t*(sc-1.0)] + 2.0;
    dc   = COUNTER(init,1.0,pre(dc=t));
    sc   = NEWCOUNTER(init,incr,false -> pre(dc)=t,reset_1);
    ock  = COUNTER(init,incr,pre(ock>=mx));
    bs   = NEWCOUNTER(init,incr,false -> pre(ock)=mx,reset);
    syf_ = R_STABLE((S(sc,i1) or S(sc,i2) or S(sc,i3) or
                    S(sc,i4)) and dc=1.0,1.0);
    count = INT_NEWCOUNTER(0,1,xedge(not syf_),reset_2);
    reset = pre(bs) >=tn and pre(ock)>=mx;
    reset_1 = pre(sc) >= tn and pre(dc)=t;
    reset_2 = false -> pre ock>=mx;
tel
```

The modules defined above can be used to model a TTP Node. The corresponding LUSTRE module for a TTP node is given in Table 4. The module NODE can be instantiated using different values for inc (drift rate) to simulate nodes in a cluster. For example,

Table 4. LUSTRE module for a TTP node.

```
--      nc                 -- node_clock
--      sc                 -- slot counter
const no = 4;             -- Number of accurate clocks
const tn = 10.0;          -- Total number of nodes
const t  = 5.0;           -- Duration of a TDMA slot
const mx = n*t;           -- Duration of a TDMA round
const init = 1.0;
const inc1 = 1.0;         --
const inc2 = 1.0004;      -- inc1..inc4 are the drift rates of the four
const inc3 = 1.002;       -- accurate clocks in the cluster
const inc4 = 1.00001; --
node NODE(inc: real) returns (local_clk: real; avg: real);
var    d:real^no; k: int;
        nc, x, j, y, sc, dc: real;
        syf, cs, reset_1: bool;

let
        nc = COUNTER(init,inc,pre nc >= mx);
        y  = COUNTER(init,1.0,pre y = mx);
        dc = COUNTER(init,1.0,pre(dc=t));
        sc = NEWCOUNTER(init,inc,false -> pre(dc)=t,reset_1);
        j  = 1.0 -> if pre nc >= mx then pre j + 1.0
                      else pre j;
        x = mx*(j-1.0) + [t*(sc-1.0)] + 2.0;
        (syf,k) = MEDL(inc);
        cs = (k=4);
        d[0] = 0.0 -> if (syf and k=1) then (nc - N-clock(inc1))
                        else pre d[0];
        d[1] = 0.0 -> if (syf and k=2) then (nc - N-clock(inc2))
                        else pre d[1];
        d[2] = 0.0 -> if (syf and k=3) then (nc - N-clock(inc3))
                        else pre d[2];
        d[3] = 0.0 -> if (syf and k=4) then (nc - N-clock(inc4))
                        else pre d[3];
        reset_1 = pre(sc) >= tn and pre(dc)=t;
        avg = 0.0 -> if k=4 then FTA(d)  else pre avg;
        local_clk = nc -> if cs then nc + a  else nc;
tel
```

```
(Node_One, avg_1) = NODE(1.00);
(Node_Two, avg_2) = NODE(1.02);
```

Simulations of TTP:

A snapshot of the simulation of TTP consisting of ten nodes using SIM2CHRO is shown in Fig. 5. In the figure, $l\_1, \ldots, l\_9$ indicate the local clock readings of the ten nodes. Here, the ten nodes were simulated assuming a drift rate of 1.0 for the non-faulty nodes (nine of them) and a drift rate of 1.04 for the faulty node (node 6 with clock reading l_6). We can see that at the end of the TDMA round, the clock l_6 deviates from the rest by a factor of around 2.0 units.

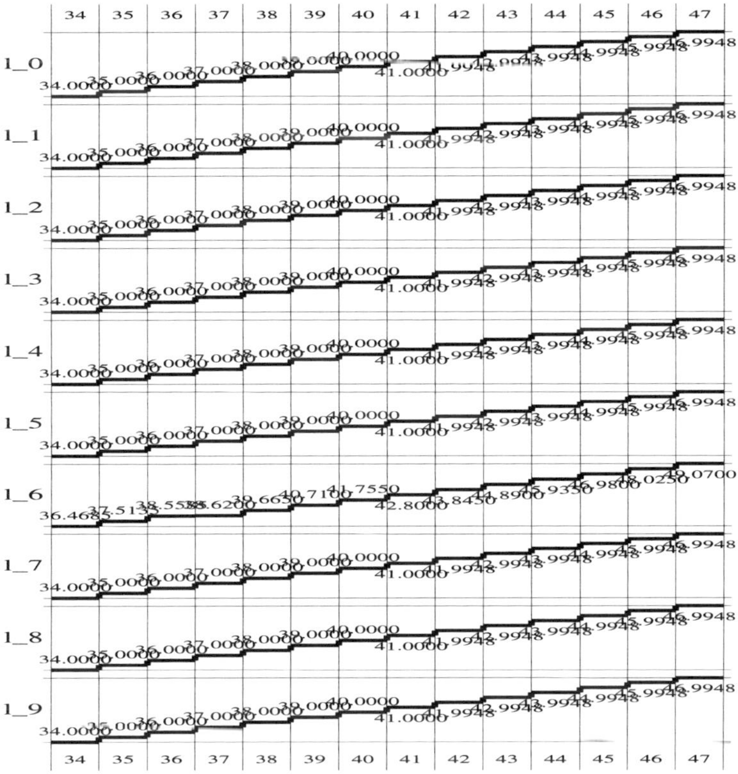

Fig. 5. Screen shot of a simulation run.

4. Verification of TTP

In this section, we establish the correctness of TTP with reference to clock synchronization and drifts. Before going into the details of verification, we shall formally describe clock synchronization and drift properties as highlighted in Ref. 2 required to be satisfied and provide a brief overview of the proof technique used.

4.1. *Clock synchronization properties*

The most trivial property that one would like to verify in synchronization algorithms is to check if the deviation of the clock readings fall within permissible limit, and that the algorithm manages to maintain it within permissible limits even in the presence of faulty clocks. A pair of clocks is said to be synchronized if their drifts are bound by a certain limit before and after the synchronization interval. Our requirement is that the synchronization algorithms keep the clocks synchronized even in the presence of faulty clocks in the cluster. Note that TTP permits at most one fault. Naturally, we need to show that there is bounded drift among clocks. As in Ref. 2, we can say that this property is satisfied if the physical clocks stay within an envelope of real time. In other words, for each non-faulty clock with clock reading PC_k, let ρ be the maximum drift rate, and $PC_k(t_1)$ and $PC_k(t_2)$ be the clock readings at t_1 and t_2 ($t_2 > t_1$). Then the bounded drift is given by:

$$\lfloor (t_2 - t_1)/(1+\rho) \rfloor \leq PC_k(t_2) - PC_k(t_1) \leq \lceil (t_2 - t_1)(1+\rho) \rceil \qquad (3)$$

As in TTP, we deal with local clocks during synchronization, rather than physical clocks, the above property can be formulated by the following properties, namely, agreement, precision and accuracy.

(1) **Agreement of local clocks:**
Let $LC_i(t)$ and $LC_j(t)$ be the local clock readings of nodes i and j at time t. Then, this corresponds to showing that at any point in the TDMA round and for any pair of clocks i and j that are non-faulty, the skew between the local clocks is bounded by a small positive value denoted ρ_{max}.

$$|LC_i(t) - LC_j(t)| \leq \rho_{\max} \qquad (4)$$

(2) **Precision enhancement:**
In TTP, FTA algorithm is applied and the clock is corrected at regular intervals defined by CS flag. Naturally, the physical clocks of the nodes will start drifting apart after the synchronization period is over. This property is a formalization of the concept that after the correction of the clocks, the clock values should be close together, i.e, within a known bound. This can be verified by checking that the time difference values collected by a TTA node during a TDMA round fall within a suitable bound. Naturally, the average of the time difference values will also obey this bound. It is now required to verify that the average value of the time differences, i.e., the correction factor of two nodes do not differ by more than a specified amount (See equation 2). Let $clock\_correction_i$ denote the correction factor for node i and let β denote the upper bound for correction factors. Then,

$$|\ clock\_correction_k - clock\_correction_l| \leq \beta \qquad (5)$$

(3) **Accuracy preservation:**
This property formalizes the notion that there should be a bound on the correction factor applied for any single node during the synchronization interval. Intuitively, this requires that the time difference values collected during any TDMA round are bound by a constant γ, which implies that their average (as computed by the FTA algorithm) would also be bound by the same constant γ. Formally, for a node k, during any synchronization interval,

$$clock\_correction_k \leq \gamma \tag{6}$$

If the above mentioned properties are satisfied, then it means that the clock readings are such that the schedule is not disturbed, and the clocks agree on each other's value during communication (i.e. synchronized). In the following section, we shall look at the verification methodology that we will use for establishing the above mentioned properties.

4.2. *Observer based verification*

An *observer*[9] is a LUSTRE program which takes as input, the main program and a safety property Ψ that is to be verified, and emits a boolean output *alarm* if the program violates the property Ψ at a precise step (trace). The observer and the main program access the same set of signals. The basic structure of an observer is given in Fig. 6. In this set up, instead of proving the property Ψ about the main program, we prove that the observer for the property Ψ, working in parallel with the main program does not emit an alarm. This scheme works only for finite traces. If we can establish that we need to consider only a finite set of traces for the property we are trying to prove, this technique leads to verification. For infinite traces, there are other techniques which we will not describe here. In the following section,

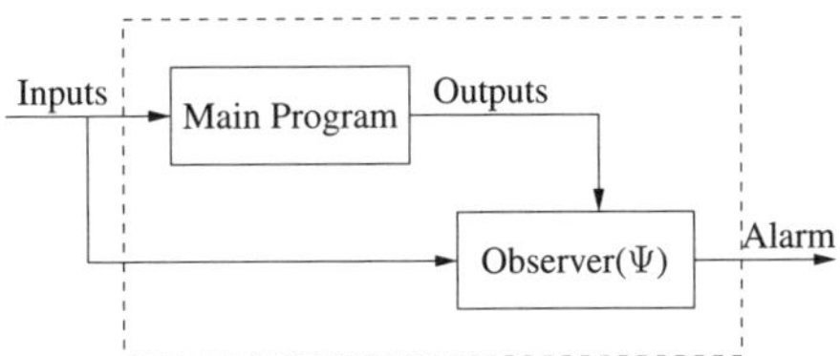

Fig. 6. Verification using an observer.

we shall see how to use the technique of observers to establish the properties of clock synchronization.

4.3. *Verification of clock synchronization properties*

Since TTP tolerates at most one fault, *a priori* we need to identify four clocks that will provide clock synchronization for the distributed control. In view of this, let us consider a TTP model in its minimum configuration, that consists of only four nodes, one of which is faulty, and a TDMA schedule shown in Fig. 7. As highlighted already, we need to construct observers for properties (1), (2) and (3). Observers for these properties are shown in Tables 5–7 respectively. Now, when the LUSTRE model for TTP cluster is run in parallel with these observers, it will emit an *alarm* signal if any of the properties are violated. Now the question is, how long should we run the model in parallel with the observers. From the fact that TTP uses a static schedule and all the clocks are synchronized simultaneously in every TDMA round, (note that initially, the properties are satisfied by the local clocks) only when the *CS* flag is set, it can be shown that testing for one TDMA round is sufficient. Due to lack of space, we shall not delve into technical details on this aspect. Thus, through simulation of the program through observers for one TDMA round, the correctness of the properties follows:

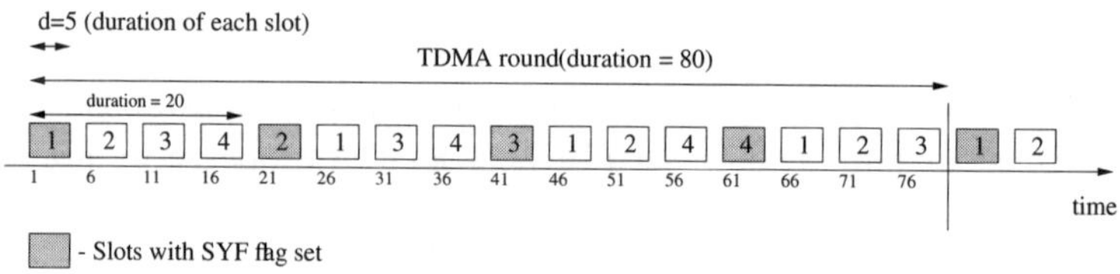

Fig. 7. TDMA Schedule

The observers corresponding to *Precision Enhancement* and *Accuracy Preservation* are given in Tables 6 and 7 respectively. Here again, for the same reasons as above, it is sufficient to consider only a single TDMA round for establishing the property. Since the traces are finite, this technique of using observers leads to a verification of the properties specified.

Table 5. Observer for verifying *Boundedness.*

```
const rho_ = -2.0;
const rho = 2.0;
node Observer_Property_Boundedness (start: bool)
                                   returns (alarm: bool);
var     avg, clk: real^4;

let
   (clk[0], avg[0]) = NODE(inc1);
   (clk[1], avg[1]) = NODE(inc2);
   (clk[2], avg[2]) = NODE(inc3);
   (clk[3], avg[3]) = NODE(inc4);
   alarm = false ->
             (rho_ >= (clk[0]-clk[1]) or (clk[0]-clk[1]) >= rho) or
             (rho_ >= (clk[1]-clk[2]) or (clk[1]-clk[2]) >= rho) or
             (rho_ >= (clk[2]-clk[3]) or (clk[2]-clk[3]) >= rho) or
             (rho_ >= (clk[3]-clk[1]) or (clk[3]-clk[1]) >= rho);
tel
```

Table 6. Observer for verifying *precision.*

```
const beta_ = -1.5;
const beta = 1.5;
node Observer_Property_Precision (start: bool) returns (alarm: bool);
var     avg, clk: real^4;

let
   (clk[0], avg[0]) = NODE(inc1);
   (clk[1], avg[1]) = NODE(inc2);
   (clk[2], avg[2]) = NODE(inc3);
   (clk[3], avg[3]) = NODE(inc4);
   alarm = false ->
         (beta_ >= (avg[0]-avg[1]) or (avg[0]-avg[1]) >= beta) or
         (beta_ >= (avg[1]-avg[2]) or (avg[1]-avg[2]) >= beta) or
         (beta_ >= (avg[2]-avg[3]) or (avg[2]-avg[3]) >= beta) or
         (beta_ >= (avg[3]-avg[1]) or (avg[3]-avg[1]) >= beta);
tel
```

Table 7. Observer for verifying *accuracy.*

```
const gamma_ = -1.5;
const gamma = 1.5;
node Observer_Property_Accuracy (start: bool) returns (alarm: bool);
var     avg, clk: real;

let
        (clk, avg) = NODE(incr);
        alarm = false -> (gamma_ >= clk or clk >= gamma);
tel
```

4.4. *Impact of clock-drifts*

Previously, we verified clock synchronization by fixing the drift rates of clocks in the cluster. This may be useful to verify an already existing system. But, for designing a new system, a number of factors have to be taken into account, like cost, reliability of the system, criticality of the application, etc. As system reliability is directly proportional to cost, in order to arrive at a balance between cost and system reliability, we should be able to choose the clocks that will be both economical and suit system requirements. As we are using an integrated simulation and verification environment, this is done by simulating the system for various values of clock drifts, and choosing the one that best suits system needs while still being of low-quality and hence economical.

For purposes of illustration, consider an example. Let us use simulation techniques to find out the maximum drift that a faulty clock can have in order not to create conflicts in the schedule. Consider the TTP model given in Fig. 3. Although only the time deviations from only four clocks are considered for clock correction, the remaining clocks in the cluster if not corrected sufficiently, can create conflicts in the TDMA schedule. All the nodes in the cluster correct their clocks when *CS* flag is set for the particular slot (here, tenth slot). Now, if we assume the fifth node to be a faulty node, it can drift at a much faster rate than the other clocks in the cluster, and by the time the tenth slot is reached, when it is supposed to correct its clock, it would be far ahead in time and will fail to collect the clock deviation during the appropriate slot, and consequently lead to a conflict in the schedule. This scenario is prevented by having a check on the maximum limit up to which a clock can drift during a TDMA round.

Now, while simulating the system, the drift rate of the faulty clock can be varied to see how bad drift rates could be accommodated in a given TDMA schedule. Let us now set the precision β to 2.0, and vary the drift rate of the faulty clock[c] to see till what value of drift, the system satisfies the desired value, and tabulate the results as shown in Table 8. A snapshot of the simulation is shown in Fig. 5.

From the tabulated figures, we see that if we have a drift that exceeds 1.04, we cannot achieve the desired precision, and that we can tolerate a drift up to 1.04, in order to achieve β of 2.0. This approach of formal verification followed by simulation is useful for practicing engineers in order to fine-tune the model for the desired parameters.

[c]The nodes were simulated with drift rate of 1.0 for all the non-faulty clocks and the drift rate of the faulty clock was varied from 1.002 to 1.045.

Table 8. Fine-tuning the precision.

Drift rate	Precision obtained
1.002	0.1212
1.02	0.9652037
1.05	>2.25
1.04	1.885
1.045	2.07

4.5. *Verification of bus-guardian*

Further, time-triggered architectures also have a "bus-guardian" that has independent information about the TDMA schedule, and it allows access to the nodes only during its corresponding time slots. When a node tries to access a slot that does not belong to it, the bus-guardian raises an "alarm" and the corresponding fault is handled using hardware or software means. The Bus Guardian is required to have independent information and does not depend on the clocks of the individual nodes, so that its role is not hampered by clock drifts. The property of the Bus Guardian is verified as a part of the schedule.

In addition to the properties mentioned above, there are other properties pertaining to the redundant nodes and membership, which are not required for the purposes of verification of clock synchronization. We have thus established the correctness of TTP with respect to clock synchronization using the integrated verification and simulation environment of LUSTRE.

5. Discussion

In this paper, we have modelled TTP using LUSTRE and have verified the clock synchronization properties. Further, we have shown that the model enables us to arrive at bounds on clock drifts of processes other than that identified for clock synchronization in TTP. In our opinion, this is advantageous, as this would have a bearing on the cost of the system, as cost of a process is dependent on the accuracy of the clocks demanded. Our experience shows that the dataflow aspect of LUSTRE, together with the integrated simulation and verification environment, provides a rich environment for the design of such complex systems. As highlighted in Ref. 9, assumptions about the environment can also be used while generating validated code. For communication architectures such as FlexRay that involve a mixture of time-triggered as well as event-triggered architectures, we need a unified modelling framework like *Multiclock* ESTEREL[20,21] that can model both synchronous as well as asynchronous tasks.

Acknowledgments

We thank Motorola for their support through the Motorola University Partnership in Research (UPR) Program. Thanks go to Dr. Srinivasa Nagaraja of Motorola for the encouragement and support.

References

1. Time-Triggered Protocol TTP/C, High-Level Specification Document, Protocol Version 1.1, www.tttech.com.
2. H. Pfeifer, D. Schwier and F. W. von Henke, *Formal Verification for Time-Triggered Clock Synchronization*, Proceedings of the 7th IFIP International Working Conference on Dependable Computing for Critical Applications, Jan. 1999.
3. J. Rushby, *An overview of formal verification for the time-triggered architecture*, Formal Techniques in Real-Time and Fault-Tolerant Systems, Lecture Notes in Computer Science Vol. 2469, pp. 83–105, Germany, September 2002.
4. J. Rushby, *Systematic Formal Verification for Fault-Tolerant Time-Triggered Algorithms*, IEEE Transactions on Software Engineering, September 1999.
5. G. Berry and G. Gonthier, *The* ESTEREL *Synchronous Programming Language: Design, semantics, Implementation*, SCP, 19 (2): 87–152, 1992.
6. H. Kopetz, *Real-Time Systems: Design Principles for Distributed Embedded Applications*, The Kluwer International Series in Engineering and Computer Science, Kluwer, The Netherlands, 1997.
7. H. Kopetz and G. Grunsteidl, *TTP — A Protocol for Fault-Tolerant Real-time Systems*, IEEE Computer, 27 (1): 14–23, January 1994.
8. H. Kopetz and W. Ochsenreiter, *Clock Synchronization in distributed real-time systems*, IEEE Trans. on Computers, 36 (8): 933–940, August 1987.
9. N. Halbwachs and P. Raymond, *Validation of Synchronous Reactive Systems: From Formal Verification to Automatic Testing*, ACSC, LNCS, 1–12, 1999.
10. N. Halbwachs, P. Caspi, P. Raymond and D. Pilaud, *The synchronous data-flow programming language* LUSTRE, Proc. IEEE, 79 (9): 1305–1320, Sept. 1991.
11. N. Halbwachs, F. Lagnier and C. Ratel, *Programming and verifying critical systems by means of the synchronous data-flow programming language* LUSTRE, IEEE Transactions on Software Engineering, 1992.
12. P. Caspi, A. Curic, A. Maignan, C. Sofronis, S. Tripakis and P. Neibert, *From simulink to* SCADE/LUSTRE *to TTA: a layered approach for distributed*

embedded applications, Proceedings of the 2003 ACM SIGPLAN conference on Language, compiler, and tool for embedded systems, San Diego, 2003.
13. L. Lamport and P. M. Melliar-Smith, *Synchronizing faults in the presence of faults*, Journal of the ACM, Vol. 32, No. 1, January 1985.
14. L. Lamport, R. Shostak and M. Pease, *The Byzantine Generals Problem*, ACM Transactions on Programming Languages and Systems, Vol. 4, No. 3, July 1982.
15. J. Lundelius and N. Lynch, *A New Fault-Tolerant Algorithm for Clock Synchronization*, Proceedings 3rd Annual ACM Symposium on Principles of Distributed Computing, pages 75–88, Vancouver, Canada, August 1984. ACM SIGACT and SIGOPS.
16. N. Shankar, *Mechanical Verification of a Generalized Protocol for Byzantine Fault-Tolerant Clock Synchronization*, Formal Techniques in Real-Time and Fault-Tolerant Systems, LNCS 571, January 1992.
17. S. Owre, J. Rushby, N. Shankar and F. von Henke, *Formal Verification of fault-tolerant architectures: Prolegomena to the design of PVS*, IEEE Transactions on Software Engineering, Vol. 21, No. 2, February 1995.
18. F. Cristian, *Understanding fault-tolerant Distributed Systems*, Communications of the ACM, Vol. 34, No. 2, February 1991.
19. FlexRay — The Communication System for Advanced Automotive Control Applications, www.flexray.com.
20. B. Rajan and R. K. Shyamasundar, *Multiclock Esterel: A Reactive Framework for Asynchronous Design*, IPDPS 2000, Cancun, May 2000.
21. B. Rajan and R. K. Shyamasundar, *Modelling Distributed Embedded Systems in Multiclock Esterel*, FORTE 2000, October 2000.

CHAPTER 13

TRIANGULAR PASTING SYSTEM

T. Kalyani*, K. Sasikala*, V. R. Dare†,‡, P. J. Abisha† and T. Robinson†

*Department of Mathematics, St. Joseph's College of Engineering, Jeppiaar Nagar, Chennai — 600 119, India

†Department of Mathematics, Madras Christian College, Chennai - 600 059, India

‡E-mail: rajkumardare@yahoo.com

We introduce a new syntactic model, called sequential tabled triangular pasting system for generating sets of two dimensional digitized geometrical patterns. This system allows two isosceles right angled triangular tiles to get glued under specified rules to form labelled or coloured patterns. Sequence of isosceles right angled triangles are generated using this system. Decidability on finiteness is obtained. Patterns with holes are generated using k-tabled pasting system (k-TPS) and it is proved that k-TPS is closed under reversal of patterns. Symmetric pasting system is introduced as a subclass of tabled triangular pasting system. Sequence of hexagons is generated using this system. Basic puzzle iso array grammar is introduced and it is compared with k-tabled triangular pasting system.

1. Introduction

The art of tiling plays an important role in the field of architecture since early civilization.[3] Over the ages intricate tiling patterns have been used to decorate and cover floors and walls.

Syntactic models play an important role in picture generation and description on account of their structure handling ability. Many models of array grammars were introduced to generate two dimensional pictures.[2,7,10] Motivated by problems in tiling, Nivat *et al.*, proposed a class of grammars called puzzle grammars for generating connected arrays of square cells and investigated theoretical questions related to their grammars.[6,9,11–13] Two dimensional recognizable languages obtained as projection of local pictures languages have been considered in Refs. 1 and 3. A pasting system using square tiles has been introduced in Ref. 8. The motivation of this paper is to find a system which generates digitized two dimensional geometrical patterns using isosceles right angled triangular tiles instead of square tiles.

In this paper we propose a parallel generating model called sequential tabled triangular pasting system which allows two isosceles right angled triangular tiles to get glued under specified rules in order to form labelled or coloured patterns over square grid. Symmetric pasting system is introduced as a subclass of two tabled triangular pasting system. Decidability result for finiteness of the system is obtained. Patterns with holes are generated using k-tabled pasting system (k-TPS) and it is proved that k-TPS is closed under reversal of patterns. Basic puzzle iso array grammar is introduced and it is compared with k-tabled triangular pasting system.

2. Notation and Preliminaries[4,5]

A tile T is a topological disk whose boundary is a single simple closed curve whose ends join up to form a loop and which has no crossing or branches. A plane tiling $\mathcal{G}$ is a countable family of topological disks $\mathcal{G} = \{T_1, T_2, \ldots\}$ which cover the Euclidean plane without gaps or overlaps.

The union of tiles $T_1, T_2, \ldots$ is the whole plane and the interior of the sets T_i are to be pairwise disjoint. From the definition of tiling we see that the intersection of any finite set of tiles of $\mathcal{G}$ has necessarily zero area. Such an intersection will consist of a set of points called vertices and lines called edges. Two tiles are called adjacent if they have an edge in common.

In this paper the study is restricted to labelled or coloured four distinct isosceles right angled triangular tiles denoted by A, B, C and D of dimensions $1/\sqrt{2}$, $1/\sqrt{2}$ and 1 unit.

The tile A is 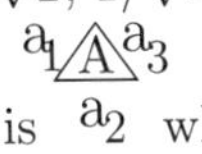

where a_1 and a_3 are the labels of the sides with equal length ($1/\sqrt{2}$ unit) and a_2 is of dimension 1 unit. Similarly edge labels for the tiles B, C and D are given as follows.

The tiles B, C and D are 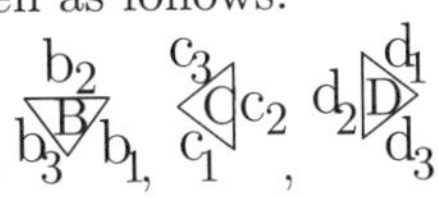

. The set of all edge labels is called an edge set, denoted by E.

An edge pasting rule or simply pasting rule is a pair (x, y) where x, $y \in E$, the edge set of all tiles. The pasting rules of tiles A, B, C and D are given below.

(1) Tile A can be glued with tile B by the pasting rules $\{(a_1, b_1), (a_2, b_2), (a_3, b_3)\}$, with tile C by the rule $\{(a_3, c_1)\}$ and with tile D by the rule $\{(a_1, d_3)\}$.
(2) Tile B can be glued with tile A by the pasting rules $\{(b_1, a_1), (b_2, a_2), (b_3, a_3)\}$, with tile C by the rule $\{(b_1, c_3)\}$ and with tile D by the rule $\{(b_3, d_1)\}$.
(3) Tile C can be glued with A by the rule $\{(c_1, a_3)\}$, with tile B by $\{(c_3, b_1)\}$ and with tile D by the pasting rules $\{(c_1, d_1), (c_2, d_2), (c_3, d_3)\}$.
(4) Tile D can be glued with tile A by the rule $\{(d_3, a_1)\}$, with B by $\{(d_1, b_3)\}$ and with C by the pasting rules $\{(d_1, c_1), (d_2, c_2), (d_3, c_3)\}$.

3. Two Tabled Triangular Pasting System

We now define a parallel generating model called two tabled triangular pasting system, which consists of two sets of symbols and two sets of pasting rules. These are used in this system in order to generate digitized two dimensional geometrical patterns.

Definition 1: A two tabled triangular pasting system (TTTPS) is a 6-tuple $S = \{\Sigma, \Sigma', E, T_1, T_2, t_0\}$, where Σ is a finite non empty set of isosceles right angled triangular tiles A, B, C and D. Σ' consists of tiles called completion tiles denoted by A', B', C' and D' which completes each generation when used such that $\Sigma \cap \Sigma' = \phi$. E is a set of edge labels of tiles in $\Sigma \cup \Sigma'$. T_1 is a finite set of pasting rules called intermediate pasting rules and T_2 is a finite set of pasting rules called final pasting rules. t_0 is the axiom, which is a finite tiling of tiles in $\Sigma \cup \Sigma'$.

A tiling pattern t_{i+1} on the square grid is generated from a pattern t_i in two stages:

(1) In stage one, pasting rules of T_1 are applied in parallel to the boundary edges of t_i giving rise to intermediate pattern It_{i+1}.
(2) and in stage two pasting rules of T_2 are applied in parallel to the boundary edges of the intermediate pattern It_{i+1} deriving t_{i+1}.

The set of all patterns derived from the axiom of the pasting system is denoted by $T(S)$.

$$T(S) = \{t_j : t_0 \overset{*}{\underset{T_1,T_2}{\Longrightarrow}} t_j / j \geq 0\}$$

The family of all patterns generated by the system is $\mathcal{F}(TTTPS)$. We will illustrate this system with the following example.

Example 1: A two tabled triangular pasting system, generating a sequence of right angled isosceles triangles, is given below.

$$S_1 = \{\Sigma, \Sigma', E, T_1, T_2, t_0\}$$

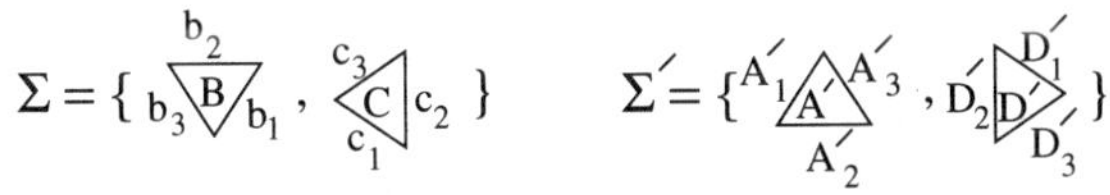

$$E = \{b_1, b_2, b_3, c_1, c_2, c_3, A'_1, A'_2, A'_3, D'_1, D'_2, D'_3\}$$

$$T_1 = \{(A'_3, b_3), (D'_1, c_1)\}$$

$$T_2 = \{(b_1, A'_1), (b_2, A'_2), (c_2, D'_2), (c_3, D'_3), (A'_1, D'_3)\}$$

$t_0 =$

$$t_0 \underset{T_1}{\Longrightarrow} It_1 \underset{T_2}{\Longrightarrow} t_1 \underset{T_1}{\Longrightarrow} It_2 \underset{T_2}{\Longrightarrow} t_2 \cdots$$

The first three members are shown in Fig. 1.

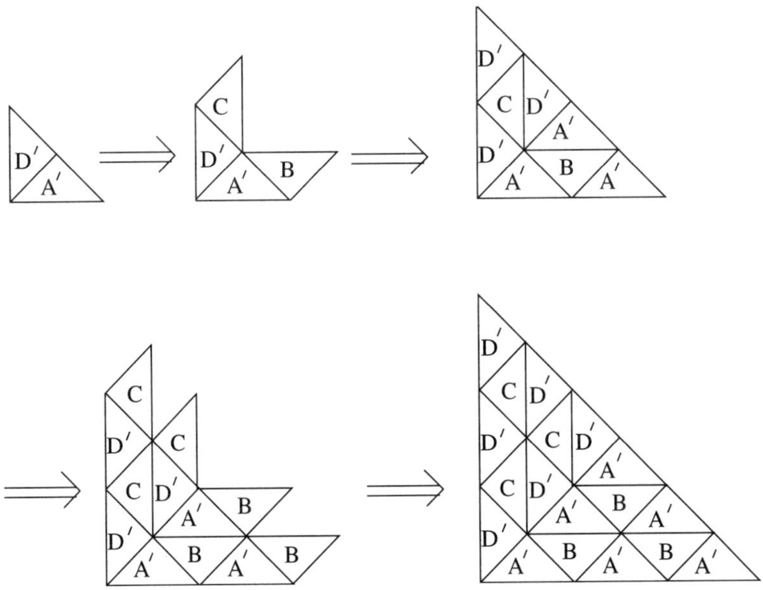

Fig. 1.

Definition 2: An iso array is an isoceles right angled triangle whose sides are denoted as S_1, S_3 (for sides of equal lengths) and S_2. An U-iso array is formed exclusively by A-tile on side S_2. Such an U-iso array formed by m A-tiles on side S_2 denoted by U_m will have m^2 tiles in total (including the m A-tiles) and it is said to be of size m.

For example the U-iso array of size 3 shown in Fig. 2 has 3 A-tiles on side S_2 and 9 tiles in total. Similarly D-iso array, R-iso array and L-iso array can be formed using exclusively the tiles B, D and C on side S_2 respectively. Iso arrays of same size can be catenated using the following catenation operations. Horizontal catenation is defined between U and D iso arrays of same size and it is denoted by the symbol $\ominus$. Right catenation is defined between any two gluable iso arrays of same size and it is denoted by the symbol $\oslash$. This catenation includes the following

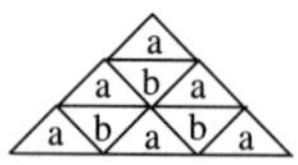

U_3

Fig. 2.

(a) $D \oslash U$ (b) $U \oslash R$ (c) $D \oslash L$ (d) $R \oslash L$
In a similar way vertical $\varobar$ and left $\obslash$ catenations can be defined.

Definition 3: Let Σ be a finite alphabet of iso triangular tiles. An iso picture of size (n, m), n, $m \geq 1$ over Σ is a picture formed by concatenating n-iso arrays of maximum size m. The number of tiles in any iso picture of size (n, m) is nm^2.

Any two iso pictures of sizes (n_1, m) and (n_2, m), n_1, n_2, $m \geq 1$ can be catenated using the rules of concatenation of iso arrays, provided the sides of iso pictures are gluable.

The patterns generated by two tabled triangular pasting system can be described in terms of catenation of iso arrays.

Example 2: The sequence of isosceles right angled triangles generated by two tabled triangular pasting system given in Example 1 can be described in terms of catenation of iso pictures as follows.

$t_3 =$ 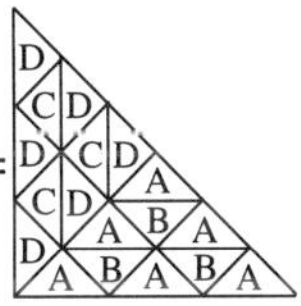 $= R_3 \oslash U_3$

Definition 4: A two tabled triangular pasting system $S = \{\Sigma, \Sigma', E, T_1, T_2, t_0\}$ is said to be deterministic if for any two pairs (x, y) and $(x, z) \in T_1 \cup T_2$ then $y = z$.

Example 1 is a deterministic pasting system.

Definition 5: Two patterns t_i and t_j of $TTTPS$ having same size and shape are said to be equivalent to one another if t_j is the identical copy of t_i. The two patterns are identical in labels as well as in shape.

For example two patterns shown in Fig. 3 are not equivalent.

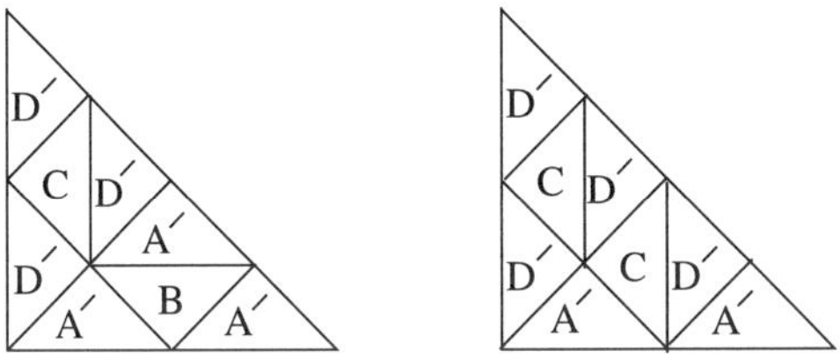

Fig. 3.

Definition 6: A two tabled triangular pasting system $S = \{\Sigma, \Sigma', T_1, T_2, t_0\}$ is said to be

(1) R-nondeterministic if there exists x, y, z such that $y \neq z$ and (x, y) and (x, z) are in $T_1 \cup T_2$.
(2) D-nondeterministic if pattern $t_i \in T(S)$ derives two distinct patterns t'_{i+1} and t''_{i+1} for any $i = 0, 1, 2, \ldots$.
The following rules give R-nondeterminisim for tiles of Σ.

$$[\{(a_1, b_1), (a_1, d_3)\}, \{(a_3, b_3), (a_3, c_1)\}, \{(b_1, a_1), (b_1, c_3)\},$$
$$\{b_3, a_3), (b_3, d_1)\}, \{(c_1, a_3), (c_1, d_1)\}, \{(c_3, b_1), (c_3, d_3)\},$$
$$\{(d_1, b_3), (d_1, c_1)\}, \{(d_3, a_1), (d_3, c_3)\}]$$

Similar rules exist for tiles belonging to Σ' and other combinations.

Remark 1: It is easily observed from the definitions of R-nondeterministic pasting system, D-nondeterministic pasting system and equality of patterns, that R-nondeterministic pasting system is equivalent to D-nondeterministic pasting system.

Definition 7: Consider a tile A, the left neighbours of A are the set of tiles that occur to the left side of A. This set is denoted by $N(l, A)$. Similarly the sets $N(r, A)$ and $N(d, A)$ are respectively the right and down neighbours of A.

$$N(l, A) = \{B, D\}, N(r, A) = \{B, C\} \text{ and } N(d, A) = \{B\}.$$

In a similar manner the neighbourhoods of the tile B can be defined as follows:

$$N(l, B) = \{A, D\}, N(r, B) = \{A, C\} \text{ and } N(u, B) = \{A\}.$$

For a tile C, the right neighbour is D, left up neighbours are B and D, left down neighbours are D and A.

$$N(r, C) = \{D\}, N(u, C) = \{B, D\} \text{ and } N(d, C) = \{D, A\}.$$

For a tile D, the left neighbour is C, right up neighbours are C and B, right down neighbours are C and A.

$$N(l, D) = \{C\}, N(u, D) = \{B, C\} \text{ and } N(d, D) = \{C, A\}.$$

Theorem 1: It is decidable whether $T(S)$ is finite for a deterministic two tabeled triangular pasting system.

Proof: We construct a directed graph G from the given pasting system S as follows. For every tile A of S there corresponds a vertex with label A. For any two tiles A and B of S there corresponds a directed arc from A to B with label r (respectively l, d) if $B \in N(r, A)$ (respectively $N(l, A)$, $N(d, A)$).

For an infinite sequence of patterns, S allows infinite growth in two possible ways. Growth take place (i) horizontally or vertically or (ii) diagonally. Horizontal growth is obtained by using the tiles A and B and it leads to a directed circuit with path label r^+ or l^+. The vertical growth is obtained by using the tiles C and D and leads to a directed circuit with path label u^+ or d^+.

Case (ii) ensures a directed circuit with path label $(r^m d^n)^+$ or $(d^n r^m)^+$ in the south east direction for some non negative integers m, $n (m + n > 0)$. Similar expressions of path label occur for other three diagonal expressions.

As finding a closed directed circuit with any of the two cases of path label at vertex is decidable, finiteness of a system is decidable. □

The next example illustrates this theorem.

Example 3: $TTTPS_3 = \{\Sigma, \Sigma', E, T_1, T_2, t_0\}$

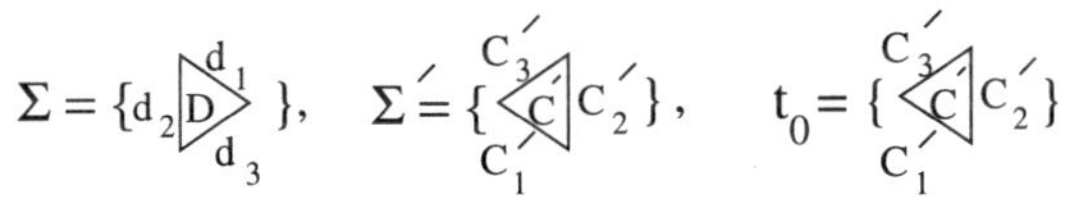

$$T_1 = \{(C_2', d_2)\}, T_2 = \{(d_3, C_3')\}, E = \{C_1', C_2', C_3', d_1, d_2, d_3\}$$

The infinite pattern generated is shown in Fig. 4. The corresponding directed graph is shown below

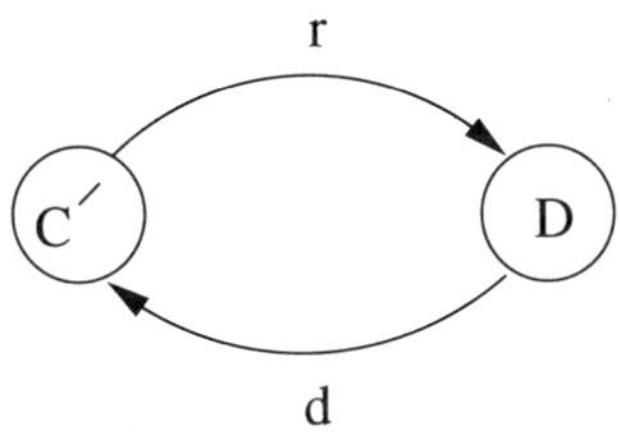

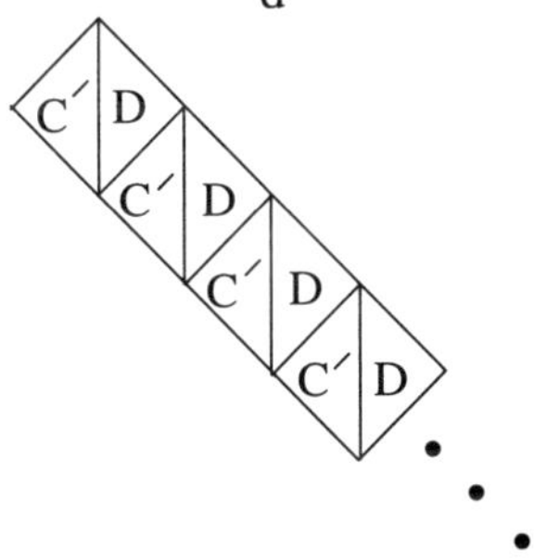

Fig. 4.

There is a directed circuit with path label $(rd)^+$ at vertex C', and the pattern grows in south east direction.

4. Sequential Tabled Triangular Pasting System

In this section we introduce a generalized tabled triangular pasting system called k-tabled triangular pasting system K-TPS in which the pasting rules are given in k-tables and the tables are applied sequentially. Using this system patterns with holes are generated.

Definition 8: A k-tabled triangular pasting system (k-TPS) is a (k + 4)-tuple $S = \{\Sigma, \Sigma', E, T_1, T_2, \ldots, T_k, t_0\}$, where Σ is a finite non empty set of isosceles right angled triangular tiles A, B, C and D. Σ' consists of tiles called completion tiles which completes each generation when used such that $\Sigma \cap \Sigma' = \phi$. E is a set of edge labels of tiles in $\Sigma \cup \Sigma'$. $T_1, T_2, \ldots, T_{k-1}$ are finite set of pasting rules called intermediate pasting rules and T_k is a finite set of pasting rules called final pasting rules. t_0 is the axiom, which is a finite tiling of tiles in $\Sigma \cup \Sigma'$.

A tiling pattern t_{i+1} on the square grid is generated from a pattern t_i in k stages:

(1) In first $(k-1)$ stages, the tables $T_1, T_2, \ldots, T_{k-1}$ are used sequentially. The rules of the tables in each stage are applied in parallel to the boundary edges of the pattern obtained in the previous stage.
(2) In the kth stage, the pasting rules of table T_k are applied in parallel to the boundary edges of the pattern obtained in the $(k-1)$th stage deriving t_{i+1}.

4.1. *Patterns with holes*

Patterns with holes are also generated by some pasting systems. If the axiom pattern does not have a hole, then due to the inherent parallel generating nature a system needs to have atleast six tiles. Hence we have the following observation.

Observation:-

There exists no pasting system $S = (\Sigma, \Sigma', E, T_1, T_2, t_0)$ to generate patterns with holes for $|\Sigma \cup \Sigma'| \leq 5$.

A triangular tile A is said to have $2N$ rules only if A has neighbours on two sides and it is said to have $3N$ rules if it has neighbours on all three sides.

Proposition 1: *A deterministic k-tables pasting system with tiles having only* $2N$ *and* $3N$ *rules generate patterns with holes if (i)* $|\Sigma \cup \Sigma'| \geq 6$ *(ii)* $k \geq 4$.

Example 4: A k-TPS $S = (\Sigma, \Sigma', E, T_1, T_2, T_3, T_4, t_0)$ generates patterns with holes.

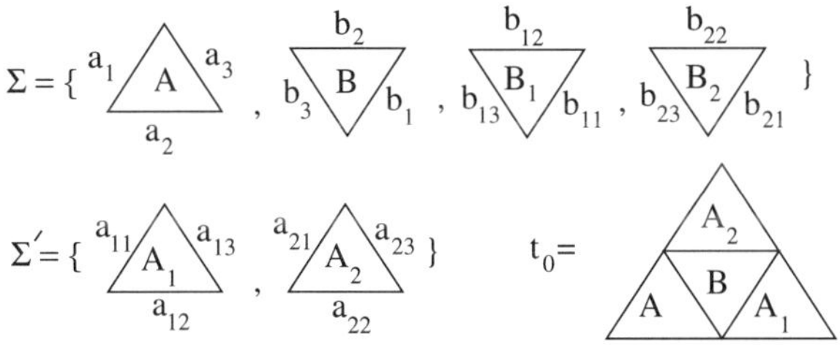

$$T_1 = \{(a_{23}, b_{23})\}, T_2 = \{(b_{12}, a_2), (b_{21}, a_1)\}$$

$$T_3 = \{(a_3, b_3)\}, T_4 = \{(b_1, a_{11}), (b_2, a_{22})\}$$

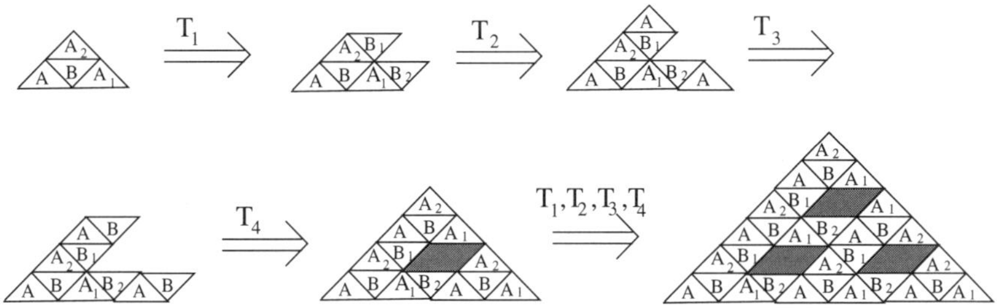

Proposition 2: *The family of patterns generated by two tabled triangular pasting system is properly included in the family of patterns generated by k-tabled triangular pasting system.*

Definition 9: Let $\Sigma = \{$ 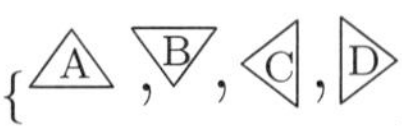 $\}$ be a finite alphabet of iso triangular tiles. The reversal of tiles, A, B, C and D are denoted by A^R, B^R, C^R and D^R and they are B, A, D and C respectively. Similarly the reversal of iso arrays are defined as follows:

The reversal of an U-iso array, denoted as U^R, is an iso array formed by the reversal of all tiles of the U iso array.

i.e., $U^R = D$, $D^R = U$, $L^R = R$, $R^R = L$.

The reversal of pasting rules are given below:

$$(a_1, b_1)^R = (b_3, a_3), (a_2, b_2)^R = (b_2, a_2), (a_3, b_3)^R = (b_1, a_1), (a_3, c_1)^R = (b_3, d_1), (a_1, d_3)^R = (b_1, c_3)\,.$$

Similarly the reversal of other pasting rules can be defined.

Theorem 2: The family of all patterns generated by k-tabled triangular pasting system is closed under reversal of patterns.

Proof: Let $P = T(S) = \{t_j/j \geq 0\}$ be a sequence of patterns generated by a k-tabled triangular pasting system $S = (\Sigma, \Sigma', E, T_1, T_2, \dots, T_k, t_0)$. We construct a k-TPS $S_1 = (\Sigma_1, \Sigma_1', E, T_{11}, T_{12}, \dots, T_{1k}, t_1)$ as follows:

$$\Sigma_1 = \Sigma^R, \quad \Sigma_1' = (\Sigma')^R,$$

$$T_{11} = T_1^R = \{(x,y)^R/(x,y) \in T_1\}$$

$$T_{12} = T_2^R = \{(a,b)^R/(a,b) \in T_2\}$$

$$\vdots$$

$$T_{1k} = T_k^R = \{(c,d)^R/(c,d) \in T_k\}$$

$$t_1 = t_0^R$$

Now the k-TPS S_1 generates the sequence of patterns $P^R = T(S_1) = \{t_j^R/t_j \in T(S)\}$. Now to show that $T(S_1) = P^R$.

Let $x \in T(S_1) = \{t_j^R/t_j \in T(S)\}$

$$\Rightarrow x = t_j^R \text{ for some } j$$

$$\Rightarrow x \in P^R \therefore T(S_1) \subseteq P^R.$$

Now conversely let $x \in P^R$

$$\Rightarrow x^R \in P = T(S) = \{t_j/j \geq 0\}$$

i.e., $x^R = t_j$ for some j
i.e., $x = t_j^R \in T(S_1)$

$$\Rightarrow P^R \subseteq T(S_1)$$

$$\therefore T(S_1) = P^R$$

hence the family of all patterns generated by k-tabled triangular pasting system is closed under reversal of patterns. □

5. Symmetric Pasting System

In this section, we introduce a sub class of k-tabled triangular pasting system called symmetric pasting system, SPS and the patterns produced by this system are symmetric either with respect to the vertical axis or horizontal axis passing through the axiom tiling, provided the axiom tiling is symmetric with respect to horizontal axis or vertical axis.

Definition 10: In a k-tabled triangular pasting system k-TPS $= \{\Sigma, \Sigma', E, T_1, T_2, \ldots, T_k, t_0\}$. A pasting rule $(a, b) \in \cup_{i=1}^{k} T_i$ is said to be symmetric if it satisfies any one of the following conditions.

(i) $(b, a) \in \cup_{i=1}^{k} T_i$.
(ii) The left neighbour of tile x is also a right neighbour of x.
(iii) Up neighbour of tile x is also down neighbour of x.

Definition 11: A k-tabled triangular pasting system k-TPS $= \{\Sigma, \Sigma', E, T_1, T_2, \ldots, T_k, t_0\}$ is said to be a symmetric pasting system if every rule in $\cup_{i=1}^{k} T_i$ are symmetric.

Example 5: Symmetric pasting system generating sequence of Hexagons is given below.

$$SPS_4 = \{\Sigma, \Sigma', E, T_1, T_2, t_0\}$$

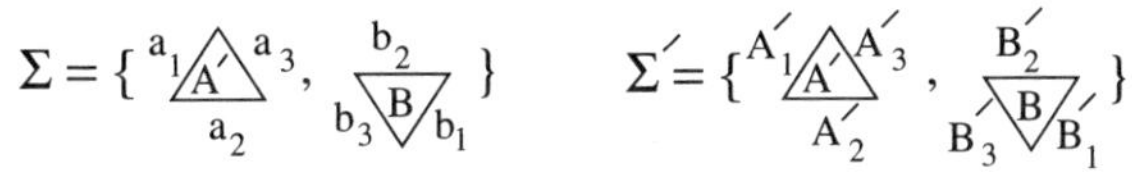

$$T_1 = \{(B_2', a_2), (A_3', b_3), (B_1', a_1), (A_2', b_2), (B_3', a_3), (A_1', b_1)\}$$

$$T_2 = \{(a_3, B_3'), (b_2, A_2'), (B_1', A_1'), (b_1, A_1'), (A_2', B_2'), (a_2, B_2'),$$
$$(B_3', A_3'), (b_3, A_3'), (A_1', B_1'), (a_1, B_1'), (B_2', A_2'), (A_3', B_3')\}$$

$t_0 =$ 

(t_0 is symmetric with respect to horiontal axis)

The first three members are given in Fig. 5. Intermediate patterns generate sequence of stars.

Proposition 3: *The family of all patterns generated by Symmetric Pasting System (SPS) is strictly included in the family of all patterns generated by Tabled Triangular Pasting System (TTPS).*

Proof: The inclusion is straight forward (since the rules of SPS are included in the rules of TTPS) sequence of Hexagons (Example 5) generated by SPS can be generated by TTPS. The proper inclusion can be seen as follows. The sequence of isosceles right angled triangles given in Example 1 cannot be generated by SPS. □

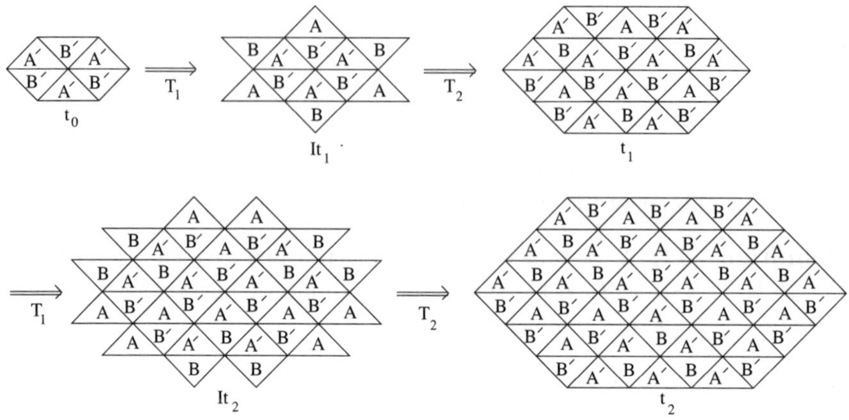

Fig. 5.

6. Basic Puzzle Iso Array Grammar

Motivated by problems in tiling, Nivat et al, proposed a class of grammars called puzzle grammars for generating connected array of unit cells. It has been shown in Ref. 11, a subclass called Basic puzzle grammars has higher generative power than regular array grammars.

The sequence of isosceles right angled triangles are generated using basic puzzle grammars. Motivated by this, in this paper, we define a grammar called Basic puzzle iso array grammar using triangular tiles as base units.

Definition 12: A basic puzzle iso array grammar (BPIG), is a structure $G = \langle N, T, R, S \rangle$ where $N = \{$$, \ldots\}$ and $T = \{$$, \ldots\}$ are finite sets of symbols (isosceles right angled triangular tiles 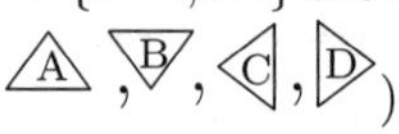); $N \cap T = \phi$. Elements of N are called nonterminals and of T terminals. $S \in N$ is the start symbol or the axiom. R consists of rules of the following forms:

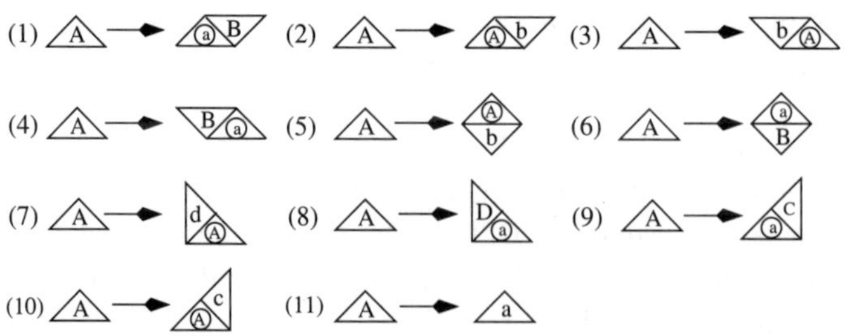

Similarly the rules can be given for the other tiles B, C and D.

Derivations begin with S written in a unit cell in the two-dimensional plane, with all other cells containing the blank symbol {#, #, #, #} not in $N \cup T$. In a derivation step, denoted $\Rightarrow$, a nonterminal A in a cell is replaced by the right hand member of a rule, whose left hand side is A In this replacement, the circled symbol of the right side of the rule used occupies the cell of the replaced symbol and the non-circled symbol of the right side occupies the cell to the right or the left or above or below the cell of the replaced symbol, depending on the type of the rule used. The replacement is possible and defined only if the cell to be filled in by the non-circled symbol contains a blank symbol.

The set of pictures or figures generated by G denoted by $L(G)$ is the set of connected digitized finite iso pictures over T (i.e., not containing non terminals) derivable in one or more steps from the axiom.

Example 6: Let $G_1 = \langle\{$A, B$\}, \{$a, b$\}, R, S\rangle$ where R consists of the following rules

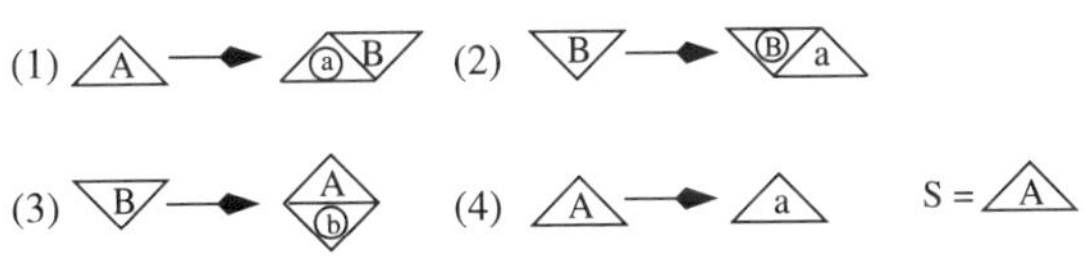

be a basic puzzle iso array grammar. A sample derivation is shown below.

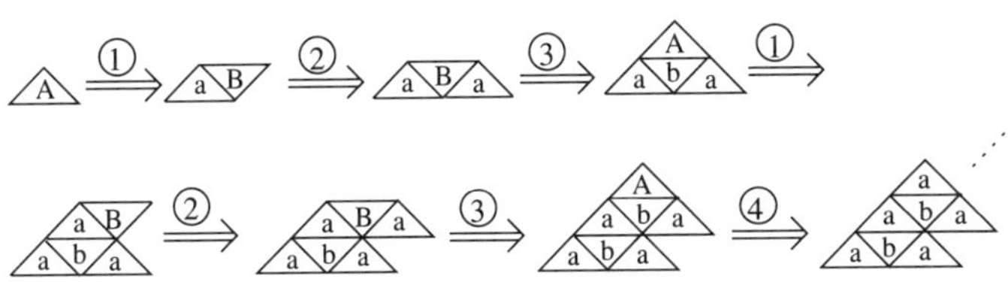

Remark 2: In a basic puzzle iso array grammar, the rules of P can be given in an equivalent form as follows: P has rules $A \rightarrow \alpha$, where A is a non terminal and α is a finite connected array of one or more triangular cells, each cell containing a symbol of $N \cup T$, with the symbol in one of the cells

of α being circled and satisfying the conditions (i) there is at most one non terminal symbol in α (ii) α is generated by a finite set of basic puzzle iso array grammar rules, the generation starting from the circled symbol in α and ending with the non terminal symbol.

Example 7: The basic puzzle iso array grammar G =

where the rules of P are

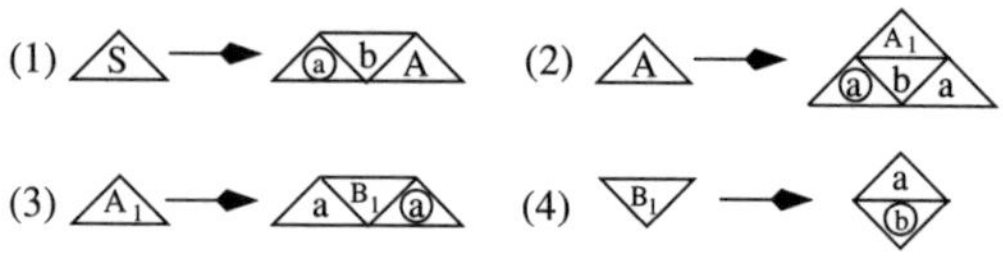

These rules can be derived from a basic puzzle iso array grammar. For example

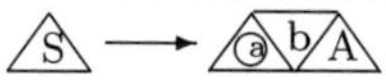

can be replaced by equivalent BPIG rules as

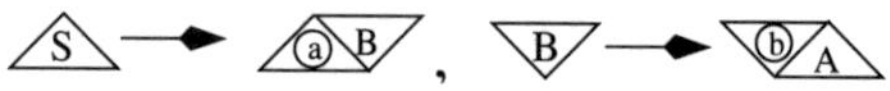

The rules of P are mentioned in the remark above. The grammar G generates isosceles right angled triangle of base 3 units.

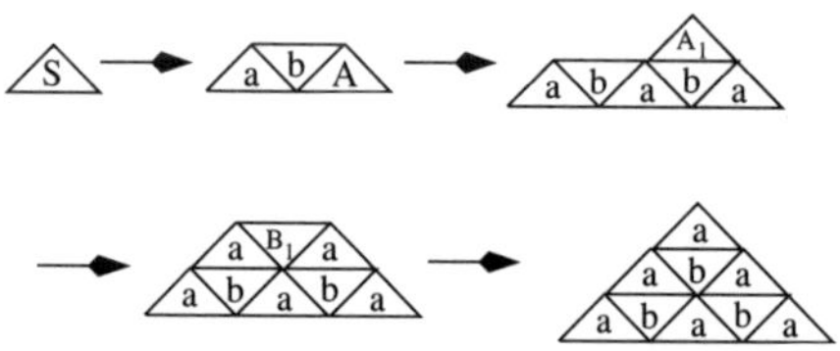

Theorem 3: The family of languages generated by k-tabled triangular pasting system (k-TPS) and the family of languages generated by basic puzzle iso array grammar (BPIG) are incomparable but not disjoint.

Proof: This is easily followed from the following figure.

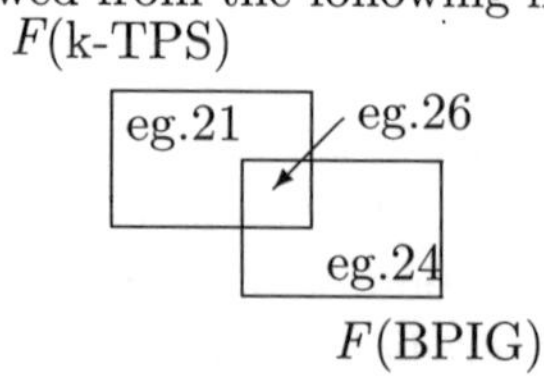

Since the pasting rules of k-tabled triangular pasting system is included in the rules of basic puzzle iso array grammar.

[For eg., the rule  can be written as (a_3, b_3), 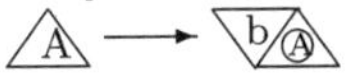 can be written as (b_1, a_1)]. Hence Example 7 can be generated by both systems.

The picture language generated by the basic puzzle iso array grammar given in Example 6 cannot be generated by k-tabled triangular pasting system, since parallel generating device is used in k-TPS.

Since BPIG generates only connected structures the pattern given in Example 5 cannot be generated by this system. □

7. Conclusion

A parallel generating model called k-tabled triangular pasting system is introduced in this paper to generate digitized geometrical patterns. Some of its properties are discussed. Basic puzzle iso array grammar is introduced and it is compared with k-tabled triangular pasting system.

Acknowledgments

The first two authors would like to thank the management of St. Josephs's College of Engineering for the encouragement and constant support to persue the research work.

The authors would like to thank Dr.Mrs. Siromoney for her valuable suggestions during the preparation of this paper.

References

1. D. Giammarresi and A. Restivo, in *Hand Book of Formal Languages*, Vol. 3, Eds. A. Salomaa and G. Rozenberg, (Springer-Verlag, Berlin, 1997), p. 215.
2. Gift Siromoney, Rani Siromoney and Kamala Krithivasan, *Computer Graphics and Image Processing*, **3**, 63 (1974).
3. B. Grunbaum and G. C. Shephard, *Tiling and Patterns*, (W.H. Freeman and Company, New York, 1987).
4. T. Kalyani, V. R. Dare and D. G. Thomas, *Lecture Notes in Computer Science*, **3316**, 738 (2004).
5. T. Kalyani, K. Sasikala and V. R. Dare, *Proceedings of 2nd National Conference on Mathematical and Computational Models*, (Allied Publishers, 2003). p. 260.
6. M. Nivat, A. Saoudi, K. G. Subramanian, R. Siromoney and V. R. Dare, *International Journal of Pattern Recognition and Artificial Intelligence*, **5**, 663, (1995).

7. R. Siromoney and G. Siromoney, *Information and Control*, **35**, (1977).
8. T. Robinson, V. R. Dare and K. G. Subramanian, *Proc. of 6th International Workshop on Parallel Image Processing and Analysis*, (Madras, 1999).
9. R. Siromoney, K. G. Subramanian, V. R. Dare and D. G. Thomas, *Pattern Recognition*, **32**, 295 (1999).
10. K. G. Subramanian, L. Revathy and R. Siromoney, *International Journal of Pattern Recognition and Artificial Intelligence*, **3**, 333 (1989).
11. K. G. Subramanian, R. Siromoney, V. R. Dare and A. Saoudi, *T.R. No. 90-6, Dept. de Mathematiques et Informatique Universite Paris - Nord C.S.P*, (1990).
12. K. G. Subramanian, R. Siromoney, V. R. Dare and A. Saoudi, *Parallel Image Analysis - Theory and Application*, 111, (World Scientific, Singapore, 1995).
13. K. G. Subramanian, R. Siromoney and V. R. Dare, *International Journal of Pattern Recognition and Artificial Intelligence*, **9**, 763 (1995).

CHAPTER 14

TOWARDS REDUCING PARALLELISM IN P SYSTEMS

Shankara Narayanan Krishna*

Department of Computer Science & Engineering,
Indian Institute of Technology, Bombay,
Powai, Mumbai, 400 076 India
E-mail: krishnas@cse.iitb.ac.in

R. Rama†

Department of Mathematics,
Indian Institute of Technology, Madras,
600 036 India
E-mail: ramar@iitm.ac.in

P Systems have an inherent non-determinism embedded in them. Hence, to implement membrane computing, we have to simulate non-determinism in a deterministic way. Further more, we have to simulate parallelism in a sequential way. To this end, we introduce two variants of P systems having a reduced parallelism and investigate their generative power.

1. Introduction

One of the central interesting features of computing with membranes is the inherent non-determinism in P systems. If we attempt to implement membrane computing on the usual computer, a big problem appears : we have to simulate non-determinism on a deterministic machine; still more, we have to simulate parallelism on a sequential machine. The aim of this paper is to study P systems with less parallelism and non-determinism.

---

*The author's work was carried out during her stay at IIT Madras.

†The author's work was partially supported by a project no. DST/MS/124/99, funded by DST, Govt. of India.

To this end, we introduce two variants of P systems which have a reduced parallelism (non-determinism) and investigate their generative power.

One of the variants considered here is called Time Dependant transition P systems, inspired from Time varying grammars which have been defined in Ref. 5. In this system, we specify a parameter called "period" which determines the sets of rules to be applied to the objects at each step. Unlike earlier systems where objects in all the membranes were allowed to evolve, we specify at each step the membranes i whose rules R_i can be applied. The objects in the other membranes remain idle. Hence, all the rules R_i cannot be applied at every step and hence the parallelism of the system comes down.

Another variant we consider here is P Systems with null parallelism. These systems are thoroughly sequential, there is no parallelism in the way of applying the rules to objects in any of the membranes. In this variant, we consider two kinds of systems: The first kind, in which an object in a membrane always corresponds to a single rule thus ruling out possible non-determinism. The second kind of systems allows having more than one rule for an object in a membrane. In both kinds of systems, the membranes also take part in the rules. To bring down the parallelism and non-determinism of the system, we allow exactly one rule to be applied to an object in any of the membranes during a transition step.

Mutisets of objects is the data structure used by both time-Dependant P systems and P systems with null parallelism.

2. Some Language Theory Prerequisites

In this section, we introduce some formal language theory notions which will be used in this paper; for further details, we refer to Ref. 6. For an alphabet V, we denote by V^* the set of all strings over V, including the empty one, denoted by λ. By CF, RE and MAT we denote the families of context-free, recursively enumerable and matrix languages without appearance checking respectively, while $ET0L$ denotes the family of languages generated by extended tabled $0L$ systems ($ET0L$ systems).

The characterization of recursively enumerable languages in many theorems is obtained by means of using matrix grammars with appearance checking.

Such a grammar is a construct $G = (N, T, S, M, F)$, where N, T are disjoint alphabets, $S \in N$, M is a finite set of sequences of the form $(A_1 \rightarrow x_1, \ldots, A_n \rightarrow x_n)$, $n \geq 1$, of context-free rules over $N \cup T$ (with $A_i \in$

$N, x_i \in (N \cup T)^*$, in all cases), and F is a set of occurrences of rules in M (we say that N is the nonterminal alphabet, T is the terminal alphabet, S is the axiom, while the elements of P are called matrices).

For w, $z \in (N \cup T)^*$, we write $w \Longrightarrow z$ if there is a matrix $(A_1 \rightarrow x_1, \ldots, A_n \rightarrow x_n)$ in M and the strings $w_i \in (N \cup T)^*$, $1 \leq i \leq n+1$, such that $w = w_1$, $z = w_{n+1}$, and, for all $1 \leq i \leq n$, either $w_i = w_i' A_i w_i''$, $w_{i+1} = w_i' x_i w_i''$, for some w_i', $w_i'' \in (N \cup T)^*$, or $w_i = w_{i+1}$, A_i does not appear in w_i, and the rule $A_i \rightarrow x_i$ appears in F. The rules of a matrix are applied in order, possibly skipping the rules in F if they cannot be applied; we say that these rules are applied in the *appearance checking mode*. If $F \neq \emptyset$, then the grammar is said to be without appearance checking (and F is no longer mentioned).

A matrix grammar $G = (N, T, S, M, F)$ is said to be in the *binary normal form* if $N = N_1 \cup N_2 \cup \{S, \dagger\}$, with these three sets mutually disjoint, and the matrices in M are of one of the following forms:

(1) $(S \rightarrow XA)$, with $X \in N_1$, $A \in N_2$,
(2) $(X \rightarrow Y, A \rightarrow x)$, with X, $Y \in N_1$, $A \in N_2$, $x \in (N_2 \cup T)^*$,
(3) $(X \rightarrow Y, A \rightarrow \dagger)$, with X, $Y \in N_1$, $A \in N_2$,
(4) $(X \rightarrow \lambda, A \rightarrow x)$, with $X \in N_1$, $A \in N_2$, $x \in T^*$.

Moreover, there is only one matrix of type 1 and F consists exactly of all rules $A \rightarrow \dagger$ appearing in matrices of type 3. The symbols in N_1 are mainly used to control the use of rules of the form $A \rightarrow x$ with $A \in N_2$, while $\dagger$ is a trap-symbol; once introduced, it is never removed. A matrix of type 4 is used only once, at the last step of a derivation.

According to Lemma 1.3.7 in Ref. 1, for each matrix grammar there is an equivalent matrix grammar in the binary normal form.

3. Time Dependent Transition P Systems

In this section, we define the first class of P systems we investigate: Time Dependant Transition P systems.

Definition 1: A *Time Dependent Transition P system* ($TDTP$ system) of degree m, $m \geq 1$ is a construct

$$\Pi = (V, T, C, \mu, w_1, w_2, \ldots, w_m, (R_1, \rho_1), (R_2, \rho_2), \ldots, (R_m, \rho_m), p, \infty)$$

where:

- V is the total alphabet of the system; its elements are called *objects*;
- $T \subseteq V$ (the output alphabet or terminal alphabet);
- $C \subseteq V$, $C \cap T = \phi$ (catalysts);
- μ is a membrane structure consisting of m membranes, labeled with $1, 2, \ldots, m$;
- w_i, $1 \leq i \leq m$, are multisets over V associated with the regions $1, 2, \ldots, m$ of μ;
- R_i, $1 \leq i \leq m$ are finite sets of *evolution rules* over V associated with the regions $1, 2, \ldots, m$ of μ; ρ_i is an irreflexive, anti-symmetric, non-transitive order relation over R_i specifying a priority relation among rules of R_i. An evolution rule is a pair (u, v) which we usually write in the form $u \to v$, where $u \in V$ and $v = v'$ or $v = v'\delta$, where v' is a string over $(V \times \{\text{here}, \text{out}\}) \cup (V \times \{in_j | 1 \leq j \leq m\})$, and $\delta \notin V$. We also consider rules involving catalysts; the rules are of the form $ca \to cv$, where $c \in C$, $a \in V - C$, and v contains no catalyst.
- p is a number between 1 and m called the "period" of the system. The period determines which membranes should work at a given instant.

In a time dependent transition P system we make the following assumptions: at the ith transition step, only the rules in R_i can be applied; the objects in all other membranes j, $j \neq i$ are put to "sleep". Now, in an m degree system, this assumption would mean that the system works for m steps: R_1 is applied in the first step, R_2 in the second step and so on till we apply R_m in the mth step. This may not be sufficient for getting a successful output every time, so we introduce periodicity in the system as follows: in a system of degree m and period p, $1 \leq p \leq m$, a membrane labeled i can be "active" during steps $i + \phi(p)$, where $\phi(p)$ is a multiple of p. This means that R_i is applicable during the transition steps i, $i + p$, $i + 2p, \ldots$ till a halting configuration is reached. So, if a $TDTP$ system of degree n has period equal to n, then there is only one set of applicable rules to the system at any point of time. $TDTP$ systems are restricted forms of transition P systems;[2] the parallelism is much less in $TDTP$ systems. By choosing the period to be as high as n in an n degree system, we are making the membranes work in a sequential way — one membrane at a time. We shall say that a membrane i is "active" in a step if R_i is applicable in that step.

The work of such a P system with catalysts and δ rules is defined as usual in the P area: in each time unit, all objects which can evolve in the active membranes obeying the priority relations should do so. The priorities are applied as follows: Let there be objects a, b and c in a membrane with rules r_a, r_b, r_c having priorities $r_a > r_b$, $r_b > r_c$. Due to the priority relations, a and c can evolve in a step, but b cannot evolve. Starting from a given configuration, we pass on to another one; a sequence of transitions form a computation and we consider as successful computations only the halting ones; the result of a halting computation consists of all objects over T which are sent out of the system during a computation.

The family of number relations $\psi_T(\Pi)$ computed by $TDTP$ systems Π of degree m and period p, with priorities, catalysts and the membrane dissolving action is denoted by $PsTDTP_m(Pri, Cat, \delta, p)$. When one of the features $\alpha \in \{Pri, Cat, \delta\}$ is not present, we replace it with $n\alpha$.

4. The Generative Power

In this section, we investigate the generative power of $TDTP$ systems. We start by looking at systems with no priorities and no catalysts, and at systems that use priorities or catalysts, and finally obtain a characterization of RE using systems having both priorities and catalysts.

Lemma 1: $PsTDTP_2(nPri, nCat, \delta, 2) - MAT \neq \phi$.

Proof: Consider the $TDTP$ system of degree two and period two,

$$\Pi = (\{S, a\}, \{a\}, \lambda, [_1[_2]_2]_1, \lambda, \{S\}, (R_1, \phi), (R_2, \phi), 2, \infty)$$

with the following sets of rules:

$$R_1 = \{a \to (a, out)\}\,,$$
$$R_2 = \{S \to a, S \to a\delta, a \to aa\delta, a \to aa\}\,.$$

Clearly, the system generates $\{a^{2^n} | n \geq 0\}$, which is not in MAT. □

Lemma 2: (i) $PsTDTP_2(Pri, nCat, n\delta, 2) - ET0L \neq \phi$,
(ii) $PsTDTP_2(nPri, Cat, \delta, 2) - ET0L \neq \phi$.

Proof: We construct two $TDTP$ systems Π_1 and Π_2 of period two, with Π_1 having priorities and Π_2 having catalysts and δ rules:

$$\Pi_1 = (\{A, B, B_1, A', a, a', a'', b\}, \{a, b\}, \lambda, [_1[_2]_2]_1, B_1, \lambda,$$
$$(R_1, \rho_1), (R_2, \rho_2), 2, \infty)\,,$$
$$\Pi_2 = (\{A, B, C, a, b\}, \{a, b\}, \{c\}, [_1[_2]_2]_1, \lambda, \{c, B\}, (R'_1, \phi), (R'_2, \phi), 2, \infty)$$

with the following sets of rules:

$$R_1 = \{B_1 \to (b, \text{out}), B_1 \to B(A, in_2), B \to bb(a', in_2), B \to bb\}$$
$$\cup \{b \to bb, b \to bb(a', in_2), b \to (b, \text{out}), a \to (a, \text{out})\},$$
$$R_2 = \{A \to aA, a' \to a'', A \to A', a \to (a, \text{out})\},$$
$$\rho_1 = \{a \to (a, \text{out}) > b \to bb, b \to bb(a', in_2);\ b \to bb, b \to bb(a', in_2),$$
$$> b \to (b, \text{out})\},$$
$$\rho_2 = \{a' \to a'' > A \to aA;\ A \to aA > a \to (a, \text{out}), A \to A'\},$$
$$R_1' = \{a \to (a, \text{out}), b \to (b, \text{out})\},$$
$$R_2' = \{B \to b\delta, B \to AC, C \to bb, A \to a, ca \to caa, C \to bb\delta,$$
$$b \to bb, b \to bb\delta\}.$$

Both systems generate $\{x | \#_b x = 2^{\#_a x}\}$ which is not an $ET0L$ language.□

Lemma 3: $PsET0L \subset PsTDTP_2(Pri, nCat, \delta, 2)$.

Proof: The properness follows from the above theorem, we have only to prove the inclusion.

Each language $L \in ET0L$ can be generated by an $ET0L$ system with only two tables, $G = (V, T, w, P_1, P_2)$.[6] Let h_1 and h_2 be morphisms defined by $h_i(a) = a_i$, $a \in V$, where a_i is a new symbol associated with a. We construct the following $TDTP$ system of degree two,

$$\Pi = (V', T, [_1[_2]_2]_1, \{Xw\}, \lambda, (R_1, \rho_1), (R_2, \emptyset), 2, \infty)$$

where

$$V' = V \cup \{X, X_1, X_2\} \cup \{a_i | a \in V, i = 1, 2\},$$
$$R_1 = \{r_i : X \to (X_i, in_2) | i = 1, 2\} \cup \{r_i' : a \to (a_i, in_2) | a \in V\}$$
$$\cup \{r_a : a \to (a, \text{out}) | a \in T\} \cup \{r_a' : a \to a | a \in V - T\},$$
$$R_2 = \{X_i \to (X, \text{out}), X_i \to X\delta | i = 1, 2\}$$
$$\cup \{a_i \to (x, \text{out}) | a \to x \in P_i\},$$
$$\rho_1 = \{r_i > r_j', i \neq j;\ r_i > r_a, r_a'\}.$$

The special symbol X decides the table to be simulated. If the rule $X \to (X_i, in_2)$ is applied, all the symbols from V are also indexed by the same subscript i and sent to membrane two. Here, the rule $a_i \rightarrow (x, \text{out})$ is applied corresponding to the rule $a \rightarrow x$ in the table P_i. The second membrane can be retained as such for continuing computations or dissolved by applying rules $X_i \rightarrow (X, \text{out})$ or $X_i \rightarrow X\delta$ respectively. In the latter case, all the terminal symbols are sent out. If any symbols $a \in V - T$ remain, the rule $a \rightarrow a$ is applied and the computation never stops.

Clearly, the terminal strings generated by the system belong to $ET0L$. □

Theorem 1: $PsRE \subseteq PsTDTP_2(Pri, Cat, n\delta, 2)$.

Proof: Let $G = (N, T, S, M, F)$ be a matrix grammar in binary normal form with appearance checking. Let there be n matrices, $m_1, m_2, \ldots, m_n$ in M. We construct a $TDTP$ system of degree two, period two with priorities and catalysts $\Pi = (V, T, \{c\}, [_1[_2]_2]_1, w_1, \lambda, (R_1, \rho_1), (R_2, \rho_2), 2, \infty)$ with

$$V = N_1 \cup N_2 \cup \{i, X_i, X_i', A_i, A_i', D'_{A_i}, e_i | 1 \leq i \leq n, X \in N_1, A \in N_2\}$$
$$\cup \{d, d', d'', e, e', Y', B', A'' | Y \in N_1, B \in N_2, A \in N_2 \cup T\} \cup \{\dagger\},$$

$$w_1 = \{XA | (S \rightarrow XA) \text{ is the initial matrix}\}, w_i = \lambda, i \neq 1,$$

R_1 consists of the rules

(1) $r_{1_i} : \{X \rightarrow Y_i, |m_i : (X \rightarrow Y, A \rightarrow x)\}$,
(2) $r_{2_i} : \{X \rightarrow Y_i' | m_i : (X \rightarrow Y, A \rightarrow \dagger)\}$,
(3) $r_{3_i} : \{X \rightarrow ei | m_i : (X \rightarrow \lambda, A \rightarrow x)\}$,
(4) $r_{4_i} : \{cA \rightarrow cA_i | m_i : (X \rightarrow Y, A \rightarrow x) \text{ or } (X \rightarrow \lambda, A \rightarrow x)\}$,
(5) $r_{5_i} : \{Y_i \rightarrow (Y_i, in_2), i \rightarrow (i, in_2) | Y \in N_1, 1 \leq i \leq n\}$,
(6) $r_{6_i} : \{A_i \rightarrow (A_i, in_2) | A \in N_2, 1 \leq i \leq n\}$,
(7) $r_{7_i} : \{Y_i' \rightarrow (Y_i', in_2) | Y \in N_1, 1 \leq i \leq n\}$,
(8) $r_{9_i} : \{A_i' \rightarrow (A_i', in_2), D'_{A_i} \rightarrow (D'_{A_i}, in_2) | A \in N_2, 1 \leq i \leq n\}$,
(9) $r_{10} : \{a \rightarrow (a, \text{out}),\ a \in T\}$,
(10) $r_{11} : d \rightarrow d',\ r_{12} : d' \rightarrow d''$,
(11) $r_{13} : \{A \rightarrow A',\ A \in N_2\},\ r_{14} : \{A' \rightarrow A',\ A \in N_2\}$,
(12) $r_{15} : e \rightarrow e,\ r_{16} : e \rightarrow \lambda$,
(13) $r_{17} : \{X \rightarrow \dagger,$ there is no rule for $X \in N_1\}$,
(14) $r_{8_{i,j\cdots l}} : \{A \rightarrow A_i' D'_{A_j} \cdots D'_{A_l} | i \leq j \leq \cdots \leq l \leq n\}$, ($m_i, m_j, \ldots, m_l$ are of the form $(X \rightarrow Y, A \rightarrow \dagger)$ and there are no type 3 matrices among $m_1, \ldots, m_{i-1},\ m_{i+1}, \ldots, m_{j-1},\ m_{j+1}, \ldots, m_{l-1},\ m_{l+1}, \ldots, m_n$).

R_2 consists of the rules

(1) $r_i : \{Y_i \to Ye_i(d, \text{out}),\ i \to e_i(d, \text{out}),\ Y'_i \to Y'(d', \text{out})\}$,
(2) $r'_i : \{A_i \to h(x) | m_i : (X \to Y, A \to x) \text{ or } (X \to \lambda, A \to x)\}$,
(3) $r''_i : \{A_i \to \dagger\}$,
(4) $R_i : \{e_i \to e'\}$,
(5) $R'_i : \{e_i \to \lambda\}$,
(6) $R''_i : \{A'_i, D'_{A_i} \to \dagger\}$,
(7) $R'''_j : \{A'_j \to A'(d, \text{out}), D'_{A_j} \to (d, \text{out})\}$,
(8) $\{Y \to Y',\ Y \in N_1\}$,
(9) $\{A' \to A'',\ Y' \to (Y, \text{out}) | Y \in N_1, A \in N_2\}$,
(10) $\{a'' \to (a, \text{out}), a \to (a, \text{out}) | a \in T\}$,
(11) $\{A'' \to (A, \text{out}) | A \in N_2\}$,
(12) $e' \to e',\ \dagger \to \dagger$.

The priority rules ρ_1 are

- $r_{1_i}, r_{3_i}, r_{5_i} > r_{8_{j,k\cdots l}}, r_{13}$,
- $r_{2_i}, r_{6_i}, r_{7_i} > r_{4_j}, r_{13}$,
- $r_{11}, r_{12} > r_{4_i}, r_{8_{j,k\cdots l}}, r_{13}, r_{16}$,
- $r_{15} > r_{4_i}, r_{8_{j,k\cdots l}}$,
- $r_{13}, r_{5_i} > r_{16}$, $1 \le i, j, k, l \le n$.

For all $1 \le i, j \le n$, the priority rules ρ_2 are

- $R''_i, R'''_j > r_i, i \ne j$,
- $r_i > r'_i, r''_i$,
- $r''_j > r_i, i \ne j$,
- $r'_i > R_i$, $R_i > R'_i$, $R'_i > r''_i$.

Let h be a homomorphism defined by $h(a) = a''$, $a \in V$ where a'' is a new symbol associated with a.

The system works as follows: In the initial configuration, only membrane one is active. Suppose we have Xw, $X \in N_1$, $w \in (N_2 \cup T)^*$ in the skin membrane.

Simulation of a type 2 matrix: If the symbol X identifying a matrix $m_i : (X \to Y, A \to x)$ is present in the skin, then the only rules which can be applied are r_{1_i} and r_{4_i}, because all other rules are of a lower priority. In the next step, the whole system "sleeps", since there are no objects in membrane two. In the next step, the applicable rules are r_{5_i}, r_{6_i} and Y_i, A_j go to membrane two. In this step, membrane two is active, while the skin membrane sleeps. Now we rewrite Y_i using r_i only if the element A of N_2 rewritten in the skin membrane corresponds to the matrix m_i as specified by the subscript of Y_i or if there were no elements of N_2 corresponding to type 2 or 4 matrices in the skin membrane. In case the element of N_2 rewritten in the skin corresponds to a matrix m_j, $j \neq i$, then r''_j is applied before r_i and the computation goes on for ever. The application of r_i sends out a symbol d which prevents evolution of any symbols of N_2 in the skin. If both Y_i and A_i are present in membrane two, r'_i, R'_i and $Y \to Y'$ are applied. Finally, the rules $A'' \to (A, \text{out})$, $Y' \to (Y, \text{out})$ are applied and the simulation of a type 2 matrix is completed correctly. If there were no elements of N_2 corresponding to type 2, 4 matrices, Y_i alone will be present in membrane two. Then R_i is applied after r_i and $e' \to e'$ can be applied for ever.

Simulation of a type 3 matrix: The rules r_{2_i} and $r_{8_{j,k,\ldots,l}}$ are applied in the skin. The rule $r_{8_{j,k,\ldots,l}}$ ensures that all symbols of N_2 corresponding to type 3 matrices are rewritten. In the next step, the system "sleeps" since membrane two is empty. Again in the next step, r_{7_i} and r_{9_j} are applied in the skin. Now in membrane two, we rewrite A'_j, D'_{A_j} corresponding to type 3 matrices m_j using R'''_j if the subscript j is not the same as the subscript specified by Y'_i. The symbols A'_i, D'_{A_i} corresponding to the same subscript as Y'_i are rewritten using R''_i and the system never halts. In case such symbols do not occur, then r_i is applied to rewrite Y'_i after applying R'''_j. Next, the rules $A' \to A''$, $A'' \to (A, \text{out})$, $Y' \to (Y, \text{out})$ are applied. The symbols d and d' which are sent to the skin membrane while applying R'''_j, r_i in membrane two, prevent the application of rules in the skin membrane. Thus, a type 3 matrix is simulated correctly. Simulation of type 4 matrices is similar to type 2 matrices. If there are elements of N_2 remaining in the skin after applying a type 4 matrix, rules r_{13} and r_{14} are applied and the system never halts. The terminals leave the system using $a \to (a, \text{out})$. It is clear that $PsRE \subseteq PsTDTP_2(Pri, Cat, n\delta, 2)$. □

5. P Systems with Null Parallelism

We now define the second class of P systems to be investigated in this paper.

Definition 2: A *P system with Null Parallelism* (PNP system) of degree m is a construct

$$\Pi = (V, T, H, \mu, w_1, \ldots, w_m, (R, \rho), \infty),$$

where:

- $m \geq 1$;
- V is an alphabet (the *total alphabet* of the system);
- $T \subseteq V$ (the *terminal* alphabet);
- H is a finite set of *labels* for membranes;
- μ is a *membrane structure*, consisting of m membranes, labeled with $1, 2, \ldots, m$;
- $w_1, \ldots, w_m$ are strings over V, describing the *multisets of objects* placed in the m regions of μ;
- R is a finite set of *developmental rules*, ρ is an irreflexive, antisymmetric, non-transitive relation over R, specifying a priority relation among rules of R. The rules are of the following forms:
  — $[_j a]_j \rightarrow [_j v]_j$, $j \in H$, $a \in V$, $v \in V^*$
  (object evolution rules)
  — $[_j a]_j \rightarrow [_j [_{j_1} v_1]_{j_1} [_{j_2} v_2]_{j_2} \cdots [_{j_n} v_n]_{j_n}]_j$ where $a \in V$, $j, j_i \in H$, $v_i \in V^*$, $1 \leq i \leq n$
  (strings are introduced in membranes $j_1, \ldots, j_n$ which are embedded within membrane j),
  — $[_j a]_j \rightarrow [_j]_j b$ for $j \in H$, $a \in V$, $b \in V^*$
  (a string is sent out),
  — $[_j a]_j \rightarrow b$ for $j \in H$, $a \in V$, $b \in V^*$
  (dissolving rules; when an object a dissolves a membrane j, all objects in j reach the immediately superior membrane and all rules involving the membrane j are lost)

The rules are applied according to the following *principle*: At any step, exactly one rule corresponding to one of the membranes $[_j]_j$ can be applied for some $j \in H$. This means that at any step, there is exactly one transition taking place in the PNP system. The transitions take place according to a possible priority relation among the rules. The priority relations are taken care as follows: Suppose there are objects o_1, o_2, o_3 in the system and rules r_1, r_2, r_3 for them with priorities $r_1 > r_2$, $r_2 > r_3$. Because of r_1, r_2 is disabled; this will remain so as long as o_1 is present in the system. But r_1 has no direct relation with r_3. Hence, we may apply r_1 or r_3 as long as r_1 is applicable. If the element o_1 disappears from the system, then r_3 will not be applicable as long as r_2 is applicable.

Now we specify two kinds of PNP systems. In PNP systems of the first kind, an object $a \in V$ will have a single rule in a membrane j. This rules out the non-determinism in having to choose between different rules for the same object in a membrane. In PNP systems of the second kind, an object can have a finite set of rules in each membrane. Both kinds of PNP systems work as follows: in each time unit, a rule corresponding to any of the membranes is applied, obeying the priority relations that may exist between the rules. A computation starts from the initial configuration, we pass to another configuration by a sequence of transition steps; each transition step consisting of the application of a single rule. Thus we get a computation as a result of a sequence of transition steps and we say that a computation is successful if it halts. We say that the system halts if there are no more rules applicable to any of the objects in any of the membranes. The result of a halting configuration consists of all objects over T sent out of the system during the computation.

The family of number relations $\psi_T(\Pi)$, computed by PNP systems Π of kinds i, $i = 1, 2$ of degree n, with priorities and the membrane dissolving action is denoted by $PsPNP_n^i(Pri, \delta)$. When one of the features $\alpha \in \{Pri, \delta\}$ is not present, we replace it with $n\alpha$. The union of all families $PsPNP_n^i(\alpha, \beta)$ is denoted by $PsPNP_*^i(\alpha, \beta)$.

6. The Generative Power

In this section, we investigate the generative power of systems with null parallelism. As in the previous section on time dependent systems, we start looking at systems having less power (in terms of priorities and dissolving actions). The last result characterizes RE, but with no bound on the number of membranes.

Lemma 4: (i) $PsCF \subseteq PsPNP_1^2(nPri, n\delta)$,
(ii) $PsPNP_2^1(nPri, \delta) - CF \neq \phi$.

Proof: (i) Given a context-free grammar $G = (N, T, S, P)$, we construct the PNP system of second kind,

$$\Pi = (N \cup T, T, [_1]_1, \{S\}, (R, \phi), \infty)\,,$$

with

$$R = \{[_1u]_1 \to [_1v]_1 | u \to v \in P\} \cup \{[_1a]_1 \to [_1]_1 a | a \in T\}$$
$$\cup \{[_1u]_1 \to [_1u]_1 | u \in V - T \text{ and } u \text{ corresponds to no rule in } P\}\,.$$

Clearly, $L(G) \subseteq L(\Pi)$.

(ii) Construct the PNP system of first kind and degree two,

$$\Pi = (\{A, B, a, b, c\}, \{a, b, c\}, [_1[_2]_2]_1, \lambda, \{AB\}, (R, \phi), \infty)$$

with

$R = \{[_1a]_1 \to [_1]_1a, [_1b]_1 \to [_1]_1b, [_1c]_1 \to [_1]_1c, [_2A]_2 \to [_2Aabc]_2, [_2B]_2 \to B\}$

In membrane two, we can apply the rule for A or B. As soon as the rule for B is applied, membrane two dissolves. The symbols a, b, c can leave the system in any order. Clearly, Π generates $\{x | \#_a x = \#_b x = \#_c x\}$, which is not in CF. □

Lemma 5: $PsET0L \subseteq PsPNP_1^2(Pri, n\delta)$.

Proof: Let $G = (V, T, w, P_1, P_2)$ be an ET0L system with only two tables as considered in Theorem 4. We construct the PNP system of second kind

$$\Pi = (V', T, [_1]_1, \{Xw\}, (R, \rho), \infty)$$

with

$$\begin{aligned} V' &= V \cup \{X, X_1, X_2\} \cup \{a_1, a_2 | a \in V\} \\ &\cup \{d, e, D\} \cup \{a' | a \in V - T\}, \\ R &= \{[_1X]_1 \to [_1X_i]_1, i = 1, 2\} \cup \{[_1X]_1 \to [_1d]_1\} \\ &\cup \{[_1d]_1 \to [_1d]_1, [_1d]_1 \to [_1]_1\} \\ &\cup \{r_{a_i} : [_1a]_1 \to [_1a_i]_1 | a \in V, i = 1, 2\} \\ &\cup \{r'_{a_i} : [_1a_i]_1 \to [_1ex]_1 | a \to x \in P_i\} \cup \{[_1X_i]_1 \to [_1X]_1 | i = 1, 2\} \\ &\cup \{[_1X_i]_1 \to [_1D]_1 | i = 1, 2\} \cup \{[_1D]_1 \to [_1D]_1\} \\ &\cup \{r_T : [_1a]_1 \to [_1]_1a | a \in T\} \cup \{r_T^c : [_1a]_1 \to [_1a']_1 | a \in V - T\} \\ &\cup \{[_1a']_1 \to [_1a']_1\}\{[_1e]_1 \to [_1e]_1, [_1e]_1 \to [_1]_1\}. \end{aligned}$$

The priority rules ρ are given by

- $[_1X]_1 \to [_1X_i]_1$, $[_1X]_1 \to [_1d]_1 > r_{a_i}$, r'_{a_i}, r_T, r_T^c,
- $[_1X_i]_1 \to [_1D]_1 > r_{a_j}$, $j \neq i$,
- $r_{a_j} > [_1X_i]_1 \to [_1X]_1, r'_{a_i}$, $\forall\ i, j$,
- $r'_{a_i} > [_1X_i]_1 \to [_1X]_1$, $[_1e]_1 \to [_1]_1$,
- r_T, $r_T^c > [_1d]_1 \to [_1]_1$,
- $[_1e]_1 \to [_1e]_1 > r_{a_i}$,
- $[_1e]_1 \to [_1]_1 > r_{a_i}$, $[_1X]_1 \to [_1X_i]_1$, $[_1X]_1 \to [_1d]_1$,
- $[_1d]_1 \to [_1d]_1 > r_{a_i}$, r'_{a_i}.

The rule $[_1X]_1 \to [_1X_i]_1$ decides the table to be simulated. The priorities ensure that the simulation of tables are done correctly. The terminals can leave the system using the rule r_T at the end of a halting configuration. If any nonterminals remain, r_T^c is applied and the system never halts. □

Lemma 6: $PsPNP_2^1(Pri, \delta) - MAT \neq \phi$.

Proof: Consider the PNP system of first kind and degree two

$$\Pi = (\{A, A', B, a\}, \{a\}, [_1[_2]_2]_1, \lambda, \{AB\}, (R, \rho), \infty)$$

with

$$R = \{[_1A]_1 \to [_1]_1a, [_1A']_1 \to [_1]_1a, [_1a]_1 \to [_1]_1a, [_2a]_2 \to [_2A'A']_2\}$$
$$\cup \{[_2A']_2 \to [_2A]_2, [_2A]_2 \to [_2a]_2, [_2B]_2 \to \lambda\},$$
$$\rho = \{[_2A]_2 \to [_2a]_2 > [_2a]_2 \to [_2A'A']_2; [_2A']_2 \to [_2A]_2 > [_2A]_2 \to [_2a]_2;$$
$$[_2a]_2 \to [_2A'A']_2 > [_2B]_2 \to \lambda, [_2A']_2 \to [_2A]_2\}.$$

Clearly, the system generates $\{a^{2^n} | n \geq 0\}$, which is not in MAT. □

Theorem 2: $PsRE \subseteq PsPNP_*^2(Pri, n\delta)$.

Proof: We omit the proof which can be found in the full version of the paper. □

References

1. J. Dassow and Gh. Păun, *Regulated Rewriting in Formal Language Theory*, Springer-Verlag, Berlin, 1989.
2. Gh. Păun, Computing with membranes, *Journal of Computer and System Sciences*, 61 (2000) and *Turku Center for Computer Science-TUCS Report* No. 208, 1998 (www.tucs.fi).
3. Gh. Păun, Computing with P Systems: Twenty Six Research Topics, *Auckland University, CDMTCS Report* No. 119, 2000 (www.cs.auckland.ac.nz/CDMTCS).
4. Gh. Păun, G. Rozenberg and A. Salomaa, Membrane computing with external output, *Fundamenta Informaticae*, 41, 3 (2000), 259–266, (www.tucs.fi).
5. A. Salomaa, *Formal Languages*, Academic Press, 1973.
6. G. Rozenberg and A. Salomaa, eds., *Handbook of Formal Languages*, Springer-Verlag, Heidelberg, 1997.

CHAPTER 15

ITERATION LEMMATA FOR RATIONAL, LINEAR, AND ALGEBRAIC LANGUAGES OVER ALGEBRAIC STRUCTURES WITH SEVERAL BINARY OPERATIONS

Manfred Kudlek
Fachbereich Informatik, Universität Hamburg, Germany
E-mail: kudlek@informatik.uni-hamburg.de

In this paper iteration lemmata for rational, linear, and algebraic languages defined by corresponding systems of equations over structures with several binary operations and a common neutral element are shown. This is a generalization of monoids with only one operation.

1. Introduction

A lot of iteration lemmata for rational, linear and algebraic languages over algebraic structures with an associative binary operation and a unit element (monoids) can be found (e.g. Ref. 5). Using a general result on normal forms in Ref. 9 such iteration lemmata can be generalized to algebraic structures with several, not necessarily associative, binary operations. Also the existence of a common neutral element of the binary operations is not necessary. If there is such an element it has to fulfill a certain nondivisibilty condition.

Rational, linear and algebraic languages are defined as least fixed point solutions of systems of equations. Such systems of equations have a strong relation to grammars or rewriting systems. In both, binary trees can be constructed, with operators and variables as vertex labels. To state iteration lemmata some norm or measure is introduced for elements of the algebraic structure and sets of them, fulfilling some conditions.

2. Systems of Equations

Definitions. In this section the definitions of rational, linear and algebraic languages as least fixed points of corresponding systems of equations are introduced.

Let $\mathcal{G}$ be a structure with a finite set of binary operations $\mathcal{O}$ and common unit element $\mathbf{1}$:

$\odot : \mathcal{G} \times \mathcal{G} \rightarrow \mathcal{P}_f(\mathcal{G})$ where $\mathcal{P}_f(\mathcal{G}) = \{A \subseteq \mathcal{G} | 0 < |A| < \infty\}$,

$\mathbf{1} \odot \{\alpha\} = \{\alpha\} \odot \mathbf{1} = \{\alpha\}$ for $\alpha \in \mathcal{G}$ and $\odot \in \mathcal{O}$.

Note that a normal binary operation $\odot : \mathcal{G} \times \mathcal{G} \rightarrow \mathcal{G}$ can also be written in this way as $\alpha \odot \beta = \{\gamma\}$.

Extend each $\odot \in \mathcal{O}$ to a binary operation $\odot : \mathcal{P}(\mathcal{G}) \times \mathcal{P}(\mathcal{G}) \rightarrow \mathcal{P}(\mathcal{G})$ by defining $A \odot B = \bigcup_{\alpha \in A, \beta \in B} (\alpha \odot \beta)$. $\odot$ is distributive with union $\cup$ (i.e. the identities $A \odot (B \cup C) = (A \odot B) \cup (A \odot C)$ and $(A \cup B) \odot C = (A \odot C) \cup (B \odot C)$ are valid), with unit element $\{\mathbf{1}\}$ ($\{\mathbf{1}\} \odot A = A \odot \{\mathbf{1}\} = A$), and zero element $\emptyset$ ($\emptyset \odot A = A \odot \emptyset = \emptyset$).

$\odot$ is an associative operation if $(\{\alpha\} \odot \{\beta\}) \odot \{\gamma\} = \{\alpha\} \odot (\{\beta\} \odot \{\gamma\})$ with the above extension. Obviously, then $\odot$ is also an associative operation on $\mathcal{P}(\mathcal{G})$, i.e. $(A \odot B) \odot C = A \odot (B \odot C)$.

Then $\mathcal{S}_\odot = (\mathcal{P}(\mathcal{G}), \cup, \odot, \emptyset, \{\mathbf{1}\})$ is an ω-complete semiring for each operation $\odot \in \mathcal{O}$, i.e. if $A_i \subseteq A_{i+1}$ for $0 \leq i$ then $B \odot \bigcup_{i \geq 0} A_i = \bigcup_{i \geq 0} (B \odot A_i)$ and $(\bigcup_{i \geq 0} A_i) \odot B = \bigcup_{i \geq 0} (A_i \odot B)$ hold.

Let $\mathcal{S} = \mathcal{S}_\mathcal{O} = (\mathcal{P}(\mathcal{G}), \cup, \mathcal{O}, \emptyset, \{\mathbf{1}\})$ denote the entire structure.

Let $p = |\mathcal{O}|$.

If $\odot$ is associative, define also

$$A^{(\odot,0)} = \{\mathbf{1}\}, \quad A^{(\odot,1)} = A, \quad A^{(\odot,k+1)} = A \odot A^{(\odot,k)},$$

and

$$A^{\odot} = \bigcup_{k \geq 0} A^{(\odot,k)}$$

for $\odot \in \mathcal{O}$.

In the sequel also prefix notation will be used sometimes, i.e. $\odot AB$ for $(A \odot B)$. With this one gets labelled binary trees over $\mathcal{P}_f(\mathcal{G})$ with vertex labels $\odot \in \mathcal{O}$ or $A \in \mathcal{P}_f(\mathcal{G})$ (for leafs).

Example 1: $\mathcal{S} = (\mathcal{P}(\Sigma^*), \cup, \{\cdot, ⧢\}, \emptyset, \{\lambda\})$ where Σ is an alphabet, $\cdot$ is normal catenation, and ⧢ the shuffle operation, and $\{\lambda\}$ the common neutral element.

Let $\mathcal{X} = \{X_1, \ldots, X_n\}$ be a set of variables such that $\mathcal{X} \cap \mathcal{G} = \emptyset$.

Define the set of *terms* $\mathcal{A} = \mathcal{A}(\mathcal{G}, \mathcal{O}, \mathcal{X})$ over $\mathcal{G}$, $\mathcal{O}$, $\mathcal{X}$ by:

$$\mathcal{P}_f(\mathcal{G}) \subseteq \mathcal{A}, \quad \mathcal{X} \subseteq \mathcal{A}, \quad f_1, f_2 \in \mathcal{A} \Rightarrow f_1 \odot f_2 \in \mathcal{A} \text{ for } \odot \in \mathcal{O},$$

and only such elements are in $\mathcal{A}$.

Let $\mathcal{P}_f(\mathcal{G})$ be called the set of *constants*.

A *monomial* over $\mathcal{S}$ is just an element $m \in \mathcal{A}$.

A *polynomial* $p(\underline{X})$ over $\mathcal{S}$ is a finite union of monomials with the notation $\underline{X} = (X_1, \ldots, X_n)$:

$$p_i(\underline{X}) = \bigcup_j m_{ij}\,.$$

Without loss of generality, the set $\mathcal{C} = \{\{\alpha\}|\alpha \in \mathcal{G}\} \subseteq \mathcal{P}_f(\mathcal{G})$ of constants suffices.

The *solution* of a system of equations $\mathcal{E}$ is a n-tuple $\underline{L} = (L_1, \ldots, L_n)$ of sets over $\mathcal{G}$, with $L_i = p_i(L_1, \ldots, L_n)$ and the n-tuple is the least one with this property, i.e. if $\underline{L'} = (L'_1, \ldots, L'_n)$ is another n-tuple satisfying $\mathcal{E}$, then $\underline{L} \leq \underline{L'}$ (where the order is defined componentwise with respect to inclusion, i.e. $\underline{A} = (A_1, \ldots, A_n) \leq (B_1, \ldots, B_n) = \underline{B} \Leftrightarrow \forall_{i=1}^{n} : A_i \subseteq B_i$).

From the theory of semirings follows that any system of equations over $\mathcal{S}$ has a unique solution, and this is the least fixed point starting with

$$\underline{X}^{(0)} = (X_1^{(0)}, \ldots, X_n^{(0)}) = (\emptyset, \ldots, \emptyset) = \underline{\emptyset}\,,$$

and

$$\underline{X}^{t+1} = \underline{p}(\underline{X}^{(t)})$$

Then the following fact holds: $\underline{X}^{(t)} \leq \underline{X}^{(t+1)}$ for $0 \leq t$.

This is seen by induction and the property of the polynomial with respect to inclusion, since

$$\underline{\emptyset} \leq \underline{X}^{(1)} \text{ and } \underline{X}^{(t+1)} = \underline{p}(\underline{X}^{(t)}) \leq \underline{p}(\underline{X}^{(t+1)}) = \underline{X}^{(t+2)}\,.$$

For the theory of semirings see Refs. 3 and 8, and for generalizations also Refs. 6 and 7.

A general system of equations is called *algebraic*, *linear* if all monomials are of the form $(A \odot_1 X) \odot_2 B$, $A \odot_1 (X \odot_2 B)$, $A \odot X$, $X \odot A$, X, or A, and *rational* if they are of the form $X \odot A$, X, or A, with $A \subseteq \mathcal{G}$. Corresponding families of languages (solutions of such systems of equations) are denoted by $\mathbf{ALG}(\mathcal{O})$, $\mathbf{LIN}(\mathcal{O})$, and $\mathbf{RAT}(\mathcal{O})$.

Grammars

Interpreting an equation $X_i = p_i(\underline{X})$ as a set of rewriting productions $X_i \to m_{ij}$ with $m_{ij} \in M(X_i)$ where $M(X_i)$ denotes the set of monomials of $p_i(\underline{X})$, *regular*, *linear*, and *context-free* grammars $G_i = (\mathcal{X}, \mathcal{C}, \mathcal{O}, X_i, P)$ using the operations $\odot \in \mathcal{O}$, can be defined. Here $\mathcal{C}$ stands for the set of all constants in the system of equations, and P for all productions defined as above. As the productions are *context-free* (*terminal*) derivation trees can also be defined. Note that the interior nodes are labelled either by pairs $(\odot, X)$ for productions of the form $X \rightarrow \odot f_1 f_2$ in prefix form, X for productions of the form $X \rightarrow Y$ or $X \rightarrow \{\alpha\}$, or by constants $\{\alpha\}$ for leafs.

3. Normal Forms

By Lemma 3.1 in Ref. 9 follows that to each system of equations an equivalent one (with additional variables) can be constructed such that any monomial on the right hand side of an equation has either the form $X \odot Y$ with $X, Y \in \mathcal{X}$ and $\odot \in \mathcal{O}$, or $\{\alpha\}$ with $\alpha \in \mathcal{C}$.

For the sequel assume the property

$$\mathbf{1} \in A \odot A \Leftrightarrow (\mathbf{1} \in A \wedge \mathbf{1} \in B) forall \odot \in \mathcal{O} .$$

This avoids the possibility that $\mathbf{1} \in \{\alpha\} \odot \{\beta\}$ for $\alpha \neq \mathbf{1}$ or $\beta \neq \mathbf{1}$, and represents some kind of nondivisibility of the unit $\mathbf{1}$.

In the following a well known construction to remove λ-productions in context-free grammars is used to remove $\mathbf{1}$ on the right hand side of equations. To achieve that define sets of variables inductively by

$$S_0 = \{X \in \mathcal{X} | \mathbf{1} \in M(X)\}$$

and

$$S_{j+1} = S_j \cup \{X \in \mathcal{X} | \exists Y, Z \in \mathcal{X} \exists \odot \in \mathbf{O} : \odot Y Z \in M(X)\} .$$

Obviously, there exists a minimal k such that $S_{k+1} = S_k$. For every $X \in S_k$ define a new variable $\overline{X}$.

For all $X \in \mathcal{X}$ consider all monomials in $M(X)$. They are of the form either $Y \odot Z$ or $\{\alpha\}$. Add to $M(X)$ the monomials Y and/or Z if $Y \in S_k$ and/or $Z \in S_k$, and remove $\{\mathbf{1}\}$ from $M(X)$ if present, yielding a set $m'(X)$. Now, define $M(\overline{X}) = M'(X) \cup \{\mathbf{1}\}$ if $\{\mathbf{1}\} \in M(X)$ and $M(\overline{X}) = M'(X)$ if $\{\mathbf{1}\} \notin M(X)$.

Then the new system of equations has identical solutions in the variables $\mathcal{X} \setminus S_k$ and $\overline{S_k}$. Interchanging the variables $\overline{X}$ and X implies that the new system has identical solutions in the variables $X \in \mathcal{X}$.

By the same construction as in Lemma 3.1 of Ref. 9 a new equivalent system of equations without monomials of the form Y with $Y \in \mathcal{X}$ can be constructed.

Thus one gets

Lemma 1: (Normal form for algebraic systems).

For any algebraic system of equations another one, possibly with additional variables, can be constructed effiently, having identical solutions in the old variables, and with monomials in $M(X)$ *of the form* $Y \odot Z$, $\{\alpha\}$ *with* $\alpha \neq \mathbf{1}$, *or* $\{\mathbf{1}\}$ *in which case* $X \notin M(X')$ *for all* $X' \in \mathcal{X}$.

The next lemma presents a relation between algebraic systems and grammars. For this terminal trees are constructed representing approximations of the least fixed point, and it is shown that the sets of terminal derivation trees with respect to $\mathcal{O}$ are equivalent.

Lemma 2: (Approximation of the least fixed point).

Terminal trees for the approximation of the least fixed point and terminal derivation trees are equivalent.

Proof: By Lemma 1 it may be assumed that variables and constants are separated.

$$\underline{X}^{(0)} = \underline{\emptyset}\,, \quad \underline{X}^{(t+1)} = \underline{p}(\underline{X}^{(t)})$$

Thus

$$X_i^{(t+1)} = \bigcup_j m'_{ij} \cup \bigcup_k \{\alpha_{ik}\}$$

where m'_{ij} are those monomials for X_i containing only variables.

Especially,

$$X_i^{(0)} = \emptyset\,, \quad X_i^{(1)} = \bigcup_k \{\alpha_{ik}\}$$

Construct forests $\mathcal{T}$ of terminal trees as follows:

$\mathcal{T}^{(1)}$ consists of all trees with roots X and children (only leafs) $\{\alpha\}$ with $\{\alpha\} \in M(X)$. Note that only monomials $\{\alpha\}$ are possible in this case.

If there are two trees, possibly identical, in $\mathcal{T}^{(1)}$ with root labels Y and Z, and $Y \odot Z \in M(X)$, then the tree with root $(\odot, X)$ and subtrees with root labels Y and Z (in this order) is in $\mathcal{T}^{(2)}$.

For $t > 1$, if there are two trees, possibly identical, in $\mathcal{T}^{(t)}$ with root labels $(\odot_1, Y)$ and $(\odot_2, Z)$, and $Y \odot Z \in M(X)$, then the tree with root $(\odot, X)$ and subtrees with root labels $(\odot_1, Y)$ and $(\odot_2, Z)$ (in this order) is in $\mathcal{T}^{(t+1)}$.

Note that all trees constructed in this way are binary trees.

Finally, define

$$\mathcal{T} = \bigcup_{t=1}^{\infty} \mathcal{T}^{(t)} .$$

On the other hand, any terminal derivation tree for X, i.e. one with constants $\{\alpha\}$ as labels for leafs, is contained in $\mathcal{T}$. This is obvious since any derivation tree just interprets the equations in one direction only. Note that the vertices are labelled by $(\odot, X)$, X (just above the leafs), or $\{\alpha\}$ (leafs). □

Removing $\{\mathbf{1}\}$ in a way analogous as for Lemma 1, and monomials Y as in Lemma 3.1 of Ref. 9, replacing monomials $\{\alpha\} \odot_1 (Y \odot_2 \{\beta\}) \in M(X)$ by $\{\alpha\} \odot_1 Z \in M(X)$ and $Y \odot_1 \{\beta\} \in M(Z)$, and $(\{\alpha \odot_1 Y) \odot_2 \{\beta\} \in M(X)$ by monomials $Z \odot_2 \{\beta\} \in M(X)$ and $\{\alpha\} \odot_1 Y \in M(Z)$, where Z is a new variable, the following two lemmata may be shown.

Lemma 3: (Normal form for rational systems).
To each rational system of equations there exists another one with monomials only of the forms $Y \odot \{\alpha\}$ with $\alpha \neq \mathbf{1}$, or $\{\alpha\}$, and with identical solutions.

Lemma 4: (Normal form for linear systems).
To each linear system of equations there exists another one with monomials only of the forms $Y \odot \{\alpha\}$, $\{\alpha\} \odot Y$ with $\alpha \neq \mathbf{1}$, or $\{\alpha\}$, and with identical solutions.

It should be remarked that the normal form lemmata also hold in the case that there is no neutral element $\mathbf{1}$.

4. Iteration Lemmata

In this section iteration lemmata will be shown. To achieve them a norm on the elements $\alpha \in \mathcal{G}$ and sets $A \subseteq \mathcal{G}$ has to be introduced.

Let a norm $\mu : \mathcal{G} \to I\!N$ be defined on $\mathcal{G}$. It can be extended to $\mathcal{P}(\mathcal{G})$ canonically by $\mu(A) = \max\{\mu(\alpha) | \alpha \in A\}$.

Assume that μ has the following properties:
$\mu(\emptyset) = \mu(\{\mathbf{1}\}) = 0$, $\mu(\{\alpha\}) > 0$ for $\alpha \neq \mathbf{1}$
$\mu(A), \mu(B) \leq \mu(A \odot B) \leq \mu(A) + \mu(B)$ for all $\odot \in \mathcal{O}$ if $A \neq \emptyset$, $B \neq \emptyset$.
Trivially, $\mu(A \cup B) = \max\{\mu(A), \mu(B)\}$.

Example 2: Consider Example 1 with the norm $\mu(a) = 1$ for $a \in \Sigma$. Then $\mu(\alpha \cdot \beta) = \mu(\alpha) + \mu(\beta)$ and $\mu(\alpha \sqcup\!\sqcup \beta) = \mu(\alpha) + \mu(\beta)$.

For a system of equation $\mathcal{E}$ with constants $\mathcal{C}$ define also

$$m = \min\{\mu(\{\alpha\}|\{\alpha\} \in \mathcal{C}\}, \quad M = \max\{\mu(\{\alpha\}|\{\alpha\} \in \mathcal{C}\}.$$

If t is the depth of a derivation tree of a rational or linear grammar in normal form corresponding to such system of equations, with α in its generated set, then

$$m \cdot t \leq \mu(\alpha) \leq M \cdot t.$$

If t is the depth of a derivation tree of a context-free grammar in normal form corresponding to an algebraic system of equations, with α in its generated set, then

$$m \cdot t \leq \mu(\alpha) \leq M \cdot 2^{t-1}.$$

In the following theorems terms are used in prefix notation. The first one presents an iteration lemma for $\mathbf{RAT}(\mathcal{O})$.

Theorem 1: For every rational language L defined by a rational system of equations there exists an integer N such that the following fact holds: if $\alpha \in L$ with $\mu(\alpha) > N$ then there exist an operation $\odot \in \mathcal{O}$ such that $\alpha \in O_1 \odot O_2 \odot O_3 v\{\gamma\} u_2\{\beta\} u_1$, $\mu(\odot O_2 \odot O_3 v\{\gamma\} u_2\{\beta\}) \leq N$, and $O_1(\odot O_2)^r \odot O_3 v\{\gamma\}(u_2\{\beta\})^r u_1 \subseteq L$ for all $r \geq 0$, and the iteration is not trivial, i.e. with $\{\mathbf{1}\}$ (O_j are sequences of operations, and u_j, v sequences of constants).

Proof: By Lemma 3 grammars in normal form and derivation trees can be used. Let $N = p \cdot n + 1$. If $\mu(\alpha) > N$ then there are two identically labelled vertices $(\odot, A)$ on the main path of the derivation tree. This means that

$$S \xrightarrow{*} O_1 A u_1 \rightarrow O_1 \odot B\{\beta\} u_1 \xrightarrow{*} O_1 \odot O_2 A u_2\{\beta\} u_1$$
$$\rightarrow O_1 \odot O_2 \odot C\{\gamma\} u_2\{\beta\} u_1 \xrightarrow{*} O_1 \odot O_2 \odot O_3 v\{\gamma\} u_2\{\beta\} u_1$$

where O_j are sequences of operations and u_j, v sequences of constants.

Then also $O_1(\odot O_2)^r \odot O_3 v\{\gamma\}(u_2\{\beta\})^r u_1 \subseteq L$ for $r \geq 0$.

Note that $\odot B\{\beta\}$, $O_2 A u_2$, $\odot C\{\gamma\}$, $\odot O_3 v\{\gamma\}$ are terms.

Considering a lower subpath of length $N+1$ gives $\mu(\odot O_2 \odot v\{\gamma\} u_2\{\beta\}) \leq N$. □

In the next an analogous iteration lemma for $\mathbf{LIN}(\mathcal{O})$ is given.

Theorem 2: For every linear language L defined by a linear system of equations there exists an integer N such that the following fact holds: if $\alpha \in L$ with $\mu(\alpha) > N$ then there exist an operation $\odot \in \mathcal{O}$ such that

$$\alpha \in u_1 \odot u_2 \odot w v_2\{\beta\} v_1, \mu(u_1 \odot u_2\{\mathbf{1}\} v_2\{\beta\} v_1) \leq N,$$

or

$$\alpha \in u_1 \odot \{\beta\}u_2 \odot wv_2v_1\,, \quad \mu(u_1 \odot \{\beta\}u_2\{\mathbf{1}\}v_2v_1) \le N\,,$$

and $u_1(\odot u_2)^r \odot w(v_2\{\beta\})^r v_1 \subseteq L$, or $u_1(\odot\{\beta\}u_2)^r \odot w(v_2)^r v_1 \subseteq L$ for all integers $r \ge 0$, and the iteration is not trivial, i.e. with $\{\mathbf{1}\}$ (u_j, v_j, w are sequences of operations and constants).

Proof: By Lemma 4 grammars in normal form and derivation trees can be used. Let $N = p \cdot n + 1$. If $\mu(\alpha) > N$ then there are two identically labelled vertices $(\odot, A)$ on the main path of the derivation tree. This means that

$$S \xrightarrow{*} u_1Av_1 \rightarrow u_1 \odot B\{\beta\}v_1 \xrightarrow{*} u_1 \odot u_2Av_2\{\beta\}v_1 \rightarrow u_1 \odot u_2 \odot C\{\gamma\}v_2\{\beta\}v_1$$

$$\xrightarrow{*} u_1 \odot u_2 \odot wv_2\{\beta\}v_1 \text{ or}$$

$$S \xrightarrow{*} u_1Av_1 \rightarrow u_1 \odot B\{\beta\}v_1 \xrightarrow{*} u_1 \odot u_2Av_2\{\beta\}v_1 \rightarrow u_1 \odot u_2 \odot \{\gamma\}Cv_2\{\beta\}v_1$$

$$\xrightarrow{*} u_1 \odot u_2 \odot wv_2\{\beta\}v_1 \text{ or}$$

$$S \xrightarrow{*} u_1Av_1 \rightarrow u_1 \odot \{\beta\}Bv_1 \xrightarrow{*} u_1 \odot \{\beta\}u_2Av_2v_1 \rightarrow u_1 \odot \{\beta\}u_2 \odot C\{\gamma\}v_2v_1$$

$$\xrightarrow{*} u_1 \odot \{\beta\}u_2 \odot wv_2v_1 \text{ or}$$

$$S \xrightarrow{*} u_1Av_1 \rightarrow u_1 \odot \{\beta\}Bv_1 \xrightarrow{*} u_1 \odot \{\beta\}u_2Av_2v_1 \rightarrow u_1 \odot \{\beta\}u_2 \odot \{\gamma\}Cv_2v_1$$

$$\xrightarrow{*} u_1 \odot \{\beta\}u_2 \odot wv_2v_1$$

where u_j, v_j, w are sequences of operations and constants.

Then also $u_1(\odot u_2)^r \odot w(v_2\{\beta\})^r v_1 \subseteq L$ or $u_1(\odot\{\beta\}u_2)^r \odot w(v_2)^r v_1 \subseteq L$ for $r \ge 0$.

Note that $\odot B\{\beta\}$, $u_2Av_2, \odot w$ are terms.

Considering an upper subpath of length $N+1$ gives

$$\mu(u_1 \odot u_2\{\mathbf{1}\}v_2\{\beta\}v_1) \le N \text{ or } \mu(u_1 \odot \{\beta\}u_2\{\mathbf{1}\}v_2v_1) \le N\,. \qquad \square$$

The last one presents an iteration lemma for $\mathbf{ALG}(\mathcal{O})$.

Theorem 3: For every algebraic language L defined by an algebraic system of equations there exists an integer N such that the following fact holds: if $\alpha \in L$ with $\mu(\alpha) > N$ then there exist an operation $\odot \in \mathcal{O}$ such that

$$\alpha \in u_1 \odot u_2 \odot wv_2v_1\,, \quad \mu(\odot u_2 \odot wv_2) \le N\,,$$

and

$$u_1(\odot u_2)^r \odot w(v_2)^r v_1 \subseteq L$$

for all $r \geq 0$, and the iteration is not trivial, i.e. with $\{\mathbf{1}\}$ (u_j, v_j, w are sequences of operations and constants).

Proof: By Lemma 1 grammars in normal form and derivation trees can be used. Let $N = 2^{p \cdot n+1}$. If $\mu(\alpha) > N$ then the depth of the derivation tree is $t > p \cdot n + 2$, and therefore there are two identically labelled vertices $(\odot, A)$ on a longest path of the derivation tree. This means that

$$S \xrightarrow{*} u_1 A v_1 \rightarrow u_1 \odot BC v_1 \xrightarrow{*} u_1 \odot u_2 A v_2 v_1 \rightarrow u_1 \odot u_2 \odot DE v_2 v_1$$

$$\xrightarrow{*} u_1 \odot u_2 \odot w v_2 v_1$$

where u_j, v_j, w are sequences of operations and constants.

Then also $u_1(\odot u_2)^r \odot w(v_2)^r v_1 \subseteq L$ for $r \geq 0$.

Note that $\odot BC$, $u_2 A v_2$, $\odot DE$, $\odot w$ are terms.

Considering a lower subpath of a longest path, of length $N + 1$, gives $\mu(\odot u_2 \odot w v_2) \leq N$. □

Again, if there is no neutral element **1**, the iteration lemmata, without **1**, hold too.

References

1. V. E. Căzănescu, *Introducere în Teoria Limbajelor Formale.* Editura Academiei RSR, Bucureşti, 1983.
2. S. Eilenberg and J. B. Wright, *Automata in General Algebras.* IC **11**, 452–470, 1967.
3. J. S. Golan, *The Theory of Semirings with Application in Mathematics and Theoretical Computer Science.* Longman Scientific and Technical, 1992.
4. M. Kudlek, *Generalized Iteration Lemmata.* PU. M. A., Vol. 6 No. 2, 211–216, 1995.
5. M. Kudlek, *Iteration Lemmata for Certain Classes of Word, Trace and Graph Languages.* Fundamenta Informaticae, Vol. 34, 249–264, 1999.
6. W. Kuich, *Semigroups and Formal Power Series: Their Relevance to Formal Language and Automata Theory.* In: Handbook of Formal Languages (eds. G. Rozenberg, A. Salomaa) Vol. 1, Chapter 9, 609–677, Springer, 1997.
7. W. Kuich, *Formal Series over Algebras.* LNCS 1893, 488–496, 2000.
8. W. Kuich and A. Salomaa, *Semirings, Automata, Languages.* EATCS Monographs on Theoretical Computer Science 5, Springer, Berlin, 1986.
9. J. Mezei and J. B. Wright, *Algebraic Automata and Context-free Sets.* IC **11**, 3–29, 1967.
10. A. Salomaa, *Formal Languages.* Academic Press, New York, London 1973.

CHAPTER 16

THE COMPUTATIONAL EFFICIENCY OF INSERTION DELETION TISSUE P SYSTEMS

K. Lakshmanan*
School of Technology and Computer Science,
Tata Institute of Fundamental Research,
Homi Bhabha Road, Colaba,
Mumbai 400 005, India
E-mail: lakshtifr.res.in

R. Rama†
Department of Mathematics,
Indian Institute of Technology Madras,
Chennai 600 036, India
E-mail: ramar@iitm.ac.in

Insertion and deletion of small strands of DNA happen frequently in all types of cells and so is a powerful operation in DNA computing area.[1] P System is a class of distributed and parallel computing model inspired from the structure and functioning of a living cell. Tissue P systems is a variant of P systems which capture the notion of inter cellular communication among the cells. The computational power of tissue P systems[8] with string-objects as the underlying data structure and insertion-deletion rules as the control structure was considered in Ref. 5. In this paper, we continue the study on insertion deletion tissue P systems towards computational efficiency point of view. We show that when these systems work in replication mode, they are able to solve NP-complete problems in polynomial time and this is exemplified by solving SAT and HPP in linear time.

*The author's work was carried out during his stay at IIT Madras.

†The author's work was partially supported in part by a Project Sanction No. DST/MS/124/99, funded by Department of Science and Technology, New Delhi.

1. Introduction

P systems introduced by Gh. Păun[9] are distributed parallel computing models which start from the observation that the processes which takes place in the complex structure of a living cell. Basically, such a system consists of a *membrane structure*, where the *regions* are separated by the membranes contain multisets of *objects* which can change (evolve) according to *rules* and can be transported from one region to another. But in most cases, since cells live together and are associated with tissues and organs, *inter-cellular* communication becomes an essential feature. This communication is done through the protein channels existing among the membranes of the neighboring cells.[6] This has been the main motivation for the introduction of tissue P systems.[8]

Tissue P systems (in short tP systems) are also motivated from the way *neurons* cooperate. A neuron has a body containing a *nucleus*; their membranes are prolonged by two classes of fibers: the *dendrites* which form a filamentary bush around the body of the neuron, and the *axon*, a unique, long filament which ends in a filamentous bush. Each of the filaments from the end of the axon is terminated with a small bulb. Neurons process impulses in the complex net established by *synapses*. A synapse is a contact between an end bulb of a neuron and the dendrites of another neuron. The neuron *synthesizes* an impulse which is transmitted to the neurons to which it is related by synapses; the synthesis of an impulse and its transmission to adjacent neurons are done according to certain *states* of the neuron. The symbols (objects or strings) are transmitted to other cells either by *replicative* or by *non-replicative* manner.

The insertion (deletion) operation means that given a pair of words (u, v) called the *context* and the insertion (deletion) of x into a word w is performed between u and v in w. This operation is a counterpart of *contextual grammars*,[10] where given a word x in w (called the *selector*) and a *context* (u, v), we adjoin u to the left of x and v to the right of x in w. Insertions and deletions of small linear DNA strands into long linear DNA strands are phenomena that happen frequently in nature and thus constitute an attractive paradigm for biomolecular computing. Gene insertion and deletion are basic phenomena found in DNA processing or RNA editing in molecular biology. The genetic mechanism and development based on these evolutionary transformations have been formulated as a formal system with two operations of insertion and deletion, called *insertion-deletion systems*.[1–3]

These systems are found very powerful, leading to characterizations of recursively enumerable language. Such results can be found in Refs. 7, 12 and 14. In Refs. 2 and 12 the characterizations of RE (the family of languages generated by recursive enumerable grammars) are obtained with a total weight being equal to 5; in Ref. 14 the total weight is improved to 4; in Ref. 7 context-free insertion-deletion systems are considered and the characterizations of RE are obtained with weight (3, 0; 3, 0), (2, 0; 3, 0) and (3, 0; 2, 0).

In Ref. 4, P systems with string objects having insertion-deletion rules as the control structure is considered and their generative power is investigated in comparison with CF, MAT, RE. In Ref. 11 the characterization of RE is obtained with one membrane and of weight (3, 1; 2, 0) and this result is improved to weight (3, 0; 2, 0) in Ref. 7. In Ref. 5 tissue P systems with insertion-deletion rules were considered and analyzed their generative power in comparison with RE, $ET0L$, $E0L$, CF.

In this paper, we renew the study on insertion-deletion tP systems and investigate their efficiency of solving NP-Complete problems in polynomial time. In order to prove the efficiency, we solve the satisfiability problem and the Hamiltonian path problem in linear time. This paper is organized as follows: In Section 2, we restate the definition of insertion-deletion tP systems which was introduced in Ref. 5. In Section 3, we first present a corollary on computational universality of the system which directly follows from Ref. 7. Then we prove the efficiency of these systems by solving NP-complete problems in linear time. Section 4 concludes the paper with the final remarks.

All formal language notions and notations we use here are elementary and standard. The reader can consult any of the monographs in this area – for instance Ref. 13 for the unexplained details.

2. Insertion-Deletion tP System

We refer to Refs. 8 and 11 for the basic elements of P systems and tP systems theory. Here, we directly present the variant of tP systems we are going to investigate.

A *insertion-deletion tissue P system* (in short InsDel tP system) *of degree* $m \geq 1$ (the degree of a system is the number of cells in the system) is a construct

$$\Pi = (O, T, \sigma_1, \ldots, \sigma_m, syn, i_{\text{out}}),$$

where:

(1) O is a finite non-empty alphabet;
(2) $T \subseteq O$ is the terminal or output alphabet;
(3) $syn \subseteq \{1, 2, \ldots, m\} \times \{1, 2, \ldots, m\}$ (synapses among cells). If $(i, j) \in syn$, then j is a *successor* of i and i is an *ancestor* of j. Also, if $(i \leftrightarrow j) \in syn$ implies $\{(i, j), (j, i)\} \in syn$;
(4) $i_{\text{out}} \in \{1, 2, \ldots, m\}$ indicates the *output cell*;
(5) $\sigma_1, \ldots, \sigma_m$ are *cells* of the form

$$\sigma_i = (Q_i, s_{i,0}, L_{i,0}, P_i), \quad 1 \leq i \leq m,$$

where:

(a) Q_i is a finite set of *states*;
(b) $s_{i,0} \in Q_i$ is the *initial state*;
(c) $L_{i,0} \in O^*$ is the set of *initial strings*;
(d) P_i is a finite set of *rules* which can be in one of the following forms:

— Insertion rules of the form $s(u, s'/x, v)_a$ or $(s(u, s'/x, v), tar)_a$
— Deletion rules of the form $s(u, x/s', v)_e$ or $(s(u, x/s', v), tar)_e$

where, s, $s' \in Q_i$, u, x, $v \in O^*$ and $tar \in \{\text{go}, \text{out}\}$, with the restriction that only $P_{i_{\text{out}}}$ can contain rules of the form $(s(u, s'/x, v), \text{out})_a$ or $(s(u, x/s', v), \text{out})_e$.

We will see how an insertion rule can be applied to a string $w \in O^*$ in a cell σ_i. If the rule $s(u, s'/x, v)_a$ is applied to a string w, then this means that x can be inserted to the left of v and to the right of u in the string w under the control state s and the resultant string $z \in O^*$ will come now under the control state s'. If the rule $(s(u, s'/x, v), \text{go})_a$ is applied to a string w, then this means that x can be inserted in between u, v in a string w, $w \in O^*$ under the state s and the resultant string z is sent to the cells related by synapses by leaving the control state as s' in cell σ_i. The resultant string z is sent to the cells according to the following modes.

- *repl:* z is sent to each of the cells σ_j such that $(i, j) \in syn$;
- *one*: z is sent to one of the cells (nondeterministically chosen) σ_j such that $(i, j) \in syn$.

If the rule $(s(u, s'/x, v), \text{out})_a$ is applied to a string w, $w \in O^*$ then this means that x can be inserted in between u, v in a string w under the control state s and the resultant string is sent out the system.

The deletion rules are applied in a similar way as told above but x is deleted from the string $w \in O^*$ when x is flanked by u on its left and v on its right under the control state s.

Any m tuple of the form $(s_1L_1, \ldots, s_mL_m)$ with $s_i \in Q_i$ and $L_i \in O^*$ is called a *configuration* of Π; thus, $(s_{1,0}L_{1,0}, \ldots, s_{m,0}L_{m,0})$ is the *initial* configuration of Π. Using the rules from the sets P_i, we can define *transitions* among the configurations of the system. During any transition, some cells can do nothing: if no rule is applicable to the available string in the current state, then the cell waits until new strings are sent to it from other cells. Each transition lasts one time unit, and the work of the net is synchronized, the same clock marks the time for all cells. A sequence of transitions among the configurations of a tP system is called a *computation* of Π. A computation which ends in a configuration where no rule in no cell can be used, is called a *halting computation.* The *language* generated by Π is the set of all strings $z \in T^*$ sent out of the system from the cell $\sigma_{i_{\text{out}}}$ during a halting computation.

For $1 \leq i \leq m$, $\tau \in \{\emptyset, \text{go}, \text{out}\}$, we say that an insertion-deletion tP system Π is of *weight* $(n, l; p, q)$ if

$$\begin{aligned}
n &= \max\{|\beta| | (s(u, s'/\beta, v), \tau)_a \in P_i\}\,, \\
l &= \max\{|u| | (s(u, s'/\beta, v), \tau)_a \in P_i \text{ or } (s(v, s'/\beta, u), \tau)_a \in P_i\}\,, \\
p &= \max\{|\alpha| | (s(u, \alpha/s', v), \tau)_e \in P_i\}\,, \\
q &= \max\{|u| | (s(u, \alpha/s', v), \tau)_e \in P_i \text{ or } (s(v, \alpha/s', u), \tau)_e \in P_i\}\,.
\end{aligned}$$

The total weight of Π is the sum $n + l + p + q$.

We denote by $L_\beta(\Pi)$, $\beta \in \{repl, \text{one}\}$, the set of all terminal strings generated by a tP system Π, in the mode β; the family of languages generated by InsDel tP systems in the mode β of weight $(n', l'; p', q')$, with at most m cells and r states such that $n' \leq n$, $l' \leq l$, $p' \leq p$, $q' \leq q$ is denoted $INS_n^l\ DEL_p^q\ tP_{m,r}(\beta)$, n, l, p, q, m, $r \geq 0$, $\beta \in \{repl, \text{one}\}$.

3. The Efficiency of the System

Before, we analyze the efficiency of the system, we first present the following corollary which states the computational universality of the system.

Corollary 1: $RE = INS_3^0\ DEL_2^0\ tP_{1,1}(\beta)$, $\beta \in \{\text{one}, repl\}$.

Proof: In Ref. 11 the characterization of RE is obtained by using insertion-deletion P systems with one membrane and of weight (3, 1; 2, 0). In Ref. 7 this result is improved to weight (3, 0; 2, 0). It is obvious that P systems with one membrane are equivalent to tP systems with one cell and one state. Hence, the characterization of recursive enumerable languages is obtained by InsDel tP systems with 1 cell and 1 state and of weight (3, 0; 2, 0).

We shall now proceed to prove that these systems hold well the computational efficiency by solving SAT problem and Hamiltonian path problem in linear time. □

3.1. *Solving satisfiability problem*

The SAT (satisfiability of propositional formulas in the conjunctive normal form) is probably the most known NP-complete problem. It asks whether or not for a given formula in the conjunctive normal form there is a truth-assignment of the variables for which the formula assumes the value *true*. A formula as above is of the form

$$\gamma = C_1 \wedge C_2 \wedge \cdots \wedge C_m ,$$

where each C_i, $1 \leq i \leq n$, is a *clause* of the form of a disjunction

$$C_i = y_1 \vee y_2 \vee \cdots \vee y_r ,$$

with each y_j being either a propositional variable, x_s, or its negation, $\sim x_s$. (Thus, we use the variables $x_1, x_2, \ldots, x_n$ and the three connectives $\vee$, $\wedge$, $\sim$: *or, and, negation*).

For example, let us consider the propositional formula

$$\beta = (x_1 \vee x_2) \wedge (\sim x_1 \vee \sim x_2) .$$

We have two variables, x_1, x_2, and two clauses. It is easy to see that it is satisfiable: any of the following truth-assignments makes the formula *true*

$$(x_1 = \text{true}, x_2 = \text{false}) , \quad (x_1 = \text{false}, x_2 = \text{true}) .$$

Theorem 1: The SAT problem can be solved by an InsDel tP system with replication mode in linear time in the number of variables and the number of clauses.

Proof. Let $\gamma = C_1 \wedge C_2 \wedge \cdots \wedge C_m$ where $C_1, C_2, \ldots, C_m$ are disjunctions, and the variables involved are $x_1, x_2, \ldots, x_n$, be the given formula. Construct a tP system

$$\Pi = (O, T, \sigma_1, \ldots, \sigma_{2n+m}, syn, 2n+m) ,$$

with the alphabet

$$O = \{a_i, \bar{a}_i, t_i, f_i | 1 | i \leq n\} ,$$

$$T - \{t_i, f_i | 1 | i | n\},$$

$$syn = \{(2i-1, 2i+1), (2i-1, 2i+2), (2i, 2i+1), (2i, 2i+2) | 1 \leq i \leq n-1\}$$
$$\cup \{(2n-1, 2n+1), (2n, 2n+1)\} \cup \{(2n+j, 2n+j+1) | 1 | j \leq m-1\}$$
(refer the Fig. 1),

For $1 \leq i \leq 2n$, $\sigma_i = (\{s, s'\}, s, L_i, P_i)$, where

$$L_1 = L_2 = \{a_1, \bar{a}_1\}, \quad L_i = \emptyset, \quad 3 \leq i \leq 2n,$$

$$P_{2i-1} = \{s(a_i, s'/t_i a_{i+1}, \lambda)_a, \quad (s'(\beta, a_i/s, t_i), go)_e, \quad s(\bar{a}_i, s'/t_i \bar{a}_{i+1}, \lambda)_a,$$
$$(s'(\beta, \bar{a}_i/s, t_i), go)_e | 1 \leq i \leq n, \quad \beta \in t_{i-1} \cup f_{i-1} \cup \lambda\},$$

$$P_{2i} = \{s(a_i, s'/f_i a_{i+1}, \lambda)_a, \quad (s'(\beta, a_i/s, f_i), go)_e, \quad s(\bar{a}_i, s'/f_i \bar{a}_{i+1}, \lambda)_a,$$
$$(s'(\beta, \bar{a}_i/s, f_i), go)_e | 1 \leq i \leq n, \quad \beta \in t_{i-1} \cup f_{i-1} \cup \lambda\},$$

$$P_{2n-1} = \{s(a_n, s'/t_n, \lambda)_a, \quad (s'(\beta, a_n/s, t_n), go)_e, \quad \beta \in t_{n-1} \cup f_{n-1} \cup \lambda\},$$

$$P_{2n} = \{s(a_n, s'/f_n, \lambda)_a, \quad (s'(\beta, a_n/s, f_n), go)_e, \quad \beta \in t_{n-1} \cup f_{n-1} \cup \lambda\}.$$

For $1 \leq j \leq m$, $\sigma_{2n+j} = (s, s, L_{2n+j}, P_{2n+j})$, where

$$L_{2n+j} = \emptyset, \quad 1 \leq j \leq m,$$

for $1 \leq j \leq m-1$,

$$P_{2n+j} = \{(s(\beta, s/\lambda, t_i), go)_a | x_i \in C_j, 1 \leq i \leq n, \beta \in t_{i-1} \cup f_{i-1} \cup \lambda\}$$
$$\cup \{(s(\beta, s/\lambda, f_i), go)_a | \bar{x}_i, 1 \in C_j, \leq i \leq n, \beta \in t_{i-1} \cup f_{i-1} \cup \lambda\},$$

$$P_{2n+m} = \{(s(\beta, s/\lambda, t_i), \text{out})_a | x_i \in C_m, \beta \in t_{i-1} \cup f_{i-1} \cup \lambda, 1 \leq i \leq n\}$$
$$\cup \{(s(\beta, s/\lambda, f_i), \text{out})_a | \bar{x}_i \in C_m, \beta \in t_{i-1} \cup f_{i-1} \cup \lambda, 1 \leq i \leq n\}.$$

In the initial configuration, the strings a_1, $\bar{a}_1$ are present in cell 1 and cell 2. Now let us see how the system works for the first $(2n-2)$ cells. Every time in odd cells, t_i is attached with both a_i, $\bar{a}_i$ and $a_i(\bar{a}_i)$ are increased to $a_{i+1}(\bar{a}_{i+1})$ under the control state s and s'. Similar thing happens in even cells, where instead of t_i, f_i is attached. The resultant strings are sent to all connected cells. In fact, if i is an odd cell, then the resultant strings will go to cells $i+2$, $i+3$ and if i is even, then the cells $i+1$, $i+2$. Note that the odd cell and the even cell can process their evolution rules in parallel. In cell $2n-1$ $(2n)$, under the control state s, t_n (f_n) is attached with a_n. In control state s', a_n is deleted, the resultant strings are sent to cell $2n+1$.

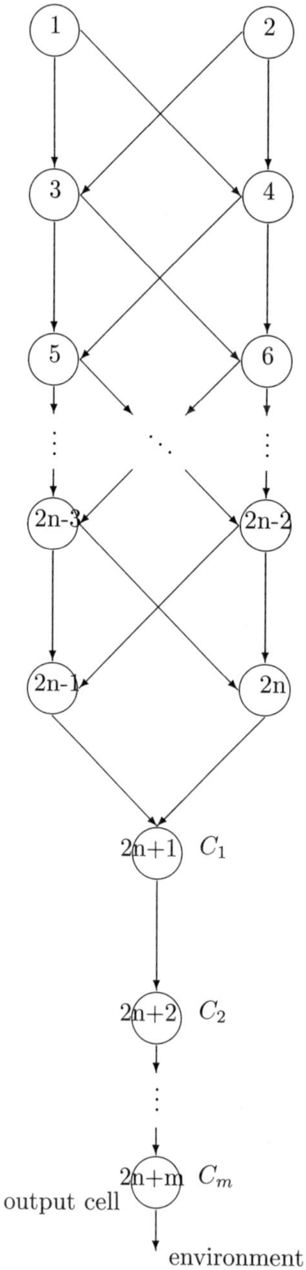

Fig. 1. Synapses relation for SAT.

As $\bar{a}_i$'s do not have evolutionary rules at cell $2n-1$ and $2n$, the strings which contain $\bar{a}_n$ can not be processed further. Though, the $\bar{a}_i$'s do not contribute to the truth assignments and even they are ignored at cells $2n-1$ and $2n$, they are important to produce 2^n possible assignment values. After $2n$ steps are over, one can observe that all the 2^n possible assignments arrive to cell $2n+1$ where t_i indicates the variable x_i getting the value *true* and f_i indicates the variable x_i getting the value *false*. In each cell σ_{2n+j}, $1 \leq j \leq m$, the string which contains t_i (f_i) is sent out of the cell provided the variable $x_i(\bar{x}_i)$ belongs to the clause C_j. In any cell σ_{2n+j}, if any string is sent to the next cell, then the clause C_j assumes the value "*true*" and therefore that string satisfies the clauses C_j and C_k, $1 \leq k \leq j-1$. Therefore, if any string that comes out of the system (environment), then that string satisfies all the clauses c_j, $1 \leq j \leq m$ and the output strings are solutions for the given SAT problem where $t_i(f_i)$ gets the value 1 (0) for the variable $x_i(\bar{x}_i)$. If no string is sent out of the system after the halting computation (the system will come to an halting stage after $2n+m$ steps are over), then the given propositional formula γ is not satisfiable for any value of x_i.

Time Complexity: The algorithm takes $2n$ steps to reach $(2n+1)$ cell to produce 2^n assignment values. From the cell $(2n+1)$, m more steps required for the strings to check each clause C_j. So, after $2n+m$ steps are over, the strings are sent out of the system. Therefore, the above algorithm takes $2n+m$ time in total (but with exponential space complexity) to check whether the given propositional formula is satisfiable or not. □

3.2. *Hamiltonian path problem*

Now we show that the Hamiltonian path problem can be solved using these systems. Given an undirected graph $G = (U, E)$, where U is the set of nodes and E the set of edges, the problem is to determine whether or not there exists a Hamiltonian path in G, that is, to determine whether or not there exists a path that passes through all the nodes in U exactly once.

Theorem 2: The undirected Hamiltonian path problem can be solved by InsDel tP systems with replication mode in linear time in the number of vertices of the given graph G.

Proof: Let $G = (U, E)$ be a graph with $U = \{a_1, a_2, \ldots, a_n\}$, $n \geq 2$ and $E \subseteq U \times U$ is set of edges. Construct an insertion-deletion tP system Π of degree $n + 2$ (with two new cells σ_p, σ_q) as follows:

$$\Pi = (O, T, \{\sigma_1, \ldots, \sigma_n, \sigma_p, \sigma_q\}, syn, q)\,,$$

with the alphabet

$$O = \{a_i, i, \varepsilon | 1 \leq i \leq n\}\,,$$

$$T = \{1, 2, \ldots, n\}\,,$$

$$syn = \{(p, i), (i, q) | 1 \leq i \leq n\} \cup \{(i \leftrightarrow j) | (a_i, a_j) \in E(G), a_i, a_j \in U\}$$

$$\text{(refer the Fig. 2 for synopses relation)}\,,$$

and the cells

$$\sigma_p = (s, s, \{a_1 a_2 \cdots a_n\}, (s(\lambda, s/\varepsilon, a_1), go)_a)\,,$$

For $1 \leq i \leq n$,

$$\sigma_i = (\{s, s'\}, s, \emptyset, \{s(\gamma_1, a_i/s', \gamma_2)_e, (s'(\beta, s/i, \varepsilon), go)_a | \gamma_1 \in a_k \cup \varepsilon\,,$$

$$\gamma_2 \in a_j \cup \lambda, \beta \in k \cup \lambda, 1 \leq i, j, k \leq n, i \neq j \neq k\})\,,$$

$$\sigma_q = (s, s, \emptyset, \{(s(i, \varepsilon/s, \lambda), \text{out})_e | 1 \leq i \leq n\})\,.$$

The system works as follows: In the initial configuration, the string $a_1 a_2 \cdots a_n$ is present in cell σ_p and no string is present in the remaining cells. In cell σ_p, ε is inserted to the left of a_1 under the state s and the resultant string $\varepsilon a_1 \cdots a_n$ is sent to all the cells i, $1 \leq i \leq n$ (i.e., vertices of the given graph G). In cell i, the symbol a_i (if it is present in the string) is deleted under the state s and now the state control will change to s'. Under the state s', i is inserted (in order to trace the vertices which are visited) to the left of ε and the resultant strings are sent to all cells connected by the edges of that vertex i of the graph and to the cell σ_q (but not again to cell σ_p anymore). When a string goes to the cell i for second time, that string will not contain a_i as that symbol was deleted already in cell i while the string visits that cell for the first time. Therefore, such strings can not be processed further. Also, when a string goes to cell σ_q with the symbols a_i, they will not be listed in the language since they are not defined as terminals. Suppose, a string visits all the cells exactly once, then the string of the form $\{(ij\cdots k)\varepsilon|$ Length of $(ij\cdots k) = n$, i, j, $k \in \{1, 2, \ldots, n\}$ with no two symbols are equal$\}$ is sent to the cell σ_q. In cell σ_q, ε is deleted and the resultant strings are sent out of the system after $2n + 2$ steps. The strings which are collected in the language are the solutions for the Hamiltonian path problem and if no string is sent to the environment after $2n+2$ steps, then the given graph has no Hamiltonian path.

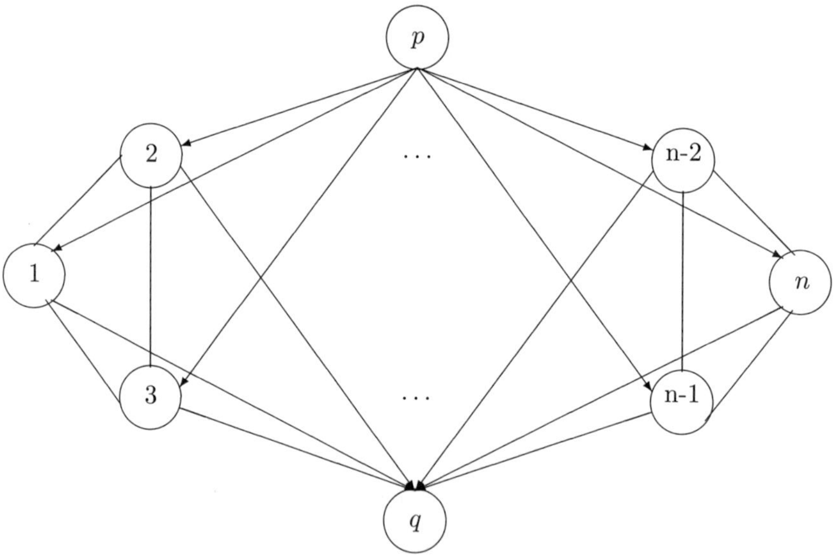

Fig. 2. Synapses relation for HPP.

Time Complexity: As there are two states s, s' in n cells and there are $n+2$ cells in total, the algorithm takes $2n+2$ steps (with exponential space) to solve the Hamiltonian path problem. □

4. Final Remarks

In this paper, we have analyzed the computational efficiency of insertion-deletion tissue P Systems. We proved the efficiency of these systems by solving the NP-complete problems in polynomial time and this is exemplified by solving SAT and HPP in linear time. Also, we proved that the characterization of recursive enumerable languages can be obtained by these systems with one cell and one state and of weight (3, 0; 2, 0) as a corollary.

References

1. M. Daley, L. Kari, G. Gloor and Rani Siromoney, Circular Contextual Insertion/Deletion with Applications to Biomolecular Computation, *SPIRE-'99*, 47–54 (1999).
2. L. Kari, Gh. Păun G. Thierrin and S. Yu, At the crossroads of DNA computing and formal languages: characterizing recursively enumerable languages by insertion-deletion systems, *DNA Based Computers III*, 318–333 (1997).
3. L. Kari and G. Thierrin, Contextual insertions/deletions and computability, *Information and Computation*, **131**, 47–61 (1996).
4. S. N. Krishna and R. Rama, Insertion-Deletion P systems, *LNCS Proceedings of DNA7 Conference*, 360–370 (2001).
5. K. Lakshmanan and R. Rama, On the Power of Tissue P Systems with Insertion and Deletion Rules, *Pre-proceedings of Workshop on Membrane Computing (WMC'03)*, 304–318 (2003).
6. W. R. Loewenstein, *The Touchstone of Life.Molecular Information, Cell Communication, and the Foundations of Life*, (Oxford Univ. Press, New York, 1999).
7. M. Margenstern, Gh. Păun, Y. Rogozhin and S. Verlan, Context-free Insertion-Deletion Systems, *Proceedings of DCFS-'03*, 265–273 (2003).
8. C. MartinVide, Gh. Păun, J. Pazos and A. Rodriguez Paton, Tissue P Systems, *Theoretical Computer Science*, **296**, 2, 295–326 (2003).
9. Gh. Păun, Computing with Membranes, *Journal of Computer and System Sciences*, **61**, 1, 108–143 (2000).
10. Gh. Păun, *Marcus Contextual Grammars*, (Kluwer Academic Publishers, Dordrecht, 1997).
11. Gh. Păun, *Membrane Computing: An Introduction*, Springer, Berlin (2002).
12. Gh. Păun, G. Rozenberg and A. Salomaa, *DNA Computing - New Computing Paradigms*, (Springer-Verlag, Berlin, 1998).
13. G. Rozenberg and A. Salomaa, eds., *Handbook of Formal Languages*, 3 volumes, (Springer-Verlag, Berlin, 1997).
14. A. Takahara, T. Yokomori, On the Computational Power of Insertion-Deletion Systems, LNCS: **2568**, 269–280 (2003).

CHAPTER 17

PETRI NETS, EVENT STRUCTURES AND ALGEBRA

Kamal Lodaya

Institute of Mathematical Sciences,
C.I.T. Campus, Taramani, Chennai 600 113, India

We define an algebraic framework for Petri nets, and prove a Myhill-Nerode theorem. As an application, we present a proof of the deterministic case of Thiagarajan's conjecture.[1] This generalizes both the trace event structure case[2] and the conflict-free case,[3] for which the conjecture has been verified.

It is more than 40 years since Petri nets have been around,[4] and there have been many algebraic attempts towards understanding them. In particular, let me mention the "Petri nets as monoids" of Meseguer and Montanari,[5,6] the "process algebra with causes" of Baeten and Bergstra (cited in a later survey[7]) and the "network algebra" of Ştefănescu.[8]

While I adopt ideas from all of these, what is new in this article is the emphasis on finite nets, following the classical treatment of finite automata on words and trees. I am indebted to Zoltán Ésik for helping to correct several errors in an earlier version of this article. The final article was prepared during a visit to Szeged supported by the Indian National Science Academy and the Hungarian Academy of Sciences.

1. Signatures and Terms

The basic transitions of automata over words are from a state to a state. When viewing automata as algebras,[9] Büchi models transitions as unary functions. Sequencing of transitions is modelled by function composition. Büchi also suggests the view of tree automata as term algebras with general k-ary functions from a signature Σ, and function composition works as before.

We generalize this slightly. The basic transitions of Petri nets[4] are multivalued functions, which take a set of i elements as argument and return a set of j elements as value.

Definition 1: A **signature** Σ consists of a finite set (the "alphabet"), with a function assigning to each element a pre-arity and a post-arity.

If $f^{j \leftarrow i}$ is an i-to-j-ary symbol, the "assignment command" $\{v_1, \ldots, v_j\} := f\{u_1, \ldots, u_i\}$ is called a transition. Here $u_1, \ldots, u_i$ ("preconditions") and $v_1, \ldots, v_j$ ("postconditions") are distinct variables, which we assume come from a suitable countable set Var.

Our syntactic entities are called "programs". These will get mapped to runs of a Petri net just as words get mapped to runs of an automaton.

Definition 2: A **Σ-program** is a sequence of transitions, satisfying the following conditions:

- All the variables occurring on the right and left hand side of a transition must be distinct. (Sets of variables, not multisets.)
- The variables on the left hand side can only occur on the right hand side of later transitions. (A variable cannot be read and then written to.)
- A variable can be assigned to only once. (A variable cannot be overwritten.)
- A variable can appear only once on the right hand side. (Conflict is ruled out.)

The input variables of the program are those which appear on the right hand side but not on the left hand side of any transition in the program. The output variables are those which appear on the left hand side but not on the right. We will call the rest of the variables internal and identify programs upto renaming of internal variables. The **arity** of a program is $o \leftarrow n$ if it has n input variables and o output variables. Such a program is called an **$n\Sigma o$-program**. We also use **$n\Sigma$-program** if all outputs are allowed. An **$n\Sigma$- ($n\Sigma o$-)language** is a set of $n\Sigma$- ($n\Sigma o$-)programs.

Programs of arbitrary length are possible, independent of $|\Sigma|$, because of the unbounded number of variables available. In a sense, every "control point" of a program is named by a unique variable.

Here is an example program. Below it are a hypergraph and a poset derived from the program, which will be defined later in this article.

$$\{q_1, buf\} := f\{p_1\}$$
$$\{r_1\} := g\{q_1\}$$
$$\{q_2\} := g\{p_2\}$$
$$\{r_2\} := h\{buf, q_2\}$$

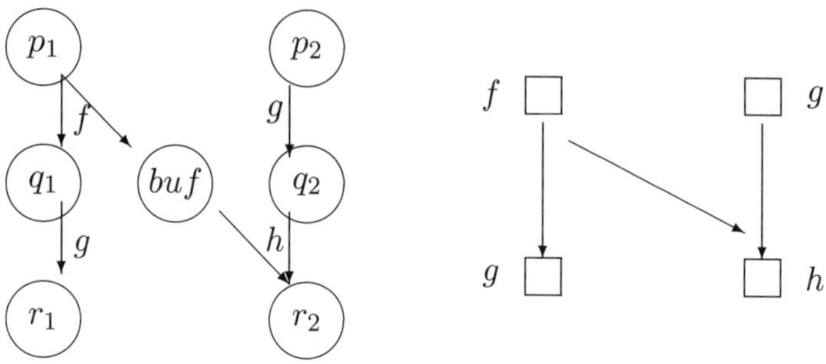

This seems fairly straightforward, but the difficulty lies in formalizing the *composition* $r; s$ of two programs (assuming the result is a program), which we have done in the example by sequencing s after r.

In earlier work,[10] we introduced the notion of a *series* Σ-*algebra* where one Σ-term s can be sequenced after another r. But the semantics there requires that the execution of r be complete before the execution of s begins.

This is inadequate to model the N-shaped execution in the example above. If r has postconditions $J \cup J_1$ and s takes preconditions J_1 to postconditions K, then their composition has postconditions $J \cup K$. Conversely, if we sequence a program s after r, we get a composition depending on the relationship between the postconditions of r and the preconditions of s. (This was studied by Goltz and Reisig.[11])

Simple projection operations π_k, $k \in \mathbf{N}$, do not work either. The names of the variables in J_1 are crucial to making the definition of composition unambiguous. But it is not *really* the names which are important, they are just "tokens" or "place-holders"!

Earlier authors have grappled with this problem in different ways: Meseguer and Montanari[5] move to categories, Ştefănescu[8] uses operators for permuting a tuple, and Baeten and Bergstra[7] introduce an explicit set of *causes* similar to our variables. The solution adopted here is to go back to Büchi's view as transitions as unary functions,[9] and declare that given an $n\Sigma o$-program r and an i-to-j transition f, $i \leq o$, there are $\binom{o}{i}$ different compositions $r;_C f$, with C ranging over the combinations. (Thus the effect of tuple permutation[8] is achieved.) Our programs seemingly use only one composition, but the notation disambiguates the different compositions.

Remark. Suppose r is the transition $\{w_1\} := f_1\{v_1\}$ and s the transition $\{w_2\} := f_2\{v_2\}$. We say the two programs are independent since they work with disjoint sets of variables. This example suggests representing programs by Mazurkiewicz traces.[12] However, note that f_1 and f_2 may or may not be independent in different contexts, so independence is not coded into the action label. The two g actions in the picture above are independent.

2. Algebras and Recognizability

We now interpret our signature not just as multiple-valued functions, but as functions from multisets to multisets. We use the notation $\wr\ldots\int$ to denote multisets and the usual $\{\cdots\}$ for sets. $X^{\wr i \int}$ denotes multisets (unordered tuples) with i elements from the set X.

Definition 3: A **Σ-multialgebra** consists of a nonempty domain X partitioned into sorts X^k, $k \in \mathbf{N}$, and for each operation $f^{j \leftarrow i}$ of Σ, an interpretation, a function $\mathcal{I}(f) : X^i \to X^j$, which extends for each $k \geq i$ and each C in $\binom{k}{i}$, to $\mathcal{I}(f_C) : X^k \to X^{k-i+j}$ by choosing the i variables using C. An **$n\Sigma$-multialgebra** has in addition a distinguished element I of X^n, and an **$n\Sigma o$-multialgebra** further has a distinguished subset O of X^o. For a **symmetric** Σ-multialgebra (possibly with distinguished input and output), we take unordered tuples instead of ordered ones (i.e., $X^{\wr m \int}$ instead of X^m) in the statements above.

The interpretation $\mathcal{I}$ can be extended in a unique way to programs, disambiguating program composition as explained above.

This definition is related to strictly symmetric monoidal categories.[5,6] But here we make do with just the composition operation rather than introducing an additional tensor product, and stay within the ambit of algebra rather than venturing into category theory.

The program Σ-multialgebra has domain the set of programs, and $\mathcal{I}(f)$ for an i-to-j operation f extends its argument program by sequencing the transition $\{v_1, \ldots, v_j\} := f\{u_1, \ldots, u_i\}$ after the program, where the names of the variables on the right are chosen from the output variables according to the combination C and the names on the left are fresh ones.

Definition 4: A **homomorphism** from a Σ-multialgebra to another is a function h which preserves the operations in the sense that $h(f_C(t)) = f_C(h(t))$. If, in addition, the signature has distinguished elements, h must preserve them: I must map to $h(I)$ and if $t \in O$ in the first algebra, then $h(t) \in O$ in the second.

Our main interest in this article is homomorphisms which map into finite multialgebras. We require the domain of such a multialgebra to be finite. This is achieved by mapping infinitely many sorts X^k into a finite set. If, in addition, we have that there is an m such that every X^{m+j} maps to a single zero element, we call the multialgebra nilpotent.

Definition 5: An $n\Sigma(n\Sigma o)$ language L is **recognizable** if there is a homomorphism h of the $n\Sigma(n\Sigma o)$ programs into a finite $n\Sigma(n\Sigma o)$ multialgebra (with a designated subset F of sort o such that for each term t, $t \in L$ iff $h(t) \in F$).

From the definition, it is clear that a recognizable $n\Sigma$-language is prefix-closed; but an $n\Sigma o$-language need not be.

3. Nets and Algebras

A Σ-program can be represented as a hypergraph $\mathcal{S} = (B, \{E_f | f \in \Sigma\})$, where B is the set of variables in the program, and each transition $\{v_1, \ldots, v_j\} := f\{u_1, \ldots, u_i\}$ is modelled by a directed hyperedge in E_f from the source nodes $u_1, \ldots, u_i$ to the target nodes $v_1, \ldots, v_j$ where f has arity $j \leftarrow i$. The conditions on a Σ-program ensure that the hypergraph is acyclic and unbranched, that is, two different hyperedges do not share source and target vertices. α-conversion yields an isomorphic hypergraph. Hypergraphs whose labelling respects the signature Σ are called Σ-hypergraphs.

Conversely, from an acyclic unbranched Σ-hypergraph we can easily write a Σ-program corresponding to it by using its nodes as names of variables.

We can define the width of a hypergraph as the size of the largest "cut" that can be made through a pictorial representation of its set of nodes without intersecting any hyperedges. A Σ-language is said to be **bounded width** if there is a bound $k \in \mathbf{N}$ such that the width of the hypergraphs corresponding to each program in it is at most k.

A hypergraph can in turn be represented as a bipartite graph $\mathcal{K} = (B, E, F, l)$ where B is as before a "sort" of nodes and E is a "sort" of transitions (hyperedges). The source and target nodes are connected by an incidence relation $F \subseteq (B \times E) \cup (E \times B)$ as follows: for the hyperedge e representing the transition above, there are edges in F from the source nodes $u_1, \ldots, u_i$ of the hyperedge to e, and from e to the target nodes $v_1, \ldots, v_j$ of the hyperedge. l labels nodes of sort E by letters from Σ: the vertex e of the graph above is labelled f.

Such graphs are known in the literature as (labelled finite) causal nets. B is the set of basic conditions of the net, E is the set of events and F is called the flow relation. A causal net is unbranched, that is, all its basic conditions b have at most one predecessor and one successor, and acyclic: the reflexive transitive closure of F is antisymmetric (that is, a partial order). Since $l : E \to \Sigma$ is an arity-respecting labelling, we call them causal Σ-nets. They give a purely relational representation of an acyclic unbranched Σ-hypergraph.

3.1. *Petri nets*

Clearly a (finite) symmetric Σ-multialgebra with domain P and interpretation T can be represented as a (finite) hypergraph $(P, \{T_f | f \in \Sigma\})$, which need be neither acyclic nor unbranched.

A relational representation of such a hypergraph is more elaborate: a bipartite weighted graph $\mathcal{N} = (P, T, W, \ell)$ where P is a set of places, T a (disjoint) set of transitions, ℓ an arity-respecting labelling of the transitions and $W : (P \times T) \cup (T \times P) \to \mathbf{N}$ defines a weighted flow relation which models hyperedges.

$\mathcal{N}$ is traditionally called a (labelled finite) Petri net.[4] For a place or transition y, its pre-set $\{x | W(x, y) > 0\}$ is conventionally denoted ${}^\bullet y$ and its post-set $\{z | W(y, z) > 0\}$ is denoted $x^\bullet$. W satisfies the condition that for each transition t, ${}^\bullet t$ and $t^\bullet$ are nonempty, and for each place p, either ${}^\bullet p$ or $p^\bullet$ is nonempty. For all transitions t, the arity of $\ell(t)$ is from the indegree of t to its outdegree $(\sum_q W(t, q) \leftarrow \sum_p W(p, t))$. If a net satisfies this condition, we call it a Σ-net.

A marking is a multiset of places. A net system is a net with a set of initial markings (and possibly a set of final markings). A finite $n\Sigma$ ($n\Sigma o$) multialgebra can be represented as a net with a single initial marking (and a set of final markings).

A "run" of a net system is described by a "token game" from an initial marking (to a final marking).[4] A net system is said to be k-safe if for all markings M reachable from the initial markings and for all places p, p occurs at most k times in M. As a consequence, the weight of the flow relation of a 1-safe system can only be 0 or 1 and we can redefine flow as a subset of $(P \times T) \cup (T \times P)$. We adopt a more abstract definition.[13]

Definition 6: A net system $\mathcal{N}$ **accepts** an $n\Sigma$-program r if there is a homomorphism from r to the net system, seen as an $n\Sigma$-multialgebra.

Conversely, any (finite) Σ-net is a hypergraph and a (finite) *deterministic* Σ-net is a symmetric partial Σ-multialgebra with domain $\bigcup_k P^k$ and a partial interpretation given by the transitions T. As for automata, a net is said to be **deterministic** if at any marking, at most one transition with the same label can be "fired". A net system is deterministic if, in addition, it has a single initial marking. If the net is k-safe, we can turn it into a nilpotent Σ-multialgebra by adding a zero element.

Remark. We can also model unlabelled nets; equip them with a labelling $\ell : T \to T$ which is the identity function. To make T into a signature, each transition is given an arity from its indegree to its outdegree. Then any (finite) unlabelled net is deterministic and is a (finite) symmetric partial T-algebra.

3.2. *Subset algebras*

Thus a net might be thought of as a multialgebra which allows nondeterministic operations. More formally, we represent a net as a **subset multialgebra**. Let $\mathcal{N} = (P, T, W, \ell)$ be a finite $n\Sigma$-net system, with set of initial markings $I \subseteq P^n$. The required algebra has as the domain of sort k all subsets $U \subseteq P^k$ of markings of $\mathcal{N}$ of size k. The interpretation of an operation $f^{j \leftarrow i}$ is given by $h(f)$, defined to take $U \subseteq P^i$ to the set V of markings M_2 such that there is a marking $M_1 \in U$ and an f-labelled transition of $\mathcal{N}$ from the marking M_1 to the marking M_2. Since Σ is a signature, f can only take the marking M_1 to a marking of size j, hence $V \subseteq P^j$. For every Σ-program r, $h(r)$ is the unique extension of h under composition starting from the subset I. h will map a program r to the set of markings reachable after executing r. It will map an $n\Sigma o$-program accepted by $\mathcal{N}$ to a subset of $O \subseteq P^o$.

The proof that the subset multialgebra accepts the same language as the net follows that of the subset construction for automata.

The subset algebra will be symmetric since the markings of a net are just multisets. The elements of this algebra (that is, subsets of markings) which consist of only reachable markings we will call **accessible**.

4. Congruences

An equivalence relation $\equiv$ on an algebra is said to be a **congruence** if it preserves the operations of the algebra. Since our operations are defined on multisets, we have to lift congruences accordingly. We say $\wr x_1, \ldots, x_i \int \equiv$

$\wr x'_1, \ldots, x'_i \wr$ if $x_m \equiv x'_m$ for $1 \leq m \leq i$. Conversely, given two such equivalent multisets of size i, we require orderings $1, \ldots, i$ of the two multisets such that $x_m \equiv x'_m$ for $1 \leq m \leq i$.

Definition 7: An equivalence relation $\equiv$ on a Σ-multialgebra is a Σ-**congruence** if for every operation $f^{j \leftarrow i}$ in Σ, $k \geq i$, $C \in \binom{k}{i}$, if $t \equiv t'$ then $t;_C f \equiv t';_C f$. It is an $n\Sigma$**-congruence** if there is a distinguished congruence class e of the domain of sort n such that for any t, $e;_C t \equiv t$.

The canonical map from an element of the domain of a Σ-multialgebra to its congruence class is a homomorphism.

From the definition of congruences, it is clear that they are closed under intersections. For two congruences of finite index, the smallest congruence which includes the union of both is a congruence of finite index.

The Myhill-Nerode congruence for an $n\Sigma$-language L is defined by: $r \approx_L s$ if for all right contexts t, we have $r;t \in L$ iff $s;t \in L$. It is the maximal congruence on $n\Sigma$-programs which saturates L.

We can now prove a Myhill-Nerode theorem.

Theorem 1: The following classes of bounded width $n\Sigma$-languages are equivalent:

(1) The set of $n\Sigma$-programs accepted by a finite $n\Sigma$-net system.
(2) The $n\Sigma$-language which is the inverse homomorphic image of a subset, not containing the zero, of a finite symmetric nilpotent $n\Sigma$-multialgebra.
(3) The $n\Sigma$-language saturated by a finite index $n\Sigma$-congruence.
(4) The $n\Sigma$-language whose Myhill-Nerode congruence has finite index.
(5) The $n\Sigma$-language accepted by a finite 1-safe deterministic $n\Sigma$-net system.

Proof: For the implication from (1) to (2), let $\mathcal{N}$ be a finite $n\Sigma$-net system accepting L, with set of initial markings I. We take the subset multialgebra for $\mathcal{N}$, which will also accept L. Since L is bounded width, we can collapse all the sorts beyond the bound into a single zero element. As $\mathcal{N}$ is finite, the set of possible markings is finite and the algebra is finite and nilpotent. The accessible elements of this algebra are the desired subset, not containing the zero, which L will map to.

For the implication from (2) to (3), we take the kernel of the homomorphism h saturating L.

(3) to (4) follows from maximality of $\approx_L$.

For the implication from (4) to (5), we need to define a finite 1-safe deterministic $n\Sigma$-net system $\mathcal{N}$ accepting L.

The places of this net are going to be congruence classes of elements of the domain.

Let the congruence class of the distinguished element e be $M_0 = \{p_1, \ldots, p_n\}$. This will be the initial marking of the net. We say the empty program (of signature $n\Sigma$) in $\mathcal{N}$ uses the places $p_1, \ldots, p_n$ for the congruence class $[\{v_1, \ldots, v_n\}]$. (Formally, this means extending the syntax of programs by this one program.)

Inductively, suppose an $O := \Sigma(I)$ program r of arity $o \leftarrow n$ using the places $p_1, \ldots, p_q$ has $O = \{u_1, \ldots, u_i, \ldots, u_o\}$. Consider now the $O' := \Sigma(I)$ program $s = (r; \{u'_1, \ldots, u'_j\} := f\{u_{i+1}, \ldots, u_o\})$ with $O' = \{u_1, \ldots, u_i, u'_1, \ldots, u'_j\}$. This defines a transition of the net labelled f. Its pre-set is the set of places corresponding to the multiset $[\{u_{i+1}, \ldots, u_o\}]$ with the weight of a place the number of u's it corresponds to, and the post-set is the set of places corresponding to $[\{u'_1, \ldots, u'_j\}]$ with the weight defined similarly. Clearly the transition respects Σ-labelling.

Suppose s has a prefix s_1 (that is, $s = s_1; s_2$) which it is congruent to — that is, s_1 is an $O' := \Sigma(I)$ program with $O' = \{v_{k_1}, \ldots, v_{k_{i+j}}\}$ given by the congruence class of places $p_{k_1}, \ldots, p_{k_{i+j}}$. Then we will also have $[\{u_1, \ldots, u_i, u'_1, \ldots, u'_j\}] = \wr p_{k_1}, \ldots, p_{k_{i+j}} \int$. But if some of the v_{k_m} are new, the set of places used has to be extended beyond $p_1, \ldots, p_q$.

In this way the infinite set of terms will map into a finite set of places, depending on the number of Myhill-Nerode congruence classes. Since the congruence is finite index, the net is finite.

Concurrency is separated out right from the initial marking $[\{v_1, \ldots, v_n\}] = \{p_1, \ldots, p_n\}$ (no repeated elements). The only thing that separates p_1 from p_2 is that the former is concurrent to $p_2, p_3, \ldots, p_n$ and the latter is concurrent to $p_1, p_3, \ldots, p_n$. The program $v' := g(v_1)$ will yield a g-transition from $[v_1]$ to $[v']$. $[v_1]$ maps to one of the places $p_1, \ldots, p_n$ by the ordering chosen by the congruence relation. There is no nondeterminism.

In fact, the program $r; \{v'_1, \ldots, v'_j\} := f\{u_{i+1}, \ldots, u_n\}$ can be renamed to the program s above, so only one transition labelled f can be enabled at the multiset of places $[\{u_{i+1}, \ldots, u_o\}]$. Hence the net is deterministic.

Finally, since the net system $\mathcal{N}$ accepts L of bounded width, there is a k-safe net system accepting L, for some k. Best and Wimmel[14] show how to produce a 1-safe net system accepting the same poset language. Both their "colouring" and "unfolding" constructions will preserve deterministic labelling. Their "balancedness" condition ensures that the result is a Σ-net. $\square$

As in the case of finite automata, the Myhill-Nerode theorem also provides a determinization. This is not that interesting a result because the usual "branching" behaviour for Petri nets is stricter than just a language of programs. In concurrency jargon, $a(b+c)$ is distinguished from $ab+ac$. We turn next to this notion of behaviour.

5. Event Structures

A (labelled) **event structure** $ES = (E, \leq, \#, \ell)$ is a (labelled) poset $(E, \leq, \ell)$ with an irreflexive symmetric conflict relation $\#$ on E, which is "inherited," that is, $e_1 \# e_2 \leq e_3$ implies $e_1 \# e_3$. Two events e_1 and e_2 of ES are said to be concurrent if they are not related by $\leq$, $\geq$ or $\#$.

We will assume an event structure to be finitary (for each element e, its left-closure $\downarrow e = \{x | x \leq e\}$ of elements preceding it is finite). This implies that the conflict relation is generated from an immediate conflict relation $\#_\mu$, where $e_1 \#_\mu e_3$ if $e_1 \# e_3$ and there is no e_2 such that $e_1 \# e_2 \leq e_3$ (and hence by symmetry no e_2 such that $e_3 \# e_2 \leq e_1$).

An event structure is said to be deterministic if $e_1 \#_\mu e_2$ implies $\ell(e_1) \neq \ell(e_2)$. An event structure is conflict-free if its conflict relation is empty. Clearly a conflict-free event structure is deterministic.

A deterministic event structure is said to be a trace event structure if there is a symmetric "dependence" relation over the set of labels such that events related by the immediate successor relation or immediate conflict relation are dependent, and conversely, dependent events are not concurrent.

A **configuration** c of ES is a left-closed subset of E ($\downarrow c = c$) which is conflict-free (that is, a poset). The "remainder" of the event structure $ES \setminus c$ is said to be a **residue** of ES. By the finiteness of left-closure, a configuration is a finite poset, but residues can of course be infinite.

From a configuration c of a Σ-labelled event structure, we can define the hypergraph $(H, \{E_f | f \in \Sigma\})$, where H is the set of edges in the Hasse diagram of c and E_f takes ${}^\bullet e$ to $e^\bullet$ precisely when e is labelled f. Since the hypergraph is acyclic and unbranched, we can further define a program t. We write $c = \text{forget}(t)$. Since the labelling of the event structure need not form a signature, t might not be a Σ-program.

It is well known[15] that a (labelled) net $\mathcal{N}$ "unfolds" into a (labelled) event structure $Unf(\mathcal{N})$. infinite. We say a (labelled) event structure ES is generated by a (labelled) net $\mathcal{N}$ if ES is isomorphic to $Unf(\mathcal{N})$.

Now we lift some definitions from infinite trees to event structures. Two configurations c and d are right-invariant (we write $c \approx_R d$) if $ES \setminus c$ and $ES \setminus d$ are isomorphic as event structures. Clearly this is an equivalence relation. An infinite event structure ES is regular if the right-invariance has finite index.

An event e is said to be enabled at a configuration c if $e \notin c$ and $c \cup \{e\}$ is a configuration. An event structure is said to have bounded enabling if there is a $b \in \mathbf{N}$ such that at any configuration of the event structure, the number of events enabled is bounded by b. Thiagarajan conjectured[1] that a well-known result linking regular infinite trees to tree automata generalizes to event structures with bounded enabling.

Conjecture 1: (*Thiagarajan's conjecture*) *An infinite regular event structure with bounded enabling is generated by a finite* 1*-safe net system.*

Thiagarajan proved the conjecture for trace event structures.[2] More recently, the conjecture was proved for the conflict-free case.[3]

We use our Myhill-Nerode result to give a proof of the deterministic case of Thiagarajan's conjecture. That the trace case follows from this is easy to see. As a corollary of our theorem, we also prove the conflict-free case.

Hence we generalize both cases. The proof does not extend to a general event structure because the Myhill-Nerode theorem collapses nondeterminism to determinism.

Theorem 2: (Deterministic case) An infinite regular deterministic event structure with bounded enabling is generated by a finite 1-safe net system.

Proof: Let $ES = (E, \leq, \#, \ell)$ be the given deterministic event structure with $\ell : E \to Dir$ ("directions"), and R be the finite set of right-invariance classes of configurations of ES.

We refine this labelling to a new labelling $\lambda : E \to \Sigma$, where $\Sigma = Dir \times R$. To each element e of E we let $\lambda(e)$ have, in addition to $\ell(e)$, the right-invariance class of $\downarrow e$ in R. Notice that since we use isomorphism to define right-invariance, a residue is different from two copies of itself (separated by conflict or concurrency). Thus, in concurrency jargon, the event structures for ab, $a(b+b)$, $a(b+b+b)$, $a(b\|b)$ and $a(b\|b+b)$ will have different sets of residues.

We still have to determine the arities for Σ. Let c be a configuration. Consider any $e \in c$. Let j be the maximum size of a configuration in $ES \setminus c$

which has elements of $e^\bullet$. This is well defined since ES has bounded enabling. The post-arity of $\lambda(e)$ is defined to be j.

Consider now a configuration $c \cup \{e\}$ where the post-arity of all $\leq$-maximal events in c has been determined. Let i be the sum of the post-arities of $\leq$-maximal elements in c which are in $^\bullet e$. The pre-arity of $\lambda(e)$ is defined to be i. Determine its post-arity as above. Because of the isomorphism defining the right-invariance, the arities of equivalent elements will be the same.

All that remains now is assigning a pre-arity to the $\leq$-minimal events e in case no other element is labelled with $\lambda(e)$. In this case, we set the pre-arity of e to be 1.

Hence $\Sigma = Dir \times R$ with these arities is a signature and ES can be seen as an event structure labelled by a signature.

Let n be the maximal sum of pre-arities of such an "initial" configuration (which only has $\leq$-minimal events). Inductively, each configuration is represented by a $n\Sigma$-program. We lift $\approx_R$ to $n\Sigma$-programs. For programs x and y such that $c = \text{forget}(x)$ and $d = \text{forget}(y)$, we let $x \approx_R y$ if $c \approx_R d$. We map programs which do not represent configurations of ES to new zero elements of the appropriate "type" (pair of arities), which are congruence classes by themselves. (This is a finite set since Σ is finite.) $\approx_R$ is an equivalence relation on $n\Sigma$-programs of finite index; it remains to show that it is a congruence.

Suppose $u_k \approx_R u'_k$, i.e., $ES \setminus \text{forget}(u_k)$ and $ES \setminus \text{forget}(u'_k)$ are isomorphic, for $1 \leq k \leq i$, and $\{v_1, \ldots, v_j\} := f\{u_1, \ldots, u_i\}$ for f in Σ. This corresponds to a configuration with a new maximal element of arity $j \leftarrow i$ labelled f. Either such an element does not exist in the event structure and both programs map to zero, or by right-invariance, $ES \setminus f\{u_1, \ldots, u_i\}$ is isomorphic to $ES \setminus f\{u'_1, \ldots, u'_i\}$. In fact, there is some ordering of variables $v'_1, \ldots, v'_j$ such that $\{v'_1, \ldots, v'_j\} := f\{u'_1, \ldots, u'_i\}$, and $ES \setminus v_k$ is isomorphic to $ES \setminus v'_k$ for $1 \leq k \leq j$. Hence the right-invariance is a congruence.

Since the event structure has bounded enabling, at any configuration at most a bounded number of events can occur in parallel. Hence the size of its antichains is bounded and the corresponding set of $n\Sigma$ programs has bounded width.

Now applying Theorem 1, there is a finite 1-safe deterministic $n\Sigma$-net system $\mathcal{N}$ accepting the language L of configurations of ES.

We use determinism to argue that ES is isomorphic to $Unf(\mathcal{N})$. Since ES is deterministically labelled by Dir, it is deterministically labelled by Σ, and each extension of a configuration is represented by a distinct program in L. The way the maximal events of the different extensions are related to each other can also be determined from L. Hence ES is determined upto isomorphism. The restriction $\mathcal{N}'$ of $\mathcal{N}$, where the R-component of the labelling is forgotten, generates ES. □

We can also use our result to give an alternate proof of the conflict-free case of Thiagarajan's conjecture, which was recently shown.[3]

Corollary 1: (*Conflict-free case*) *An infinite regular conflict-free event structure with bounded enabling is generated by a finite* 1*-safe forward unbranched net system.*

Proof: Applying Theorem 2, we get a finite unlabelled 1-safe net system generating ES.

Suppose the net obtained is forward branched. That is, there is a place p with at least two transitions t_1, t_2 in $p^\bullet$. (That is, $t_1 \#_\mu t_2$.) Then there is a program accepted by the net in which the transition t_i occurs once but t_j does not occur (for $i \neq j \in \{1, 2\}$), but there is no program accepted by the net in which t_1, t_2 both occur once.

Corresponding to each of these programs, there is a configuration of ES in which the event corresponding to transition t_i occurs once as a maximal event but that corresponding to t_j does not occur (for $i \neq j \in \{1, 2\}$). But then there is a configuration of ES in which both these events are maximal and the program for this configuration too must be accepted by the net, a contradiction.

Hence the net is forward unbranched. □

Remarks. The earlier proofs of Thiagarajan and Nielsen[2,3] take up several pages of difficult combinatorial argument, and have an explicit treatment of concurrency in the form of a trace labelling. The arguments in our two main theorems separate out into congruences and their labellings. The combinatorics and concurrency is left to the proof of Best and Wimmel[14] which we use. It would be interesting to find a proof of (4) to (5) in Theorem 1 which is independent of this.

Our approach should be of interest to the process algebra community. In particular, one can attempt to tackle the general conjecture by working with a syntax of terms with an explicit sum operation.

References

1. P. S. Thiagarajan, Regular event structures and finite Petri nets: a conjecture, in *Formal and natural computing – essays dedicated to Grzegorz Rozenberg* (W. Brauer, H. Ehrig, J. Karhumäki and A. Salomaa, eds.), LNCS 2300 (2002) 244–256.
2. P. S. Thiagarajan, Regular trace event structures, BRICS Research Abstracts (1996), http://www.brics.dk/RS/96/32/BRICS-RS-96-32.ps.gz.
3. M. Nielsen and P. S. Thiagarajan, Regular event structures and finite Petri nets: the conflict-free case, *Proc. ICATPN*, Adelaide (J. Esparza and C. Lakos, eds.), LNCS 2360 (2002) 335–351.
4. C.-A. Petri, Fundamentals of a theory of asynchronous information flow, *Proc. IFIP*, Munich (C. M. Popplewell, ed.), North-Holland (1962) 386–390.
5. J. Meseguer and U. Montanari, Petri nets are monoids, *Inform. Comput.* 88 (1990) 105–155.
6. J. Meseguer, U. Montanari and V. Sassone, Representation theorems for Petri nets, in *Foundations of computer science — festschrift for W. Brauer* (C. Freksa, M. Jantzen and R. Valk, eds.) LNCS 1337 (1997) 239–249.
7. J. C. M. Baeten and T. Basten, Partial order process algebra (and its relation to Petri nets), in *Handbook of process algebra* (J. A. Bergstra, A. Ponse and S. A. Smolka, eds.), Elsevier (2001) 769–872.
8. G. Ştefănescu, *Network algebra*, Springer (2000).
9. J. R. Büchi, *Finite automata, their algebras and grammars: Towards a theory of formal expressions* (D. Siefkes, ed.), Springer (1989).
10. K. Lodaya and P. Weil, Rationality in algebras with a series operation, *Inform. Comput.* 171,2 (2001) 269–293.
11. U. Goltz and W. Reisig, The non-sequential behaviour of Petri nets, *Inform. Comput.* 57 (1983) 125–147.
12. V. Diekert and G. Rozenberg, eds. *The book of traces*, World Scientific (1995).
13. W. Thomas, Uniform and nonuniform recognizability, *TCS* 292 (2003) 283–298.
14. E. Best and H. Wimmel, Reducing k-safe Petri nets to pomset-equivalent 1-safe Petri nets, *Proc. ATPN*, Aarhus (M. Nielsen and D. Simpson, eds.), LNCS 1825 (2000) 146–165.
15. M. Nielsen, G. D. Plotkin and G. Winskel, Petri nets, event structures and domains I, *TCS* 13 (1981) 85–108.

CHAPTER 18

PATTERN GENERATION AND PARSING BY ARRAY GRAMMARS

Kenichi Morita, Jin-Shan Qi and Katsunobu Imai

Department of Information Engineering, Hiroshima University, Higashi-Hiroshima, 739-8527, Japan

E-mail: {morita, qi, imai}@iec.hiroshima-u.ac.jp

We give a survey on the studies of pattern generation and parsing problems using isometric array grammars (IAGs) and their subclasses. Among various subclasses of IAGs, we focus on regular array grammars (RAGs), and uniquely parsable array grammars (UPAGs). RAGs are the lowest subclass of Chomsky-like hierarchy in IAGs, where each rewriting rule is restricted to a very simple one. In spite of such a strong constraint to the form of rewriting rules, RAGs have a rich generating ability. On the other hand, several decision problems for RAGs become very hard. A UPAG remedies such shortcomings, where any derivation process of a pattern has a "backward deterministic" nature, and hence parsing can be performed deterministically. We show that UPAGs can be used to recognize certain topological properties of a pattern, such as connectedness and simple-connectedness.

1. Introduction

From the early stage of development of formal language theory, the notion of "picture languages" attracted many researchers. It is in fact an important problem to give useful and interesting frameworks to generate two- or higher-dimensional pictures. In the pioneering works of Siromoney *et al.*,[8–11] various grammatical frameworks for pictures were introduced and studied. Especially, they proposed several classes of matrix grammars, which are formal models for generating two-dimensional symbol arrays, and gave interesting applications of them.

An isometric array grammar (IAG) introduced by Rosenfeld[3,7] is another interesting grammatical model for picture languages. An isometric regular array grammar (RAG)[1] is a subclass of IAGs having very simple array rewriting rules. In spite of the strong constraint to the form of rewriting rules, RAGs have a rich ability of generating patterns.[13,12] On the other hand, several decision problems for RAGs become very hard. Especially, the membership problem for RAGs is NP-complete, and thus analysis (parsing) of patterns is intractable.[4] A uniquely parsable isometric array grammar (UPAG)[14] remedies such shortcomings, where any derivation process of a pattern has a "backward deterministic" nature, and hence parsing can be performed deterministically.

In this paper, we give a survey on the studies on IAGs, especially, generating ability of RAGs and UPAGs. We also show how UPAGs are used to recognize some topological properties of a pattern, such as connectedness and simple-connectedness.

2. Pattern Generation in Array Grammars

An isometric array grammar (IAG) introduced by Rosenfeld[3,7] is a formal grammar for two-dimensional languages. An IAG has a set of rules to rewrite symbol arrays. Each rule has an "isometric" property, *i.e.*, both sides of the rule must be the same shape of symbol arrays. This condition is required to avoid a distortion (shear) of an array when applying the rule to a host array.

In this section, after giving definitions on IAGs, we discuss generating abilities of subclasses of IAGs.

2.1. *Definitions on isometric array grammars (IAGs)*

Let Σ be a finite set of symbols called an *alphabet*. A *two-dimensional word* over Σ is a non-empty connected array of symbols in Σ. The set of all two-dimensional words over Σ is denoted by Σ^{2+}. Similarly, the sets of all two-dimensional rectangular words and square words are denoted by Σ_R^{2+} and Σ_S^{2+}, respectively.

Definition 1:[3,7] An *isometric array grammar* (IAG) is defined by the following 5-tuple.

$$G = (N, T, P, S, \#)$$

N: A finite set of nonterminal symbols.
T: A finite set of terminal symbols ($N \cap T = \emptyset$).
P: A finite set of rewriting rules.
S: A start symbol ($S \in N$).

#: A blank symbol ($\# \notin N \cup T$).

Each rewriting rule in P is of the form $\alpha \to \beta$, and $\alpha, \beta \in (N \cup T \cup \{\#\})^{2+}$ must satisfy the following conditions (to be more precise see Ref. 7):

(1) The shapes of α and β are geometrically identical (*i.e.*, isomeric).
(2) α contains at least one nonterminal symbol.
(3) Terminal symbols in α are not rewritten by the rule $\alpha \to \beta$.
(4) The application of the rule $\alpha \to \beta$ preserves the connectivity of the host array.

A *#-embedded array* of a word $\xi \in (N \cup T)^{2+}$ is an infinite array over $N \cup T \cup \{\#\}$ obtained by embedding ξ in a two-dimensional infinite array of #'s, and is denoted by $\xi_\#$. (Formally, a #-embedded array is a mapping $\mathbf{Z}^2 \to (N \cup T \cup \{\#\})$.) We say that a word η is *directly derived* from a word ξ in G if $\xi_\#$ contains α and $\eta_\#$ is obtained by replacing one of the occurrences of α in $\xi_\#$ with β for some rewriting rule $\alpha \to \beta$ in G. This is denoted by $\xi \underset{G}{\Rightarrow} \eta$. The reflexive and transitive closure of the relation $\underset{G}{\Rightarrow}$ is denoted by $\overset{*}{\underset{G}{\Rightarrow}}$. We say that a word η is *derived* from a word ξ in G if $\xi \overset{*}{\underset{G}{\Rightarrow}} \eta$. The *array language* generated by G is defined by $L(G) = \{w | S \overset{*}{\Rightarrow} w,\ \text{and } w \in T^{2+}\}$.

Let $G = (N, T, P, S, \#)$ be an IAG. By restricting the form of a rewriting rule $\alpha \to \beta$ of G, we can obtain three subclasses of IAGs.

Definition 2:[3] If non-# symbols in α are not rewritten into #'s, then G is called a *monotonic array grammar* (MAG).

Definition 3:[1] If α consists of exactly one nonterminal and possibly some #'s, then G is called a *context-free array grammar* (CFAG).

Definition 4:[1] If each rewriting rule is one of the following forms, then G is called a *regular array grammar* (RAG), where $A, B \in N$, and $a \in T$.

$$\# A \to B a, \quad A \# \to a B, \quad \begin{matrix}\# \\ A\end{matrix} \to \begin{matrix}B \\ a\end{matrix}, \quad \begin{matrix}A \\ \#\end{matrix} \to \begin{matrix}a \\ B\end{matrix}, \quad A \to a\,.$$

2.2. *Pattern generation in RAGs*

It is known that the class of IAGs and its three subclasses form a Chomsky-like hierarchy.[1] The class of RAGs is the smallest one in this hierarchy. However, RAGs have relatively high pattern generating ability in spite of the very restricted form of their rewriting rules. As we shall see later, this generating power comes from the "#-context-sensing ability" of an RAG (*i.e.*, the left-hand side of a rule may have # besides a nonterminal symbol).

Since each rule of an RAG rewrites at most one blank symbol (#) into a non-blank symbol, a large number of rules may be needed to generate a meaningful two-dimensional language. So, it is convenient to introduce a useful subclass of IAGs equivalent to that of RAGs.

Let $r = \alpha \to \beta$ be a rule of a CFAG. r is called *strongly linear* if the following conditions hold (to be more precise, see Ref. 13).

(1) β contains at most one nonterminal.
(2) There is a single-stroke path covering all the symbols of α starting from the position of the nonterminal in α to the (corresponding) position of the nonterminal in β (or to some appropriate position if β has no nonterminal).

Definition 5:[13] Let $G = (N, T, P, S, \#)$ be a CFAG. If every rule in P is strongly linear, then G is called a *strongly linear array grammar* (SLAG).

Example 1: Consider the following rule, where X, $Y \in N$, a, $b \in T$.

$$\begin{array}{cc} \# & \# \\ \# & \# \\ \# & X \end{array} \quad \to \quad \begin{array}{cc} b & Y \\ a & a \\ b & a \end{array}$$

It is easy to see that it is strongly linear. In fact, there is a single-stroke path covering all the six symbols of the left-hand side starting from the X to the upper-right # whose position corresponds to Y in the right-hand side. We can decompose the above rule into the following ones of an RAG along the single-stroke path, where X_1, X_2, X_3 and X_4 are new nonterminals.

$$\# X \to X_1\, a\,, \qquad \begin{array}{c} \# \\ X_1 \end{array} \to \begin{array}{c} X_2 \\ b \end{array}, \qquad X_2\, \# \to a\, X_3\,,$$

$$\begin{array}{c} \# \\ X_3 \end{array} \to \begin{array}{c} X_4 \\ a \end{array}, \qquad X_4\, \# \to b\, Y$$

It is clear that the above five rules of an RAG correctly simulates the original rule of an SLAG.

Generalizing the method in Example 1, the following theorem is obtained. It states that the generating abilities of SLAGs and RAGs are the same (note that the class of RAGs is a subclass of SLAGs).

Theorem 1:[13] For any SLAG G, we can construct an RAG G' such that $L(G) = L(G')$.

With the aid of SLAGs, we can show that various geometrical patterns such as all rectangles, all squares, *etc.* are generated by RAGs.

Example 2:[13] An SLAG that generates the set of rectangles over $\{a\}$ of size $(6i+4) \times (4j+8)$ $(i, j \in \{0, 1, \cdots\})$.

$$G_R = (\{S, T, L, I, R, B\}, \{a\}, P_R, S, \#)$$

The set P_R consists of the following 12 rules. It is easily verified that all these rules are strongly linear.

(S)

$$\begin{array}{cccc} S & \# & \# & \# \\ \# & \# & & \\ \# & \# & & \end{array} \rightarrow \begin{array}{cccc} a & a & a & T \\ a & a & & \\ a & a & & \end{array}$$

(T1)

$$\begin{array}{ccccc} T & \# & \# & \# & \# \\ & & & \# & \# \\ & & & \# & \# \end{array} \rightarrow \begin{array}{cccc} a & a & a & T \\ & & a & a \\ & & a & a \end{array}$$

(T2)

$$\begin{array}{ccccc} T & \# & \# & \# & \# \\ & \# & \# & & \\ & \# & \# & & \end{array} \rightarrow \begin{array}{ccccc} a & a & a & a & R \\ & a & a & & \\ & a & a & & \end{array}$$

(I2)

$$\begin{array}{ccccc} & & \# & \# & \\ & & \# & \# & \\ \# & \# & \# & \# & I \\ \# & \# & & & \\ \# & \# & & & \end{array} \rightarrow \begin{array}{ccccc} & & a & a & \\ & & a & a & \\ a & a & a & a & a \\ a & a & & & \\ L & a & & & \end{array}$$

(I1)

$$\begin{array}{ccccc} \# & \# & & & \\ \# & \# & & & \\ \# & \# & \# & \# & I \\ & & \# & \# & \\ & & \# & \# & \end{array} \rightarrow \begin{array}{ccccc} a & a & & & \\ a & a & & & \\ I & a & a & a & a \\ & & & a & a \\ & & & a & a \end{array}$$

(R1)

$$\begin{array}{cccc} & & & R \\ & & \# & \# \\ & & \# & \# \\ \# & \# & \# & \# \\ \# & \# & & \\ \# & \# & & \end{array} \rightarrow \begin{array}{cccc} & & & a \\ & & a & a \\ & & a & a \\ I & a & a & a \\ a & a & & \\ a & a & & \end{array}$$

(L)

$$\begin{array}{cccc} & & \# & \# \\ L & & \# & \# \\ \# & \# & \# & \# \\ \# & \# & & \\ \# & \# & & \end{array} \rightarrow \begin{array}{cccc} & & a & a \\ & & a & a \\ a & a & a & I \\ a & a & & \\ a & a & & \end{array}$$

(I3)

$$\begin{array}{ccccc} & \# & \# & & \\ & \# & \# & & \\ I & \# & \# & \# & \# \\ & & & \# & \# \\ & & & \# & \# \end{array} \rightarrow \begin{array}{ccccc} & a & a & & \\ & a & a & & \\ a & a & a & a & I \\ & & & a & a \\ & & & a & a \end{array}$$

(I4)

$$\begin{array}{ccccc} & & & \# & \# \\ & & & \# & \# \\ I & \# & \# & \# & \# \\ & \# & \# & & \\ & \# & \# & & \end{array} \rightarrow \begin{array}{ccccc} & & & a & a \\ & & & a & a \\ a & a & a & a & R \\ & a & a & & \\ & a & a & & \end{array}$$

(B2)

$$\begin{array}{ccccc} & & \# & \# & \\ & & \# & \# & \\ \# & \# & \# & \# & B \end{array} \rightarrow \begin{array}{ccccc} & & a & a & \\ & & a & a & \\ a & a & a & a & a \end{array}$$

(B1)

$$\begin{array}{ccccc} \# & \# & & & \\ \# & \# & & & \\ \# & \# & \# & \# & B \end{array} \rightarrow \begin{array}{ccccc} a & a & & & \\ a & a & & & \\ B & a & a & a & a \end{array}$$

(R2)

$$\begin{array}{cccc} & & & R \\ & & \# & \# \\ & & \# & \# \\ \# & \# & \# & \# \end{array} \rightarrow \begin{array}{cccc} & & & a \\ & & a & a \\ & & a & a \\ B & a & a & a \end{array}$$

Figure 1 shows a derivation of a rectangular word of size 10×12.

A derivation process of a rectangular word is as follows. First, the rule (S) is used. Then, (T1) is applied repeatedly (0 times or more) to form the top edge of a rectangle. If (T2) is used, rightward growth of the top edge terminates. At this point "shape codes" are formed on the second and the third rows of the generated array. A shape code consists of a projection and a notch formed by the symbol a's. One bit of information is represented by a pair [projection, notch] or [notch, projection]. The left/right end and the inner part of a word are distinguished by such a pair.

At the right end, either (R1) or (R2) can be used. If (R1) is used, then (I1) is repeatedly applied to grow the inside of a rectangle. It should be noted that the rule (I2) cannot be used in the inside, since the positions of projections and notches do not match between the host array and the left-hand side of the rule. The rule (I2) is used only at the left end to terminate

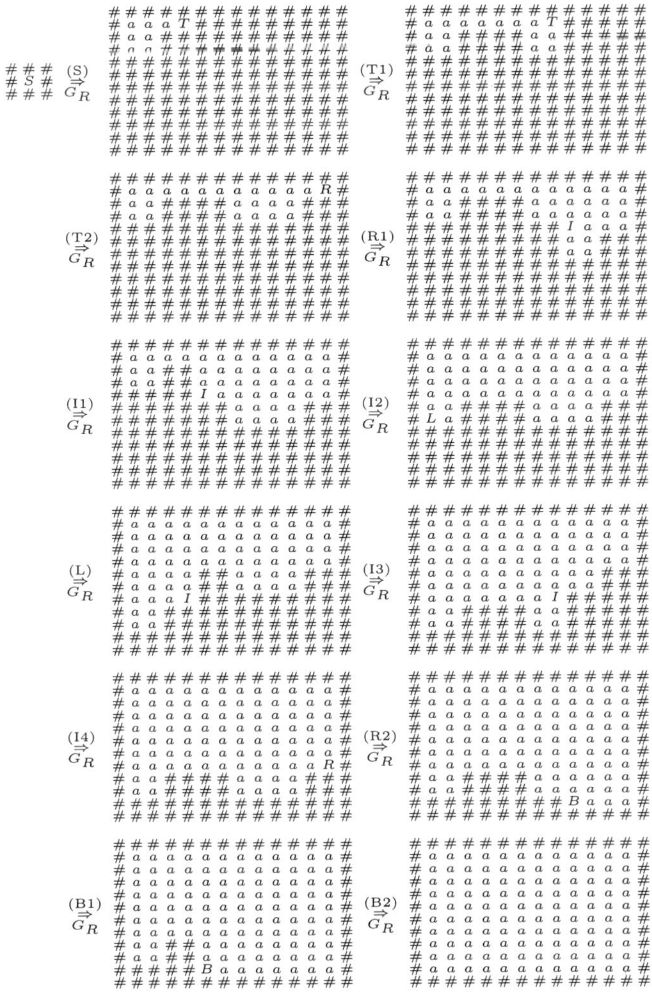

Fig. 1. A derivation process of a rectangular word by G_R of Example 2.

the leftward growth. Note that the shape codes are transmitted to the lower rows after the applications of these rules.

At the left end the rule (L) is used, and then (I3) is repeatedly applied. The rule (I4) is used at the right end to terminate the rightward growth.

If (R2) is applied at the right end, then the downward growth stops. Repeated applications of (B1) make the bottom edge of a rectangle. The derivation process terminates by applying (B2) at the south-west corner.

By adding appropriate rules to G_R in Example 2, we can obtain an SLAG (hence, RAG) that generates $\{a\}_R^{2+}$, the set of all sizes of rectangles. It is also possible to give an SLAG (RAG) that generates the set of all squares.

Theorem 2:[13] There are RAGs that generate $\{a\}_R^{2+}$ and $\{a\}_S^{2+}$.

2.3. *Uniquely parsable array grammars (UPAGs)*

As shown in the previous subsection, RAGs have relatively high generating ability of geometrical patterns. On the other hand, however, several decision problems on RAGs become very hard to solve. It is also due to the #-context-sensing ability. For example, emptiness problem for RAG languages is undecidable.[4] As for the membership problem, the following result is known. Hence, in general, pattern analysis (or parsing) based on RAGs is not performed efficiently.

Theorem 3:[4] The membership problem (given an IAG G and a word $x \in T^{2+}$, decide whether $x \in L(G)$) is NP-complete for the class of RAGs.

In order to remedy such inefficiency of parsing, a uniquely parsable array grammar (UPAG) was introduced.[14] In this subsection we give definitions and basic properties on UPAGs.

Let $\alpha \to \beta$ be a rule of an IAG. The subarray of α whose symbols are not changed (*i.e.* rewritten to the same symbols) by the application of $\alpha \to \beta$ is called the *context portion* of α. The subarray of α where each symbol is rewritten to a different symbol is called the *rewritten portion* of α. The context portion and the rewritten portion of β are also defined similarly.

Definition 6:[14] Let $G = (N, T, P, S, \#)$ be an IAG. If P satisfies the following conditions, G is called a *uniquely parsable array grammar* (UPAG).

(1) The right-hand side of each rule in P contains a symbol other than # and S.

(2) Let $r_1 = \alpha_1 \to \beta_1$ and $r_2 = \alpha_2 \to \beta_2$ be two rules in P (may be $r_1 = r_2$). Superpose β_1 and β_2 at all the possible positions variously translating them. For any superposition of β_1 and β_2, if all the symbols in overlapping portions of them match, then

   (a) these overlapping portions are contained in the context portions of β_1 and β_2, or

   (b) the whole β_1 and β_2 are overlapping, and $r_1 = r_2$.

For example, the pair of rules $aB \rightarrow ab$ and $Ca \rightarrow ca$ satisfies the condition 2(a) of Definition 6, but the pair $\#B \rightarrow ab$ and $Ca \rightarrow ca$ does not.

Example 3:[14] A UPAG that generates the set of all squares over $\{a\}$ of size larger than or equal to 2×2.

$$G_S = (\{S, D, G, E\}, \{a\}, P_S, S, \#)$$

The set P_S consists of the following 9 rules.

$$\begin{array}{cc}\# & \# \\ S & \# \\ \# & \end{array} \rightarrow \begin{array}{cc}\# & \# \\ a & S \\ S & \end{array} \qquad \begin{array}{ccc} & \# & \\ a & S & \# \\ & \# & \end{array} \rightarrow \begin{array}{ccc} & \# & \\ a & a & \# \\ & G & \end{array} \qquad \begin{array}{ccc}\# & S & S \\ & \# & \end{array} \rightarrow \begin{array}{ccc}\# & a & D \\ & S & \end{array}$$

$$\begin{array}{ccc}a & D & S \\ & \# & \end{array} \rightarrow \begin{array}{ccc}a & a & D \\ & S & \end{array} \qquad \begin{array}{cc}D & G \\ \# & \end{array} \rightarrow \begin{array}{cc}a & D \\ G & \end{array} \qquad \begin{array}{cc} & \# \\ D & \# \\ \# & \end{array} \rightarrow \begin{array}{cc} & \# \\ a & \# \\ S & \end{array}$$

$$\# \, S \, G \rightarrow \# \, a \, E \qquad a \, E \, S \rightarrow a \, a \, E \qquad \begin{array}{cc}E & \# \\ \# & \end{array} \rightarrow \begin{array}{cc}a & \# \\ \# & \end{array}$$

We can verify that G_S is a UPAG (since it is rather tedious to check it, we did it by computer). The following is a derivation example in G_S.

$$S \Rightarrow \begin{array}{cc}a & S \\ S & \end{array} \Rightarrow \begin{array}{ccc}a & a & S \\ S & S & \end{array} \Rightarrow \begin{array}{cccc}a & a & a & S \\ S & S & S & \end{array} \Rightarrow \begin{array}{cccc}a & a & a & a \\ S & S & S & G \end{array} \Rightarrow \begin{array}{cccc}a & a & a & a \\ a & D & S & G \\ S & & & \end{array} \Rightarrow \begin{array}{cccc}a & a & a & a \\ a & a & D & G \\ S & S & & \end{array}$$

$$\Rightarrow \begin{array}{cccc}a & a & a & a \\ a & a & a & D \\ S & S & G & \end{array} \Rightarrow \begin{array}{cccc}a & a & a & a \\ a & a & a & a \\ S & S & G & S \end{array} \Rightarrow \begin{array}{cccc}a & a & a & a \\ a & a & a & a \\ a & D & G & S \\ S & & & \end{array} \Rightarrow \begin{array}{cccc}a & a & a & a \\ a & a & a & a \\ a & a & D & S \\ S & G & & \end{array} \Rightarrow \begin{array}{cccc}a & a & a & a \\ a & a & a & a \\ a & a & a & D \\ S & G & S & \end{array}$$

$$\Rightarrow \begin{array}{cccc}a & a & a & a \\ a & a & a & a \\ a & a & a & a \\ S & G & S & S \end{array} \Rightarrow \begin{array}{cccc}a & a & a & a \\ a & a & a & a \\ a & a & a & a \\ a & E & S & S \end{array} \Rightarrow \begin{array}{cccc}a & a & a & a \\ a & a & a & a \\ a & a & a & a \\ a & a & E & S \end{array} \Rightarrow \begin{array}{cccc}a & a & a & a \\ a & a & a & a \\ a & a & a & a \\ a & a & a & E \end{array} \Rightarrow \begin{array}{cccc}a & a & a & a \\ a & a & a & a \\ a & a & a & a \\ a & a & a & a \end{array}$$

A rewriting rule $\alpha \rightarrow \beta$ is called *reversely applicable* to η *at* (i, j), iff β occurs in $\eta_\#$ at the position (i, j), where the position of an occurrence means the x-y coordinates of the leftmost symbol of its uppermost row. If $\xi_\#$ is obtained by reversely applying $\alpha \rightarrow \beta$ at (i, j), we say ξ is *directly reduced* from η by the reverse rewriting with the *label* $L = [\alpha \rightarrow \beta, (i, j)]$. This is denoted by $\eta \overset{L}{\Leftarrow} \xi$. Apparently, $\eta \overset{L}{\Leftarrow} \xi$ iff $\xi \overset{L}{\Rightarrow} \eta$. If $\eta \overset{L_1}{\Leftarrow} \zeta_1 \overset{L_2}{\Leftarrow} \zeta_2 \cdots \zeta_{n-1} \overset{L_n}{\Leftarrow} \xi$ for some $\zeta_1, \zeta_2, \ldots, \zeta_{n-1}$, we also write it by $\eta \overset{n}{\Leftarrow} \xi$.

The following theorem states that if $\eta \overset{n}{\Leftarrow} S$, then *every* reduction starting from η always reaches the symbol S in n steps without backtracking.

Theorem 4:[14] Let $G = (N, T, P, S, \#)$ be a UPAG. Let $\alpha \to \beta$ be any rule in P that is reversely applicable to $\eta \in (N \cup T)^{2+}$ at (i, j). If $\eta \overset{n}{\Leftarrow} S$, then there exists a reduction $\eta \overset{L}{\Leftarrow} \zeta \overset{n-1}{\Longleftarrow} S$ for some ζ, where $L = [\alpha \to \beta, (i, j)]$.

This theorem can be generalized to the case of parallel reduction.

Let $G = (N, T, P, S, \#)$ be a UPAG, and let $\alpha_1 \to \beta_1, \ldots, \alpha_m \to \beta_m$ be rewriting rules in P that are reversely applicable to $\eta \in (N \cup T)^{2+}$ at the positions $(i_1, j_1), \ldots, (i_m, j_m)$, respectively, and let $L_k = [\alpha_k \to \beta_k, (i_k, j_k)] (k = 1, \ldots, m)$. We assume these labels differ each other. Since G is a UPAG, any two of these reverse applications do not overlap except in their context portions. Therefore, these reverse applications can be performed simultaneously (*i.e.* in parallel). We write such parallel reduction by $\eta \overset{\{L_1, \ldots, L_m\}}{\Longleftarrow} \zeta$.

Theorem 5:[14] Let $G = (N, T, P, S, \#)$ be a UPAG. Let $L_1, \ldots, L_m$ be different labels which are reversely applicable to $\eta \in (N \cup T)^{2+}$. If $\eta \overset{n}{\Leftarrow} S$, then the following reduction exists for some ζ.

$$\eta \overset{\{L_1, \ldots, L_m\}}{\Longleftarrow} \zeta \overset{n-m}{\Longleftarrow} S$$

It is possible to extend the framework of two-dimensional IAGs to three-dimensional ones. Imai *et al.*[2] gave a three-dimensional UPAG that generates all cubes. Figure 2 shows a parallel parsing process of a cube.

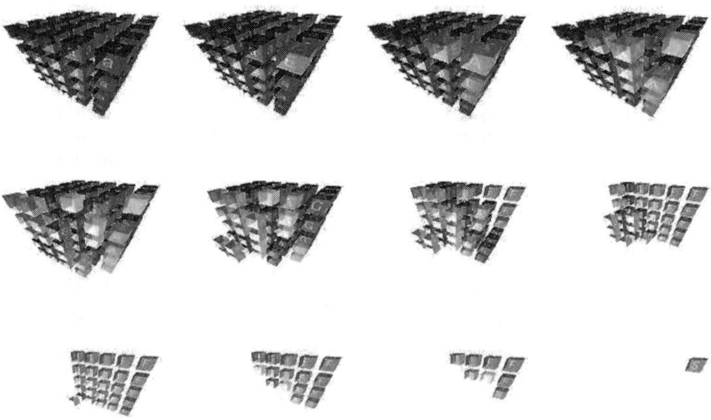

Fig. 2. Parallel parsing of a cube based on a three-dimensional UPAG.

3. Generating Connected and Simply-Connected Words by UPAGs

In this section, we investigate how UPAGs can generate patterns with certain topological properties. Especially, we consider the problem of designing UPAGs that generates all connected words (that may contain holes) and all simply-connected words (that contain no hole). (Here, we employ *4-connectedness*,[7] which is defined based on 4-adjacency.) Once such UPAGs are given, they can be used as an efficient recognition (or parsing) tools for connectedness and simple-connectedness because of their property of unique parsability (Theorem 4) or parallel parsability (Theorem 5).

Theorem 6:[5] The following UPAG generates all connected words over the alphabet $\{a\}$ and only those.

$$G_{\text{connect}} = (\{S, A\}, \{a\}, P_{\text{connect}}, S, \#)\,,$$

where P_{connect} consists of the following rewriting rules.

$$(1)\ \begin{array}{ccc} & \# & \\ \# & S & \# \\ & \# & \end{array} \rightarrow \begin{array}{ccc} & \# & \\ \# & A & \# \\ & \# & \end{array} \qquad (5a)\ \begin{array}{cccc} & \# & & \\ \# & A & A & \\ & A & \# & \# \\ & & \# & \end{array} \rightarrow \begin{array}{cccc} & \# & & \\ \# & \# & A & \\ & A & A & \# \\ & & \# & \end{array} \qquad (5d)\ \begin{array}{cccc} & A & A & \\ A & A & A & \\ A & A & \# & \# \\ & & \# & \end{array} \rightarrow \begin{array}{cccc} & A & A & \\ A & \# & A & \\ A & A & A & \# \\ & & \# & \end{array}$$

$$(2)\ \begin{array}{ccc} & A & \\ \# & \# & \# \\ & \# & \end{array} \rightarrow \begin{array}{ccc} & A & \\ \# & A & \# \\ & \# & \end{array} \qquad (5b)\ \begin{array}{cccc} & A & A & \\ \# & A & A & \\ & A & \# & \# \\ & & \# & \end{array} \rightarrow \begin{array}{cccc} & A & A & \\ \# & \# & A & \\ & A & A & \# \\ & & \# & \end{array} \qquad (6)\ A \rightarrow a$$

$$(3)\ \begin{array}{ccc} & \# & \\ A & \# & \# \\ & \# & \end{array} \rightarrow \begin{array}{ccc} & \# & \\ A & A & \# \\ & \# & \end{array} \qquad (5c)\ \begin{array}{cccc} & \# & & \\ A & A & A & \\ A & A & \# & \# \\ & & \# & \end{array} \rightarrow \begin{array}{cccc} & \# & & \\ A & \# & A & \\ A & A & A & \# \\ & & \# & \end{array}$$

$$(4)\ \begin{array}{ccc} A & A & \\ A & \# & \# \\ & \# & \end{array} \rightarrow \begin{array}{ccc} A & A & \\ A & A & \# \\ & \# & \end{array}$$

Theorem 7:[6] The following UPAG generates all simply-connected words over the alphabet $\{a\}$ and only those.

$$G_{\text{s-connect}} = (\{S, A\}, \{a\}, P_{\text{s-connect}}, S, \#)\,,$$

where $P_{\text{s-connect}} = P_{\text{connect}} - \{(5d)\} \cup \{(5d')\}$ (*i.e.*, $P_{\text{s-connect}}$ is obtained by replacing the rewriting rule $(5d)$ in P_{connect} by the rule $(5d')$ below).

$$(5d')\ \begin{array}{cccc} \# & A & A & \\ A & A & A & \\ A & A & \# & \# \\ & & \# & \end{array} \rightarrow \begin{array}{cccc} \# & A & A & \\ A & \# & A & \\ A & A & A & \# \\ & & \# & \end{array}$$

In the following, we describe a proof of Theorem 7, which was first given by Qi *et al.*[6]

To prove this theorem, we make the following preparations. Let η be an arbitrary word over $\{A\}$. An *SE-cell* (that is a "south-east corner cell") in η is a cell with a symbol A such that its south and east neighbor cells are both #'s. We can classify SE-cells into five cases as shown in Fig. 3 (SE-cells are indicated by $\boxed{A}$).

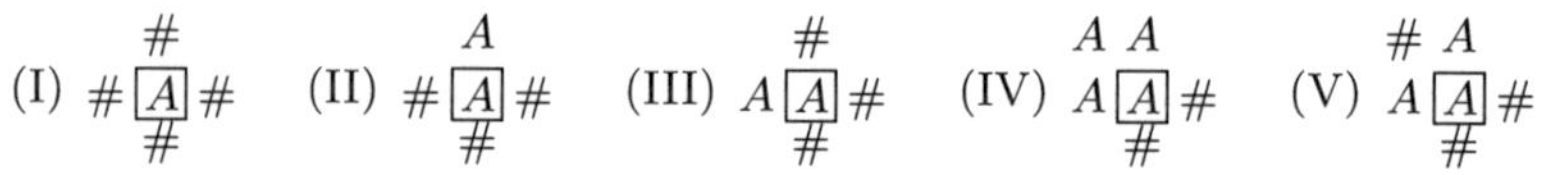

Fig. 3. Classification of SE-cells.

It is also easy to see that the case (V) can be further classified into 10 sub-cases (a)–(j) as in Fig. 4. Note that, in the cases (f)–(j) of Fig. 4, cells indicated by $\underline{A}$ are also SE-cells.

Fig. 4. Sub-classification of SE-cells of the case (V) in Fig. 3.

Let Σ be a finite nonempty set of symbols, and $p : \mathbf{Z}^2 \to \Sigma \cup \{\#\}$ be an infinite array. The *support* of p is defined as follows: $\mathrm{supp}(p) = \{(x,y) | p(x,y) \neq \#\}$. We consider only of p such that $\mathrm{supp}(p)$ is nonempty and finite. $x^p_{\min}$ and $y^p_{\max}$ are defined as follows: $x^p_{\min} = \min\{x | p(x,y) \neq \#\}$, and $y^p_{\max} = \max\{y | p(x,y) \neq \#\}$. We define a function $\mathrm{ind}_p : \mathrm{supp}(p) \to \mathbf{Z}$ as follows:

$$\mathrm{ind}_p(x,y) = |x - x^p_{\min}| + |y - y^p_{\max}| .$$

The function ind gives each point in supp(p) an index. Furthermore, we define an index function for p as follows:

$$\mathrm{ind}_p^* = \sum_{(x,y)\in \mathrm{supp}(p)} \mathrm{ind}_p(x,y)\,.$$

Lemma 1:[6] *Let $p : \mathbf{Z}^2 \to \{\#, A\}$ be an arbitrary two-dimensional infinite array, such that* supp(p) *forms a simply-connected word. Then, p contains at least one of the patterns of the cases (I)–(IV) in Fig.* 3 *or the cases (a)–(d) in Fig.* 4 *as a sub-pattern.*

Proof: It is clear that there is at least one SE-cell, because supp(p) is nonempty and finite. Moreover, since supp(p) is a simply-connected word (that has no hole), the sub-pattern (e) does not appear. Here, we assume (on the contrary) that every SE-cell in p is in one of the cases (f)–(j). Let (x_0, y_0) be the SE-cell having the smallest index among them. Consider the case that (x_0, y_0) is the cell $\boxed{A}$ in the sub-case (f) (the proof is similar for the cases (g)–(j)). Then, the cell $\underline{A}$ that is on the north-west direction of (x_0, y_0) in Fig. 4(f) is also an SE-cell. It has the index $\mathrm{ind}_p(x_0, y_0) - 3$, which contradicts the assumption that (x_0, y_0) has the least index. Thus, the lemma holds. □

Lemma 2:[6] *Let $p : \mathbf{Z}^2 \to \{\#, A\}$ be an arbitrary two-dimensional infinite array such that* supp(p) *forms a simply-connected word. Then, at least one of the rewriting rules* (1)–(4), (5a)–(5c), *or* (5d') *is reversely applicable to p. Let p' be the array which is obtained by reversely applying one of those rules to p. Then,* supp(p') *also forms a simply-connected word and* $\mathrm{ind}_{p'}^* < \mathrm{ind}_p^*$ *or* $\mathrm{ind}_{p'}^* = \mathrm{ind}_p^* = 0$ *holds.*

Proof: We can say, from Lemma 1, that one of the rewriting rules (1)–(4), (5a)–(5c), or (5d') is reversely applicable to p. Because the cases (I)–(IV) and the sub-cases (a)–(d) of the case (V) exactly correspond to the right-hand sides of these rewriting rules. It is easily verified that a reverse application of any one of these rewriting rules neither changes the connectivity of a word nor creates a hole in a word. Hence, supp(p') also forms a simply-connected word. Moreover, by comparing the left-hand and right-hand sides of each rewriting rule, we can see that a reverse application of each rewriting rules other than (1) makes $\mathrm{ind}_{p'}^* < \mathrm{ind}_p^*$. Rewriting rule (1) can be reversely applicable only when supp(p) consists of just one point. In this case, $\mathrm{ind}_{p'}^* = \mathrm{ind}_p^* = 0$. By above, the lemma holds. □

Proof of Theorem 7. It is clear that UPAG $G_{\text{s-connect}}$ generates only simply-connected words consisting of a's. Because, the rewriting rule (1) of $P_{\text{s-connect}}$ generates the simply-connected word consisting of only one A, and each rewriting rule other than (1) neither changes the connectivity of a word (consisting of A's and a's), nor creates a hole.

Next, we show that $G_{\text{s-connect}}$ generates *all* simply-connected words consisting of a's. For this purpose, it is sufficient to show that there is a reduction $w \overset{*}{\Leftarrow} S$ for an arbitrary simply-connected word $w \in \{A\}^{2+}$. (Because, by using the rule (6) repeatedly, w becomes the word $x \in \{a\}^{2+}$ having same shape as w, and thus $w \overset{*}{\Rightarrow} x$. Hence, we can say that if $w \overset{*}{\Leftarrow} S$ then $S \overset{*}{\Rightarrow} x$). Let $p : \mathbf{Z}^2 \rightarrow \{\#, A\}$ be a pattern representing $w_{\#}$. We show $w \overset{*}{\Leftarrow} S$ by the mathematical induction on the value ind_p^*.

By Lemma 2, at least one of the rewriting rules (1)–(4), (5a)–(5c), or (5d') is reversely applicable to p. In the case $\text{ind}_p^* = 0$, the rewriting rule (1) is reversely applicable, and thus $w \Leftarrow S$. In the case $\text{ind}_p^* = k > 0$, one of the rewriting rules (2)–(4), (5a)–(5c), or (5d') is reversely applicable, and p' is obtained by using that rule. p' satisfies $\text{ind}_{p'}^* < k$ and $\text{supp}(p')$ is again a simply-connected word. Hence, from the assumption of mathematical induction, $w \overset{*}{\Leftarrow} S$. By above, the theorem holds. □

4. Concluding Remarks

Here, we discussed several aspects of pattern generation and parsing problems in isometric array grammars and their subclasses. It is left for the future study to give simple and interesting uniquely parsable array grammars that generate patterns with some other topological properties that are not discussed in this paper.

References

1. C. R. Cook and P. S. P. Wang, A Chomsky hierarchy of isotonic array grammars and languages, *Computer Graphics and Image Processing*, **8**, 144–152 (1978).
2. K. Imai, Y. Matsuda, C. Iwamoto and K. Morita, A three-dimensional uniquely parsable array grammar that generates and parses cubes, *Electronic Notes in Theoretical Computer Science*, **46** (2001).
3. D. L. Milgram and A. Rosenfeld, Array automata and array grammars, *Information Processing 71*, North-Holland, 69–74 (1972).
4. K. Morita, Y. Yamamoto and K. Sugata, The complexity of some decision problems about two-dimensional array grammars, *Information Sciences*, **30**, 241–264 (1983).

5. K. Morita and K. Imai, Uniquely parsable array grammars for generating and parsing connected patterns, *Pattern Recognition*, **32**, 269–276 (1999).
6. J. S. Qi, R. L. A. Shauri and K. Morita, Generation of simply-connected patterns and simple closed curves by uniquely parsable array grammars (in Japanese), *Trans. IEICE*, **J85-D-I**, 168–172 (2002).
7. A. Rosenfeld, *Picture Languages*, Academic Press, New York (1979).
8. R. Siromoney, On equal matrix languages, *Information and Control*, **14**, 135–151 (1969).
9. G. Siromoney, R. Siromoney and K. Krithivasan, Abstract families of matrices and picture languages, *Computer Graphics and Image Processing*, **1**, 284–307 (1972).
10. G. Siromoney, R. Siromoney and K. Krithivasan, Picture languages with array rewriting rules, *Information and Control*, **22**, 447–470 (1973).
11. G. Siromoney, R. Siromoney and K. Krithivasan, Array grammars and kolam, *Computer Graphics and Image Processing*, **3**, 63–82 (1974).
12. P. S. P. Wang (ed.), *Array Grammars, Patterns and Recognizers*, World Scientific, Singapore (1989).
13. Y. Yamamoto, K. Morita and K. Sugata, Context-sensitivity of two-dimensional regular array grammars, *Int. J. Pattern Recognition and Artificial Intelligence*, **3**, 295–319 (1989).
14. Y. Yamamoto and K. Morita, Two-dimensional uniquely parsable isometric array grammars, *Int. J. Pattern Recognition and Artificial Intelligence*, **6**, 301–313 (1992).

CHAPTER 19

ANCHORED CONCATENATION OF MSCs

Madhavan Mukund*, K. Narayan Kumar*, P. S. Thiagarajan† and Shaofa Yang†

*Chennai Mathematical Institute, Chennai, India
E-mail: {madhavan, kumar}@cmi.ac.in

†School of Computing, National University of Singapore, Singapore
E-mail: {thiagu, yangsf}@comp.nus.edu.sg

We study collections of Message Sequence Charts (MSCs) defined by High-level MSCs (HMSCs) under a new type of concatenation operation called *anchored concatenation*. We show that there is no decision procedure for determining if the MSC language defined by an HMSC is regular and that it is undecidable if an HMSC admits an implied scenario. Further, the languages defined by locally synchronized HMSCs are precisely the finitely generated regular MSC languages. These results mirror the ones for the asynchronous concatenation case. On the other hand, the MSC language obtained by closing under implied scenarios is regular for *every* HMSC. Secondly, one can effectively determine whether a locally synchronized HMSC admits an implied scenario. Neither of these results hold in the asynchronous concatenation case.

1. Introduction

Message Sequence Charts (MSCs) are an appealing visual formalism that is suitable for modelling telecommunication software.[12] They are used in a number of software engineering notational frameworks such as SDL[18] and UML.[5,7] A collection of MSCs is used to capture the scenarios that a designer might want the system to exhibit (or avoid). Hence it is fruitful to have suitable mechanisms to specify a collection of MSCs.

A common way to specify a collection of MSCs is to use a High-level (or Hierarchical) Message Sequence Chart (HMSC).[14] An HMSC is a directed graph where each node is labelled an HMSC or an MSC. The HMSCs labelling the nodes are not allowed to reference each other. Hence, without loss of expressiveness, we shall conveniently assume that each node is labelled by just an MSC. From an HMSC one obtains MSCs by walking from an initial vertex to a terminal one, while *concatenating* the MSCs at the vertices visited. The collection of MSCs thus obtained is defined to be the MSC language of the HMSC.

In the literature, one encounters two extreme types of MSC concatenation, *asynchronous* and *synchronous concatenation.* In *asynchronous concatenation* the MSCs are concatenated along lifelines. If $M = M_1 \circ M_2$, then no event of an instance in M_2 may execute until all the events of the same instance in M_1 have finished executing. In *synchronous concatenation* one demands that *all the events* of M_1 must be executed before *any* event in M_2 can be executed. Asynchronous concatenation leads to a very expressive class of HMSC-definable MSC collections while synchronous concatenation gives rise to very restricted and impractical MSC collections.

We propose here a new and natural MSC concatenation termed *anchored concatenation.* In this operation, we demand that an agent which is active in both M_1 and M_2 can start executing in M_2 only after *all* the events in M_1 have finished executing; in effect, all — *and only* — the agents participating in M_1 must synchronize before any agent of M_2 that was also active in M_1 can start executing again. This is a weaker form of synchronous concatenation since we impose no restrictions on the agents of M_2 that do not participate in M_1.

We present here the resulting theory of MSC languages generated by HMSCs. We pay particular attention to their closures with respect to *implied scenarios.*[1,2,20] Briefly, implied scenarios arise naturally when one implements a collection of MSCs in a distributed setting. One of our main results is that the closure (with respect to implied scenarios) of *every* HMSC is a regular MSC language. This establishes that HMSCs can be a fruitful specification formalism if we interpret the set of scenarios defined by an HMSC to be its implied scenarios-closure under anchored concatenation. Such collections can be easily realized as a network of finite state automata with local acceptance conditions; they will communicate with each other via bounded fifoes as well as by performing common synchronization actions.

In common with the theory under asynchronous concatenation, there is no decision procedure for determining if the MSC language defined by an HMSC is regular or for determining if an HMSC admits an implied scenario. It turns out that the languages defined by HMSCs that satisfy the syntactic condition of being locally synchronized are precisely the finitely generated regular languages.

On the other hand, the language of MSCs obtained by closing under implied scenarios is both regular and finitely generated for *every* HMSC. Moreover, one can decide whether a locally synchronized HMSC admits an implied scenario. None of these results holds in the case of asynchronous concatenation.

There is a substantial theory of the MSC languages defined by HMSCs under asynchronous concatenation.[1–3,9–11,13,16] Synchronous concatenation of MSCs is informally defined and some related verification problems and their complexities are discussed in Ref. 3. In the framework of Live Sequence Charts,[8] a restricted type of concatenation that is much closer to anchored and not synchronous concatenation is implicitly assumed.

In the next section we extend the usual notion of MSCs in order to admit synchronizations. This gives a convenient handle on the anchored concatenation operation. We then use a restricted type of these enriched MSCs to define the MSC languages generated by HMSCs under anchored concatenation. In Section 3, we present the related automaton model called *product* Message Passing Automata. In the subsequent two sections we establish our main results. In the final section, we briefly discuss the prospects for future work.

2. Message Sequence Charts

Let $\mathcal{P} = \{p, q, r, \ldots\}$ be a finite set of *agents* (processes). These agents communicate with each other via fifo channels as well as multi-way synchronizations. The set of *channels* is $Ch = \{(p,q) \in \mathcal{P} \times \mathcal{P} | p \neq q\}$. Let Δ be a finite alphabet of *messages*. We define the *communication alphabet* to be $\Sigma_{com} = \{p!q(m), p?q(m) | (p,q) \in Ch, m \in \Delta\}$ and the *synchronization alphabet* to be $\Sigma_{syn} = \{P \subseteq \mathcal{P} || P| > 0\}$. We set $\Sigma = \Sigma_{com} \cup \Sigma_{syn}$. The action $p!q(m)$ denotes p sending a message m to q, while the action $p?q(m)$ denotes p receiving a message m from q. The action $P \in \Sigma_{syn}$ represents the processes in P performing a multi-way synchronization. We do not explicitly model the exchange of information that takes place during such a synchronization. A singleton synchronization $\{p\}$ represents an internal action performed by p. Henceforth, we fix $\mathcal{P}$, Δ, Ch, Σ and let p, q range over $\mathcal{P}$, m over Δ and P over Σ_{syn}.

For $a \in \Sigma$, we define loc(a), the *locations* of a, as follows: $\text{loc}(p!q(m)) = \text{loc}(p?q(m)) = \{p\}$ and $\text{loc}(P) = P$. Thus loc(a) is the set of processes that take part in a. For $p \in \mathcal{P}$, we define $\Sigma_p = \{a \in \Sigma | p \in \text{loc}(a)\}$.

Message sequence charts (MSCs) are restricted Σ-labelled posets. A Σ-labelled poset is a structure $M = (E, \leq, \lambda)$ where $(E, \leq)$ is a poset and $\lambda : E \to \Sigma$ a labelling function. For $e \in E$, we define $\downarrow e = \{e' \in E | e' \leq e\}$. For $p \in \mathcal{P}$, we define $E_p = \{e \in E | p \in \text{loc}(\lambda(e))\}$. Also, for $a \in \Sigma$, we let $E_a = \{e \in E | \lambda(e) = a\}$. We set $E_{com} = \{e \in E | \lambda(e) \in \Sigma_{com}\}$ and $E_{syn} = \{e \in E | \lambda(e) \in \Sigma_{syn}\}$.

For $(p, q) \in Ch$ and $m \in \Delta$, we define the relation $<_{pqm} \subseteq E \times E$ to capture the causal relationship between the send and receive actions of each message. For e, $e' \in E$, $e <_{pqm} e'$ iff $\lambda(e) = p!q(m)$, $\lambda(e') = q?p(m)$ and $|{\downarrow e} \cap E_{p!q(m)}| = |{\downarrow e'} \cap E_{q?p(m)}|$.

For $(p, q) \in Ch$, define $<_{pq} = \bigcup_{m \in \Delta} <_{pqm}$. For $p \in \mathcal{P}$, define $\leq_{pp} = (E_p \times E_p) \cap \leq$, with $<_{pp}$ standing for the largest irreflexive subset of $\leq_{pp}$. An event e is classified as a *send*, *receive* or *synchronization event* in the obvious way.

We are now ready to define MSCs.

An *MSC* (over $\mathcal{P}$) is a *finite* Σ-labelled poset $M = (E, \leq, \lambda)$ which satisfies the following conditions:

- $\leq_{pp}$ is a linear order for each p.
- For each $(p, q) \in Ch$ and $m \in \Delta$, $|E_{p!q(m)}| = |E_{q?p(m)}|$.
- $\leq$ is the reflexive, transitive closure of $\bigcup_{p,q \in \mathcal{P}} <_{pq}$.
- If $e_1 <_{pqm} e_2$ and $f_1 <_{pqm'} f_2$ where $m \neq m'$, then $e_1 <_{pp} f_1$ iff $e_2 <_{qq} f_2$.
- If e_1, $e_2 \in E_{com}$, $e \in E_{syn}$ such that $e_1 <_{pq} e_2$, $p \neq q$, and $\{p, q\} \subseteq \lambda(e)$, then either $e < e_1 < e_2$ or $e_1 < e_2 < e$.

The fourth clause ensures that each channel (p, q) is fifo. The last clause ensures that no message from p to q crosses a synchronization involving p and q.

Figure 1 shows an MSC. We depict the events of the MSC in *visual order*. The communication actions of each process are arranged in a vertical line. Members of $<_{pq}$ are shown with horizontal or downward-sloping arrows from the vertical line of p to that of q. The labels on these arrows indicate the message transmitted. A synchronization action is drawn as a rectangle that disconnects the vertical lines of the processes participating in this synchronization. In what follows, unless stated otherwise, by an "MSC" we shall mean an object defined as above.

We identify an MSC with its isomorphism class. Let $\mathcal{M}_{\mathcal{P}}$ be the set of MSCs over $\mathcal{P}$. The subscript $\mathcal{P}$ will often be dropped. Let $M = (E, \leq, \lambda) \in \mathcal{M}$. Set $\text{loc}(e) = \text{loc}(\lambda(e))$ for $e \in E$ and $\text{loc}(M) = \bigcup\{\text{loc}(e) | e \in E\}$. The processes in $\text{loc}(M)$ are said to be *active* in M. We refer to the set of

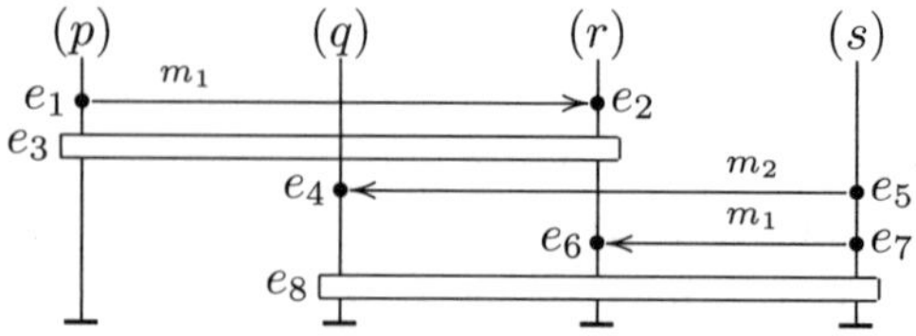

Fig. 1. A simple MSC over $\{p, q, r, s\}$.

linearizations of M as $lin(M)$ — that is, $\sigma \in lin(M)$ iff $\sigma = \lambda(e_1) \cdots \lambda(e_n)$, $E = \{e_1, \ldots, e_n\}$ and for each pair e_i, e_j with $i < j$, $e_j \not\leq e_i$.

An *MSC language* (over $\mathcal{P}$) is a subset of $\mathcal{M}$. Let $\mathcal{L}$ be an MSC language. Set $lin(\mathcal{L}) = \bigcup\{lin(M) | M \in \mathcal{L}\}$. We say $\mathcal{L}$ is *regular* iff $lin(\mathcal{L})$ is a regular subset of Σ^*.

Concatenation of MSCs

Let $M_1 = (E_1, \leq_1, \lambda_1)$ and $M_2 = (E_2, \leq_2, \lambda_2)$ be MSCs. The *concatenation* $M_1 \circ M_2$ of M_1 and M_2 is the MSC $M = (E, \leq, \lambda)$ defined as follows:

- E is the disjoint union of E_1 and E_2.
- $\leq$ is the reflexive, transitive closure of $\leq_1 \cup \leq_2 \cup \sqsubset$, where $\sqsubset = \{(e_1, e_2) | e_1 \in E_1, e_2 \in E_2, \mathrm{loc}(e_1) \cap \mathrm{loc}(e_2) \neq \emptyset\}$.

We note that $M_1 \circ M_2$ is also an MSC. In what follows, by "concatenation" we shall always mean the operation $\circ$ defined above.

Let $M = (E, \leq, \lambda)$ be an MSC. We say that M is *plain* iff $E_{syn} = \emptyset$. Plain MSCs correspond to the standard definition of MSCs in the literature.[12] For plain MSCs, the operation defined above corresponds to the usual definition of asynchronous concatenation.

Let $M_i = (E_i, \leq_i, \lambda_i)$, $i = 1, 2$, be a pair of plain MSCs. The *synchronous concatenation* of M_1 and M_2 is the MSC $M = (E, \leq, \lambda)$ where E is the disjoint union of E_1 and E_2 and $\leq$ is the reflexive, transitive closure of $\leq_1 \cup \leq_2 \cup (E_1 \times E_2)$ (see, for instance[3]). Thus synchronous concatenation for plain MSCs requires *all* events in M_1 be completed before *any* event in M_2 is executed. This can be captured in our setting by inserting a synchronous event involving the entire set of processes $\mathcal{P}$ between M_1 and M_2.

Synchronous concatenation is often the intended interpretation when describing a communication protocol as a sequence of phases, with a common set of participating agents across the different phases. However, if M_1 and M_2 are phases involving disjoint sets of agents, it is unnatural to force all events in M_1 to occur before those of M_2. A more natural version of synchronous concatenation is the anchored version.

Let $M_i = (E_i, \leq_i, \lambda_i)$ with $i = 1, 2$ be plain MSCs. The *anchored concatenation* $M_1 \circledcirc M_2$ of M_1 and M_2 is the MSC $M = (E, \leq, \lambda)$ where E is the disjoint union of E_1 and E_2 and $\leq$ is the reflexive, transitive closure of $\leq_1 \cup \leq_2 \cup \prec$, where $\prec = \{(e_1, e_2) | e_1 \in E_1, e_2 \in E_2, \text{loc}(e_2) \subseteq \text{loc}(M_1)\}$.

To study anchored concatenation, we shall work with a specific subclass of our MSCs called *episodes.* An *episode* is an MSC $M = (E, \leq, \lambda)$ which contains a synchronization event e such that $E_{syn} = \{e\}$, $\downarrow e = E$ and $\lambda(e) = \text{loc}(E \setminus \{e\})$. In other words, an episode is a plain MSC equipped with a terminal synchronization event involving all the processes that participate in the "body" of the MSC. The requirement that the body of an episode should be a plain MSC is only for technical ease and is not an essential restriction.

Observe that for episodes, concatenation coincides with anchored concatenation. Hence, while working with episodes, we dispense with $\circledcirc$ and just use $\circ$ to denote (anchored) concatenation.

We are now ready to define the main objects of our study in this new setting, namely, HMSCs.

HMSCs

An HMSC (over $\mathcal{X}$) is a structure $\mathcal{G} = (Q, \rightarrow, Q_{\text{in}}, F, \mathcal{X}, \Phi)$ where

- Q is a finite and nonempty set of states.
- $\rightarrow \subseteq Q \times Q$.
- $Q_{\text{in}} \subseteq Q$ is a set of initial states.
- $F \subseteq Q$ is a set of final states.
- $\mathcal{X}$ is a finite set of episodes.
- $\Phi : Q \rightarrow \mathcal{X}$ is a labelling function.

A path π through an HMSC $\mathcal{G}$ is a sequence $q_0 \rightarrow q_1 \rightarrow \cdots \rightarrow q_n$ such that $(q_{i-1}, q_i) \in \rightarrow$ for $i \in \{1, 2, \ldots, n\}$. The MSC generated by π is $M(\pi) = M_0 \circ M_1 \circ \cdots \circ M_n$ where $M_i = \Phi(q_i)$. We say π is a *run* iff $q_0 \in Q_{\text{in}}$ and $q_n \in F$. The *MSC language* of $\mathcal{G}$ is $\mathcal{L}(\mathcal{G}) = \{M(\pi) | \pi \text{ is a run through } \mathcal{G}\}$.

For an MSC M, we define the *communication graph* CG_M of M to be the *undirected* graph $(\mathcal{P}, \mapsto)$, where $(p, q) \in \mapsto$ iff there exists $e \in E$ with $\lambda(e) = p!q(m)$ or $\lambda(e) = p?q(m)$ or $\{p, q\} \subseteq \lambda(e)$. Note that this definition of CG_M is slightly different from the one used for asynchronous concatenation,[3,9] where a *directed* graph is constructed reflecting the flow of information through messages between processes. We say an HMSC $\mathcal{G}$ is *locally synchronized* iff for every cycle $\pi = q \rightarrow q_1 \rightarrow q_2 \rightarrow \cdots \rightarrow q_n \rightarrow q$, the communication graph of $M(\pi)$ consists of a single connected component (and isolated vertices).

We extend the concatenation operation $\circ$ to MSC languages in the obvious way. That is, for $\mathcal{L}_1, \mathcal{L}_2 \subseteq \mathcal{M}$, $\mathcal{L}_1 \circ \mathcal{L}_2 = \{M_1 \circ M_2 | M_1 \in \mathcal{L}_1, M_2 \in \mathcal{L}_2\}$. Let $\mathcal{X}$ be a set of episodes. Define $\mathcal{X}^1 = \mathcal{X}$ and $\mathcal{X}^{n+1} = \mathcal{X}^n \circ \mathcal{X}$. The MSC language $\mathcal{X}^{\circledast} = \cup_{n \geq 1} \mathcal{X}^n$ is the *iteration* of $\mathcal{X}$. An MSC language $\mathcal{L}$ is said to be *finitely generated* iff $\mathcal{L} \subseteq \mathcal{X}^{\circledast}$ for some finite set $\mathcal{X}$ of episodes.

Implied scenarios

For $\sigma \in A^*$ and $B \subseteq A$, let $\sigma \restriction B$ denote the projection of σ onto B — that is, the string obtained from σ by erasing letters not in B. Let $M = (E, \leq, \lambda)$ be an MSC. For $p \in \mathcal{P}$, $\leq_{pp}$ is a linear order. Hence, all linearizations $\sigma \in lin(M)$ generate the same sequence $\sigma \restriction \Sigma_p$. We denote this sequence by $M \restriction p$. We say that an MSC M is *implied* by the MSC language $\mathcal{L}$ iff for each $p \in \mathcal{P}$, there exists $M_p \in \mathcal{L}$ with $M \restriction p = M_p \restriction p$. The MSC language $\mathcal{L}$ is *closed* with respect to implied scenarios iff every MSC implied by $\mathcal{L}$ is in $\mathcal{L}$. The *closure* of $\mathcal{L}$ is the smallest closed set of MSCs which contains $\mathcal{L}$. For an HMSC $\mathcal{G}$, we denote the closure of $\mathcal{L}(\mathcal{G})$ by $\hat{\mathcal{L}}(\mathcal{G})$ and call it the *closure* of $\mathcal{G}$. The MSCs in $\hat{\mathcal{L}}(\mathcal{G}) \backslash \mathcal{L}(\mathcal{G})$ are called *implied scenarios* of $\mathcal{G}$. Figure 2 shows an HMSC with an implied scenario.

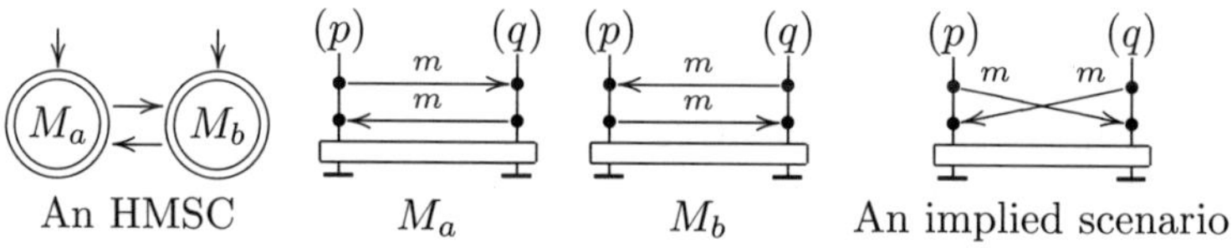

Fig. 2. An implied scenario.

3. Preliminaries

To avoid tedious repetition, we adopt the following linguistic convention for the rest of the paper.

- By "*our setting*", we mean the framework in which all HMSC nodes are labelled by episodes and all MSCs are concatenations of episodes. Further, unless stated otherwise, we assume we are in our setting.

- By "*conventional setting*", we mean the framework where the nodes of HMSCs are labelled by plain MSCs and all the MSCs are asynchronous concatenations of plain MSCs (and are hence themselves plain MSCs.)

We begin by characterizing the linearizations of our MSCs, using a straightforward extension of the results in Ref. 9. For a word σ and a letter a, let $|\sigma|_a$ denote the number of occurences of a in σ. Recall that Σ denotes our alphabet of communication and synchronization actions. A word $\sigma = a_1 \cdots a_n \in \Sigma^*$ is *proper* iff for every $k \in \{1, \ldots, n\}$, if $a_k = p?q(m)$, then there exists $j < k$ such that $a_j = q!p(m)$ and $\sum_{m' \in \Delta} |a_1 \cdots a_j|_{q!p(m')} = \sum_{m' \in \Delta} |a_1 \cdots a_j \cdots a_k|_{p?q(m')}$. And further, if $a_k = P \in \Sigma_{syn}$, then for every $\{r, s\} \subseteq P$, $m' \in \Delta$, we have $|a_1 \cdots a_k|_{r!s(m')} = |a_1 \cdots a_k|_{s?r(m')}$. We say σ is *complete* iff it is proper and $|\sigma|_{p!q(m)} = |\sigma|_{q?p(m)}$ for $(p, q) \in Ch$, $m \in \Delta$. Let Σ° denote the set of complete words over Σ.

Define a *context-sensitive independence* relation $\mathcal{I} \subseteq \Sigma^* \times (\Sigma \times \Sigma)$ as follows: $(\sigma, a, b) \in \mathcal{I}$ iff σab is proper, $\text{loc}(a) \cap \text{loc}(b) = \emptyset$, and $|\sigma|_{p!q(m)} > |\sigma|_{q?p(m)}$ whenever $a = p!q(m)$, $b = q?p(m)$. Note that if $(\sigma, a, b) \in \mathcal{I}$, then $(\sigma, b, a) \in \mathcal{I}$. Define $\approx \subseteq \Sigma^\circ \times \Sigma^\circ$ to be the least equivalence relation such that $\sigma ab\sigma' \approx \sigma ba\sigma'$ whenever $\sigma ab\sigma', \sigma ba\sigma' \in \Sigma^\circ$ and $(\sigma, a, b) \in \mathcal{I}$. It is straightforward to establish that $\mathcal{M}$ and $\Sigma^\circ/\approx$ are in one-to-one correspondence via the mapping $M \mapsto lin(M)$. Thus MSCs can be identified with equivalence classes in $\Sigma^\circ/\approx$.

In the conventional setting, the machine model for recognizing a set of MSCs is a *message-passing automaton* (MPA).[9] We modify this model to handle multi-way synchronization actions and local acceptance conditions. A *product* MPA (over Σ) is a structure $\mathcal{A} = \{\mathcal{A}_p = (S_p, S_p^{\text{in}}, \rightarrow_p, F_p) | p \in \mathcal{P}\}$ where for each p, S_p is a finite set of local states, $S_p^{\text{in}} \subseteq S_p$ a finite set of local initial states, $\rightarrow_p \subseteq S_p \times \Sigma_p \times S_p$ the p-local transition relation, and $F_p \subseteq S_p$ a finite set of local final states.

The set of *global states* of $\mathcal{A}$ is $\Pi_{p \in \mathcal{P}} S_p$. For a global state s, we let s_p denote the local state of p in s. A *configuration* is a pair (s, χ) where $s \in \Pi_{p \in \mathcal{P}} S_p$ and $\chi : Ch \rightarrow \Delta^*$ specifies the queue of messages currently residing in each channel. The set of *initial configurations* is $Conf_{\mathcal{A}}^{\text{in}} = \{(s, \chi_\varepsilon) | s \in \Pi_{p \in \mathcal{P}} S_p^{\text{in}}\}$, where $\chi_\varepsilon : (p, q) \mapsto \varepsilon$ assigns every channel an empty queue. The set of *final configurations* is $\{(s, \chi_\varepsilon) | s \in \Pi_{p \in \mathcal{P}} F_p\}$. The product MPA $\mathcal{A}$ defines a transition system $(Conf_{\mathcal{A}}, \Sigma, Conf_{\mathcal{A}}^{\text{in}}, \Longrightarrow_{\mathcal{A}})$ where the set of *reachable* configurations $Conf_{\mathcal{A}}$ and the transition relation $\Longrightarrow_{\mathcal{A}} \subseteq Conf_{\mathcal{A}} \times \Sigma \times Conf_{\mathcal{A}}$ are defined inductively as follows.

- $Conf_{\mathcal{A}}^{\text{in}} \subseteq Conf_{\mathcal{A}}$.
- Suppose $(s, \chi) \in Conf_{\mathcal{A}}$, (s', χ') is a configuration and $p!q(m) \in \Sigma$ such that $(s_p, p!q(m), s'_p) \in \rightarrow_p$, $s_r = s'_r$ for $r \neq p$, $\chi'((p,q)) = \chi((p,q)) \cdot m$ and $\chi'(c) = \chi(c)$ for $c \neq (p,q)$. Then $(s', \chi') \in Conf_{\mathcal{A}}$ and $(s, \chi) \stackrel{p!q(m)}{\Longrightarrow}_{\mathcal{A}} (s', \chi')$.
- Suppose $(s, \chi) \in Conf_{\mathcal{A}}$, (s', χ') is a configuration and $p?q(m) \in \Sigma$ such that $(s_p, p?q(m), s'_p) \in \rightarrow_p$, $s_r = s'_r$ for $r \neq p$, $\chi((q,p)) = m \cdot \chi'((q,p))$ and $\chi'(c) = \chi(c)$ for $c \neq (q,p)$. Then $(s', \chi') \in Conf_{\mathcal{A}}$ and $(s, \chi) \stackrel{p?q(m)}{\Longrightarrow}_{\mathcal{A}} (s', \chi')$.
- Suppose $(s, \chi) \in Conf_{\mathcal{A}}$, (s', χ') is a configuration and $P \in \Sigma_{syn}$ such that $(s_p, P, s'_p) \in \rightarrow_p$ for $p \in P$, $s_r = s'_r$ for $r \notin P$, $\chi = \chi'$, and further, for $c \in Ch \cap (P \times P)$, $\chi(c) = \varepsilon$. Then $(s', \chi') \in Conf_{\mathcal{A}}$ and $(s, \chi) \stackrel{P}{\Longrightarrow}_{\mathcal{A}} (s', \chi')$.

A run of $\mathcal{A}$ over $\sigma \in \Sigma^*$ is a map ρ from the set of prefixes of σ to the reachable configurations of $\mathcal{A}$ such that $\rho(\varepsilon) \in Conf_{\mathcal{A}}^{\text{in}}$ and for each prefix τa of σ, $\rho(\tau) \stackrel{a}{\Longrightarrow}_{\mathcal{A}} \rho(\tau a)$. We say that ρ is *accepting* iff $\rho(\sigma)$ is a final configuration. The *language* $L(\mathcal{A})$ accepted by $\mathcal{A}$ is the set of words in Σ^* which have an accepting run. It is easy to observe that $L(\mathcal{A})$ is a $\approx$-closed subset of Σ° and hence can be viewed as an MSC language. For an integer B, we say that $\mathcal{A}$ is B*-bounded* iff for every channel $c \in Ch$ and for every reachable configuration (s, χ) of $\mathcal{A}$, it is the case that $|\chi(c)| \leq B$. It is clear that if $\mathcal{A}$ is B-bounded, then $L(\mathcal{A})$ is a regular subset of Σ°. It is also easy to see that the following holds.

Proposition 1: *The MSC language accepted by a product MPA is closed (under implied scenarios).*

4. MSC Languages of HMSCs

We shall show that it is undecidable whether the MSC language of an HMSC is regular whereas the MSC language of a locally synchronized HMSC is always regular. We shall also show that locally synchronized HMSCs capture exactly the class of finitely generated regular MSC languages.

Let $\mathcal{G} = (Q, \rightarrow, Q_{\text{in}}, F, \mathcal{X}, \Phi)$ be an HMSC over a set of episodes $\mathcal{X}$. We define an independence relation $I_{\mathcal{X}}$ over $\mathcal{X}$ as follows: $(X, Y) \in I_{\mathcal{X}}$ iff $\text{loc}(X) \cap \text{loc}(Y) = \emptyset$. We can then interpret $(\mathcal{X}, I_{\mathcal{X}})$ as a (Mazurkiewicz) trace alphabet. Let $\sim_{\mathcal{X}} \subseteq \mathcal{X}^* \times \mathcal{X}^*$ be the trace equivalence relation induced by $(\mathcal{X}, I_{\mathcal{X}})$. For $L \subseteq \mathcal{X}^*$, the *trace closure* of L with respect to $I_{\mathcal{X}}$ is denoted by $[L]_{I_{\mathcal{X}}}$.

It will be convenient to work with the strings of MSCs generated by an HMSC. To distinguish this language from the language of all linearizations of the MSCs generated by the HMSC, we use the term "episodic-string language" or "e-string language" for short. We define the *e-string language* of $\mathcal{G}$, $L_e(\mathcal{G})$, to be the set of strings $M_0 M_1 \cdots M_n \in \mathcal{X}^*$ for which there exists a run $q_0 \to q_1 \to \cdots \to q_n$ with $M_i = \Phi(q_i)$ for $i \in \{0, 1, \ldots, n\}$.

Lemma 1: *Let $\mathcal{G}$ be an HMSC over a set of episodes $\mathcal{X}$. Its MSC language $\mathcal{L}(\mathcal{G})$ is regular iff the trace closure of its e-string language $L_e(\mathcal{G})$ with respect to $I_{\mathcal{X}}$ is a regular subset of $\mathcal{X}^*$.*

Proof: The proof is immediate from two basic observations.

Firstly, for $M_1 M_2 \cdots M_n$, $M_1' M_2' \cdots M_n' \in \mathcal{X}^*$, $M_1 M_2 \cdots M_n \sim_{\mathcal{X}} M_1' M_2' \cdots M_n'$ iff $M_1 \circ M_2 \circ \cdots \circ M_n = M_1' \circ M_2' \circ \cdots \circ M_n'$. It follows that $\mathcal{L}(\mathcal{G}) = \{M_1 \circ M_2 \cdots \circ M_n | M_1 M_2 \cdots M_n \in [L_e(\mathcal{G})]_{I_{\mathcal{X}}}\}$.

Secondly, we can effectively construct a *finite transduction*[20] $\varphi : lin(\mathcal{X}^{\circledast}) \to \mathcal{X}^*$ such that for $\tau = b_1 \cdots b_n \in lin(\mathcal{X}^{\circledast})$, $\varphi(\tau) = M_1 \cdots M_n \in \mathcal{X}^*$ where $\tau \in lin(M_1 \circ \cdots \circ M_n)$ and $\tau \restriction \Sigma_{syn} = P_1 \cdots P_n$ with $P_i = M_i \restriction \Sigma_{syn}$ for $i \in \{1, \ldots, n\}$. It then follows that $\varphi(lin(\mathcal{L}(G))) = [L_e(\mathcal{G})]_{I_{\mathcal{X}}}$.

In $\tau = b_1 \cdots b_n$, let j be the least index such that $b_j \in \Sigma_{syn}$. We can effectively identify a *unique* episode $X \in \mathcal{X}$ such that $lin(X)$ is a subsequence of $b_1 \cdots b_j$. Further, for any action b_i in $b_1 \cdots b_j$ that is not from X, we have $\mathrm{loc}(b_i) \cap \mathrm{loc}(X) = \emptyset$. Thus, we can reorder τ as $w_X w' b_{j+1} \cdots b_n$ where $w_X \in lin(X)$ and w' is the subsequence of $b_1 \cdots b_j$ obtained by erasing all the actions from $lin(X)$. For $w' b_{j+1} \cdots b_n$, we can inductively identify a sequence $M_2 \cdots M_n \in \mathcal{X}^*$, as required. For τ, the corresponding sequence is then $X M_2 \cdots M_n$. □

Theorem 1: There is no effective decision procedure to determine if the MSC language of an HMSC is regular.

Proof: It is known[19] that it is undecidable if the trace closure of a regular language $L \subseteq A^*$ with respect to a trace alphabet (A, I) is regular. We reduce this problem to ours. Let $(A_1, \ldots, A_n)$ be a distributed alphabet implementing (A, I). Create a set of processes $\mathcal{P} = \{p_i, p_i' | i \in \{1, \ldots, n\}\}$ and a message alphabet $\Delta = A$. Encode each $a \in A$ by an episode M_a shown in Fig. 3, where $A_{i_1}, A_{i_2}, \ldots, A_{i_k}$ are the components containing a. Construct an HMSC $\mathcal{G}$ over $\mathcal{X} = \{M_a | a \in A\}$ with $L_e(\mathcal{G}) = L$. It follows that $I = I_{\mathcal{X}}$. By Lemma 1, $[L]_I$ is regular iff $\mathcal{L}(\mathcal{G})$ is regular. □

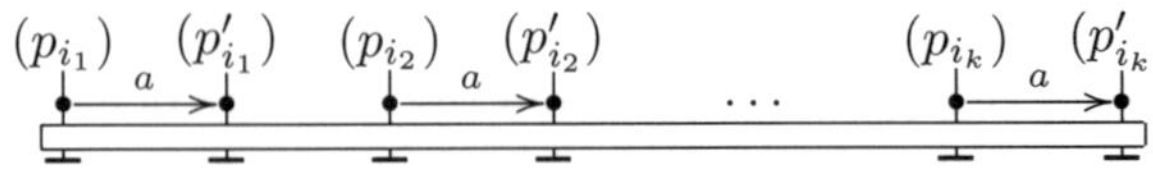

Fig. 3. The episode M_a.

Theorem 2: The MSC language of a locally synchronized HMSC is regular.

Proof: Let $\mathcal{G} = (Q, \rightarrow, Q_{\text{in}}, F, \mathcal{X}, \Phi)$ be a locally synchronized HMSC. By Lemma 1, it suffices to show that $[L(\mathcal{G})]_{I_\mathcal{X}}$ is regular. Observe that the communication graph of every episode is a complete graph. Hence, for $\sigma = M_1 \cdots M_n \in \mathcal{X}^*$, the communication graph of $M_1 \circ \cdots \circ M_n$ is connected iff σ is a *connected trace.*[6] It is known that if $L \subseteq \mathcal{X}^*$ is regular and every word in L is connected, then $[L^*]_{I_\mathcal{X}}$ is also regular.[6] The claim then follows. □

Theorem 3: Every finitely generated regular MSC language can be represented as the MSC language of a locally synchronized HMSC.

Proof: Let $\mathcal{L} \subseteq \mathcal{X}^{\circledast}$ be a regular MSC language where $\mathcal{X}$ is a finite set of episodes. Following the proof of Lemma 1, there exists a regular trace language $L \subseteq \mathcal{X}^*$ such that $\mathcal{L} = \{M_1 \circ \cdots \circ M_n | M_1 \cdots M_n \in L\}$. Fix a strict linear order on $\mathcal{X}$, which then induces a lexicographic order $\sqsubseteq$ on $\mathcal{X}^*$. Define $LEX \subseteq \mathcal{X}^*$ as follows: $\sigma \in LEX$ iff σ is the $\sqsubseteq$-least element in the trace containing σ. Set $lex(L) = L \cap LEX$. Following,[6] we have the following:

- $lex(L)$ is a regular subset of $\mathcal{X}^*$ and $L = [lex(L)]_{I_\mathcal{X}}$.
- If $\sigma_1\sigma\sigma_2 \in LEX$, then $\sigma \in LEX$.
- If $\sigma \in \mathcal{X}^*$ is *not* connected, then $\sigma\sigma \notin LEX$.

Create an HMSC $\mathcal{G}$ such that $L(\mathcal{G}) = lex(L)$. It then follows that $\mathcal{L} = \mathcal{L}(\mathcal{G})$ and $\mathcal{G}$ is locally synchronized. □

5. Closure of HMSCs with Respect to Implied Scenarios

In the conventional setting, it is easy to observe that the closure of an MSC language defined by an HMSC is, in general, *not* regular. A trivial example is the HMSC whose MSC language is $\{M\}^{\circledast}$, where M is the MSC whose sole linearization is $p!q(m)q?p(m)$. The closure of this language is itself and it is obviously not regular. In fact, it is not difficult to show it is undecidable if the closure of a (locally synchronized) HMSC is regular. However, in our setting, the closure of an HMSC language is *always* regular.

Theorem 4: The closure of every HMSC language is regular.

Proof: Let $\mathcal{G} = (Q, \rightarrow, Q_{\text{in}}, F, \mathcal{X}, \Phi)$ be an HMSC. We construct a *bounded* product MPA $\mathcal{A} = \{\mathcal{A}_p = (S_p, S_p^{\text{in}}, \rightarrow_p, F_p) | p \in \mathcal{P}\}$ accepting $\widehat{\mathcal{L}}(\mathcal{G})$ as follows. For $p \in \mathcal{P}$, set L_p to be the projection of $lin(\mathcal{L}(\mathcal{G}))$ onto Σ_p. It is easy to see that each L_p is regular. Set $\mathcal{A}_p$ to be the minimal deterministic finite state automaton accepting L_p. It follows that $\mathcal{A}$ accepts $\widehat{\mathcal{L}}(\mathcal{G})$. It is easy to observe that $\mathcal{A}$ is bounded by the maximum length of $\{X \restriction p | X \in \mathcal{X}\}$. □

From the proof of Theorem 4, it follows that the closure of an HMSC language can be effectively represented as a bounded product MPA. Hence the set of linearizations of the MSCs in the closure of an HMSC language can also be effectively computed. From Theorem 2 and the fact that the equivalence of regular string languages can be effectively determined, the next result is immediate.

Corollary 1: *We can effectively decide whether a locally synchronized HMSC admits an implied scenario.*

In the conventional setting, it is easy to observe that the closure of an HMSC language is in general *not* finitely generated. A simple example is the HMSC whose MSC language is $\{M_1, M_2\}^{\circledast}$, where M_1 (respectively M_2) is the MSC whose sole linearization is $p!q(m)\ q?p(m)$ (respectively $q!p(m)\ p?q(m)$). However, in our setting, the closure of an HMSC is always finitely generated.

Theorem 5: The closure of every HMSC language is finitely generated.

Proof: Let $\mathcal{G} = (Q, \rightarrow, Q_{\text{in}}, F, \mathcal{X}, \Phi)$ be an HMSC. Let $\mathcal{Y}$ be the set of episodes M such that for each $p \in \mathcal{P}$, there exists $M_p \in \mathcal{X}$ with $M \restriction p = M_p \restriction p$. Let $\mathcal{H}$ be an HMSC with $L(\mathcal{H}) = \mathcal{X}^*$. Since $\widehat{\mathcal{L}}(\mathcal{G}) \subseteq \widehat{\mathcal{L}}(\mathcal{H})$, it suffices to show that $\widehat{\mathcal{L}}(\mathcal{H}) \subseteq \mathcal{Y}^{\circledast}$.

Let $M = (E, \leq, \lambda) \in \widehat{\mathcal{L}}(\mathcal{H})$. Note that for any $M' \in \mathcal{L}(\mathcal{H})$, all maximal events in M' are synchronization events. Hence all maximal events in M are synchronization events too. Pick $e \in E_{syn}$ such that $\downarrow e \cap E_{syn} = \{e\}$. We shall show that $Y = (\downarrow e, \leq_{\downarrow e}, \lambda_{\downarrow e}) \in \mathcal{Y}$, where, $\leq_{\downarrow e}$ and $\lambda_{\downarrow e}$ are, respectively, the restrictions of $\leq$ and λ to $\downarrow e$. With this, we can remove Y from M, and it is clear that inductively $M \in \mathcal{Y}^{\circledast}$.

It remains to prove that Y is an episode. Set $P = \lambda(e)$ and pick $p \in P$. There must exist $X \in \mathcal{X}$ such that $X \restriction p = Y \restriction p$ and $\mathrm{loc}(X) = P$. Hence for any $e' < e$, if $\lambda(e') = p!q(m)$ or $\lambda(e') = p?q(m)$, then $q \in P$. It follows that $P = \mathrm{loc}(Y)$. □

The proof above also yields the following useful observation.

Corollary 2: *Let $\mathcal{G}$ be an HMSC over a set of episodes $\mathcal{X}$ such that $\mathcal{L}(\mathcal{G}) = \mathcal{X}^{\circledast}$. Then $\mathcal{G}$ admits no implied scenario iff $\mathcal{X} = \{M | M$ is an episode and $\forall\, p \exists\, X_p \in \mathcal{X}, X_p \restriction p = M \restriction p\}$.*

The following result however mirrors the situation in the conventional setting.

Theorem 6: It is undecidable whether an HMSC admits an implied scenario.

Proof: We shall make use of the reduction from the Post Correspondence Problem (PCP) in Ref. 16 for proving the undecidability of determining if the trace closure of a star-free language remains star-free. An instance of PCP consists of two morphisms g, $h : K^* \to \Gamma^*$ where K, Γ are disjoint finite alphabets. A solution is a word $w \in K^+$ such that $g(w) = h(w)$.

We briefly describe the main ingredients of the reduction in Ref. 16. Create a trace alphabet (A, I) where $A = K \cup \Gamma \cup \{c\}$, $c \notin K \cup \Gamma$ and $I = \{(x, c), (c, x) | x \in K \cup \Gamma\}$. Define W_g to be the trace closure with respect to I of $\{w \cdot g(w) \cdot c^{|g(w)|} | w \in K^+\}$ and a regular language $L_g \subseteq A^*$ such that $[L_g]_I = A^* \backslash W_g$. Analogously define W_h and L_h. The construction has the following property. If the PCP instance has no solution, then $[L_g \cup L_h]_I = A^*$. Otherwise, $[L_g \cup L_h]_I$ is *not regular.*

As in the proof of Theorem 1, we construct an HMSC $\mathcal{G}$ over $\mathcal{X} = \{M_a | a \in A\}$ using *the distributed alphabet* $(K \cup \Gamma, \{c\})$. If $[L_g \cup L_h]_I = A^*$, then $\mathcal{L}(\mathcal{G}) = \mathcal{X}^{\circledast}$, and $\mathcal{L}(\mathcal{G})$ is easily seen to admit no implied scenario by Corollary 2. If not, then $[L_g \cup L_h]_I$ is not regular and thus $\mathcal{L}(\mathcal{G})$ is not regular. Consequently $\mathcal{G}$ must admit an implied scenario, by Theorem 4. Thus $\mathcal{G}$ admits an implied scenario iff the original instance of PCP has a solution. □

6. Conclusions

We have proposed here the notion of anchored concatenation and studied MSC languages defined by HMSCs under this operation. Our results show that the resulting theory is non-trivial and bears both commonalities and differences with the corresponding theory in the conventional setting.

We have considered here only finite MSCs. It will be interesting to explore our theory for infinite MSCs by adapting the techniques developed in Ref. 13. It will also be worthwhile to consider realizations in the form of netcharts[4,15] instead of product MPAs.

References

1. R. Alur, K. Etessami and M. Yannakakis, Inference of message sequence graphs. In *Proc. of ICSE '00*, pages 304–313. ACM, 2000.
2. R. Alur, K. Etessami and M. Yannakakis, Realizability and verification of MSC graphs. In *ICALP '01, LNCS 2076*, pages 797–808. Springer, 2001.
3. R. Alur and M. Yannakakis, Model checking of message sequence charts, In *CONCUR '99, LNCS 1664*, pages 114–129. Springer, 1999.
4. N. Baudru and R. Morin, The pros and cons of netcharts. In *CONCUR '04, LNCS 3170*, pages 99–114. Springer, 2004.
5. G. Booch, I. Jacobson and J. Rumbaugh, *Unified Modeling Language User Guide.* Addison-Wesley, 1997.
6. V. Diekert and G. Rozenberg, editors. *The Book of Traces.* World Scientific, 1995.
7. D. Harel and E. Gery, Executable object modeling with statecharts. *IEEE Computer*, 31(7): 31–42, 1997.
8. D. Harel and R. Marelly, *Come, Let's Play: Scenario-Based Programming Using LSCs and the Play-Engine.* Springer, 2003.
9. J. G. Henriksen, M. Mukund, K. Narayan Kumar, M. Sohoni and P. S. Thiagarajan, A theory of regular MSC languages. *Information and Computation*, 202(1): 1–38, 2005.
10. J. G. Henriksen, M. Mukund, K. Narayan Kumar and P. S. Thiagarajan, Regular collections of message sequence charts. In *MFCS '00, LNCS 1893*, pages 405–414. Springer, 2000.
11. ITU-TS, ITU-TS Recommendation Z.120: Message sequence charts. 1997.
12. D. Kuske, A further step towards a theory of regular MSC languages. In *STACS '02, LNCS 2285*, pages 489–500. Springer, 2002.
13. S. Mauw and M. A. Renier, High-level message sequence charts. In *Proc. of SDL '97: Time for Testing – SDL, MSC and Trends*, pages 291–306. Elsevier, 1997.
14. M. Mukund, K. Narayan Kumar and P. S. Thiagarajan, Netcharts: Bridging the gap between HMSCs and executable specifications. In *CONCUR '03, LNCS 2761*, pages 296–310. Springer, 2003.
15. A. Muscholl and D. Peled, Message sequence graphs and decision problems on Mazurkiewicz traces. In *MFCS '99, LNCS 1672*, pages 81–91. Springer, 1999.
16. A. Muscholl and H. Peterson, A note on the commutative closure of star-free languages. *Information Processing Letters*, 57(2): 71–74, 1996.

17. E. Rudolph, P. Graubmann and J. Grabowski, Tutorial on message sequence charts. In *Comp. Networks and ISDN Sys. — SDL and MSC* **28**. 1996.
18. J. Sakarovitch, The "last" decision problem for rational trace languages. In *LATIN'92, LNCS 583*, pages 460–473. Springer, 1992.
19. S. Uchitel, J. Kramer and J. Magee, Detecting implied scenarios in message sequence chart specifications. In *Proc. of FSE '01*. ACM, 2001.
20. S. Yu, Regular languages. In *Handbook of Formal Languages, Vol. 1*. 1997.

CHAPTER 20

SIMPLE DEFORMATION OF 4D DIGITAL PICTURES

Akira Nakamura
Hiroshima University, Japan

1. Introduction

In Ref. 1, we have considered topology-preserving deformations of two-valued 2D digital pictures. This deformation (called SD) was defined as a finite sequence of operations of "addition" or "deletion" of a simple pixel. By making use of this deformation, in Refs. 1 and 2, we defined " magnification method" of two-valued 2D and 3D pictures. In Ref. 3, Kong introduced the concept of simple 4-xels of two-valued 4D digital pictures. Also, in Ref. 4 the author considered magnifications of various digital pictures as well as their applications.

In this paper, we define an SD of 4D digital picture P that is an extension of 2D (or 3D) case. This deformation is "topology-preserving" (in the sense of homotopy). Further, we describe a magnification method of P based on this SD. Although the simple deformation is topology-preserving, it is not animality-preserving. We show this fact by considering a counter-example. In the last section, we propose some of open problems concerned with to the subject.

We assume that readers are familiar with the basic concepts of digital topology.

2. Definition

We consider a two-valued digital 4D pictures P that is denoted by $P = (Z^4, 80, 8, B)$. In other words, we put 1 or 0 at each lattice point of Z^4, where the set of 1's is finite. B is the set of 1's. To treat digital pictures in continuous analog, usually we center a closed unit hypercube at each of lattice points such that a closed unit white hypercube is put to 0 and a closed unit black hypercube is to 1. Such a unit hypercube is also called a 4-*xel*. From B, we have a set of closed unit black hypercubes that is denotes by $[B]$. From $P = (Z^4, 80, 8, B)$, we can stipulate here the following rule (R):

(R) If a unit white hypercube and a unit black one have a common border, then the border is black.

Unless the special mention provided, we use the same notation B for $[B]$. In general, 4D pictures are not visible. To avoid this invisibility, hereafter, we use a coordinate to represent a 4-xel (i.e., a closed unit hypercube). The fourth coordinate is called the *t-coordinate.*

We use the concepts in Kong.[3] He introduced a concept of attachment of a 4-xel q in B as well as simple 4-xels. That is, *attachment* (denoted by Attach (q, B) of a 4-xel q in B is defined as the (possibly empty) xel complex Boundary $(q) \cap \bigcup\{\text{Boundary}(X) | X \epsilon B - \{q\}\}$. We use the meaning of simple 4-xels that is given in Ref. 3. That is, a 4-xel q (i.e., hypercube) of B is *simple* in B iff the following conditions all hold:

(a) $\cup$ Attach (q, B) is nonempty and connected,
(b) $\cup$ Boundary $(q) - \cup$ Attach (q, B) is nonempty and connected,
(c) $\cup$ Attach (q, B) is simply connected.

The above definition is for a "black" 4-xel. A "white" simple 4-xel is dually defined as follows: Let q be a white 4-xel. Assuming that q were black, if q is a black simple 4-xel, the white q is called a *white simple 4-xel.* In other words, if Attach $(q, B \cup \{q\})$ satisfies

(a') $\cup$ Attach $(q, B \cup \{q\})$ is nonempty and connected,
(b') $\cup$ Boundary $(q) - \cup$ Attach $(q, B \cup \{q\})$ is nonempty and connected,
(c') $\cup$ Attach $(q, B \cup \{q\})$ is simply connected.

then q is a white simple 4-xel.

In the paper,[3] Kong proved that change of values of simple 4-xels is topology-preserving (in the sense of homotopy). We define a *simple deformation* (abbreviated to SD) of 4D pictures by the quite same way as 2D (or 3D) case.

In the paper, we provide a magnification method of 4D digital pictures. This method is an extension of the 2D (or 3D) case.[1,2] We show that the magnification is obtained by SD.

Here, we consider adjacency relation between two 4-xels. Let $p(x_1, y_1, z_1, t_1)$ and $q(x_2, y_2, z_2, t_2)$ be 4-xels of B such that

(*) $|x_1 - x_2| \leq 1$, $|y_1 - y_2| \leq 1$, $|z_1 - z_2| \leq 1$, and $|t_1 - t_2| \leq 1$.

Since our picture P is $P = (Z^4, 80, 8, B)$, we have the following facts:

(1) If $|x_1 - x_2| + |y_1 - y_2| + |z_1 - z_2| + |t_1 - t_2| = 4$, then the unit hypercube p is point-adjacent to the unit hypercube p; that is, $p \cap q$ is one (real) point.
(2) If $|x_1 - x_2| + |y_1 - y_2| + |z_1 - z_2| + |t_1 - t_2| = 3$, then the unit hypercube p is point-adjacent to the unit hypercube p; that is, edge-adjacent to the unit hypercube q.
(3) If $|x_1 - x_2| + |y_1 - y_2| + |z_1 - z_2| + |t_1 - t_2| = 2$, then the unit hypercube p is face-adjacent to the unit hypercube q.
(4) If $|x_1 - x_2| + |y_1 - y_2| + |z_1 - z_2| + |t_1 - t_2| = 1$, then the unit hypercube p is cube-adjacent to the unit hypercube q.
(5) If $|x_1 - x_2| + |y_1 - y_2| + |z_1 - z_2| + |t_1 - t_2| = 0$, then the unit hypercube p is identical to the unit hypercube q.

Note that if p and q don't satisfy the above assumption $(*)$, the unit hypercube p and the unit hypercube q are disjoint.

Let us use the standard notation $N_{80}(q)$ that is the set of 4-xels 80-adjacent to q, where it doesn't contain q itself. $N(q)$ is defined as $N_{80}(q) \cup \{q\}$. To make our picture visible, we use the "moving pictures method" that consists of cross sections (called *t-levels*) of a picture by the fourth coordinate t. See Fig. 1 that represents $N(q)$. Also, the Schlegel diagram of a 4-xel is very useful for our discussion. Figure 2 shows a Schlegel diagram of Boundary$(q) - f$, where f is a 3D face of q. See Fig. 2 that shows common borders of black 4-xels (x, y, z, t) and $q(0, 0, 0, 0)$.

Let us consider three 4-xels $q(x, y, z, t)$, $p(x, y, z, t + 1)$, $r(x, y, z, r - 1)$. Then, we say that p is a 4-xel *t-above* q and r is a 4-xel *t-below* q. IN the following discussion, we treat a case where a 4-xel t-above q is black and a 4-xel t-below q is white, and vice versa.

3. Main Theorem

Before proving the main theorem, we investigate some properties of 4-xels. First, note that $\cup$ Attach (q, B) is "black" and $\cup$ Boundary $(q) - \cup$ Attach (q, B) is "white".

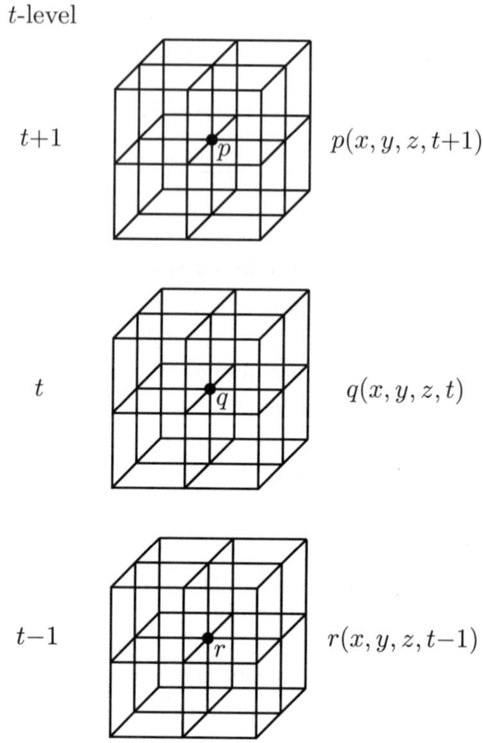

Fig. 1.

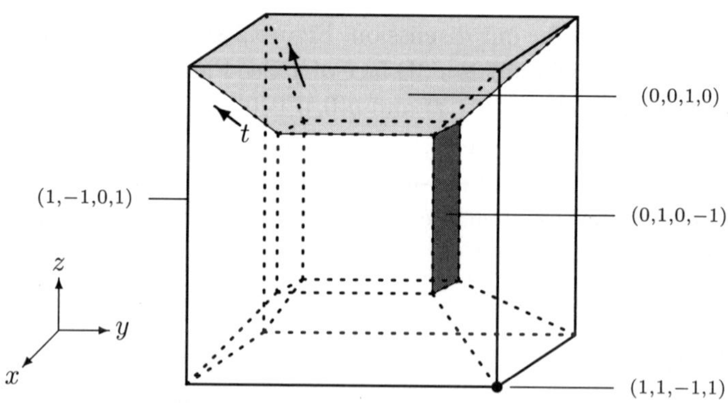

Fig. 2. Common border between a black 4-xel (x, y, z, t) and $q(0, 0, 0, 0)$.

Claim 1: $\cup$ Attach (q, B) consists of common borders of q and each black 4-xel (i.e., black hypercube) in $N_{80}(q)$.

Proof: A 4-xel that is not in $N_{80}(q)$ is disjoint with q. Since each black 4-xel in $N_{80}(q)$ is 80-adjacent to q, this claim is immediate. □

Claim 2: If all black 4-xels in $N_80(q)$ are 80-connected in $N_{80}(q)$, then $\cup$ Attach (q, B) is connected.

Proof: If all black 4-xels in $N_{80}(q)$ are 80-connected, there is at least one black digital 80-path in $N_{80}(q)$ (e.g., b_1, $b_2, \ldots, b_k$) from a black 4-xel to another black 4-xel. From Claim 1, we can get a real (no-digital) path that goes through the common border between q and b_i, $(i = 1, 2, \ldots, k)$.

Therefore we have this claim. □

Claim 3: Let r be a black 4-xel t-below $q(x, y, z, t)$. Then, black 4-xels whose t-level are $t - 1$ is connected in the border of q. A (white) border of each white 4-xel whose t-level is $t - 1$ is excluded from the border of q.

Proof: The black 4-xels at level $t - 1$ are 80-connected through r. Hence, from Claim 2 we have the first half of this claim.

From the assumption, the common border of an arbitrary white 4-xel with q is a point, a line, or a face. But, by the rule (R) these points, lines and faces do not appear in the border of q. This is the second half of this claim. □

Let w be a white 4-xel in $N_{80}(q)$. The common border between w and q is denoted by com-bd (w, q).

Theorem 1: The magnification of P is done by SD.

Proof: Let P be a given 4D picture. We assume that 1's (black 4-xels) of P are between t-coordinates h and 1. In other words, the highest t-coordinate of black 4-xels of P is h and the lowest t-coordinate of black 4-xels is 1. This level h is called the $t-top$ of P. This assumption is always valid since we can re coordinate the t-coordinate. First, we consider magnification of P in the direction of t-coordinate (for short, $t - direction$) by a factor of an integer $k(> 1)$. After that, we successively repeat the magnification to x-direction, to y-direction, and z-direction. This is the same as the magnification in

3D case. That is, in 3D case we first considered upward (i.e., z-direction) magnification and then repeat it to x-direction and to y-direction.

Now, let us explain about dilation of P to t-direction by a factor k. This method is done inductively on the t-coordinate, t-level by t-level, from the t-top. □

(I) Procedure for the t-top: (1) Let us consider an arbitrary black 4-xel q_1 whose t-coordinate is h. That is, q_1 is one of 4-xels of the highest t-coordinate. Note that all 4-xels whose t-coordinate is $h+1$ are white 4-xels. See Fig. 3. Let p_1 be a white 4-xel t-above q_1. Let us consider attachment of p_1. By making use of Claims 2, 3 we have (a). Also, we have (b) from the situation. Since q_1 is black and we are considering t-top level, the condition (c) is satisfied. More exactly, let A be the union of a Schlegel diagram of

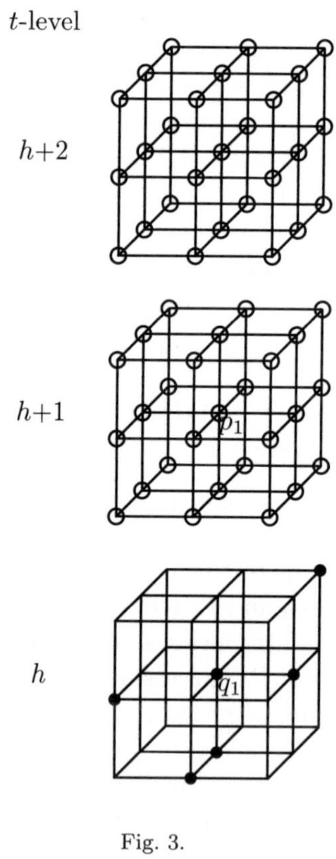

Fig. 3.

h+2

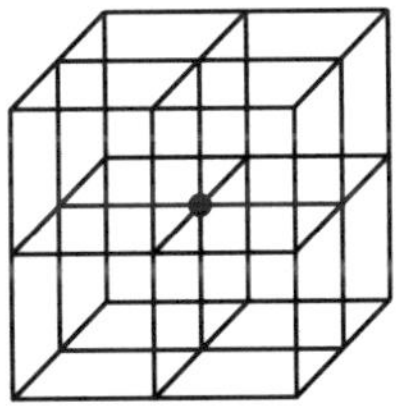

h+1

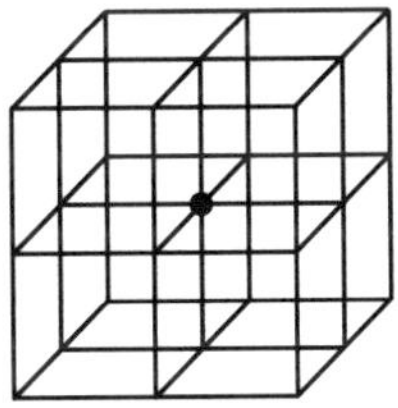

h

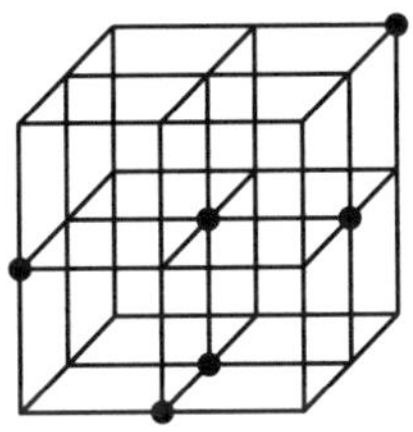

Fig. 4.

Attach $(p_1, B \cup \{p_1\})$. Since there are no annulus/doughnut-type hole in A, $\bigcup$ Attach $(p_1, B \cup \{p_1\})$ is simply connected.

Hence, p_1 is simple. Therefore, we can SD-change p_1 to a black 4-xel. We repeat this dilation of q_1 until the t-coordinate becomes $h \times k$. See Fig 4. (2) After (1), we consider another arbitrary black 4-xel q_2 whose t-coordinates is h. Let p_2 be a white 4-xel t-above q_2. See Fig. 5. In this case, from the attachment of p_2 it is also known that p_2 is a simple white 4-xel. The reason is as follows:

Proof of (a). For any black 4-xel at level $h+1$, a 4-xel (say, q_1) t-below it also black. But, q_1 is 80-connected to black q_2. Hence, we have (a). (The non-emptiness is obvious.) □

Proof of (b). Since a 4-xel t-above p_2 is white, the nonemptiness is obvious. For a white 4-xel p whose t-coordinate is h, there is no common border

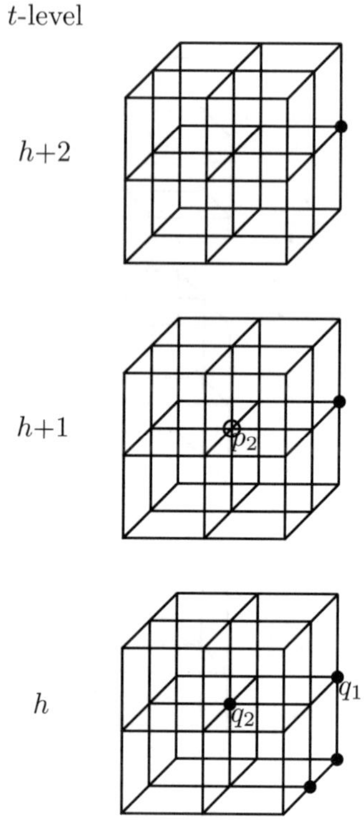

Fig. 5.

between p and p_2. This follows from Claim 3. Let w_1 and w_2 be white 4-xels on level $h+1$ or $h+2$ such that both com-bd (w_1, p_2) and com-bd (w_2, p_2) are nonempty. In this time, com-bd (w_1, p_2) and com-bd (w_2, p_2) are (white) connected in the border of p_2. This follows from the following fact; the common border between p_2 and the 4-xel t-above p_2 is white. □

Proof of (c). If a 4-xel at $(x, y, z, h+2)$ in $N_{80}(p_2)$ is black then a 4-xel at $(x, y, z, h+1)$ and a 4-xel at (x, y, z, h) are also black and (x, y, z, h) are 8-connected to the black 4-xel q_2. hence, we cannot have any annulus/doughnut-type hole in $N_{80}(p_2)$. Therefore, we can SD-change p_2 to a black 4-xel. □

We repeat t-upward this dilation of q_2 until the t-coordinate becomes $h \times k$. See Fig. 6.

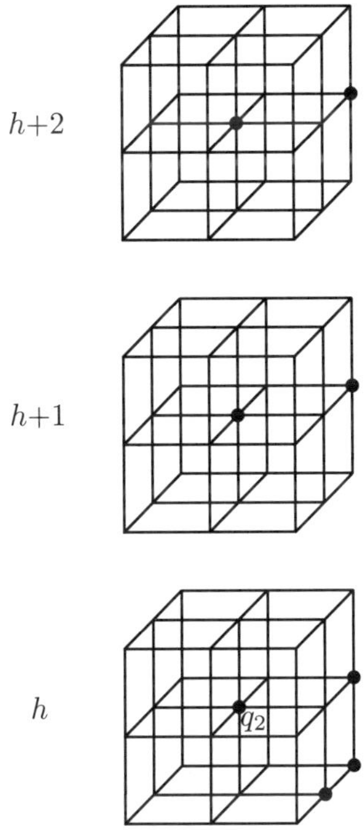

Fig. 6.

(3) We repeat the procedure (2) for all black 4-xels whose t-coordinates are h. See Fig. 7.

(4) Then, we consider an arbitrary white 4-xel $w_1(x, y, z, h)$ whose t-coordinate is h. That is, w_1 is one of white 4-xels of the highest t-coordinate is larger than h are all white. Of course, 4-xels (x, y, z, j) where $h < j \leq h \times k$ are all white. hence, for this w_1 we do nothing. The same thing goes to all other white 4-xels whose t-coordinate are h. See Fig. 8.

Therefore, our t-upward dilation is finished for the top level. At this stage, all black 4-xels whose t-coordinate is highest (i.e., t-topmost) are dilated until $h \times k$, and also all white 4-xels whose t-coordinate is highest (i.e., t-topmost) are dilated until $h \times k$.

Induction Step Assume that the t-upward dilation of all 4-xels at t-level $i + 1$ has been finished. We want to t-upward SD-dilate also black 4-xels at t-level i before white 4-xels at t-level i. If not so, the dilation of this

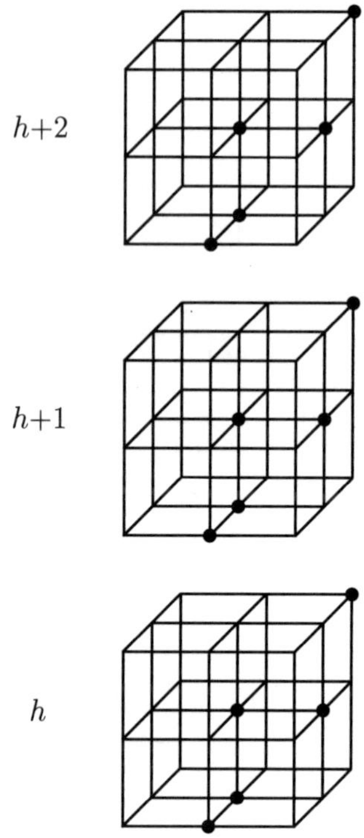

Fig. 7.

step is not always simple. Here, from the induction hypothesis we have the following situation (α) and (β):

(α) If a 4-xel $q(x, y, z, i+1)$ is black, then for every j such that for $i+1 < j \leq k \times (i+1)$ a 4-xel $p(x, y, z, j)$ are black.
(β) If a 4-xel $q(x, y, z, i+1)$ is white, then for every j such that for $i+1 < j \leq k \times (i+1)$ a 4-xel $p(x, y, z, j)$ are white.

(5) Let us consider an arbitrary black 4-xel r_1 at level i, and let a 4-xel t-above r_1 be s_1. If s_1 is black, then we do nothing. We consider a Case where s_1 is white. See Fig. 9. Then, from the attachment of s_1 it is known that s_1 is simple.

Without difficulty, we can show (a) from (α). By the similar argument to the proof of (b) in the step (2), we have also (b) in this case.

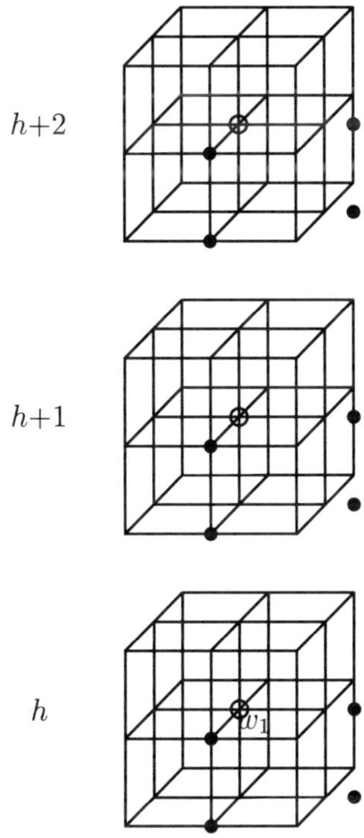

Fig. 8.

Proof of (c). We can use the same argument as in the step (2). Let A be the union of a Schlegel diagram of Attach $(s_1, B \cup \{s_1\})$ is simply connected. Therefore, we can SD-change s_1 to black. This dilation of t-direction is repeated until we arrive at $k \times i$. See Fig. 10.

(6) After finishing (5), we consider another arbitrary black 4-xel r_2 at level i. Let s_2 be a 4-xel t-above r_2. If an s_2 is black, then we do nothing. We consider a case where s_2 is white. Then, we consider the attachment of Attach $(s_2, B \cup \{s_2\})$. Then, from the induction hypothesis (α) and (β) it is known that s_2 is simple. This is the same reason as in (5).

Hence, we can SD-change s_2 to black. This dilation of t-direction. Th dilation of tA-direction is repeated until we arrive at $k \times i$.

(7) We repeat the above procedure to every black 4-xel at level i:

(8) After that, we consider an arbitrary white 4-xel, v_1 at t-level i. Let u_2 be a 4-xel t-above v_1.

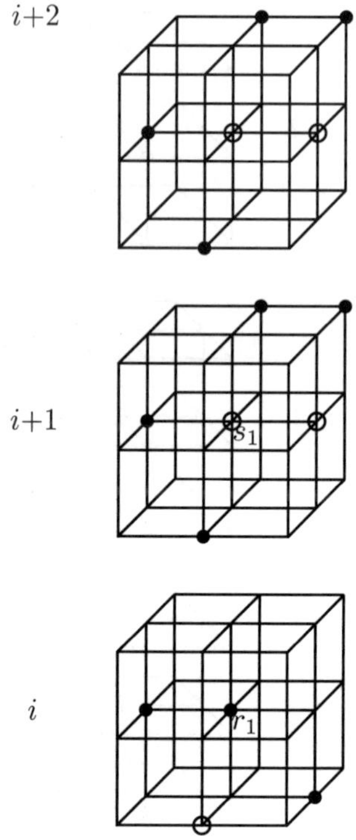

Fig. 9.

If u_2 is white, we do nothing. Let us consider a case where u_2 is black. See Fig. 11. By the same reason as mentioned in the previous steps, we know that u_2 is simple. Hence, we can SD-change u_2 to white. The proof of (b) may be rather difficult. But, it follows the fact: If com-bd (w, u_2) is nonempty, it is connected to com-bd (v_1, u_2).

Further, this procedure can be applied until we arrive at a 4-xel $(x, y, z, i \times k)$. In this case, note that a 4-xel $(x, y, z, (i+1) \times k)$ is black. See Fig. 12.

(9) By repeating the above (8), we can SD-dilate every white 4-xel at t-level in P until we arrive at the y-level $i \times k$.

Therefore, the obtained picture (denoted by $P^{(t)}$) is a picture that is a magnified one of P to t-direction. Since $(i+1) \times k - i \times k = k$ the magnified amount is k. By the same method, we can magnify to x-direction by a factor k. By repeating this procedure to y-direction and z-direction, we have a magnified picture of P to each direction by a factor k. □

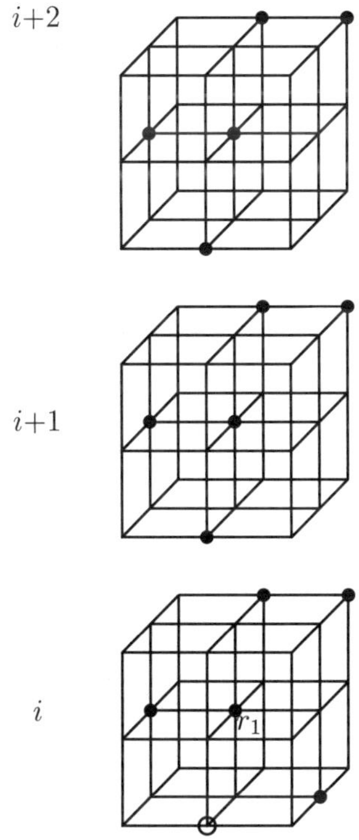

Fig. 10.

4. Further Problems

There are some interesting applications of magnification. An animal — according to János Pach — is any topological 3-ball in $\boldsymbol{R}^3$ consisting of unit cubes. In general, w can define animal in $\boldsymbol{R}^n$ (where n is a positive integers) that are called an *n-animal.* The question called "animal problem" is whether every 3-animal can be reduced to a single unit cube by a finite sequence of either adding or removing a cube, while maintaining the animal property throughout. This question is fairly well-known as an open problem.

It is not so difficult to solve the 2-animal problem. There are various methods to prove this problem. For example, it is enough to use our magnification technique in Ref. 4. But, these methods are not applicable to the "3-animal problem" since there is a local pattern in an animal. A such that we can upward dilate A by SD but not deform A in animality-preserving.

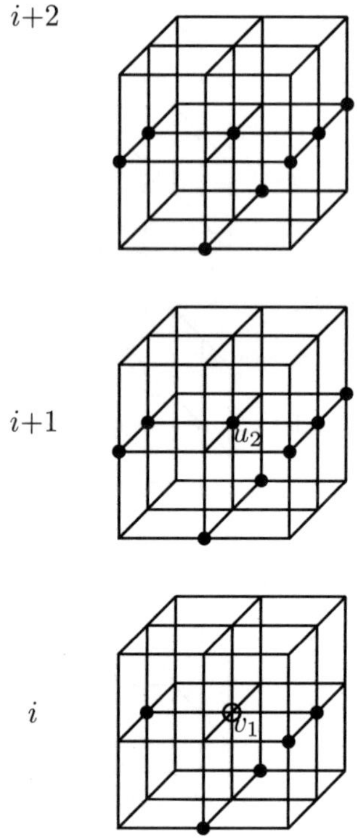

Fig. 11.

Such a local pattern is: $\{(0,0,0),(0,0,1),(1,0,0),(1,1,0),(2,1,0),(2,1,1)\}$. A difficult point is in "animality-preserving". However, if we permit SD instead of the animality-preserving, the problem seems to be solvable. When the author was collaborating with the late Professor A. Rosenfeld, we called it "B-problem".

There are the following open problems in 4D pictures:

(i) The 4D B-problem.
(ii) The 4-animal problem.

It may be possible to solve the problem (i) by making use the 4D magnification technique of this paper. But, the (ii) will be an extremely hard problem.

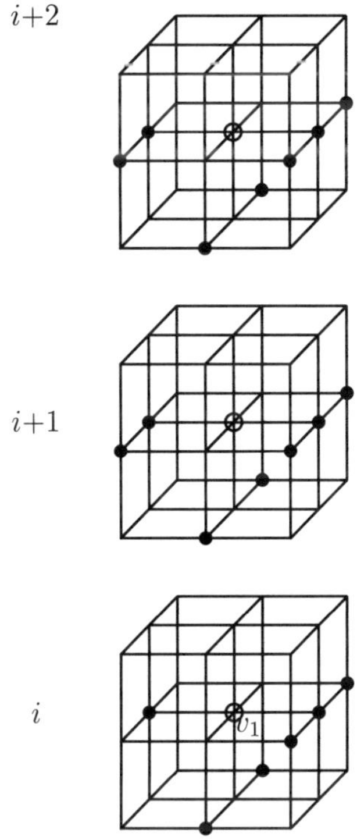

Fig. 12.

Acknowledgment

The author wishes to thank Prof. T. Y. Kong for his comments on earlier version of this paper.

References

1. A. Rosenfeld, T. Y. Kong and A. Nakamura, Topology-preserving deformations of two-valued digital pictures, *Graphical Models and Image Processing*, **60** (1998), 24–34.
2. A. Nakamura and A. Rosenfeld, Digital knots, *Pattern Recognition*, **33** (2000), 1541–1553.
3. T. Y. Knog, Topology-preserving deletions of 1's from 2-, 3- and 4-dimensional binary images, *Lecture Notes in Computer Science*, **1347** (1997), 3–18.
4. A. Nakamura, Magnifications of digital topology (invited paper), *Lecture Notes in Computer Science*, **3322** (2004), 260–275.

CHAPTER 21

PROBABILISTIC INFERENCE IN TEST TUBE AND ITS APPLICATION TO GENE EXPRESSION PROFILES

Yasubumi Sakakibara

Department of Biosciences and Informatics, Keio University, 3-14-1 Hiyoshi, Kohoku-ku, Yokohama, 223-8522, Japan
E-mail: yasubio.keio.ac.jp

Takashi Yokomori

Department of Mathematics, Faculty of Education and Integrated Arts and Sciences, Waseda University, Japan

Satoshi Kobayashi

Department of Computer Science, University of Electro-Communications, Tokyo, Japan

Akira Suyama

Institute of Physics and Department of Life Sciences, University of Tokyo, Japan

We propose a probabilistic interpretation for the test tube with a large amount of DNA strands and consider a probabilistic logical inference based on the probabilistic interpretation by combining with our previous work to represent and evaluate Boolean formulae on DNA computing. Second, we propose a new method for analyses of gene expression profiles based on the probabilistic logical inference. By employing the DNA Coded Number method, we propose *in-vitro* gene expression analyses which not only detect gene expressions but also find logical formulae of gene expressions. An important advantage of our method is that the intensity of fluorescence with a corresponding color is not only proportional to *expression level* of each gene in a sample but also proportional to *satisfiability level* of a Boolean formula for the gene expression pattern. These features of the in-vitro analyses and the DCN method allow us more quantitative analyses of gene expression profiles and the logical operations.

1. Introduction

We consider probabilistic computations and robust computations executed in the test tube based on DNA computing. Our fundamental idea is the use of a large number of DNA strands in the test tube where each individual DNA strand computes a function by itself.

First, we consider the following probabilistic interpretation of the test tube. We simply represent a "probability (weight)" by the volume (number) of copies of a DNA strand which encodes the probabilistic attribute. Approximately, 2^{40} DNA strands of length around several hundreds are stored in 1.5 ml of a standard test tube, and by considering the test tube of 1.5 ml as the unit, we can represent the probabilistic values using the quantities of DNA strands with precision up to 2^{40}. For example, let the volume (concentration) of the DNA strands for representing the attribute "A" be 5/10 of the test tube, the volume of DNA strands for "B" be 3/10, and the volume of DNA strands for "C" be 2/10. In this case, we can consider the probabilistic value of "A" is 0.5 (50%), the probabilistic value of "B" is 0.3 (30%) and the probabilistic value of "C" is 0.2 (20%).

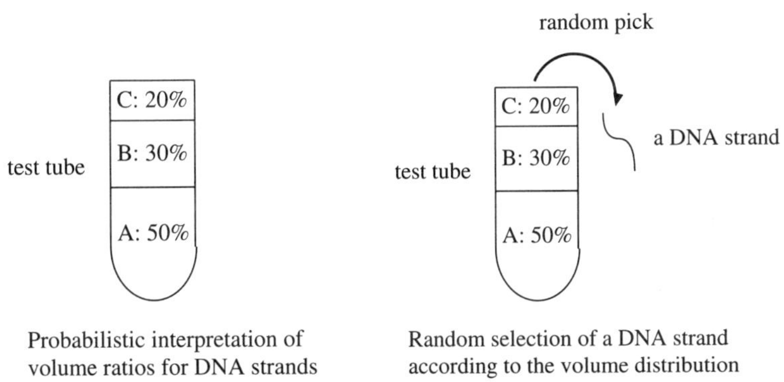

Fig. 1. (left:) The probabilistic interpretation of the test tube, and (right:) randomized prediction with probability proportional to the volumes of DNA strands.

This probabilistic interpretation of the test tube is utilized and executed by "randomized prediction". That is, a prediction by choosing (picking out) a DNA strand in the test tube at random with probability (frequency) proportional to its current volume of each DNA strands. For example, the probability of randomly picking out a DNA strand for "A" (randomized prediction of "A") from the test tube is 0.5.

On the other hand, Sakakibara[5,6] has recently proposed new methods to encode any DNF (disjunctive normal form) Boolean formula to a DNA strand, evaluate the encoded Boolean formula for a truth-value assignment by using hybridization and primer extension with DNA polymerase. By employing this evaluation methods, we are able to deal with logical operations such as logical-"and" and logical-"or" in the test tube.

Based on the probabilistic interpretation of the test tube and combined with the method to represent and evaluate Boolean formulae in DNA, we execute a probabilistic logical inference in test tube such as *probabilistic* logical-and and *probabilistic* logical-or.

Second, we apply the probabilistic logical inference in test tube to *in-vitro* analyses of gene expression profiles.

Recently, DNA chip[3] or Microarray[2,7] technologies have been developed and considered as an important tool for detecting the gene expression levels. A most fascinating feature of the DNA chip is the massive simultaneous detection of expressions for a large number of genes. Moreover, DNA chip technology has much potential for various applications including gene discovery and disease diagnosis. This is done by using a simple technology of the hybridizations to complementary DNA strands bonded to a glass surface in an array format.

On the other hand, Suyama *et al.*[8] have developed the DNA Coded Number (DCN) method with the purpose to apply DNA-based computers to genome information processing. In the DCN method, genome information is first converted into data expressions in DCNs using a conversion table written with DNA molecules. DCNs are numbers represented by orthonormal DNA base sequences. The orthonormal sequences have uniform melting temperature and no mishybridization or folding potential to minimize computational error in DNA computing. A set of orthonormal sequences with such features can be designed by using coding theory and string algorithms to search a set of DNA sequences with a large Hamming distance and a same number of "G" and "C" contents.[1] For example, a set of over 200 orthonormal sequences of length 25 nt has been designed using a greedy algorithm.[10] This set is sufficient to uniquely represent the truth-value assignments of 100 distinct genes in 1-digit and and 5×10^3 distinct genes in 2-digit DCNs, respectively.

DCN-encoded genome information is then analyzed by using various DNA-computing operations such as logical operations with a power of the massive parallelism of DNA computing. The results of the analysis are finally obtained by reading out a sequence of DCNs.

Based on these observation, we propose a new method for analysing gene expression profiles *in vitro* by combining the probabilistic logical inference method with the DCN method. Our *in-vitro* gene expression analyses not only detect gene expressions but also find logical formulae of gene expressions.

2. Evaluation of Boolean Formulae in DNA

In this section, we review our previous work[5,6] of encoding and evaluating Boolean formulae on DNA strands.

The Boolean function is a mathematical function defined on attributes (Boolean variables) which is often used to define gene regulation rules for gene regulation networks. A Boolean formula consists of attributes, logical-"and", logical-"or" and "negation". More formally, there are n Boolean variables (or attributes) and we denote the set of such variables as $X_n = \{x_1, x_2, \ldots, x_n\}$. A *truth-value assignment* $a = (b_1, b_2, \ldots, b_n)$ is a mapping from X_n to the set $\{0, 1\}$ or a binary string of length n where $b_i \in \{0, 1\}$ for $1 \leq i \leq n$. Note that *the Boolean variables correspond to the gene expressions (that is, the expression for a gene to be "ON" or "OFF") and the assignments correspond to the gene expression patterns. When a gene is expressed, the truth-value of a Boolean variable which corresponds to the gene becomes 1 and when the gene is unexpressed, the truth-value of the Boolean variable becomes 0.* A *Boolean function* is defined to be a mapping from $\{0, 1\}^n$ to $\{0, 1\}$. *Boolean formulae* are useful representations for Boolean functions. The simplest Boolean formula is just a single variable. Each variable x_i $(1 \leq i \leq n)$ is associated with two *literals*: x_i itself and its negation $\neg x_i$. A *term* is a conjunction of literals. A Boolean formula is in *disjunctive normal form* (DNF, for short) if it is a disjunction of terms. Every Boolean function can be represented by a DNF Boolean formula. For any constant k, a k-term DNF formula is a DNF Boolean formula with at most k terms. We denote the truth value of a Boolean formula β for an assignment $a \in \{0, 1\}^n$ by $\beta(a)$.

In our previous work,[5,6] we have proposed an evaluation algorithm for DNF Boolean formulae using DNA strands and biological operations.

First, we encode a k-term DNF formula β into a DNA single-strand as follows:

Let $\beta = t_1 \vee t_2 \vee \cdots t_k$ be a k-term DNF formula.

(1) For each term $t = l_1 \wedge l_2 \wedge \cdots l_j$ in the DNF formula β where l_i $(1 \leq i \leq j)$ is a literal, we use the DNA single strand of the form:

$$5' - \textbf{stopper} - \textbf{marker} - seqlit_1 - \cdots - seqlit_j - 3'$$

where $seqlit_i$ $(1 \leq i \leq j)$ is the encoded sequence for a literal l_i. The **stopper** is a *stopper sequence* for the polymerization stop that is a technique developed by Hagiya *et al.*[4] The **marker** is a special sequence for a extraction used later at the evaluation step.

(2) We concatenate all of these sequences encoding terms t_j $(1 \leq j \leq k)$ in β and denote by $e(\beta)$ the concatenated sequence encoding β.

For example, the 2-term DNF formula $(x_1 \wedge \neg x_2) \vee (\neg x_3 \wedge x_4)$ on four variables $X_4 = \{x_1, x_2, x_3, x_4\}$ is encoded as follows:

$$5' - \textbf{marker} - x_1 - \neg x_2 - \textbf{stopper} - \textbf{marker} - \neg x_3 - x_4 - 3'$$

Second, we put the DNA strand $e(\beta)$ encoding the DNF formula β into the test tube and do the following biological operations to evaluate β for the truth-value assignment $a = (b_1, b_2, \ldots, b_n)$.

Algorithm $B(T, a)$:

(1) Let the test tube T contain the DNA single-strand $e(\beta)$ for the DNF formula β.

(2) Let $a = (b_1, b_2, \ldots, b_n)$ be the truth-value assignment. For each b_i $(1 \leq i \leq n)$, if $b_i = 0$ then put the Watson-Crick complement $\overline{x_i}$ of the DNA substrand encoding x_i into the test tube T, and if $b_i = 1$ then put the complement $\overline{\neg x_i}$ of $\neg x_i$ into T.

(3) Cool down the test tube T for annealing these complements to complementary substrands in $e(\beta)$.

(4) Apply the primer extension with DNA polymerase to the test tube T with these annealed complements as the primers. As a result, if the substrand for a term t_j in β contains a literal lit_i and the bit b_i makes lit_i 0 (that is, if b_i is 0 then the truth-value of lit_i equal to x_i becomes 0, and if b_i is 1 then the truth-value of lit_i equal to $\neg x_i$ becomes 0), then the complement $\overline{seqlit_i}$ of the substrand $seqlit_i$ has been put in Step

(2) and is annealed to $seqlit_i$. The primer extension with DNA polymorase extends the primer $\overline{seqlit_i}$ and the subsequence for the marker in the term t_j becomes double-stranded, and the extension stops at the stopper sequence. Otherwise, the subsequence for the marker remains single-stranded. This means that the truth-value of the term t_j is 1 for the assignment a.

(5) Extract the DNA (partially double-stranded) sequences that contains single-stranded subsequences for markers. These DNA sequences represent the DNF formulae β whose truth-value is 1 for the assignment a.

The Fig. 2 illustrates the behavior of the algorithm B for $\beta = (x_1 \wedge \neg x_2) \vee (\neg x_3 \wedge x_4)$ and a truth-value assignment $a = (1011)$ on $X_4 = \{x_1, x_2, x_3, x_4\}$.

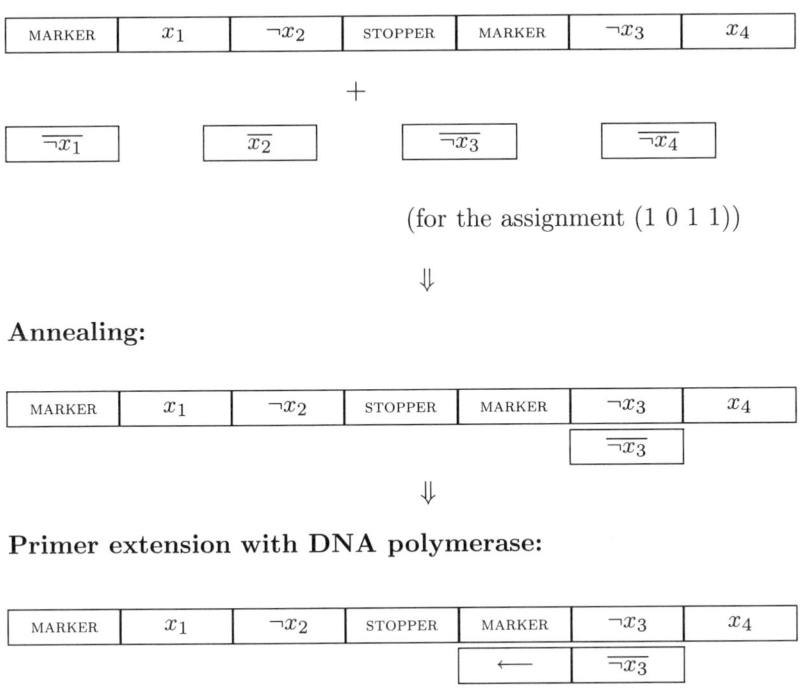

Fig. 2. (upper:) For the assignment (1 0 1 1), the Watson-Crick complements $\overline{\neg x_1}$, $\overline{x_2}$, $\overline{\neg x_3}$ and $\overline{\neg x_4}$ of the encodings for $\neg x_1$, x_2, $\neg x_3$ and $\neg x_4$ are put to the test tube and (middle:) $\overline{\neg x_3}$ is annealed to the DNA strand encoding $(x_1 \wedge \neg x_2) \vee (\neg x_3 \wedge x_4)$. (lower:) Primer extension with DNA polymerase extends the primer $\overline{\neg x_3}$, and the right marker becomes double-stranded and the left marker remains single-stranded.

The truth-value of β is 1 for the assignment $a = (1011)$. We call the algorithm $B(T, a)$ the *logical evaluation operation* for a DNA strand encoding a DNF formula.

We have already verified the biological feasibilities for the evaluation method of Boolean formulae. Yamamoto *et al.*[9] have done the following biological experiments to confirm the effects of the evaluation algorithm $B(T, a)$ for DNF Boolean formulae:

(1) for a simple 2-term DNF Boolean formula on three variables, we have generated DNA sequences encoding the DNF formula by using DNA ligase in the test tube,
(2) the DNA sequences are amplified by PCR,
(3) for a truth-value assignment, we have put the Watson-Crick complements of DNA substrands encoding the assignment, applied the primer extension with DNA polymerase, and confirmed the primer extension and the polymerization stop at the stopper sequences,
(4) we have extracted the DNA sequences encoding the DNF formula with magnetic beads through biotin at the 5'-end of primer and washing.

3. Probabilistic Inference in DNA

3.1. *Probability represented by volumes of DNA strands and randomized prediction*

First, we consider the following three problems:

- representation of (non-binary, multiple) numbers using quantities (volumes) of DNA strands,
- extension from $\{0, 1\}$ truth-values to multiple (probabilistic) truth-values of assignments,
- randomized prediction according to the volumes of DNA strands.

An usual method to represent the truth (binary) value for some attribute, say "A" (for example, some Boolean variable), by using DNA strands in the test tube is to prepare a DNA strand to represent the attribute "A" and to check whether the corresponding DNA strands are present in the tube. The value is 1 if there exists at least one and the value is 0 otherwise. We extend this to representing quantitative (non-binary) values using large quantities of DNA strands. We simply represent a "probability (weight)" by the volume (number) of copies of a DNA strand which encodes the probabilistic attribute. Approximately, 2^{40} DNA strands of length around several hundreds are stored in 1.5 ml of a standard test tube, and by considering the test tube of 1.5 ml as the unit, we can represent the probabilistic values using the quantities of DNA strands with precision up to 2^{40}.

This probabilistic interpretation of the test tube is utilized and executed by prediction by sampling the tube at random, that is, selecting a DNA strand with probability (frequency) proportional to its current volume of each DNA strands. For example, the probability of predicting "A", "B", or "C" by randomly picking out the corresponding strand is 0.7, 0.2, and 0.1, respectively.

3.2. *Probabilistic logical inference using volumes of DNA strands*

In probabilistic logic, the logical variable "x" takes a real truth-value between 0 and 1. Further, when the value of the variable x is c ($0 \leq c \leq 1$), the negation "$\neg x$" of the variable x takes the value $1 - c$.

Combining the representation method for probabilistic values using quantities of DNA strands with the method for representing and evaluating Boolean formulae, we can execute the following probabilistic logical inference:

(1) We extend the truth-value assignment $a = (b_1, b_2, \ldots, b_n)$ to the probabilistic truth-value assignment $a' = (c_1, c_2, \ldots, c_n)$ where each c_i is a real value between 0 and 1 to represent the probability that the variable x_i becomes 1.
(2) We execute a modified algorithm $B(T, a')$ for the probabilistic truth-value assignment $a' = (c_1, c_2, \ldots, c_n)$ such that for each c_i ($1 \leq i \leq n$) and the unit volume Z of the test tube, we put $(1 - c_i)Z$ amount of the Watson-Crick complement $\overline{\neg x_i}$ of the negation $\neg x_i$ into the test tube T and put $c_i Z$ amount of the complement $\overline{x_i}$ of x_i into T.

Example 1: We consider two Boolean variables $\{x, y\}$ and a Boolean formula "$x \wedge \neg y$" which is encoded as follows:

$$5' - \mathbf{marker} - x - \neg y - 3'$$

We prepare enough amount Z of copies of this DNA strand and let the probabilistic assignment be $a' = (c_1, c_2)$.

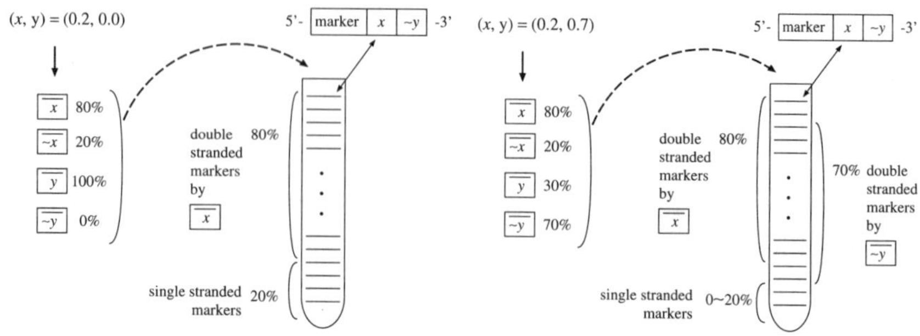

Fig. 3. Probabilistic logical inferences with a Boolean formula $x \wedge \neg y$.

- Case $c_1 = 1.0$ (100%) and $c_2 = 0.0$ (0%):
  The execution of the algorithm $B(T, a')$ implies that all DNA strands representing $x \wedge \neg y$ have single-stranded markers and hence the probability that the truth-value of $x \wedge \neg y$ is 1 is 1.
- Case $c_1 = 1.0$ (100%) and $c_2 = 1.0$ (100%):
  The execution of the algorithm $B(T, a')$ implies that all markers of DNA strands for $x \wedge \neg y$ become double-stranded and hence the probability that the truth-value of $x \wedge \neg y$ is 1 is 0.
- Case $c_1 = 0.2$ (20%) and $c_2 = 0.0$ (0%): (illustrated in the upper side of Fig. 3)
  The execution of the algorithm $B(T, a')$ implies that 20% amount (that is, $0.2Z$) of DNA strands for $x \wedge \neg y$ have single-stranded markers and hence the probability that the truth-value of $x \wedge \neg y$ is 1 is 0.2.
- Case $c_1 = 0.2$ (20%) and $c_2 = 0.7$ (70%): (illustrated in the lower side of Fig. 3)
  The execution of the algorithm $B(T, a')$ implies that the amount between 0% and 20% of DNA strands for $x \wedge \neg y$ have single-stranded markers (the expected amount is 6%) and hence the probability that the truth-value of $x \wedge \neg y$ is 1 is between 0.0 and 0.2.

Example 2: We consider a Boolean formula "$x \vee \neg y$" which is encoded as follows:

$$5' - \mathbf{marker} - x - \mathbf{stopper} - \mathbf{marker} - \neg y - 3'$$

- Let the probabilistic assignment be $a' = (1.0, 0.0)$.
  The execution of the algorithm $B(T, a')$ implies that all left markers of DNA strands representing $x \vee \neg y$ remains single-stranded while all

right markers become double-stranded, and hence the probability that the truth-value of $x \vee \neg y$ is 1 is 1.

- Let the probabilistic assignment be $a' = (0.2, 0.7)$.
  The execution of the algorithm $B'(T, a')$ implies that 80% left markers of DNA strands for $x \vee \neg y$ become double-stranded and 70% right markers become double-stranded, and hence the amount between 30% and 50% of DNA strands have at least one single-stranded marker. Thus the probabilistic truth-value of $x \vee \neg y$ is between 0.3 and 0.5.

After these probabilistic inferences inside the test tube, we extract the result of the probabilistic inference by simply picking out one DNA strand from the test tube as "randomized prediction".

4. Application to *in-vitro* Gene Expression Analyses

In this section, we apply the probabilistic logical inference in test tube combined with the DNA Coded Number method[8] to *in-vitro* analyses of gene expression profiles with logical operations.

4.1. *DNA coded number*

DNA coded numbers (DCNs) are representations of numbers in DNA sequences chosen from a set of orthonormal DNA base sequences, which have uniform melting temperature and no mishybridization or folding potential. A set of orthonormal sequences with such features can be designed by using coding theory and string algorithms to search a set of DNA sequences with a large Hamming distance and a same number of "G" and "C" contents.[1] For example, a set of over 200 orthonormal sequences of length 25 nt has been designed using a greedy algorithm.[10] This set is sufficient to uniquely represent the truth-value assignments of 100 distinct genes in 1-digit and and 5×10^3 distinct genes in 2-digit DCNs, respectively.

DCNs associated with expressed or unexpressed genes are generated using DNA molecular reaction as shown in Fig. 4. First, an expressed gene transcript is converted into a corresponding DCN with a partially double-stranded DNA adapter molecule A and a single-stranded DNA anchor molecule a. The adapter contains a single-stranded region, which is the right half of a unique sequence of target transcript, and a double-stranded region encoding a unique DCN with flanking common sequences SD and ED. The anchor has a single-stranded region, which is the left half of a unique sequence of target transcript, and a biotin molecule at the 5' end.

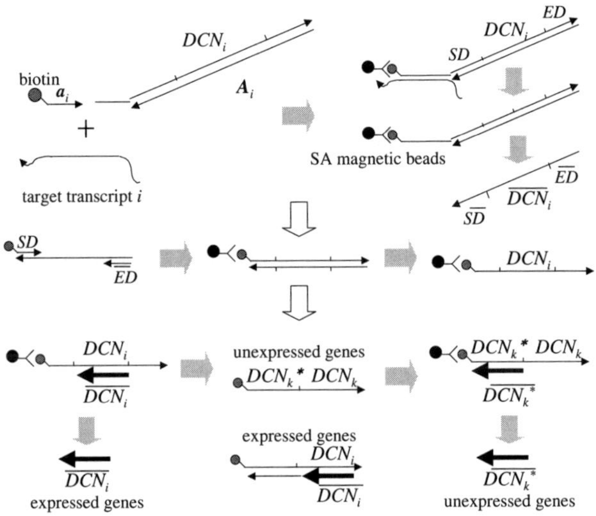

Fig. 4. Generation of DCN strands, $\overline{DCN_i}$ and $\overline{DCN*_i}$, corresponding to expressed and unexpressed genes, respectively.

The sequence of cDNA complementary to a unique sequence of expressed gene transcript facilitates ligation of adapter A to anchor a with Taq DNA ligase. This operation is identical to the append operation, which has been used to solve an instance of 3-SAT problems on DNA-computers.[10] All adapter molecules ligated to biotinylated anchors are captured on streptavidin (SA) magnetic beads and are then melted into single strands to obtain a set of single-stranded DNA molecules representing DCNs corresponding to expressed genes.

DNA single strands representing DCNs are then amplified by PCR with a primer pair of SD and $\overline{ED}$. The use of the common primer pair SD and $\overline{ED}$ and the orthonormality of base sequences representing DCN facilitate the uniform amplification, which is needed for quantitative gene expression profiling. Amplified DCNs with flanking SD and ED sequences are captured on SA magnetic beads through biotin at the 5'-end of SD primer. They are then melted into single strands to serve as probes for the get operation to extract DCNs corresponding to expressed genes. The get operation starts with addition of the magnetic beads with single-stranded SD-DCN-ED sequences to a solution mixture of $\overline{DCN}$ single strands of all target genes. After hybridization and washing, only $\overline{DCN}$ single strands of expressed genes are extracted.

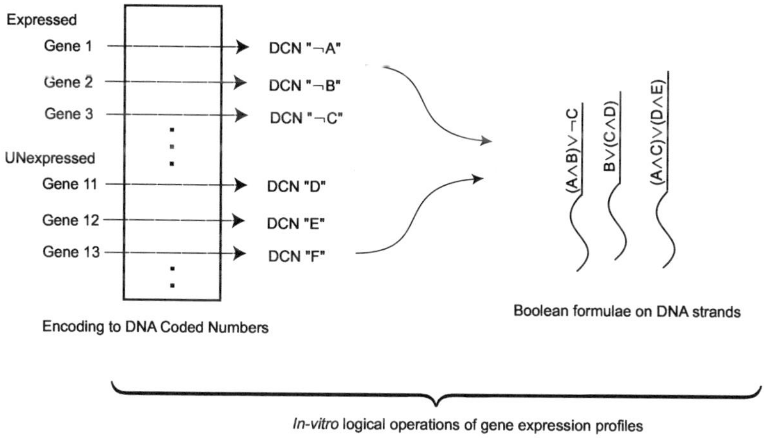

Fig. 5. *In-vitro* gene expression analyses with logical operations executable.

Part of the extracted DCN solution is used to generate DCNs of *unexpressed genes.* $\overline{DCN}$ strands of expressed genes are annealed to 5'-biotinylated single strands of $DCN*$-DCN sequences, and then subjected to primer extension with DNA polymerase. $DCN*$-DCN single strands corresponding to expressed genes are converted into double strands while those strands corresponding to unexpressed genes remain single-stranded.

Double-stranded and single-stranded $DCN*$-DCN sequences are separated with hydroxyapatite beads, which have different affinity to single- and double-stranded DNA. Single-stranded $DCN*$-DCN sequences are then used for the get operation to extract $\overline{DCN*}$ sequences of unexpressed genes, i. e., DCNs corresponding to unexpressed genes, from a mixture of $\overline{DCN*}$ strands of all target genes.

4.2. *Applications of gene expression analyses*

We illustrate *in-vitro* gene expression analyses with logical operations executable in Fig. 5. For example, a Boolean formula $(\mathrm{A} \wedge \mathrm{B}) \vee \neg \mathrm{C}$ in the figure means that if the gene A is expressed and the gene B is expressed or if the gene C is not expressed, the formula is satisfied.

The volume of each DCN sequences which is extracted from the corresponding gene in the sample represents the probabilistic truth-value of the DCN and is proportional to the *expression level* of the gene. These probabilistic truth-value assignments are applied to the mechanism of the probabilistic logical inference.

We describe the process of operations on *in-vitro* gene expression analyses:

(1) The messenger RNA (mRNA) is extracted from the sample, and a complementary DNA (cDNA) sequence is generated. The target sequences (transcripts) represent all of the genes expressed in the reference sample.
(2) (Case 1: expressed genes)
For an expressed gene, the truth-value of a Boolean variable for the gene becomes 1. Therefore, those cDNA sequences generated at Step 1 are translated into DCN sequences so that each gene expression is translated into an unique DCN sequence encoding the "negation" of a Boolean variable representing the gene.
(3) (Case 2: unexpressed genes)
For an unexpressed gene, the truth-value of a Boolean variable for the gene becomes 0. Therefore, for each unexpressed gene, an unique DCN sequence which encodes a Boolean variable representing the gene is generated.
(4) Those DCN sequences are simultaneously applied to a test tube with DNA strands encoding various Boolean formulae, called *logical test tube*, and the logical evaluation operation is executed in the logical test tube.
(5) The complementary marker sequences *fluorescently tagged* with different colors are applied to the logical test tube and annealed to marker subsequences which remain single-stranded after the logical evaluation operation.
(6) If the logical test tube shows some color, it indicates that the truth-value of a Boolean formula corresponding to the color is 1 and hence the Boolean formula of the color is satisfied with the gene expressions. Further, the intensity of the fluorescence of the color is proportional to the *satisfiability level* of the Boolean formula of the color with the gene expression pattern.

Thus, in the logical test tube, the results of the probabilistic logical inference are extracted in the form of the intensity of the fluorescence of the color. Figure 6 illustrates these operations for the *in-vitro* gene expression analyses.

5. Conclusions

In this paper, we have considered a probabilistic interpretation of the test tube, and proposed *in-vitro* gene expression analyses by combining the

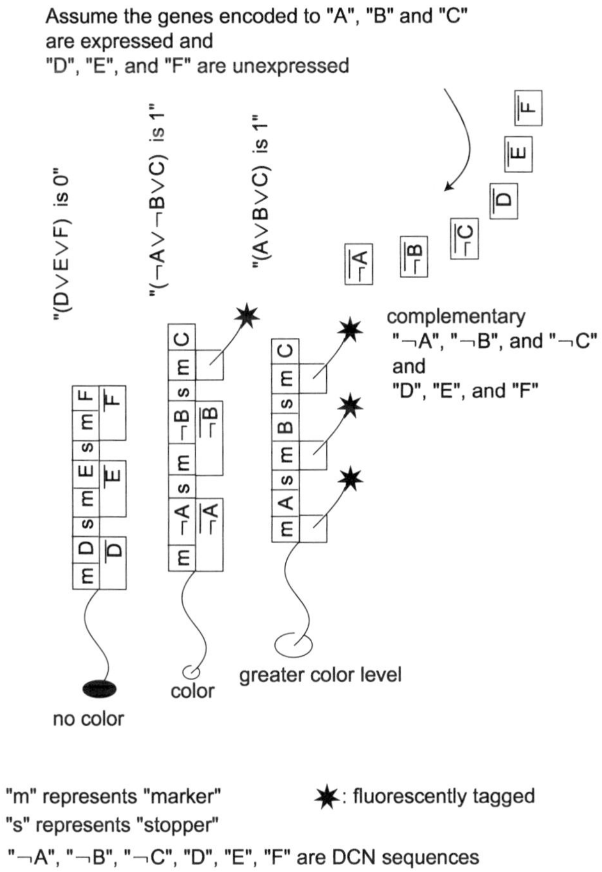

Fig. 6. (upper:) the gene expressions generated from mRNA in the sample are translated to DCNs which are Watson-Crick complementary sequences encoding "¬ A", "¬ B" and "¬ C", and the unexpressed genes "D", "E" and "F" are translated to DCNs encoding them respectively. (middle:) the complementary "D", "E" and "F" are annealed to the DNA single strands encoding Boolean formulae in the logical test tube and the primer extension with DNA polymerase is applied with the primers. As a result, all marker subsequences in the formula $(D \vee E \vee F)$ become double-stranded, which means the truth-value of the formula is 0, and it shows no corresponding color. Two marker subsequences in the formula $(\neg A \vee \neg B \vee C)$ become double-stranded and one marker subsequence remains single-stranded, which means the truth-value of the formula is 1, and the complementary marker sequences fluorescently tagged are annealed to the single-stranded marker subsequence and it shows a corresponding fluorescent color. All marker subsequences in the formula $(A \vee B \vee C)$ remain single-stranded, which means all terms are satisfied with the expression pattern, and three complementary marker sequences fluorescently tagged are annealed and it shows a corresponding fluorescent color with greater level.

DNA-computing method for representing and evaluating Boolean functions with the DCN method. We have established that, in principle, this method not only allows detection of gene expression, but also that a logical expression describing the gene expression itself could be ascertained as well. This means that a DNA chip designed by this method also has information processing capabilities on chip, a new feature that may hold considerable interest for further applications.

While the biological feasibilities for the evaluation method of Boolean formulae[9] and the DCN method[8] have already been verified, a practical implementation and the test of the in-vitro gene expression analyses will be significantly important for a convincing argument.

Acknowledgments

This work was performed through Special Coordination Funds for Promoting Science and Technology, and Grant-in-Aid for Scientific Research on Priority Area no. 14085205, from the Ministry of Education, Culture, Sports, Science and Technology, the Japanese Government. This work was also performed in part through Special Coordination Funds for Promoting Science and Technology from the Ministry of Education, Culture, Sports, Science and Technology, the Japanese Government.

References

1. M. Arita and S. Kobayashi, DNA Sequence Design Using Templates. *New Generation Computing*, 20: 263–277, 2002.
2. J. L. DeRisi, V. R. Lyer and P. O. Brown, Exploring the metabolic and genetic control of gene expression on a genomic scale. *Science*, 278: 680–686, 1997.
3. S. P. A. Fodor, Massively parallel genomics. *Science*, 277: 393–395, 1997.
4. M. Hagiya, M. Arita, D. Kiga, K. Sakamoto and S. Yokoyama, Towards parallel evaluation and learning of Boolean μ-formulas with molecules. In H. Rubin and D. H. Wood, editors, *DNA Based Computers III*, DIMACS Series in Discrete Mathematics and Theoretical Computer Science, Vol. 48, 57–72, 1999. American Mathematical Society.
5. Y. Sakakibara, Solving computational learning problems of Boolean formulae on DNA computers. In A. Condon and G. Rozenberg, editors, *Proceedings of 6th International Workshop on DNA-Based Computers*, Leiden, The Netherlands, 193–204, 2000. Springer Verlag, Lecture Notes in Computer Science, Vol. 2054, Heidelberg.
6. Y. Sakakibara, DNA-based algorithms for learning Boolean formulae. *Natural Computing*, 2: 153–171, 2003.

7. M. Schena, D. Shalon, R. Heller, A. Chai, P. O. Brown and R. W. Davis, Parallel human genome analysis: Microarray-based expression monitoring of 1000 genes. *Proceedings of the National Academy of Sciences*, 93(20): 10614–10619, 1996.
8. A. Suyama, N. Nishida, K. Kurata and K. Omagari, Gene expression analysis by DNA computing. In S. Miyano, R. Shamir and T. Takagi, editors, *Currents in Computational Molecular Biology*, 20–21, 2000. University Academy Press.
9. Y. Yamamoto, S. Komiya, Y. Sakakibara and Y. Husimi, Application of 3SR reaction to DNA computer (in Japanese). In *Seibutu-Buturi*, 40(S198), 2000.
10. H. Yoshida and A. Suyama, Solution to 3-SAT by breadth first search. In E. Winfree and D. K. Gifford, editors, *DNA Based Computers V*, DIMACS Series in Discrete Mathematics and Theoretical Computer Science, Vol. 54, 9–20, 2000. American Mathematical Society.

CHAPTER 22

ON LANGUAGES DEFINED BY NUMERICAL PARAMETERS*

Arto Salomaa
Turku Centre for Computer Science,
Lemminkäisenkatu 14, 20520 Turku, Finland
E-mail: asalomaa@it.utu.fi

The paper investigates definitions of languages based on Boolean combinations of equations dealing with the number of subword occurrences. Complete characterizations are obtained for a certain class of subwords (a-*separated*). Interconnections to the theory of Parikh-matrices, as well as applications of some known results, are also studied.

1. Introduction

Formal languages are customarily defined either by generative devices (rewriting systems, grammars), or by accepting devices (machines, automata). However, sometimes also descriptional devices are used, a typical example being regular expressions. This paper undertakes the study of certain numerical descriptional devices: one considers sets of words satisfying certain numerical conditions. A powerful tool will be the number of certain subword occurrences. For many languages surprisingly simple characterizations are obtained in this fashion. Moreover, the numerical characterizations eliminate some undesirable effects of noncommutativity.

The most direct numerical fact about a word w is its *length* $|w|$. Languages over a one-letter alphabet can be identified with their length sets. In case of arbitrary alphabets, length sets give only a very rude

*Dedicated to *Professor Rani Siromoney* on her 75th Birthday. I have been fortunate to know Rani Siromoney already for more than three decades. Although we have never worked together for any longer period, our paths have crossed every now and then. Of the many-faceted research of Rani Siromoney, I have had similar interests especially in the theory of L systems and cryptography. I hope that my present contribution to the very basics of language theory will be of interest for her and her associates.

characterization of a language. The components i_j of the *Parikh vector*,[2,6,8] $\Psi(w) = (i_1, \ldots, i_k)$ indicate the number of occurrences of the letter a_j, $1 \leq j \leq k$, in w, provided w is over the alphabet $\Sigma = \{a_1, \ldots, a_k\}$. The set of Parikh vectors associated to the words in a language gives considerably more information about the language,[8] than its length set. To get still more information, one has to focus the attention to *subwords and factors*. In this paper, these notions are understood as follows.

Definition 1: A word u is a *subword* of a word w if there exist words $x_1, \ldots, x_n$ and $y_0, \ldots, y_n$, some of them possibly empty, such that

$$u = x_1 \cdots x_n \text{ and } w = y_0 x_1 y_1 \cdots x_n y_n \,.$$

The word u is a *factor* of w if there are words x and y such that $w = xuy$. If the word x (resp. y) is empty, then u is also called a *prefix* (resp. *suffix*) of w. A subword or factor u of w is termed *proper* if u is not empty and $u \neq w$.

In classical language theory,[8] our subwords are usually called "scattered subwords", whereas our factors are called "subwords". The notation used throughout the article is $|w|_u$, the number of occurrences of the word u as a subword of the word w. Two occurrences are considered different if at least one letter of u occurs in a different position in w. Occurrences of u in w can be viewed as $|u|$-dimensional vectors, with strictly increasing coordinates i, $1 \leq i \leq |w|$. This gives rise to an obvious formal definition.

Clearly, $|w|_u = 0$ if $|w| < |u|$. We also make the *convention* that, for any w and the empty word λ,

$$|w|_\lambda = 1 \,.$$

In Ref. 9 the number $|w|_u$ is denoted as a "binomial coefficient" $|w|_u = \binom{w}{u}$. Indeed, if w and u are words over a one-letter alphabet, $|w|_u$ reduces to the ordinary binomial coefficient.

Consider the set of all words w over the binary alphabet $\{a, b\}$ satisfying the equation $|w|_a = |w|_b$. Clearly, the set of all such words is a nonregular language, definable by a context-free grammar with the productions

$$S \to \lambda\,, \quad S \to SS\,, \quad S \to aSb\,, \quad S \to bSa\,.$$

Thus, the equation $|w|_a = |w|_b$ constitutes an alternative definitional device for this language. The purpose of this paper is to consider definitions of languages based on similar equations. After some preliminary examples in the next section, the fundamental notions are defined in Section 3. The general theory is closely connected with *Parikh matrices*.[1,3–5,10–14] Languages defined by such numerical parameters are, in general, difficult to define by other means. We will perform a detailed study in the case of *a-separated words*.

We assume that the reader is familiar with the basics of formal languages. Whenever necessary,[8] may be consulted. As customary, we use small letters from the beginning of the English alphabet a, b, c, d, possibly with indices, to denote letters of our formal alphabet Σ. Words are usually denoted by small letters from the end of the English alphabet.

2. Preliminary Considerations

Before the formal definitions given in the next section, we begin with some explanations and examples. We consider in this paper equations expressed in terms of numbers $|w|_u$. Here w is viewed as an unknown, and the u's (there may be several of them) are specific words over an alphabet Σ. There may be several equations. In general, we are dealing with a Boolean combination of such equations. We are looking for the language of all words w satisfying the Boolean combination.

We already considered above the language of all words w satisfying the equation $|w|_a = |w|_b$. Whenever the alphabet Σ is not specified, it is understood to be the minimal alphabet containing the letters of each of the words u. Thus, in this case the alphabet is $\{a, b\}$. Consider next the equation $|w|_{ab} = 4$. It is not difficult to see the language of all words w satisfying this equation is the regular language

$$b^*(a^2b^2 + a^4b + ab^4 + abaab + abbab)a^* .$$

Thus, the former equation defines a more complicated language than the latter equation. This holds in spite of the fact that the subword ab is more complicated than single letters. However, the right side of the latter equation is a constant, which is a decisive factor contributing to the complexity of the language.

Consider then the conjunction $|w|_{ab} = 4 \wedge |w|_a = 2$. The language obtained is $b^*(a^2b^2 + ab^4a + abbab)$, still infinite. But the further conjunction

$$|w|_{ab} = 4 \wedge |w|_a = 2 \wedge |w|_{ba} = 2$$

defines the language $\{ba^2b^2, ab^2ab\}$. (Clearly, it is not of interest to consider alphabets bigger than the minimal alphabet determined by the u's. The additional letters could be inserted anywhere in the word, without affecting the validity of the equations.)

Our next example is the language L defined by the conjunction

$$|w|_a = |w|_b \wedge |w|_b = |w|_c \wedge |w|_{abc} = (|w|_a)^3 .$$

It is not difficult to see that $L = \{a^n b^n c^n | n \geq 0\}$. Indeed, each of the three letters a, b, c has the same number $n \geq 0$ of occurrences in the words of L. For such words, the number of occurrences of abc cannot exceed n^3, and this maximal number is achieved only when each a precedes each b, and each b precedes each c. Clearly, the language

$$\{a_1^n a_2^n \cdots a_k^n | n \geq 0\} , \quad k \geq 2 ,$$

can be defined in the same way.

The conjunction

$$|w|_a = 2|w|_b \wedge |w|_{aba} = (|w|_b)^3$$

leads to similar considerations. Clearly, the defined language L' contains all words of the form $a^n b^n a^n$, $n \geq 0$. But are there any further words in L'? Is it possible that also some other words satisfy the two equations? Choosing $|w|_b = 4$, the possible candidates

$$w = a^5 b^4 a^3 , \quad a^3 babab^2 a^3 , \quad a^4 b^2 ab^2 a^3 , \quad a^4 b^3 aba^3$$

yield the values

$$|w|_{aba} = 60 , \quad 61 , \quad 62 , \quad 63 ,$$

respectively, all values being less than the required 64. Indeed, L' contains no further words, which is seen by the following simple argument. Assume that $|w|_b = n$ and $|w|_a = 2n$. Consider a specific occurrence of b in w. If

$$n - i(\text{resp. } n + i) , \quad -n \leq i \leq n ,$$

occurrences of a lie to the left (resp. right) of this specific occurrence of b, then this b takes part of $n^2 - i^2$ occurrences of aba in w. Thus, the maximal number n^3 of the latter occurrences is reached only if $i = 0$ for each b. This means that $w = a^n b^n a^n$.

Finally, we consider the two languages L_1 and L_2 defined by the single equations

$$|w|_a = |w|_{ab} \text{ and } |w|_a = |w|_{aba} ,$$

respectively. Since ab is "simpler" than aba, one might think that also L_1 is "simpler" than L_2. However, the converse is the case, this being due to the fact that aba is *a-separated.* (The definition of this notion, as well as the corresponding results, will be presented in Section 5.)

In fact, L_2 is the regular language $b^*(\lambda + a^2ba^2 + ab^2a)b^*$. Indeed, a prefix or suffix of w consisting of b's affects neither $|w|_a$ nor $|w|_{aba}$. The regular expression for L_2 results by an analysis of the number of b's in a word $w = aua$, so that the equation $|w|_a = |w|_{aba}$ will be satisfied. For instance, if $|w|_b = 2$ and $i_1, i_2 \geq 1$ (resp. $j_1, j_2 \geq 1$) denote the number of a's to the left (resp. right) of the first and second b, then

$$i_1 + j_1 = i_2 + j_2 = i_1 j_1 + i_2 j_2 ,$$

yielding $i_1 = j_1 = i_2 = j_2 = 1$, which leads to the word ab^2a. The values $|w|_b = 0, 1$ yield similarly the words λ and a^2ba^2, whereas no word results from the values $|w|_b \geq 3$.

The language L_1 is not context-free because

$$L_1 \cap a^*b^*a^* = \{a^i b^j a^{ij-i} | i, j \geq 1\} \cup \{\lambda\}$$

which is not a context-free language.

3. Basic Definitions

The preceding section serves as an intuitive background for the formal definitions given below. A *Boolean subword condition*, BSC, is a general device for defining languages, based on numerical parameters. We will first define the notion of a *subword history*, SH, essentially following.[4] It is a numerical quantity, associated to a variable word w, polynomial in some numbers $|w|_u$, where each u is a word over the basic alphabet Σ. The notion SH leads naturally to the notions of a *subword history equation*, SHE, and *Boolean subword condition*, BSC. The words *satisfying* a given BSC constitute a language, $L(BSC)$. An important special case will be the *elementary* Boolean subword conditions, and the languages defined by them.

Definition 2: Let Σ be an alphabet and $w \in \Sigma^*$. A *subword history* in Σ and its *value* in w are defined recursively as follows. For every $u \in \Sigma^*$, $\|_u$ is a subword history in Σ, referred to as *monomial*, and its value in w equals $|w|_u$. Assume that SH_1 and SH_2 are subword histories in Σ, with values α_1 and α_2 in w, respectively. Then so are

$$-(SH_1), \quad (SH_1) + (SH_2), \text{ and } (SH_1) \times (SH_2),$$

with values in w

$$-\alpha_1\,, \quad \alpha_1+\alpha_2\,, \text{ and } \alpha_1\alpha_2\,,$$

respectively.

A subword history is *linear* if it is obtained without using the operation $\times$. Two subword histories SH_1 and SH_2 are termed *equivalent*, written $SH_1 = SH_2$, if they assume the same value in any w.

We will use natural abbreviations in the sequel. For instance, instead of $\|_{ab} + \|_{ab} + \|_{ab}$ we write $3\|_{ab}$. The alphabet Σ is understood as the minimal alphabet for the words u appearing in the given SH. Thus,

$$SH = \|_{ab} \times \|_{bc} - \|_{abc} - \|_{babc} - 2\|_c$$

is a subword history over the alphabet $\{a, b, c\}$. For the word $w = abcabc^2$ it assumes the value $3 \cdot 5 - 7 - 2 - 2 \cdot 3 = 0$.

Definition 3: Consider a subword history SH and an integer i. A word w *satisfies the subword history equation* (abbreviated SHE)

$$SH = i$$

if the value of SH in w equals i. A subword history equation is *elementary* if SH is monomial and i nonnegative.

Thus, the word $w = abcabc^2$ satisfies the subword history equation $SH = 0$, where SH is the subword history (not elementary) introduced before Definition 3. It would be no loss of generality to restrict Definition 3 to the case $i = 0$, because any positive integer i can be expressed as the sum with i copies of $\|_\lambda$. (Recall that $|w|_\lambda = 1$, for any w.)

We are now ready for the following fundamental definition. The notion is more general than the one defined in Ref. 13.

Definition 4: A *Boolean subword condition* (over an alphabet Σ), BSC, is defined recursively as follows.

- A subword history equation (over Σ) is a BSC. A word $w \in \Sigma^*$ *satisfies* this BSC if it satisfies the equation.
- If BSC_1 and BSC_2 are Boolean subword conditions, then so are $(BSC_1) \vee (BSC_2)$, $(BSC_1) \wedge (BSC_2)$ and $\neg(BSC_1)$. A word $w \in \Sigma^*$ *satisfies*

  $$(BSC_1) \vee (BSC_2)(\text{resp. } (BSC_1) \wedge (BSC_2))$$

  if it satisfies at least one of (resp. both of) BSC_1 and BSC_2. Finally, w *satisfies* $\neg(BSC_1)$ if it does not satisfy BSC_1.

A Boolean subword condition is *elementary* if each subword history equation appearing in it is elementary.

The *language* $L(BSC)$ *defined* (or *generated*) by a Boolean subword condition BSC consists of all words satisfying BSC.

Some additional remarks are in order. Again, the alphabet Σ is implicitly defined by the words appearing in a BSC. The negation $\neg$ can be expressed also by the inequality sign, and unnecessary parentheses can be omitted. Conjunctions of equations can be expressed as chains of equations. We may also move terms in an equation from one side to another in the natural way.

For instance, it is easy to see that every word $w \in \{a,b\}^*$ satisfies the BSC defined by the single equation $\|_a \times \|_b = \|_{ab} + \|_{ba}$. Hence, $L(BSC) = \{a,b\}^*$. We know from the preceding section that the language defined by the Boolean subword condition

$$\|_a = \|_b = \|_c \wedge \|_{abc} = (\|_a)^3 (\text{resp.} \|_a = 2\|_b \wedge \|_{aba} = (\|_b)^3)$$

equals $\{a^n b^n c^n | n \geq 0\}$ (resp. $\{a^n b^n a^n | n \geq 0\}$).

In conclusion, we present a couple of further results based on the preceding section. The (elementary) Boolean subword condition

$$\|_{ab} = 4 \wedge \|_a = 2 \wedge \|_{ba} = 2$$

defines the finite language $\{ba^2b^2, ab^2ab\}$. If BSC is the Boolean subword condition (not elementary!)

$$\|_a = \|_{aba}\,,$$

then $L(BSC) = b^*(\lambda + a^2ba^2 + ab^2a)b^*$.

4. Useful Reductions

In general, Boolean subword conditions constitute a very simple descriptive way of defining languages. Often it is very difficult to characterize languages $L(BSC)$ by other means. However, some reduction results can be presented, BSC's can be simplified. One such result will be presented below. Also, the characterization succeeds in some special cases. Such a case, based on an earlier result, will be presented in this section, and another case in the next section.

Making use of constructions involving the *shuffle operation*, $u \sqcup\!\sqcup v$, the following result was established in Ref. 4.

Lemma 1: *Every subword history is equivalent to a linear subword history. Moreover, a linear subword history equivalent to a given subword history can be effectively constructed.*

Clearly, two linear subword histories are equivalent if and only if they are identical, apart from the order of terms. Thus, we have a decision method for the equivalence of subword histories. Moreover, we obtain now the following theorem, as a consequence of Lemma 1.

Theorem 1: Given a Boolean subword condition BSC, another Boolean subword condition BSC' can be effectively constructed such that

$$L(BSC) = L(BSC')$$

and, moreover, every subword history equation in BSC' is linear.

Observe that, although the equivalence problem is decidable for subword histories, Theorem 1 does not give a decision method for the equivalence of languages $L(BSC)$. Indeed, such a decision method would also decide the inclusion problem for subword histories, known to be a very hard problem.[4,13]

For the techniques used in Lemma 1, the reader is referred to Ref. 4. We present here some examples.

Making use of the linear subword history equivalent to $(\|_a)^3$, the language $\{a^n b^n c^n | n \geq 0\}$ can be defined by the Boolean subword condition

$$\|_a = \|_b = \|_c \wedge \|_{abc} = 6\|_{a^3} + 6\|_{a^2} + \|_a \,.$$

Similarly, the language $\{a^n b^n c^n d^n | n \geq 0\}$ can be defined by the Boolean subword condition

$$\|_a = \|_b = \|_c = \|_d \wedge \|_{abcd} = 24\|_{a^4} + 36\|_{a^3} + 14\|_{a^2} + \|_a \,.$$

The subword histories

$$(\|_{ab})^2 \text{ and } 2\|_{abab} + 4\|_{a^2b^2} + 2\|_{a^2b} + 2\|_{ab^2} + \|_{ab}$$

are equivalent.

It is not difficult to construct, for a subword history equation, a linear bounded automaton accepting the set of words satisfying the equation. Therefore, we obtain the following result by the closure properties of context-sensitive languages.

Theorem 2: Every language defined by a Boolean subword condition is context-sensitive.

Quasi-uniform languages introduced in Ref. 7 play a central role in the theory of elementary subword history equations.

Definition 5: A language L over an alphabet Σ is *quasi-uniform* if, for some $m \geq 0$,

$$L = B_0^* b_1 B_2^* b_3 \cdots b_{2m-1} B_{2m}^* ,$$

where each b_i is a letter of the alphabet Σ, and each B_i is a subset (possibly empty) of Σ.

Observe that B_i^* reduces to the empty word when B_i is empty. Thus, there may be several consecutive letters in the regular expression but the subsets are always separated by a letter. It was shown in Ref. 13 that the set of words satisfying a given elementary subword history equation $SH = i$, $i > 0$, is a finite union of quasi-uniform languages and, hence, a star-free regular language. Moreover, a regular expression for it can be effectively constructed. Clearly, the set of words satisfying an elementary subword history equation $SH = 0$ is also effectively a star-free regular language. Hence, we obtain the following result, by the closure properties of star-free languages.

Theorem 3: If BSC is an elementary Boolean subword condition, then $L(BSC)$ is a star-free regular language. Moreover, a star-free regular expression can be effectively constructed for $L(BSC)$.

5. The Case of a-Separated Words

We have already pointed out that, in general, it is not easy to characterize languages defined by Boolean subword conditions using some other means. In this section we will present a detailed analysis in a specific case.

A subword history equation

$$\|_a = \|_u , \quad a \in \Sigma, \quad u \in \Sigma^+, \quad u \neq a ,$$

will be referred to as an *a-equation.* We will investigate Boolean subword conditions BSC determined by a single a-equation. The language $L(BSC)$ will in this case be denoted by $L(a, u)$. Recall that the languages $L(a, ab)$ and $L(a, aba)$ were already studied at the end of Section 2.

We have excluded the values $u = \lambda$ and $u = a$. Clearly, their inclusion would result into the simple languages

$$L(a, a) = \Sigma^* \text{ and } L(a, \lambda) = (\Sigma - \{a\})^* a (\Sigma - \{a\})^* .$$

It will turn out that the language $L(a, u)$ is essentially different if the word u is (resp. is not) *a-separated.* This notion will now be defined.

Definition 6: Let Σ be an alphabet and $a \in \Sigma$. A word $u \in \Sigma^+$ is *a-separated* if a is both a prefix and suffix of u and, moreover, u has no factor u_1 with the properties $|u_1| = 2$ and $|u_1|_a = 0$. An a-equation $\|_a = \|_u$ is termed a-separated if the word u is a-separated.

Thus, an a-separated word contains no two consecutive letters $\neq a$. If u is a-separated, then $|u|_a > |u|/2$.

The word u being a-separated affects an a-equation in the following way. Whenever u is a-separated and $w \in L(a,u)$, then no word w' is in $L(a,u)$, where

$$w = w_1 w_2 \,, \quad w' = w_1 a w_2 \,.$$

Thus, it is not possible to insert anywhere in w the letter a, and still stay in the language $L(a,u)$. We still need the following definition.

Definition 7: A word w is *minimal* for the a-equation $\|_a = \|_u$ if $w \in L(a,u)$ but no proper subword of w is in $L(a,u)$.

Thus neither one of two minimal words for the equation $\|_a = \|_u$ is a subword of the other. Minimal words need not be unique. For instance, both of the words a^2ba^2 and ab^2a are minimal for the equation $\|_a = \|_{aba}$.

Lemma 2: *Assume that the equation $\|_a = \|_u$ is a-separated, $w \in L(a,u)$ and $w = w_1 w_2$, for some (possibly empty) words w_1 and w_2. Then $w_1 a w_2 \notin L(a,u)$. Moreover, if w is minimal for the equation $\|_a = \|_u$, then $|w| < 2|u|$.*

Proof: Consider the first claim. We know that

$$|w|_a = |w|_u \,, \quad u = a u_1 a \,,$$

where u_1 does not contain two consecutive letters $\neq a$. (The possibility $u = a$ is excluded in the definition of an a-equation.) Thus, $|w|_a = |w|_u \geq 2$. Clearly,

$$|w_1 a w_2|_a = |w|_a + 1 \,.$$

We assert that

$$|w_1 a w_2|_u \geq |w|_u + 2 \,,$$

whence the first claim follows. Indeed, if w_1 (resp. w_2) does not contain an occurrence of a, then by replacing the first (resp. last) occurrence of a in w with the new occurrence of a, we get at least two new occurrences of u. The same holds true if both w_1 and w_2 contain an occurrence of a. Then we use the fact that u_1 does not contain two consecutive letters $\neq a$, and replace the closest among the a's in u with the new occurrence of a. (For instance, if

$$u = aba\,, \quad w = ab^2a\,, \quad w_1 = ab\,, \quad w_2 = ba\,,$$

then in *ababa* the middle a creates a new occurrence of *aba* both with the first and the last a.)

Consider next the second claim, and let w be minimal. Since u is a subword of w, the word w results from u by inserting letters successively. Let u contain t (≥ 2) occurrences of a. Thus, we have initially

$$|u| \geq |u|_a = t \geq 2 \text{ and } |u|_u = 1\,,$$

and finally, after inserting letters to u,

$$|w|_a = |w|_u\,.$$

On the other hand, the insertion of each letter $b \neq a$ increases the number of occurrences of u at least by one, whereas the number of occurrences of a remains unaltered. (If the number of occurrences of u does not increase, we have a contradiction with the minimality.) As seen in the first part of the proof, the insertion of a always increases the number of occurrences of u. The increase is at least two beginning with the second insertion of a. Consequently, the insertion of each letter (with the possible exception of the first a) increases the (originally negative) difference $|u|_u - |u|_a$ at least by one, whence the estimate $|w| < 2|u|$ follows. □

Lemma 3: *If the word w is minimal for an a-separated equation $||_a = ||_u$, then the subset $L_w(a,u)$ of $L(a,u)$, consisting of all words that contain w as a subword, is quasi-uniform.*

Proof: We know from Lemma 2 that we cannot insert the letter a to w and stay in the language $L(a,u)$. If we insert a letter $b \neq a$, the number of occurrences of u as a subword should not change. This means that we can insert to the position in question the entire set B^*, where B is the subalphabet of such letters b. Thus, a quasi-uniform language results.

We are now ready for the main result. □

Theorem 4: The language $L(a,u)$ defined by an a-equation $||_a = ||_u$ is

(1) A finite union of quasi-uniform languages if u is a-separated,
(2) Context-free and nonregular if u is not a-separated and $|u| = 1$,
(3) Non-context-free but context-sensitive, otherwise.

Proof: Clearly, every word in $L(a,u)$ contains a minimal subword. Hence, (1) is a direct consequence of the last sentence of Lemma 2, and Lemma 3. In the case of (2), a context-free grammar was given already in the Introduction. (Clearly, the language is not regular.) In the case of (3), the language $L(a,u)$ is context-sensitive by Theorem 2. We will prove that it is not context-free.

Thus, assume that u is not a-separated and $|u| \geq 2$. Suppose first that a is not a suffix of u. (The case of a being not a prefix is handled similarly.) Thus,

$$u = b_1 \cdots b_t b\,, \quad b \neq a\,, \quad t \geq 1\,,$$

where each b is a letter. We assume for simplicity that b_1 and b are different from their neighbors. If this is not the case, the argument below will remain the same but the definition of the function γ has to be slightly modified.

Consider now the intersection

$$L' = L(a,u) \cap b_1^+ b_2 \cdots b_t b^+ a^*\,.$$

Assume that $r(\geq 0)$ of the letters $b_2, \ldots, b_t$ are equal to a, and define, for $i,\, j \geq 1$,

$$\gamma(i,j) = \begin{cases} ij - i - r & \text{if } a = b_1\,, \\ ij - r & \text{if } a \neq b_1\,. \end{cases}$$

Then

$$L' = \{b_1^i b_2 \cdots b_t b^j a^{\gamma(i,j)} | i,j \geq 1\}\,.$$

(Only words with a nonnegative value of $\gamma(i,j)$ are included in L'.) By the Pumping Lemma, L' is not context-free. Hence, $L(a,u)$ is not context-free.

Assume then that a is both a prefix and suffix of u but u contains two consecutive letters $\neq a$. Thus, we may write u in the form

$$u = ab_1 \cdots b_s bcc_1 \cdots c_t a\,, \quad s,t \geq 0\,, \quad b \neq a\,, \quad c \neq a\,,$$

where the b's and c's are letters and possibly $b = c$. As in the first part of the proof, we assume here for simplicity that $a \neq b_1$ and $c \neq c_1$. We consider now the intersection

$$L' = L(a,u) \cap a^+ b_1 \cdots b_s b a^* c^+ c_1 \cdots c_t a\,.$$

Assume that $r \geq 0$ of the letters $b_1, \ldots, b_s, c_1 \ldots, c_t$ equal a, and define, for $i,\, j \geq 1$,

$$\gamma(i,j) = \begin{cases} ij - i - r & \text{if } b \neq c\,, \\ i\binom{j+1}{2} - i - r & \text{if } b = c\,. \end{cases}$$

Then

$$L' = \{a^i b_1 \cdots b_s b a^{\gamma(i,j)} c^j c_1 \cdots c_t a | i, j \geq 1\}.$$

We conclude as before that $L(a, u)$ is not context-free. This completes the proof of the Theorem. □

We conclude this section with some examples. If $u = a^i$, $i \geq 2$, then $L(a, u)$ is the singleton $\{a^{i+1}\}$. (In this case it is natural to assume that the alphabet consists of the letter a.) The previously considered language $L(a, aba)$ is the union of three quasi-uniform languages:

$$L(a, aba) = b^* \cup b^* a^2 b a^2 b^* \cup b^* a b^2 a b^*.$$

Observe that $|a^2ba^2| < 2|aba|$, as it should be by Lemma 2. Another example is

$$L(a, a^2ba) = b^* \cup b^* a^2 b^3 a b^* \cup b^* a^2 b^2 a^2 b^*.$$

The union of quasi-uniform languages defining the language $L(a, abaca)$ is quite complicated, one of the terms of the union being

$$\{b, c\}^* a c^* b c^* b c^* b c^* a b^* c b^* a \{b, c\}^*.$$

We know that the language $La, ab)$ is not context-free. An explicit expression for this language is

$$\{\lambda\} \cup b^* \{a b^{r_1} \cdots a b^{r_k} a^{\Sigma_{j=1}^{k} j r_j - k} | k \geq 1, \quad r_j \geq 0\}.$$

6. Languages Associated with Parikh Matrices

Boolean subword conditions can be expressed as properties of entries in certain upper triangular square matrices. Such matrices, nowadays generally called *Parikh matrices*, were originally introduced in Ref. 3, and the generalized version in Ref. 14. They are very closely connected with the topic of the present paper but are by no means the only generalizations of Parikh vectors introduced in the past. We mention here the generalization introduced and discussed in Refs. 15 and 16. It characterizes a word completely but, unlike the Parikh matrix, it is not directly applicable to monoid morphisms because, in catenations, one has to take care of the appropriate translation.

Consider upper triangular square matrices, with nonnegative integer entries, 1's on the main diagonal and 0's below it. The set of all such matrices is denoted by $\mathcal{M}$, and the subset of all matrices of dimension

$k \geq 1$ is denoted by $\mathcal{M}_k$. We will define below the generalized version of the Parikh matrix. We first recall the definition of the "Kronecker delta". For letters a and b,

$$\delta_{a,b} = \begin{cases} 1 & \text{if } a = b\,, \\ 0 & \text{if } a \neq b\,. \end{cases}$$

Definition 8: Let $u = b_1 \cdots b_t$ be a word, where each b_i, $1 \leq i \leq t$, is a letter of the alphabet Σ. The *Parikh matrix mapping with respect to* u, denoted Ψ_u, is the morphism:

$$\Psi_u : \Sigma^* \to \mathcal{M}_{t+1}\,,$$

defined, for $a \in \Sigma$, by the condition: if $\Psi_u(a) = M_u(a) = (m_{i,j})_{1 \leq i,j \leq (t+1)}$, then for each $1 \leq i \leq (t+1)$, $m_{i,i} = 1$, and for each $1 \leq i \leq t$, $m_{i,i+1} = \delta_{a,b_i}$, all other elements of the matrix $M_u(a)$ being 0. Matrices of the form $\Psi_u(w)$, $w \in \Sigma^*$, are referred to as *generalized Parikh matrices.*

Thus, the Parikh matrix $M_u(w)$ associated to a word w is obtained by multiplying the matrices $M_u(a)$ associated to the letters a of w, in the order in which the letters appear in w. The above definition implies that if a letter a does not occur in u, then the matrix $M_u(a)$ is the identity matrix.

For instance, if $u = abcba$, then

$$M_u(a) = \begin{pmatrix} 1 & 1 & 0 & 0 & 0 & 0 \\ 0 & 1 & 0 & 0 & 0 & 0 \\ 0 & 0 & 1 & 0 & 0 & 0 \\ 0 & 0 & 0 & 1 & 0 & 0 \\ 0 & 0 & 0 & 0 & 1 & 1 \\ 0 & 0 & 0 & 0 & 0 & 1 \end{pmatrix}.$$

Similarly,

$$M_u(b) = \begin{pmatrix} 1 & 0 & 0 & 0 & 0 & 0 \\ 0 & 1 & 1 & 0 & 0 & 0 \\ 0 & 0 & 1 & 0 & 0 & 0 \\ 0 & 0 & 0 & 1 & 1 & 0 \\ 0 & 0 & 0 & 0 & 1 & 0 \\ 0 & 0 & 0 & 0 & 0 & 1 \end{pmatrix}, \quad M_u(c) = \begin{pmatrix} 1 & 0 & 0 & 0 & 0 & 0 \\ 0 & 1 & 0 & 0 & 0 & 0 \\ 0 & 0 & 1 & 1 & 0 & 0 \\ 0 & 0 & 0 & 1 & 0 & 0 \\ 0 & 0 & 0 & 0 & 1 & 0 \\ 0 & 0 & 0 & 0 & 0 & 1 \end{pmatrix}.$$

In the original definition of a Parikh matrix,[3] the word u was chosen to be $u = a_1 \cdots a_k$, for the alphabet $\Sigma = \{a_1, \ldots, a_k\}$. In the general setup, the main result can be formulated as follows. For $1 \leq i \leq j \leq t$, denote $\beta_{i,j} = b_i \cdots b_j$. Denote the entries of the matrix $M_u(w)$ by $m_{i,j}$.

Theorem 5: For all i and j, $1 \le i \le j \le t$, we have $m_{i,1+j} = |w|_{\beta_{i,j}}$.

Going back to our example $u = abcba$, we infer from Theorem 5 that, for any word w,

$$M_u(w) = \begin{pmatrix} 1 & |w|_a & |w|_{ab} & |w|_{abc} & |w|_{abcb} & |w|_{abcba} \\ 0 & 1 & |w|_b & |w|_{bc} & |w|_{bcb} & |w|_{bcba} \\ 0 & 0 & 1 & |w|_c & |w|_{cb} & |w|_{cba} \\ 0 & 0 & 0 & 1 & |w|_b & |w|_{ba} \\ 0 & 0 & 0 & 0 & 1 & |w|_a \\ 0 & 0 & 0 & 0 & 0 & 1 \end{pmatrix}.$$

For $w = a(bc)^5ba$ we obtain

$$M_u(w) = \begin{pmatrix} 1 & 2 & 6 & 15 & 35 & 35 \\ 0 & 1 & 6 & 15 & 35 & 35 \\ 0 & 0 & 1 & 5 & 15 & 15 \\ 0 & 0 & 0 & 1 & 6 & 6 \\ 0 & 0 & 0 & 0 & 1 & 2 \\ 0 & 0 & 0 & 0 & 0 & 1 \end{pmatrix}.$$

By Theorem 5, Boolean subword conditions can be expressed in terms of generalized Parikh matrices as follows. Let BSC be a given Boolean subword condition. Consider the (finite) set of words u such that $\|_u$ appears in BSC. Let v, $|v| = t$, be a word such that each of these words u appears as a *factor* of v. We can choose v to be the catenation of all such words u, although in most cases a much shorter v will suffice. Consider the generalized Parikh matrices M_v of dimension $t+1$. By Theorem 5, for each word u such that $\|_u$ appears in BSC, a specific entry in the matrix $M_v(w)$ equals the value $|w|_u$. This happens for all words w, and the entry depends on u but is independent of w. (Indeed, there may be several such entries, since u may appear several times as a factor of v.) These considerations lead to the following result.

Theorem 6: For a given Boolean subword condition BSC, a word v, $|v| = t$, can be constructed such that the generalized Parikh matrix mapping Ψ_v has the following property. To every item $\|_u$ in BSC, there corresponds a specific entry in the matrices in $\mathcal{M}_{t+1}$. A word w is in $L(BSC)$ if and only if BSC is satisfied when the entries in the in the matrix $\Psi_v(w)$ are substituted for the corresponding items $\|_u$ in BSC.

We conclude with a couple of applications of Theorem 6. The language $L(a, ab)$ (considered at the end of the last section) consists of all words w

such that in the generalized Parikh matrix $M_{ab}(w)$ the entries (1, 2) and (1, 3) coincide.

Consider the Boolean subword condition BSC defined by

$$(\|_{ab} = \|_{ba} = \|_{b}) \wedge (\|_{bc} = \|_{cb} = \|_{abc} = \|_{cba}) \wedge (\|_{abcb} = \|_{bcba} = \|_{bcb} = \|_{abcba}) \,.$$

A word w is in $L(BSC)$ if and only if the entries of the matrix $\Psi_{abcba}(w)$ coincide in each of the following three sets:

$$\{(1,3),(2,3),(4,6)\},\ \{(1,4),(2,4),(3,5),(3,6)\},\ \{(1,5),(1,6),(2,5),(2,6)\}.$$

Each of the words $a(bc)^i ba$, $i \geq 0$, is in $L(BSC)$.

Considering the matrices $\Psi_{abcba}(w)$, one can also prove that the language defined by the Boolean subword condition

$$\|_{abcb} \times \|_{cba} + 1 = \|_{abcba} \times \|_{cb}$$

is empty.

References

1. S. Fossé and G. Richomme, Some characterizations of Parikh matrix equivalent binary words. Manuscript (2003).
2. W. Kuich and A. Salomaa, *Semirings, Automata, Languages.* Springer-Verlag, Berlin, Heidelberg, New York, 1986.
3. A. Mateescu, A. Salomaa, K. Salomaa and S. Yu, A sharpening of the Parikh mapping. *Theoret. Informatics Appl.* 35 (2001) 551–564.
4. A. Mateescu, A. Salomaa and S. Yu, Subword histories and Parikh matrices. *J. Comput. Syst. Sci.* 68 (2004) 1–21.
5. A. Mateescu and A. Salomaa, Matrix indicators for subword occurrences and ambiguity. *Int. J. Found. Comput. Sci* 15 (2004) 277–292.
6. R. J. Parikh, On context-free languages. *J. Assoc. Comput. Mach.* 13 (1966) 570–581.
7. G. Rozenberg, Decision problems for quasi-uniform events. *Bull. Acad. Polon. Sci.* XV (1967) 745–752.
8. G. Rozenberg and A. Salomaa (eds.), *Handbook of Formal Languages 1–3.* Springer-Verlag, Berlin, Heidelberg, New York (1997).
9. J. Sakarovitch and I. Simon, Subwords. In M. Lothaire: *Combinatorics on Words*, Addison-Wesley, Reading, Mass. (1983) 105–142.
10. A. Salomaa, Counting (scattered) subwords. *EATCS Bulletin* 81 (2003) 165–179.
11. A. Salomaa, On the injectivity of Parikh matrix mappings. TUCS Technical Report 601 (2004), to appear in *Fundamenta Informaticae.*
12. A. Salomaa, Connections between subwords and certain matrix mappings. TUCS Technical Report 620 (2004), to appear in *Theoretical Computer Science.*

13. A. Salomaa and S. Yu, Subword conditions and subword histories. TUCS Technical Report 633 (2004), submitted for publication.
14. T.-F. Şerbănuţă, Extending Parikh matrices. *Theoretical Computer Science* 310 (2004) 233–246.
15. R. Siromoney and V. R. Dare, A generalization of the Parikh vector for finite and infinite words. *Springer Lecture Notes in Computer Science* 206 (1985) 290–302.
16. G. Siromoney, R. Siromoney, K. G. Subramanian, V. R. Dare and P. J. Abisha, Generalized Parikh vector and public key cryptosystems. In Narasimhan, R. (ed.) *A Perspective in Theoretical Computer Science, Commemorative Volume for Gift Siromoney*, World Scientific (1989) 301–323.

CHAPTER 23

AN APPLICATION OF REGULAR TREE GRAMMARS

Priti Shankar

Department of Computer Science and Automation,
Indian Institute of Science, Bangalore 560012, India

We describe a technique for the automatic generation of instruction selectors from tree grammar specifications of machine instructions. The technique is an extension of the LR parsing approach and constructs a finite state automaton that controls the tree-parsing process. The specification of actions along with the rules of the tree grammar enables a syntax directed translation into machine level instructions.

1. Introduction

One of the final phases in a typical compiler is the *instruction selection* phase. This traverses an intermediate representation of the source code and selects a sequence of target machine instructions that implement the code. There are two aspects to this task. The first one has to do with finding efficient algorithms for generating an optimal instruction sequence with reference to some measure of optimality. The second has to do with the automatic generation of instruction selection programs from precise specifications of machine instructions. Achieving the second aim is a first step towards retargetabiltiy of code generators. The seminal work of Hoffman and O'Donnell[4] and Chase[3] provided new approaches that could be adopted for retargetable code generation. They considered the general problem of pattern matching in trees with operators of fixed arity and presented algorithms for both top-down and bottom-up tree pattern matching. Hoffmann and O'Donnell showed that if tables encoding the automaton could be precomputed, then matching could be achieved in linear time. Several tools for generating retargetable code generators were designed based on these ideas; these are described in Ref. 6. Matching in the context of this paper is actually parsing of an input subject tree, which is an intermediate representation (IR) tree. The tree is said to have been *reduced* to the start symbol of a regular tree grammar by a tree parsing process, which implicitly constructs a derivation tree for the subject tree. The sequence of productions used is a *cover* for the tree. In general, there are several covers, given a set of productions, and we aim to obtain the best one according to some measure of optimality. A simplified form of the dynamic programming algorithm of Aho and Johnson[1] is used in most code generator tools where what is computed at each node is a set of (rule, scalar cost) pairs. The rule is the production used at that node in the cover and the cost is the cost of the computation of the subtree rooted at that node. The cost associated with a subtree is computed either at compile time (i.e. dynamically), by using cost rules provided in the grammar specification, or by simply adding the costs of the children to the cost of the operation at the root, or at compiler generation time (i.e. statically), by precomputing differential costs and storing them along with the instructions that match as part of the state information of a tree pattern matching automaton. How exactly this is done will become clear in the following sections.

2. Regular Tree Grammars and Tree Parsing

Let A be a finite alphabet consisting of a set of operators OP and a set of terminals T. Each operator *op* in OP is associated with an *arity*, $arity(op)$. Elements of T have arity 0. The set $TREES(A)$ consists of all trees with internal nodes labeled with elements of OP, and leaves with labels from T. Such trees are called *subject trees* in this chapter. The number of children of a node labeled *op* is $arity(op)$. Special symbols called *wildcards* are assumed to have arity 0. If N is a set of wildcards, the set $TREES(A \cup N)$ is the set of all trees with wildcards also allowed as labels of leaves.

We begin with a few definitions.

Definition 1: A *regular cost augmented tree grammar* G is a four tuple (N, A, P, S) where:

(1) N is a finite set of *nonterminal* symbols.
(2) $A = T \cup OP$ is a *ranked alphabet*, with the ranking function denoted by arity. T is the set of *terminal* symbols and OP is the set of *operators*.

(3) P is a finite set of *production rules* of the form $X \to t[c]$ where $X \in N$ and t is an encoding of a tree in $TREES(A \cup N)$, and c is a cost, which is a non negative integer.
(4) S is the *start symbol* of the grammar.

A *tree pattern* is thus represented by the righthand side of a production of P in the grammar above. A production of P is called a *chain rule*, if it is of the form $A \to B$, where both A and B are nonterminals.

Definition 2: A production is said to be in normal form if it is in one of the three forms below.

(1) $A \to op(B_1, B_2, \ldots, B_k)[c]$ where A, B_i, $i = 1, 2, \ldots, k$ are all non terminals, and op has arity k.
(2) $A \to B[c]$, where A and B are non terminals. Such a production is called a *chain rule*.
(3) $B \to b[c]$, where b is a terminal.

A grammar is in normal form if all its productions are in normal form. Any regular tree grammar can be put into normal form by the introduction of extra nonterminals and zero-cost rules.

Below is an example of a cost augmented regular tree grammar in normal form. Arities of symbols in the alphabet are shown in parentheses next to the symbol.

Example 1: $G = (\{V, B, G\}, \{a(2), b(0)\}, P, V)$

$$
\begin{array}{lll}
P: & & \\
& V \to a(V, B) & [0] \\
& V \to a(G, V) & [1] \\
& V \to G & [1] \\
& G \to B & [1] \\
& V \to b & [7] \\
& B \to b & [4]
\end{array}
$$

Definition 3: For t, $t' \in TREES(A \cup N)$, t directly derives t', written as $t \Rightarrow t'$ if t' can be obtained from t by replacement of a leaf of t labeled X by a tree p where $X \to p \in P$. We write $\Rightarrow_r$ if we wish to specify that rule r is used in a derivation step. The relations $\Rightarrow^+$ and $\Rightarrow^*$ are the transitive closure and reflexive-transitive closure respectively of $\Rightarrow$.

An X-derivation tree, D_X, for G has the following properties:

- The root of the tree has label X.
- If X is an internal node, then the subtree rooted at X is one of the following three types; (For describing trees we use the usual list notation)
  (1) $X(D_Y)$ if $X \to Y$ is a chain rule and D_Y is a derivation tree rooted at Y.
  (2) $X(a)$ if $X \to a$, $a \in T$ is a production of P.
  (3) $X(op(D_{X_1}, D_{X_2}, \ldots, D_{X_k}))$ if $X \to op(X_1, X_2 \cdots X_k)$ is an element of P.

The language defined by the grammar is the set

$$L(G) = \{t | t \in TREES(A)\,,\ \text{and } S \Longrightarrow^* t\}$$

With each derivation tree, is associated a cost, namely, the sum of the costs of all the productions used in constructing the derivation tree. We label each nonterminal in the derivation tree with the cost of the subtree below it. Four cost augmented derivation trees for the subject tree $a(a(b, b), b)$ in the language generated by the regular tree grammar of Example 1 above, are displayed in Fig. 1.

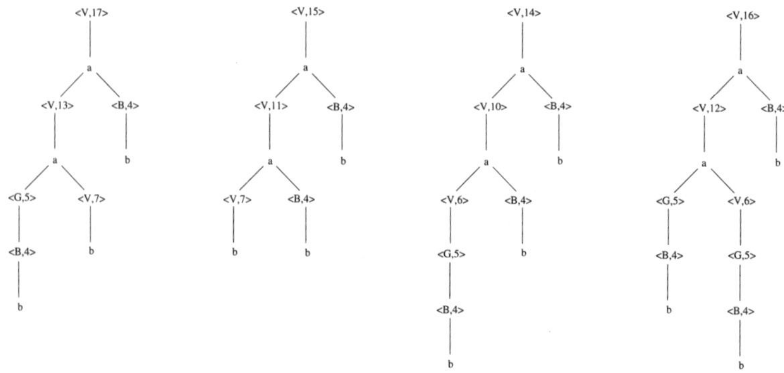

Fig. 1. Four cost-augmented derivation trees for the subject tree $a(a(b, b), b)$ in the grammar of Example 1.

Definition 4: A rule $r : X \to p$ matches a tree t if there exists a derivation $X \Rightarrow_r p \Rightarrow^* t$.

Definition 5: A nonterminal X matches a tree t if there exists a rule of the form $X \to p$ which matches t

Definition 6: A rule or nonterminal matches a tree t at node n if the rule or nonterminal matches the subtree rooted at the node n.

Each derivation tree for a subject tree thus defines a set of matching rules at each node in the subject tree, (a *set* because there may be chain rules that also match at the node).

Example 2: For all the derivation trees of Fig. 1 the rule $V \rightarrow a(V, B)$ matches at the root.

For a rule $r : X \rightarrow p$ matching a tree t at node n, where t_1 is the subtree rooted at node n, we define

(1) the cost of rule r matching t at node n. It is the minimum of the cost of all possible derivations of the form $X \Rightarrow_r p \Rightarrow^* t_1$.
(2) the cost of nonterminal X matching t at node n as the minimum of the cost of all rules r of the form $X \rightarrow p$ which match t_1.

Typically, any algorithm that does dynamic cost computations, compares the costs of all possible derivation trees and selects one with minimal costs while computing matches. To do this it has to compute for each nonterminal that matches at a node, the minimal cost of reducing to that nonterminal (or equivalently, deriving the portion of the subject tree rooted at that node from the nonterminal.) In contrast, algorithms that perform static cost computations, precompute relative costs, and store differential costs for nonterminals. Thus, the cost associated with a rule r at a particular node in a subject tree, is the difference between the minimum cost of deriving the subtree of the subject tree rooted at that node using rule r at the first step, and the minimum cost of deriving it using any other rule at the first step. Figure 2 shows the matching rules with relative costs at the nodes of the subject tree for which derivation trees are displayed in Fig. 1. Assuming such differences are bounded for all possible derivation trees of the grammar, they can be stored as part of the information in the states of a finite state tree parsing automaton. Thus no cost analysis need be done at matching time. Clearly, tables encoding the tree automaton with static costs tend to be larger than those without cost information in the states.

The *tree-parsing problem* we will address in this paper is:

Given a regular tree grammar $G = (N, T, P, S)$, and a subject tree t in $TREES(A)$, find (a representation of) all S-derivation trees for t.

The problem of computing an optimal derivation tree has to take into account costs as well. We will describing an algorithm based on LR-parsing

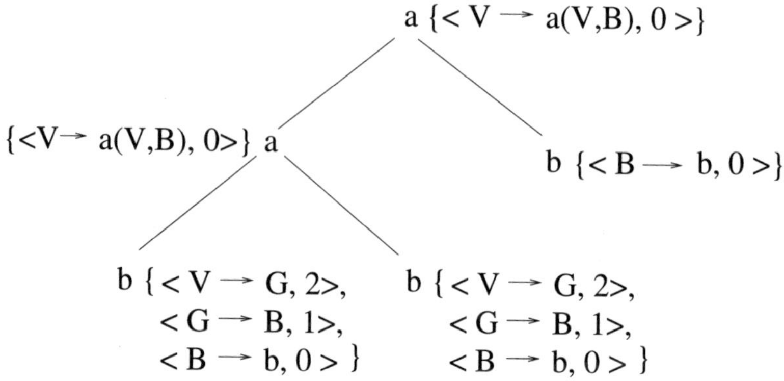

Fig. 2. Subject tree of Fig. 1 shown with <matching rule,relative cost> pairs.

for solving this problem. The algorithm we will present will solve the following problem, which we will call the *optimal tree-parsing problem*:

Given a cost augmented regular tree grammar G and a subject tree t in $TREES(A)$, *find a representation of a cheapest derivation tree for t in G.*

Given an specification of the target machine by a regular tree grammar at the semantic level of a target machine, and an IR tree, we distinguish between the following two times when we solve the optimal tree-parsing problem for the IR tree.

(1) **Preprocessing time:** This is the time required to process the input grammar, independent of the IR tree. It typically includes the time taken to build the matching automaton or the tables.
(2) **Matching Time:** This involves all IR tree dependent operations, and captures the time taken by the driver to match a given IR tree using the tables created during the preprocessing phase. The matching phase typically folllowed by an instruction selection pass where a suitable machine instruction or a sequence of machine instructions is output for the selected match at each node.

For the application of instruction selection, minimizing matching time is important since it adds to compile time, whereas preprocessing is done only once at compiler generation time.

3. Techniques Extending LR-Parsers

The technique described here can be viewed as an extension of the $LR(0)$ parsing strategy and is based on the work reported in Ref. 6. Let G' be the context free grammar obtained by replacing all right-hand sides of productions of G by postorder listings of the corresponding trees in $TREES(A \cup N)$. Note that G is a regular tree grammar whose associated language contains trees, whereas G' is a context free grammar whose language contains strings with symbols from A. Of course, these strings are just the linear encodings of trees.

Let $post(t)$ denote the postorder listing of the nodes of a tree t. The following (rather obvious) claim underlies the algorithm:

A tree t is in $L(G)$ if and only if $post(t)$ is in $L(G')$. Also any tree α in $TREES(A \cup N)$ that has an associated $S-$derivation tree in G has an unique sentential form $post(\alpha)$ of G' associated with it.

The problem of finding matches at any node of a subject tree t is equivalent to that of parsing the string corresponding to the postorder listing of the nodes of t. Assuming a bottom up parsing strategy is used, parsing corresponds to reducing the string to the start symbol, by a sequence of *shift* and *reduce* moves on the parsing stack, with a match of rule r being reported at node j whenever r is used to reduce by at the corresponding position in the string.Thus a *deterministic pushdown automaton* is constructed for the purpose.

3.1. *Extension of the LR(0) Parsing Algorithm*

We assume that the reader is familiar with the notions of rightmost derivation sequences, handles, viable prefixes of right sentential forms, and items being valid for viable prefixes. Definitions may be found in Ref. 5. The meaning of an *item* in this section corresponds to that understood in LR parsing theory. By a viable prefix *induced* by an input string is the stack contents that result from processing the input string during an LR parsing sequence. If the grammar is ambiguous, then there may be several viable prefixes induced by an input string.

The key idea used in the algorithm is contained in the theorem stated below.[7]

Theorem 1: Let G' be a normal form context free grammar derived from a regular tree grammar. Then all viable prefixes induced by an input string are of the same length.

In order to apply the algorithm to the problem of tree pattern matching, the notion of *matching*, is refined to one of *matching in a left context.*

Definition 7: Let n be any node in a tree t. A subtree t_i is said to be to the left of node n in the tree, if the node m at which the subtree t_i is rooted occurs before n in a postorder listing of t. t_i is said to be a maximal subtree to the left of n if it is not a proper subtree of any subtree that is also to the left of n.

Definition 8: Let $G = (N, T, P, S)$ be a regular tree grammar in normal form, and t be a subject tree. Then rule $X \rightarrow \beta$ matches at node j in left context α, $\alpha \in N^*$ if

(1) $X \rightarrow \beta$ matches at node j or equivalently, $X \Rightarrow \beta \Rightarrow^* t'$ where t' is the subtree rooted at j.
(2) If α is not ϵ, then the sequence of maximal complete subtrees of t to the left of j, listed from left to right is $t_1, t_2, \ldots, t_k$, with t_i having an X_i-derivation tree, $1 \leq i \leq k$, where $\alpha = X_1 X_2 \cdots X_k$.
(3) The string $X_1 X_2 \cdots X_k X$ is a prefix of the postorder listing of some tree in $TREES(A \cup N)$ with an $S-$derivation.

Example 3: Consider the context free grammar below.

$$\begin{array}{ll}
1.\ stmt \rightarrow addr\ reg := & [1] \\
2.\ addr \rightarrow reg\ con\ + & [0] \\
3.\ addr \rightarrow reg & [0] \\
4.\ reg \rightarrow reg\ con+ & [1] \\
5.\ reg \rightarrow con & [1] \\
6.\ con \rightarrow CONST & [0]
\end{array}$$

Consider the subject tree of Fig. 3 and the derivation tree alongside. The rule $con \rightarrow CONST$ matches at node 2 in left context ϵ. The rule $con \rightarrow CONST$ matches at node 3 in left context $addr$. The rule $reg \rightarrow reg\ con\ +$ matches at node 5 in left context $addr$.

The following property forms the basis of the algorithm.

Let t a subject tree with postorder listing $a_1 \cdots a_j w$, $a_i \in A, w \in A^*$. Then rule $X \rightarrow \beta$ matches at node j in left context α if and only if there is a rightmost derivation in the grammar G' of the form

$$S \Rightarrow^* \alpha X z \Rightarrow^* \alpha post(\beta) z \Rightarrow^* \alpha a_h \cdots a_j z \Rightarrow^* a_1 \cdots a_j z\,, \quad z \in A^*$$

where $a_h \cdots a_j$ is the subtree rooted at node j.

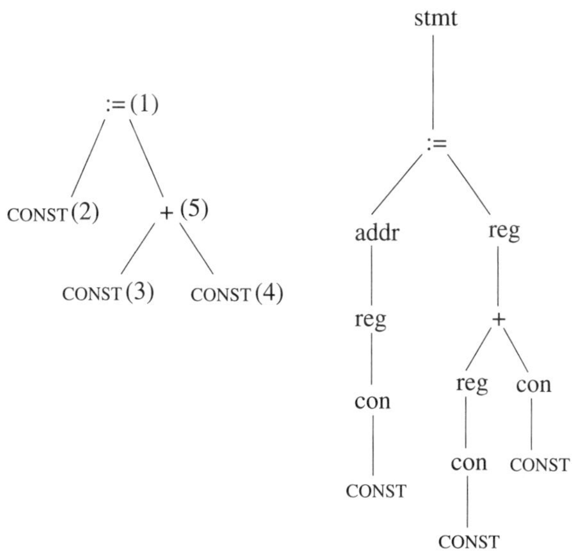

Fig. 3. A derivation tree for a subject tree derived by the grammar of Example 3.

Since there is a direct correspondence between obtaining rightmost derivation sequences in G' and finding matches of rules in G, the possibility of using an LR-like parsing strategy for tree parsing is obvious. Since all viable prefixes are of the same length a deterministic finite automaton (DFA) can be constructed that recognizes *sets* of viable prefixes. We call this device the *auxiliary automaton.* The grammar is first augmented with the production $Z \to S\$$ to make it prefix free. Next, the auxiliary automaton is constructed; this plays the role that a DFA for canonical set of LR items does in an LR parsing process. We first explain how this automaton is constructed without costs. The automaton M is defined as follows:

$$M = (Q, \Sigma, \delta, q_0, F)$$

where each state of Q contains a set of items of the grammar:

$\Sigma = A \cup 2^N$

$q_0 \in Q$ is the start state

F is the state containing the item $Z \longrightarrow S\$$.

$\delta : Q \times (A \cup 2^N) \mapsto Q$

Transitions of the automaton are thus either on terminals or on sets of nonterminals. A set of nonterminals will label an edge iff all the nonterminals in the set match some subtree of a tree in the language generated by the regular tree grammar *in the same left context.* The precomputation of M is similar to the precomputation of the states of the DFA for canonical sets of $LR(0)$ items for a context free grammar. However there is one important difference. In the DFA for $LR(0)$ items, transitions on nonterminals are determined just by looking at the sets of items in any state. Here we have transitions on *sets* of non terminals. These can not be determined in advance, as we do not know a priori, which rules are matched simultaneously when matching is begun from a given state. Therefore, transitions on sets of non terminals are added as and when these sets are determined.

Informally, at each step, we compute the set of items generated by making a transition on some element of A. Because the grammar is in normal form, each such transition leads to a state, termed a *matchset* which calls for a reduction by one or more productions called *match_rules*. Since all productions corresponding to a given operator are of the same length (because operator arities are fixed and the grammar is in normal form), a reduction involves popping off a set of right-hand sides from the parsing stack, and making a transition on a set of nonterminals corresponding to the left-hand sides of all productions by which we have performed reductions, from each state (called an *LCset*) that can be exposed on stack after popping off the set of handles. This gives us, perhaps, a new state, which is then added to the collection if it is not present. Two tables encode the automaton. The first, δ_A, encodes the transitions on elements of A. Thus it has, as row indices, the indices of the *LCsets*, and as columns, elements of A. The second, δ_{LC}, encodes the transitions of the automaton on sets of non terminals. The rows are indexed by *LCsets*, and the columns by indices of sets of nonterminals. The operation of the matcher, which is effectively a tree parser, is defined in Fig. 4.

Clearly, the algorithm is linear in the size of the subject tree. It remains to describe the precomputation of the auxiliary automaton coded by the tables δ_A and δ_{LC}.

3.2. *Precomputation of tables*

The start state of the auxiliary automaton contains the same set of items as would the start state of the DFA for sets of $LR(0)$ items. From each state, say q, identified to be a state of the auxiliary automaton, we find the state entered on a symbol of A, say a. (This depends only on the set of items in the first state). The second state, say m (which we will refer to as

procedure $TreeParser(a, M, matchpairs)$
// The input string of length $n+1$ including the end marker is in array a
// M is the DFA (constructed from the context free grammar) which controls the parsing process with transition functions δ_A and δ_{LC}.
// $matchpairs$ is a set of pairs (i, m) such that the set of rules in m matches at node i in a left context induced by the sequence of complete subtrees to the left of i.
$stack = q_0$; $matchpairs = \emptyset$
$current\_state = q_0$
for $i = 1$ **to** n **do**
  $current\_state := \delta_A(current\_state, a[i])$;
  $match\_rules = current\_state.match\_rules$
  // The entry in the table δ_A directly gives the set of rules matched.
  $pop(stack)$ $arity(a[i]) + 1$ times;
  $current\_state := \delta_{LC}(topstack, S_m)$;
  //S_m is the set of nonterminals matched after chain rule application
  $match\_rules = match\_rules \cup current\_state.match\_rules$
  // add matching rules corresponding to chain rules that are matched
  $matchpairs = matchpairs \cup \{(i, match\_rules)\}$
  $push(current\_state)$
end for
end procedure

Fig. 4. Procedure for tree parsing using bottom up context free parsing approach.

a matchstate), will contain only complete items. We then set $\delta_A(q, a)$ to the pair $(match\_rules(m), S_m)$, where $match\_rules(m)$ is the set of rules that match at this point, and S_m is the set of left-hand side nonterminals of the associated productions of the context free grammar. Next we determine all states that have paths of length $arity(a) + 1$ to q. We refer to such states as *valid left context* states, for q. These are the states that can be exposed on stack while performing a reduction, after the handle is popped off the stack. If p is such a state then we compute the state r corresponding to the itemset got by making transitions on elements of S_m augmented by all nonterminals that can be reduced to because of chain rules. These new item sets are computed using the usual rules that are used for computing sets of $LR(0)$ items. Finally, the *closure* operation on resulting items completes the new item set associated with r. The closure operation here is the conventional one used for constructing canonical sets of LR items.[2]

Computing states that have paths of the appropriate length to a given state is expensive. A very good approximation is computed by the function $Validlc$ in Fig. 5. This function just examines the sets of items in a

```
function Validlc(p, m)
if NTSET(p, rhs(m)) = S_m then
  Validlc := true
else
  Validlc := false
end if
end function
```

Fig. 5. Function to compute valid left contexts.

matchstate and a candidate left context state and decides whether the candidate is a valid left context state. For a matchstate m let $rhs(m)$ be the set of right-hand sides of productions corresponding to complete items in m.

For a matchstate m and a candidate left context state p, define

$$NTSET(p, rhs(m)) = \{B | B \to \cdot\alpha \in itemset(p), \alpha \in rhs(m)\}$$

Then a necessary, but not a sufficient condition for p to be a valid left context state for a matchstate corresponding to a matchset m is $NTSET(p, rhs(m)) = S_m$. (The condition is only necessary, because there may be another production that always matches in this left context when the others do, but which is not in the matchset.)

Before we describe the preprocessing algorithm, we have to define the costs that we will associate with items. The definitions involve keeping track of costs associated with rules partially matched (as that is what an item encodes) in addition to costs associated with rules fully matched.

Definition 9: The absolute cost of a nonterminal X matching an input symbol a in left context ϵ is represented by $abscost(\epsilon, X, a)$. For a derivation sequence d represented by $X \Rightarrow X_1 \Rightarrow X_2 \cdots \Rightarrow X_n \Rightarrow a$, let $C_d = rulecost(X_n \to a) + \sum_{i=1}^{n-1} rulecost(X_i \to X_{i+1}) + rulecost(X \to X_1)$; then $abscost(\epsilon, X, a) = \min_d(C_d)$.

Definition 10: The *absolute cost* of a nonterminal X matching a symbol a in left context α is defined as follows:

$$abscost(\alpha, X, a) = abscost(\epsilon, X, a) \text{ if } X \text{ matches in left context } \alpha$$
$$abscost(\alpha, X, a) = \infty \text{otherwise}$$

Definition 11: The *relative cost* of a nonterminal X matching a symbol a in left context α is $cost(\alpha, X, a) = abscost(\alpha, X, a) - \min_{y \in N} \{abscost(\alpha, Y, a)\}$.

Having defined costs for trees of height one we next look at trees of height greater than one. Let t be a tree of height greater than one.

Definition 12: The cost $abscost(\alpha, X, t) = \infty$ if X does not match t in left context α. If X matches t in left context α, let $t = a(t_1, t_2, \ldots, t_q)$ and $X \longrightarrow Y_1 Y_2 \cdots Y_q a$ where Y_i matches t_i, $1 \leq i \leq q$.

Let $abscost(\alpha, X \rightarrow Y_1 Y_2 \cdots Y_q a, t) = rulecost(X \rightarrow Y_1 \cdots Y_q a) + cost(\alpha, Y_1, t_1) + cost(\alpha Y_1, Y_2, t_2) + \cdots + cost(\alpha Y_1 Y_2 \cdots Y_{q-1}, Y_q, t_q)$. Hence define

$$abscost(\alpha, X, t) = \min_{X \Rightarrow \beta \Rightarrow^* t} \{abscost(\alpha, X \Rightarrow \beta, t)\}\,.$$

Definition 13: The relative cost of a nonterminal X matching a tree t in left context α is $cost(\alpha, X, t) = abscost(\alpha, X, t) - \min_{Y \Rightarrow^* t} \{abscost(\alpha, Y, t)\}$.

We now proceed to define a few functions that will be used by the algorithm. The function *Goto* makes a transition from a state on a terminal symbol in A and computes normalized costs. Each such transition always reaches a match state as the grammar is in normal form.

function *Goto(itemset, a)*
$Goto = \{[A \rightarrow \alpha\, a\,., c] \mid\ [A \rightarrow \alpha.a, c'] \in itemset$ and
$c = c' + rule\_cost(A \rightarrow \alpha\, a) -$
$\min\{c'' + rule\_cost(B \rightarrow \beta\, a) \mid\ [B \rightarrow \beta.a, c''] \in itemset\}\}$
end function

Fig. 6. The function to compute transitions on elements of A.

The *reduction* operation on a set of complete augmented items $itemset_1$ with respect to another set of augmented items, $itemset_2$ is encoded in the function *Reduction* in Fig. 7.

The function *Closure* is displayed in Fig. 8 and encodes the usual closure operation on sets of items.

The function *ClosureReduction* is shown in Fig. 9.

Having defined these functions, we now present the routine for precomputation in Fig. 10.

The procedure *LRMain* will produce the auxiliary automaton for states with cost information included in the items. Equivalence relations that can be used to compress tables are described in Ref. 6. We display the automa-

function $Reduction(itemset_2, itemset_1)$
//First compute costs of nonterminals in matchsets
$\mathcal{S} = S_{itemset_1}$
$cost(X) = \min\{c_i | \; [X \to \alpha_i., c_i] \in itemset_1\}$ if $X \in \mathcal{S}$ ∞ otherwise
// Process chain rules and obtain updated costs of nonterminals
$temp = \bigcup\{[A \to B., c] | \; \exists [A \to .B, 0] \in itemset_2 \wedge [B \to \gamma., c_1] \in itemset_1 \wedge c = c_1 + rule\_cost(A \to B)\}$
repeat
  $\mathcal{S} = \mathcal{S} \cup \{X | \; [X \to Y., c] \in temp\}$
  for $X \in \mathcal{S}$ **do**
    $cost(X) = \min(cost(X), \min\{c_i | \; \exists [X \to Y_i., c_i] \in temp\})$
    $temp = \{[A \to B., c] | \; \exists [A \to .B, 0] \in itemset_2 \wedge [B \to Y., c_1] \in temp \wedge c = c_1 + rule\_cost(A \to B)\}$
  end for
until no change to *cost* array or $temp = \phi$
//Compute reduction
$Reduction = \bigcup\{[A \to \alpha B.\beta, c] | \; [A \to \alpha.B\beta, c_1] \in itemset_2 \wedge B \in \mathcal{S} \wedge c = cost(B) + c_1$ if $\beta \neq \epsilon$ else
//This is a complete item corresponding to a chain rule
$c = rule\_cost(A \to B) - \min\{c_i | \; \exists [X \to .Y, 0] \in itemset_2, \wedge c_i = rule\_cost(X \to Y)\}$
end function

Fig. 7. Function that performs reduction by a set of rules given the LCstate and the matchstate.

function $Closure(itemset)$
repeat
  $itemset = itemset \bigcup\{[A \to .\alpha, 0] | \; [B \to .A\beta, c] \in itemset\}$
until no change to itemset
$Closure = itemset$
end function

Fig. 8. Function to compute the closure of a set of items

function $ClosureReduction(itemset)$
$ClosureReduction = Closure(Reduction(itemset))$
end function

Fig. 9. Function to compute *ClosureReduction* of a set of items.

```
procedure LRMain()
lcsets := ∅
matchsets := ∅
list := Closure({[S → .α, 0] | S → α ∈ P})
while list is not empty do
  delete next element q from list and add it to lcsets
  for each a ∈ A such there is a transition on a from q do
    m := Goto(q, a)
    δ_A(q, a) := (match(m), S_m)
    if m is not in matchsets then
      matchsets := matchsets ∪ {m}
      for each state r in lcsets do
        if Validlc(r, m) then
          p := ClosureReduction(r, m)
          δ_LC(r, S_m) := (match(p), p)
          if p is not in list or lcsets then
            append p to list
          end if
        end if
      end for
    end if
  end for
  for each state t in matchsets do
    if Validlc(q, t) then
      s := ClosureReduction(q, t)
      δ_LC(q, S_t) := (match(s), s)
      if s is not in list or lcsets then
        append s to list
      end if
    end if
  end for
end while
end procedure
```

Fig. 10. Algorithm to construct the auxiliary automaton.

ton constructed for the post-order form of the grammar in Example 1 in Fig. 11 below:

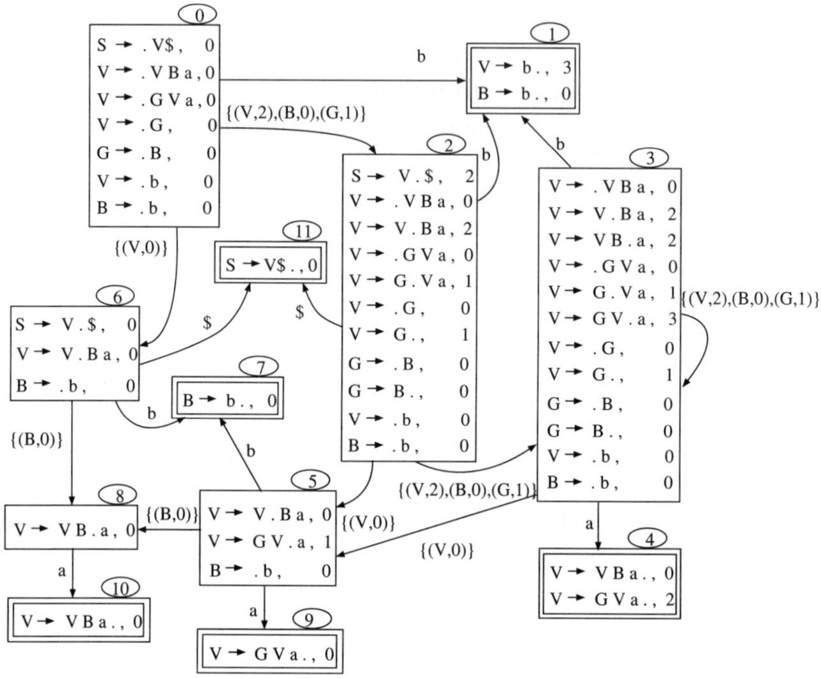

Fig. 11. Auxiliary automaton for post-order form of grammar of Example 1.

4. Conclusion

We have described a practical application of regular tree grammars and shown how instruction selectors can be automatically generated from tree grammar specifications of machine instructions. The automaton generated is a pushdown automaton. Augmentation of the specifications with attributes and actions can produce powerful tree translation systems.

References

1. A. V Aho and S. C. Johnson, Optimal code generation for expression trees. *Journal of the ACM*, 23(3): 146–160, 1976.

2. A. V. Aho, R. Sethi and J. D. Ullman, *Compilers: Principles, Techniques, and Tools.* Addison Wesley, 1986.
3. D. Chase, An improvement to bottom up tree pattern matching. In *Proc. of the 14th ACM Symp. on Principles of Programming Languages*, pages 168–177, 1987.
4. C. Hoffman and M. J. O'Donnell, Pattern matching in trees. *Journal of the ACM*, 29(1): 68–95, 1982.
5. J. E. Hopcroft and J. D. Ullman, *An Introduction to Automata Theory, Languages and Computation.* Addison Wesley, 1979.
6. Maya Madhavan, Priti Shankar, S. Rai and U. Ramakrishna, Extending Graham-Glanville techniques for optimal code generation. *ACM Transactions on Prog. Lang. and Systems*, 22(6): 973–1001, 2000.
7. P. Shankar, A. Gantait, A. R. Yuvaraj and M. Madhavan, A new algorithm for linear regular tree pattern matching. *Theoretical Computer Science*, 242: 125–142, 2000.

CHAPTER 24

DIGITALIZATION OF KOLAM PATTERNS AND TACTILE KOLAM TOOLS

Shojiro Nagata* and Robinson Thamburaj†

*InterVision Institute,
4-24, Katase 5,Fujisawa, 251-0032 Japan
E-mail: intvsn@cityfujisawa.ne.jp

†Department of Mathematics, Madras Christian College,
Chennai 600059, Tamil Nadu, India
E-mail: robin.mcc@gmail.com

Kolam is a traditional and popular graphical folk art practiced in the southern part of India using rice flour for decorating courtyards. Haptic identification of Kolam however is not possible by the visually challenged people. This paper describes two tactile line drawing tools, which make these patterns accessible to the visually challenged. One of the two tools was developed as a Universal Designed Cube with 6 primitive patterns on each of 6 sides. These primitive patterns were found by researching how to draw Kolam and other similar traditional patterns of Celtic knot in Europe or Soma paintings in Africa.

1. Kolam Patterns

In southern Indian villages, the courtyard in front of each house is decorated every morning by drawing of traditional designs called Kolam. The decoration of the floor with Kolam designs (Fig. 1) is carried out by women, who deftly draw with pinches of rice flour or limestone powder held between the thumb and the first finger and letting the powder fall in a continuous line by moving the hand in desired directions. On festive occasions, the Kolam designs are more elaborate and complicated. Initially a regularly arranged dot array is drawn and then lines are drawn around the dots or connecting them. A Kolam could be made up of a single, un-segmented, closed thread of line or it could be made up of superimposition of two or more closed threads of lines, each constituting one component of the global Kolam pattern. Many Kolam designs are geometric patterns formed by means

Fig. 1. Simple kolam patterns.

of interleaving straight and curved lines. These patterns can be classified as recursive designs and non-recursive designs.

2. Picture Language

Two-dimensional picture generating models are of interest in the area of pattern recognition by computers. Graph grammars and array grammars have been studied extensively for the description and analysis of two-dimensional structures. Rosenfeld advocated cycle grammars, as early as 1974 for the generation and description of pictures having rotational symmetry.[9,10]

Motivated by the Kolam patterns, Siromoney et al have introduced, different types of array grammars generating array languages[11–13,15,16] and have given specific instructions for drawing certain kinds of Kolam patterns namely, Kambi Kolam — literally meaning wire decoration with dots-which can be represented as a single strand. Each Kambi begins and ends at the same point, i.e. each Kambi is an unending line or a closed curve with or without loops (cycles).[14] The approach was syntactic and the emphasis was on considering each pattern as made up of sub patterns. Siromoney Kolam array grammar can generate digital rectangular arrays of different sizes, but with same proportion between the length and breadth. This property is a requirement when a camera on a robot does not maintain a fixed distance from the object of interest and the grammar has proved to be useful in an inference scheme.

Experiments were conducted by Siromoney to find out how the Kolam practitioners store such complicated patterns in their memory and retrieve them with ease while drawing the Kolam. In the course of the study, it was found that Kolam practitioners remember, describe and draw the designs in terms of "moves" such as "going forward", "taking a right turn", "taking a

U — turn to the right and so on reminiscent of the "interpretations" which are used in computer graphics as sequences of commands which control a "turtle". Treating each kind of a move as a terminal sign, each Kambi Kolam represented a picture cycle. A Kambi Kolam is a closed curve with or without loops represented in the form of cycle, which is a string, joined at two ends. Each element of the string belongs to the set K = {F, R(1), R(2), R(3), L(1), L(2), L(3)} where F stands for "move forward one unit", $R(1)$ represents a "half turn to the right", R(2) a "U-turn to the right," R(3) a "complete loop to the right" and similarly L(1), L(2), and L(3) for turns to the left. These picture cycle languages can be viewed and generated in several ways — (i) some of them may be regarded as cycles in the graph theoretic sense — as a sequence of nodes and arcs, or (ii) they may be converted into strings and generated by string grammars either Chomskian or Lindenmayer type, or (iii) as necklaces of terminal symbols. The terminal symbols may be of different types — each symbol may have a graphic interpretation or represent simpler turtle moves or chain code alphabet with coordinates specified or not or "Kolam moves".

3. Digitalization of Kolam Patterns

Of the many types of Kolam patterns, a certain family of patterns (Kambi Kolam) over square grid, is expressed with regular dotted square tiles. The kolam line expressed on a tile either crosses the edge of the tile or turns around the center dot of the tile. Nagata et al have given new digital representation to denote the crossing of kolam line across the edge of the tile and turning of the kolam line about the center dot respectively.[6] Therefore each tile has a four digit representation taken in anti-clockwise sense. The 16 possible primitives (including the isomorphic shapes) named in 6 categories namely circle, drop, saddle, pupil, fan and diamond and their digital representaion are shown in Fig. 2.

A sample of Swastika Kolam pattern formed with a single string and a knot expression of Takara_Musubi (Copyright by KASF 2003) are shown in Fig. 3.

Catenations of these primitives drawn on the tiles produce single or multiple Kambi Kolam patterns. The simple Kolam pattern that resembles the numeral "8" is represented by two "drop" tiles and is represented by the string "00100010" starting at the top edge of a tile. The other regular polygons (triangle, hexagon) allow us make other type tiles with linear

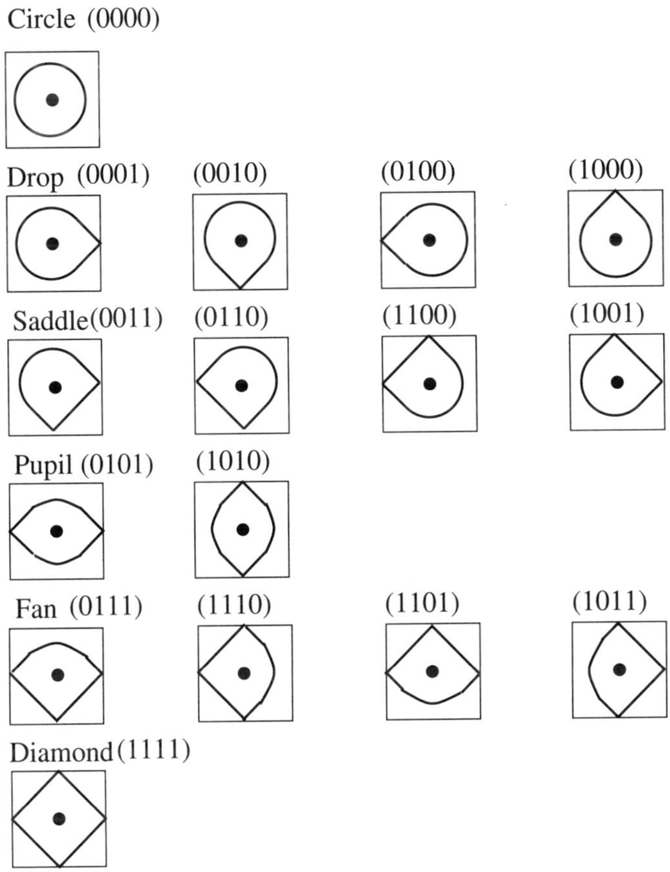

Fig. 2. Primitive patterns.

lines crossing at edges and arc-lines. This square tiling also was discussed as Mirror-light ray curves by Gerdes[2,3] and then Jablan.[4]

In the above representation, Nagata et al also expressed on a cycle problem based on a "smooth pass" rule of tracing[6] and have developed Kolam-designer software that shows an animation of the tracing pattern in a computer as drawn by Kolam practitioners.[7]

4. Universal Kolam Cube (UKC/PsyKolo)

As the only 6 primitive patterns were found to be enough to make Kolam patterns, Nagata et al embodied the idea of those primitive tiles into a

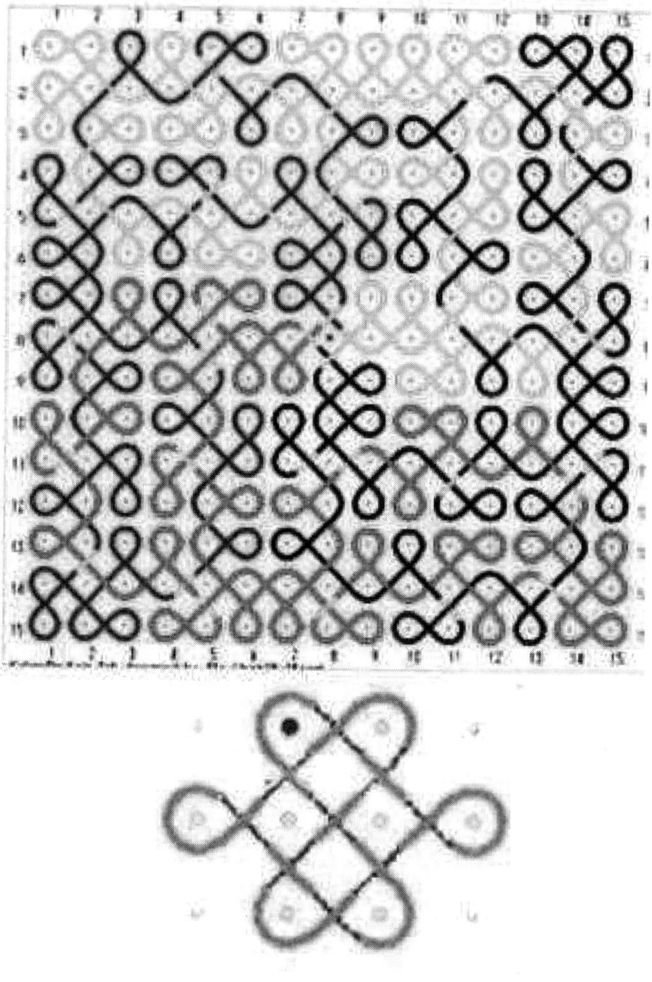

Fig. 3.

tangible educational tool named KoMa (acronym for Kolam Magic, later renamed PsyKolo for Psychological Kolam, meaning cube in Japanese). PsyKolo consists of a set of wooden cubes (of 4.5 cm size each) with basic primitive shapes embossed on each of all the six sides of a cube (Fig. 4) with embossed lines on Microcapsule paper accessible to the disabled people. With a small magnetic element concealed in each of the 6 sides of a cube, many cubes can be attached side by side without repulsion to form linear or

Fig. 4. Universal Kolam Cube / PsyKolo

planar formations. The cubes thus arranged can be rotated easily to form different symmetric closed curves and Kolam patterns. They can be formed in Matrix formations of N × M of rectangular shaped Kolam patterns (e.g. 3×3 cubes, Fig. 4) or any other formations. The cubes can be rotated to form new Kolam patterns.

The authors have improved PsyKolo cube with discrete-stimulus dotted tactile lines, which is more effective to recognize the lines, and filled each primitive with a specific colour. The modified Psykolo (named as Universal Kolam Cube (UKC)) gives better stimulation while tracing for the visual disability and the coloured Kolam patterns thus formed attract children with learning disabilities (LD), sighted as well as low vision children. Case studies conducted with Attention Deficient Hyperactivity Disorder (ADHD) and Autistic pupil showed their preference for forming single Kambi pattern and their ability to distinguish between different coloured patterns.

5. Tactile Kolam Sheets

Tactual shape perception is a synthesis of many parameters that lead visually challenged people to make sense of external stimuli. There are many methods by which tactile diagrams can be produced. One such method is using a microcapsule paper. It is a special paper coated with alcohol-filled microcapsules, which expand when heated. A few experiments have

Fig. 5. Kolam pattern formation

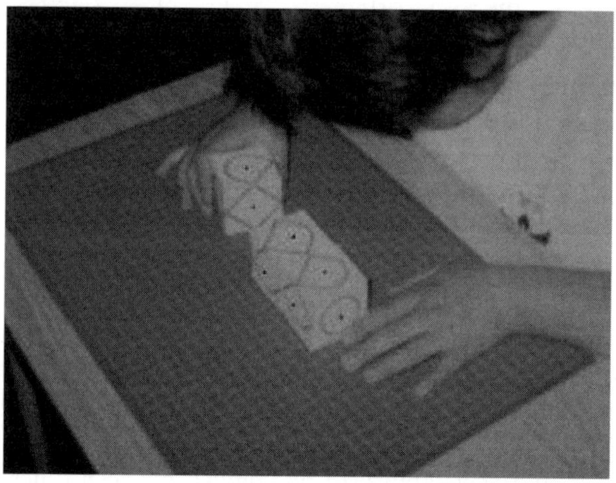

Fig. 6. A child with learning disability arranging a pattern.

investigated the effectiveness of microcapsule paper for producing diagrams (Aldrich *et al.*, Kirkwood and Pike *et al.*[1,5,8]).

The intricate Kolam patterns which give a great appeal to visual sense is a difficult art form for the people with visual impairment to understand and appreciate. The patterns drawn with rice flour or limestone powder get erased when a visually challenged person tries to sense it through his/her fingers. The Kolam pattern drawn with black ink on the microcapsule paper protrudes to form a tactile line when heated. The tactile drawings as tangible line graphics make this art form accessible to the visually challenged.

Viewing the Kambi Kolam pattern as a chain code representation on a square grid, a new technique of representing the hand movements in four directions is considered. Denoting by the symbol n the movement of one unit northward (e, w, s for other three directions), the pattern is represented as a word over $\{n, e, w, s\}$ (Fig. 7). Representation over $\{n, e, w, s\}$ is found to be easier by the visually challenged to remember the design than the other pen command representations used in picture descriptions. They preferred this technique to record and create new Kolam designs by themselves.

Fig. 7. Tactile recognition of a kambi kolam pattern

6. Summary

The Universal Kolam Cube (UKC) also called PsyKolo, is an educational toy developed to express traditional designs found in South India (Kolam patterns), Europe (Celtic patterns) and Africa (Sona patterns). It assists the visual challenged people to learn these traditional drawings and appreciate the geometrical features. Any disabled person has the access to understand an experience formation of new patterns that emerge from simple recursive primitives.

The authors conducted experiments in South India and Japan with visually challenged and disabled people on the pattern recognition using the Universal Kolam Cube.

The drawing of Kolam patterns practiced purely as an art form earlier is now opening new avenues in the area of computer graphics, textile industry, rehabilitating the disabled of the aged persons, special education for visually challenged, ethno-mathematics etc. The second author has an ongoing work of decorating the wall ceiling with illuminated bulbs foming Kolam patterns.

Acknowledgments

The authors would like to thank Prof. Yoshiko Toriyama of University of Tsukuba for her suggestions, The University of Tsukuba School for the Visually Impaired, Tokyo for the support while conducting the experiments, and Ms. Kitayama Shizuko for the cooperation in experimenting with her students with learning disability. The first author would like to thank the members of KASF (Kolam Art and Science Forum), especially Prof. Ken Shiina, Prof. Kiwamu Yanagisawa, and Mr. Tetsuya Asano for useful discussion with them and also acknowledges the partial grant-in-aid support by Nakayama Hayao Foundation for Science, Technology and Culture, Japan for his research work including the research tour in Tamil Nadu, India.

References

1. F. K. Aldrich and A. J. Parkin, Tangible line graphs: an experimental investigation of three formats using capsule paper, Human Factors, Vol. 29 (1987), 301–309.
2. P. Gerdes, Reconstruction and Extension of Lost Symmetries: Examples from the Tamil of South India, Computers Math. Applic., Vol. 17, No. 4–6, (1989), 791–813.
3. P. Gerdes, On Mirror Curves and Lunda-Designs, Comput. & Graphics, Vol. 21–3 (1997), 371–378.
4. S. V. Jablan, Mirror Generated Curves, Symmetry: Culture and Science Vol. 6–2, (1995), 275–278.
5. R. Kirkwood, Tactile diagrams: their production by current-day methods and their relative suitability in use, The British Journal of Visual Impairment, 4 (1986), 95–99.
6. S. Nagata and K. Yanagisawa, Attractiveness of Kolam design — Characteristics of single stroke cycle, Bulletin of the Society for Science on Form in Japan, Vol. 19–2 (2004), 221–222.
7. S. Nagata and K. Yanagisawa, Kolam Design Software and Tangible Universal Design Tools, Proc. of 58th Symposium of Science on Forms, Japan (2004), Bulletin of the Society for Science on Form in Japan, Vol. 19–2 (2004), 276. http://intervision.aadau.net
8. E. Pike, M. Blades and C. Spencer, Maps on microcapsule paper: the performance of visually impaired children, The British Journal of Visual Impairment, 11: 1 (1993), 18–20.

9. A. Rosenfeld, A note on cycle grammars, Information control 27 (1975) 374–377.
10. A. Rosenfeld and R. Siromoney, Picture languages -A survey, Languages of Design Vol. 1 (1993), 229–245.
11. G. Siromoney and R. Siromoney, Rosenfeld's cycle grammar and Kolam. Lecture Notes in Computer Science 291 (1987), 564–579.
12. G. Siromoney, R. Siromoney and K. Krithivasan, Array grammars and Kolam, Comp. Graphics and Image Proc. 3 (1974), 63–82.
13. G. Siromoney, R. Siromoney and K. Krithivasan, Picture languages with array rewriting rules, Inform. Control, 22 (1992), 447–470.
14. G. Siromoney, R. Siromoney and T. Robinson, Kambi Kolam and cycle grammars, In "A Perspective in Theoretical Computer Science" (Ed: R. Narasimhan) Series in Computer Science Vol. 16, World Scientific (1989), 267–300.
15. R. Siromoney, Array languages and Lindenmayer systems — a survey, In "The Book of L" (Eds: G. Rozenberg, A. Salomaa) Springer-Verlag (1985).
16. R. Siromoney and G. Siromoney, Extended controlled table-L-arrays, Inform. Control 35 (2) (1977), 119–138.

CHAPTER 25

HEXAGONAL ARRAY ACCEPTORS AND LEARNING

D. G. Thomas*, M. H. Begam†, N. G. David* and Colin de la Higuera‡

*Department of Mathematics,
Madras Christian College, Tambaram, India
E-mail: dgthomasmcc@yahoo.com

†Department of Mathematics,
Arignar Anna Government Arts College, Walajapet, India

‡EURISE, Universite de Saint-Etienne
23 rue du Docteur Paul Michelon, 42023 Saint-Etienne, France

In this paper, we construct 3 directions online tessellation automata to recognize hexagonal picture languages. We study the inference of certain classes of hexagonal picture languages.

1. Introduction

Picture languages generated by grammars or recognized by automata have been advocated since the seventies for problems arising in the framework of pattern recognition and image analysis.[2–4,7] Hexagonal patterns are known to occur in the literature on picture processing and scene analysis. Siromoney *et al.*[6,9] constructed grammars for generating hexagonal arrays and hexagonal patterns.

Recently Dersanambika *et al.*[1] have introduced two interesting classes of hexagonal picture languages, viz., local hexagonal picture languages (HLOC) and recognizable hexagonal picture languages (HREC) and studied their properties. In this paper, we develop a recognizing device called 3 directions online tessellation automata to recognize these languages and provide examples. We show that the class of all hexagonal picture languages recognized by 3 directions online tessellation automata is exactly the family of hexagonal picture languages recognizable by hexagonal tiling systems (HTS).

On the other hand, machine learning has been of great interest and much study has centered around the inductive inference of finite automata recognizing linear strings.[5] In Ref. 8, learning of certain classes of two dimensional picture languages is considered. In this paper, we provide a linear time algorithm that learns in the limit from positive data the class of local hexagonal picture languages. We present a polynomial time algorithm that learns the class of hexagonal recognizable picture languages from positive data with restricted subset queries.

2. Preliminaries

In this section, we review some basic definitions introduced in Ref. 1.

We consider hexagons of the type:

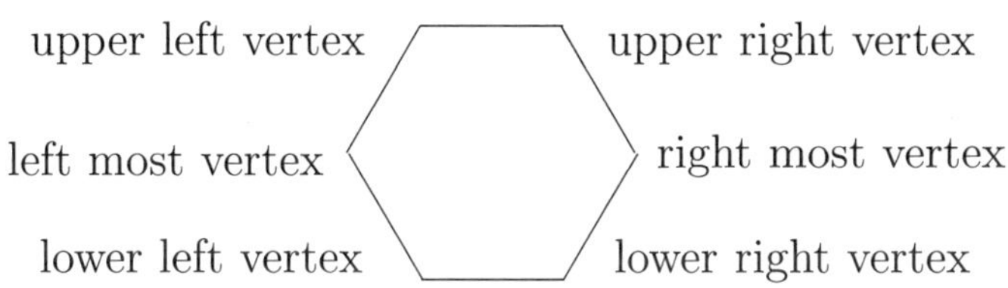

Let Σ be a finite alphabet of symbols. A hexagonal picture p over Σ is a hexagonal array of symbols of Σ. For example, a hexagonal picture over the alphabet $\{a, b\}$ is:

$$\begin{array}{ccccc} & a & & a & \\ a & & b & & b \\ & b & & a & \end{array} \tag{1}$$

The set of all hexagonal arrays of the alphabet Σ is denoted by Σ^{**H}. A hexagonal picture language L over Σ is a subset of Σ^{**H}.

With respect to a triad 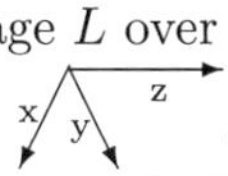 of triangular axes x, y, z the coordinates of each element of hexagonal picture can be fixed.

For example, for the hexagonal array of Eq. (1), we have

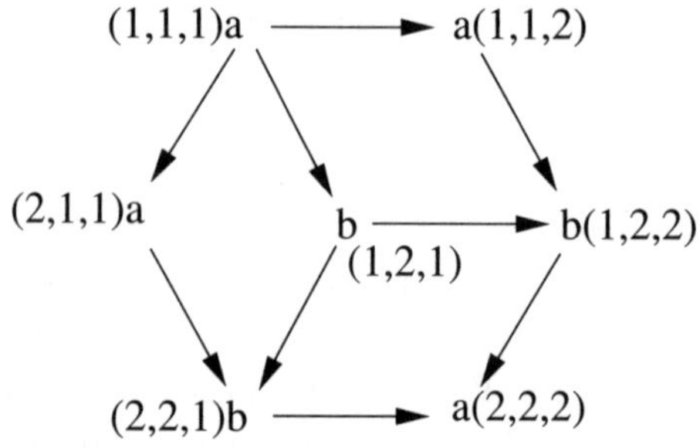

For $p \in \Sigma^{**H}$, let $\hat{p}$ be the hexagonal array obtained by surrounding p with a special boundary symbold $\# \neq \Sigma$.

$$\begin{array}{ccccccccc} & & \# & & \# & & \# & & \\ & \# & & a & & a & & \# & \\ \hat{p} = \# & & a & & b & & b & & \# \\ & \# & & b & & a & & \# & \\ & & \# & & \# & & \# & & \end{array}$$

Given a picture $p \in \Sigma^{**H}$, let $l_1(p)$ denote the number of elements in the border of p from upper left vertex to left most vertex in the direction $\swarrow$ called x direction, $l_2(p)$ denote the number of elements in the border of p from upper right vertex to right most vertex in the direction $\searrow$ called y direction and $l_3(p)$ denote the number of elements in the border of p from upper left vertex to upper right vertex in the direction $\rightarrow$ called z direction.

The directions are fixed with origin of reference as the upper left vertex, having coordinates (1, 1, 1). The triple $(l_1(p), l_2(p), l_3(p))$ is called the size of the picture p. Furthermore, if $1 \leq i \leq l_1(p)$, $1 \leq j \leq l_2(p)$, $1 \leq k \leq l_3(p)$, let p_{ijk} denote the symbol in p with coordinates (i, j, k). For example, the hexagonal array given in Eq. (1) is of size (2, 2, 2) and $p_{111} = a$, $p_{221} = b$, etc.

Given a hexagonal picture p of size (l, m, n) for $g \leq l$, $h \leq m$ and $k \leq n$, we denote by $B_{g,h,k}(p)$ the set of all hexagonal blocks (or hexagonal subpictures) of p of size (g, h, k). Each member of $B_{2,2,2}(p)$ is called a hexagonal tile.

The family HLOC

Let Σ be a finite alphabet. A hexagonal picture language $L \subseteq \Sigma^{**H}$ is called local if there exists a finite set Δ of hexagonal tiles over $\Sigma \cup \{\#\}$ such that $L = \{p \in \Sigma^{**H} / B_{2,2,2}(\hat{p}) \subseteq \Delta\}$. L is denoted by $L(\Delta)$.

The family of local hexagonal picture languages will be denoted by HLOC.

The family HREC

Let Σ be a finite alphabet. A hexagonal picture language $L \subseteq \Sigma^{**H}$ is called recognizable if there exists a local hexagonal picture language L' over an alphabet Γ and a mapping $\pi : \Gamma \to \Sigma$ such that $L = \pi(L')$.

Example 1: Let $\Sigma = \{1, 2, 3\}$;

$$\Delta = \left\{ \begin{array}{ccccc} & \# & & \# & \\ \# & & 1 & & 1 \\ & 2 & & 2 & \end{array}, \begin{array}{ccccc} & \# & & \# & \\ 1 & & 1 & & 1 \\ & 2 & & 2 & \end{array}, \begin{array}{ccccc} & \# & & \# & \\ 1 & & 1 & & \# \\ & 2 & & 2 & \end{array}, \right.$$

$$\begin{array}{ccccc} & \# & & 1 & \\ \# & & 2 & & 2 \\ & \# & & 3 & \end{array}, \begin{array}{ccccc} & 1 & & 1 & \\ 2 & & 2 & & 2 \\ & 3 & & 3 & \end{array}, \begin{array}{ccccc} & 1 & & \# & \\ 2 & & 2 & & \# \\ & 3 & & \# & \end{array},$$

$$\left. \begin{array}{ccccc} & 2 & & 2 & \\ \# & & 3 & & 3 \\ & \# & & \# & \end{array}, \begin{array}{ccccc} & 2 & & 2 & \\ 3 & & 3 & & 3 \\ & \# & & \# & \end{array}, \begin{array}{ccccc} & 2 & & 2 & \\ 3 & & 3 & & \# \\ & \# & & \# & \end{array} \right\}.$$

Then

$$L_1 = L(\Delta) = \left\{ \begin{array}{ccccc} & 1 & & 1 & \\ 2 & & 2 & & 2 \\ & 3 & & 3 & \end{array}, \begin{array}{ccccccc} & 1 & & 1 & & 1 & \\ 2 & & 2 & & 2 & & 2 \\ & 3 & & 3 & & 3 & \end{array}, \right.$$

$$\left. \begin{array}{ccccccccc} & 1 & & 1 & & 1 & & 1 & \\ 2 & & 2 & & 2 & & 2 & & 2 \\ & 3 & & 3 & & 3 & & 3 & \end{array}, \ldots \right\}$$

= The set of all hexagons of sizes $(2, 2, k)(k \geq 2)$ with z direction elements respectively at the top are 1, at the middle are 2 and at the bottom are 3.

Clearly $L(\Delta)$ is local.

Example 2: Let $\Sigma = \{a\}$. It is shown[1] that the language of hexagonal pictures over Σ with all sides of equal length is not local, but, recognizable.

The family $\mathcal{L}(HTS)$

A hexagonal tiling system T is a 4-tuple $(\Sigma, \Gamma, \pi, \theta)$ where Σ and Γ are two finite sets of symbols, $\pi : \Gamma \to \Sigma$ is a projection and θ is a set of hexagonal tiles over the alphabet $\Gamma \cup \{\#\}$.

The hexagonal picture language $L \subseteq \Sigma^{**H}$ is tiling recognizable if there exists a tiling system $T = (\Sigma, \Gamma, \pi, \theta)$ such that $L = \pi(L(\theta))$. It is denoted by $L(T)$. The family of hexagonal picture languages recognizable by hexagonal tiling systems is denoted by $\mathcal{L}(HTS)$.

It is easy to see that HREC is exactly the family of hexagonal picture languages recognizable by hexagonal tiling sytems ($\mathcal{L}(HTS)$).

3. Automata for Languages of HREC

We define a 3 directions online tessellation automaton referred to as 3OTA, to accept languages of HREC.

Definition 1: A non-deterministic (deterministic) 3 directions online tessellation automaton is defined by $\mathcal{A} = (\Sigma, Q, q_0, F, \delta)$ where

- Σ is the input alphabet
- Q is a finite set of states
- $q_0 \in Q$ is the initial state
- $F \subseteq Q$ is the set of final states
- $\delta : Q \times Q \times Q \times \Sigma \to 2^Q (\delta : Q \times Q \times Q \times \Sigma \to Q)$ is the transition function.

A run of $\mathcal{A}$ on a hexagonal picture $p \in \Sigma^{**H}$ consists of associating a state (from the set Q) to each position (i, j, k) of p. Such state is given by the transition function δ and depends on the states already associated.

For p, consider $\hat{p}$ and let all the border letters $\#$ in p be associated with state q_0.

The computation of the automaton starts at time $t = 1$, by reading p_{111} and associating the state $\delta(q_0, q_0, q_0, p_{111})$ to position $(1, 1, 1)$. In general, we view $\delta(q_1, q_2, q_3, p_{ijk})$ as

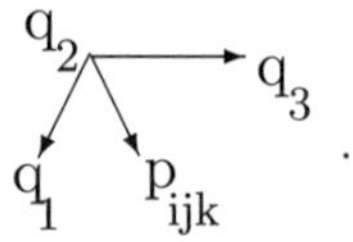

At time $t = 2$, states are simultaneously associated to positions p_{211} and p_{112}. This process continues till a state is associated to position $(l_1(p),$

$l_2(p), l_3(p))$. A 3OTA $\mathcal{A}$ recognizes a hexagonal picture p if there exists a run of $\mathcal{A}$ on $\hat{p}$ such that the state associated to position $(l_1(p), l_2(p), l_3(p))$ is a final state. The set of all hexagonal pictures recognized by $\mathcal{A}$ is denoted by $\mathcal{L}(A)$.

Let $\mathcal{L}(3OTA)$ be the set of hexagonal picture languages recognized by $3OTA$s.

4. Examples

(1) A 3 directions online tessellation automaton to recognize the local hexagonal picture language $L(\Delta)$ shown in example 2.1 is given by:

$$\mathcal{A}_1 = (\Sigma_1, Q_1, q_0, F_1, \delta_1)$$

where $\Sigma_1 = \{1, 2, 3\}$; $Q_1 = \{q_0, q_1, q_2, q_3\}$; $F_1 = \{q_3\}$ and

$$\delta_1(q_0, q_0, q_0, 1) = q_1$$

$$\delta_1(q_0, q_0, q_1, 2) = q_2$$

$$\delta_1(q_1, q_0, q_0, 1) = q_1$$

$$\delta_1(q_2, q_1, q_1, 2) = q_2$$

$$\delta_1(q_0, q_2, q_2, 3) = q_3$$

$$\delta_1(q_3, q_2, q_2, 3) = q_3$$

$$\delta_1(q_2, q_1, q_0, 2) = q_2$$

$$\delta_1(q_3, q_2, q_2, 3) = q_3\,.$$

(2) A 3 directions online tessellation automaton to recognize the recognizable hexagonal picture language over one letter alphabet $\{a\}$ with all sides of equal length is given by: $\mathcal{A}_2 = (\Sigma_2, Q_2, q_0, F_2, \delta_2)$ where $\Sigma_2 = \{a\}$; $Q_2 = \{q_0, q_1\}$; $F_2 = \{q_1\}$ and

$$\delta_2(q_0, q_0, q_0, a) = q_1$$

$$\delta_2(q_0, q_0, q_1, a) = q_0$$

$$\delta_2(q_1, q_0, q_0, a) = q_0$$

$$\delta_2(q_0, q_1, q_0, a) = q_1$$

$$\delta_2(q_1, q_0, q_1, a) = q_0\,.$$

Remark 1: 1. Consider the picture:

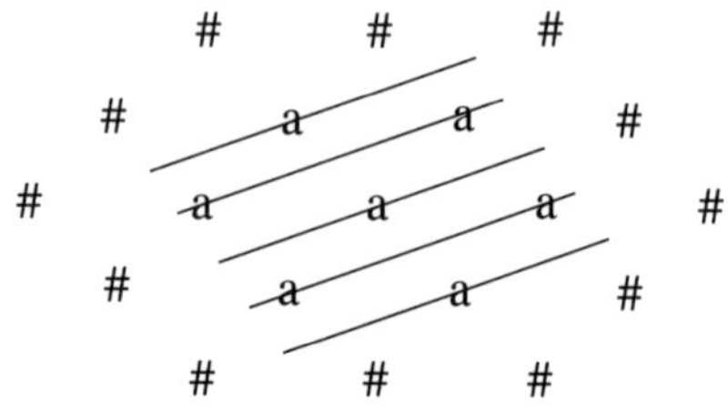

The five lines on the above picture explain five steps of computation done by the automaton given in Example 2, for testing whether or not this hexagonal array of size (2, 2, 2) can be accepted.

2.

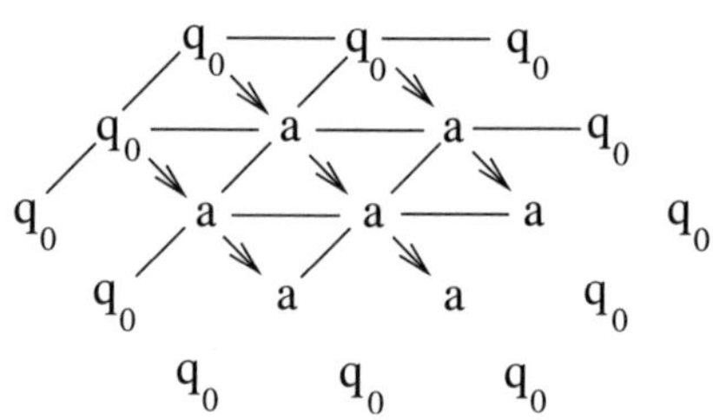

The arrows explain how do we apply δ function on the hexagon, considered in 1 of this remark.

5. Results

In this section, we show that $\mathcal{L}(3OTA) = \mathcal{L}(HTS)$. To prove this result, we have the following two lemmas.

Lemma 1: *If a hexagonal picture language is recognized by a 3OTA, then it is recognized by a finite hexagonal tiling system. i.e.,* $\mathcal{L}(3OTA) \subseteq \mathcal{L}(HTS)$.

Proof: Let $L \in \Sigma^{**H}$ be a language recognized by a three-directional on-line tessellation automaton $\mathcal{A} = (\Sigma, Q, I, F, \delta)$. We have to show that there exists a tiling system T that recognizes L.

Let $T = (\Sigma, \Gamma, \theta, \pi)$ be a tiling system such that

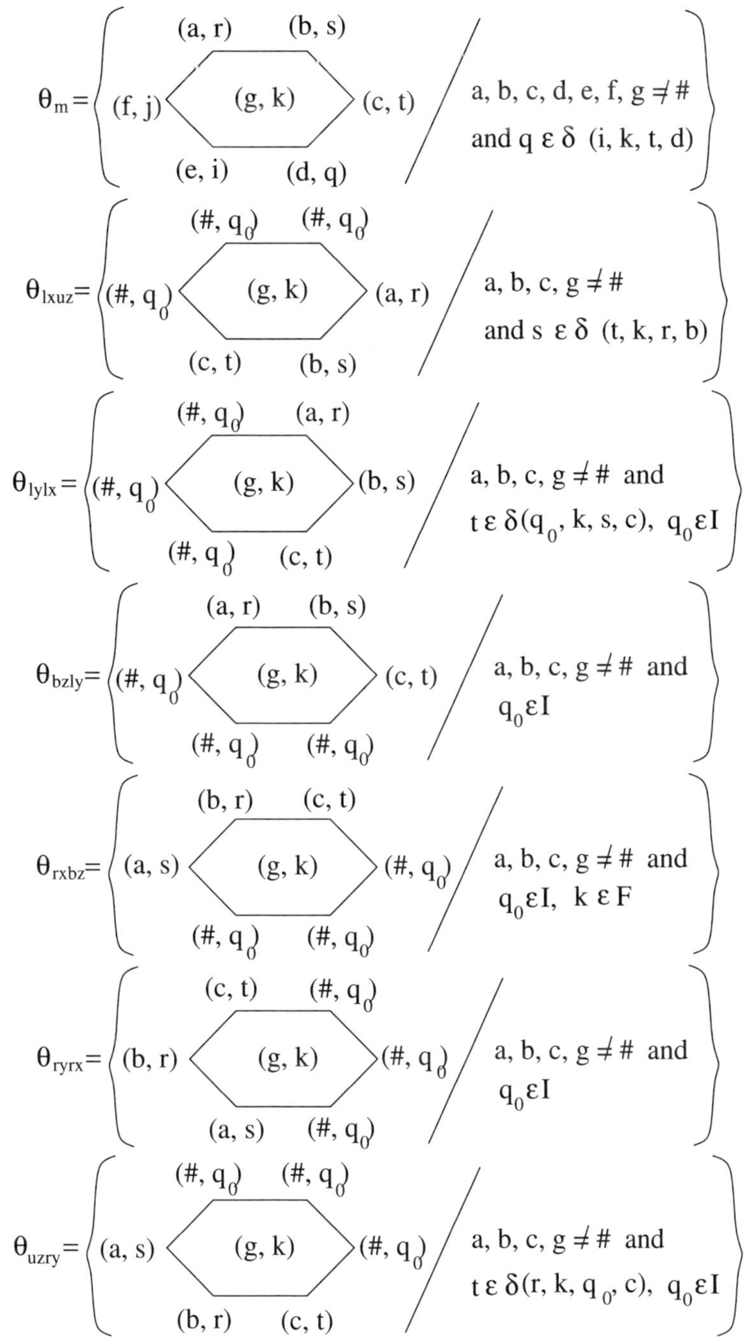
θm =
(a, r) (b, s)
(f, j) (g, k) (c, t)
(e, i) (d, q)
a, b, c, d, e, f, g ≠ #
and q ε δ (i, k, t, d)
θlxuz =
(#, q0) (#, q0)
(#, q0) (g, k) (a, r)
(c, t) (b, s)
a, b, c, g ≠ #
and s ε δ (t, k, r, b)
θlylx =
(#, q0) (a, r)
(#, q0) (g, k) (b, s)
(#, q0) (c, t)
a, b, c, g ≠ # and
t ε δ(q0, k, s, c), q0 ε I
θbzly =
(a, r) (b, s)
(#, q0) (g, k) (c, t)
(#, q0) (#, q0)
a, b, c, g ≠ # and
q0 ε I
θrxbz =
(b, r) (c, t)
(a, s) (g, k) (#, q0)
(#, q0) (#, q0)
a, b, c, g ≠ # and
q0 ε I, k ε F
θryrx =
(c, t) (#, q0)
(b, r) (g, k) (#, q0)
(a, s) (#, q0)
a, b, c, g ≠ # and
q0 ε I
θuzry =
(#, q0) (#, q0)
(a, s) (g, k) (#, q0)
(b, r) (c, t)
a, b, c, g ≠ # and
t ε δ(r, k, q0, c), q0 ε I

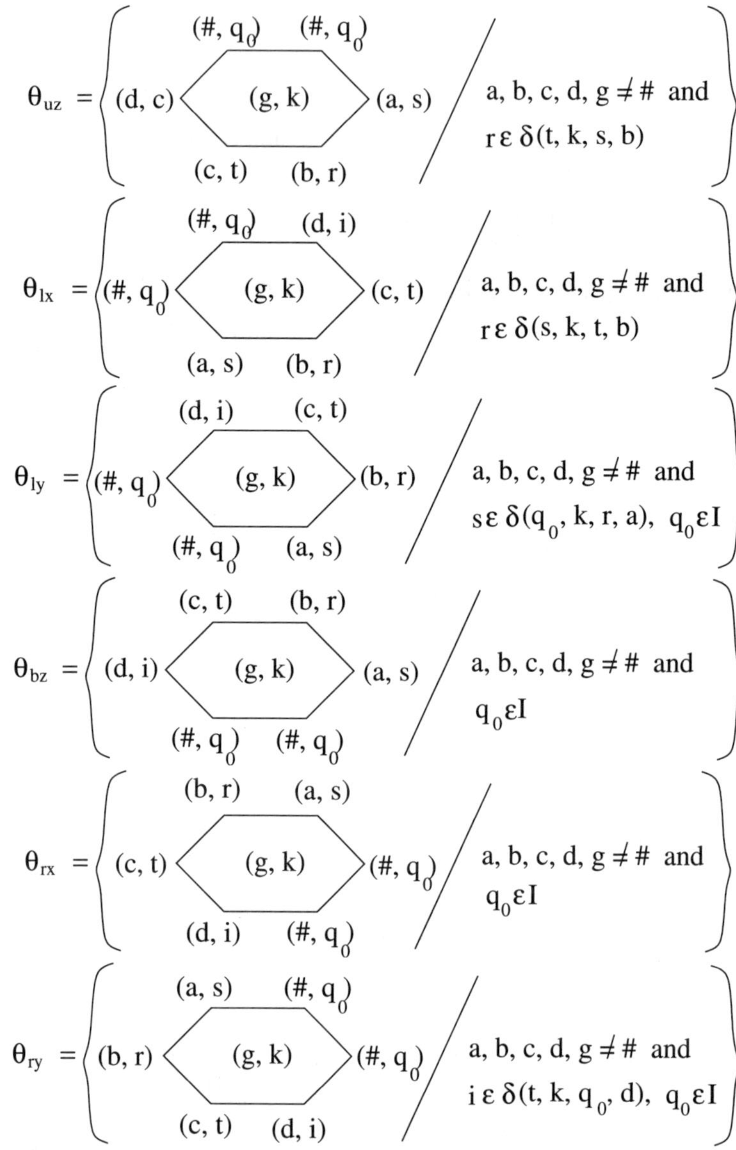
θuz =
(#, q0) (#, q0)
(d, c) (g, k) (a, s)
(c, t) (b, r)
a, b, c, d, g ≠ # and
r ε δ(t, k, s, b)
θlx =
(#, q0) (d, i)
(#, q0) (g, k) (c, t)
(a, s) (b, r)
a, b, c, d, g ≠ # and
r ε δ(s, k, t, b)
θly =
(d, i) (c, t)
(#, q0) (g, k) (b, r)
(#, q0) (a, s)
a, b, c, d, g ≠ # and
s ε δ(q0, k, r, a), q0 ε I
θbz =
(c, t) (b, r)
(d, i) (g, k) (a, s)
(#, q0) (#, q0)
a, b, c, d, g ≠ # and
q0 ε I
θrx =
(b, r) (a, s)
(c, t) (g, k) (#, q0)
(d, i) (#, q0)
a, b, c, d, g ≠ # and
q0 ε I
θry =
(a, s) (#, q0)
(b, r) (g, k) (#, q0)
(c, t) (d, i)
a, b, c, d, g ≠ # and
i ε δ(t, k, q0, d), q0 ε I

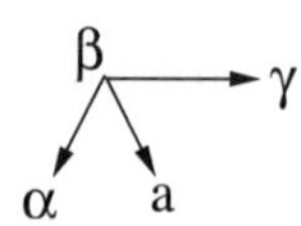
β
γ
α
a

$\Gamma = (\Sigma \cup \{\#\}) \times Q$

$\theta = \theta_m \cup \theta_{lxuz} \cup \theta_{lylx} \cup \theta_{bzly} \cup \theta_{rxbz} \cup \theta_{ryrx} \cup \theta_{uzry} \cup \theta_{uz} \cup \theta_{lx} \cup \theta_{ly}$
$\cup\, \theta_{bz} \cup \theta_{rx} \cup \theta_{ry}$

(Here m, b, l, r, u mean "middle", "bottom", "left", "right", "upper" respectively and $lxuz$ means left x direction with upper z direction and so on) with

$$\pi : \Sigma \cup \{\#\} \times Q \to \Sigma$$

is such that

$$\pi(a, q) = a \;\forall\; a \in \Sigma \cup \{\#\}, q \in Q$$

We notice that the set θ is defined in a way that a picture p' of the underlying local hexagonal picture language of $L(T)$ describes exactly a run of the 3OTA $\mathcal{A}$ on $p = \pi(p')$.

Then it is easy to verify that $\mathcal{L}(\mathcal{A}) = L(T)$. □

Lemma 2: *If a language is recognizable by a finite tiling system then it is recognizable by a three directions online tessellation automaton* ($\mathcal{L}(HTS) \subseteq \mathcal{L}(3OTA)$).

Proof: Let $L \subseteq \Sigma^{**H}$ be a language recognized by the tiling sytem $(\Sigma, \Gamma, \theta, \pi)$ and L' the underlying local language represented by the set of tiles θ i.e., $\pi(L') = L$. It suffices to show that there exists a 3OTA recognizing $L' \subseteq \Gamma^{**H}$. □

Lemma 3: *If L is a local hexagonal picture language then it is recognizable by a 3OTA. i.e., $HLOC \subseteq \mathcal{L}(3OTA)$.*

Proof: Let $L \subseteq \Sigma^{**H}$ be a local hexagonal picture language. Then $L = L(\Delta)$ where Δ is a finite set of hexagonal tiles over $\Sigma \cup \{\#\}$.

We construct a 3OTA as follows:

$\mathcal{A} = (\Sigma, Q, I, F, \delta)$

- $Q = \Delta$;
- $$I = \left\{ \begin{array}{ccc} \# \; g & & e \; \# \\ f \;\; a \;\; b \; , & h \;\; k \;\; l \\ c \; d & & m \; n \end{array} \middle| \; b, c, d, f, g, e, h, m, n, l \in \Sigma \cup \{\#\} \text{ and} \right.$$
$$\left. \begin{array}{ccc} \# \; g & & e \; \# \\ f \;\; a \;\; b \; , & h \;\; k \;\; l \\ c \; d & & m \; n \end{array} \quad \in \Delta \right\}$$

- $F = \left\{ \begin{array}{ccc} & a\ b & \\ c & d & \# \\ & \#\ \# & \end{array} \middle| \begin{array}{ccc} & a\ b & \\ c & d & \# \\ & \#\ \# & \end{array} \in \Delta \right\}$

The transition $\delta : Q \times Q \times Q \times \Sigma \to 2^Q$ is defined in a way that the run of $\mathcal{A}$ over a picture p simulates a tiling of p by elements of $Q = \Delta$. We explain this briefly.

Given a borded picture $\hat{p}$ with $p \in L(\Delta)$, for each symbol a in the (i, j, k)th position of p, we first find three symbols α, β, γ of $\Sigma \cup \{\#\}$ in $\hat{p}$, asociated with "a" using the diagram

If $\alpha \in \Sigma$, we choose the tile in $\hat{p}$ with α as the middle element. If $\alpha = \#$, we choose the tile in $\hat{p}$ with a as the middle element.

We do similarly for β and γ separately.

Suppose the tiles chosen for α, β, γ are t_1, t_2, t_3 respectively. Then we define, $\delta(t_1, t_2, t_3, a) = t_4$, a tile with "a" as the middle point. We observe that t_1, t_2, t_3, $t_4 \in \Delta$. For example, the transition

$$\delta \left(\begin{array}{ccc} & a\ b & \\ c & d & e \\ & f\ g & \end{array}, \begin{array}{ccc} & b\ r & \\ d & e & s \\ & g\ t & \end{array}, \begin{array}{ccc} & c\ d & \\ p & f & g \\ & w\ v & \end{array}, g \right)$$

that computes the state for the symbol g in the position (i, j, k) corresponds to the following diagram of tiling of p.

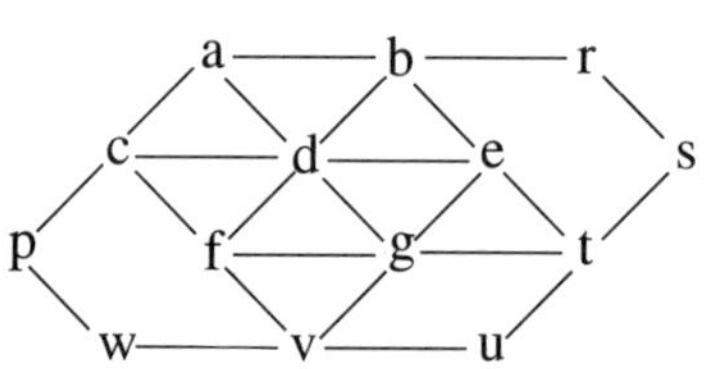

Here

$$\delta \left(\begin{array}{ccc} & a\ b & \\ c & d & e \\ & f\ g & \end{array}, \begin{array}{ccc} & b\ r & \\ d & e & s \\ & g\ t & \end{array}, \begin{array}{ccc} & c\ d & \\ p & f & g \\ & w\ v & \end{array}, g \right) = \begin{array}{ccc} & d\ e & \\ f & g & t \\ & v\ u & \end{array}, \text{ provided } f, d, e \in \Sigma,$$

$$\begin{array}{ccc} & d\ e & \\ f & g & t \\ & v\ u & \end{array}, \begin{array}{ccc} & a\ b & \\ c & d & e \\ & f\ g & \end{array}, \begin{array}{ccc} & b\ r & \\ d & e & s \\ & g\ t & \end{array} \text{ and } \begin{array}{ccc} & c\ d & \\ p & f & g \\ & w\ v & \end{array} \text{ are in } \Delta.$$

It can be easily verified that $L = L(\mathcal{A})$. □

6. Learning of Local Hexagonal Array Languages

In this section we introduce the notion of the characteristic sample for a local hexagonal array language and provide an algorithm to learn local hexagonal picture languages through identification in the limit using positive data.

Definition 2: Let L be a local hexagonal picture language over Σ and suppose $L = L(\Delta)$ for some $\Delta \subseteq (\Sigma \cup \{\#\})^{2\times 2\times 2}$. Δ is said to be minimal if $L = L(\Delta')$ for some finite $\Delta' \subseteq (\Sigma \cup \{\#\})^{2\times 2\times 2}$ implies $\Delta \subseteq \Delta'$.

Lemma 4: *Let L be a local hexagonal picture language over Σ. Then there exists a minimal Δ for L such that $L = L(\Delta)$.*

Remark 2: We assume hereafter that Δ is minimal for any local hexagonal picture language $L = L(\Delta)$.

Definition 3: Let T be a finite subset of Σ^{**H}. Let $\Delta_T = \{B_{2,2,2}(\hat{p})/p \in T\}$. The set $L = L(\Delta_T)$ is called local hexagonal picture language associated with T.

Lemma 5: *Let T, T' be finite subsets of Σ^{**H}. Then*

(i) $T \subseteq L(\Delta_T)$
(ii) *if $T \subseteq T'$, then $L(\Delta_T) \subseteq L(\Delta_{T'})$ and*
(iii) *if L is an arbitrary local hexagonal picture language and T, a finite subset of L then $L(\Delta_T) \subseteq L$.*

Definition 4: Let L be a local hexagonal picture language. A finite subset U of L is called a characteristic sample for L iff L is the smallest local hexagonal picture language containing U.

Lemma 6: *Let U be the characteristic sample for a local hexagonal picture language L. Then*

(1) $L = L(\Delta_U)$
(2) *If $U \subseteq T \subseteq L$ for a finite set T, then $L = L(\Delta_T)$*

Theorem 1: There exists a characteristic sample for any local hexagonal picture language L.

We now present an algorithm that learns an unknown local hexagonal picture language, in the limit from positive data

Algorithm HL

Input: A sequence E_i of positive presentations of L.

Output: An increasing sequence Δ_i such that $L(\Delta_i)$ are local hexagonal picture languages.

Procedure:

Initialize E_0 to ϕ
Construct the initial $\Delta_0 = \phi$
repeat(forever)
  let Δ_i be the current conjecture
  read the next positive example p
  scan p to obtain $B_{2,2,2}(\hat{p})$
  $\Delta_{i+1} = \Delta_i \cup B_{2,2,2}(\hat{p})$
  $E_{i+1} = E_i \cup \{p\}$
  output Δ_{i+1} as new conjecture

Lemma 7: *Let Δ_0, $\Delta_1, \ldots, \Delta_i, \ldots$ be the sequence of conjectures by the algorithm HL. Then*

(1) *for all $i \geq 0$, $L(\Delta_i) \subseteq L(\Delta_{i+1}) \subseteq L$ and*
(2) *there exists $r \geq 0$ such that for all $i \geq 0$, $L(\Delta_r) = L(\Delta_{r+i}) = L$.*

Summarizing all the lemmas, we obtain the following theorem.

Theorem 2: Given an local hexagonal picture language L, the algorithm HL learns, in the limit, a set Δ_i such that $L(\Delta_i) = L$.

Time Analysis: The time complexity of the algorithm HL depends on the size of the positive data provided. The product measure $V(p)$ of an example p, where p is a hexagonal picture of size (l, m, n) is lmn. Hence the running time of the algorithm is a function of N, the sum of product measures of all the positive data provided. Each time a new example p is provided, $B_{2,2,2}(\hat{p})$ and hence the new conjecture Δ_{i+1} is computed in time $O(V(p))$. Hence the total time required is $\Sigma_{p \in E_r} O(V(p)) = O(N)$ where E_r is the set of positive data with which the algorithm converges to a correct conjecture.

7. Learning of Recognizable Hexagonal Picture Languages

Let $M = (\Sigma, Q, q_0, F, \delta)$ be a 3OTA such that $L(M) = L \in HREC$. Let $\Gamma = \Sigma \times Q$ and h_1, h_2 be alphabetic mappings on Γ given by $h_1(a, q) = a$, $h_2(a, q) = q$. A hexagonal picture P over Γ is called a computation description picture if $h_2(P)$ is a run of M on $h_1(P)$, and is called an accepting computation description picture if $h_2(P)$ is an accepting run.

The following lemma can be proved as in the case of strings.

Lemma 8:

(1) *The alphabet* Γ *contains* $O(mn)$ *elements where* n = *number of states of the minimal 3OTA* M_L *for* L, *and* $m = |\Sigma|$.
(2) *For* $p \in L$, *let* $d(p)$ *be a picture over* Γ *representing an accepting computation description for* p. $X(p) = h_2(d(p))$ *is called a valid picture for* p. *Let* $Val(p) = \{X(p)/X(p)$ *is a valid picture for* $p\}$. *Then* $|Val(p)| = O(n^{V(p)})$ *where* $V(p)$ *is the product measure.*
(3) *Let* S *be a local hexagonal picture language over* Q *such that* $L = h(S)$ *and* R_S *be a characteristic sample for* S. *Then there is a finite subset* S_L *of* L *such that* $R_S \subseteq Val(S_L)$.

From lemma 7.1 we obtain a learning algorithm for languages of HREC.

Algorithm HR
Input : A positive presentation of L, $n = |Q|$ for the minimal 3OTA for L.
Output : A sequence of conjectures of the form $h(L(\Delta))$.
Query : Restricted subset query.
Procedure :

Initialize E_0 to ϕ
Construct the initial $\Delta_0 = \phi$
repeat(forever)
  Let Δ_i be the current conjecture
  read the next positive example p
  compute $Val(p) = \{\alpha_1, \alpha_2, \ldots, \alpha_t\}$
  for each j scan α_j to compute $\Delta_{ij} = B_{2,2,2}(\hat{\alpha}_j)$
  ask if $h(L(\Delta_{ij})) \subset L$ or not
  $Val(p) = Val(p) \backslash \{\alpha_j$ / the answer is no$\}$
  $E_{i+1} = E_i \cup Val(p)$
  $\Delta_{i+1} = \Delta_i \cup \{B_{2,2,2}(\hat{\alpha})/\alpha \in Val(p)\}$
  Output Δ_{i+1} as new conjecture.

Lemma 9: *Let* n *be the number of states of the minimal 3OTA accepting the recognizable hexagonal picture language. After at most* $t(n)$ *subset queries, the algorithm HR produces a conjecture* Δ_i *such that* E_i *includes a characteristic sample for a local hexagonal picture language* U *such that* $L = h(U)$ *where* $t(n)$ *is a polynomial in* n, *which depends on* U.

This is a consequence of lemma 7.1 and the fact that the maximum size for pictures in L is bounded by a polynomial in n. Summarizing, we obtain the following theorem.

Theorem 3: Given an unknown recognizable hexagonal picture language L, the algorithm HR efficiently learns in the limit from positive data and restricted subset queries, a subset Δ of $(\Sigma \cup \{\#\})^{2\times 2\times 2}$ such that $L = h(L(\Delta))$.

Acknowledgments

The authors thank Dr. K. G. Subramanian for useful comments. The first author acknowledges the funding by the University of Saint-Etienne, France for his earlier visits to the University and fruitful discussion there on the topic of learning theory with faculty of EURISE.

References

1. K. S. Dersanambika, K. Krithivasan, C. Martin-Vide and K. G. Subramanian, *Lecture Notes in Computer Science* **3322**, 52 (2004).
2. K. S. Fu, *Syntactic Pattern Recognition and Applications*, (Prentice Hall Inc., 1982).
3. D. Giammarresi and A. Restivo, *Fundamenta Informatica* **25**, 399 (1996).
4. D. Giammarresi and A. Restivo, in *Hand Book of Formal Languages, Vol. 3*, Eds. G. Rozenberg and A. Salomaa, (Springer-Verlag, Berlin, 1997), p. 215.
5. Y. Sakakibara, *Theoretical Computer Science* **185**, 15 (1997).
6. G. Siromoney and R. Siromoney, *Computer Graphics and Image Processing* **5**, 353 (1976).
7. G. Siromoney, R. Siromoney and K. Krithivasan, *Computer Graphics and Image Processing* **1**, 284 (1982).
8. R. Siromoney, Lisa Mathew, K. G. Subramanian and V. R. Dare, *International Journal of Pattern Recognition and Artificial Intelligence* **8**, 627 (1994).
9. K. G. Subramanian, *Computer Graphics and Image Processing* **10**, 338 (1979).

CHAPTER 26

POLLARD'S RHO SPLIT KNOWLEDGE SCHEME

M. K. Viswanath and K. P. Vidya*

Department of Mathematics, Madras Christian College (Autonomous), Affiliated to University of Madras, Chennai 600 059, Tamil Nadu, India
**E-mail: kpvidya@hotmail.com*

In a Split Knowledge Scheme or a (2, 2) Threshold Scheme, a secret S that controls a critical action is divided into two pieces called shares or shadows. These shares are distributed to the two participants of the scheme such that, the secret may be recovered only if both participants input their shares. This security scheme plays a significant role in inter bank/branch payment systems in which critical payment instructions are carried out for customer(s). In this paper, we propose a Split Knowledge Scheme that is based on the Pollard rho attack on the Elliptic Curve Discrete Logarithm Problem (ECDLP). Our scheme proves itself in computational efficiency and also guarantees the authenticity of the shares at the time of reconstruction of the secret. An illustration of our scheme with its application to Wired Payment Systems in Banks is discussed here.

1. Introduction

A threshold scheme having t participants with a threshold value k is a scheme in which a secret S is divided into t pieces called shares. These shares are distributed among the t participants where a coalition of $k \leq t$ participants can reconstruct the secret while the same is impossible for a coalition of $k - 1$ or fewer participants. Our scheme, that is based on the Pollard rho attack[7] of the ECDLP is a Split Knowledge Scheme where a maximum of only two persons are allowed to participate in the scheme. The secret that is shared between the two participants may be recovered only if both participants pool in their shares since knowledge of only one share is inadequate for the reconstruction of the secret.

To give a brief outline on the mathematics of our scheme we first define the elliptic curve discrete logarithm problem (ECDLP): Given an elliptic curve E defined over a finite field F_q, a point $P \in E(F_q)$ of order n, and a point $Q \in \langle P \rangle$, find the integer $l \in [0, n-1]$ such that $Q = lP$. The integer l is called the discrete logarithm of Q to the base P, denoted $l = \log_P Q$. Now, the Pollard rho attack on the ECDLP finds two distinct pairs (c', d'), (c'', d'') of integers modulo n such that the points $X' = c'P + d'Q$ and $X'' = c''P + d''Q$ collide. That is, a suitable iterating function $f : \langle P \rangle \rightarrow \langle P \rangle$ is defined so that any point X_0 in $\langle P \rangle$ determines a sequence $\{X_i\}_{i \geq 0}$ of points where $X_i = f(X_{i-1})$ for $i \geq 1$. Now, since $\langle P \rangle$ is finite, the sequence will collide at some ith iteration and then cycle for the remaining iterations forming a ρ-like shape. Then l can be obtained by computing $l = (c' - c'')(d'' - d')^{-1} \mod n$. We set l as the secret of our threshold scheme. To generate the shares or shadows, $\langle P \rangle$ is partitioned into two sets of roughly the same size and these shares are distributed to the participants A_1 and A_2 of the scheme.

Section 1 of this paper describes the purpose, motivation and background and gives a brief outline of the mathematics of our scheme. Section 2 deals with the notion of elliptic curves while Section 3 discusses the main theme of the paper. An application of our scheme to Wired Payment Systems in banks is explained in Section 4.

2. Elliptic Curves

An elliptic curve E defined over a finite prime field F_p of characteristic greater than three is given by the set of points that satisfy the equation $y^2 = x^3 + ax + b$, a, $b \in F_p$ where, discriminant $\Delta = -16(4a^3 + 27b^2) \neq 0$ together with the point at infinity O. It forms an abelian group over a special type of addition, where, O serves as the identity element of the group and the inverse of a point $R = (x_1, y_1)$ on the curve is given by $-R = (x_1, -y_1)$. The Group law for addition of two points $R = (x_1, y_1)$ and $S = (x_2, y_2)$ for $R \neq S$ and $S \neq -R$, is given by the co-ordinates $(x_3, y_3) \in E(F_p)$ where, $x_3 = \lambda^2 - x_1 - x_2$, $y_3 = \lambda(x_1 - x_3) - y_1$ and the slope λ is given by $(y_2 - y_1)/(x_2 - x_1)$ if $R \neq S$ and $S \neq -R$ and $(3x_1^2 + a)/2y_1$ if $R = S$. The order n of the elliptic curve over F_p, i.e., the number of elements in the abelian group is determined by the bounds stated in Hasse's Theorem $p + 1 - 2\sqrt{p} < n < p + 1 + 2\sqrt{p}$ while the order of a point $R \in E(F_p)$ is the smallest positive integer α for which

$\alpha R = O$. Further, if the group is of prime order it implies that the group is cyclic and every element of the group other than O is a generator of the group.

3. Pollard's Rho Split Knowledge Scheme

In our security scheme, a trusted entity T divides a secret S such that it can be distributed to the participants A_1 and A_2 of the scheme. The secret S is chosen to be an integer $l \in [0, n-1]$ and $P, Q = lP$ are points on a randomly chosen elliptic curve E. The curve E of prime order n defined over a finite prime field F_p is generated by the point P. The trusted entity T then selects random integers $a_j, b_j \in [0, n-1]$, computes the value $R_j = a_jP + b_jQ$, for $j = 1$ and 2, and distributes the tuple $S_j = (a_j, b_j, R_j)$ to the participants A_1 and A_2 respectively. T keeps the parameters P and Q secret. The S_j serve as the shares or shadows of the scheme while P and Q are set as the verification parameters that are later used by T to verify these S_j at the time of reconstruction of the secret.

Suppose that, the secret S is to be reconstructed from the knowledge of the shares S_1 and S_2 that are received from A_1 and A_2 respectively. The shares S_1 and S_2 are first verified for correctness using the verification parameters P and Q by computing $a_jP + b_jQ = V_j$ and comparing the value of V_j with that of the corresponding R_j in S_j for $j = 1$ and 2. Now, Σa_j, Σb_j, ΣR_j, are computed from the knowledge of S_1 and S_2 and are set as c', d', X', respectively where X' satisfies $X' = \Sigma R_j = c'P + d'Q$. A suitable partition function $H : \langle P \rangle \to L = \{1, 2\}$ is chosen such that it spans both partitions of $\langle P \rangle$. The iterating function $f : \langle P \rangle \to \langle P \rangle$ defined by $f(X') = X' + a_jP + b_jQ$ where $j = H(X')$, determines two distinct pairs (c', d') and (c'', d'') of integers modulo n such that the two points $X' = c'P + d'Q$ and $X'' = c''P + d''Q$ on E collide. Then the pairs (c', d') and (c'', d'') are used to compute $l = (c' - c'')(d'' - d')^{-1} \mod n$ which is the secret S.

Thus the Pollard's rho attack on the Elliptic curve discrete logarithm problem allows an efficient partitioning of the elliptic curve group. Moreover, as the knowledge of only one share does not reveal the secret, both participants of the scheme have to necessarily collude to reconstruct S. The mechanism also provides a means to trace the rightful owner of the share using verification parameters P and Q.

3.1. *Mechanism: Pollard's rho split knowledge scheme*

SUMMARY A secret S is distributed between two participants A_1 and A_2 of the $(2,2)$-threshold scheme.

RESULT S is reconstructed using the shares of both participants.

(I) *Setup*: A trusted entity T

(1) Selects an elliptic curve E over a finite prime field F_p of prime order n generated by a point P.

(2) Sets the secret S as a random integer l and determines the point $Q = lP$ on E.

(3) Selects random integers a_j, $b_j \in [0, n-1]$ and computes $R_j = a_jP + b_jQ$, $j = 1, 2$.

(4) Sets $c' = \Sigma a_j$, $d' = \Sigma b_j$, and $X' = \Sigma R_j = c'P + d'Q$.

(5) Distributes the shares S_j to the participants A_j where the tuple $S_j = (a_j, b_j, R_j)$.

(6) Keeps the verification parameters (P, Q) secret.

(II) *Pooling of shares*

(1) T receives the shares $S_j = (a_j, b_j, R_j)$ from the participants A_j.

(2) Computes $a_jP + b_jQ = V_j$ using verification parameters P and Q and verifies if V_j equals R_j for $j = 1$ and 2 respectively.

(3) T proceeds with step 4 if $V_1 = R_1$ and $V_2 = R_2$ or else exits from the application after sending a warning to A_1 or A_2 or both depending on who has entered the wrong input.

(4) T defines a partition function $H : \langle P \rangle \to L = \{1, 2\}$ where $H(X') = H(x, y) = x(\mod 2) + 1$.

(5) Repeat

(a) Compute $j = H(X')$.

(b) Set $X' = X' + R_j$, $c' = c' + a_j \mod n$, $d' = d' + b_j \mod n$.

(c) For i from 1 to 2 do

(d) Compute $j = H(X'')$.

(e) Set $X'' = X'' + R_j$, $c'' = c'' + a_j \mod n$, $d'' = d'' + b_j \mod n$.

(6) Until $X'' = X'$.

(7) Compute $l = (c' - c'')(d'' - d')^{-1} \mod n$ which is the secret S.

(8) Exit

4. Wired Payment System

Wired Payment Systems are Agency Services offered by banks to transfer funds from one branch office to another at the request of a customer. The branch office that originates the transaction is called the originator and that which responds to the transaction is called the responder. The transactions involve the transmission of highly sensitive data that need to be protected from adversaries. This necessitates the use of security techniques where both entities share control of the transaction process. In the following section we discuss an application of Mechanism 3.1 to Wired Payment System in banks from an Indian context.

4.1. *Protocol*

In Wired Payment Systems (WPS), let us suppose that, Alice, an account holder at the Branch Office B_1 of a bank approaches the authorized official of B_1 with a request to transfer funds from her account to Bob's account where it is assumed that Bob is an account holder at Branch Office B_2 of the same bank. The authorized official at B_1 debits Alice's account with B_1 and encrypts the message using symmetric key techniques. The cipher text is then sent to the Branch Office B_2. The honesty of the concerned official at B_2 in revealing his/her identity to the official at B_1 is assumed. The official at B_2 decrypts the cipher text and credits Bob's account with B_2 for the sum of money indicated in the message. Now, Bob can withdraw the sum against the balance in his account on producing a cheque for the same amount. The officials of the two Branch Offices then send the confirmations of the transaction to each other by post. They also record the transaction in the Inter Branch General ledger (IBGL) and report all such inter branch transactions to the Reconciliation Office (IBRO) by means of a daily statement.

In the protocol that we propose, the account holder may request a WPS transfer of funds using online banking facilities provided by the Inter Branch Reconciliation Office (IBRO). A successful transaction is illustrated in Fig. 1.

On submission of the request, the secret S is set typically as the string that consists of Transaction ID, Transaction Date (day/month/year), Transaction Time (hh:mm:ss), Bank Code, Originating Branch Code (B_1), Name and Account Number of Account holder at the branch where transaction originates, Responding Branch Code (B_2), Name and Account Number of Account holder at the branch which responds to the transaction, Currency, and Amount. Now the shares $S_j = (a_j, b_j, R_j)$ are generated and the tuple (Transaction ID, Branch Code, S_j) are distributed to the authorized officials of B_j for $j = 1, 2$ respectively. Here, it is to be mentioned that the

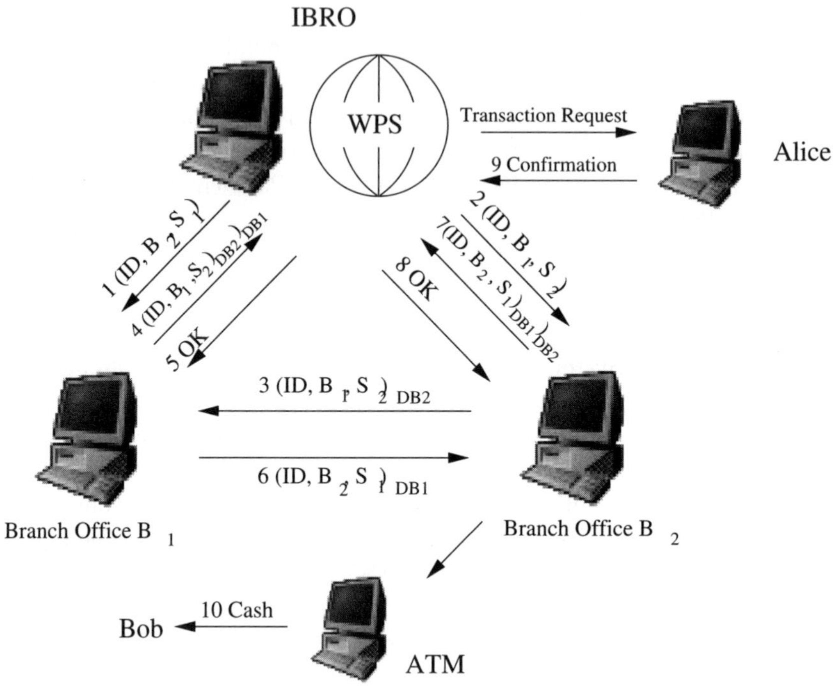

Fig. 1. Illustration of a successful transaction using the proposed scheme for Wired Payment Systems.

Branch Code in the tuple sent to B_1 who is the originator of the transaction is that of the Responding Branch B_2 and in the tuple that is sent to B_2 who responds to the transaction, the Branch Code corresponds to that of the originator B_1. Both offices B_1 and B_2 are thus alerted to the existence of a high value transaction that is to take place between them.

4.2. *Algorithm wired payment system*

SUMMARY An amount of S Dollars is transferred from Branch Offices B_1 to B_2 of a bank using Split Knowledge Scheme.

NOTATION IBRO is the Inter Branch Reconciliation Office. IBGL is the Inter Branch General ledger. $DB1$ and $DB2$ represent the digital signatures of the officials at B_1 and B_2 respectively, where B_1 is the originator and B_2 the responder. v is used to denote any verification function used by IBRO. IBGL-OrigCr and IBGL-RespDr denotes IBGL Originating Credit and Responding Debit entries respectively.

RESULT Alice transfers an amount of S dollars from her account to Bob's account by means of secure online banking facilities.

Steps

(1) Alice requests for a transfer of funds from her account to Bob's account
(2) The secret is set as a number which typically consists of the following information: ID, Date (dd/mm/yy), Time (hh:mm:ss), Bank Code, Originating Branch Code (B_1), Account Number and Name of Account holder at B_1, Responding Branch Code (B_2), Account Number and Name of Account holder at B_2, Currency, and Amount S.
(3) IBRO generates the shares of the secret as S_j for $j = 1$ and 2 using mechanism 3.1.
(4) IBRO sends (ID, B_2, S_1) and (ID, B_1, S_2) to Branch Offices B_1 and B_2 respectively
(5) B_2 then sends $(ID, B_1, S_2)DB2$ to B_1.
(6) B_1 computes the secret using the function f and extracts S from it, then debits Alice's account for the amount S and sends $((ID, B_1, S_2)_{DB2})_{DB1}$ to IBRO.
(7) IBRO verifies the digital signature $DB1$ of B_1 and then using the value of S_2 in $((ID, B_1, S_2)_{DB2})_{DB1}$ it verifies the identity of B_2

    (a) If $v(DB1)$ and $v(S_2)$ return OK, IBRO records (IBGL-Orig) and confirms transaction to B_1 who proceeds with step 8.
    (b) else If $v(DB1)$ and $v(S_2)$ return NOT OK then IBRO sends warning to B_1 and cancels the transaction. B_1 reverses all entries that were recorded prior to the cancellation and ends the transaction (Step 13).

(8) B_1 sends $(ID, B_2, S_1)_{DB1}$ to B_2.
(9) B_2 sends $((ID, B_2, S_1)_{DB1})_{DB2}$ to IBRO.
(10) IBRO verifies the identity of B_2 from $DB2$ and also the identity of B_1 from S_1 in $((ID, B_2, S_1)_{DB1})_{DB2}$

    (a) If $v(DB2)$ and $v(S_1)$ return OK and If v(IBGL-Orig) exists then IBRO confirms transaction to B_2 who proceeds with step 11.
    (b) If one of $v(DB2)$, $v(S_1)$, v(IBGL-Orig) returns NOT OK then IBRO sends a warning message to B_1 and B_2. In the case of a fraudulent transaction B_1 and B_2 reverse all recorded entries and end the transaction (Step 13).

(11) If IBRO confirms the transaction to B_2 then B_2 computes the secret, credits Bob's account to the amount S and confirms credit to IBRO else B_2 withholds the credit to Bob's account.
(12) If IBRO receives confirmation from B_2 then IBRO records (IBGL-Resp) and sends transaction confirmation to Alice else IBRO sends request cancelled to Alice.
(13) End of transaction.

Now, the official at the responding branch B_2 sends a copy of (ID, B_1, S_2) to Branch Office B_1. A suitable digital signature scheme is used to sign the share before it is transmitted to B_1. On receiving the share at B_1 the digital signature is first verified. It is ensured that there are no mismatches regarding the ID and Branch Code before the message is decrypted using Mechanism 3.1. Now, Alice's account with B_1 is debited and the corresponding credit to the Inter Branch General Ledger (IBGL) is intimated to the IBRO. This message to IBRO consists of a signed copy of the share received from B_2 duly countersigned by the official at B_1. The IBRO verifies if $a_2P + b_2Q = V_2$ equals the value of R_2 in S_2 using the verification parameters P and Q. If V_2 is found to be equal to R_2, then IBRO records the originating credit entry pertaining to B_1 and sends the confirmation to B_1. Now B_1 is assured that the share sent by B_2 is authentic and sends (ID, B_2, S_1) to B_2 countersigned with its signature. B_2 confirms the authenticity of this share with IBRO by the same process that was adopted by B_1. The IBRO verifies the share and also searches its records for a corresponding originating credit entry from B_1. If such an entry exists IBRO confirms the debit to B_2. Thus B_2 is assured of the credibility of the transaction and proceeds with decrypting the message. Bob's account with B_2 is now credited with the amount, which may be withdrawn by him at any time. Then B_2 sends confirmation to IBRO who records the responding debit entry of the transaction pertaining to B_2. If the transaction fails at any stage then IBRO sends a transaction-cancelled message to Alice and reverses the entries in its records. On the other hand on a successful completion of the transaction Alice receives a confirmation from IBRO.

The following section illustrates the application with an example. For academic purpose, we consider only numbers with small numerical values and set the secret S as the amount involved in the transaction.

4.3. *Illustration*

Suppose that, Alice wishes to transfer an amount of thirty dollars from her account in branch office B_1 to Bob's account in branch office B_2. Alice may access the fill out form from the server at the reconciliation office (IBRO) using the online banking facilities and submit the same after furnishing the required details. Suppose next that, to set the secret S, the trusted entity T selects at random the elliptic curve $E(F_{29})$ given by $y^2 = x^3 + 4x + 20$ where the discriminant $\Delta = -16(4a^3 + 27b^2) = -176896 \not\equiv 0 (\bmod\ 29)$. The number of elements in the elliptic curve group is 37 a prime, and so, $E(F_{29})$ is a cyclic group. Therefore, every element of the group except the point at infinity O is a generator of all the other elements of the group.

$0P = O$	$10P = (13, 23)$	$20P = (27, 27)$	$30P = (24, 7)$
$1P = (1, 5)$	$11P = (10, 25)$	$21P = (0, 7)$	$31P = (17, 10)$
$2P = (4, 19)$	$12P = (19, 13)$	$22P = (3, 28)$	$32P = (6, 17)$
$3P = (20, 3)$	$13P = (16, 27)$	$23P = (5, 7)$	$33P = (15, 2)$
$4P = (15, 27)$	$14P = (5, 22)$	$24P = (16, 2)$	$34P = (20, 26)$
$5P = (6, 12)$	$15P = (3, 1)$	$25P = (19, 16)$	$35P = (4, 10)$
$6P = (17, 19)$	$16P = (0, 22)$	$26P = (10, 4)$	$36P = (1, 24)$
$7P = (24, 22)$	$17P = (27, 2)$	$27P = (13, 6)$	
$8P = (8, 10)$	$18P = (2, 23)$	$28P = (14, 6)$	
$9P = (14, 23)$	$19P = (2, 6)$	$29P = (8, 19)$	

Now, the secret S is set as 30. If the point P is chosen to be the pair $(1, 5)$ which is a generator of the group the point Q would be $30P = (24, 7)$. The trusted entity T, in this case, the IBRO chooses random integers a_j, $b_j \in [0, 36]$ and computes the points $R_j = a_jP + b_jQ$ for $j = 1$ and 2. The shares $S_j = (a_j, b_j, R_j)$ for $j = 1$ and 2 are set as:

$$S_1 = (3, 4, (19, 13)), S_2 = (5, 2, (14, 6))$$

Then, T distributes the tuple (ID, B_2, S_1) and (ID, B_1, S_2) to B_1 and B_2 respectively.

At the time of reconstruction of the secret S, the initial values required for the iterative process defined by the function f are set as follows: the tuple (c', d', X') is set as $(8, 6, (20, 3))$ where c', $d' \in [0, 36]$ and $X' = c'P + d'Q = 8P + 6(30P) = 3P$ modulo 37, where 37 is the order of the elliptic curve group. It can be seen from above that the value of $3P$ is $(20, 3)$.

Table 1.

Iteration	c'	d'	X'	c''	d''	X''
—	8	6	3P = (20, 3)	8	6	3P = (20, 3)
1	11	10	15P = (3, 1)	16	12	6P = (17, 19)
2	16	12	6P = (17, 19)	24	18	9P = (14, 23)
3	21	14	34P = (20, 26)	30	26	33P = (15, 2)
4	24	18	9P = (14, 23)	1	32	36P = (1, 24)
5	27	22	21P = (0, 7)	11	36	18P = (2, 23)
6	30	26	33P = (15, 2)	17	7	5P = (6, 12)
7	35	28	24P = (16, 2)	25	13	8P = (8, 10)
8	1	32	36P = (1, 24)	33	19	11P = (10, 25)
9	6	34	27P = (13, 6)	4	35	14P = (5, 22)
10	11	36	18P = (2, 23)	12	31	17P = (27, 2)
11	14	3	30P = (24, 7)	20	0	20P = (27, 27)
12	17	7	5P = (6, 12)	20	6	23P = (5, 7)
13	20	11	17P = (27, 2)	1	10	5P = (6, 12)
14	25	13	8P = (8, 10)	9	16	8P = (8, 10)

The values of c', d', X', c'', d'', X'' tabulated for the different iterations are shown in Table 1. The process terminates when a collision occurs in the values of X' and X''. It can be seen that in this case the values of X' and X'' are equal in the fourteenth iteration. The corresponding values of c', d', c'', d'', are 25, 13, 9, 16 respectively. Now, $(c' - c'')(d'' - d')^{-1} \mod n$ is computed for $n = 37$.

That is, $l = (c' - c'')(d'' - d')^{-1} \mod n = (25 - 9)(16 - 13)^{-1} (\mod 37) = 30$ which is the value of the secret S. This reconstruction of S at the branch office B_1 sets off the debit entry in Alice's account with B_1 and the corresponding IBGL credit entry is also recorded at IBRO. Branch Office B_1 waits for confirmation from the IBRO before it sends the share S_1 across to branch office B_2. Now, B_2 verifies the originating credit entry with the IBRO. On receiving a positive response from the reconciliation office, B_2 credits Bob's account with it, for the required sum. Then B_2 sends its confirmation to IBRO who in turn records the IBGL debit entry for the corresponding transaction ID and sends the confirmation to Alice. This completes the transaction. If there is an error at any stage the transaction is cancelled and the bank sends a transaction-cancelled message to Alice.

5. Conclusion

The proposed protocol and mechanism ensures a higher degree of security than the symmetric key techniques that are followed today by most Indian banks. In our scheme, the messages are encrypted at the Reconciliation Office and it thus relieves the bank official from the difficult process of encrypting and decrypting messages using a codebook. Nevertheless, their involvement in the transaction cannot be denied at a later date as their digital signatures on the messages may be verified. As our scheme requires only half the message to be conveyed by officials the high security risk involved in the transmission of sensitive data is minimized. An adversary who may have access to information that is transmitted from one office cannot determine the amount transacted with the knowledge of only one half of the message. In addition to this, the branch office that responds to the transaction has the convenience of verifying the existence of the corresponding originating credit entry at the reconciliation office, before making payment of the amount. This safeguards the bank from heavy losses caused by adversaries who may withdraw large sums of money from an account that might have been credited against a fraudulent message received through telex, telephone or email. Since such fraudulent transactions can be detected only at the time of reconciliation of records it results in the fraud going unnoticed till it is too late to recover the amount.

The security technique used in our scheme also provides a fairly simple method of computation of shares for the participants of the scheme and uses negligible memory space during the iterative process. Although the suggested protocol requires a few more messages to be transmitted between the reconciliation office and branch offices, it is possible to verify the authenticity of the shares and the credibility of the transaction before the payment is made. This high level of security in our scheme ensures the safety of transaction of those customers who use sophisticated techniques of online banking.

References

1. G. R. Blakley, *Proc. Nat. Computer Conf. AFIPS Conf. Proc.*, **48** 313 (1979).
2. Y. Desmedt, *Lecture Notes in Computer Science*, **293** 120 (1988).
3. Y. Desmedt, *Proceedings of the 3rd Symposium on: State and Progress of Research in Cryptography*, **110** (1993).
4. N. Koblitz, *Math. Comp.*, **48(177)** 203 (1987).
5. K. Kuhn and R. Struik, *Lecture Notes in Computer Science*, **2259** 212 (2001).
6. P. Oorschot van and M. Weiner, *Journal of Cryptology*, **12** 1 (1999).
7. J. M. Pollard, *Math. Comp.*, **32(143)** 918 (1978).
8. A. Shamir, *Communications of ACM*, **22** 612 (1979).
9. J. H. Silverman, *The Arithmetic of elliptic curves*, Vol. 106, (Graduate Texts in Mathematics, Springer-Verlag, 1986).

10. N. Smart, *Journal of Cryptology,* **12** 193 (1999).
11. E. Teske, *Lecture Notes in Computer Science,* **1423** 541 (1998).
12. E. Teske, *Mathematics of Computation,* **70**, 809 (2001).
13. K. P. Vidya and M. K. Viswanath, *Computational Mathematics* Eds. K. Thangavel and P. Balasubramaniam, (Narosa Publishing House, New Delhi, India, 2005), p 37.

CHAPTER 27

CHARACTERIZATIONS FOR SOME CLASSES OF CODES DEFINED BY BINARY RELATIONS

Do Long Van* and Kieu Van Hung†

**Institute of Mathematics,*
18 Hoang Quoc Viet Road, 10307 Hanoi, Vietnam
E-mail: dlvan@math.ac.vn

†Hanoi Pedagogical University 2, Vinh Phuc, Vietnam
E-mail: hungkv@hn.vnn.vn

Superinfix codes (p-superinfix codes, s-superinfix codes), sucypercodes and supercodes have been introduced and considered by the authors in earlier papers. In particular, it has been proved that the embedding problem for these classes of codes has positive solution in both the finite and regular case. In this paper, characterizations of these codes, especially of the maximal ones, by means of Parikh vectors and their appropriate generalizations are given. Also a procedure to generate all the maximal supercodes on a two-letter alphabet is exhibited.

1. Introduction

Defining codes by binary relations was initiated by G. Thierrin and H. Shyr in the middle of 1970s.[7] It appeared that this is a good method in introducing new classes of codes. The idea of this comes from the notion of independent sets in universal algebra.[2]

One of the interesting problems in the theory of codes is that of embedding a code in a given class C of codes into a code maximal in the same class (not necessarily maximal as a code) which preserves some property (usually, the finiteness or the regularity) of the given code. This is called the *embedding problem* for the class C of codes.

Until now the answer for the embedding problem is known only for several cases using different combinatorial techniques. In Ref. 8 (see also Ref. 9) it is proposed a general embedding schema for the classes of codes, which can be defined by length-increasing transitive binary relations. This allows to solve positively, in a unified way, the embedding problem for many classes of codes well-known as well as new (see Refs. 3, 8–10).

In this paper, we consider in details several among the new classes of codes mentioned above, namely those of p-superinfix codes, s-superinfix codes, superinfix codes, sucypercodes and supercodes, which can be all defined by length-increasing transitive binary relations. Characterizations of these codes, especially of the maximal ones, by means of Parikh vectors and their appropriate generalizations are established. For the case of two-letter alphabets, a procedure to generate all the maximal supercodes and an algorithm to embed a supercode in a maximal one, are proposed.

We now recall some notions and notations, which will be used in the sequel. Let A throughout be a finite alphabet. We denote by A^* the free monoid generated by A whose elements are called *words* on A. The *empty word* is denoted by 1 and $A^+ = A^* - 1$. The number of all occurrences of letters in a word u is the *length* of u, denoted by $|u|$.

A word u is a *prefix* (*suffix*) of a word v if $v = ux$ ($v = xu$, resp.), for some $x \in A^*$. If $x \neq 1$ then u is a *proper prefix* (*proper suffix*, resp.) of v. An *infix* or *factor* of a word v is a word u such that $v = xuy$ for some $x, y \in A^*$; the infix is *proper* if $xy \neq 1$. We say that u is a *subword* of v if $u = u_1 \cdots u_n$, $v = x_0u_1x_1 \cdots u_nx_n$ for some $n \geq 1$ and $u_1, \ldots, u_n$, $x_0, \ldots, x_n \in A^*$. If $x_0 \cdots x_n \neq 1$ then u is called a *proper subword* of v. If u is a subword (proper subword) of v we also say that v is a *superword* (*proper superword*) of u. A word u is a *permutation* of a word v if $|u|_a = |v|_a$ for all $a \in A$, where $|u|_a$ denotes the number of occurrences of a in u. And u is a *cyclic permutation* of v if there exist x, y such that $u = xy$ and $v = yx$.

Any subset of A^* is a *language* over A. A language X is a *code* over A if for all integers $n, m \geq 1$ and for all $x_1, \ldots, x_n, y_1, \ldots, y_m \in X$, the equality

$$x_1x_2 \cdots x_n = y_1y_2 \cdots y_m ,$$

implies $n = m$ and $x_i = y_i$ for $i = 1, \ldots, n$. A code X is *maximal* over A if it is not properly contained in another code over A. Let C be a class of codes over A and $X \in C$. The code X is *maximal in* C (not necessarily maximal as a code) if X is not properly contained in another code in C. For further details of the theory of codes we refer to Ref. 1, 5 and 6.

Given a binary relation $\prec$ on A^*. A subset X in A^* is an *independent set* with respect to the relation $\prec$ if any two elements of X are not in this relation. We say that a class C of codes is *defined by* $\prec$ if the codes in this class are exactly the independent sets w.r.t. $\prec$. Then, we denote the class C by $C_\prec$. Very often, the relation $\prec$ characterizes some property α of words.

In this case, we write $\prec_\alpha$ instead of $\prec$ and also C_α instead of $C_{\prec_\alpha}$. The relation $\prec$ is said to be *length-increasing* if for any $u, v \in A^*$, $u \prec v$ implies $|u| < |v|$. We denote by $\preceq$ the reflexive closure of $\prec$, i.e. for any $u, v \in A^*$, $u \preceq v$ iff $u = v$ or $u \prec v$.

It is easy to verify that the following binary relations on A^* are transitive (except for $\prec_b$) and length-increasing.

$u \prec_p v \Leftrightarrow v = ux$ with $x \neq 1$;
$u \prec_s v \Leftrightarrow v = xu$ with $x \neq 1$;
$u \prec_b v \Leftrightarrow (u \prec_p v) \vee (u \prec_s v)$;
$u \prec_{p.i} v \Leftrightarrow v = xuy$ with $y \neq 1$;
$u \prec_{s.i} v \Leftrightarrow v = xuy$ with $x \neq 1$;
$u \prec_i v \Leftrightarrow v = xuy$ with $xy \neq 1$;
$u \prec_{p.h} v \Leftrightarrow \exists n \geq 1 : u = u_1...u_n \wedge v = x_0u_1x_1...u_nx_n$ with $x_1...x_n \neq 1$;
$u \prec_{s.h} v \Leftrightarrow \exists n \geq 1 : u = u_1...u_n \wedge v = x_0u_1x_1...u_nx_n$ with $x_0...x_{n-1} \neq 1$;
$u \prec_h v \Leftrightarrow \exists n \geq 1 : u = u_1...u_n \wedge v = x_0u_1x_1...u_nx_n$ with $x_0...x_n \neq 1$;
$u \prec_{p.si} v \Leftrightarrow \exists w \in A^* : w \prec_p v \wedge u \preceq_h w$;
$u \prec_{s.si} v \Leftrightarrow \exists w \in A^* : w \prec_s v \wedge u \preceq_h w$;
$u \prec_{si} v \Leftrightarrow \exists w \in A^* : w \prec_i v \wedge u \preceq_h w$;
$u \prec_{p.scpi} v \Leftrightarrow (\exists v' : v' \prec_p v)(\exists v'' \in \sigma(v')) : u \preceq_h v''$;
$u \prec_{s.scpi} v \Leftrightarrow (\exists v' : v' \prec_s v)(\exists v'' \in \sigma(v')) : u \preceq_h v''$;
$u \prec_{scpi} v \Leftrightarrow (\exists v' : v' \prec_i v)(\exists v'' \in \sigma(v')) : u \preceq_h v''$;
$u \prec_{p.spi} v \Leftrightarrow (\exists v' : v' \prec_p v)(\exists v'' \in \pi(v')) : u \preceq_h v''$;
$u \prec_{s.spi} v \Leftrightarrow (\exists v' : v' \prec_s v)(\exists v'' \in \pi(v')) : u \preceq_h v''$;
$u \prec_{spi} v \Leftrightarrow (\exists v' : v' \prec_i v)(\exists v'' \in \pi(v')) : u \preceq_h v''$;
$u \prec_{scp} v \Leftrightarrow \exists v' \in \sigma(v) : u \prec_h v'$;
$u \prec_{sp} v \Leftrightarrow \exists v' \in \pi(v) : u \prec_h v'$;

where $\pi(v)$ and $\sigma(v)$ are the sets of all permutations and all cyclic permutations of v respectively. In the sequel, for any $X \subseteq A^*$, we put $\pi(X) = \bigcup_{u \in X} \pi(u)$ and $\sigma(X) = \bigcup_{u \in X} \sigma(u)$.

The mentioned above relations define corresponding classes of codes which are named respectively as the classes C_p of *prefix codes*, C_s of *suffix codes*, C_b of *bifix codes*, $C_{p.i}$ of *p-infix codes*, $C_{s.i}$ of *s-infix codes*, C_i of *infix codes*, $C_{p.h}$ of *p-hypercodes*, $C_{s.h}$ of *s-hypercodes*, C_h of *hypercodes*, $C_{p.si}$ of *p-subinfix codes*, $C_{s.si}$ of *s-subinfix codes*, C_{si} of *subinfix codes*, $C_{p.scpi}$ of *p-sucyperinfix codes*, $C_{s.spci}$ of *s-sucyperinfix codes*, C_{spci} of *sucyperinfix codes*,

$C_{p.spi}$ of *p-superinfix codes*, $C_{s.spi}$ of *s-superinfix codes*, C_{spi} of *superinfix codes*, C_{scp} of *sucypercodes* and C_{sp} of *supercodes*.

To facilitate understanding we give now intuitive definitions of the classes of codes introduced above which are the main research subject of this paper. This explains also the way we named these kinds of codes.

A subset $X \subseteq A^+$ is a *superinfix* (*p-superinfix, s-superinfix*) *code*, $X \in C_{spi}$ ($X \in C_{p.spi}, X \in C_{s.spi}$, resp.), if no word in X is a **su**bword of a **per**mutation of a proper **infix** (i.e. factor) (**p**refix, **s**uffix, resp.) of another word in X. And a subset X of A^+ is a *supercode* (*sucypercode*), $X \in C_{sp}$ ($X \in C_{scp}$, resp.), if no word in X is a proper **su**bword of a **per**mutation (**cy**clic **per**mutation, resp.) of another word in X. Thus supercodes and sucypercodes are hypercodes. Hence, all the supercodes and sucypercodes over a finite alphabet are finite.

2. Characterizations

Let $A = \{a_1, a_2, \ldots, a_k\}$ and $K = \{1, 2, \ldots, k\}$. For every $u \in A^*$, we denote by $p(u)$ the Parikh vector of u, namely

$$p(u) = (|u|_{a_1}, |u|_{a_2}, \ldots, |u|_{a_k}) \,.$$

where $|u|_{a_i}$ denotes the number of occurrences of a_i in u. Thus p is a mapping from A^* into the set V^k of all the k-vectors of non-negative integers.

The following fact is useful in the sequel.

Lemma 1: *For any u, $v \in A^+$, the following conditions are equivalent*

(i) *u is a subword (a proper subword, resp.) of a permutation of v;*
(ii) *v is a superword (a proper superword, resp.) of a permutation of u;*
(iii) *$p(u) \leq p(v)$ ($p(u) < p(v)$, resp.).*

Proof: (i) $\Leftrightarrow$ (iii) Let u be a subword of a permutation of v. By definition, there exists $v' \in \pi(v)$ such that u is a subword of v'. Then we have $p(u) \leq p(v') = p(v)$. Conversely, let $p(u) \leq p(v)$. We shall prove by induction on $|v|$ that u is a subword of a permutation of v. If $|v| = 1$ then $u = v \in A$, the assertion is trivial. Let $|v| = n + 1$ and suppose that the assertion is true for all v' with $|v'| = n$. If $p(u) = p(v)$ then u is a permutation and therefore a subword of a permutation of v. Let now $p(u) < p(v)$. There exists then $a \in A$ such that $|u|_a < |v|_a$. Then there is $v' \in \pi(v)$ such that $v' = v''a$. We have $p(u) \leq p(v'')$. By the induction hypothesis, u is a subword of a permutation of v''. Hence, u is a subword of a permutation of v' and therefore of v.

(ii) $\Leftrightarrow$ (iii) The argument is similar. $\square$

For any subset $X \subseteq A^*$ we denote by $p(X)$ the set of all Parikh vectors of the words in X, $p(X) = \{p \in V^k | p = p(u) \text{ for some } u \in X\}$.

The following result gives an interesting characterization of supercodes.

Theorem 1: For any subset $X \subseteq A^+$ the following assertions are equivalent

(i) X is a supercode;
(ii) $\pi(X)$ is a supercode;
(iii) $p(X)$ is an independent set w.r.t. the relation $<$ on V^k.

Proof: (i) $\Leftrightarrow$ (iii) By definition, X is a supercode iff it is an independent set w.r.t. the relation $\prec_{sp}$. The later is equivalent to the fact that $\forall\, u, v \in X$: $p(u) \not< p(v)$, which in turn is equivalent to the fact that $p(X)$ is an independent set w.r.t. the relation $<$ on V^k.

(iii) $\Rightarrow$ (ii) Let $p(X)$ be an independent set w.r.t. $<$. Since $p(X) = p(\pi(X))$, by the above, $\pi(X)$ is a supercode.

(ii) $\Rightarrow$ (i) Evident. $\square$

The following fact, proved in Ref. 10, allows us to establish a simple characterization of sucypercodes.

Lemma 2: *For any* u, $v \in A^*$ *we have* $\exists v' \in \sigma(v) : u \preceq_h v'$ *iff* $\exists u' \in \sigma(u) : u' \preceq_h v$.

Proposition 1: *For any subset* X *of* A^+, X *is a sucypercode iff so is* $\sigma(X)$.

Proof: The sufficiency is trivial. Let X be a sucypercode. If $\sigma(X)$ were not a sucypercode, there would exist u, $v \in \sigma(X)$ and $v' \in \sigma(v)$ such that $u \prec_h v'$. Then we have $u \in \sigma(x)$, $v \in \sigma(y)$ for some x, $y \in X$. Thus $u \prec_h v'$ with $v' \in \sigma(y)$. By Lemma 2, there exists $u' \in \sigma(u)$ such that $u' \prec_h y$. Since $u' \in \sigma(x)$, again by Lemma 2, there exists $y' \in \sigma(y)$ such that $x \prec_h y'$. This means that $x \prec_{scp} y$, a contradiction. $\square$

Now, to every $u \in A^+$ we associate two elements of the cartesian product $V^k \times K$, denoted by $p_L(u)$ and $p_F(u)$, and one element of $V^k \times K^2$, denoted by $p_{LF}(u)$, which are defined as follows

$$p_L(u) = (p(u), l)\,; \quad p_F(u) = (p(u), f)\,; \quad p_{LF}(u) = (p(u), l, f)\,;$$

where l and f are the indices of the last and the first letter in u, respectively. Thus p_L and p_F are mappings from A^+ into $V^k \times K$, while p_{LF} is a mapping from A^+ into $V^k \times K^2$. These mappings are then extended to languages in a standard way: $p_L(X) = \{p_L(u)|u \in X\}$, $p_F(X) = \{p_F(u)|u \in X\}$ and $p_{LF}(X) = \{p_{LF}(u)|u \in X\}$.

Put $U = \{(\xi, i) \in V^k \times K | p_i(\xi) \neq 0\}$ and $W = \{(\xi, i, j) \in V^k \times K^2 | p_i(\xi), p_j(\xi) \neq 0\}$. To each of the sets U and W we associate a binary relation, denoted both by $\prec$, which are defined by

$$(\xi, i) \prec (\eta, j) \Leftrightarrow (\xi \leq \eta) \wedge (p_j(\xi) < p_j(\eta)),$$

$$(\xi, m, n) \prec (\eta, i, j) \Leftrightarrow (\xi \leq \eta) \wedge (p_i(\xi) < p_i(\eta) \vee p_j(\xi) < p_j(\eta)),$$

where $p_i(\xi)$, $1 \leq i \leq k$, denotes the ith component of ξ. These relations on U and on W, as easily verified, are transitive. Notice that for all language $X \subseteq A^+$, $p_L(X)$ and $p_F(X)$ are subsets of U while $p_{LF}(X)$ is a subset of W.

The following fact is easily verified.

Lemma 3: *For any u, $v \in A^+$ we have*

(i) $u \prec_{p.spi} v$ *iff* $p_L(u) \prec p_L(v)$;
(ii) $u \prec_{s.spi} v$ *iff* $p_F(u) \prec p_F(v)$;
(iii) $u \prec_{spi} v$ *iff* $p_{LF}(u) \prec p_{LF}(v)$.

To every subset X of A^+, we associate the sets

$$E_X = \{x \in X | \exists\, y \in X : p(y) < p(x)\} \text{ and } O_X = X - E_X .$$

Clearly, if $E_X = \emptyset$ then X is a supercode.

Let u be a word in A^+, we define the following operations

$$\pi_L(u) = \pi(u')b, \text{ with } u = u'b, b \in A;$$

$$\pi_F(u) = a\pi(u'), \text{ with } u = au', a \in A;$$

$$\pi_{LF}(u) = \begin{cases} a\pi(u')b, & \text{if } |u| \geq 2 \text{ and } u = au'b, \text{ with } a, b \in A; \\ u, & \text{if } u \in A; \end{cases}$$

which are extended to languages in a normal way: $\pi_L(X) = \bigcup_{u \in X} \pi_L(u)$, $\pi_F(X) = \bigcup_{u \in X} \pi_F(u)$ and $\pi_{LF}(X) = \bigcup_{u \in X} \pi_{LF}(u)$.

Lemma 4: *Let X be a subset of A^+. If $p_L(X)$ ($p_F(X)$) is an independent set w.r.t. the relation $\prec$ on U then so is $p_L(\pi(O_X) \cup \pi_L(E_X))$ ($p_F(\pi(O_X) \cup \pi_F(E_X))$, resp.). If $p_{LF}(X)$ is an independent set w.r.t. the relation $\prec$ on W then so is $p_{LF}(\pi(O_X) \cup \pi_{LF}(E_X))$.*

Proof: We treat only the case of $p_L(X)$. The reasonements for the other cases are similar. Let $p_L(X)$ be an independent set w.r.t. $\prec$ on U. If $p_L(\pi(O_X) \cup \pi_L(E_X))$ were not an independent set w.r.t. $\prec$ on U then there would exist s, $t \in p_L(\pi(O_X) \cup \pi_L(E_X))$ such that $s \prec t$. Since s, $t \in p_L(\pi(O_X) \cup \pi_L(E_X))$, we have $s = p_L(u)$, $t = p_L(v)$ for some u, $v \in \pi(O_X) \cup \pi_L(E_X)$. Because $p_L(u) \prec p_L(v)$, we must have $v \in \pi_L(E_X)$. If $u \in \pi_L(E_X)$ then $p_L(u)$, $p_L(v) \in p_L(\pi_L(E_X)) = p_L(E_X) \subseteq p_L(X)$, a contradiction. If $u \in \pi(O_X)$ then on one hand there exists $u' \in O_X$ such that $p(u') = p(u)$ with $p_L(u') \in p_L(O_X) \subseteq p_L(X)$, and on the other hand $p_L(v) \in p_L(E_X) \subseteq p_L(X)$. From $p_L(u) \prec p_L(v)$ it follows $p_L(u') \prec p_L(v)$, which contradicts the hypothesis that $p_L(X)$ is an independent set w.r.t. $\prec$. □

To end this section, we give characterizations of p-superinfix codes, s-superinfix codes and superinfix codes.

Theorem 2: For any subset X of A^+, the following assertions are equivalent

(i) X is a p-superinfix code (resp., a s-superinfix code, a superinfix code);
(ii) $\pi(O_X) \cup \pi_L(E_X)$ is a p-superinfix code (resp., $\pi(O_X) \cup \pi_F(E_X)$ is a s-superinfix code, $\pi(O_X) \cup \pi_{LF}(E_X)$ is a superinfix code);
(iii) $p_L(X)$ is an independent set w.r.t. the relation $\prec$ on U (resp., $p_F(X)$ is an independent set w.r.t. the relation $\prec$ on U, $p_{LF}(X)$ is an independent set w.r.t. the relation $\prec$ on W).

Proof: We treat only the case of p-superinfix codes. For the other cases the argument is similar.

(i) $\Leftrightarrow$ (iii) By definition, X is a p-superinfix code iff it is an independent set w.r.t. $\prec_{p.spi}$. By Lemma 3(i), the later is equivalent to the fact that $p_L(u) \not\prec p_L(v)$ for all u, $v \in X$, or equivalently $p_L(X)$ is an independent set w.r.t. $\prec$ on U.

(iii) $\Rightarrow$ (ii) Let $p_L(X)$ be an independent set w.r.t. $\prec$ on U. According to Lemma 4, $p_L(\pi(O_X) \cup \pi_L(E_X))$ is also an independent set w.r.t. $\prec$ on U. Hence, by the above, $\pi(O_X) \cup \pi_L(E_X)$ is a p-superinfix code.

(ii) $\Rightarrow$ (i) It is evident because any subset of a p-superinfix code is also a p-superinfix code. □

Example 1: Consider the language $X = \{a^2ba, aba^2, ab^3, ba^3, bab^2, b^2ab, a^2b^2a, a^2b^3, ababa, abab^2, ab^2a^2, ab^2ab, ba^2ba, ba^2b^2, baba^2, babab, b^2a^3, b^2a^2b\}$

over the alphabet $A = \{a, b\}$. It is easy to check that $p_L(X) = \{((3,1),1),((3,2),1),((2,3),2),((1,3),2)\}$ and that it is an independent set w.r.t. $\prec$ on $U = \{(\xi, j) \in V^2 \times \{1,2\} | p_j(\xi) \neq 0\}$. By Theorem 2, X is a p-superinfix code.

3. Maximality

First we formulate a characterization of the maximal supercodes by means of independent sets w.r.t. the relation $<$ on V^k.

Theorem 3: For any subset X of A^+, X is a maximal supercode iff $p(X)$ is a maximal independent set w.r.t. $<$ on V^k and $\pi(X) = X$.

Proof: Let X be a maximal supercode. If $\pi(X) \neq X$ then, by Theorem 1, $\pi(X)$ is a supercode containing strictly X, a contradiction with the maximality of X. Thus $\pi(X) = X$. Next, we prove that $p(X)$ is a maximal independent set w.r.t. $<$ on V^k. Indeed, by Theorem 1, $p(X)$ is an independent set w.r.t. $<$. If it is not maximal then $\exists p \notin p(X)$ such that $p(X) \cup \{p\}$ is still an independent set w.r.t. $<$. Choose u to be any word with $p(u) = p$ (such a word always exists). Then, $p(X \cup \{u\}) = p(X) \cup \{p\}$. Again by Theorem 1 this implies that $X \cup \{u\}$ is still a supercode, a contradiction with the maximality of the supercode X.

Conversely, let $p(X)$ be a maximal independent set w.r.t. $<$ on V^k and $\pi(X) = X$. By Theorem 1, X is a supercode. Suppose X is not a maximal supercode. There exists a word u not in X and therefore not in $\pi(X)$ such that $X \cup \{u\}$ is still a supercode. Because $u \notin \pi(X)$, $p = p(u)$ is not in $p(X)$. Again by Theorem 1, $p(X \cup \{u\}) = p(X) \cup \{p\}$ is still an independent set w.r.t. $<$, a contradiction. □

Next we characterize the maximal p-superinfix, s-superinfix and superinfix codes by means of independent sets w.r.t. the relation $\prec$ on U and on W.

Theorem 4: For any subset X of A^+, we have

(i) X is a maximal p-superinfix (s-superinfix) code iff $p_L(X)$ (resp., $p_F(X)$) is a maximal independent set w.r.t. the relation $\prec$ on U and $\pi(O_X) \cup \pi_L(E_X) = X$ (resp., $\pi(O_X) \cup \pi_F(E_X) = X$).

(ii) X is a maximal superinfix code iff $p_{LF}(X)$ is a maximal independent set w.r.t. the relation $\prec$ on W and $\pi(O_X) \cup \pi_{LF}(E_X) = X$.

Proof: (i) We prove only the case of p-superinfix codes. For the case of s-superinfix codes the argument is similar. Let X be a maximal p-superinfix code. If $\pi(O_X) \cup \pi_L(E_X) \neq X$ then, by Theorem 2, $\pi(O_X) \cup \pi_L(E_X)$ would be a p-superinfix code strictly containing X, a contradiction with the maximality of X. Hence, $\pi(O_X) \cup \pi_L(E_X) = X$. We next show that $p_L(X)$ is a maximal independent set w.r.t. the relation $\prec$ on U. Indeed, by Theorem 2, $p_L(X)$ is an independent set w.r.t. $\prec$ on U. If $p_L(X)$ were not maximal then $\exists t \in U - p_L(X)$ such that $p_L(X) \cup \{t\}$ is still an independent set w.r.t. $\prec$. Let $t = (\xi, j)$. Since $p_j(\xi) \neq 0$, we can choose a word u such that $p(u) = \xi$ and the last letter of u has index j. Thus $p_L(u) = t$. Evidently $u \notin X$. We have $p_L(X \cup \{u\}) = p_L(X) \cup \{t\}$. Again by Theorem 2, $X \cup \{u\}$ is still a p-superinfix code, a contradiction with the maximality of X.

Conversely, let $p_L(X)$ be a maximal independent set w.r.t. $\prec$ on U and $\pi(O_X) \cup \pi_L(E_X) = X$. By Theorem 2, X is a p-superinfix code. Suppose X is not maximal as a p-superinfix code. Then, there exists $u \notin X$ such that $X \cup \{u\}$ is still a p-superinfix code. If $p_L(u) \in p_L(X)$ then $p_L(u) = p_L(x)$ for some $x \in X$. This implies $p(u) = p(x)$ and the last letters of u and x are the same. Therefore $u \in \pi_L(x) \subseteq \pi(O_X) \cup \pi_L(E_X) = X$, a contradiction. Thus $t = p_L(u) \notin p_L(X)$. Again by Theorem 2, $p_L(X \cup \{u\}) = p_L(X) \cup \{t\}$ is still an independent set w.r.t. $\prec$, a contradiction with the maximality of $p_L(X)$. Thus X must be maximal as a p-superinfix code.

(ii) Let X be a maximal superinfix code. If $\pi(O_X) \cup \pi_{LF}(E_X) \neq X$ then, by Theorem 2, $\pi(O_X) \cup \pi_{LF}(E_X)$ would be a superinfix code strictly containing X, a contradiction. So, $\pi(O_X) \cup \pi_{LF}(E_X) = X$. Now we show that $p_{LF}(X)$ is a maximal independent set w.r.t. the relation $\prec$ on W. By Theorem 2, $p_{LF}(X)$ is an independent set w.r.t. $\prec$ on W. If $p_{LF}(X)$ were not maximal then $\exists t \in W - p_{LF}(X)$ such that $p_{LF}(X) \cup \{t\}$ is still an independent set. Let $t = (\xi, i, j)$. Since $p_i(\xi) \neq 0$ and $p_j(\xi) \neq 0$, we can choose a word u, whose the last and the first letter are a_i and a_j respectively, and such that $p(u) = \xi$. Thus $p_{LF}(u) = t$. Evidently $u \notin X$. We have $p_{LF}(X \cup \{u\}) = p_{LF}(X) \cup \{t\}$. Again by Theorem 2, $X \cup \{u\}$ is still a superinfix code, a contradiction with the maximality of X.

Conversely, let $p_{LF}(X)$ be a maximal independent set w.r.t. $\prec$ on W and $\pi(O_X) \cup \pi_{LF}(E_X) = X$. By Theorem 2, X is a superinfix code. Suppose X is not maximal as a superinfix code. Then, there exists $u \notin X$ such that $X \cup \{u\}$ is still a superinfix code. If $p_{LF}(u) \in p_{LF}(X)$ then $p_{LF}(u) = p_{LF}(x)$ for some $x \in X$. This implies $p(u) = p(x)$, and that u and x have the same last and first letters. Therefore $u \in \pi_{LF}(x) \subseteq \pi(O_X) \cup \pi_{LF}(E_X) = X$, a contradiction. Thus $t = p_{LF}(u) \notin p_{LF}(X)$. Again by Theorem 2,

$p_{LF}(X \cup \{u\}) = p_{LF}(X) \cup \{t\}$ is still an independent set w.r.t. $\prec$ on W, a contradiction with the maximality of $p_{LF}(X)$. Thus X must be maximal as a superinfix code. □

Example 2: (i) Let $X = \{a^3, ab^2, bab, b^2a, b^3, a^2ba, a^2b^2, aba^2, abab, ba^3, ba^2b\}$. It is easy to see that $X = \pi(O_X) \cup \pi_L(E_X)$ and $p_L(X) = \{((3,0),1), ((3,1),1), ((2,2),2), ((1,2),1), ((1,2),2), ((0,3),2)\}$, which is easily verified to be a maximal independent set w.r.t. $\prec$ on $U = \{(\xi, i) \in V^2 \times \{1,2\} | p_i(\xi) \neq 0\}$. By virtue of Theorem 4(i), we may conclude that X is a maximal p-superinfix code over $A = \{a, b\}$.

(ii) Let's consider the set $X = \{a^3, a^2ba, aba^2, b^4, a^2b^2a, ababa, ab^2a^2, bab^3, b^2ab^2, b^3ab, a^2b^3a, abab^2a, ab^2aba, ab^3a^2, ba^2b^3, babab^2, bab^2ab, b^2a^2b^2, b^2abab, b^3a^2b\}$ over $A = \{a, b\}$. We have evidently $O_X = \{a^3, b^4\}$. A simple verification leads to $X = \pi(O_X) \cup \pi_{LF}(E_X)$ and also $p_{LF}(X) = \{((3,0),1,1), ((3,1),1,1), ((3,2),1,1), ((3,3),1,1), ((2,4),2,2), ((1,4),2,2) ((0,4),2,2)\}$. It is easy to see that the latter is a maximal independent set w.r.t. $\prec$ on $W = \{(\xi, i, j) \in V^2 \times \{1,2\}^2 | p_i(\xi), p_j(\xi) \neq 0\}$. By Theorem 4(ii), it follows that X is a maximal superinfix code over A.

Recall that a subset X of A^+ is an *infix* (*p-infix, s-infix*) code if no word in X is an infix of a proper infix (prefix, suffix, resp.) of another word in X. The subset X is called a *sucyperinfix* (*p-sucyperinfix, s-sucyperinfix*) code if no word in X is a **su**bword of a **cy**clic **per**mutation of a proper **infix** (**p**refix, **s**uffix, resp.) of another word in X.

The following result establishes relationship between maximal p-superinfix (s-superinfix, superinfix) codes and p-infix (s-infix, sucyperinfix, resp.) codes.

Theorem 5: For any subset X of A^+, we have

(i) X is a maximal p-superinfix (s-superinfix, resp.) code iff X is a maximal p-infix (s-infix, resp.) code and $\pi(O_X) \cup \pi_L(E_X) = X$ ($\pi(O_X) \cup \pi_F(E_X) = X$, resp.).

(ii) X is a maximal superinfix code iff X is a maximal sucyperinfix code and $\pi(O_X) \cup \pi_{LF}(E_X) = X$ ($\pi(O_X) \cup \pi_F(E_X) = X$, resp.).

Proof: (i) We treat only the case of p-superinfix codes. Let X be a maximal p-superinfix code. By Theorem 4(i), $\pi(O_X) \cup \pi_L(E_X) = X$. If X is not a maximal p-infix code then there exists a word $y, 1 \neq y \notin X$, such that $Y = X \cup \{y\}$ is still a p-infix code. By Theorem 4(i), we have $\pi(O_X) \cup \pi_L(E_X) = X$ and $p_L(X)$ is a maximal independent set w.r.t. $\prec$ on U. If

$p_L(y) \in p_L(X)$ then there is an $x \in X$ such that $p(y) = p(x)$ and the last letters of y and x are the same. Then, $y \in \pi_L(x) \subseteq \pi(O_X) \cup \pi_L(E_X) = X$, a contradiction with $y \notin X$. Thus we must have $p_L(y) \notin p_L(X)$ and therefore $p_L(X) \cup \{p_L(y)\}$ is not an independent set w.r.t. $\prec$ on U, i.e. either $p_L(y) \prec p_L(x)$ or $p_L(x) \prec p_L(y)$, for some $x \in X$. Suppose $p_L(y) \prec p_L(x)$, and let a_j be the last letter of x. Since $p(y) \leq p(x)$ and $p_j(y) < p_j(x)$, there exists $x' \in \pi_L(x) \subseteq \pi(O_X) \cup \pi_L(E_X) = X$ such that x' is of the form $x' = zya_j$ with $z \in A^*$. This is impossible because Y is a p-infix code. Suppose now $p_L(x) \prec p_L(y)$. Without loss of generality we may assume $x \in O_X$. Let a_j be the last letter of y. We have $p(x) \leq p(y)$ and $p_j(x) < p_j(y)$. Therefore there exists $x'' \in \pi(x) \subseteq \pi(O_X) \subseteq X$ such that y has the form $y = zx''a_j$, a contradiction. Thus X must be maximal as a p-infix code that required to prove.

Conversely, let X be a maximal p-infix code with $\pi(O_X) \cup \pi_L(E_X) = X$. We first show that $p_L(X)$ is an independent set w.r.t. $\prec$ on U. Suppose the contrary that there exist $u, v \in X$ such that $p_L(u) \prec p_L(v)$, and let a_j be the last letter of v. By definition, $p(u) \leq p(v)$ and $p_j(u) < p_j(v)$. Therefore, there is $v' \in \pi_L(v) \subseteq X$ such that $v' = zua_j$, which contradicts the hypothesis that X is a p-infix code. Thus $p_L(X)$ must be an independent set w.r.t. $\prec$ on U and hence X is a p-superinfix code. The maximality of X as a p-superinfix code is then evident.

(ii) Let X be a maximal superinfix code. By Theorem 4(ii), $\pi(O_X) \cup \pi_{LF}(E_X) = X$. Assume that X is not a maximal sucyperinfix code. Then, there exists a word y, $1 \neq y \notin X$, such that $Y = X \cup \{y\}$ is a sucyperinfix code. By Theorem 4(ii), $\pi(O_X) \cup \pi_{LF}(E_X) = X$ and $p_{LF}(X)$ is a maximal independent set w.r.t. $\prec$ on W. If $p_{LF}(y) \in p_{LF}(X)$ then there exists $x \in X$ such that $p(y) = p(x)$, and the first and last letters of y and x are the same. Then, $y \in \pi_{LF}(x) \subseteq \pi(O_X) \cup \pi_{LF}(E_X) = X$, a contradiction with $y \notin X$. Thus we must have $p_{LF}(y) \notin p_{LF}(X)$ and therefore $p_{LF}(X) \cup \{p_{LF}(y)\}$ is not an independent set w.r.t. $\prec$ on W, i.e. either $p_{LF}(y) \prec p_{LF}(x)$ or $p_{LF}(x) \prec p_{LF}(y)$, for some $x \in X$. Suppose $p_{LF}(y) \prec p_{LF}(x)$, and let a_i and a_j be the first letter and last letter of x respectively. Since $p(y) \leq p(x)$ and $p_i(y) < p_i(x)$ or $p_j(y) < p_j(x)$, either there exists $x' \in \pi_F(x)$ such that x' is of the form $x' = a_iyz$ or there is $x'' \in \pi_L(x)$, $x'' = zya_j$, with $z \in A^*$. Assume $x' = a_iyz$, and let $yz = y_1y_2$ with a_j is the last letter of y_1. Then, the word $w = a_iy_2y_1 \in \pi_{LF}(x) \subseteq \pi(O_X) \cup \pi_{LF}(E_X) = X$ and therefore $y \prec_{scpi} w$, which contraditcs the fact that Y is a sucyperinfix code. Assume now $x'' = zya_j$, and let $zy = y'_1y'_2$ with a_i is the first letter of y'_2. We have $w' = y'_2y'_1a_j \in \pi_{LF}(x) \subseteq X$ and hence $y \prec_{scpi} w'$, a contradiction.

Next, suppose $p_{LF}(x) \prec p_{LF}(y)$. Without loss of generality we may assume $x \in O_X$. Let a_i and a_j be the first letter and last letter of y respectively. By definition, $p(x) \leq p(y)$ and $p_i(x) < p_i(y)$ or $p_j(x) < p_j(y)$. Therefore either there exists $u \in \pi(x) \subseteq \pi(O_X) \subseteq X$ or there is $v \in \pi(x) \subseteq X$ such that y has the form either $y = a_i uz$ or $y = z'va_j$, a contradiction. Thus X must be maximal as a sucyperinfix code that required to prove.

Conversely, let X be a maximal sucyperinfix code with $\pi(O_X) \cup \pi_{LF}(E_X) = X$. We show that $p_{LF}(X)$ is an independent set w.r.t. $\prec$ on W. Assume the contrary that there exist $u, v \in X$ such that $p_{LF}(u) \prec p_{LF}(v)$, and let a_i and a_j be the first letter and last letter of v respectively. Then, we have $p(u) \leq p(v)$ and $p_i(u) < p_i(v)$ or $p_j(u) < p_j(v)$. Therefore, either there is $v' \in \pi_F(v)$ such that $v' = a_i uz$ or there exists $v'' \in \pi_L(v)$, $v'' = zua_j$, with $z \in A^*$. Suppose $v' = a_i uz$ and let $uz = u_1u_2$ with a_j is the last letter of u_1. Then, the word $w = a_i u_2 u_1 \in \pi_{LF}(v) \subseteq \pi(O_X) \cup \pi_{LF}(E_X) = X$ and therefore $u \prec_{scpi} w$, which contraditcs the hypothesis that X is a sucyperinfix code. Suppose now $v'' = zua_j$ and let $zu = u_1'u_2'$ with a_i is the first letter of u_2'. We have $w' = u_2'u_1'a_j \in \pi_{LF}(v) \subseteq X$ and hence $u \prec_{scpi} w'$, a contradiction. Thus $p_{LF}(X)$ must be an independent set w.r.t. $\prec$ on W and hence X is a superinfix code. The maximality of X as a superinfix code is then trivial. □

A subset X in A^+ is a *subinfix* (*p-subinfix, s-subinfix*) code if no word in X is a **sub**word of a proper **infix** (**p**refix, **s**uffix, resp.) of another word in X. We have evidently $C_{spi} \subset C_{scpi} \subset C_{si} \subset C_i$ as well as similar inclusions for the corresponding p-classes and s-classes of codes.

As a direct consequence of Theorem 5 we obtain

Corollary 1: *For any subset X of A^+, X is a maximal p-superinfix (s-superinfix, resp.) code iff X is a maximal p-subinfix/p-sucyperinfix (s-subinfix/s-sucyperinfix, resp.) code and $\pi(O_X) \cup \pi_L(E_X) = X$ ($\pi(O_X) \cup \pi_F(E_X) = X$, resp.).*

We have moreover

Corollary 2: *Every maximal p-superinfix (s-superinfix) code is a maximal code.*

Proof: Recall that a code X is *thin* if there is a word w, which cannot be a factor of any word in X. Any p-infix code (s-infix code) X is thin because any word of the form axa with $x \in X, a \in A$ cannot be a factor of any word in X. Every maximal p-infix code (s-infix code) is a maximal prefix code (suffix code, resp.).[4] Thus, by Theorem 5(i), every maximal p-superinfix code (s-superinfix code) is a maximal prefix code (suffix code, resp.) which is thin. As well-known, for a thin code X, it is a maximal prefix code (suffix code) if and only if it is a maximal code (see Ref. 1). Hence, every maximal p-superinfix code (s-superinfix code) is a maximal code. □

This corollary in combination with Theorems 2.1 and 2.2 in Ref. 3 give us immediately

Corollary 3: *Every finite (regular) p-superinfix code (s-superinfix code) is included in a finite (regular, resp.) p-superinfix code (s-superinfix code) which is maximal as a code.*

Remark 1: While, as seen above, a maximal p-superinfix code (s-superinfix code) is always a maximal prefix code (suffix code, resp.), a maximal superinfix code is not necessarily a maximal subinfix code. Indeed, consider the code $X = ab^*a$ over the alphabet $A = \{a, b\}$ which is easily verified to be a maximal superinfix code. But it is not a maximal subinfix code because $X \cup \{bab\}$ is still a subinfix code.

Now we consider some properties of maximal sucypercodes and their relationship with other kinds of codes, namely with supercodes and hypercodes. Recall that a subset X of A^+ is a *hypercode*, $X \in C_h$, if no word in X is a proper subword of another word in it. Note that $C_{sp} \subset C_{scp} \subset C_h$. Supercodes have been first considered in Ref. 9.

Theorem 6: For any subset X of A^+, we have the following

(i) X is a maximal supercode iff X is a maximal hypercode and $\pi(X) = X$.
(ii) X is a maximal sucypercode iff X is a maximal hypercode and $\sigma(X) = X$.
(iii) X is a maximal supercode iff X is a maximal sucypercode and $\pi(X) = \sigma(X)$.

Proof: (i) Let X be a maximal supercode. We have $\pi(X) = X$ by Theorem 3. Suppose that X is not a maximal hypercode. Then, there is a word u not in X such that $X \cup \{u\}$ is still a hypercode. By Theorem 3, $\pi(X) = X$. Thus $Y = \pi(X) \cup \{u\}$ is a hypercode. If Y is not a supercode then either $p(u) < p(v)$ or $p(v) < p(u)$ for some $v \in \pi(X)$. By Lemma 1, u must be a proper subword of a permutation of v or a proper superword of a permutation of v. This means that there exists $v' \in \pi(v)$ such that u is either a proper subword of v' or a proper superword of v'. But v' is in Y too, which contradicts the fact that Y is a hypercode. The set Y and therefore the set $X \cup \{u\}$ must be a supercode, a contradiction. Thus X is a maximal hypercode that required to prove.

Conversely, let X be a maximal hypercode with $\pi(X) = X$. Being a hypercode, no word in X is a proper subword of another word in X. Moreover, since $\pi(X) = X$, no word in X can be a proper subword of a permutation of another word in X, i.e. X is a supercode. The maximality of X as a supercode is then evident.

(ii) Let X be a maximal sucypercode. If $\sigma(X) \neq X$ then, by Proposition 1, $\sigma(X)$ is a sucypercode strictly containing X, a contradiction with the maximality of X. Next, if X is not a maximal hypercode then there exists $1 \neq y \notin X$ such that $X \cup \{y\}$ is still a hypercode. Hence $Y = \sigma(X) \cup \{y\}$ is a hypercode. We now prove that Y is still a sucypercode. Suppose the contrary that it is not the case. Then either $y \prec_{scp} x$ or $x \prec_{scp} y$, for some $x \in \sigma(X)$. If $y \prec_{scp} x$ then there is $x' \in \sigma(x) \subseteq Y$ such that $y \prec_h x'$, which contradicts the fact that Y is a hypercode. If $x \prec_{scp} y$ then there exists $y' \in \sigma(y)$ such that $x \prec_h y'$. By Lemma 2, there exists $x'' \in \sigma(x)$ such that $x'' \prec_h y$, again a contradiction. Thus $Y = X \cup \{y\}$ is a sucypercode, which contradicts the maximality of X as a sucypercode. This contradiction shows that X must be a maximal hypercode.

Conversely, let X be a maximal hypercode with $\sigma(X) = X$. As X is a hypercode, we have $u \not\prec_h v$ for all $u, v \in X$. Since $\sigma(X) = X$ this implies $u \not\prec_{scp} v$ for all $u, v \in X$. Thus X is a sucypercode and hence a maximal sucypercode.

(iii) By (i), X be a maximal supercode iff X is a maximal hypercode and $\pi(X) = X$. Since $X \subseteq \sigma(X) \subseteq \pi(X)$ and by (ii), the later is equivalent to X is a maximal sucypercode and $\pi(X) = \sigma(X)$. □

4. Supercodes over Two-Letter Alphabets

Let's fix a two-letter alphabet $A = \{a, b\}$. On V^2 we introduce the relation $\prec_{2.v}$ defined by

$$u \prec_{2.v} w \Leftrightarrow p_1(u) > p_1(w) \wedge p_2(u) < p_2(w)\,,$$

where $p_i(u)$ denotes the i-th component of u. For simplicity, in this section we write $\prec$ instead of $\prec_{2.v}$.

A finite sequence (may be empty) S: $u_1, u_2, \ldots, u_n$ of elements in V^2 is a *chain* if

$$u_1 \prec u_2 \prec \cdots \prec u_n\,.$$

The chain S is *full* if

$$\forall\, i, 1 \leq i \leq n-1, \nexists v : u_i \prec v \prec u_{i+1}\,.$$

If the full chain S satisfies moreover the condition

$$p_2(u_1) = p_1(u_n) = 0\,,$$

then it is said to be *complete*. A finite subset T of V^2 is *complete* if it can be arranged to become a complete chain. For $1 \leq i < j \leq n$ we denote by $[u_i, u_j]$ the subsequence u_i, $u_{i+1}, \ldots, u_j$ of the sequence S.

Theorem 7: For any finite subset X of A^+, X is a maximal supercode iff $p(X)$ is complete and $X = \pi(X)$.

Proof: Let X be a maximal supercode with $|p(X)| = n$. By Theorem 3, $p(X)$ is a maximal independent set w.r.t. $<$ on V^2 and $X = \pi(X)$. So, for any different u, v in $p(X)$, $p_1(u) \neq p_1(v)$, $p_2(u) \neq p_2(v)$. Arrange $p(X)$ to become a sequence $u_1, u_2, \ldots, u_n$ such that $p_1(u_1) > p_1(u_2) > \cdots > p_1(u_n)$. We must have $p_2(u_1) < p_2(u_2) < \cdots < p_2(u_n)$. That is $u_1 \prec u_2 \prec \cdots \prec u_n$. If $p_2(u_1) \neq 0$ then, choosing u to be any 2-vector with $p_1(u) > p_1(u_1)$ and $p_2(u) = 0$, the set $p(X) \cup \{u\}$ is still an independent set w.r.t. $<$, a contradiction. Thus $p_2(u_1) = 0$. Similarly we have $p_1(u_n) = 0$. Now if there exists v such that $u_i \prec v \prec u_{i+1}$ for some i, $1 \leq i \leq n-1$, then $p(X) \cup \{v\}$ is an independent set w.r.t. $<$, which contradicts again the maximality of $p(X)$. Thus, the sequence u_1, $u_2, \ldots, u_n$ is a complete chain and, therefore, the set $p(X)$ is complete.

Conversely, since, as it is easily verified, every complete set is a maximal independent set w.r.t. $<$, and $X = \pi(X)$, again by Theorem 3, we have X is a maximal supercode. □

Example 3: For any $n \geq 1$, the sequence

$$(n, 0), (n-1, 2), \ldots, (n-i, 2i), \ldots, (0, 2n)$$

is obviously a complete chain. Therefore, the set $V_n = \{(n,0), (n-1,2), \ldots, (0,2n)\}$ is complete. With $n = 3$ for example, $V_3 = \{(3,0), (2,2), (1,4), (0,6)\}$. By Theorem 7 it follows that the set $X = \pi(\{a^3, a^2b^2, ab^4, b^6\}) = \{a^3, a^2b^2, abab, ab^2a, ba^2b, baba, b^2a^2, ab^4, bab^3, b^2ab^2, b^3ab, b^4a, b^6\}$ is a maximal supercode.

By Theorem 7, in order to characterize the maximal supercodes over $A = \{a, b\}$ we may characterize the complete sets instead. For this we first consider some transformations on complete chains. Let S: $u_1, u_2, \ldots, u_n$ be a complete chain.

(T1) (*extension*). It consists in doing consecutively the following:

- Add on the left of S a 2-vector u with $p_1(u) > p_1(u_1)$;
- Delete from S all the u_is with $p_2(u_i) \leq p_2(u)$;
- If u_{i_0} is the first among the u_is remained, then insert between u and u_{i_0} any chain such that $[u, u_{i_0}]$ is a full chain;
- If there is no such a u_{i_0}, then add on the right of u any chain ending with a v, $p_1(v) = 0$, and such that $[u, v]$ is a full chain;
- Add on the left of u any chain begining with a v, $p_2(v) = 0$, and such that $[v, u]$ is a full chain.

(T2) (*replacement*). The following steps will be done successively:

- Replacing some element u_i in S by an element u with $p_1(u) = p_1(u_i)$;
- If $p_2(u) < p_2(u_i)$, then delete all the u_js on the left of u with $p_2(u_j) \geq p_2(u)$;
- If u_{j_0} is the last among the u_j remained, then insert between u_{j_0} and u any sequence such that $[u_{j_0}, u]$ is a full chain;
- If there is no such a u_{j_0}, then add on the left of u any chain commencing with a v, $p_2(v) = 0$, and such that $[v, u]$ is a full chain;
- If $i < n$ then insert between u and u_{i+1} any chain such that $[u, u_{i+1}]$ is a full chain;
- If $p_2(u) > p_2(u_i)$, then delete all the u_js on the right of u with $p_2(u_j) \leq p_2(u)$;
- If u_{j_0} is the first among the u_js remained, then insert between u and u_{j_0} any chain such that $[u, u_{j_0}]$ is a full chain;
- If there is no such a u_{j_0}, then add on the right of u any chain ending with a v, $p_1(v) = 0$, and such that $[u, v]$ is a full chain;
- If $i > 1$ then insert between u_{i-1} and u any chain such that $[u_{i-1}, u]$ is a full chain;
- If $i = 1$ then add on the left of u any chain begining with a v, $p_2(v) = 0$, and such that $[v, u]$ is a full chain.

(T3) (*insertion*). This consists of the following successive steps:

- For some i, insert in the middle of u_i and u_{i+1}, $1 \leq i \leq n-1$, an element u with $p_1(u_i) > p_1(u) > p_1(u_{i+1})$;
- If $p_2(u) \leq p_2(u_i)$, then delete all the u_js on the left of u with $p_2(u_j) \geq p_2(u)$;

• If u_{j_0} is the last among the u_js remained, then insert between u_{j_0} and u any chain such that $[u_{j_0}, u]$ is a full chain;

• If there is no such a u_{j_0}, then add on the left of u any chain commencing with a v, $p_2(v) = 0$, and such that $[v, u]$ is a full chain;

• Insert between u and u_{i+1} any chain such that $[u, u_{i+1}]$ is a full chain;

• If $p_2(u) \geq p_2(u_{i+1})$, then delete all the u_js on the right of u with $p_2(u_j) \leq p_2(u)$;

• If u_{j_0} is the first among the u_js remained, then insert between u and u_{j_0} any chain such that $[u, u_{j_0}]$ is a full chain;

• If there is no such u_{j_0}, then add on the right of u any sequence ending with a v, $p_1(v) = 0$, and such that $[u, v]$ is a full chain;

• Insert between u_i and u any chain such that $[u_i, u]$ become a full chain.

Theorem 8: The following assertions hold true

(i) The transformations (T1)–(T3) preserve the completeness of a chain.

(ii) Any complete chain can be obtained from another one by a finite number of applications of the transformations (T1)–(T3).

(iii) Every chain S can be embedded in a complete chain by a finite number of applications of the transformations (T1)–(T3).

Proof: (i) Easily seen by the definitions of (T1)–(T3).

(ii) Let $S : u_1, u_2, \ldots, u_n$ and $S' : v_1, v_2, \ldots, v_m$ be two complete chains. To obtain S' from S we can do as follows. According as $p_1(v_1)$ greater, equal or less than $p_1(u_1)$ we apply to S the transformations (T1), (T2) or (T3) in an appropriate way with $u = v_1$. In any case we obtain a complete chain $S^{(1)}$ commencing with v_1. Suppose $S^{(k)}$, $1 \leq k \leq m-1$, have been constructed, which is a complete chain commencing with $v_1, \ldots, v_k$. Let $S^{(k)} : v_1, \ldots, v_k, w_{k+1}, \ldots, w_r$. We construct $S^{(k+1)}$ as follows. If $p_1(v_{k+1}) > p_1(w_{k+1})$ then, since $p_1(v_{k+1}) < p_1(v_k)$, we may apply (T3) to insert v_{k+1} in the middle of v_k and w_{k+1}. Because S' is complete, in the chain obtained, v_{k+1} must be next to v_k. If $p_1(v_{k+1}) = p_1(w_{k+1})$, then we may apply (T2) to replace w_{k+1} by v_{k+1}. Again by the completeness of S', in the chain obtained, v_{k+1} must be next to v_k. Let now $p_1(v_{k+1}) < p_1(w_{k+1})$. There exists then an integer $t \geq 1$ such that $p_1(w_{k+t+1}) \leq p_1(v_{k+1}) < p_1(w_{k+t})$. If $p_2(v_{k+1}) > p_2(w_{k+1})$ then it follows that $v_k < w_{k+1} < v_{k+1}$, a contradiction with the completeness of S'. So we have $p_2(v_{k+1}) \leq p_2(w_{k+1})$. According as $p_1(w_{k+t+1}) = p_1(v_{k+1})$ or $p_1(w_{k+t+1}) < p_1(v_{k+1})$, we may apply (T2) or (T3) to replace w_{k+t+1} by v_{k+1}, or to insert v_{k+1} in the middle of w_{k+t} and w_{k+t+1}. Because $p_2(v_{k+1}) \leq p_2(w_{k+1})$, w_{k+1} will be deleted and in the chain obtained, v_{k+1} must be next to v_k. Thus, in any case, the chain obtained is complete and commences with $v_1, v_2, \ldots, v_{k+1}$. We take this chain to be $S^{(k+1)}$. As $p_1(v_m) = 0$, $S^{(m)}$ must coincide with S'.

(iii) Given a chain $S : v_1, v_2, \ldots, v_n$. Choose S' to be any complete chain. Similarly as above, we may apply to S' appropriate transformations (T1)–(T3), to "enter" $v_1, v_2, \ldots, v_n$ consecutively. Notice that entering v_{i+1}, $i \geq 1$, does not delete any of $v_1, \ldots, v_i$ which have been entered previously. □

Example 4: Consider the chain $S : (5,2), (3,4), (1,7)$. We try to embed S in a complete chain by using (T1)–(T3). For this, we choose an arbitrary complete chain S', say $S' : (2,0), (1,2), (0,4)$, and manipulate like this:

- Applying (T1) to S' with $u = (5,2)$ we obtain from step to step the following sequences, where underline indicates the 2-vectors added in every step.

$$\underline{(5,2)}, (2,0), (1,2), (0,4);$$
$$(5,2), (0,4);$$
$$(5,2), \underline{(2,3)}, (0,4);$$
$$\underline{(6,0)}, (5,2), (2,3), (0,4);$$

- Applying (T3) to the last chain with $u = (3,4)$ we obtain successively:

$$(6,0), (5,2), \underline{(3,4)}, (2,3), (0,4);$$
$$(6,0), (5,2), (3,4);$$
$$(6,0), (5,2), (3,4), \underline{(1,5)}, \underline{(0,6)};$$
$$(6,0), (5,2), \underline{(4,3)}, (3,4), (1,5), (0,6);$$

- Applying (T2) to the last chain with $u = (1,7)$ we obtain:

$$(6,0), (5,2), (4,3), (3,4), \underline{(1,7)}, (0,6);$$
$$(6,0), (5,2), (4,3), (3,4), (1,7);$$
$$(6,0), (5,2), (4,3), (3,4), (1,7), \underline{(0,8)};$$
$$(6,0), (5,2), (4,3), (3,4), \underline{(2,6)}, (1,7), (0,8).$$

The last chain is a complete chain containing S.

As a consequence of Theorem 8 we have

Theorem 9: Let A be a two-letter alphabet. Then, we have

(i) There exists a procedure to generate all the maximal supercodes over A starting from an arbitrary given maximal supercode.
(ii) There is an algorithm allowing to construct, for every supercode X over A, a maximal supercode Y containing X.

Proof: (i) Let X be a given maximal supercode. Compute first $p(X)$, which is a complete set. Arrange $p(X)$ to become a complete chain S. By Theorem 8(ii), every possible complete chain, hence every complete set, can be obtained from S by a finite number of applications of the transformations (T1)–(T3). The inverse images of all such sets w.r.t. the morphism p give all the possible maximal supercodes.

(ii) $p(X)$ is an independent set w.r.t. $<$. So it can be arranged to become a chain S. By Theorem 8(iii), we can construct a complete chain S' containing S. Let T be the complete set corresponding to S'. Put $Y = p^{-1}(T)$. Evidently Y contains X and $p(Y) = T$. By Theorem 7, Y is a maximal supercode. □

Example 5: Let $X = \{b^2a^2bab, a^3ba^2b, b^4ab^3\}$. Since $p(X) = \{(3,4),(5,2),(1,7)\}$ is an independent set w.r.t. $<$ on V^2, by Theorem 1, X is a supercode over $A = \{a, b\}$. The corresponding chain of $p(X)$ is

$$S : (5,2),(3,4),(1,7)\,.$$

As has been shown in Example 4, the sequence

$$S' : (6,0),(5,2),(4,3),(3,4),(2,6),(1,7),(0,8)$$

is a complete chain containing S. The corresponding complete set of S' is

$$T = \{(6,0),(5,2),(4,3),(3,4),(2,6),(1,7),(0,8)\}\,.$$

So $Y = p^{-1}(T)$ is a maximal supercode containing X. More explicitly, $Y = \pi(Z)$ with $Z = \{a^6, a^5b^2, a^4b^3, a^3b^4, a^2b^6, ab^7, b^8\}$.

References

1. J. Berstel and D. Perrin, *Theory of Codes.* Academic Press, New York, 1985.
2. G. Grätzer, *Universal Algebra.* Van Nostrand, Princeton, NJ, 1968.
3. K. V. Hung, P. T. Huy and D. L. Van, On some classes of codes defined by binary relations. *Acta Mathematica Vietnamica* **29** (2004), 163–176.
4. M. Ito, H. Jürgensen, H. Shyr and G. Thierrin, Outfix and infix codes and related classes of languages. *Journal of Computer and System Sciences* **43** (1991), 484–508.

5. H. Jürgensen and S. Konstatinidis, Codes. In: G. Rozenberg, A. Salomaa (eds.), *Handbook of Formal Languages.* Springer, Berlin, 1997, 511–607.
6. H. Shyr, *Free Monoids and Languages.* Hon Min Book Company, Taichung, 1991.
7. H. Shyr and G. Thierrin, Codes and binary relations. *Lecture Notes 586 "Sèminarie d'Algèbre, Paul Dubreil, Paris (1975-1976)"*, Springer-Verlag, 180–188.
8. D. L. Van, Embedding problem for codes defined by binary relations. *Preprint 98/A22*, Institute of Mathematics, Hanoi, 1998.
9. D. L. Van, On a class of hypercodes. In: M. Ito, T. Imaoka (eds.), *Words, Languages and Combinatorics III.* (Proceedings of the 3rd International Colloquium, Kyoto, 2000), World Scientific, 2003, 171–183.
10. D. L. Van and K. V. Hung, An approach to the embedding problem for codes defined by binary relations (submitted).